Complete Guide to

Outdoor

PROJECTS

Sunset Books, Menlo Park, California

The Consultants

Kenneth A. Long, a licensed master plumber, is co-owner and chief executive officer of Long's Corporation in northern Virginia and a past president of the Virginia Association of Plumbing, Heating, and Cooling Contractors. "Plumbing," says Long, " is the art of running pipe."

Jeff Palumbo is a registered journeyman carpenter who has a home-building and remodeling business in northern Virginia. His interest in carpentry was sparked by his grandfather, a master carpenter with more than 50 years' experience. Palumbo teaches in the Fairfax County Adult Education Program.

Mark M. Steele is a professional home inspector in the Washington, D.C., area. He has developed and conducted training programs in home-ownership skills for first-time homeowners. He appears frequently on television and radio as an expert in home repair and consumer topics.

J. Paul Trueblood consults and teaches in the civil engineering field. He served in the U.S. Marine Corps as a civil engineer for 25 years before retiring in 1983.

Guy Morgan Williams is a landscape architect whose experience ranges from small urban gardens to large-scale master plans and estate design. He is president and co-owner of DCA Landscape Architects, Inc., in Washington, D.C.

Complete Guide to Outdoor PROJECTS

Sunset Books, Menlo Park, California

CONTENTS

1 Rustic Decks and Elegant Porches

The outdoor additions described in this chapter range from a relatively simple-to-build freestanding deck to a wraparound porch with a hip roof anchored to the house. These ambitious structures can challenge an experienced carpenter, yet all are within your reach if you plan ahead, take your time, and proceed in the orderly fashion described on the following pages.

Measuring rise for steps to a deck →

Building a Simple Deck

A low, freestanding deck like the 10-foot-square example shown on the following pages combines simplicity and elegance. Supported entirely on posts set well within the perimeter, the structure appears to float above the ground. The basic design applies to any size deck you may want to build and is easily customized with finishing touches that appeal to you *(pages 38-45)*. And because this kind of deck requires no connection to the house, you can build it anywhere in your yard.

Design Considerations: Alongside a house, a door onto the deck is a must. If possible, build at an existing door, removing any steps that might hinder construction.

Determine the size and spacing of structural elements for your deck from the charts on page 9. Decking is ordinarily laid over joists spaced 16 inches apart, but diagonal decking calls for 12-inch joist spacing. A railing—mandatory on all decks over 2 feet high and recommended on lower decks—requires the addition of special bridging to keep the posts from twisting the joists they are attached to.

Sketch a plan of your deck that shows all the dimensions. You may need to submit the plan and apply for a building permit; if not, it's wise nonetheless to confirm with local authorities that the design complies with building codes.

At the Lumberyard: Examine each board individually. Avoid curved or twisted planks; they are hard to work with, and the defects can worsen over time, weakening the deck. And while you may prefer redwood or cedar for the decking *(page 14)*, choose posts of pressure-treated southern pine rated for ground contact.

Special Materials: Galvanized joist hangers and a variety of other framing connectors greatly simplify deck construction. Galvanized hangers are widely available—as are nails of appropriate diameter and length. Do not substitute common nails, which will make joints that lack the necessary strength. Other fasteners should also be galvanized to prevent rust. Redwood decking, however, requires acid-resistant aluminum nails.

Equipment for the Job: Besides common carpentry tools, you will need a posthole digger and a water level for a day; consider renting them. Your circular saw must be powerful enough to cut heavy, wet pressure-treated wood. Use a carbide-tipped crosscut blade, and back off if the motor slows.

CAUTION *Before excavating, establish the locations of underground obstacles such as electric, water, and sewer lines, and dry wells, septic tanks, and cesspools.*

TOOLS

- Measuring tape (25-foot)
- Plumb bob
- Posthole digger
- Carpenter's level
- Mortar tub
- Hoe
- Trowel
- Water level
- Circular saw
- Framing square
- Drill with $\frac{1}{2}$-inch bit

MATERIALS

- Mason's cord
- Concrete mix
- 4-by-4 posts
- 2-by-6 or larger framing lumber
- 2-by-4 or 2-by-6 decking
- 2-by-4 rails
- 2-by-2 pickets
- Common nails (3-inch and $3\frac{1}{2}$-inch)
- Carriage bolts ($\frac{1}{2}$- by 6-inch)
- Framing connectors and nails

SAFETY TIPS

Protect your eyes when hammering nails or using a circular saw. Wear a dust mask when cutting pressure-treated lumber, and wash hands thoroughly after handling it.

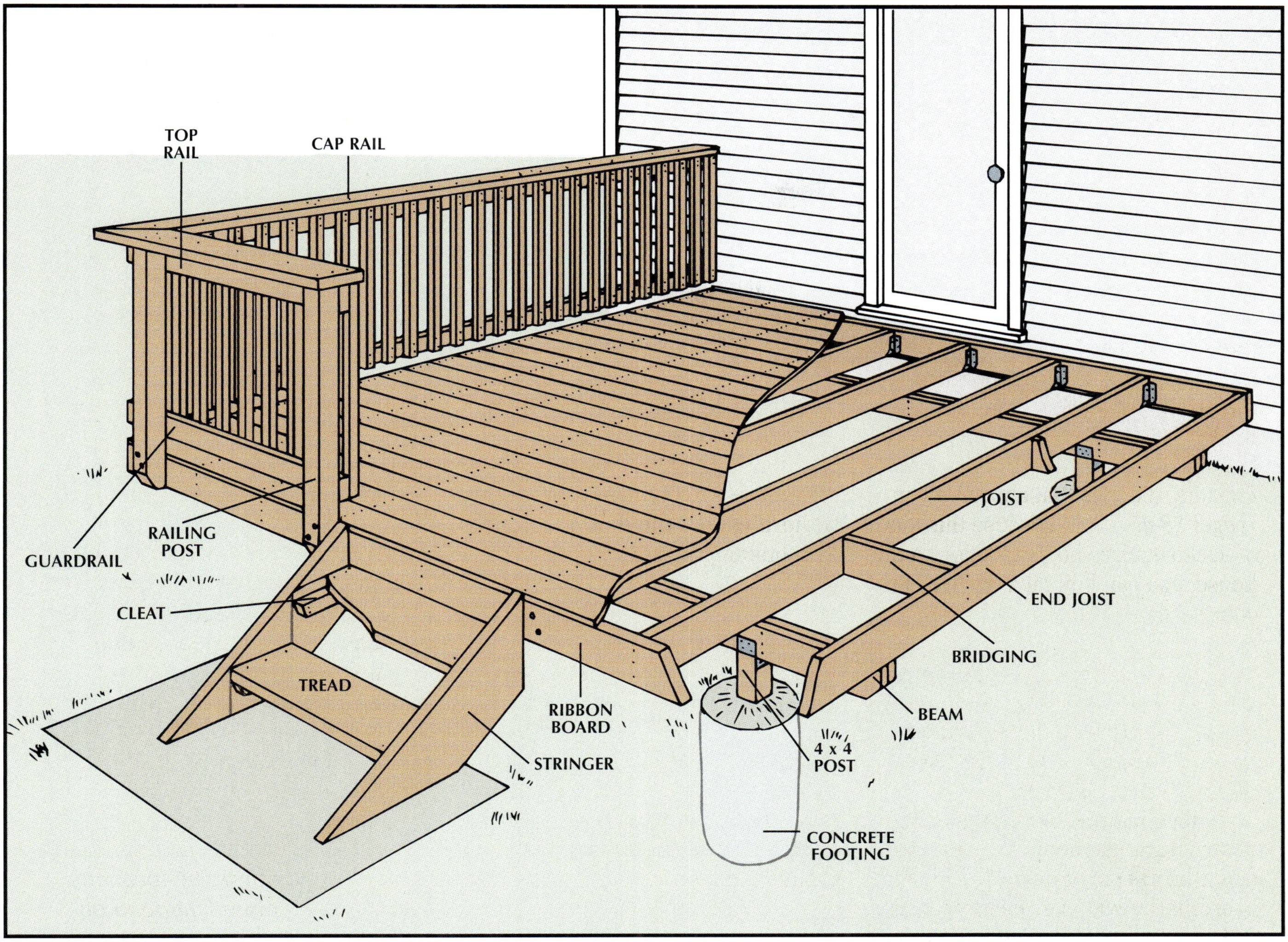

Anatomy of a deck. This freestanding deck stands next to the house on 4-by-4 posts embedded in concrete footings reaching below the frostline. The posts support beams of doubled boards secured to the tops of the posts with metal framing connectors. Resting on the beams is a frame nailed together with joist hangers as well as other framing connectors and covered with boards nailed to each joist. Bridging pieces brace end joists against twisting by forces exerted by railing posts bolted to the outside of the frame. The railing consists of guardrail, top rail, and cap rail nailed to these posts and filled in with vertical pickets. Easy-to-make steps, consisting of treads on cleats nailed to stringers, lead from the deck to a concrete slab on the ground.

Maximum Joist Span		
JOIST SIZE	**JOIST SPACING**	
	12"	16"
2" x 6"	11' 7"	9' 9"
2" x 8"	15' 0"	12' 10"
2" x 10"	19' 6"	16' 5"

Maximum Beam Span				
BEAM SIZE	**JOIST SPAN**			
	6'	8'	10'	12'
2 x 6s (2)	8'	7'	6'	5'
2 x 8s (2)	10'	9'	8'	7'
2 x 10s (2)	12'	11'	10'	9'
2 x 12s (2)	14'	13'	12'	11'

Spans for joists and beams. From the chart above choose a joist size for the width of the deck you would like to construct, then use the chart shown at right, above, to select a beam, which is made of two boards nailed together. Joists may extend beyond beams—and beams beyond posts—by $\frac{1}{3}$ the length of the spans in the charts. With this information, you will be able to calculate the number and spacing of posts needed to support the structure.

ERECTING POSTS AND BEAMS

1. Squaring the layout.

Use triangulation to establish post positions square to the house wall.

◆ Make two marks to indicate the width of the deck on the house. Between these marks make two other marks to indicate post positions.

◆ Hammer a nail partway into the wall at one of the inner marks. Six feet from the nail, drive another. Tie a length of mason's cord to this nail and mark it 10 feet from the nail.

◆ Tie one end of one end of another length of cord to the nail at the post-position mark and the other end to a 1-by-2 stake. Mark this cord 8 feet from the nail.

◆ Pull the cords taut and maneuver them until the marks touch, then drive the stake into the ground. Repeat the process at the other side of the deck. Mark each cord where the outside faces of each post will lie.

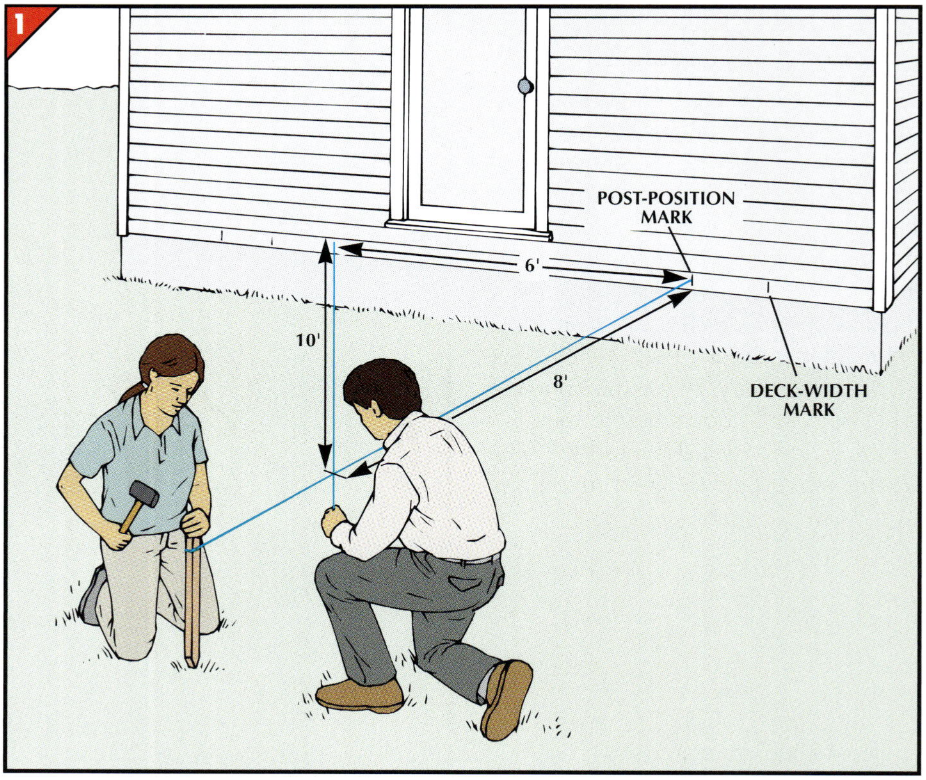

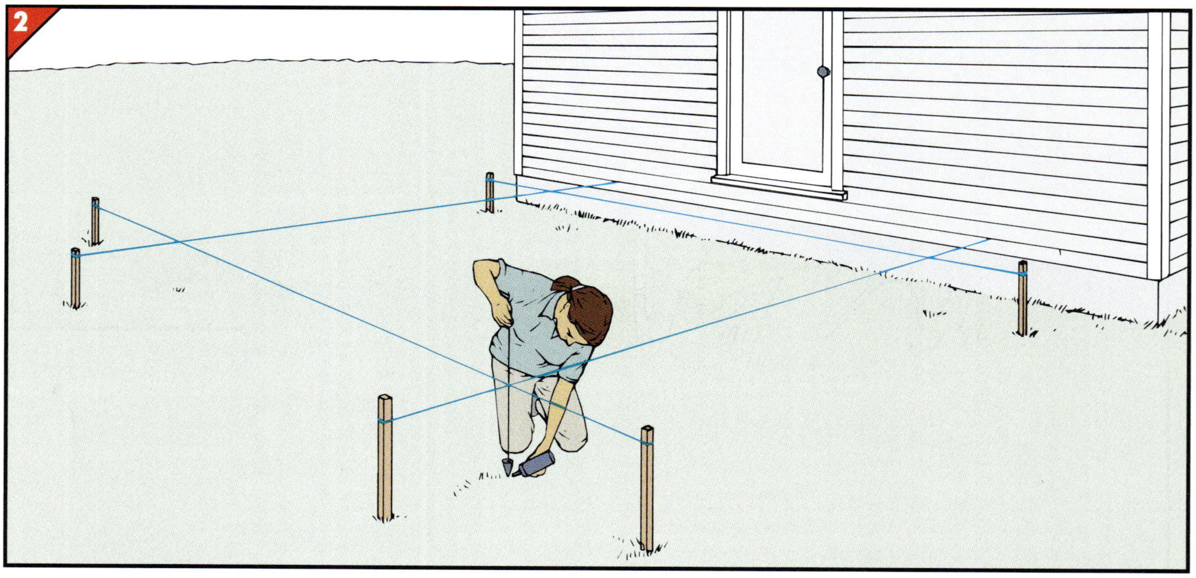

2. Chalking post positions.

◆ Stake 2 cords so they cross the beam marks made in Step 1.

◆ Use a plumb line and chalk mark the ground at the 4 string intersections; remove the strings, leaving the nails and stakes.

◆ With a posthole digger, dig footing holes at the chalk marks. Make each 12 inches across at the top, widening to 16 inches at the bottom. Dig down 24 inches—or 8 inches below the frostline, whichever is greater.

◆ Pour 8 inches of concrete into the holes and let it set up to 48 hours; retie the strings that you took down to dig the hole.

3. Plumbing the posts.

◆ Set a 4-by-4 post of ample length in one of the holes. Position it at the intersection of the strings as shown at right, taking care not to push the cords out of line. Fasten a 1-by-2 brace to one side of the post with a single nail, then drive a stake into the ground within reach of the brace. While a helper with a level holds the post vertical, nail the brace to the stake. Use the same method to plumb and brace the adjacent side of the post.

◆ After plumbing the other posts, pour concrete into the holes, stopping a few inches below the lip, then replumb the posts as necessary. Allow the concrete to set at least 24 hours before removing the braces. Pack dirt into the hole, sloping the surface to direct runoff away from the post.

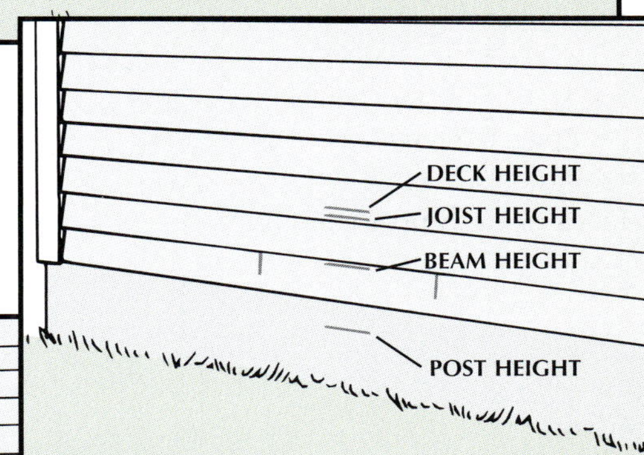

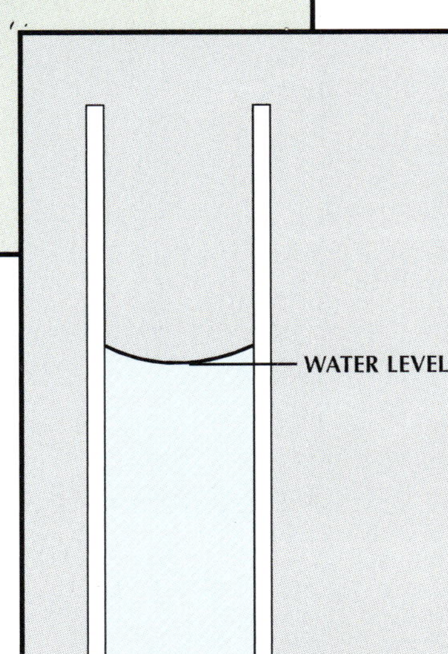

4. Preparing posts for cutting.

◆ Mark the house with the height of the deck floor, then measure down a distance equal to the thickness of the decking plus the depth of a joist and a beam *(top inset)*.

◆ Fill a water level. With a helper, adjust the level so that the water comes to the post-height mark on the house *(bottom inset)*. At the other end of the level, mark the post at the height of the water.

◆ Place a combination square at the post-height mark and draw cutting lines on each face of the post. Repeat this process on the remaining posts.

5. Preparing a post for a beam.
Set a circular saw to cut 2 inches deep. Position the lower edge of the blade at the post-height mark and cut across one face of the post. Repeat the process on the other side of the post, then nail a post-and-beam connector *(inset)* to the top of the post.

6. Making and mounting beams.
◆ Cut 4 beam boards the width of the deck, then fasten the boards together in pairs to form beams. Nail the beams with 3-inch galvanized common nails driven in rows of 3 into both sides of the beam at 16-inch intervals. Stagger the nails so that rows on one side fall midway between rows on the other.
◆ Bevel the bottom corners of each beam by cutting along a diagonal line drawn between marks 2 inches from the corner.
◆ Center the beams in the connectors atop the posts, and nail them in place.

A SKELETON OF JOISTS

1. Building the outer frame.
◆ Cut end joists and ribbon boards to length.
◆ To make the frame, drive three $3\frac{1}{2}$-inch nails through the faces of the ribbon boards into the ends of the joists.
◆ With a helper, set the frame on the beams $\frac{1}{2}$ inch from the house wall, end joists even with the ends of the beams.
◆ To square the frame, measure the diagonals *(left)*. If they are not equal, tap the frame with a heavy hammer to make them so.
◆ Use galvanized framing connectors to secure the end joists to the beams *(inset)*, and inside the corners to stiffen the frame.

2. Marking joist locations.

Measuring from the inner face of one end joist, mark one of the ribbon boards at 16-inch intervals, then extend the marks down the face of the board with a framing square. Pencil an X on the side of the line nearest to the starting point. Mark the other ribbon board in the same manner, starting from the same end joist.

◆ Align the inner edge of a joist hanger with each mark, positioning the opening of the hanger over the X and flush with the bottom of the ribbon board *(inset)*. Nail this side of the hanger in place.

◆ Cut all inner joists to length.

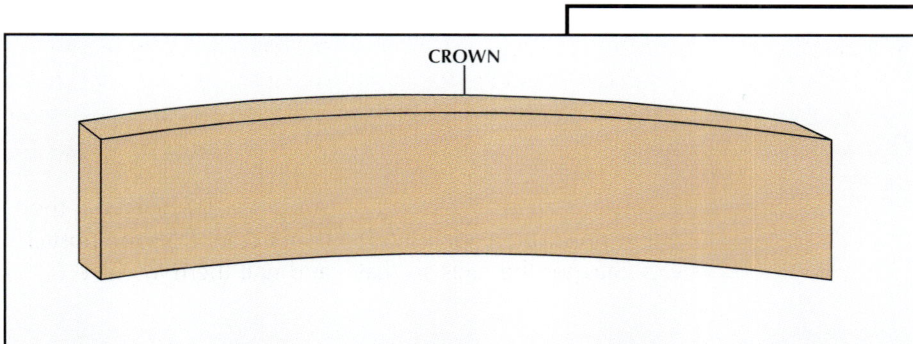

A crowned joist.

Most lumber used for deck framing is slightly curved along its length, as shown in the exaggerated depiction at left. Sight down the edge of a board to detect such a curve. Install joists crown up.

3. Installing joists and bridging.

◆ Slide the first inner joist into its joist hangers. Secure each end by holding the hanger closed and nailing it to the ribbon board, then to each side of the new joist.

◆ For a deck that will have a railing, add pieces of bridging to reinforce the end joists after installing the adjacent inner joists. Position the bridging between the joists, offset about 4 inches from each railing-post location *(page 9)*. Drive three $3\frac{1}{2}$-inch common nails through each joist into the ends of the bridging.

◆ Install the remaining inner joists.

SIMPLE FLOORING

Types of decking.
You can surface a deck with 2-by-4s, 2-by-6s, or decking stock 1 inch thick with rounded edges *(above, top)*. Pressure-treated pine is the most economical; the greenish tinge often seen in this material bleaches slowly to gray. Alternatives are redwood and cedar, which resist rot naturally. Left untreated, redwood weathers to a dark gray, cedar to a silvery gray. Select decking board by board if possible. Avoid boards that are twisted, crooked, or cupped. If you must use cupped boards, lay them convex side up to shed water.

1. Laying the first boards.
◆ Trim a decking board to the width of the deck and lay it about $\frac{1}{8}$ inch from the house wall. Secure it with three 3-inch nails.
◆ Attach subsequent boards, $\frac{1}{8}$ inch apart, with one end flush with one edge of the deck.

2. Laying bowed boards and the final rows.
◆ Position the convex edge of a bowed board against the straight edge of the preceding one. Nail one end to the joist with the usual spacing. Place $\frac{1}{8}$-inch spacers at several joists. Push the board against the spacers and nail the other end in place. Nail the board to the intermediate joists and remove the spacers.
◆ Adjust the spacing of the final 3 feet of decking—or trim one or more boards up to $\frac{1}{4}$ of their width—to bring the last board flush with the edge of the deck.

3. Trimming board ends.

◆ Snap a chalk line across the ends of the boards where they extend beyond the edge of the deck. Use the pretrimmed board at the house to help position the line at the face of the end joist.

◆ Tack a straight board alongside the line as a saw guide, then trim all the decking with a circular saw set to cut slightly deeper than the thickness of the boards.

ALTERNATIVE DECKING PATTERNS

Diagonal decking.

◆ Measuring from an outer corner of the deck frame, mark off equal distances—about half a joist length—on an end joist and the ribbon board.

◆ Nail a decking board at the marks.

◆ Lay subsequent boards on both sides of the first with a $\frac{1}{8}$-inch gap. To span a distance greater than the length of a decking board, cut the ends of two boards to join at the center of a joist.

◆ Within 1 foot of the house—and where boards abut the wall—precut the boards at a 45° angle.

◆ Trim the boards flush with the frame *(Step 3, above)*.

TRICKS OF THE TRADE

A Jig for Quick and Easy Angle Cuts

A straight 2-by-2 a couple of feet long and a scrap of plywood with 10 inches of factory edge are the components of a jig for trimming boards at a 45° angle. To make the jig, use a combination square to mark a 45° angle across the middle of the 2-by-2, then screw the plywood to the board with the factory edge along the line *(left)*. Trim away excess plywood.

Hold the jig against a decking board and position the saw with its base against the plywood and its blade aligned with the cutting mark. On the first cut, saw across both the decking and the jig *(dotted line, below)*, using the plywood as a guide. For subsequent cuts, set the end of the jig at the cutting line.

Herringbone decking.

This style of decking is achieved by dividing the deck into two parts and covering each diagonally *(page 15)* in opposite directions.

◆ In a deck that has no joist at the center, install one if you want a symmetrical pattern.

◆ Cover one side of the frame with diagonal decking boards, precutting 45° angles only on those near the house. Nail the decking to all but the center joist.

◆ Cut the overhanging ends flush with deck sides and along the midline of the center joist, then nail the trimmed ends to the center joist.

◆ For the other side of the deck *(above)*, cut a 45° angle on one end of all the decking boards *(both ends of boards near the house)*. At the center joist, butt the boards against the ones that have already been installed, then nail them to the center joist and to all the others.

◆ Mark and cut the overhanging ends flush with the frame.

PICKET RAILINGS FOR SAFETY

1. Cutting a post bevel.

Cut 4-by-4 railing posts to length, then bevel one corner of each.

◆ Determine post length by adding together the height above the deck of the finished railing, the thickness of the decking, and the width of a joist, and then subtracting the thickness of the cap rail. Cut all of the posts to this dimension.

◆ Mark a line across one face of each post, 2 inches from the bottom. Set the base plate of the circular saw to make a 45° bevel and cut along the lines *(right)*.

2. Plumbing and drilling posts.

◆ Draw a line on each post at the point where the top of the decking will meet it. Drive a large finishing nail halfway into each post above the line and just touching it.

◆ Have a helper hold each post in position with its weight resting on the nail while you drill a $\frac{1}{2}$-inch hole through the post and the deck frame. Insert a carriage bolt, fit a washer and nut onto the end, and tighten the assembly so the post moves only when tapped with a hammer.

◆ While the helper plumbs the post with a level, drill another hole and insert a carriage bolt. Tighten both bolts, then remove the finishing nail.

3. Attaching the rails.

◆ Cut 2-by-4 top rails and guardrails; nail them to the inside of the posts, flush with the tops and 2 inches above the deck surface. Secure the butt joints at the corners with 3-inch nails.

◆ Cut 2-by-8 cap rails with 45° angle mitered ends and secure them to the posts and the top rails using $3\frac{1}{2}$-inch nails.

4. Nailing pickets to rails.

Cut 2-by-2 pickets to extend from the underside of the cap rail to the bottom of the lower guardrail, then nail them to both guardrails with $2\frac{1}{2}$-inch nails. Use a piece of 2-by-4 as a spacer to ensure a uniform gap between pickets no more than 4 inches wide.

Stairs to a Low-Lying Deck

Steps for a deck built less than 2 feet above ground level are relatively easy to build, usually requiring no railing or anchors to the ground. Loads imposed on stairs are carried by treads that span descending boards called stringers, usually 2-by-12s. The top of the steps is fastened to the deck; the bottom rests on a concrete slab.

The Math of Stairs: The riddles of steps are how many will be needed and where they will meet the ground. As a first step toward solving them, measure total rise—the distance from the ground to the surface of the deck.

To find the number of steps, divide the total rise by 7 inches—the ideal height of a stair. For the 21-inch-high deck shown on pages 14-17, the number is 3. *(For fractional values, plan for a slightly higher or lower step, add a step, or subtract one).* Divide the total rise by the number of steps to get unit rise—the actual height of each step.

Allow for steps between 10 and $11\frac{1}{2}$ inches deep, a dimension called the unit run. Multiply this figure by the number of steps to get total run, the horizontal distance between the deck and the front edge of the bottom tread.

If your yard slopes slightly or the slab for the bottom of the steps rises higher than ground level, you may need to refine rise and run figures by repeating the foregoing measurements and calculations.

Meeting the Codes: Stairs are strictly regulated by building codes. Stringers carrying treads made from 2-by-10s, like those shown here, should be separated by no more than 30 inches. Check with local authorities to determine whether you need a stair railing *(pages 40-41)* or anchors for the bottoms of the stringers *(page 59)*.

TOOLS

- Folding rule
- Carpenter's level
- Framing square
- Circular saw
- Hammer
- Mortar tub
- Spade

MATERIALS

- 2-by-12s
- 2-by-10s
- 2-by-3s
- 1-by-4s
- Galvanized common nails (3- and $3\frac{1}{2}$-inch)
- Concrete mix

1. Establishing rise and run.

◆ Measure the approximate total rise of the steps from the top of the decking to the ground and divide by 7. Multiply the result by the tread depth to get total run. Mark this distance on a carpenter's level with tape.

◆ Rest the level on the deck, aligning the tape with the edge of the decking, then measure actual total rise at the end of the level *(left)*. Chalk a mark on the ground at this point, then measure another 15 inches out from this mark to determine where the front edge of the slab will fall.

2. Preparing the slab.

◆ Dig a hole 6 inches deep for the slab, about 1 foot wider than the stairs and 30 inches from front to back.

◆ Construct a rectangular form of 1-by-4s to fit in the top of the hole, with 1-by-4s nailed to the sides to keep it from falling in. Shim the form to level it.

◆ Fill the hole with concrete and finish it level with the top of the form *(pages 97 and 98)*.

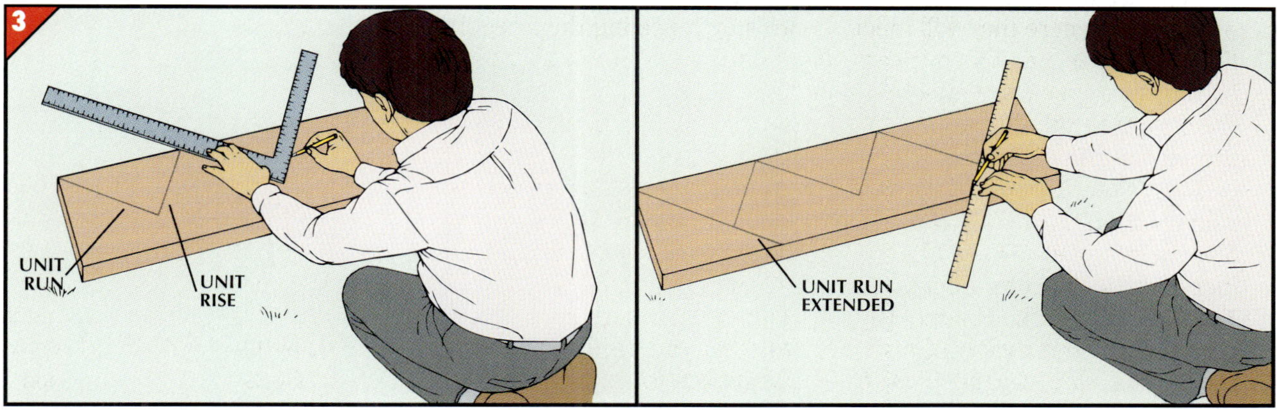

3. Marking unit rise and run.

◆ Recheck rise and run; from a 2-by-12, cut 2 stringers a bit longer than the distance from the top edge of the deck to the slab's front edge.

◆ Position a framing square on one of the boards so that the value for unit run on one arm of the square meets the corner of the board and the value for unit rise on the other arm meets the edge. Draw the unit rise and run on the board as shown above, left, and repeat the procedure for each step. *(Since the deck serves as the top step, only 2 stair treads are necessary.)*

◆ Extend the first unit-run line you drew and the last unit-rise mark across the board *(above, right)*.

◆ Mark the other stringer board as a mirror image of the first.

4. Cutting stringers.

Lay each stringer board across scraps of 4-by-4 or sawhorses. Cut off the ends of the board along the lines extended in the preceding step to produce the trapezoid shape shown in the inset at right.

5. Attaching cleats to stringers.

◆ Draw a line $1\frac{1}{2}$ inches below each unit-run line.

◆ Cut 2-by-3 cleats, mitering the ends for a neat appearance. Position each cleat as shown at right, then secure it with three 3-inch nails.

6. Installing stair treads.

◆ Secure the stringers to the inside faces of the deck railing posts with $3\frac{1}{2}$-inch nails. If you have not built a railing, use framing connectors to attach the stringers to the ribbon board.

◆ Cut 2-by-10 treads to span the distance between the stringers. Position the treads atop the cleats, flush with the front edge of the stringers, and fasten them with 3-inch nails driven into the cleats.

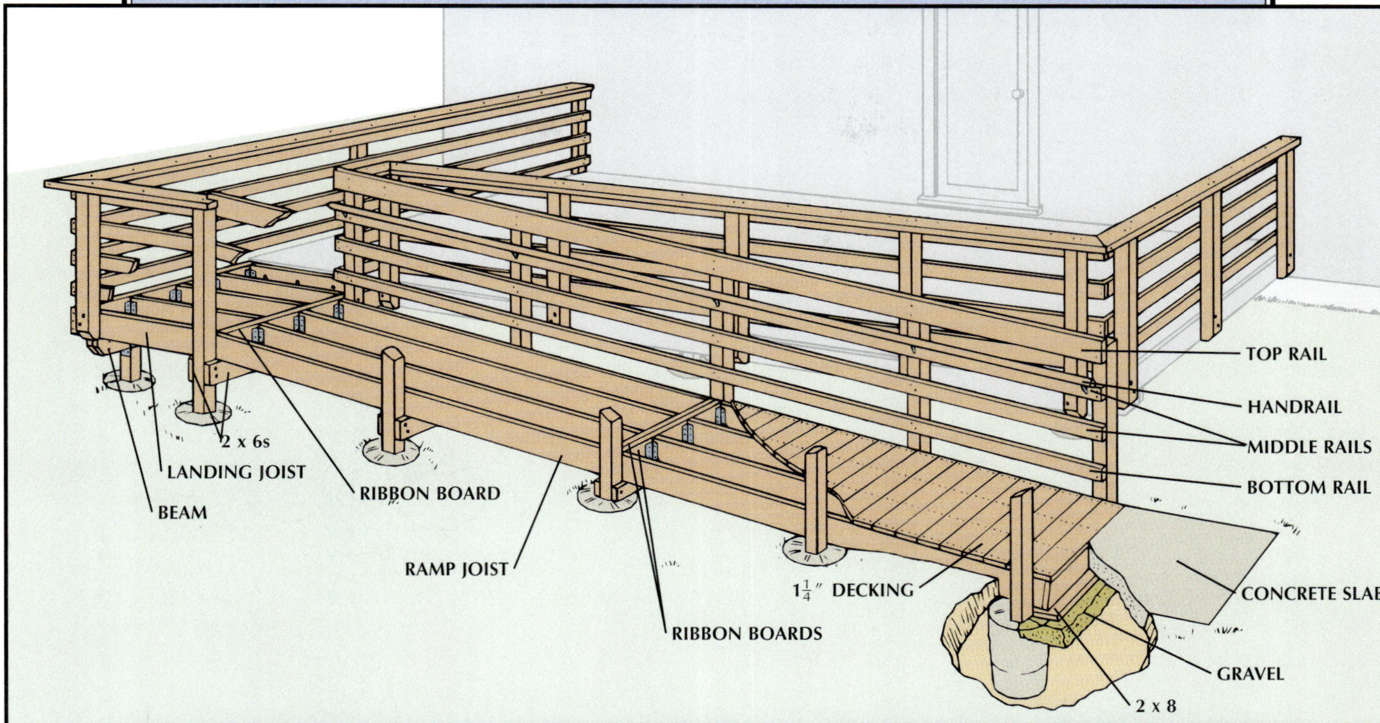

Sloping Access from the Ground

For those who get around with a wheelchair or crutches, a ramp can transform a deck from an obstacle into a delight. Most building codes specify that ramps rise no more than 1 inch for every 12 inches of run (1 in 20 is ideal), so they are practical only for low decks. For example, the 21-inch-high deck shown on the preceding pages would require a slope 21 feet long.

A ramp includes an upper landing at least 36 inches square (42 inches for wheelchairs), a concrete slab at the bottom, and the sloping platform between them. For small decks, a second landing midway in the slope allows a turn for a compact appearance. By augmenting the methods shown beginning on page 10, you can build landings as freestanding additions to any deck.

Landing joists are supported at one end by a beam atop 4-by-4 posts. A ribbon board covers the other ends of the joists and rests on a 2-by-6, one of two attached with $\frac{1}{2}$-inch carriage bolts to opposite sides of a pair of 4-by-4 posts. These posts—and others spaced no more than 5 feet apart along the ramp and joined by 2-by-6s—rest on concrete footings in earth-filled holes and serve as railing posts as well as support for the ramp.

The ramp is framed in modules made of 2-by-6 joists attached to ribbon boards with joist hangers. The top module has an angled end that fits flush against the landing; all other module ends are square. Joints between modules fall at the posts, each module resting on one of the 2-by-6s attached there.

At the bottom of the ramp, joists enter narrow trenches and rest on 2-by-8s laid flat atop undisturbed earth or 2 inches of gravel. The slab rises 1 inch above grade to provide a smooth transition to the $1\frac{1}{4}$-inch decking.

Railings are nailed to the inner faces of the posts. A 2-by-6, rounded to provide a firm grip, forms a top rail 36 inches above the ramp surface and 2 inches higher than the post tops. The space between the 2-by-4 bottom rail and the ramp surface is no more than 4 inches; middle rails are no more than 6 inches apart. A $1\frac{1}{2}$-inch round handrail is attached at a height convenient for a wheelchair user.

Overhead Coverings for Shade

Adding an overhead covering to a deck serves two purposes: It shields the outdoor living space from the sun, and it helps to integrate the deck with the architecture of the house. The covering can be a leafy bower, a simple arrangement of snow fencing unrolled on top of cleats, or a permanent structure of sun-filtering wooden louvers.

Building the Frame: The 8- by 10-foot frame illustrated on the following pages can be used to support these coverings and others. It will bear a moderate snow load of 20 pounds per square foot; if you live in an area of heavy snow, you should consult your local building department or a structural engineer for appropriate modifications.

Although the frame here is shown attached to a deck, you can adapt it for a concrete patio by securing the posts to the slab with post anchors and expansion shields. You can also build a covering if there is no underlying structure; in that case, the posts rest on concrete footings *(page 11)*.

In preparing to build the frame, buy posts somewhat longer than needed, so they can be cut to the right length once they are in place. You may also want to cut simple decorative ends on the beam and rafters, as shown on pages 23 and 24, before beginning construction.

Covering Options: The choice of covering depends largely on orientation and ventilation. If the deck or patio faces south and is heated by daylong sun, you may prefer a very dense covering for maximum shade. On the other hand, ventilation may be a concern; a solid cover attached to two or more house walls, for example, can trap hot air. In such a case, a more open covering would be a better choice. A deck or patio facing north is usually shaded by the house, so the covering can be chosen for its looks alone.

For decks with an eastern or western exposure, a covering that offers partial shade should be sufficient. A 24-inch eggcrate grid *(page 26)* gives moderate shade, especially in the midmorning and midafternoon. For more shade, install a checkerboard of 2-by-2 slats over the grid. Other choices for deep shade include snow fencing and fixed louvers.

In winter, a dense covering can keep warming sunlight from reaching the house. One solution to this problem is a covering that can be removed and stored. Another option is a deciduous vine *(page 27)*, which will lose its leaves in winter.

TOOLS

- Water level
- Protractor or T bevel
- Circular saw
- Chalk line
- Staple gun
- Saber saw
- Combination square
- Nail set

MATERIALS

- Flashing
- 4-by-4 posts
- 2-by-6 or larger framing lumber
- 1-by-6 lumber for spacers
- 2-by-2 slats
- Snow-fencing or woven-reed panels
- Post-and-beam connectors
- Joist hangers
- Carriage bolts ($\frac{1}{2}$- by 6-inch)
- Galvanized nails (2-inch and 3-inch)
- Galvanized finishing nails ($2\frac{1}{2}$-inch and 3-inch)
- Copper staples ($\frac{1}{2}$-inch)

SAFETY TIPS

Protect your eyes when hammering nails and when using a circular saw. Earplugs reduce the noise of this tool to a safe level, and a dust mask is advisable when sawing pressure-treated lumber, which contains arsenic compounds as a preservative. Wash any exposed skin thoroughly after handling pressure-treated lumber.

Choosing Lumber of the Right Size

When building a framework over a deck, the standard post size is 4-by-4. Lumber for the beam and rafters varies in dimension, depending on the distances they span. Use the chart below to determine the correct lumber for your needs.

BEAM

Distance between posts	Beam size
6 feet	two 2 x 6s
8 feet	two 2 x 8s

RAFTERS

Distance between ledger and beam	Rafter size
10 feet	2 x 6
12 feet	2 x 8
16 feet	2 x 10

ERECTING A STRUCTURAL SUPPORT

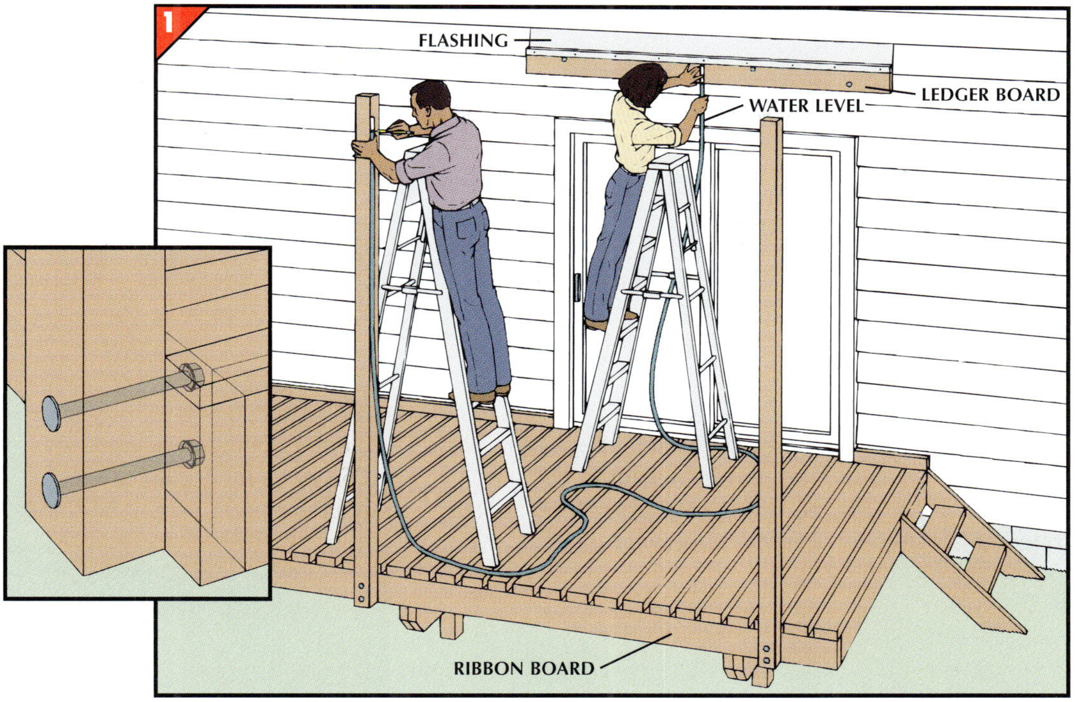

1. Securing the posts.

◆ Bolt a ledger board on the side of the house and add flashing *(page 33)*.

◆ On the outside edge of the deck, position two 4-by-4 posts flush with the bottom of the ribbon board, aligning the outer edges of the posts so that they are 2 inches in from the ends of the ledger; this leaves room to nail the outermost joist hangers to the ledger. Attach the posts to the ribbon board with 6-inch-long $\frac{1}{2}$-inch carriage bolts *(inset)*.

◆ With a helper, use a water level to mark each post at the height of the ledger's bottom edge. Then subtract the width of the beam lumber and cut the posts to that height.

2. Attaching the beam.

◆ Cut 2 boards for the beam, each 2 feet longer than the distance between posts to allow for an overhang on both sides.

◆ Nail the boards together at 16-inch intervals, using 3-inch galvanized nails and working from alternate sides of the assembly.

◆ Attach post-and-beam connectors to the top of each post and, with a helper, lift the assembled beam into them. Center the beam and nail it to the brackets.

3. Installing the rafters.

◆ Draw a vertical pencil line $2\frac{3}{4}$ inches in from each end of the ledger board to mark where the end rafters will be centered; this measure includes 2 inches for the joist hangers, plus half the thickness of the rafter.

◆ Subdivide the distance between the lines so that the interior rafters will be evenly spaced and no more than 2 feet apart. Center and nail a joist hanger over each mark.

◆ Mark corresponding lines on top of the beam, beginning $\frac{3}{4}$ inch in from the outer face of each post.

◆ Cut the rafters to length, allowing for a decorative overhang beyond the beam. Slip one end of each rafter into a joist hanger, and center the rafter over the corresponding line on the beam. Nail the rafter end to the joist hanger, then toenail the rafter to the beam using two 3-inch nails on each side.

◆ From the same size lumber you used for the rafters, cut blocking boards that will fit on top of the beam between the rafters to prevent them from twisting. Stagger the boards so you can end-nail them through the sides of the rafters.

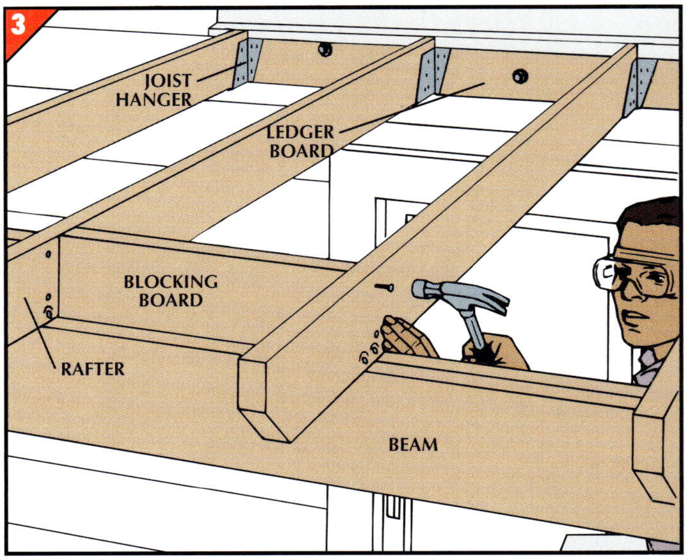

SHADE FROM SLANTED LOUVERS

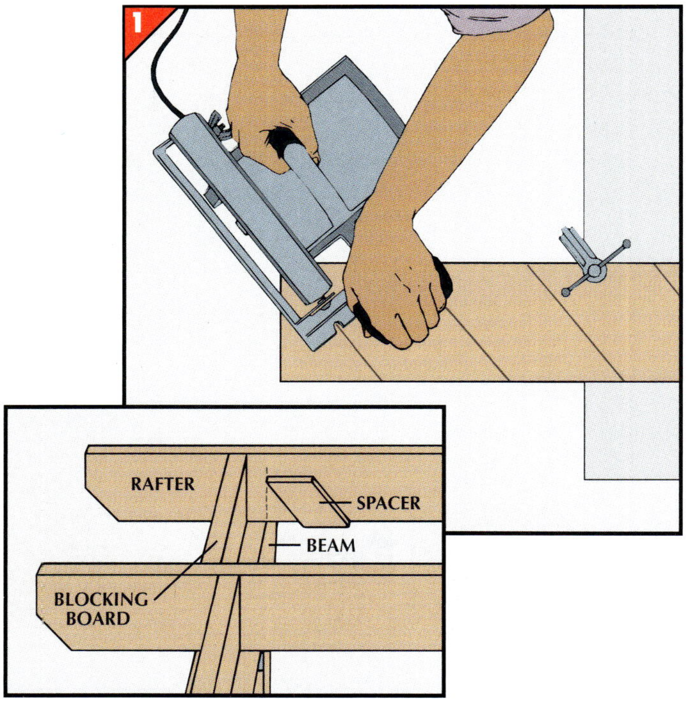

1. Cutting the spacers.

◆ With a protractor or a T bevel, mark a length of 1-by-4 lumber with parallel lines spaced 4 inches apart and angled to the desired slant of the louvers *(box, right)*. Then cut along the lines with a circular saw.

◆ Nail spacers to the beam ends of a pair of rafters with 2-inch galvanized finishing nails. The spacers should extend only as far as the inner edge of the beam *(inset)*.

Planning for Louvers

Shade provided by louvers depends mainly on two factors. One is the direction of the louvers. For decks with a southern exposure, louvers that slope down toward the house admit more sunlight, while louvers that slope up toward the house provide more shade. For an eastern exposure, downward-slanted louvers give the most sunlight in the morning; reversing the tilt offers more sun in the afternoon. The opposite holds for decks facing west.

The other consideration is louver angle. Although louvers are commonly angled between 40° and 50°, you may wish to calculate a louver angle that will capture maximum winter sun for your house. Find your latitude in an atlas. Round it to the nearest degree, and subtract it from 66° (the latitude of the Arctic Circle). Installing your louvers at the resulting angle will give you the greatest warmth in winter. This setting also blocks about 75 percent of solar radiation on the longest day of summer. To let in more summer sun, increase the louver angle; for less, decrease it.

2. Installing the louvers.

◆ Cut a 1-by-6 louver to fit between the two rafters, and nail it to the spacers with 3-inch nails. Place a second pair of spacers snugly against the louver and face-nail them to the rafters with 2-inch galvanized finishing nails. Attach a second louver to the spacers.

◆ Continue adding spacers and louvers until the entire row has been filled.

◆ Cut two filler-spacers shaped to fit between the last louver and the vertical face of the ledger, then nail them to the rafters.

◆ Add spacers and louvers between each pair of rafters in the same way *(inset)*.

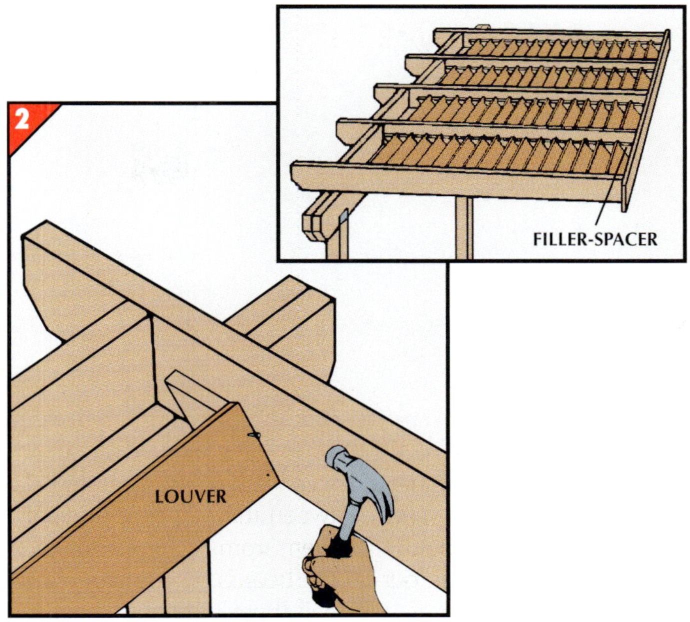

SUN SHIELDS OF WOVEN REEDS OR SNOW FENCING

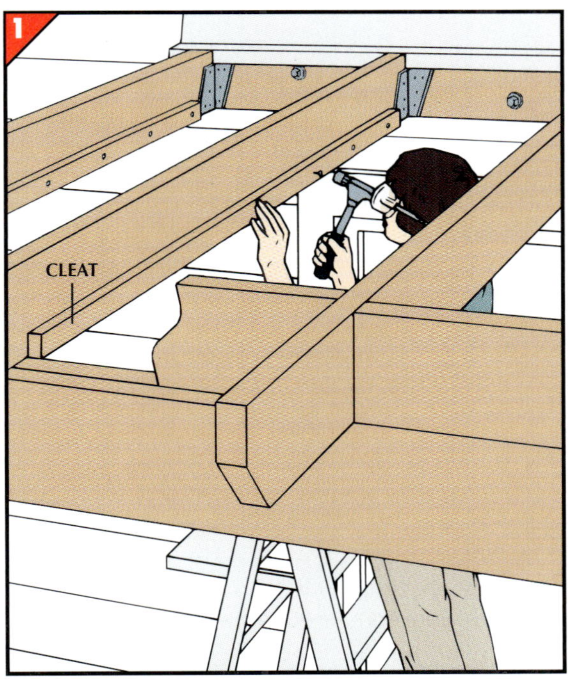

1. Installing cleats.

◆ To support frames for woven-reed panels, nail 1-by-2 cleats along the lower edge of each rafter with 2-inch nails. Make the cleats long enough to extend from the inner face of the beam to the joist hanger.

◆ Build rectangular frames of 2-by-2s to rest securely on the cleats, but fit them loosely enough to be removed in winter. The frame pieces can simply be butt-nailed to each other at the corners with 3-inch nails.

2. Attaching the reed.

◆ Lay a roll of woven-reed fencing over a frame and fasten it in place *(above)* with $\frac{1}{2}$-inch copper-plated staples spaced 2 inches apart. Trim away all of the excess fencing with a saber saw. Repeat this procedure for each frame.

◆ Lower the frames into place on top of the cleats *(inset)*.

◆ In windy areas, secure the frames with screw eyes set into the underside of the frames and screw hooks fastened into the cleats.

Shading with snow fencing.
◆ Install cleats in the same manner as for woven-reed panels *(page 25)*.
◆ Cut the fencing to fit between the rafters, leaving intact one of the two binding wires that hold the fence pickets together. Lay the trimmed fencing directly on top of the cleats.
◆ Nail a second set of 1-by-2 cleats on top of the fencing to hold it in place.

THE VERSATILITY OF ORDINARY LUMBER

Constructing an airy eggcrate.
◆ Beginning 2 feet from the ledger board, mark the bottoms of the end rafters at 2-foot intervals. Snap a chalk line between the pairs of marks to transfer the measurements to interior rafters. Then use a combination square to extend these marks to the vertical faces of each rafter.
◆ Cut crosspieces of rafter lumber to fit between the rafters.
◆ Nail the crosspieces between rafters at the marks with 3-inch galvanized finishing nails. Butt-nail the crosspieces through the sides of the rafters wherever possible, and use a nail set to sink nail heads into the rafter so they will not interfere with the installation of other crosspieces. Where butt-nailing is not possible, toenail the crosspieces to the rafters.

Adding a checkerboard grid.

For deeper shade, top each square of an eggcrate covering with eight 2-by-2 slats, each cut 24 inches long.

◆ Starting with a corner square at the ledger, place the first slat across 2 rafters so that its ends overlap half of each rafter and its inner edge overlaps half the ledger. Nail each end to a rafter with $2\frac{1}{2}$-inch galvanized finishing nails; make sure the nails do not angle back toward the ledger and pierce the flashing.

◆ Center the second slat between the rafters at the opposite end of the square, aligning its outer edge with the midpoint of the crosspiece. Nail its ends to the rafters.

◆ Fill the intervening area with 6 more slats, evenly spaced and nailed in the same manner. For less shade, use fewer, more widely spaced boards.

◆ On the adjacent squares, reverse the direction of the slats. To protect the top of the ledger flashing, face-nail a 2-by-2 nailing board to the ledger between the rafters. Nail the slats to the nailing board and the crosspiece.

◆ Continue in this fashion, alternating the direction of the slats on adjacent squares, to create a checkerboard pattern *(inset)*.

A LEAFY BOWER

Chosen and placed with care, a vine trained over an eggcrate covering, as shown at left, will control not only how much shade you get but when you get it.

There are many varieties to choose from. Some survive for years, but may develop slowly; others, such as morning glory or moonflower, grow as much as 25 feet in their single season of life, providing nearly instant cover.

Wisteria, grape, and other deciduous vines will cool a patio in summer; in the fall they will drop their leaves to let the winter sun reach the house. Evergreens, such as jasmine and Cape honeysuckle, will shelter decks and patios in southern climates all year long.

How much shade a vine will provide depends both on its growth habits and on its leaves. Vines that cling by means of hooks, thorns, or tendrils do not offer as much shade as those that twist densely around themselves and their supports. Vines with small, translucent leaves like those of the silver-lace simply filter the sunshine, while the large, opaque leaves of the English ivy or hop vine can overlap one another to blot out the sun.

Many vines have decorative fruits and flowers—but these can be a mixed blessing. Keep in mind that flowers, fruits, and berries tend to litter a deck or patio. They also attract bees and birds, a nuisance to some. And beware of some intriguing flowers, such as those of the Dutchman's pipe, which have an objectionable smell.

Decks for the Second Story

A deck that rises 8 or more feet above the ground shares much with similar structures built nearer the ground. For example, joist spans and spacing *(page 9)* are identical to those for a low-lying deck. Decking is also the same.

However, these taller structures require additional rigidity. Some comes from thicker, stiffer posts at the outer edge of the deck, the rest from a piece of lumber called a ledger board. Fastened directly to the house, the ledger board allows the deck to borrow strength from the larger structure.

Design Considerations: The layout of your house is an important factor in planning a high deck. The wall next to the deck must have a door—or a place where a new door can be added. Consider siting the deck with the door close to one end of the deck, to allow you to make the most of your outdoor space.

The overall height of the deck is dictated by the level of the framing for the adjacent house floor, to which the ledger is anchored. The deck surface is positioned 3 inches below the door. Any deck higher than a couple of feet off the ground requires a railing.

Structural Concerns: The technique for attaching the ledger varies according to the type of framing members in the house floor. If your house was built before 1970, it probably has a solid band of lumber for securing the ledger. A newer house, however, may have prefabricated framing components that lack the solid wood needed for anchoring the ledger. In such cases, you will need to strengthen the house framing before building the deck.

If your house has an unfinished basement or a crawlspace, look there to identify the type of framing you have. *(Without such accessibility, check with your local building authorities. They may have the builder's plans on file.)* If the boards resting on the foundation are solid lumber—usually 2-by-10 or 2-by-12—the framing will require no reinforcement.

The opposite is true if you see either I-beams or floor trusses *(page 33)*. I-beams look like their name: A cross section shows top and bottom 2-by-3s or 2-by-4s called flanges joined by a web of plywood or flake board about 10 inches high. Floor trusses are equally recognizable. Between the flanges runs a web of short diagonal pieces that form a zigzag pattern.

Building Codes: All the structural elements of your deck are governed by local building codes. Check them well as you plan your deck—before beginning construction. The design shown here conforms to most codes for decks from 8 feet to 3 stories high. Keep in mind that an inspector will want to check the deck framing and any house reinforcements that you make to accommodate the ledger. Leave your work visible until the inspection is completed.

CAUTION

Before excavating, establish the locations of underground obstacles such as electric, water, and sewer lines, and dry wells, septic tanks, and cesspools.

TOOLS

- Plumb bob
- Measuring tape (25-foot)
- Posthole digger
- Carpenter's level
- Chalk line
- Ladders
- Water level
- Circular saw
- Framing square
- Combination square
- Drill with $\frac{9}{16}$-inch and $\frac{3}{8}$-inch bits
- Hand ripsaw

MATERIALS

- Mason's cord
- Powdered chalk
- Concrete mix
- 6-by-6s
- 2-by-8s, 2-by-10s, or 2-by-12s
- Lag screws ($\frac{1}{2}$- by $3\frac{1}{2}$-inch)
- Carriage bolts ($\frac{1}{2}$- by 6-inch)
- Galvanized common nails (3- and $3\frac{1}{2}$-inch)
- Framing connectors and nails
- Aluminum flashing (7-inch)
- Decking

SAFETY TIPS

Wear goggles when hammering nails or sawing. Use a dust mask when sawing pressure-treated lumber, and wash your hands thoroughly after handling it. When you are sawing or drilling an unfastened board, have a helper steady it.

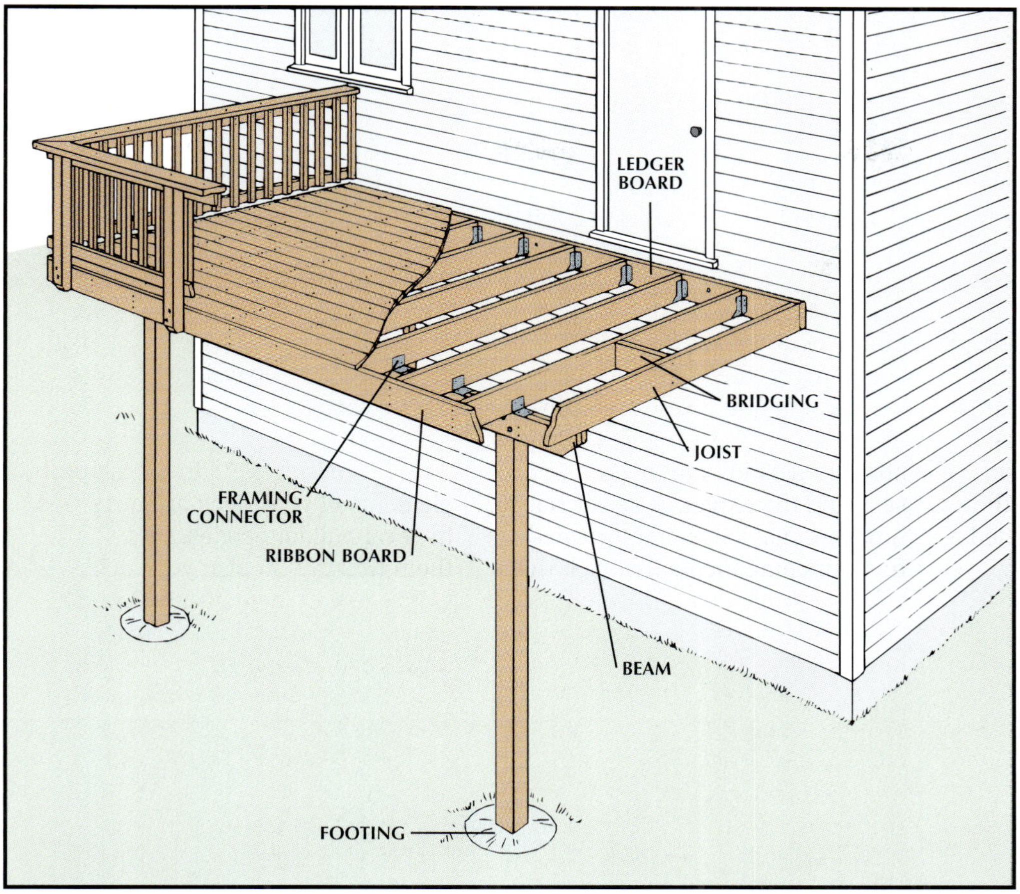

Components of a second-story deck.
This second-story deck is attached to the side of the house by a ledger board bolted directly to the house framing. Notched 6-by-6 posts embedded in concrete footings that reach below the frostline support a beam of doubled boards, which is bolted to the posts. The deck's joists are fastened to the ledger with joist hangers and to the beam with nails or framing connectors. A ribbon board covers joist ends. The decking and railing are identical to those shown on the freestanding deck *(pages 14-17)*.

ERECTING THE POSTS

1. Laying out the deck.

◆ Drop a plumb bob from the center of the door threshold and mark a reference line on the foundation. To do so, hold one arm of a framing square against the foundation with the outer edge of the other arm touching the plumb bob string. Mark the foundation at the corner of the square *(right)*.

◆ With this mark as a reference point, measure in each direction along the foundation to establish the width of the deck. Drive stakes at these points.

◆ Cut 2 pieces of mason's cord at least as long the planned depth of the deck. Tie a string to each stake, then use the squaring technique shown on page 10 to stake the strings at right angles to the house wall.

2. Marking footing positions.

◆ Measuring from the house, mark the beam's outer edge on each string. Stake a third string so that it crosses the first two at these points.

◆ Beginning at a deck-edge string, mark the length of the beam overhang *(page 9)*, on the beam string. Drop a plumb bob from that point and spray a chalk mark *(right)*. After repeating this process on the other side of the deck, take down the beam string, leaving the stakes in place.

◆ At each chalk mark, dig a hole 16 inches square, extending below the frostline. Pour 8 inches of concrete into each hole. Replace the beam string and allow the concrete to harden up to 48 hours.

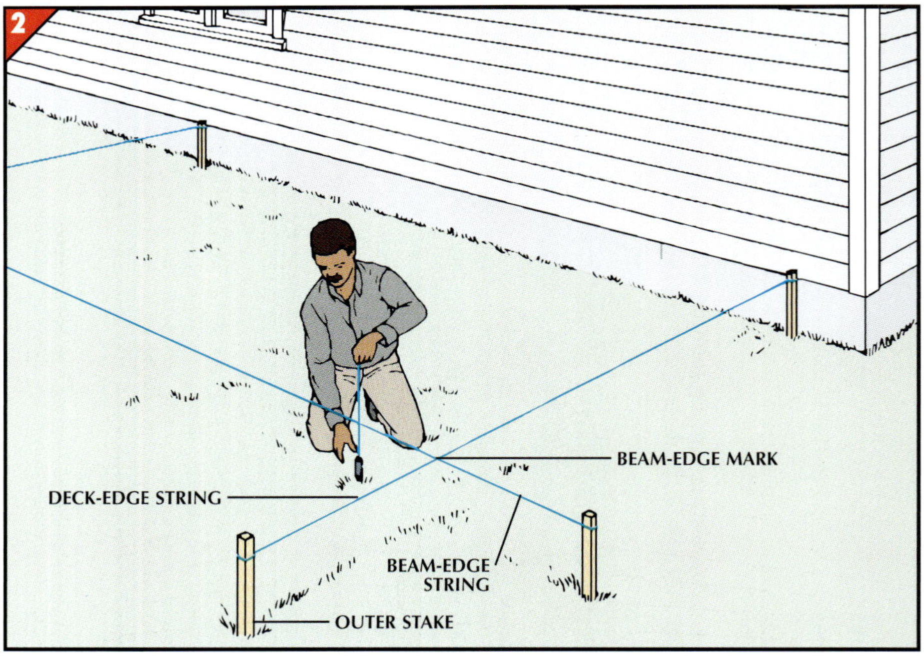

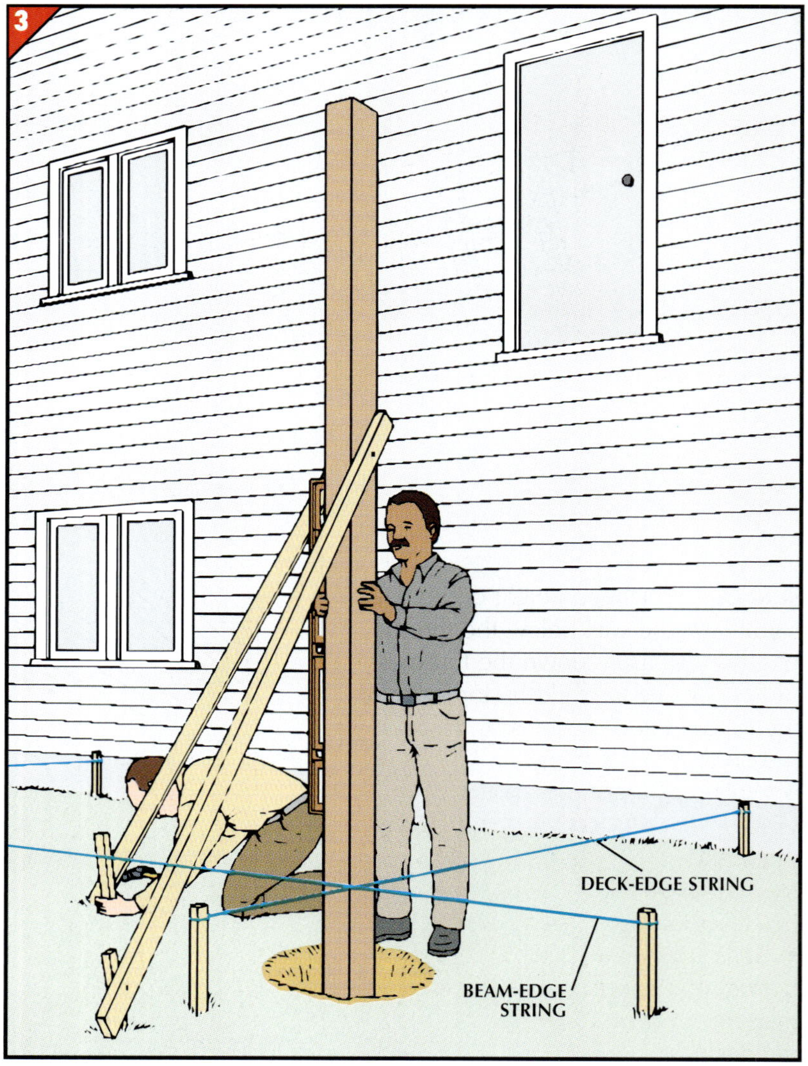

3. Setting the posts.

◆ Set an uncut post on each footing, with the post corner at the intesection of the deck-edge and beam-edge strings. Pour 4 inches of concrete around the post.

◆ Fasten a 2-by-3 brace, 6 to 8 feet long, to one side of a post with a single nail or screw. Drive a stake into the ground within reach of the brace. While a helper with a 4-foot level holds the post vertical, fasten the brace to the stake. Attach a brace to an adjacent side of the post in the same way, then plumb and brace the other post.

◆ Pack dirt tightly around the posts and allow 24 hours for the concrete to harden.

1. Marking the width on the wall.
Have a helper hold a long, straight board upright against the wall and touching a deck-edge string. While the helper plumbs the board with a 4-foot level, draw a line on the house from a point several inches above the door threshold and extending more than 1 foot below it. Repeat this step at the other side of the deck.

2. Measuring for the cut.
◆ Mark the planned height of the deck surface on the wall below the threshold, then measure down the thickness of the decking to mark the top edge of the ledger. Pencil a similar mark for the bottom of the ledger.
◆ While a helper holds one end of a water level at the ledger top, hold the other end at the vertical line drawn on the wall in Step 1. Mark the line at the height of the water *(page 11)*.
◆ Transfer the height of the ledger bottom by the same means, then repeat the process at the other side of the deck.
◆ Snap chalk lines for the top and bottom of the ledger.

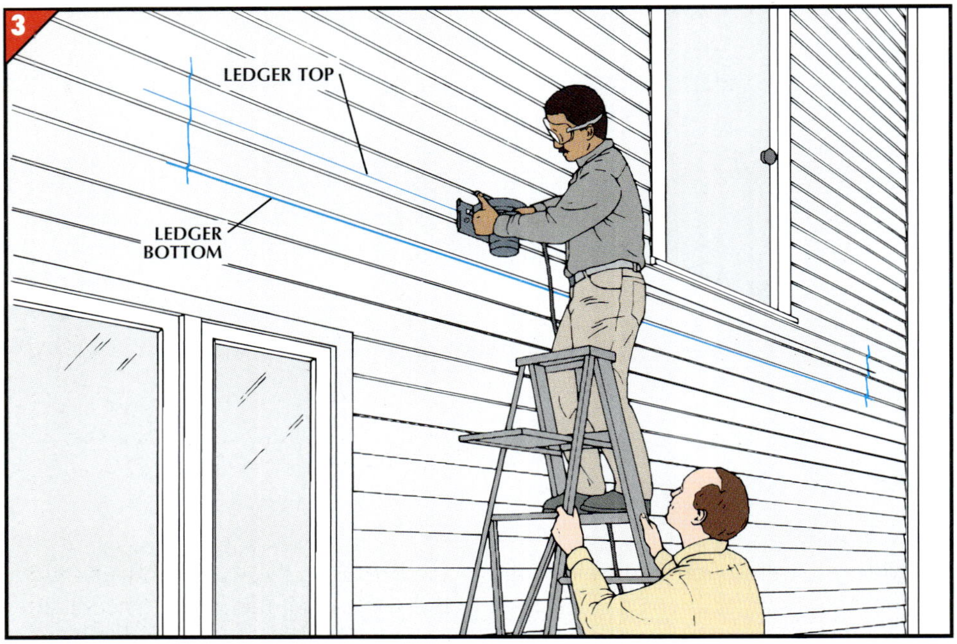

3. Cutting the siding.

◆ For wood siding, set a circular saw to cut through the siding but no deeper. Begin with a plunge cut *(box, below)* at one end of the area marked for removal. Next, saw along the ledger-top line as far as you can without leaning, then start a similar cut at the ledger-bottom line. Move the ladder and cut along both lines, continuing to the end of the ledger. There, make a vertical cut.

◆ With aluminum siding, follow the same procedure using a metal-cutting blade in the saw. Vinyl siding can be sawed with a blade intended for wood or cut with a utility knife guided by a straightedge.

TRICKS OF THE TRADE

Beginning a Cut in Siding

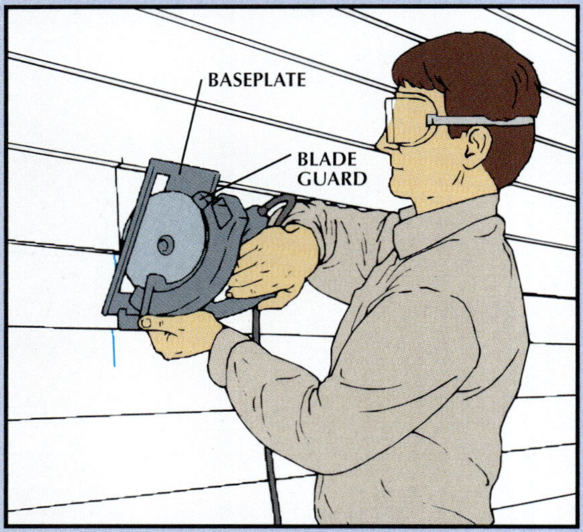

With your finger off the trigger, retract the blade guard with your thumb. Hold the saw with the back of the blade about 2 inches from the beginning of the cutting line, then rest the front edge of the baseplate on the board and tilt the saw so that the blade is about 1 inch above the line. Grip the saw tightly, switch it on, and pivot the blade slowly into the board. Turn off the saw, and after the blade stops turning, lift it from the cut. Reposition the saw and make another plunge cut to the beginning of the cutting line, and without turning off the saw, push it forward to complete the cut.

Make vertical cuts from the top down. Restart a saw in a cut 1 inch back from your farthest progress. If you hit a nail, back off and start a new plunge cut beyond it. Later, remove wood around the nail with a knife and pull or cut the nail.

4. Prying off the siding.

◆ Insert the flat end of a pry bar into the lower cut and lift the siding—wood, aluminum, or vinyl—away from the sheathing. Reach under the siding with wire cutters to sever the exposed nails.

◆ If the nails are too thick to cut, place a wood block under the pry bar to gain enough leverage to pull the siding farther from the wall, freeing the nails.

◆ Discard the siding, and hammer the cut ends of the siding nails flush with the sheathing.

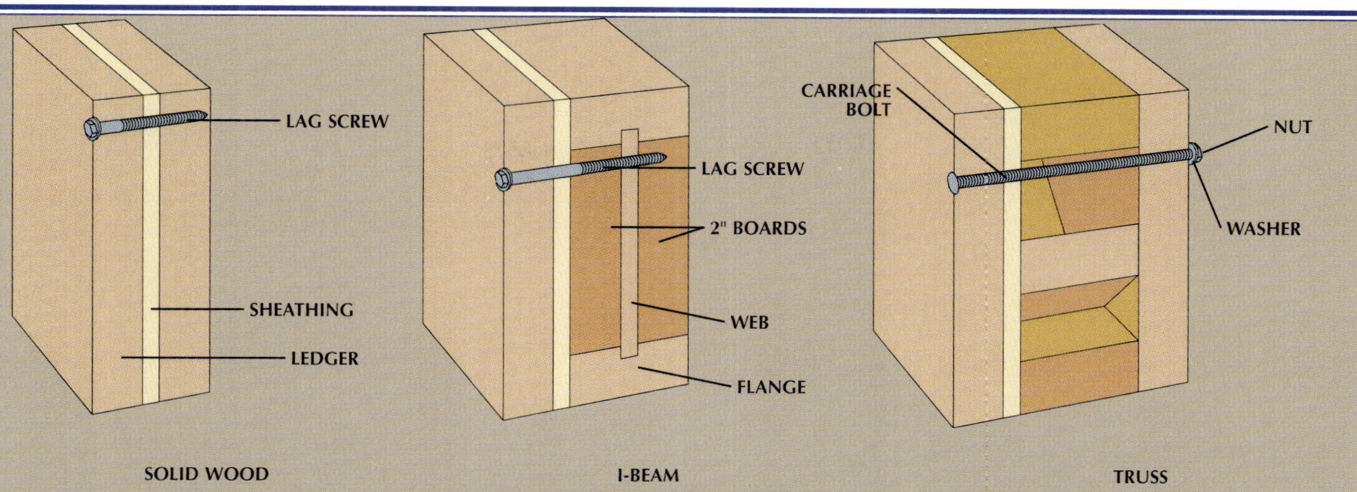

Attachments for Different Framing

In most cases a ledger is fastened with lag screws to the solid wood of a joist or ribbon board in the floor *(above, left)*. Some houses, however, are built with wood I-beams *(above, center)* or trusses *(above, right)*, which require reinforcement. The first step is to expose the inner sides of I-beams and trusses where the ledger will attach to the house. To do so, cut away the ceiling in the room below. Make an opening about 2 feet wide, measured from the wall, to allow room for hammering.

Reinforcing an I-beam.
Buttress this kind of framing inside and out, the full length of the ledger. Measure the distance between the flanges of the I-beam, and select 2-inch boards to fit. Working through holes in the ceiling, tack them to the plywood web. Outside, cut away sheathing to expose the web. Secure the boards to the web with carriage bolts, then nail the strip of sheathing back in place. Attach the ledger with lag screws.

Reinforcing a truss.
Strengthen a section at least as long as the ledger with 2-by-10s or 2-by-12s, whichever match the truss height. Attach the boards to the truss with 3-inch nails. Fasten the ledger to this board with carriage bolts.

5. Installing flashing.

◆ Cut strips of 7-inch-wide flashing to span the ledger opening, allowing for a 3-inch overlap between sections. Make a strip approximately 12 inches long for each end of the ledger.

◆ Bend each strip lengthwise, 4 inches from the edge. Push the 4-inch leg of the flashing under the siding, cutting slots for siding nails you encounter. Cut the end pieces so they can be folded to enclose the top corners of the ledger *(inset)*. Friction will hold the flashing in place until the ledger is installed.

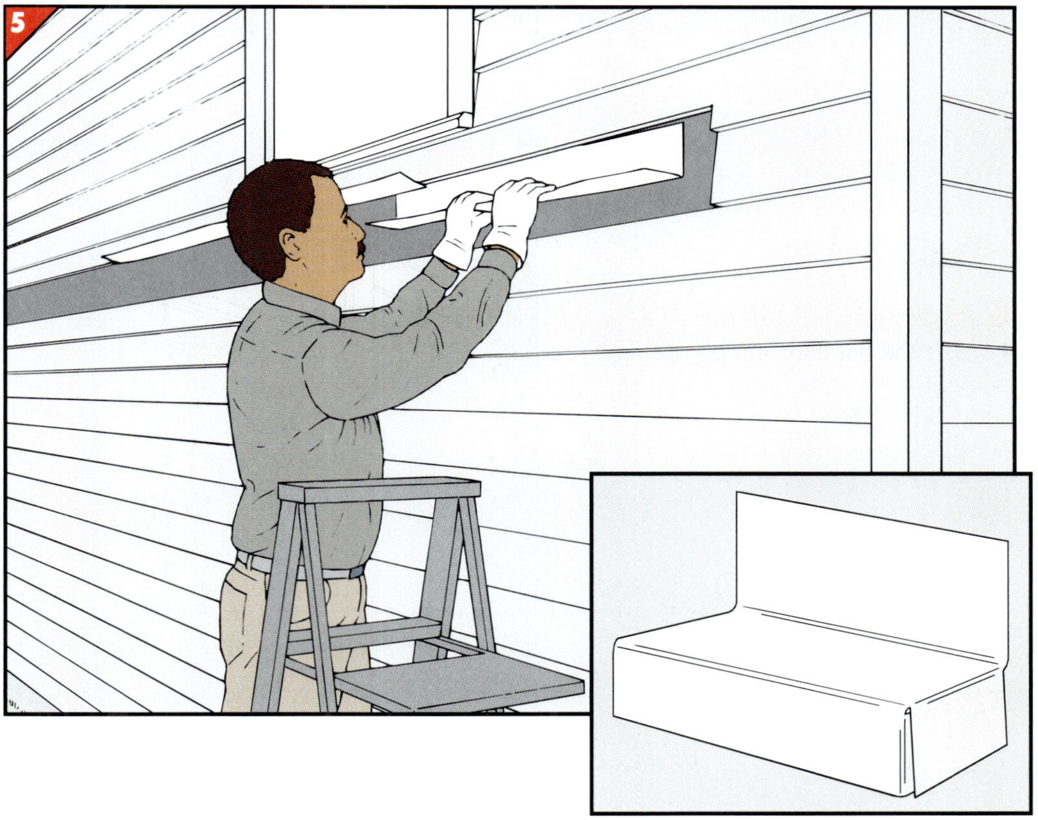

HANGING A LEDGER BOARD

1. Marking joist locations.

◆ Cut 4 straight pieces of joist lumber to deck width, one for the ledger, one for the ribbon board, and two for the beam. Clamp the pieces together, edges and ends aligned.

◆ With a combination square, mark the edges of the boards at 16-inch intervals, then pencil an X beside each line, away from the starting point.

◆ Unclamp the boards and extend the lines down the face of the one to be used as the ledger board. Install joist hangers as described on page 13, and attach an all-purpose hanger $1\frac{1}{2}$ inches from each end of the ledger.

◆ Starting 6 inches from one end, drill $\frac{9}{16}$-inch holes at 2-foot intervals, staggered as shown here *(inset)*.

2. Attaching the ledger.

◆ With a helper, lift the ledger into position under the flashing. Drive 3-inch nails at 2-foot intervals to hold the ledger in place.

◆ Fold the flashing over the face and corners of the ledger. To secure the flashing, nail it to the face and ends of the ledger with common nails.

◆ For mounting the ledger to a joist or reinforced I-beam in a house, bore $\frac{3}{8}$-inch holes for $\frac{1}{2}$- by $3\frac{1}{2}$-inch lag screws, using the holes already drilled in the ledger as guides. With trusses, bore $\frac{9}{16}$-inch holes for carriage bolts.

NOTCHING POSTS AND CONSTRUCTING A FRAME

1. Marking and cutting posts to height.

◆ With a water level, mark each post at the height of the bottom of the ledger board. Extend the mark around all four sides of each post.

◆ Trim the posts to height, beginning with a circular saw and finishing the job with a hand saw.

2. Marking post tops.

With a square, mark the top of each post for a beam notch as shown at left, taking care that the notch faces away from the house *(below)*. The width of the notch is always 3 inches, and the depth is equal to the width of the ledger board.

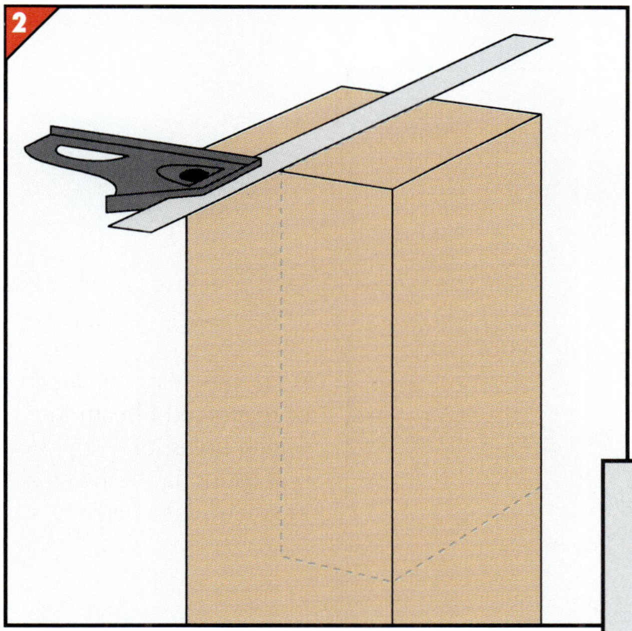

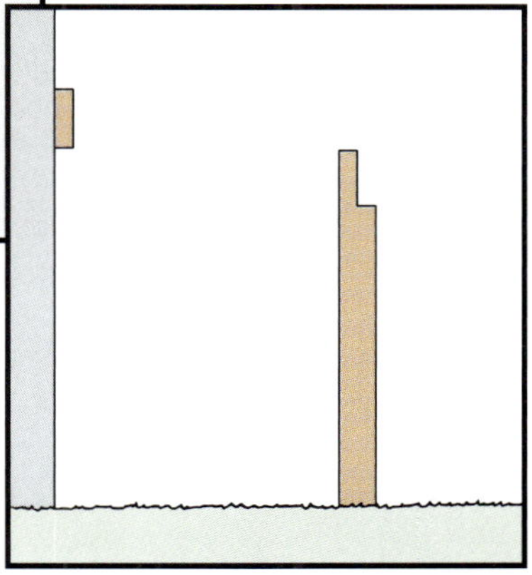

3. Cutting the notches.

◆ With a circular saw set to its maximum depth, cut across the top of the post and the side facing away from the house along the lines drawn in Step 2.

◆ Finish cutting out the notch with a handsaw. A ripsaw with about 8 teeth per inch is the most efficient tool for the vertical cut; nearly any saw will do for the small amount of wood remaining in the horizontal cut.

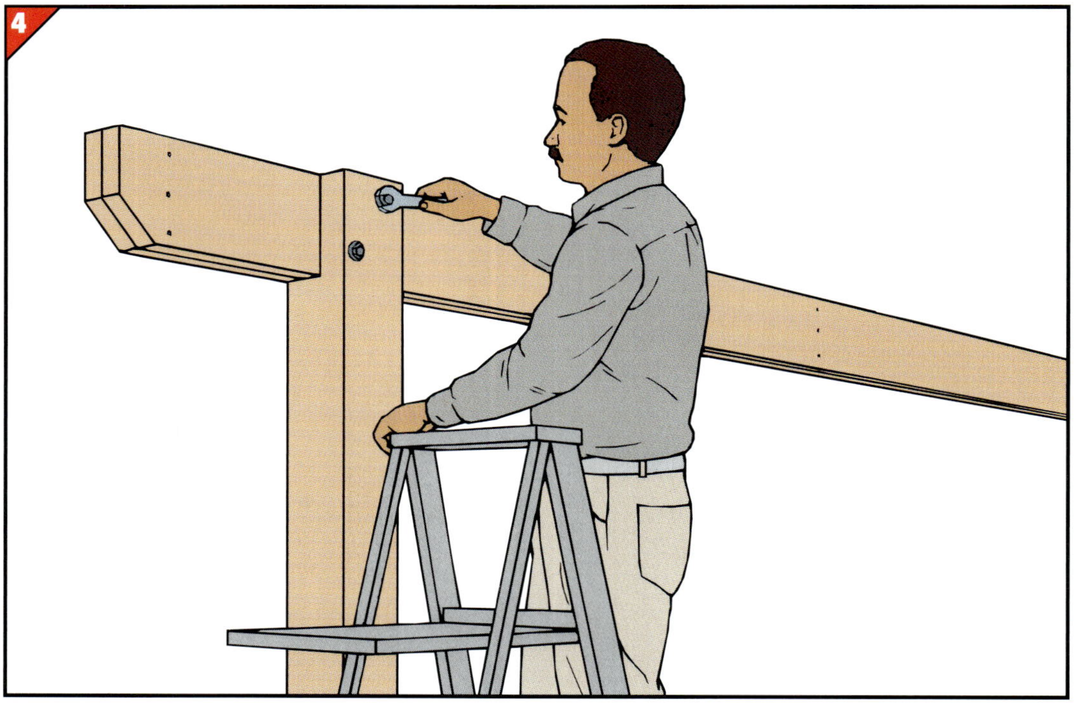

4. Attaching the beam.

◆ Make a beam *(page 12, Step 6)* with the boards' marked edges at the top. Set it in the notches of the posts, with equal overhangs. Toenail a 3-inch nail through the bottom of the beam into each post.

◆ On a diagonal across the notch—and at least 2 inches from the top or sides of the post—drill two $\frac{1}{2}$-inch holes through the beam and post. Secure the beam with $\frac{1}{2}$- by 6-inch carriage bolts.

◆ If the deck has more than 2 posts, drill and bolt the beam to interior posts after tightening the bolts at the ends.

5. Attaching the joists.

◆ Nail a multipurpose framing anchor to one end of a joist. Rest the board on the beam and nail the anchor to the ledger *(right)*.

◆ To install interior joists, place one end on the beam and the other in a joist hanger. Hold the hanger closed, then nail it first to the ledger, then to the joist.

◆ Use the marks atop the beam to align the joists perpendicular to the ledger. Secure each joist to the beam with a right-angle framing connector or with 3-inch nails toenailed through the joist into the beam, two on one side and one on the other.

6. Trimming the joists.

◆ Mark the joist length atop the two end joists, then snap a chalk line between these points across the tops of the interior joists. Use a square to extend the chalk marks down one side of each joist.

◆ Lay a 4- by 8-foot sheet of $\frac{1}{2}$-inch plywood on the joists as a work platform. Kneeling on the plywood, trim the joist ends with a circular saw, always cutting on the same side of the lines to ensure equal joist lengths.

7. Nailing the ribbon board.

◆ With the ribbon board on the ground, hammer three $3\frac{1}{2}$-inch nails into the board as follows: Below each mark made on page 34, Step 1, place one nail 1 inch from the top, one 1 inch from the bottom, and the third midway between the first two. The nail tips should barely protrude from the other side.

◆ With a helper to support one end of the ribbon board, nail it to the other end joist. While the helper raises or lowers the ribbon board to align it, nail it to the next joist and then to the remaining joists in succession.

Adding Custom Details to a Deck

Modifications to the structure of a deck allow you to adapt it to your own tastes. A stairway provides access to the yard from a second-story deck. An angled railing adds a touch of elegance, and benches provide built-in convenience. Joists cut to different lengths allow variations in deck shape. You can even frame a hole to accommodate a favorite shade tree.

Any option you add must conform to building codes, which govern everything from the spacing of stair rails to the method of attaching a bench. Submit plans to local authorities early to avoid last-minute changes at inspection time.

Variations in Technique: Any of these options may call for unusual construction methods. A hole or a cutaway corner, for example, requires adjustments to the framing before the deck is surfaced. The angled railing, on the other hand, is installed in holes cut through the decking. And stairs, whose stringers may be no more than 30 inches apart, should precede deck railings because railing posts at the top of the stairs can help support the deck railing as well.

Building a Landing: Most codes require a landing for stairs higher than 8 feet. Base the height of the landing on a multiple of the unit rise *(page 18)*. A landing must be at least 36 inches square. The distance between landing and deck is determined by the number of risers above the landing multiplied by the unit run—typically about 10 inches. Subtracting 15 inches from the result lets the upper section of the stairs rest on the landing. If the calculations produce an awkward position for the landing, you may want to modify the deck plans.

TOOLS

Deck-building tools *(pages 8, 18, and 28)*
Carpenter's protractor
T bevel

MATERIALS

Galvanized common nails ($3\frac{1}{4}$-inch)
Galvanized finishing nails (2-, 3-, and $3\frac{1}{4}$-inch)
Masonry nails (3-inch)
Carriage bolts ($\frac{1}{2}$-inch)
Joist hangers, single and double
Concrete
Mason's cord
1-by-2s
2-by-6, 2-by-10, and 2-by-12 framing stock
4-by-4 and 6-by-6 posts

VARIATIONS ON THE RECTANGLE

1. Altering the frame.

To shape the corners or edges of a deck, construct the framing as shown on pages 10-13 or 29-37, then cut away portions for the profile you want.

◆ For an angled corner, mark the end joist for cutting between the outside corner and the supporting beam, then make a mark on the ribbon board at the same distance from the corner. Cut both boards at the marks you have just made, removing the corner of the frame.

◆ Measure the distance between the outside edges of the cut frame members *(inset),* and transfer this measurement to a length of ribbon-board stock.

2. Closing the cutaway corner.

◆ To make a corner board, cut along the marks with a circular saw set at a 45° angle. Bevel the board so the outer face is longer than the inner one.

◆ Drill pilot holes in the ends of the corner board, then secure it to the end joist and ribbon board with $3\frac{1}{2}$-inch nails.

By cutting the frame elsewhere along the deck edge, you can create different shapes. Shortening a joist near the midpoint of an edge and adding angled ribbon boards creates a notch. Cutting the joists progressively longer from two corners of the deck out to the midpoint of one edge creates a curve *(inset)*.

3. Fitting an angled railing.

◆ After installing decking, add at least two 4-by-4 railing posts to each railing segment *(pages 16-17)*.

◆ Cut top rails slightly long and support a side top rail on nails driven partway into the posts. Hold the corner top-rail under the side rail, and mark the intersection points on both faces of each board.

◆ Take down the rails and connect the points with a line across the edge, then bevel both rails with a circular saw.

ADDING A STAIRWAY

1. Locating the bottom of the stairs.

◆ From a scrap of 2-by-12 lumber, cut a pitch block—a right-angle triangle with a 50° angle at one corner.

◆ Tack the pitch block to the deck where you plan to install a stair carriage *(inset)*. Stretch a string along the edge of the pitch block, and chalk a mark where the string meets the ground. Do the same for the other carriage.

◆ Enclose the chalk marks in a rectangle 6 inches wider and longer than a stair tread, with the front of the rectangle 2 inches in front of the marks *(dotted line)*. Dig a 6-inch-deep hole, pour and finish a slab *(page 19)*, and wait 24 hours before proceeding.

2. Installing the stairs.

◆ Cut 2-by-10 carriages *(page 58)*, making the first tread below the stair top $1\frac{1}{2}$ inches deeper than the others. Cut 2 facing boards, using a carriage as a template for cutting the ends.

◆ Nail the facing boards to the carriages, then nail each assembly to the deck, tops against the underside of the decking *(right)*.

◆ Nail the carriages to a 2-by-6 fitted between them on the slab, then drive four 3-inch masonry nails through the 2-by-6 into the slab. Add stair treads to the carriages *(page 20)*.

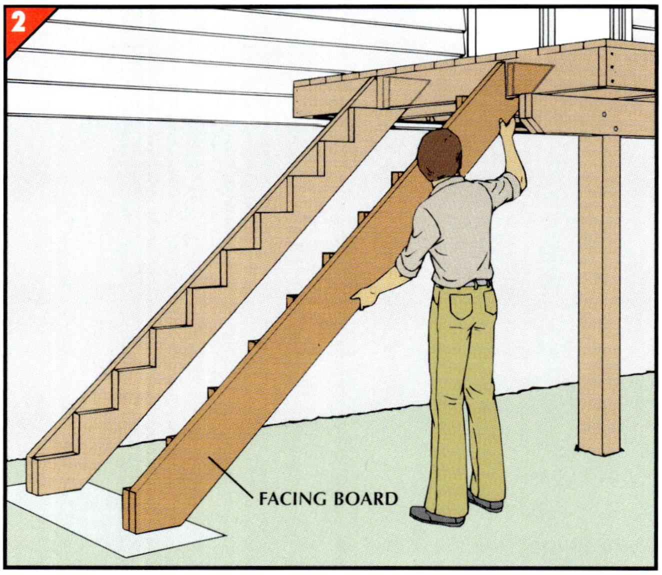

3. Adding stair-railing posts.

◆ At intervals less than 5 feet, bolt 4-by-4 railing posts to the carriages *(page 17)*. Set posts with the bottom edge nearest the deck aligned with the bottom carriage edge. *(At the top of the stairs, the stair railing shares posts with the deck railing.)*

◆ Use a framing square to mark the carriage-post tops for cutting; rest the tongue *(short arm)* on the edge of the facing board and pencil a line along the end of the body *(right)*.

4. Attaching the rails.

◆ Tack a 2-by-6 top rail to the posts, edge flush with the post tops. Draw lines across the rail at the outer edges of the top and bottom posts.

◆ Remove the board, cut it along the lines, and attach it with three 3-inch nails into each post.

◆ Mark and cut lower rails in the same manner, allowing gaps of no more than 4 inches between them.

5. Attaching the handrail.

◆ On the top rail, rest a 2-by-6 handrail long enough to extend about 4 inches beyond the bottom stair post.
◆ Mark the edge of the board on both sides of the top post and draw lines at these marks across the face of the handrail board. Between these lines draw another line $3\frac{1}{2}$ inches from the railing edge and parallel to it.
◆ Use these marks as guides for a 2-sided notch in the end of the handrail *(inset),* cut so that the end and the outside edge of the handrail fit flush with the top post.
◆ Mark and notch the other handrail in the same way, then nail the handrails to the posts and top rails.

BUILDING TO FIT THE SPACE

A stairway landing.

A landing is a miniature deck with doubled ribbon boards in lieu of a beam, joists spaced at 16-inch intervals, and standard decking. The ledger is anchored to wall studs with lag screws, and notched 6-by-6 posts support the ribbon board. For a freestanding landing, a second pair of posts can substitute for a ledger board, as long as postholes are dug more than 8 inches from the house foundation. The height of a landing is a whole-number multiple of the height of a step.

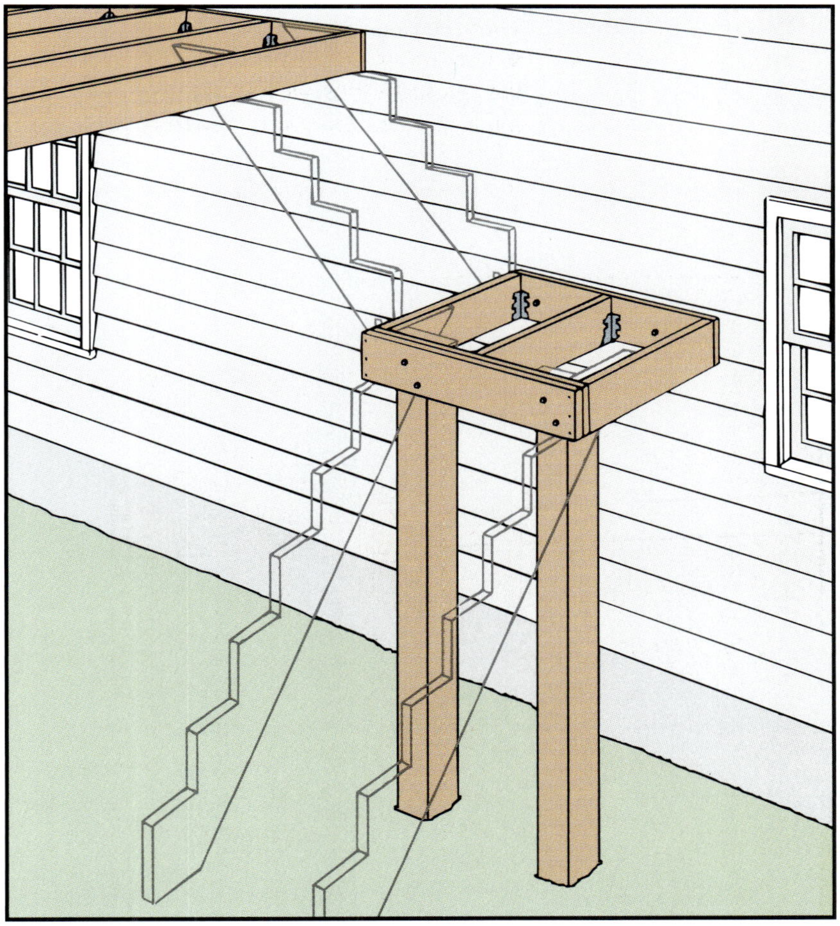

An aperture in a deck.

◆ To frame an opening—around a tree, for example—begin by doubling the joists on both sides of the hole. Double-wide joist hangers are available for this purpose.

◆ Between the doubled joists, insert headers, also made of two thicknesses of joist stock.

◆ For every joist location spanned by the headers, place a partial joist between the header and the ledger board on one side of the opening and, on the other side, between the header and the ribbon board.

◆ After the decking is in place, erect a railing around the opening.

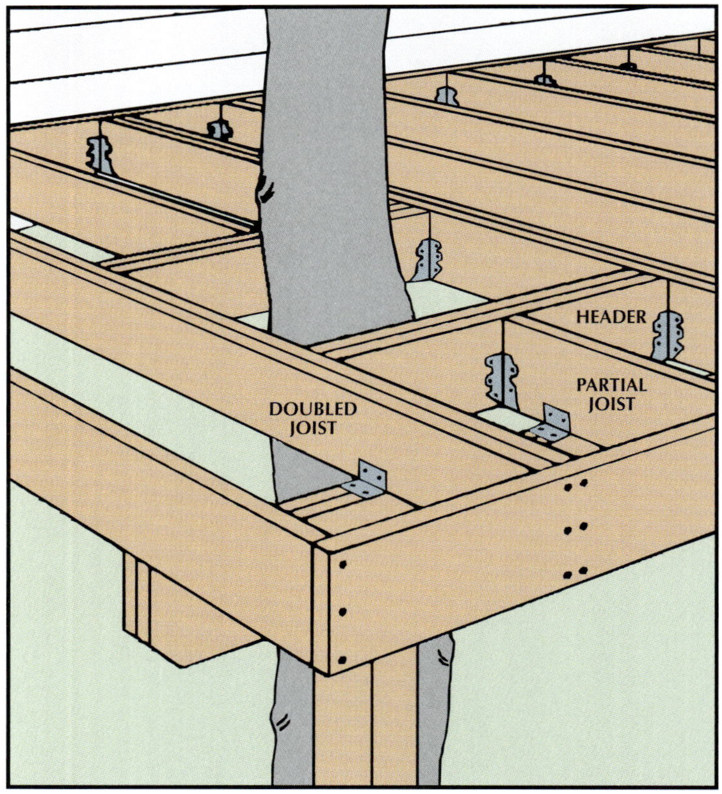

SLANTED RAILINGS FOR A DECK

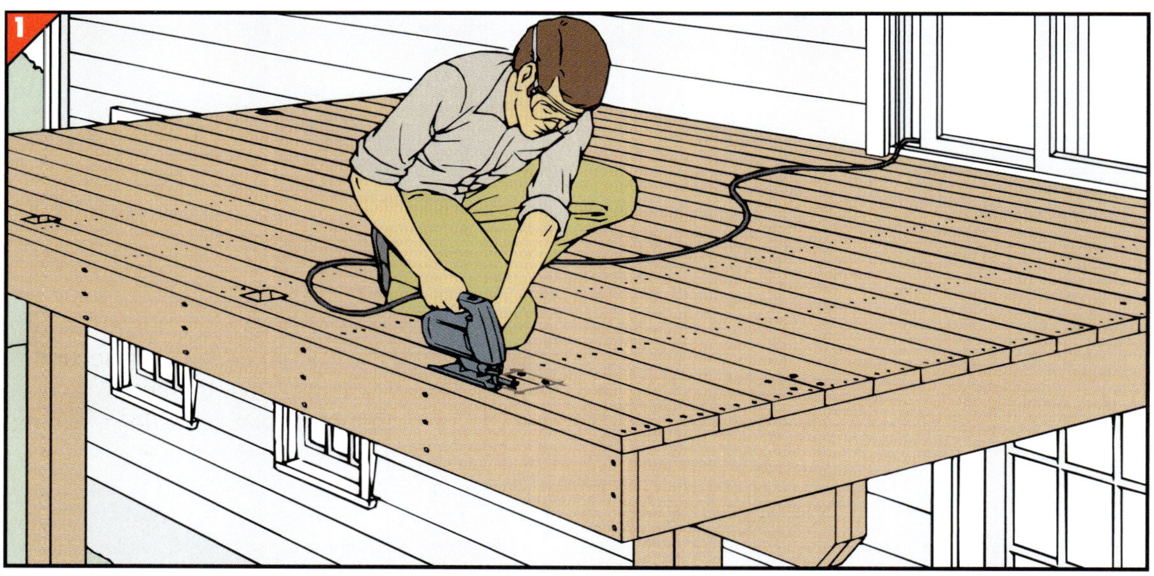

1. Cutting postholes.

◆ On the decking, mark openings $3\frac{3}{4}$ inches wide and $3\frac{7}{8}$ inches long, with the shorter dimension $1\frac{1}{4}$ inch from the deck edge. Position openings within 16 inches of the corners and no more than 5 feet apart. Along the ribbon board, each opening must have one long side adjacent to a joist.

◆ Drill 15° angled holes at the corners of each rectangle, tilting the top of the drill toward the edge of the deck. Saw the long sides with a saber saw set for a vertical cut; on the short sides, set the saw for a 15° cut.

◆ Nail bridging *(page 13)* next to one edge of each opening along the end joists.

2. Attaching the posts.

Follow the procedure on page 17 to install a 4-by-4 post in each corner hole, bolting each one to a joist or bridging. However, instead of anchoring the posts in a vertical position, use a carpenter's protractor to slant them at an angle of 15° *(left)*. Under the deck, align the inner corner of the post with the bottom of the adjacent joist or bridging.

◆ Measure 36 inches up from the deck surface on the inner face of each post. Stretch a string between the marks and use it to align the inner faces of the remaining posts as you install them.

◆ Make a cutting mark across each post at the height of the string, then set a circular saw for a 15° cut and trim the post tops level.

3. Adding the rails.

◆ Drive a nail partway into each post $5\frac{1}{2}$ inches from the top to support a 2-by-6 rail.

◆ Butt a rail board against the house, its end extending beyond the deck corner. Set the adjoining rail against the first. Mark the first board where the second touches its lower edge *(left)*. Mark the bottom edge of the second board 3 inches from the end.

◆ With a protractor set at $14\frac{1}{2}$°, extend cutting lines from the marks across the faces of the rails, making the top edges longer than the bottom ones.

◆ Miter the boards along these lines with a circular saw set at 44°, cutting so that the outer face of the board is the longer.

◆ Nail the rails to the posts and to each other, then add more rails, spaced no more than 4 inches apart, in the same manner *(inset)*.

BENCHES FOR THE PERIMETER

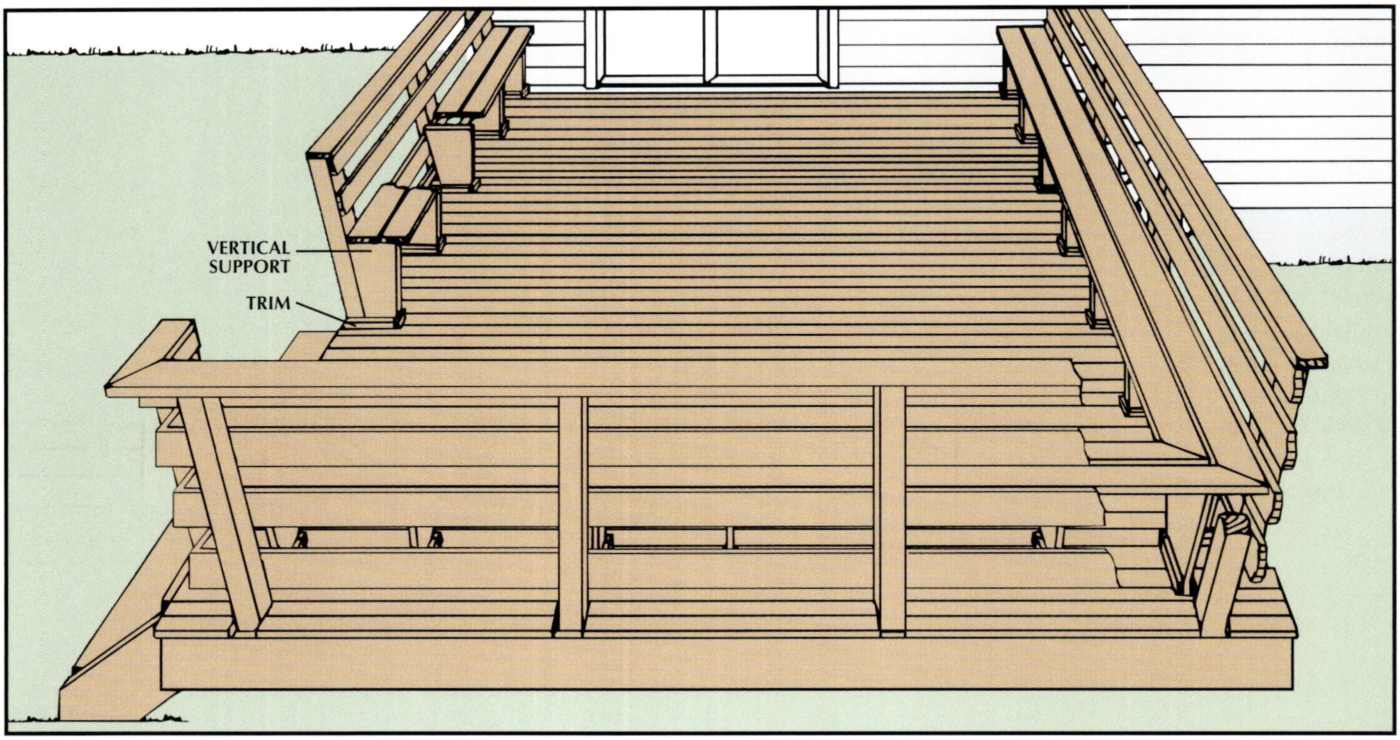

Elements of a built-in bench.
This wraparound bench uses an angled railing *(pages 42-43)* for a backrest. The lower rails on each side of the stair opening are cut away to accommodate vertical supports cut from 2-by-12s to match the angles of the railing posts and trimmed in 1-by-2 lumber at the base. Seat planks made of 2-by-6s rest on the supports, which are set at 30-inch intervals and nailed to the railings and decking.

1. Making bench supports.

◆ Cut 17-inch-long pieces of 2-by-12, one for each support required.

◆ Set the handle of a T bevel on the decking and align the blade with the bottom rail. Draw a line at this angle passing through a corner and across the face of a 2-by-12 support blank. Clamp the blank to a work surface and cut along the line.

◆ Use this support as a template for the others. Make one of them the same shape as the first; cut the others $1\frac{1}{2}$ inches narrower to account for railing thickness *(inset)*.

2. Installing the supports.

◆ With a circular saw, trim $1\frac{1}{2}$ inches from the 2 bottom rails at the stair opening. Position an end support against the post and the rail ends, and drive two $3\frac{1}{4}$-inch nails through the support into the end of each rail. Toenail the support to the decking with 3 nails angled through each side.

◆ Install intermediate supports at intervals of 30 inches or less. If a support falls at a post, move it far enough to one side to allow nailing through railings. Toenail support bottoms to the decking *(inset)*.

◆ Hide the toenails with strips of 1-by-2 lumber fastened to the supports with 2-inch finishing nails.

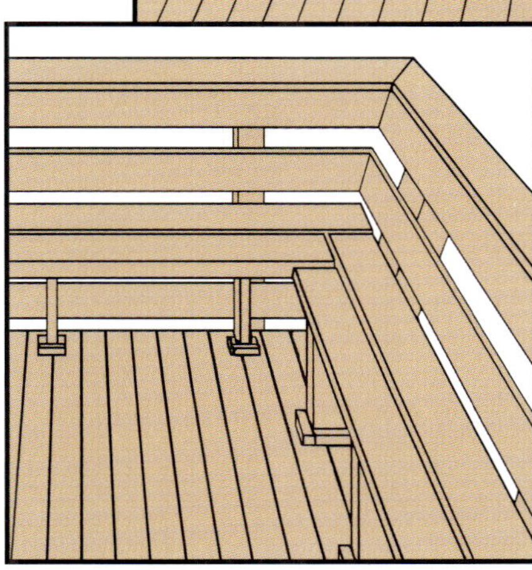

3. Attaching seat planks.

◆ Miter one end of four 2-by-6s at a 45° angle to fit together at a corner. Tack the planks to the supports leaving $\frac{1}{8}$ inch between the boards. Over the midpoint of each support, pencil a mark on the unmitered end, staggering the marks to fall at different supports.

◆ Remove the planks, cut them, and nail them in place with three $3\frac{1}{4}$-inch nails at each support.

◆ Plank the other corners in the same way, then measure, cut, and install intermediate planks.

◆ To make a herringbone corner *(inset)*, leave the plank ends square and butt them end to edge.

Spacious Porches with a Choice of Views

A porch can improve the appearance and increase the value of your home. The wraparound design shown on the following pages goes best with a large house, but you can easily modify the design to build a porch along one side of your house.

Either structure is a major undertaking. Before you break ground to begin construction, contact your local building authority for a building permit and the required schedule of site inspections.

Planning a Porch: Regardless of the shape you intend for your porch, draw a detailed sketch of the structure, making sure that it satisfies local codes. Position piers so that the concrete footings beneath them will not encounter underground utilities. Ideally, piers and the roof supports above them should frame rather than block doors and windows. If your property slopes more than 3 feet in 8, have a professional excavator level it. Concrete steps or sidewalks may need to be partially demolished.

In most porches, the floor lies one step—6 to $7\frac{1}{2}$ inches—below the threshold of the door into the house. For a wraparound porch, plan wings of equal depth no greater than 10 feet. Doing so will enable you to build a roof with the relatively simple techniques shown on pages 60-71.

Lumber for the Frame: A porch 10 feet deep is supported on joists and beams of 2-by-8s. For narrower structures, consult the chart on page 9. Pressure-treated southern pine is the wood of choice. For every running foot of porch, you'll need 12 to 15 feet of 2-by-8.

Estimating Materials for Piers: Use the depth of your footing *(page 50)* in the formula on page 88 to calculate how much concrete to buy. Dry concrete mix is available in bags or you can buy it from a ready-mix company *(page 96)*.

Build the piers with standard construction-grade cored bricks. Pier height is the finished height of the porch floor, less the thickness of a floor board, the height of a joist, and a small amount to slope the porch for drainage *(page 88)*.

After calculating pier height, use a mason's rule—marked in inches on one side and in courses (rows) of brick on the other—to determine how many courses of brick each pier will require. Add one course to compensate for starting the pier below grade. Multiply the number of rows by the number of bricks in each *(page 51)* and again by the number of piers, then add 5 percent for waste.

Lay the bricks with mortar mix formulated for outdoor use. One cubic foot of mortar will bond 25 to 30 bricks.

Beyond the Basic Structure: Once the floor and stairs are in place, you can add a roof *(pages 60-69)* and a ceiling *(page 70)*, as well as a railing and columns *(page 71)*. When the porch is completed, paint the floor and the stairs with a finish coat made especially for porches and decks.

CAUTION

Before excavating, establish the locations of underground obstacles such as electric, water, and sewer lines, and dry wells, septic tanks, and cesspools.

TOOLS

- Hammer drill
- Circular saw
- Hammer
- Mason's level
- Plumb bob
- Try square
- Framing square
- Water level
- Power screwdriver
- Spade
- Posthole digger
- Mason's trowel
- Convex jointer
- Mason's rule
- Utility knife
- Caulk gun
- Power floor nailer and mallet

MATERIALS

- Concrete
- Bricks
- Mortar
- Powdered chalk
- 2-by-4s
- 1-by-6s
- 2-inch framing lumber
- 1-inch fascia board
- Tongue-and-groove flooring
- Aluminum flashing
- Silicone caulk
- Wood preservative
- Wood putty
- Joist hangers
- Joist-hanger nails
- Framing anchors
- Lag screws ($\frac{1}{2}$- by 4-inch)
- Lag shields ($\frac{1}{2}$-inch)
- Masonry drill bit ($\frac{3}{4}$-inch)
- Drill bit ($\frac{9}{16}$-inch)

SAFETY TIPS

Wear goggles or other eye protection when hammering or using a power saw, a dust mask when cutting pressure-treated lumber, and gloves when working with wet mortar.

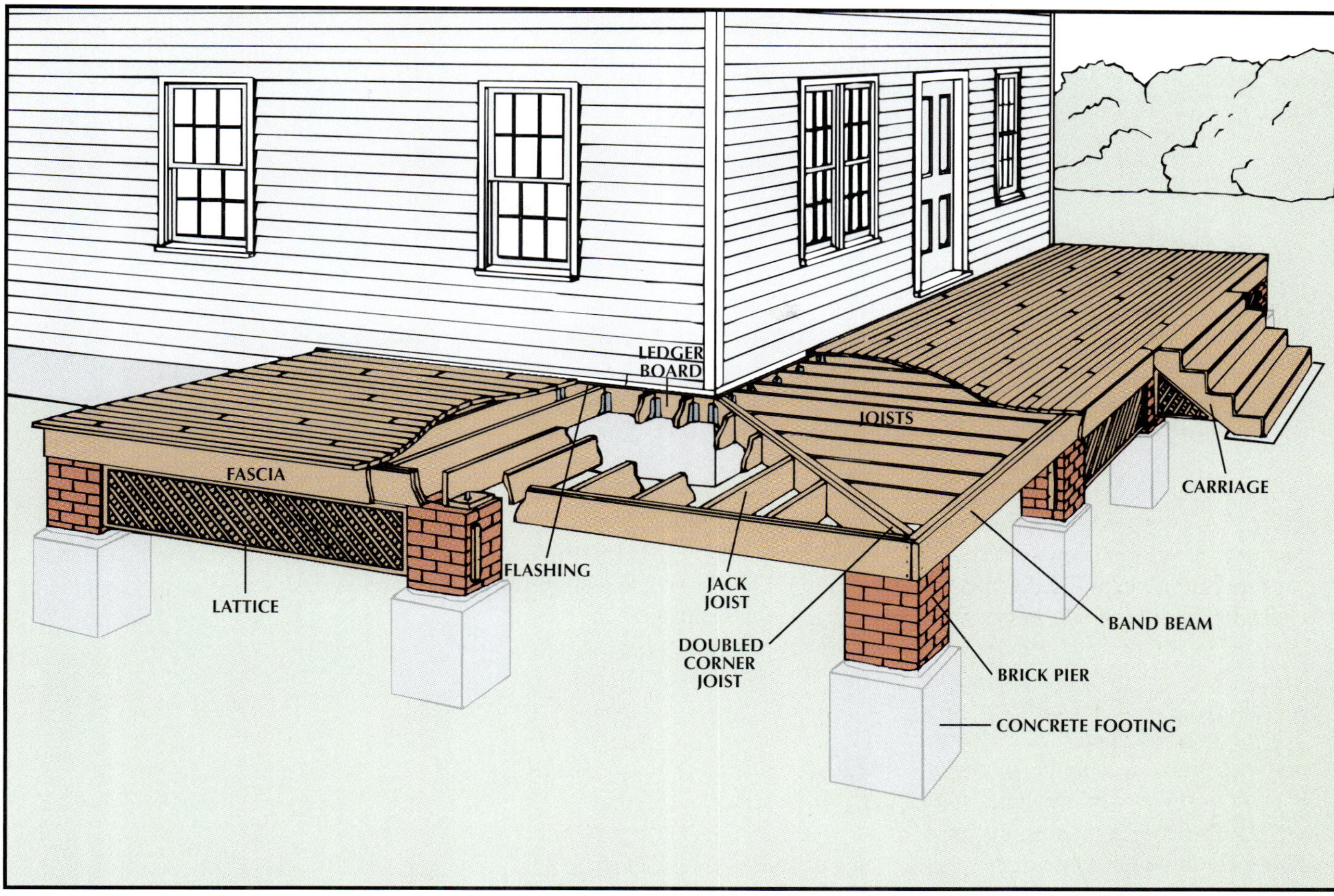

Anatomy of a wraparound porch. Brick piers built on concrete footings support a doubled band beam at the perimeter of the 8-foot-wide porch shown above. The larger central corner pier bears the additional load carried by a doubled corner joist. A ledger board bolted to the house wall supports the inner edge of the porch. Flashing prevents water from seeping behind the ledger board. Joists of 2-by-8 lumber between the ledger and the band beam—and shorter jack joists between the band beam and the corner joist—underlie a floor made of $\frac{3}{4}$- by $3\frac{1}{4}$-inch tongue-and-groove boards. The carriages that support a wide set of steps are fastened at the top to the band beam and rest at the bottom on a shallow concrete footing. A fascia board covers the rough lumber of the band beam, and lattice skirts enclose the crawl space underneath the porch.

CONSTRUCTING A LEDGER BOARD

1. Marking hole positions.

◆ Cut away house siding with a circular saw $\frac{1}{4}$ inch above the planned height of the porch floor *(page 32).*

◆ From the straightest lengths of joist lumber available, cut ledger-board pieces for each porch wing. Make one ledger board $1\frac{1}{2}$ inches longer than the length of the wing it will support.

◆ Four inches from one end of each ledger board—and every 16 inches thereafter—make a pencil mark on the centerline.

◆ Alternating 2 inches above and below the centerline, drill a $\frac{9}{16}$-inch bolt hole opposite each mark.

2. Installing the ledger board.

◆ Nail the board to the house wall—level, and $\frac{3}{4}$ inch below the porch-floor height.

◆ For a concrete foundation, bore $2\frac{1}{2}$ inches into the concrete through the lower holes with a hammer drill and a $\frac{3}{4}$-inch masonry bit, then seat expansion shields in the holes with the bit. Other foundation materials require a different approach *(box, below)*.

◆ Fasten the ledger to the concrete with $\frac{1}{2}$- by 4-inch lag screws and washers.

◆ Secure the upper half of the ledger board according to your house framing *(page 33)*.

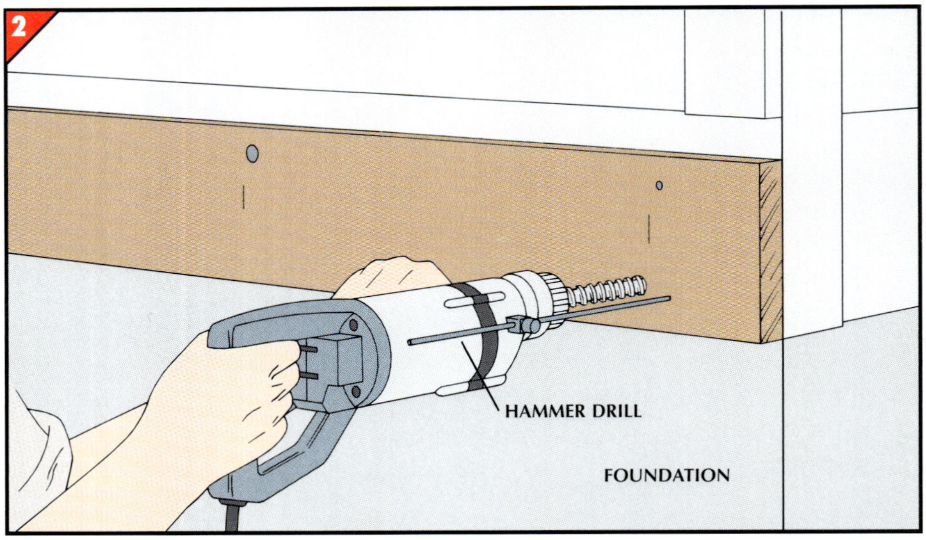

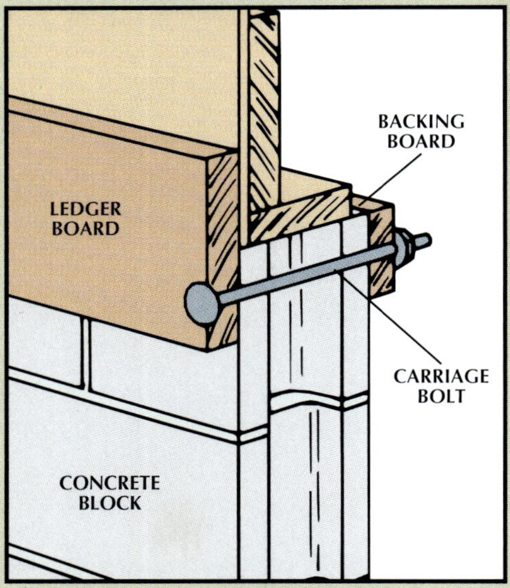

Dealing with Other Types of Masonry

To attach a ledger board to brick, hollow block, or a veneered surface, bolt it through a backing board on the other side of the foundation. Doing so requires access to the ledger location from inside the foundation—simple enough in an unfinished basement or tall crawlspace, more challenging in a finished basement.

Proceed by nailing the ledger in place and using ledger bolt holes *(page 47)* as guides to bore $\frac{3}{4}$-inch holes through the foundation with a hammer drill. Tack a 2-by-4 or wider backing board over the row of holes in the house interior, and use the foundation holes as guides to drill through the backing board. Place a $\frac{1}{2}$- by 12-inch carriage bolt in each hole. Inside the foundation, put a washer and nut on each bolt, and tighten securely.

PLANNING AND POURING FOOTINGS

1. Stakes for batter boards.

◆ Lay out a pattern of 5 small stakes as rough perimeter, or boundary, markers. Place stakes at the 3 corners of the porch and at the 2 points where the house walls, if extended, would intersect the perimeter *(dotted lines)*.

◆ Cut sixteen 2-by-4 stakes about 1 foot longer than porch height for batter boards. Drive pairs of stakes about 2 feet outside the perimeter markers, then remove the markers.

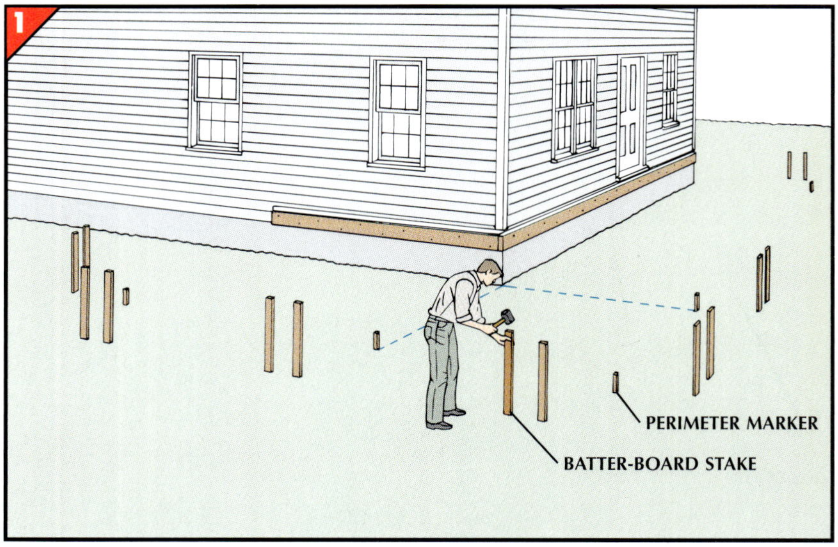

2. Erecting batter boards.

◆ With a water level *(page 11)*, mark the height of the top of the ledger board on the 2-by-4 stakes.

◆ Measure down from this mark a distance equal to the width of the ledger board ($7\frac{1}{2}$ inches for a 2-by-8) plus an amount for drainage—$\frac{1}{8}$ inch for each foot that the porch extends from the house. A mark at this point establishes pier height.

◆ Screw a 1-by-6 batter board to each pair of stakes with the top at pier height, making sure that the board is level.

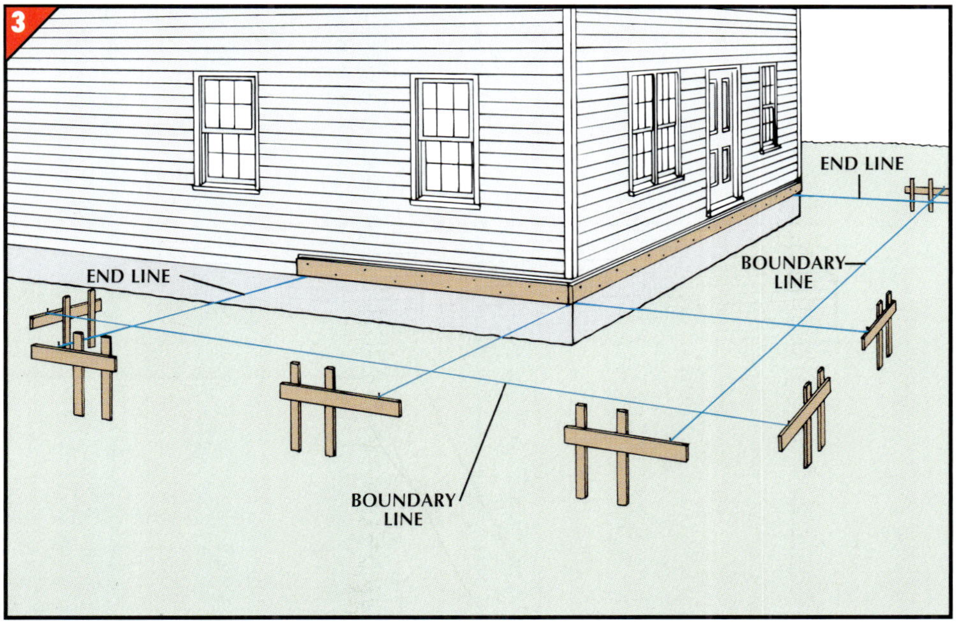

3. Stringing boundary lines.

◆ Hammer nails partway into the bottom of the ledger, one nail 8 inches from each end and one at the central corner.

◆ Tie 2 lengths of mason's cord to the corner nail, then use the squaring method described on page 10, Step 1 to align each string perpendicular to a house wall. Where each string crosses a batter board, hammer a small nail and loop the string around it.

◆ To establish the perimeter of the porch *(left)*, adapt the method for squaring a layout shown on page 30. Measure the diagonals of the two rectangles and one square formed by the strings as on page 12, Step 7 to make sure the layout is square.

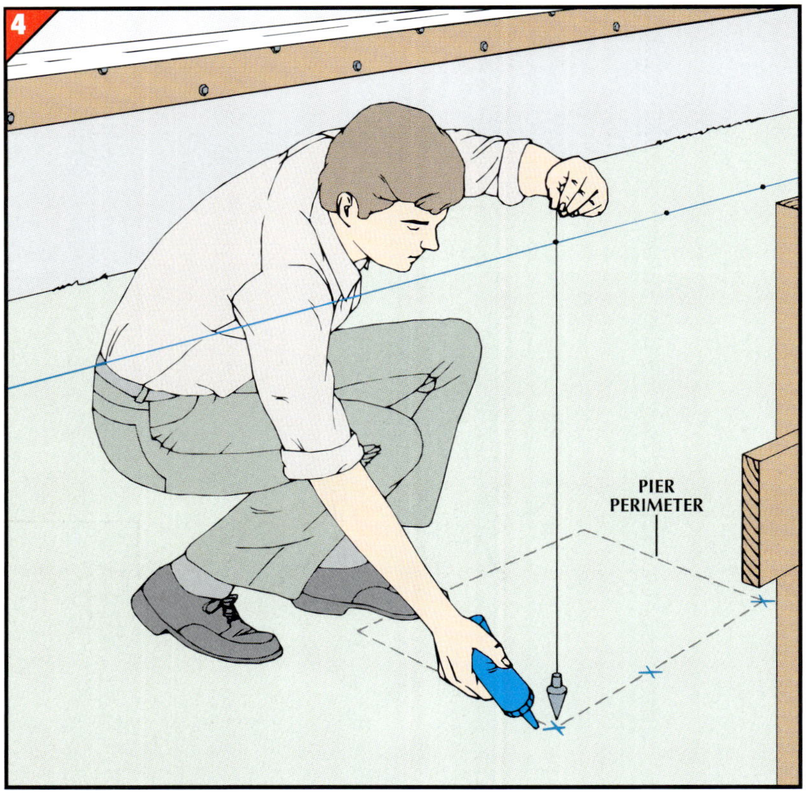

4. Establishing footing locations.

◆ For footings between corners, mark evenly spaced pier centers on the boundary and end lines of each wing. Space them no farther apart than the maximum span allowed for doubled beams of your joist lumber—9 feet for 2-by-8s *(page 9)*. Drop a plumb line 8 inches to either side of each mark and chalk an X as shown at left, then outline a 12- by 16-inch rectangle at each pier position.

◆ For the pier at the end of each wing, drop a plumb bob from the intersection of the boundary and end strings to establish the center of the pier. Chalk an X at that point, then outline a 12- by 16-inch rectangle on the ground, straddling the end line.

◆ Repeat the process at the boundary-line intersection to mark the corner of the pier at the central corner, but chalk a 16- by 16-inch square on the ground.

5. Constructing the footings.

◆ Unhook one end of each batter-board string.

◆ With a spade and a posthole digger, excavate footing holes at least 4 inches larger in each dimension than the outlines chalked on the ground. Dig 24 inches deep or 8 inches below the frostline, whichever is greater, then tamp the soil at the bottom to compact it.

◆ Pour concrete into each hole to a height 3 inches below ground level. Slice through the wet concrete with a spade in order to remove air bubbles and push large pebbles below the surface.

◆ Cover the footings with moist burlap and allow them to set for 24 to 48 hours.

6. Marking footings for piers.

◆ Reattach the boundary lines to the batter boards.

◆ Outline the shapes of the piers on the footings as you did on the ground in Step 4 above, using a try square to make accurate corners. Take down the boundary strings.

BUILDING BRICK PIERS

1. Laying the bricks.

◆ With a mason's trowel, spread a $\frac{3}{8}$-inch layer of mortar inside the pier outline. Furrow the mortar with the point of the trowel. Lay the first course of well-dampened bricks, buttering adjoining surfaces with $\frac{3}{8}$ inch of mortar. *(For a 16- by 16-inch pier, duplicate the pattern that is shown in the top inset at right.)*

◆ Trowel away excess mortar, then level and square the first course before laying the next.

◆ Stagger the joints in succeeding courses as shown in the bottom inset at right. At the end of each course, shape and smooth the joints with a convex jointer.

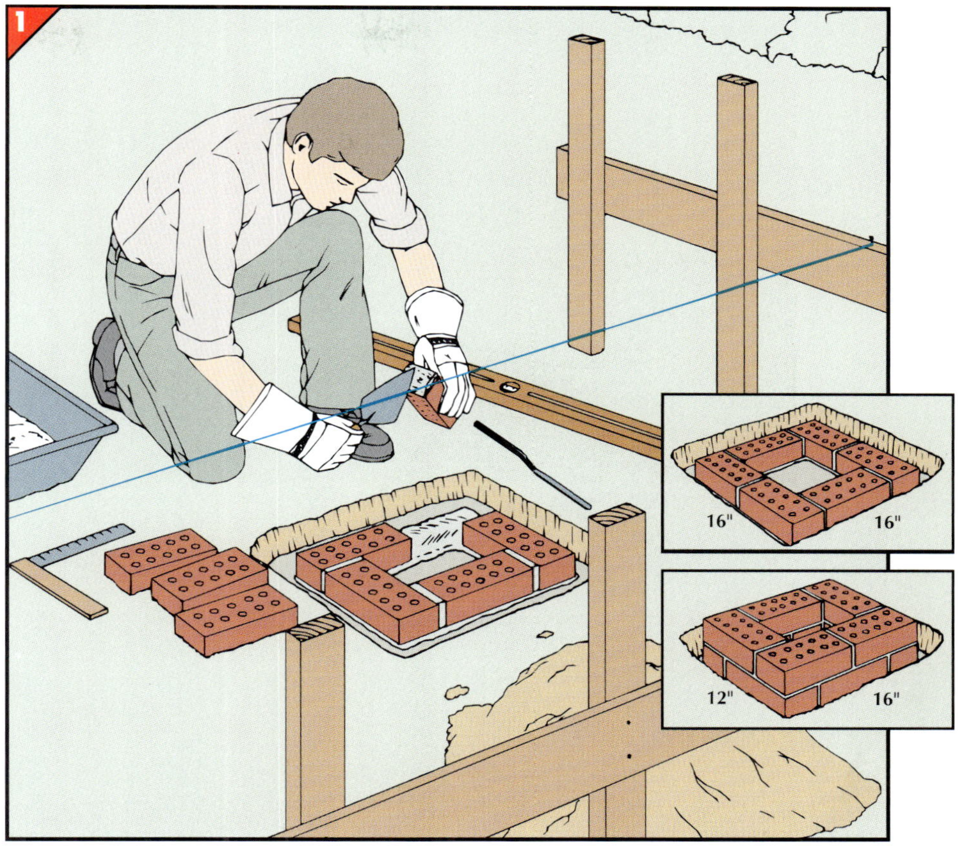

2. Completing the piers.

◆ When you have laid bricks to a point 4 or 5 courses below the planned height of the pier, gauge your progress with a mason's rule and a level set atop a batter board—or reattach the boundary line as a guide. If the distance to build is not an even multiple of the average height per course of the bricks you've already laid, adjust the thickness of the mortar joints on the remaining courses to compensate.

◆ After you have built all the piers, remove the batter boards and stakes.

3. Installing J-bolt anchors.

◆ Fill the piers to a point 8 inches below the top with rubble such as stones and chipped brick, then with mortar to the top.

◆ Before the mortar dries, insert a $\frac{1}{2}$- by 8-inch J bolt in each pier. For the large corner pier *(left)*, position the J bolt so it will not obstruct the porch's corner joist. Elsewhere, plant the bolt in the center of the pier. In every case, allow $2\frac{1}{2}$ inches of bolt threads to protrude from the mortar.

WEATHERPROOFING THE LEDGER

1. Flashing the top and ends.

◆ Loosen or remove house siding above the ledger to allow for flashing installation.

◆ Follow the instructions on page 33 to install flashing at both ends of the ledger and along the top of both wings to within 3 inches of the house corner.

◆ Cut 2 pieces of flashing to make a cap for the ledger corner: Make one piece $7\frac{1}{2}$ inches by 6 inches, and the other $7\frac{1}{2}$ inches by 10 inches.

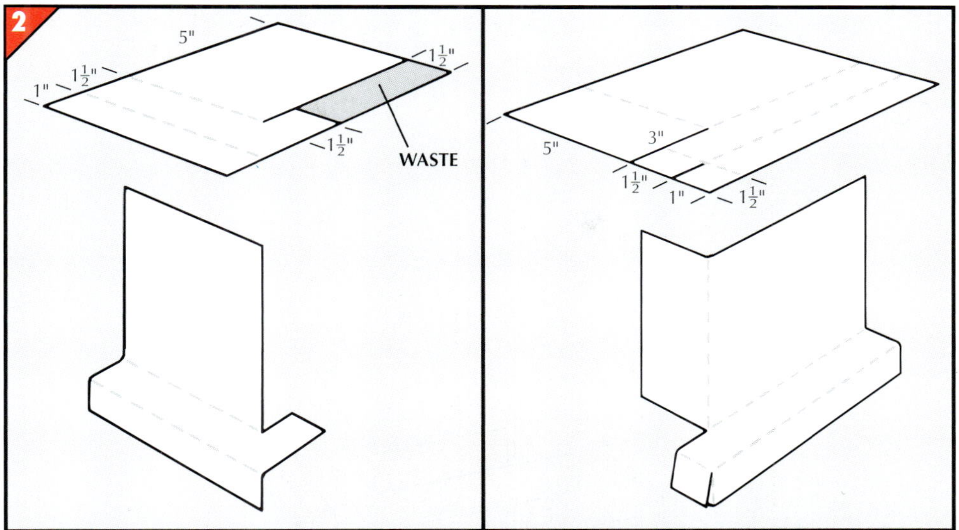

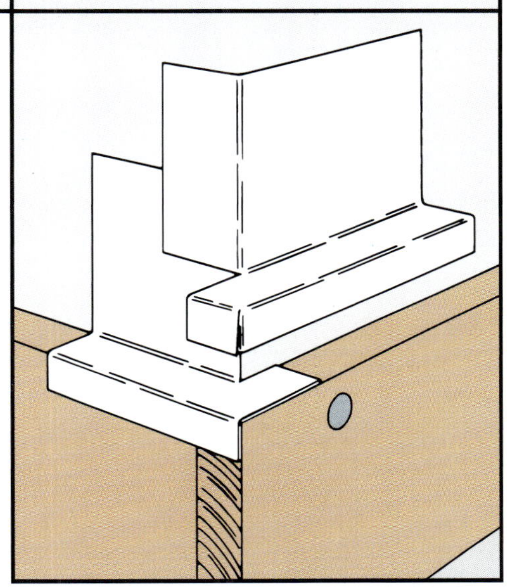

2. Fabricating corner pieces.

◆ Measure and mark the smaller piece of flashing as shown above, top. Cut along the solid lines with a utility knife, then using the edge of a table or a level, bend the flashing along the dotted lines to form the shape shown above, bottom.

◆ Follow the same procedure to mark, cut, and fold the larger piece of flashing into the shape in the illustration above right.

◆ The illustration at right shows how the 2 pieces overlap to protect the ledger corner.

3. Installing corner flashing

◆ Slip the upper edge of the smaller piece under the house siding at the ledger corner. Nail the flashing to the face of the ledger.

◆ Lay a bead of caulk where the seam between the two corner pieces will lie.

◆ Install the larger corner flashing piece. Fit it snugly over the smaller piece of flashing and the corner of the ledger. Nail it to the ledger face.

◆ Caulk all flashing seams.

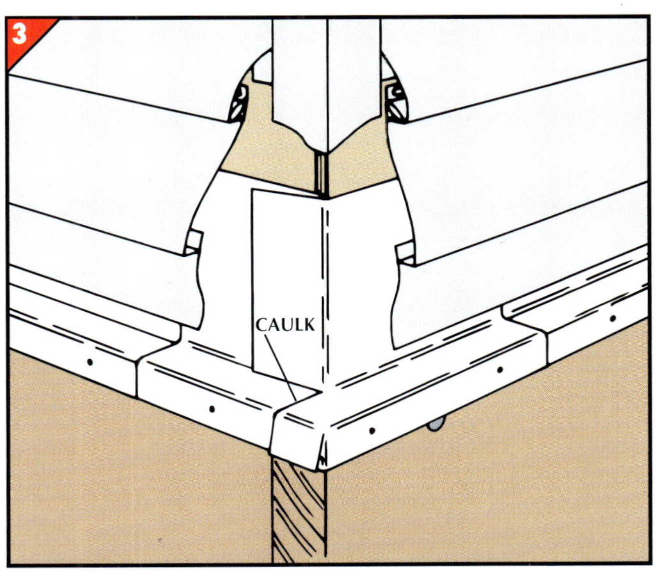

ASSEMBLING THE SUBSTRUCTURE

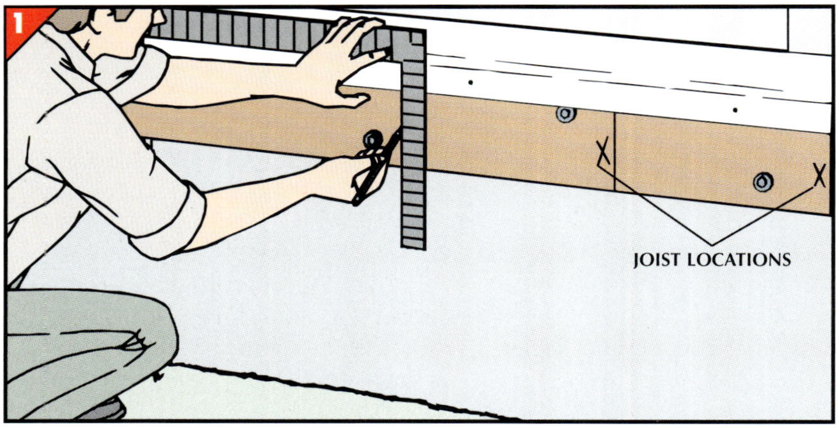

1. Establishing joist positions.
Align the body of a framing square with the top edge of the ledger at the end of one wing. Mark the sides of joist positions every 16 inches from the end of the ledger. To allow room for the installation of the doubled corner joist, adjust the position of the last full-length joist, if necessary, so it is no closer than 5 inches to the ledger corner.

2. Installing the first joists.
◆ On the top and the side of each pier, scribe a line 3 inches from the outer face of the pier and parallel to the house to mark the thickness of the double band beam.
◆ Select a piece of lumber for an end joist, crown it *(page 13),* and position it as shown at left. Make a cut mark where the board crosses the line scribed on the pier.
◆ Cut the joist to length. Attach a multipurpose framing anchor to the end with joist-hanger nails, then nail the hanger to the ledger. Repeat the procedure for the joist at the end of the other wing.
◆ Install a joist at each of the remaining 12- by 16-inch piers, attaching them to the ledger with joist hangers. Pier joists may pass no closer than 2 inches from J bolts; shift the joists slightly along the ledger as needed to satisfy this requirement.

3. Starting the inner band beam.
◆ Cut a piece of joist lumber to extend from an end joist to a point 3 inches beyond the joist resting on the adjacent pier, then nail it to the ends of both joists with three $3\frac{1}{2}$-inch nails *(left).*
◆ Trim another beam section to reach 3 inches past the next joist and nail it in place. Work along both wings of the porch toward the corner pier. Where the band beams meet, nail through the face of one into the end of the other. *(Loose joints between band-beam sections will be secured in the next step when the band beam is doubled.)*
◆ Measure and cut joists to fit between the ledger board and the band beam *(above right).* Attach one end of each joist to the ledger with a joist hanger and nail the band beam to the other end.

TRICKS OF THE TRADE

Compensating for an Uneven House Wall

A band beam will mimic undulations in a house wall unless you cut joists to compensate. To find the length for each joist, tie a string above the ledger to nails tapped into the narrow space between the ledger and the joists resting on the first and last small pier of each wing. Sight past the string to a tape measure at each joist location. Note how far the ledger bows in or out and add the distance to—or subtract it from—the length of either end joist, then cut a joist to that measure.

4. Securing the frame.

◆ To anchor the porch, select a scrap of joist lumber to serve as blocking. At the small piers *(above, left),* set the piece on top of the J bolt and against the band beam. Tap the blocking with a hammer and drill a $\frac{3}{4}$-inch hole at the resulting mark. Fasten the board to the bolt with a nut and a washer, then drive 3 nails through the band beam into the blocking.

◆ At the corner pier *(above, right),* fit blocking against one arm of the band beam, trimming as necessary to fit the blocking between the beam and the space to be occupied by the corner joist. Bolt the blocking in place, then nail the beam to it.

Finish the band beam by installing a second, outer set of boards alongside those that are already nailed to the blocking. Cut the outer boards to offset the joints between them from the joints between the inner set. Nail the inner and outer beam boards to each other every 8 inches from alternate sides with three $2\frac{1}{2}$-inch nails. Drive additional nails on both sides of every joint.

5. Making a doubled corner joist.

◆ Measure the distance between the ledger corner and inside corner of the band beam. Mark this distance, plus $1\frac{1}{2}$ inches, on 2 pieces of joist lumber.
◆ Lay the boards edge to edge, crowns outward. Without turning the boards over, cut parallel 45° miters at the ends of each board, then set the boards face to face so that the miters form a point at one end and a V at the other. Nail the boards together from both sides at 16-inch intervals, staggering the rows of nails *(right).*
◆ Nail a multipurpose framing anchor to each side of the joist at the V-shaped end *(inset).*
◆ Install the joist, bending the hangers to fit the ledger. Use joist-hanger nails at the ledger, and drive 4-inch nails through the band beam into the pointed end of the joist.

6. Installing jack joists.

◆ Starting at the corner, mark jack-joist positions, 16 inches apart, on the band beams.
◆ Measure from each mark to the corner joist and cut jack joists with one end mitered to a 45° angle.
◆ Tap a U-shaped joist hanger onto the outer end of each jack joist. While a helper holds the joist in place, nail the mitered end to the corner joist. Then nail the joist hanger to the beam and the joist.
◆ Install the rest of the jack joists, alternating sides as you work.

LAYING FLOORBOARDS

1. Installing the outer rows.

◆ Cut the grooved edge from boards for the first row on one of the porch wings. Paint the cut edges with wood preservative.

◆ Starting where the wings meet, nail the first row of boards to the band beam, tongued edges toward the house, with $2\frac{1}{2}$-inch galvinized finishing nails every 16 inches. Position the boards so that their cut edges overhang the band beam by $1\frac{1}{2}$ inches, and allow the two end boards to overhang the corners about 3 inches.

◆ Trim the next few rows of boards so that their ends meet over joists, randomizing the joints. Before nailing a row of boards in place, measure their distance from the house wall at several points. Adjust the tongue-and-groove joint to make the boards parallel to the wall. Then tongue-nail each board in the row to every joist *(page 119, inset).*

2. Using a power nailer.

When you have installed at least 4 rows of boards, speed up the installation by using a power floor nailer. Continue to measure the distance between the boards and the house wall every few rows to be sure they are still parallel. Do not install the last 3 rows against the house.

3. Mitering floorboards at the corner.

◆ Tack a straight board to the floor parallel to the corner joist to serve as a saw guide. Position the guide so that the saw cuts the boards at the seam in the 2-piece joist.

◆ Install flooring for the second wing, precutting 45° angles on board ends that abut the first wing *(page 15).*

◆ Precut and install the last 3 rows of boards on both wings. Nail through the face of each board into the joists below, taking care not to pierce the ledger flashing. If necessary, trim the last row of boards lengthwise to fit under the siding.

◆ Trim the boards at the end of each wing, leaving a $1\frac{3}{4}$-inch overhang.

◆ Sink exposed nailheads; fill the holes with wood putty.

Building a Porch Stairway

To do a large porch justice, a stairway should be wide enough to span the distance between the centers of two piers. For solidity underfoot, plan to install the carriages that support the steps no more than 30 inches apart. Although dimensions can vary, a stairway with carriages cut for steps 7 to 8 inches high and 10 inches deep are the safest and most comfortable to climb.

Getting Ready: Have on hand all the materials you need before beginning the job. In all likelihood, you will have to not only crosscut tread stock—$1\frac{1}{4}$-by-12 lumber with one edge rounded—and risers to length but also rip them to width. Coat with wood preservative any lumber that is not pressure treated. Plan to install the carriages and blocking within 48 hours of pouring the concrete base for the stairs.

MATERIALS

- 2-by-2s
- 2-by-12s
- $1\frac{1}{4}$-inch tread stock
- 1-inch fascia and riser stock
- $1\frac{5}{8}$-inch lath
- Wood lattice

1. Positioning the base.

◆ Mark the total run of the stairway on top of a mason's level with tape.
◆ Butt the level against the band beam under the flooring, and hold a folding ruler perpendicular to the level at the tape. Set the level aside and chalk an X where the ruler touches the ground. Connect this mark and two others made the same way with a line the width of the stairway, then outline a trench 2 inches in front of the line, 12 inches behind it, and 6 inches beyond each end.
◆ Dig the trench 4 inches deep and fill it with concrete to grade *(page 19)*.
◆ Recalculate the total rise from the concrete surface and make any necessary adjustments in riser height.

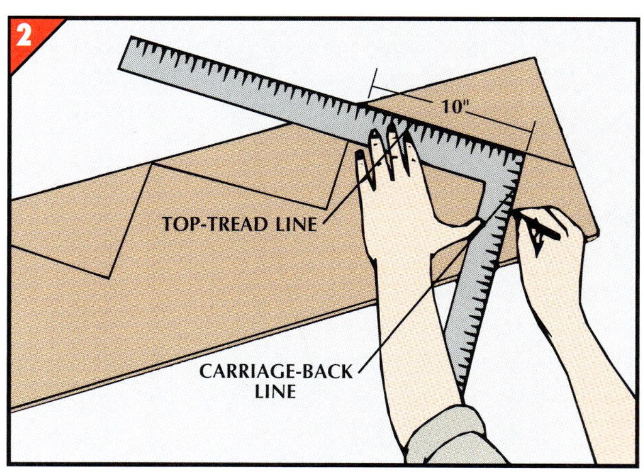

2. Making the carriages.

◆ Mark a 2-by-12 with the unit rise and unit run—7 inches and 10 inches in this case—as shown on page 19, making the bottom riser shorter than the others by the thickness of the tread stock. Draw the carriage-back line as shown at right.
◆ Cut out the carriage and check the fit. Remake the piece if the distance between the top tread and the surface of the porch floor is not exactly equal to the thickness of the tread stock.
◆ Use the carriage as a template for the others.

3. Attaching the carriages.

◆ Cut 8 pieces of blocking from joist stock to fit between carriages when they are evenly spaced across the width of the stairway.

◆ Rest the center carriage against the band beam. Nail a piece of blocking to the band beam so that the blocking touches the carriage, then nail through the carriage into the blocking. Fasten another length of blocking to the band beam to sandwich the center carriage.

◆ Working from the center outward, anchor the tops of the remaining carriages to blocking.

◆ At the bottom of the stairway, set blocking between an end carriage and an adjacent one. Nail the blocking to the concrete base with $2\frac{1}{2}$-inch masonry nails, then fasten the carriages to the blocking. Install the remaining three pieces of blocking.

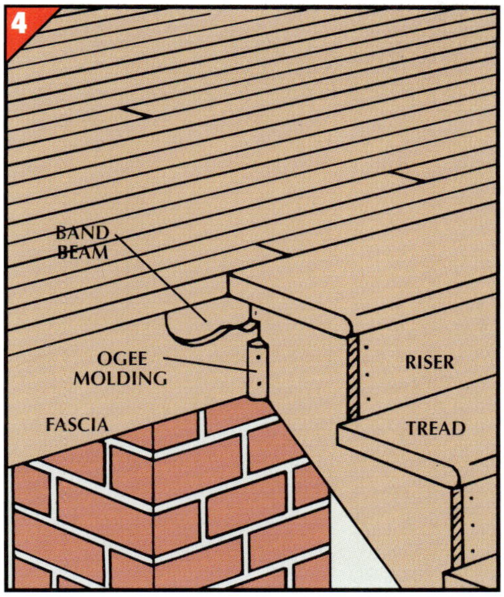

4. Adding risers and treads.

◆ From 1-inch stock, cut risers to fit as shown above, and fasten them with $3\frac{1}{2}$-inch galvanized finishing nails.

◆ Trim tread stock for a 1-inch overhang at the front and sides of each step; nail the treads to the carriages.

◆ Make fascia boards from 1-inch lumber, mitering the ends at porch corners for a finished appearance. Attach the fascia to the band beam with galvanized finishing nails.

◆ Cover the seam between the fascia and carriages with ogee molding.

◆ Countersink all nailheads and fill the holes with wood putty.

SKIRTS TO HIDE A CRAWLSPACE

Constructing lattice screens.

◆ Build a 2-by-2 frame to fit between adjacent piers. Nail a section of prefabricated lattice to the frame, then trim the lattice flush. Cover lattice edges with strips of $1\frac{5}{8}$-inch lath.

◆ Attach 2-by-4 furring strips to the sides of the brick piers with masonry nails driven into mortar joints. Position the furring strips so the screen fits snugly against the inner face of the overhanging fascia.

◆ Nail the lattice frame to the furring strips and the fascia.

◆ Countersink all exposed nailheads and fill the holes with wood putty.

◆ Adapt this procedure to make triangular-shaped lattice screens for the sides of the stairway.

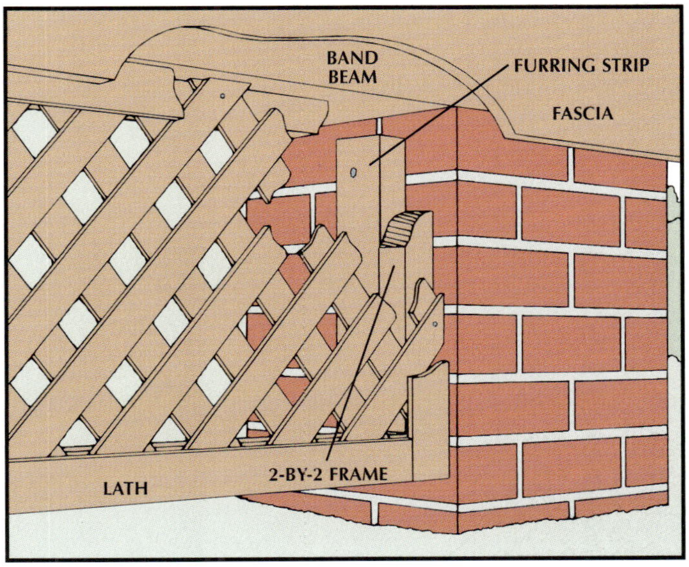

A Hip Roof for a Wraparound Porch

The real trick to roof framing is cutting rafters—common and jack rafters for the wings and a hip rafter at the corner. There is more to these angled boards than meets the eye. The main challenge is to cut a notch called a bird's mouth where the outer end of the rafter rests on a header that supports the roof at the eaves.

The Ideal Pitch: For a porch of a given width, the location and depth of the bird's mouth depend primarily on the pitch of the roof. Most porch roofs have the same slope as the roof of the house they are attached to. To measure the slope of an existing roof, adapt the technique on page 58, Step 1 to measure the number of inches rise per foot of run, a figure called the unit rise.

Because a porch roof may approach second-story window sills no closer than 3 inches, you may have to settle for a gentler slope. The box opposite explains how to predict this outcome, once you know the dimensions of the rafter stock you need. For a porch up to 8 feet wide use 2-by-6s. Porches between 8 feet and 11 feet wide demand 2-by-8s.

Adjusting Pitch: Decrease the slope if the ideal pitch brings the roof too close to second-story windows. Roofing materials impose limits on this reduction. With a unit rise of 4 or more you may use any material you like—tile, slate, cedar shakes, or asphalt shingles. But a unit rise of 3 disqualifies all but asphalt shingles. Shallower slopes require a built-up roof. Consider lowering the porch-ceiling height—8 feet is standard— slightly to meet the 3-inch limit—or consult a roofer.

Lumber Sizes: Use common-rafter stock for the header, joists, ledger boards, and jack rafters. The hip rafter at the corner and rafter plates attached to the house require boards 2 inches wider.

Porch posts are generally 4-by-4s, but if piers are more than 9 feet apart, use 6-by-6s.

TOOLS

- Framing square
- Plumb bob
- Circular saw
- Carpenter's level
- Handsaw or saber saw

MATERIALS

- 2-by-4s
- 2-by-6s, 2-by-8s, or 2-by-10s
- 1-by-6s or 1-by-8s
- Plywood ($\frac{1}{2}$-inch)
- Lag screws ($\frac{1}{2}$- by $3\frac{1}{2}$-inch and $\frac{3}{8}$- by 5-inch)
- Joist hangers
- Framing, post, and rafter anchors
- 15-pound roofing felt and nails
- Aluminum drip edge
- Asphalt shingles
- Ridge venting
- Aluminum flashing
- Self-sealing roofing nails
- Galvanized common nails ($1\frac{1}{2}$-, $2\frac{1}{2}$-, and 3-inch)
- Gutters and downspouts

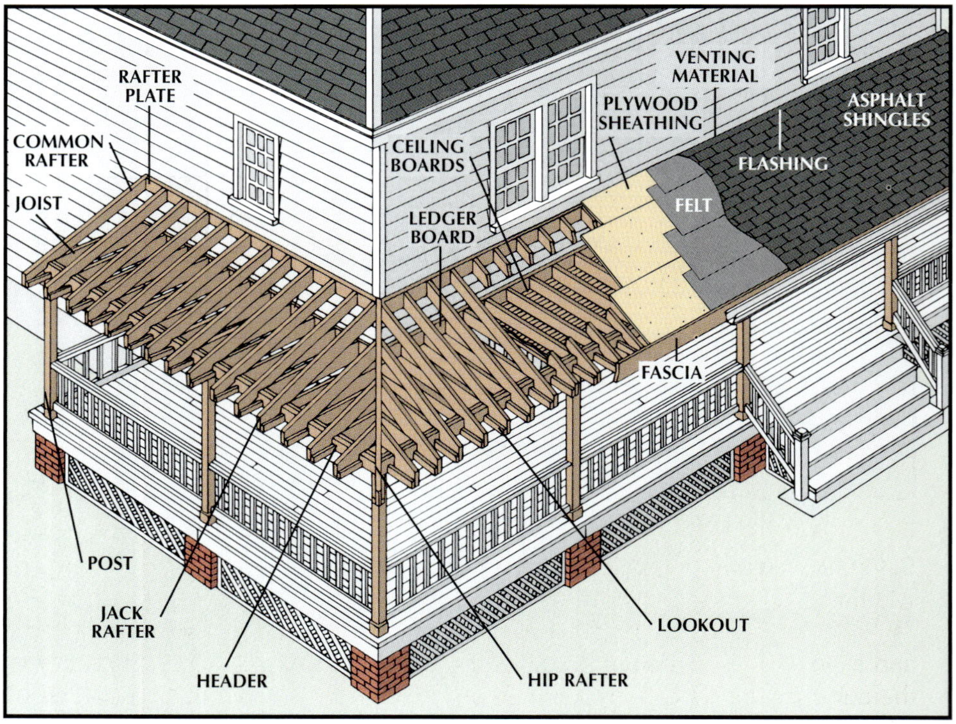

Anatomy of a wraparound porch roof.

Joists and sloping boards called common rafters form the skeleton of a porch roof. The corner is shaped by a hip rafter and shorter jack rafters, elements mimicked by a corner joist and jack joists below them. Joists and rafters are anchored at one end to plates fastened to the house wall, and at the other to a header supported by posts centered over brick piers. Asphalt shingles laid over roofing felt and $\frac{1}{2}$-inch plywood sheathing keep out the weather. At the rafter plate, a strip of venting material covered by aluminum flashing promotes air circulation between rafters and joists. A tongue-and-groove ceiling hides the joists. Horizontal boards called lookouts give a nailing surface for the ceiling along the eaves and for the fascia.

Previewing a Roof

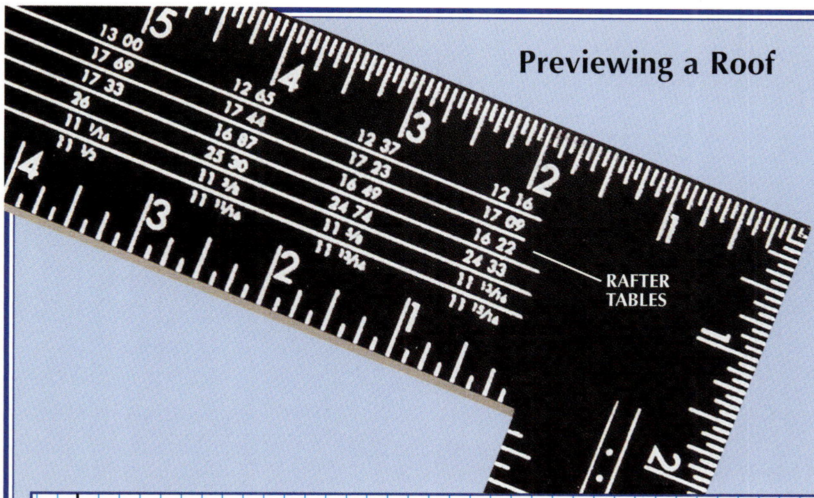

To create the planning diagram at left, draw the house wall on 12-to-the-inch graph paper. Half an inch above ceiling height, add a ledger board, a joist, and a $3\frac{1}{2}$-inch-wide header. Extend the joist bottom to the right, and mark the height of second-story windows on the wall.

Multiply unit rise by total run in inches, then divide by 12 to get total rise. Mark this distance on the wall, up from the ledger's top. Through this point and the corner of the header, draw a rafter line to the extended joist. Indicate the bottom of the rafter with a line parallel to the rafter line. Find the rafter-length factor in the top line of the rafter table on a framing square *(left, top)*, under the unit-rise inch mark. For a unit rise of 4, the factor is 12.65. Multiply the factor by the width of your rafters and divide by 12. Mark this distance plus 2 inches for roofing on the wall above the rafter bottom. If this point is less than 3 inches below the window sill, decrease roof slope or lower the porch ceiling.

Use the formula below to find the rafter length, then measure the overhang run and use it in the formula to find overhang length. Add the two lengths, and buy rafter stock longer than the sum.

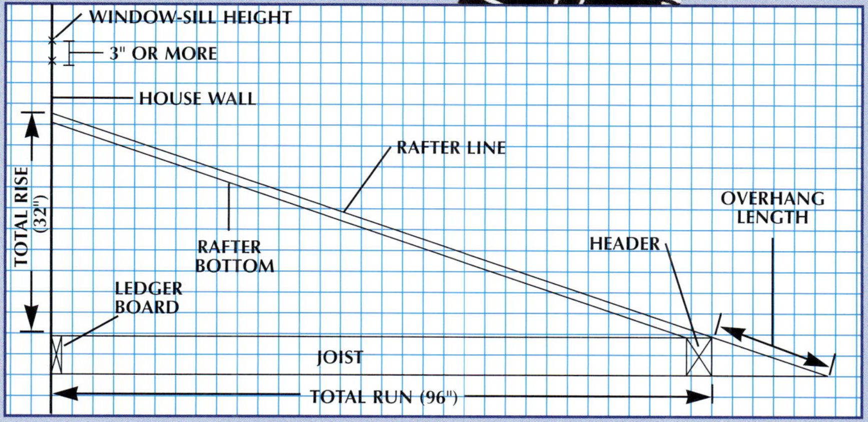

Run (in inches)		Rafter-length factor		Rafter length
____________	x	____________	÷ 12 =	____________

THE CORRECT HEIGHT FOR A RAFTER PLATE

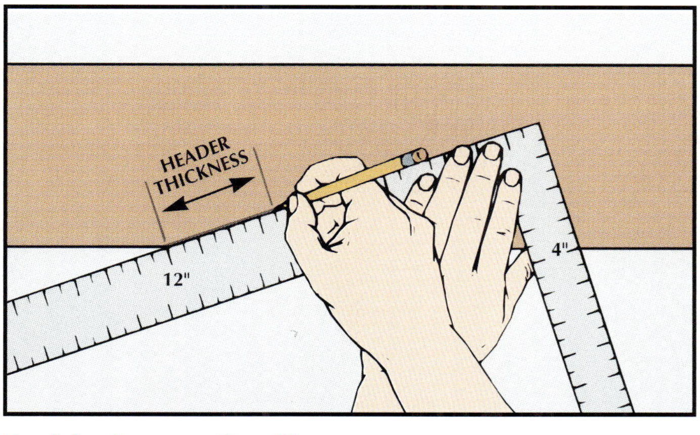

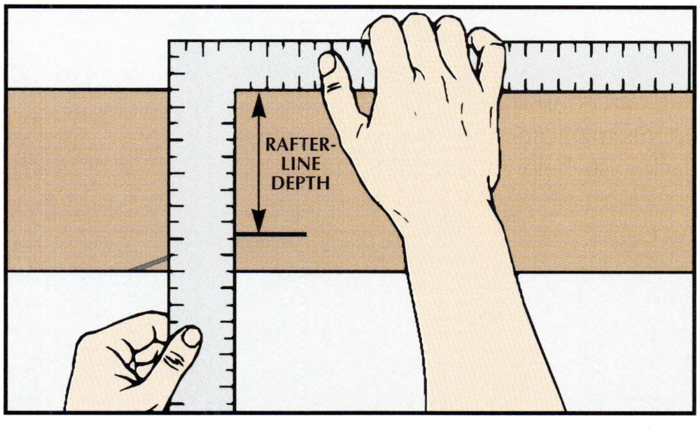

Positioning a rafter line.

Before erecting the rafter plate, determine how much of the width of a rafter will lie above the theoretical roof rise.

◆ Set a framing square on a board of common-rafter stock and align the unit run on the outside of the body—12—and the unit rise—in this case 4—on the outer edge of the tongue with the edge of the board as shown *(above, left)*. Starting at the 12, draw a line of a length equal to the thickness of the header—$3\frac{1}{2}$ inches in this example.

◆ Place the square as shown above, and measure the vertical distance from the top edge of the board to the end of the slanted line. This is the rafter-line depth.

SUPPORTS FOR THE ROOF

1. Snapping chalk lines for plates.

◆ For each wing of the porch, snap two plumb chalk lines on the house wall—one 3 inches in from the end of the wing, the other near the house corner. Snap a horizontal chalk line 8 feet, $\frac{1}{2}$ inch above the porch floor to mark the bottom of the ledger board, then add a line to mark the top of the ledger board.

◆ Measure up from this line a distance equal to the sum of the total rise and the rafter-line depth *(page 61)*—plus 2 inches to allow for roofing materials. Snap a horizontal chalk line at this height. Two inches plus the width of the rafter plate lower on the wall, snap another.

◆ Remove the siding at the ledger-board and rafter-plate positions *(page 32)*.

◆ Cut ledgers and rafter plates to overlap at the corner, and attach them to floor framing *(page 33)* or fasten them to studs in the wall with lag screws. Set the bottom edge of the rafter plate against the bottom of the opening in the siding.

2. Installing post anchors.

◆ On each wing, snap a chalk line along the floor, directly above the outer face of the band beam. Set post anchors at the lines *(inset)*: 3 inches in from the end of each wing, one at the intersection of chalk lines above the large corner pier, and one above the center of each noncorner pier.

◆ Place an offset washer in the base of each anchor, and mark the washer hole on the floor. Drill a $\frac{5}{16}$-inch hole 5 inches deep through the floor into the band beam.

◆ Fasten each anchor to the porch with a 5- by $\frac{3}{8}$-inch lag screw. Set a post support in each anchor.

3. Erecting posts.

◆ Set a post, slightly taller than porch-ceiling height, in the anchor at the end of one wing; brace it plumb with scrap 2-by-4s.

◆ Tack a joist to the end of the ledger board. While a helper holds the board level, mark the position of its bottom edge on the post. Take down the post and the joist. Similarly, mark a post for the outer end of the other porch wing. Cut and compare the two posts. If they are the same length, cut all of the posts to that length. Otherwise, custom measure and cut each post.

◆ Nail a post-and-beam connector to the top of each post except the one at the corner, then set each post in its anchor and drive nails partway through the anchor and into the wood. Brace the posts plumb with 2-by-4s.

4. Installing headers.

◆ Cut a pair of joist-stock boards to fit between the outside edge of one wing's end post and the middle of the adjacent post. Put a piece of $\frac{1}{2}$-inch plywood between the boards, and nail the assembly every 8 inches on alternate sides with three 3-inch nails. Make other headers to fit between the centers of adjacent posts, ending at the last post before the corner.

◆ Set the headers atop the posts, and nail them to the post connectors; toenail the abutting ends of adjacent headers together. Install headers on the other wing.

◆ For the corner, build header sections long enough to extend across the top of the corner post, then miter the ends of the headers at a 45° angle *(inset)*; nail the headers to each other and toenail them to the post.

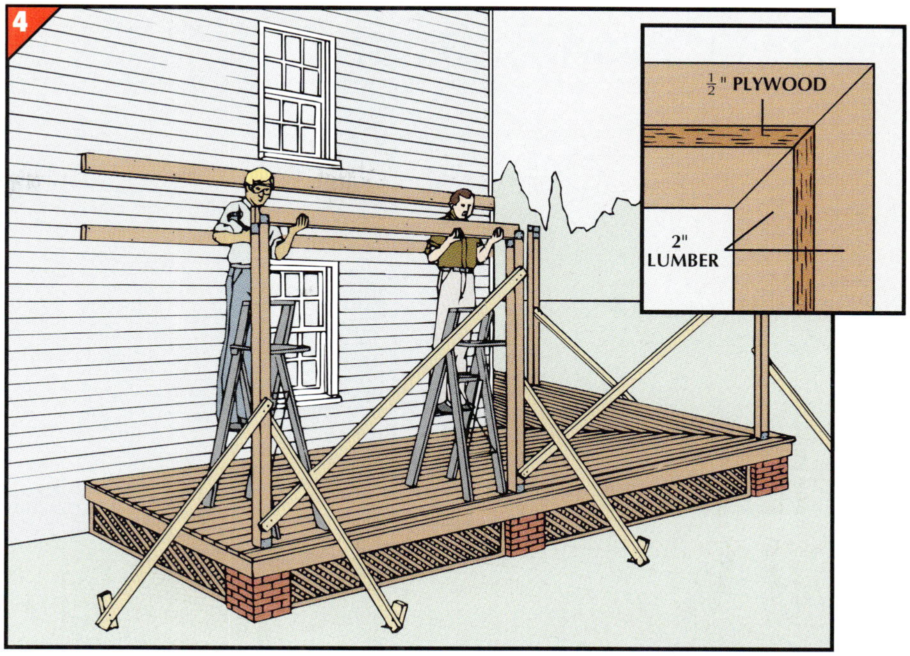

5. Squaring the frame.

◆ Tack a 2-by-4 to the ledger board and the header *(above)*. Lay a second 2-by-4 on the first and tack one end 4 feet along the ledger board to make a diagonal brace for the header. Remove the braces installed at the end post in Step 3 *(left)*.

◆ Mark the header and the floor 1 foot from the end post, then use a plumb line to align the marks. Nail the diagonal brace to the 2-by-4 linking the ledger board and header. Add a second brace at the midpoint of the wing. Steady the other wing in the same way, then finish the nailing begun in Step 3 to secure the posts to the anchors.

◆ Beginning 4 inches from the corner of the house, install ceiling joists every 16 inches along each wing, attaching them with joist hangers. Remove header braces as you approach them. Toenail end joists to the ledger and header. Install corner joists and jack joists as for a floor *(page 56, Steps 4 and 5)*. When all joists are in place, remove the remaining post braces.

CUTTING AND INSTALLING COMMON RAFTERS

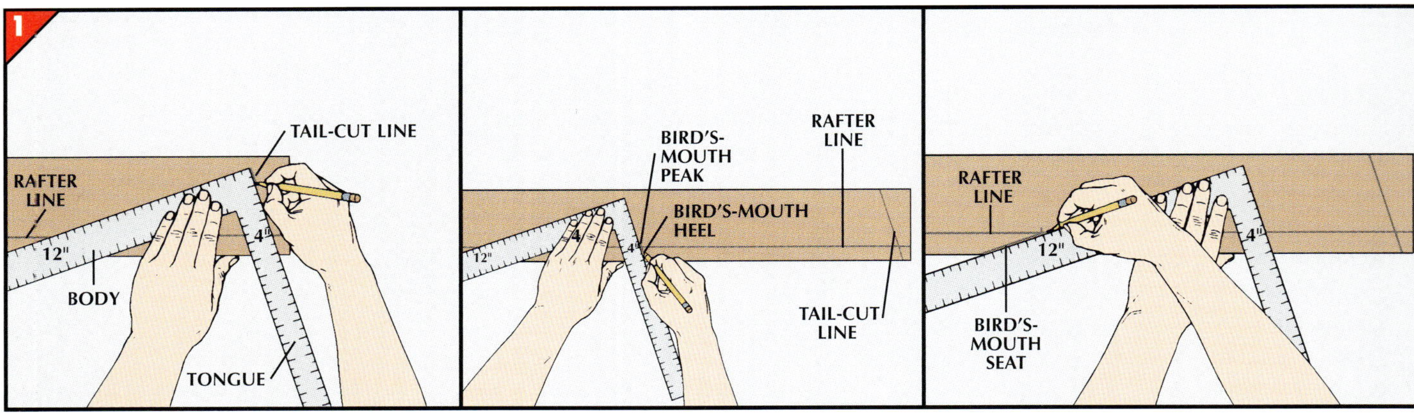

1. Marking tail and bird's-mouth cuts.

◆ With a chalk line, snap a rafter line along a rafter board at the depth established on page 61.

◆ Place a framing square near one end of the board, with the 12 on the body and the unit rise on the tongue touching the rafter line. Draw a line along the tongue, then extend it across the board to establish the tail-cut line *(above, left).*

◆ Measuring from the tail-cut line, mark the overhang length on the rafter line to establish the peak of the bird's mouth. Set the unit-rise number at the peak and the 12 on the rafter line, and draw the heel of the bird's mouth —a line from the peak to the bottom edge of the rafter *(above, center).* Next, set the 12 at the peak and the unit-rise number on the rafter line, and draw the seat of the bird's mouth *(above, right).*

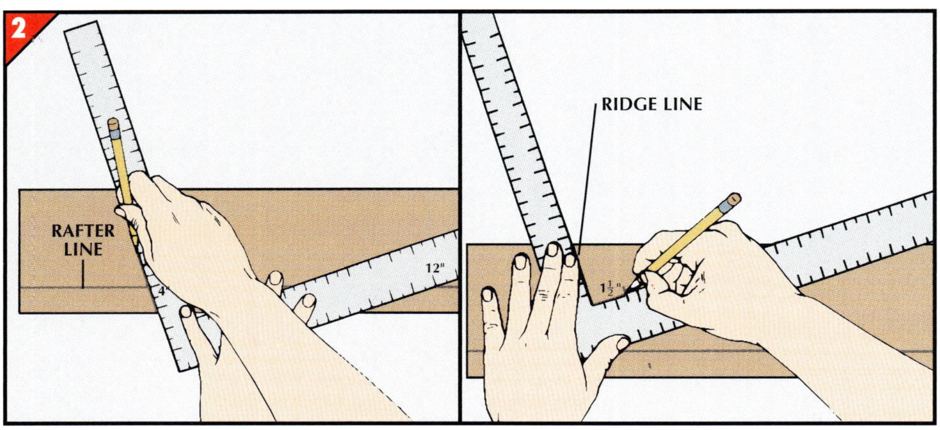

2. Establishing the ridge cut.

◆ Mark the rafter length, measured from the bird's-mouth peak, on the rafter line. Place the unit-rise number on the framing square at the rafter-length mark and the 12 on the rafter line, then draw a ridge line along the tongue *(far left).*

◆ To adjust rafter length for rafter-plate thickness, lay the tongue's inner edge along the ridge line as shown at left and mark two points $1\frac{1}{2}$ inches from the ridge line. Draw the ridge-cut line through the points.

3. Testing the rafter for fit.

◆ Make the ridge cut and the tail cut on the rafter with a circular saw. Use a saber saw or a handsaw to cut the bird's mouth.

◆ With a helper holding the rafter flush with the face and the end of the rafter plate, set the bird's mouth on the header. Recut the rafter if you find any gaps greater than $\frac{1}{8}$ inch at the rafter plate or bird's mouth *(the tip of the rafter may be higher than the top edge of the rafter plate).* When you have a rafter that fits properly, use it as a template for the remaining common rafters *(inset).*

4. Installing common rafters.

◆ Use a plumb bob to help mark the rafter plate directly above the side of each joist facing the porch corner, except for the two joists nearest the corner. For them, mark the plates $1\frac{1}{2}$ inches from the corner.

◆ At each rafter position, nail a multipurpose framing anchor to the rafter plate so that it will not intrude between plate and rafter. Fasten wing-shaped rafter anchors to the header to meet the opposite face of each rafter.

◆ Attach each rafter to the plate and the header, nailing into the rafter face through the framing anchor and through the wing-shaped rafter anchor at the header *(inset).*

ADDING HIP AND JACK RAFTERS

1. Making a hip rafter.

◆ Find the length of the hip rafter and its overhang with the formula on page 61. Use common-rafter total run and overhang run in the calculation, but consult the second line of the framing square's rafter table for the reference number.

◆ With a chalk line, snap a rafter line along the rafter board at the depth from the rafter's top edge established on page 61, less $\frac{1}{4}$ inch to compensate for roof sheathing. Using the number 17 on the body of the square, draw the tail line, the bird's mouth, and the ridge line on the rafter *(page 64, Step 1).*

◆ For the ridge cut, adjust the ridge line *(page 64, Step 2)* by $3\frac{5}{8}$ inches instead of $1\frac{1}{2}$ inches to compensate for the thickness of the rafter-plate corner. Apply the same procedure to draw a tail-cut line $\frac{3}{4}$ inch closer to the bird's mouth than the tail line. Extend the tail- and ridge-cut lines across the top and bottom edges of the rafter board with a try square, then connect these lines on the other face of the board.

◆ Cut out the bird's mouth with a saber saw. Set a circular saw at 45° and trim the rafter board along the ridge- and tail-cut lines on both faces to form V-shaped ends on the rafter.

◆ Install the hip rafter by nailing through the common rafters into the ridge end of the hip rafter, then toenailing it to the header.

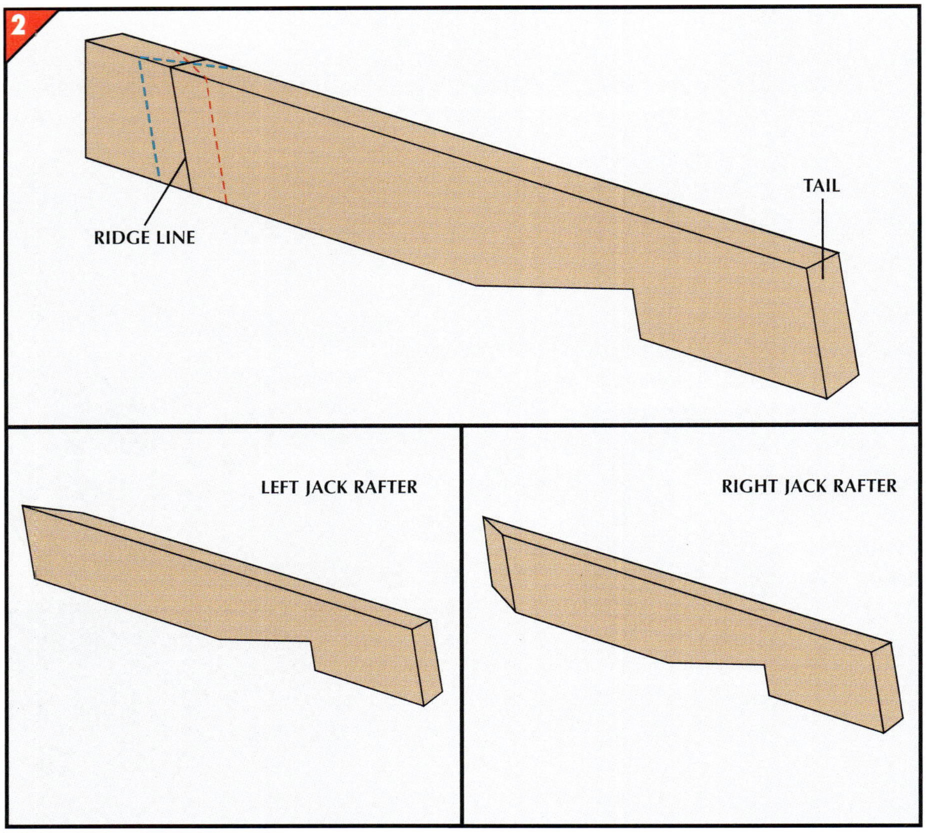

2. Cutting the first jack rafters.

◆ Find the length in inches of the two shortest jack rafters under the unit-rise number in the third line of the rafter table, and add to it the overhang length of a common rafter. On boards slightly longer than this sum, mark rafter-line depth, then cut a bird's mouth and the rafter tail cut—all as for a common rafter *(pages 61 and 64)*. Locate and draw the ridge line *(left, top)* at rafter length minus $1\frac{1}{8}$ inches—half the diagonal thickness of the hip rafter—from the peak of the bird's mouth.

◆ On the rafter destined for the left side of the hip rafter, adjust the ridge line away from the tail $\frac{3}{4}$ inch *(blue dotted line)* as shown on page 64, Step 2. On the right-side joist, move the ridge line $\frac{3}{4}$ inch toward the tail *(red dotted line)*.

◆ Set a circular saw at 45° and make the ridge cuts for each side of the hip rafter as shown at left, bottom.

3. Installing the jack rafters.

◆ Cut the remaining jack rafters using one of the short jacks as a template for the tail and bird's-mouth cuts. Mark and cut the ridge bevels as in Step 2, increasing the length of each successive rafter by the number under the unit rise on the third line of the rafter table on the framing square.

◆ Starting with the shortest jack rafters, install each pair in succession, taking care not to bow the hip rafter. Face-nail the jacks to the hip rafter and attach them to the header with rafter anchors.

SHEATHING AND SHINGLES

1. A foundation for shingles.
◆ Lay sheets of Type C-D $\frac{1}{2}$-inch plywood horizontally, C side up, overhanging the rafter tails by $\frac{3}{4}$ inch and the end rafters by 3 inches. Leave $\frac{1}{16}$-inch—$\frac{1}{8}$-inch in very humid climates—expansion gaps between courses. Trim sheets so the ends rest on rafters and the joints of successive courses are staggered. Nail the plywood to the rafters with $1\frac{1}{2}$-inch nails, spacing the nails 6 inches apart at joints and 1 foot apart elsewhere. At the porch corner, trim the sheets for a $\frac{1}{8}$-inch gap at the center of the hip rafter. Leave a 1-inch ventilation opening between the top edge of the sheathing and the rafter plate.

◆ Unroll 15-pound roofing felt even with bottom edge of the plywood and tack the felt to the sheathing every few feet with wide-headed paper nails, ending 1 foot past the hip. Lay succeeding courses of felt to overlap earlier ones by 2 inches.

◆ Along the eave line, install an aluminum drip edge *(inset)*. Secure it with roofing nails driven every foot.

CAUTION *Install temporary 2-by-4 footholds for added security when working on the roof.*

2. Laying the first row of shingles.
◆ Trim the tabs from a section of roofing to make a starter strip *(inset)*, then cut 6 inches from one end. Lay the strip in the corner formed by the drip edge and the end of a wing, then fasten it with three roofing nails along the center. Cut and lay full-length starter strips end to end along the eaves.

◆ Lay the first row of shingles on top of the starter course, overhanging porch-wing ends by $\frac{1}{2}$ inch. Fasten each section with $1\frac{1}{4}$-inch roofing nails driven $\frac{5}{8}$ inch above the slots that divide the strip into tabs. Place a nail above each slot and 1 inch from each end. At the corner, trim the shingles along the hip rafter.

3. Working up the roof.
◆ Shorten by 6 inches—half a tab—the first section of shingles in each successive course. Align the cut end with the end of the first shingle in the previous course, adjusting overlap to match the house roof. If the tab at the hip will be shorter than 6 inches, cut half a tab from the preceding section of shingles before laying the last section next to it.

◆ Adjust shingle overlap on the last few courses, if necessary, so that the top row will be at least 6 inches wide. Trim the shingles along the top edge of the sheathing.

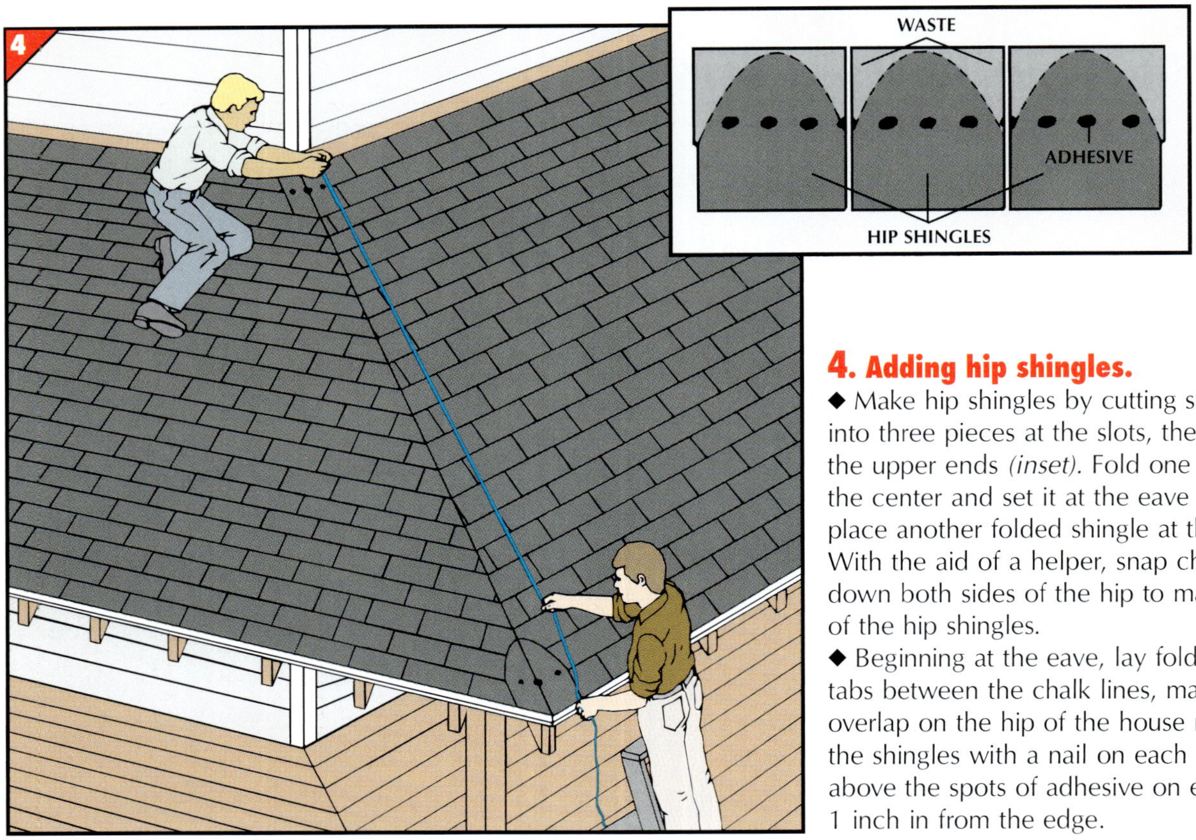

4. Adding hip shingles.

◆ Make hip shingles by cutting shingle sections into three pieces at the slots, then rounding the upper ends *(inset)*. Fold one shingle down the center and set it at the eave line, then place another folded shingle at the house wall. With the aid of a helper, snap chalk lines down both sides of the hip to mark the edges of the hip shingles.

◆ Beginning at the eave, lay folded shingle tabs between the chalk lines, matching the overlap on the hip of the house roof. Fasten the shingles with a nail on each side, 2 inches above the spots of adhesive on each tab and 1 inch in from the edge.

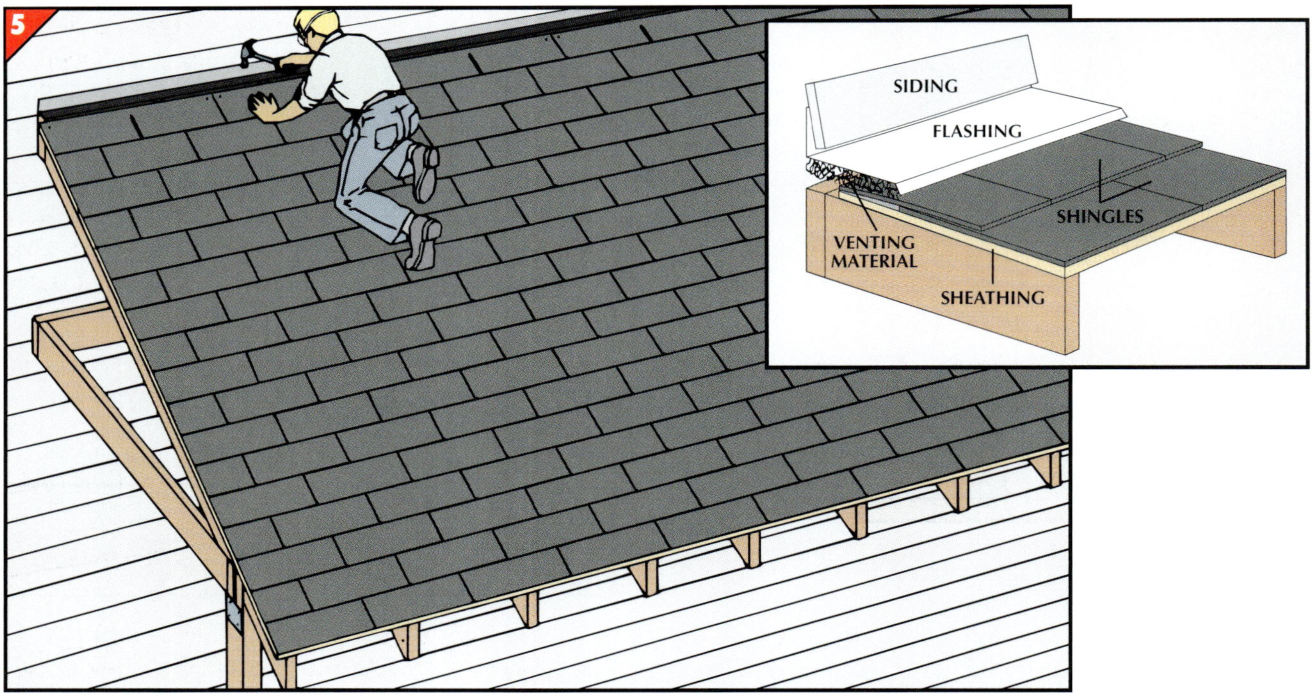

5. Venting and flashing.

◆ Nail a strip of venting material along the top edge of the roof as shown above, following the manufacturer's instructions.

◆ Install aluminum flashing over the venting material *(inset)*. Buy flashing wide enough to extend 4 inches under the house siding and 1 inch beyond the venting material.

◆ Nail the flashing through the venting material and shingles, and into the roof sheathing at 1-foot intervals. Use self-sealing roofing nails, which are fitted with silicone or neoprene washers.

CAUTION *Overhammering the nails will crush the venting material.*

SIDE ENCLOSURES AND SOFFIT SUPPORTS

1. Installing lookouts.

◆ Use a level to mark the tail of each rafter flush with the bottom edge of the header, then saw the rafter along the line. Cut 2-by-4 lookouts to fit against the header and even with each rafter tail.

◆ Set the lower edge of the lookout flush with the bottom of the header and the newly cut edge at the rafter overhang. Face-nail the lookout to the rafter, then toenail it to the header *(top inset)*.

◆ Cut a lookout for each side of the hip rafter *(bottom inset)*, making parallel 45° bevels on both ends. Fit the lookouts to the header and hip rafter as in the bottom inset.

2. Enclosing the ends of the roof.

◆ Cut a piece of $\frac{1}{2}$-inch exterior-grade plywood to cover the triangular space created by the rafter and the joist at the end of each wing. Extend the plywood $\frac{1}{2}$ inch below the bottom of the joist to cover the ends of ceiling boards *(page 71)*. Nail the plywood cover to the rafter and the joist.

◆ From a 1-inch board the same width as a rafter, cut a rake board that matches the common rafters both in length and in the angle of the ridge and tail cuts. Butt the rake against the underside of the plywood sheathing and nail it to the plywood cover. If the plywood sheathing on the roof extends past the outer face of the rake, trim the corner with a strip of quarter-round molding.

3. Adding a fascia and gutters.

◆ Make fascia boards from 1-inch lumber about 2 inches wider than the depth of rafter tails. Cut the boards so that joints fall at the centers of the tails.

◆ Slip the fascia into the space between the tails and the drip edge, lining up the outer end of the fascia with the outer face of the rake board. Nail the fascia to the rafter tails. At the corner where the two wings meet, miter the ends of the fascia board at a 45° angle.

◆ Attach gutters to the fascia and downspouts to the corner post and end posts according to the manufacturer's instructions *(inset)*.

Ceilings and Railings

Ceilings and railings, the finishing touches to a porch, are made of specially milled lumber called porch stock. For ceilings, it consists of tongue-and-groove boards $\frac{1}{2}$ inch thick and 3 inches wide with a bead down the center. These are generally installed from the house wall to the eaves, forming one continuous surface *(below)*.

To allow air to circulate within the enclosed space above the ceiling, screened vents are installed in the ceiling boards of the overhang. The vents are available in several shapes and sizes at hardware stores; your local building code will specify the correct size and spacing for your area.

Wood for Railings: Cap-rail stock for the upper railing is milled with a 1-inch-wide groove on the underside to accept the tops of 1-by-1 pickets. The picket bottoms fit against the angled face of bottom-rail stock as shown on the facing page. All three elements can be purchased specially milled for decorative effect, but they also come in the standard stock shown here, available in 16-foot lengths that can be cut to fit any porch.

MATERIALS

- Ceiling boards
- 4-by-4s
- Parting bead
- Vents
- Cap-rail stock
- Bottom-rail stock
- Pickets
- Post caps
- Ogee molding

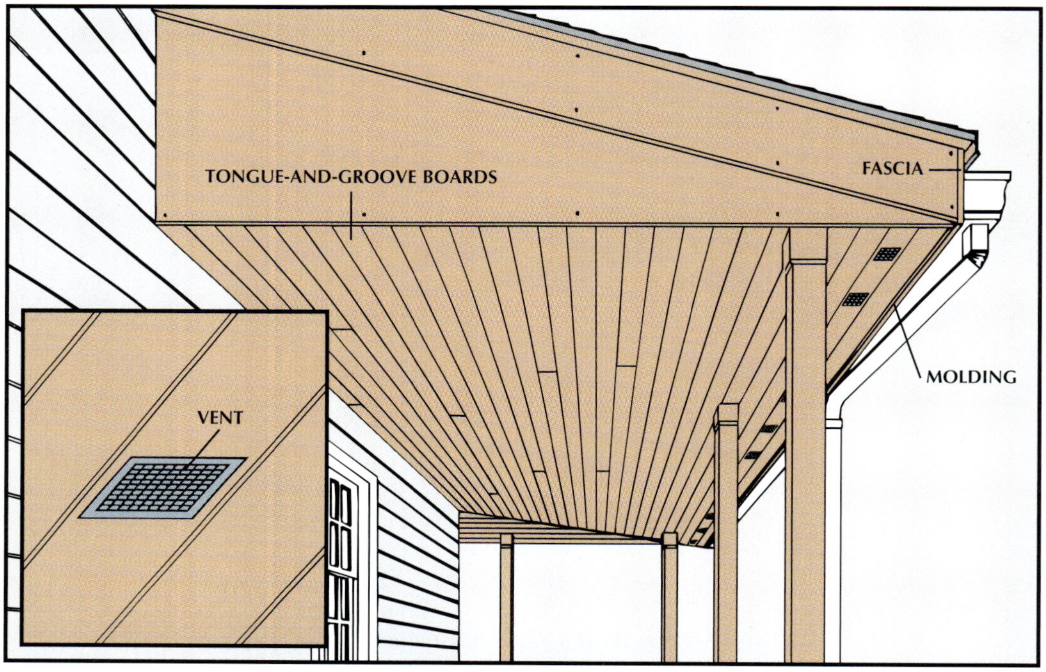

A tongue-and-groove porch ceiling.

◆ Starting at the wall of the house, face-nail tongue-and-groove boards to the ceiling joists with 2-inch finishing nails. Where the two wings meet, miter the ceiling boards to join at a 45° angle. At the ends of the porch, butt the ceiling boards against the inside of the plywood triangle that encloses the roof. Notch the ceiling boards to fit around porch posts.

◆ Finish the ceiling by nailing flat molding such as parting bead around the perimeter of the ceiling to conceal ceiling board joints with the plywood triangles and fascia boards.

◆ Cut holes in the ceiling at the center of the overhang for placement of screened vents *(inset)*.

◆ Before painting, set all nails and fill the holes with putty.

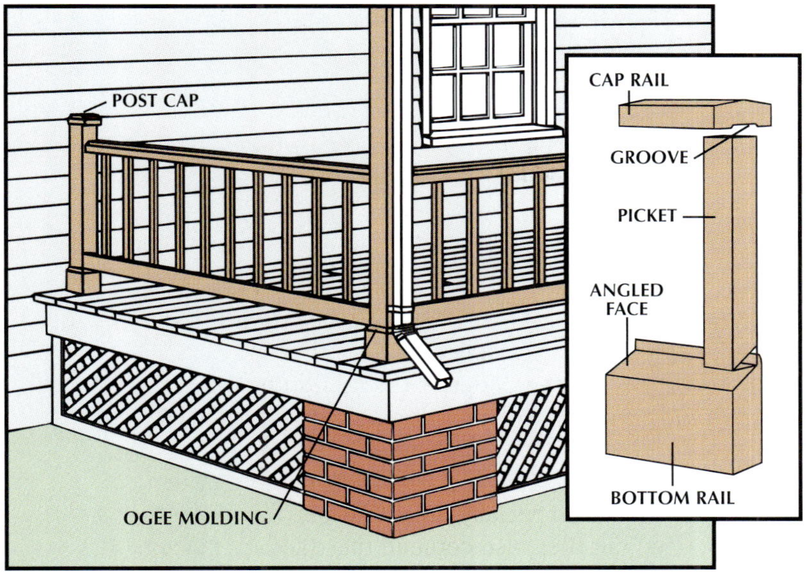

A railing to surround the porch.

◆ Between porch posts, install 4-by-4 railing posts cut 2 inches longer than the height of the railing as specified by building codes. Mount the uprights on post anchors, placing one post flush against the house at the end of each wing. Install others between porch posts as required by code. Cover the post anchors with 1-by-4 lumber finished with $\frac{1}{2}$-inch ogee molding, and top each post with a post cap.

◆ Toenail the bottom rails to the posts above the molding and with the angled face toward the house, then toenail cap rails to the posts.

◆ Cut a 1-by-1 picket to fit between the rails, mitering one end to the angle of the bottom rail *(inset)*. Use the first picket as a template for marking others. Drill pilot holes to prevent splitting, then toenail the pickets to the rails so that the gaps between pickets are less than 4 inches wide.

A railing for the porch stairs.

◆ Cut posts for the bottom of the stairs to the same height as the other railing posts *(left)*, and fasten them with post anchors to the concrete footing directly against each side of the bottom step, notching the bottom tread as needed. Cover the anchor with trim.

◆ Miter the bottom and cap rails to fit snugly between the posts at the top and bottom of the stairs.

◆ Cut pickets as for the porch railing, then miter the tops and bottoms to match the slope of the railing *(inset)*. Toenail the pickets into place.

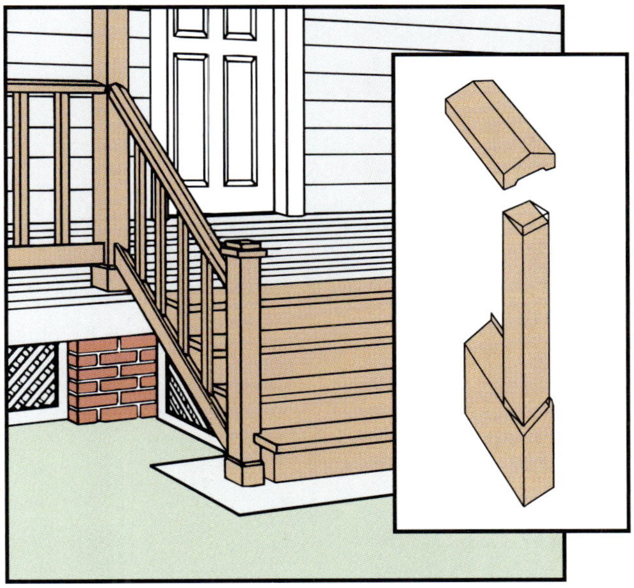

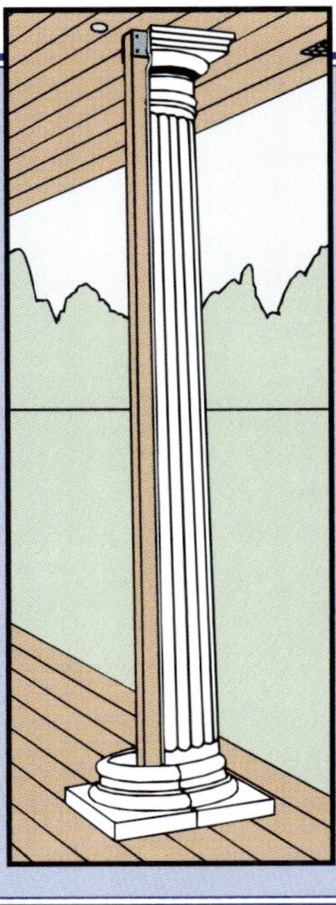

Classical Columns for Purists

A porch on a large house can benefit from posts that are more substantial in appearance than the basic 4-by-4 supports. The simplest to add are the hollow variety that enclose existing posts *(left)*. Available from most large lumberyards in lengths from 8 to 20 feet, they can be ordered made of wood or aluminum, with plain or fluted columns, and topped with a choice of capitals, including some styled after ancient Greek architecture *(right)*. All such columns come split in half for ease of installation.

Columns require weatherproofing whether made of aluminum or wood. Coat the inside with roofing compound to a height of 2 feet. Ventilate the column with two holes in the porch ceiling, one inside the column, the other within 1 foot of the exterior. If the capital protrudes past the fascia, install a strip of aluminum flashing to deflect rain.

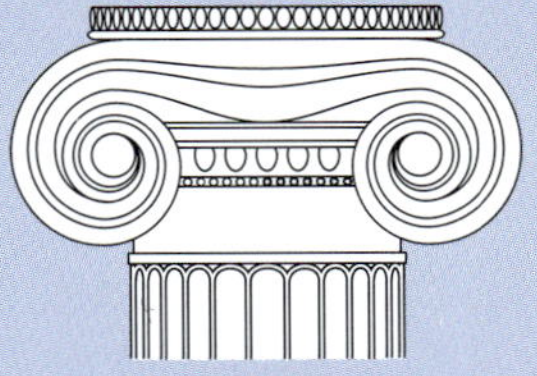

IONIC

CORINTHIAN

Adding Screens to Bugproof a Porch

Enclosing a porch with screens requires a suitable framework for attaching the mesh. If your porch has a knee wall—a partition approximately 3 feet high around the perimeter of the porch—and square posts no more than 5 feet apart, you may need to add only a doorframe and studs against the house wall at the ends of the porch. To keep flying insects out, notch the studs to match the siding *(opposite)*. Build the doorframe to fit the width of the door, but buy a door slightly taller than you need so it can be trimmed to fit.

Porches without knee walls vary in the amount of construction needed for screening. In addition to a doorframe, some may lack only a few uprights. Others may need a complete set of vertical and horizontal supports. Pick the elements that are appropriate for your porch from the ones shown on the following pages.

Attaching the Mesh: No matter what type of screening you choose *(page 114)*, there are a number of ways to attach it to the porch. The simplest is to staple the screen directly to the supporting structure and cover the seams with molding.

Or you can install screen-spline channels that fasten to the porch. The channels anchor the mesh with a flexible spline identical to that used in aluminum screens *(page 114)*. A decorative cover hides the spline and the screen edges.

A third option is wood-framed screens *(page 116)*. Although more expensive and time-consuming than the preceding methods, framed screens complement a large, elegant porch better than the others.

TOOLS

- Crosscut or circular saw
- Saber saw
- Compass
- Chalk line
- Miter box and backsaw
- Staple gun
- Hammer
- Utility knife
- Belt sander
- Drill
- Screwdriver
- Screen-spline roller

MATERIALS

- 2-by-4s
- Doorstop molding
- Screen bead
- Screen door
- Door hinges and latch
- Screening
- Screen spline and molding
- Galvanized common nails (3-inch)
- Galvanized finishing nails (2-inch)
- Screws
- Copper-coated staples ($\frac{1}{4}$-inch)
- Brads ($\frac{3}{4}$-inch)
- Turn buttons

FRAMING ALTERNATIVES

A screened porch that stands alone.
The framework for enclosing a porch consists of 2-by-4 studs toenailed to the floor and ceiling. If you wish to attach screening to this supporting structure, space the studs no more than 5 feet apart, 3 feet if you plan wood-framed screens. Blocking between the studs at the floor and ceiling helps to keep the uprights from warping, while knee rails 3 feet above the floor help anchor the mesh.

A porch with decorative columns or posts *(right)* demands that the framework be recessed from the edges of the porch to accommodate doubled corner studs. If the porch has posts with flat surfaces *(inset)*, they can serve as the corner studs.

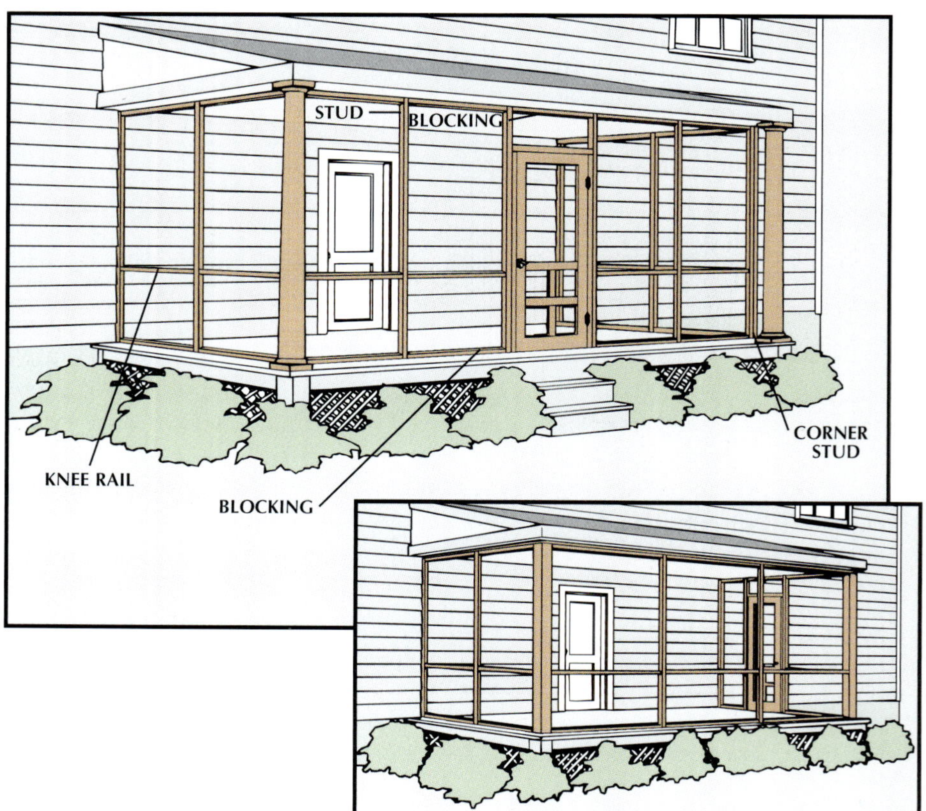

STUDS AND KNEE RAILS

1. Notching an end stud.

◆ To notch a stud for siding, place the face of the board against the house wall. Open a compass to the thickness of the siding, then move the metal point of the compass vertically down the siding so that the pencil transfers the siding profile to the stud *(below)*. Cut out the profile with a saber saw.

◆ Snap a chalk line along the edges of the porch as a guide to installing studs, allowing for corner studs if you must add them.

◆ Nail the notched stud to the house with 3-inch galvanized nails set at 8-inch intervals, then install additional studs along the chalk lines, toenailing them to floor and ceiling.

2. The remaining studs and doorframe.

◆ Cut 2 jack studs the height of the doorway and nail them to full-length studs, called king studs *(above)*. For a door at the front of the porch, the studs on both sides of the frame are equal in length. For a side door, they are different lengths to compensate for the drainage slope of the porch floor.

◆ Toenail the 2 stud assemblies, jack studs facing each other, to the floor and ceiling so that the distance between them is $\frac{1}{4}$ inch greater than the width of the door you plan to install.

◆ Measure and cut a 2-by-4 header to fit atop the jack studs. Fasten it with nails driven through each king stud into the header's ends.

3. Adding blocking and a knee rail.

Cut 2-by-4s to fit between the studs at the ceiling, at a height of about 3 feet, and at the floor. Between each pair of studs, nail one blocking board to the floor and another to the ceiling. End-nail the knee-rail pieces through the studs where possible; otherwise toe-nail them to the studs.

4. Installing stops for framed screens.

Molding nailed to all four sides of each porch opening prevents the frame from falling inward and positions the frame flush with the exterior face of the supporting structure.

◆ Rule a line around each opening as a guide to recessing the molding a distance equal to the thickness of the frame you will build.

◆ Cut pieces of doorstop molding—mitered ends result in the most craftsmanlike appearance—to fit along the sides, top, and bottom of each porch opening, then fasten the molding with a 2-inch galvanized finishing nail every 8 inches.

◆ Fasten a pair of turn buttons *(inset)* to both sides of each opening to hold the frame against the stops.

ATTACHING SCREENING DIRECTLY TO THE PORCH

1. Stapling the screening.

◆ Cut a length of screening larger than the opening, and fasten the top of the piece to the porch with $\frac{1}{4}$-inch staples driven $\frac{1}{4}$ inch from the opening. Staple one top corner and then the other, restapling as needed to make sure that the top edge is taut and straight. Next, staple the rest of the upper edge at 2-inch intervals.

◆ Pull the screen down evenly over the opening and staple along the bottom at 2-inch intervals, beginning with the corners; then staple from the top to the bottom of the studs and across the knee rail.

◆ Cut away the excess screening $\frac{1}{4}$ inch outside the lines of staples.

2. Trimming with screen bead.

◆ Miter-cut 4 lengths of $\frac{5}{8}$-inch screen bead to cover the staples and to frame the opening flush with its edges. Nail the screen bead around the opening with $\frac{3}{4}$-inch brads every 6 inches. To prevent the bead from warping, alternate the brads from one edge of the bead to the other.

◆ Square-cut a length of bead to fit the knee rail and nail it in place.

SECURING THE MESH WITH SPLINE MOLDING

Unusual cuts at intersections.

◆ To install dual-channel screen-spline molding so that neither channel is blocked *(right),* miter corners of the molding and its cover as shown for a wood frame on page 116.
◆ Where a stud crosses the knee rail, cut a 45° point on each piece of molding. The 4 points meet at the center of the intersection.
◆ At T intersections, cut a point on the molding piece that represents the upright of the T and use it to mark a notch on the crosspiece *(inset).*
◆ After screwing the molding to the frame, secure the mesh with a screen-spline roller *(page 114)* one opening at a time, first across the top, then at the bottom, and finally along the sides.
◆ Trim away the excess screening, and snap the spline cover into place *(far right).*

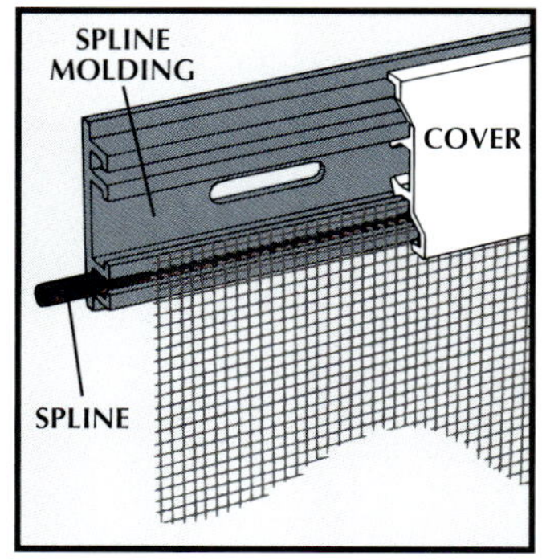

HANGING A WOOD-FRAMED SCREEN DOOR

1. Trimming the door to fit.

◆ With a helper, measure from the header to the porch floor on both sides of the doorframe. Then subtract $\frac{1}{4}$ inch from each measurement to give the door $\frac{1}{8}$-inch clearance, top and bottom.
◆ Transfer the results to the edges of the door, working from the top down.
◆ Connect the 2 marks *(inset),* and trim the door to the line with a saw or, if the adjustment is too small for sawing, with a belt sander.

2. Hanging the door.

◆ Screw 2 hinges to the outer face of the door—1 foot from the top and 1 foot from the bottom. To ensure clearance between door and frame, tape $\frac{1}{8}$-inch-thick spacers above both hinges on the door's edge and on top of the door. Nickels, strips of corrugated cardboard, or $2\frac{1}{2}$-inch-long common nails work well as spacers.

◆ Have a helper hold the door in the frame so that the spacers touch the top and side of the frame. Shim the door to support it or use a block of wood and a pry bar as a foot lever *(left)*. On the doorframe, mark the holes for hinge screws.

◆ Set the door aside and drill pilot holes at the marks, then position the door in the opening and screw the hinges to the frame.

◆ Untape the spacers, and check the door's operation. Shave any edges that bind with a block plane or a wood rasp.

3. Installing a doorstop and latch.

To keep the door from closing too far, nail a band of molding to the doorframe.

◆ While a helper holds the door flush with the outside of the doorframe, mark a line on the frame along the top and sides of the door.

◆ Cut 3 strips of doorstop molding to fit along the top and sides of the frame. Miter the top molding and the upper ends of the side moldings; then cut the bottom ends of the side moldings square.

◆ With the door swung open, place the pieces along the guidelines drawn earlier, and nail them to the doorframe with 2-inch finishing nails set 8 inches apart *(inset)*.

◆ Finally, install a latch according to the manufacturer's directions.

2 Patios of Brick and Concrete

Masonry surfaces actually float on the surface of the ground, rising and subsiding with spring thaws and winter frosts. In the case of concrete, the slab floats on a layer of gravel, while bricks and stone embedded in sand shift individually to adapt to changing contours. Either structure requires considerable excavation, heavy work lightened by a rotary tiller used to loosen soil for easier removal.

Edging a brick patio →

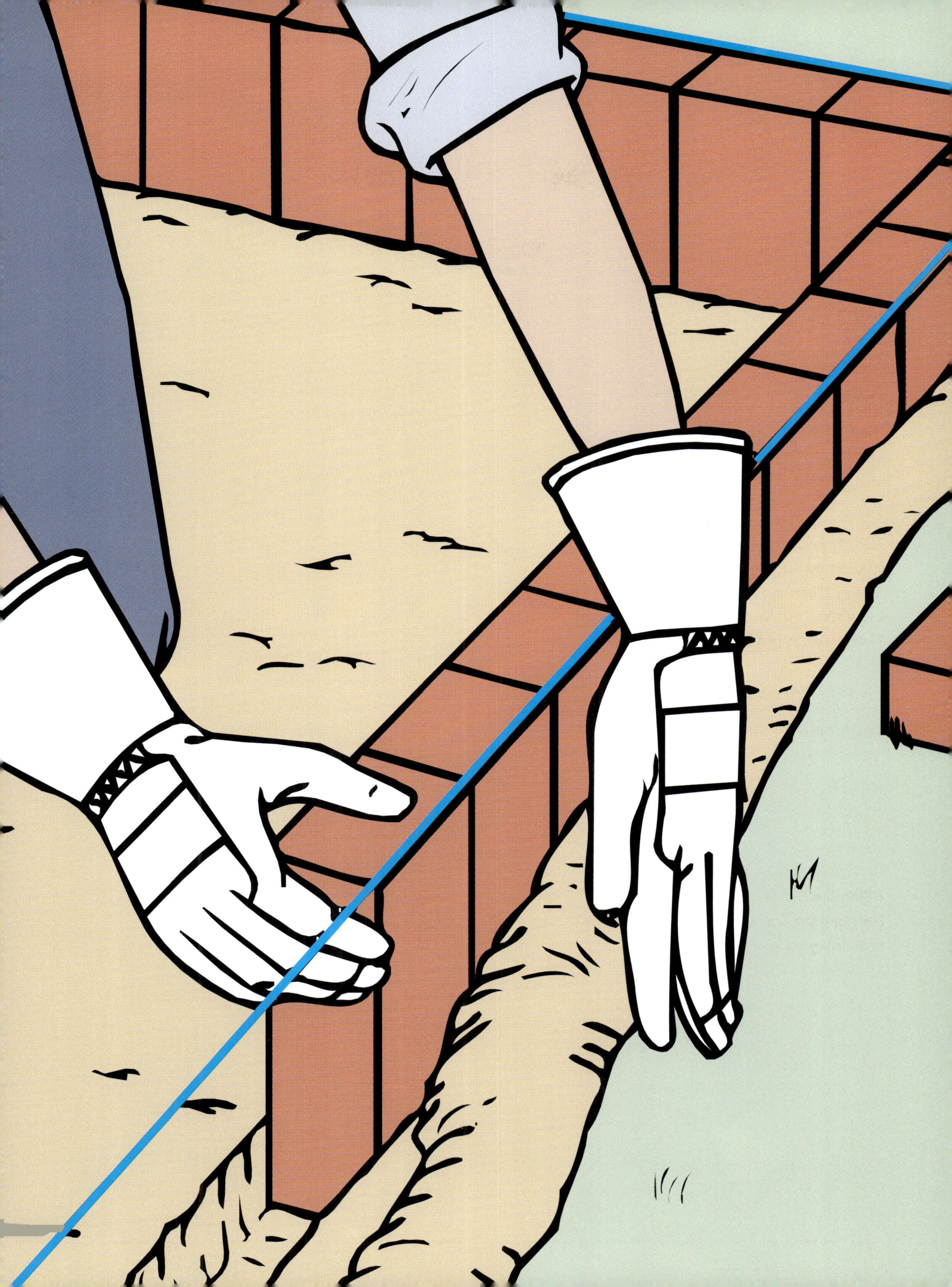

Patterns to Set in Sand or Mortar

A patio with a surface of bricks or concrete paving blocks is weather-resistant and enduring. Because the brick or concrete pavers are small and uniform in size, such a patio is also easy to install and maintain.

The Spectrum of Materials: Standing water and changing temperatures are tough on brick patios; buy paving bricks, which are stronger than those used to build vertical structures. As shown opposite, you can combine them in a number of patterns. Molded concrete paving blocks, on the other hand, are designed to interlock.

Choosing Sand or Concrete: Both brick and concrete pavers may be set on a tightly compacted bed of sand *(pages 82-87)* or on a concrete slab with mortar *(page 103)*. Sand is self-draining and lets the pavers move independently as the earth shifts, and pavers set on sand can be leveled or replaced individually. Patios of mortared bricks or blocks, however, last longer, need less upkeep, and rarely have weeds.

Maintaining the Patio: Whether the pavers are on sand or concrete, moss may be a problem. Although it can be attractive, moss can also be a slippery hazard. To eliminate it, apply moss killer, sold at garden-supply stores. If your patio develops mildew stains, scrub it with household bleach. Finally, weeds can grow between pavers laid on sand, even when a weed-control barrier has been placed underneath. If that happens, you may need to spray all gaps with herbicide, taking care not to spray near trees and other desirable plants.

SAFETY TIPS

Wear hard-toed shoes when you are transporting brick or concrete pavers. If you are working with mortar, leather-palmed work gloves will protect your hands from irritants.

PAVERS FOR PATIOS

Brick pavers.
The paving brick at near right measures about $3\frac{5}{8}$ inches wide by $7\frac{5}{8}$ inches long; these dimensions allow for ample mortar joints between bricks. You can also purchase paving bricks like the one above it, which is exactly twice as long as it is wide. For use on a sand bed, these bricks fit together without gaps to help keep weeds from poking through. In climates where the ground freezes, use paving bricks that are rated SX, which means they can withstand severe weather.

Concrete pavers.
Molded concrete paving blocks come in numerous shapes; the three shown at right are among the more common. Because the blocks are laid down in interlocking patterns, they are less likely to shift position during or after installation.

STACK BOND

RUNNING BOND

BASKET WEAVE

HERRINGBONE

An emphasis on regularity. You can set rectangular bricks in any of the four classic patterns shown above, or combine the patterns to give varied surface designs. Avoid the stack-bond arrangement for large patios, since it is difficult to align; instead, frame other patterns with a stack-bond border. A running-bond pattern, in which the bricks are staggered, is easier to lay uniformly over a broad area.

Interlocking patterns like basket weave and herringbone, in which brick orientation varies, increase the durability of a sand-bed patio, since each brick is held in place by its neighbors. The basket weave above has brick faces exposed; another version has the bricks set on their sides, three to a square. Herringbone, with its directional nature, is useful for directing a viewer's eye to a particular spot.

Layouts based on circles.
To accommodate a tree, a fountain, or other fixed object, lay a circular pattern *(far left)*. Begin at the center with two rings of half bricks, then add rings of full-size bricks to fill an area of any size *(page 86)*.

A scalloped effect like that used on European boulevards *(near left)* is achieved with overlapping arcs of brick as shown on page 87. Loosely fill the scallops with whole and half bricks.

Bricks without Mortar

By far the easiest patio to build is one made of bricks set into a bed of sand. A sand base allows rainwater to seep down to tree or shrub roots, and sand lets bricks accommodate the earth below as it settles or shifts with freezing and thawing.

When planning a patio, consider the stability of the ground. Recent landfill more than 3 feet deep or water found within 1 foot of the surface may cause settling problems. If such conditions exist—or if you live in an earthquake zone—consult a landscape architect.

Laying Out a Sand Bed: To minimize brick cutting, lay a dry run around the patio perimeter before excavating, adjusting the patio dimensions to incorporate as many whole bricks as possible. Be sure to plan for a permanent edging *(page 84)*, required to keep sand-laid bricks from shifting. Chop out tree roots near the surface that would prevent bricks from lying flat. Before digging, check with a building inspector to see if you must erect a silt fence to keep eroded soil on your property.

Drainage: Usually, 2 inches of sand on well-tamped earth offers adequate drainage. Dense clay soils or heavy rainfall, however, often require the added drainage of a 4-inch layer of gravel under the sand. Use the estimator on page 88 to figure the amounts you need. To prevent sand from sifting down into the gravel, cover it with 15-pound roofing felt or 6-mil polyethylene sheeting punctured to let rainwater through. If drainage is a particular problem, slope the sand bed away from the house about 1 inch every 4 to 6 feet. Perforated drain tile or plastic tubing laid in the gravel layer helps drain water away from wet spots.

Choosing the Right Bricks: Untextured, exterior-grade bricks are best; rough or grooved surfaces collect water that can crack bricks when it freezes. But avoid glazed bricks, which become slippery when wet. "Bricks" of molded concrete, which come in a wide array of colors and shapes, offer an alternative to traditional clay brick.

With Gaps or Without: Patterns of bricks laid tight against one another control weeds better than bricks laid with gaps between them. For a gapless patio, buy special paving bricks exactly half as wide as they are long.

Other paving bricks are sized for mortar joints between them. The gap both accentuates the pattern and channels rainwater down the long side of the brick—away from the house, if you align the long edges with any slope the site may have. Plastic sheeting laid on the sand bed before the bricks are laid helps keep weeds from growing in the gaps, and sand swept into the gaps keeps the bricks from moving.

CAUTION *Before excavating, establish the locations of underground obstacles such as electric, water, and sewer lines, and dry wells, septic tanks, and cesspools.*

TOOLS

Brickset
4-pound maul
Mason's hammer
Rubber mallet
Level
Framing square
Circular saw with a carbide masonry blade

MATERIALS

Bricks
Washed gravel ($\frac{3}{4}$-inch)
Polyethylene sheeting
Sand
2-by-2 stakes
String

SAFETY TIPS

Wear eye protection when cutting bricks. A dust mask is recommended when trimming brick with a circular saw. Gloves help prevent blisters and abrasions.

TWO METHODS FOR CUTTING BRICKS

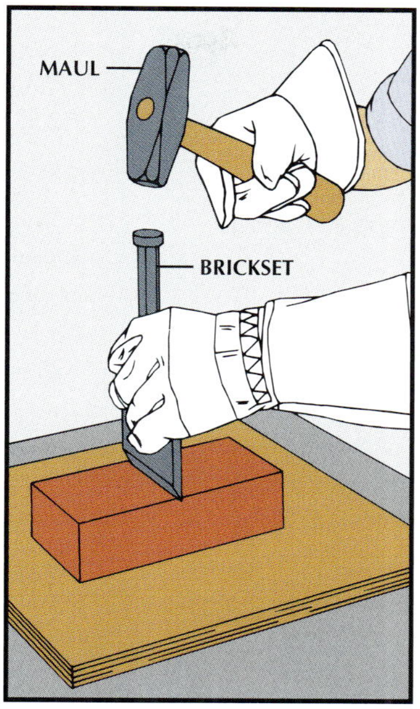

Using a brickset.
To cut a small number of bricks, use a wide chisel—called a brickset—and a 4-pound maul. Draw a cutting line on the brick, then cushion the brick on sand or a board. Hold the brickset vertically with the beveled edge facing away from you and strike the tool sharply. Then tilt the brickset slightly toward you and strike again, thus splitting the brick. Practice on a few broken bricks before you cut the bricks you will use.

Scoring bricks with a circular saw.
Large numbers of bricks are more easily cut with the help of a circular saw fitted with a carbide masonry blade. Hold the brick in a simple jig made of 2-by-4 scraps, spaced a brick's width apart and nailed to a piece of plywood. Set the saw for a $\frac{1}{4}$-inch cut, then slowly guide the blade along the cutting line, grooving the brick. Make a matching groove on the other side, then hold the brick in your hand and break off the unwanted portion with the blunt end of a mason's hammer *(inset).*

EXCAVATING FOR A PATIO

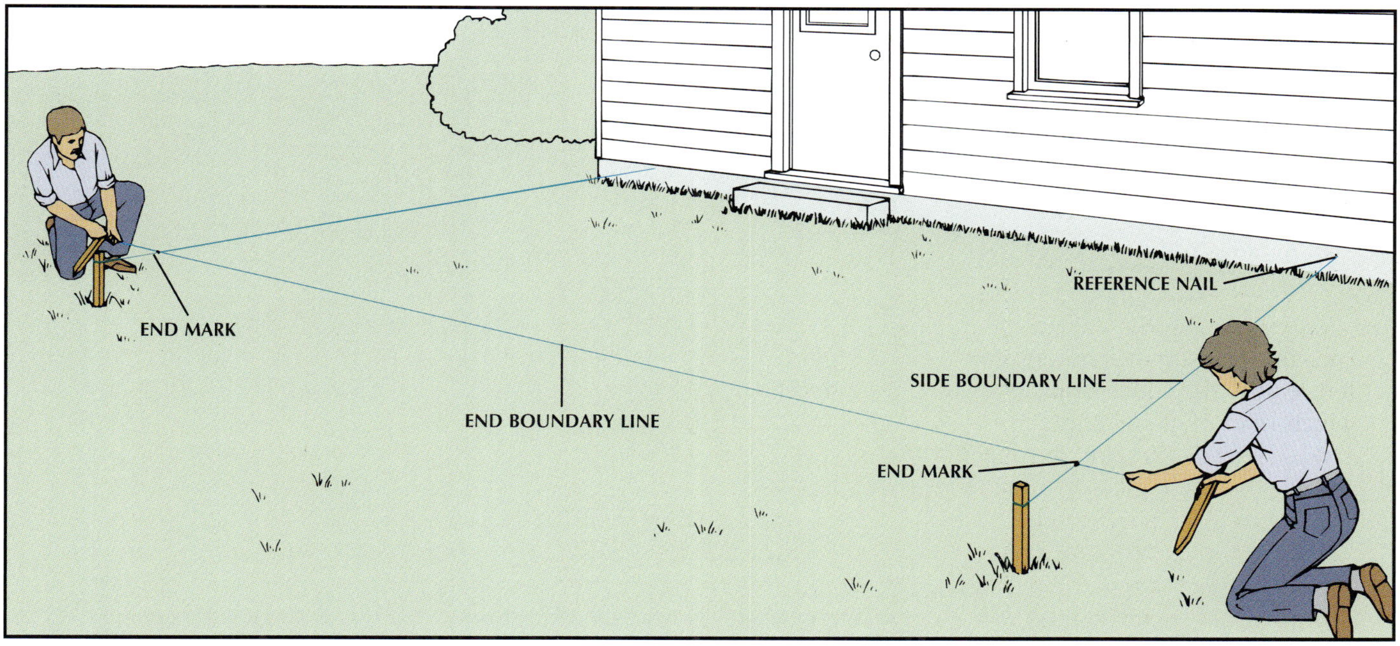

Laying out a rectangular site.
◆ Drive reference nails into the wall of the house to mark both sides of the patio.
◆ Use the method shown on page 10 to establish positions for 2-by-2 stakes opposite the nails and 2 feet beyond the end of the future patio.
◆ Tie string between the nails and stakes to establish side boundary lines for the patio and mark each string where the patio will end.
◆ With a helper *(above),* stake a third string so that it crosses the marks you made on the side boundary lines.
◆ To excavate the area, first dig a trench along the boundary lines. Make the trench deep enough to accommodate the bricks, sand, and gravel if any. Work in parallel rows, back and forth between the perimeter trenches.

Laying out an irregular shape.

◆ Draw the patio on graph paper, with each square representing 1 square foot. To estimate the area of the patio, assign a rough fractional value to parts of squares inside the outline. Then add up the full squares and the fractions. Use this figure when buying brick, sand, and gravel.

◆ Lay out a garden hose in the shape of the patio, then outline the perimeter on the ground with a dispenser of powdered chalk *(page 94)*. Trench around the perimeter, then excavate.

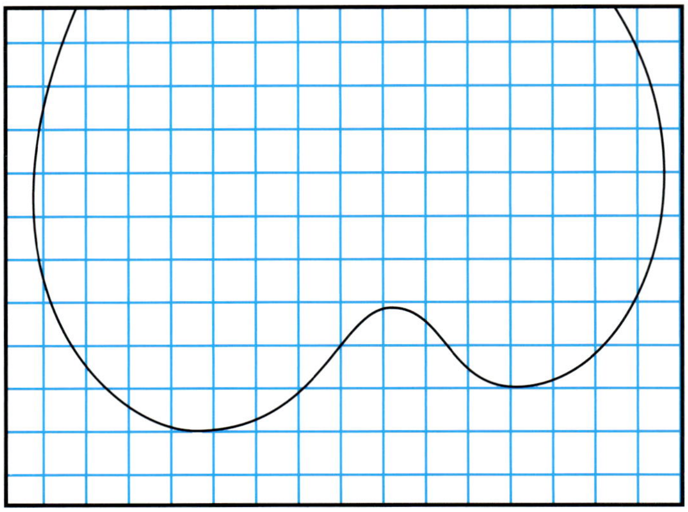

LAYING BRICKS IN SAND

1. Edging the perimeter.

◆ First, compact the earth inside the excavation with a tamper *(page 89)*.

◆ Around the perimeter, dig a narrow trench such that the top of a brick stood on end in the trench will be even with the patio surface. *(If a side of the patio will border a flower bed, let the edging extend 2 inches higher.)*

◆ Tamp the bottom of the trench with the end of a 2-by-4, then stretch reference strings as guides for aligning the tops of the edging bricks with one another. Next, stand bricks upright around the perimeter *(above)*, with their top edges touching the strings. Press earth against the bricks to hold them up.

◆ Add washed gravel as necessary, distributing it evenly over the surface with a rake. Cover the gravel with roofing felt, or polyethylene sheeting that has been punctured with drainage holes at 4- to 6-inch intervals.

◆ Spread a 2-inch layer of sand over the bed. Dampen the sand, then tamp the surface again.

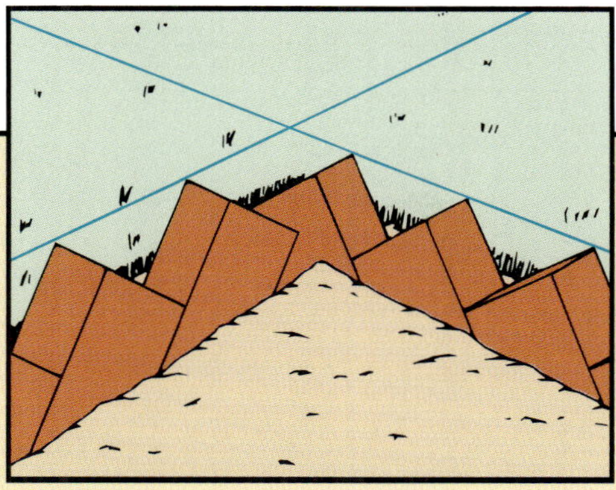

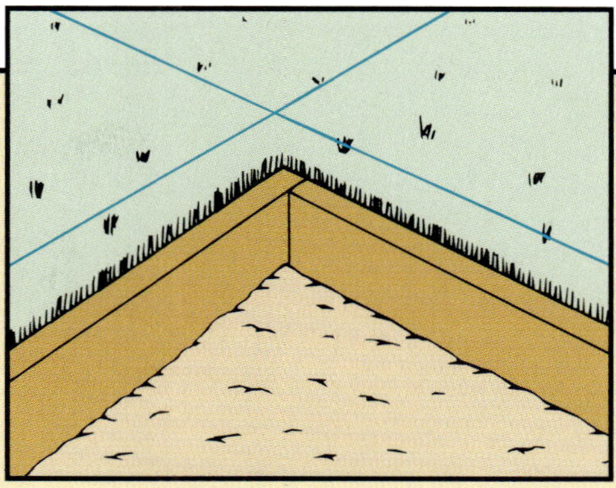

Alternative edgings.
To make a sawtooth pattern with teeth protruding 2 inches above the patio surface *(above)*, set the bricks at an angle of 45° in the trench. Other choices for edgings include rot-resistant redwood or pressure-treated 2-by-6s *(above, right)* set in a narrower trench, or upright bricks set in a curve *(right)* for a rounded corner. To lay out a curved corner, use a level to align the tops of the bricks.

2. Laying the bricks.

◆ Use a reference string to help align bricks in the pattern you choose for your patio. Begin a herringbone pattern, for example, with a brick set at a 45° angle to the edging in each of two adjacent patio corners. Tap the bricks into the sand with a rubber mallet to make them flush with the edging bricks.

◆ Stretch a string between two spare bricks, set just outside the edging, so that the string passes over the corners of the two corner bricks. As you set bricks in the first row, align corners with the string. Use the mallet or adjust the sand bed to keep the bricks even with one another.

◆ To begin a new row, lay a brick at each end as a guide for positioning the reference string. Fill in the row, smoothing any sand you may have disturbed. Repeat for each row.

◆ Fill triangular spaces along the patio edges with brick that you have cut to fit, then gently sweep sand into any gaps that remain. Add more sand if necessary after it rains.

A CIRCULAR PATIO TO SURROUND A TREE

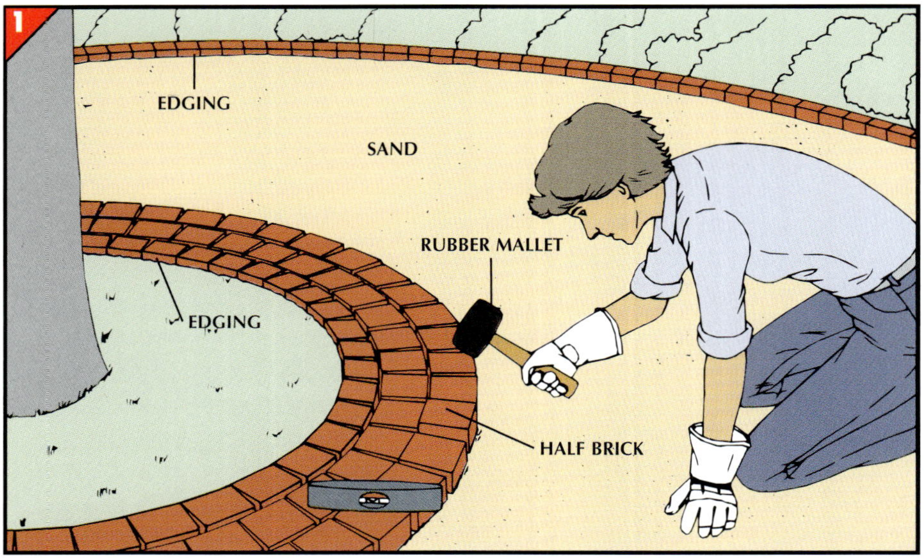

1. Starting with half bricks.

◆ Loop a garden hose around the tree to mark inner and outer perimeters for the patio. Make the inner circle at least 3 feet in diameter to avoid wide gaps between the half bricks used in the first two courses.

◆ Excavate and edge the area to be paved, then prepare the sand bed.

◆ Cut half bricks for the first course and tap them into place with a rubber mallet, wedging the inner corners of the bricks tight against each other *(left).* Use a level to align the tops of the bricks. Trim the last half brick in each course as needed for a snug fit.

◆ Lay a second course of half bricks against the first.

2. Setting the whole bricks.

◆ Place concentric circles of whole bricks in the sand bed so that their inner edges touch at the corners and butt against the preceding course. Tap each brick into place with a rubber mallet. Use a 4-foot mason's level to align the brick, adding or removing sand as necessary.

◆ Continue laying whole bricks in concentric circles out to the edging.

3. Filling gaps at the edge.

◆ Mark a brick to fit each oddly shaped nook along the patio's outer perimeter. Cut the brick with a brickset as shown on page 83, then trim as needed by chipping it with the sharp end of a mason's hammer. Set the brick into place with a rubber mallet.

◆ Gently brush sand into the gaps between bricks, repeating the process as necessary to refill the cracks after a rain.

SETTING BRICKS IN OVERLAPPING SCALLOPS

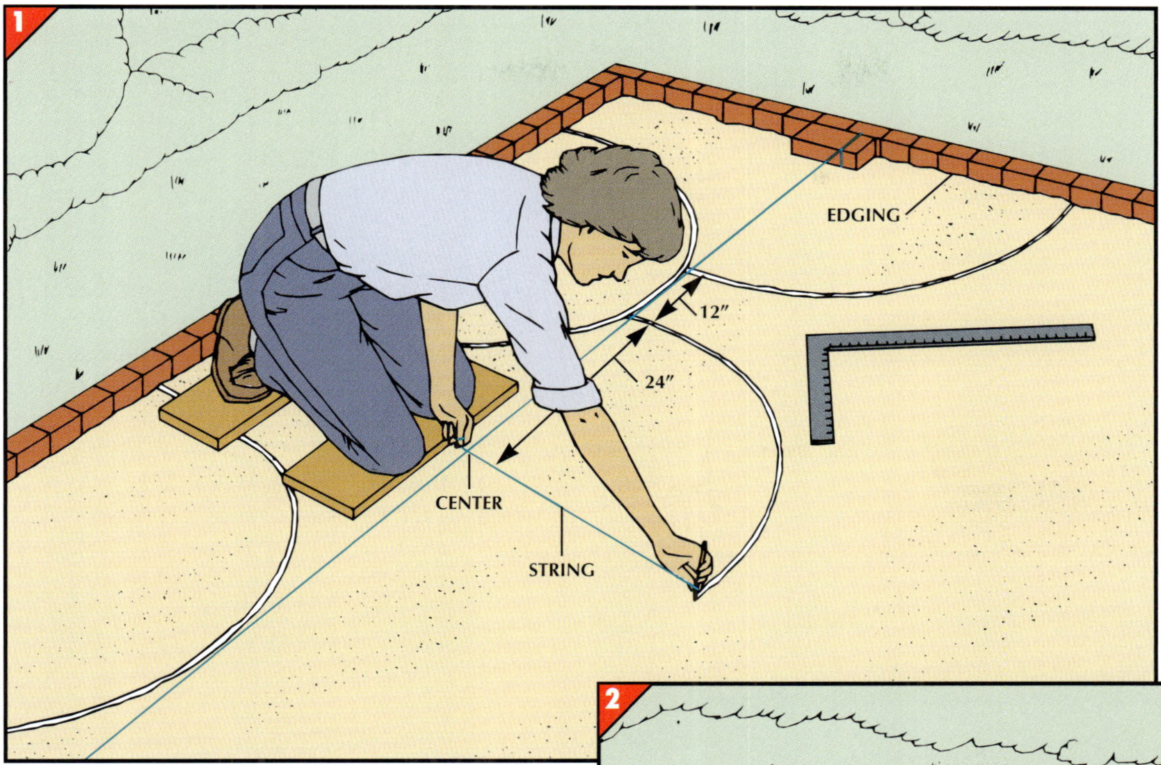

1. Scribing scallop arcs.

◆ Use the edging of a sand bed to establish a base line for drawing semicircles in the sand. Arcs that have a radius of 24 inches and are spaced with their centers 60 inches apart make an attractive pattern. Scribe arcs across one end of the sand bed, with partial arcs at the sides if necessary.

◆ Stretch a string between two bricks so that it crosses the tops of the arcs in the first row *(above)*. Kneeling on boards to avoid disturbing arcs already drawn, scribe another row of arcs with centers midway between those in the first row. A framing square helps in marking these centers and those in subsequent rows. Use partial arcs in the last row if necessary.

2. Paving the scallops.

◆ Arrange whole bricks along each arc *(right)*, then with a partial brick, start filling each scallop at the narrow space between arcs. Half a brick, followed by three-quarters of a brick in the next course, works well with 24-inch arcs.

◆ Pave the rest of each scallop with whole bricks laid in slightly curving rows *(inset)*. Fill partial scallops with whole bricks and any cavities with cut bricks or sand.

◆ Sweep sand into any gaps that remain.

Groundwork for a Concrete Slab

A concrete slab consists of a layer of concrete, usually reinforced with wire mesh, that rests on a drainage bed of gravel. Although the 4-inch reinforced slab on 4 inches of gravel described on the following pages satisfies many building codes, always check with local authorities for the correct specifications.

Building codes may also specify the degree of slope required for water runoff and whether a silt fence is needed during construction to limit soil erosion. Local zoning laws may dictate the location, design, and size of a slab.

Getting Started: Selecting a site for a slab requires the same care as choosing one for a brick patio *(page 82)*. When your plan is completed use the estimator below to calculate how much concrete and gravel you'll use, based on the area of the slab and the thickness of the concrete plus the gravel bed.

To prepare the site for a rectangular slab, lay out boundaries with wood stakes and string as shown on page 83, and excavate the site. Dig 2 feet beyond the strings to accommodate form boards and braces, then proceed as shown here. Site preparation for a free-form slab appears on pages 94-95. Save sod and dirt to fill in at the sides of the finished slab.

Expansion Joints: Many local codes require a strip of asphalt-impregnated expansion-joint filler in the concrete every 8 to 10 feet of a slab's length and between the slab and the house foundation *(page 92, Step 7)*. The purpose of the joints is to prevent damage as concrete expands and contracts with changes in temperature. Try to buy joint filler as wide as the thickness of the slab. If unavailable, somewhat narrower or wider filler is satisfactory.

Forms to Shape Concrete: Unless you plan on a decorative pattern of permanent form boards *(page 93)*, build forms from inexpensive woods such as fir, spruce, or pine. Plywood, made flexible with the technique shown on page 94, is used to mold the curves of a free-form slab. Double-headed nails allow both types of temporary forms to be quickly disassembled.

TOOLS

- Common carpentry tools
- Spade
- Tamper
- Screed
- Rake
- 4-pound maul
- Line level
- Wire cutters

MATERIALS

- 1-by-2s
- 2-by-4s
- Plywood ($\frac{3}{4}$-inch)
- 2-by-2 stakes
- Mason's cord
- Double-headed nails (2-inch)
- Common nails (3-inch)
- Spikes (6-inch)
- Masonry nails ($1\frac{1}{2}$-inch)
- Washed gravel ($\frac{3}{4}$-inch)
- Expansion-joint filler
- Reinforcing mesh
- Binding wire
- Concrete blocks
- Powdered chalk
- Lath

SAFETY TIPS

Wear goggles when nailing form boards together and joint filler to the house. Gloves protect your hands from blisters, splinters, and especially cuts when handling wire mesh.

CALCULATIONS FOR SLOPE AND VOLUME

Length of a side boundary line in feet				
________	x 0.25	=	______	inches

Calculating slope.
For a slope of $\frac{1}{4}$ inch per foot, use the formula above to determine the difference in height between the edge of the slab that abuts the house and the edge parallel to it. Multiply by 0.125 instead of 0.25 for a slope of $\frac{1}{8}$ inch per foot.

Area in square feet		Thickness in inches				
______	x	______	x 0.0033	=	______	cubic yards

Estimating cubic yardage.
Use the estimator above to find the amount of concrete or gravel needed for a slab or drainage bed. The result in cubic yards—the bulk measure in which such materials are sold—includes an 8 percent allowance for waste and spillage.

TILTING A SLAB FOR DRAINAGE

1. Leveling the excavated area.

◆ Using a rake, break up any clods of earth; then, with a helper, pull an 8-foot-long 2-by-4 leveling board across the area to smooth it *(above)*.

◆ Dampen the area with a hose, and compact the surface by pounding it with a tamper. You can rent one or build one from a 2-foot square of $\frac{3}{4}$-inch plywood with a braced handle, 4 feet high, made of 2-by-4s.

◆ After tamping, pull the leveling board across the area again, using it as a straightedge to make sure that the surface is reasonably even.

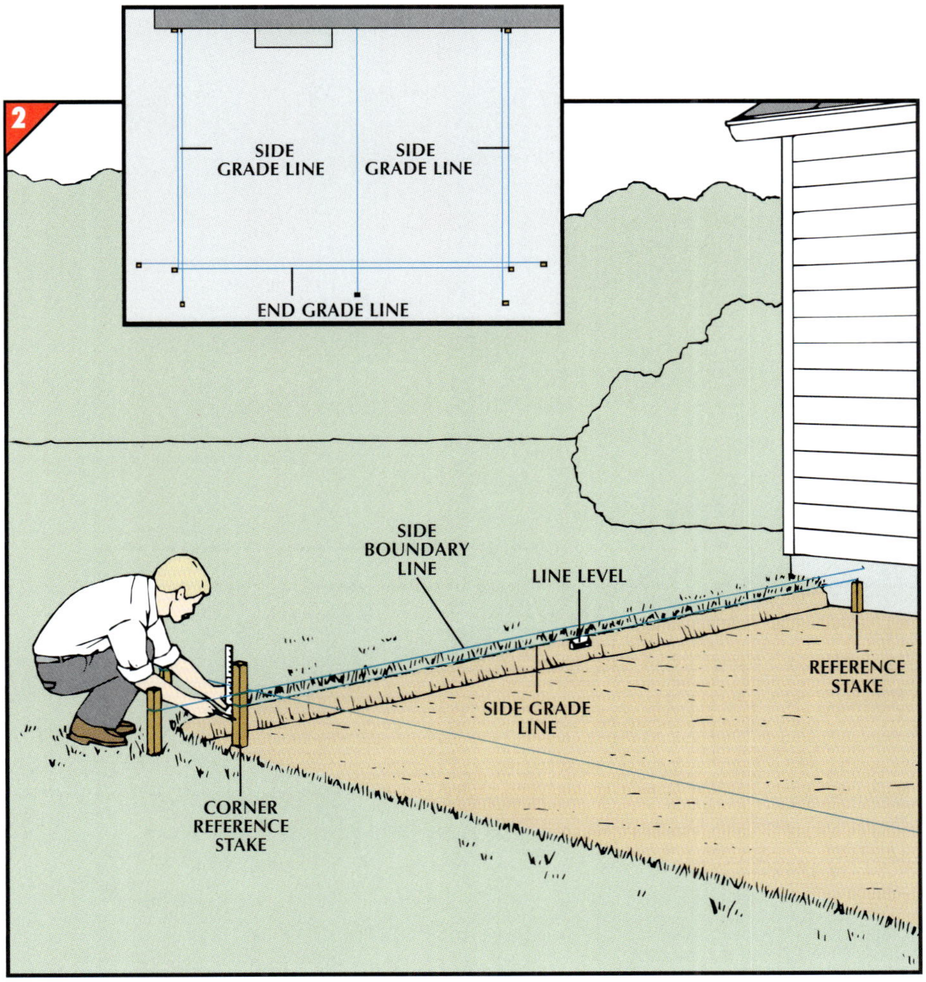

2. Establishing the grade.

◆ Mark the slab height—the sum of the slab and gravel-bed thicknesses—on the house wall, 2 inches outside a side boundary line. Center a 2-by-2 reference stake on the mark and drive it into the ground next to the house wall, bringing the top even with the slab-height mark. Center a nail on top of the stake and hammer it in partway.

◆ Measure along the side boundary line to a point 2 inches beyond the end boundary line, and drive a corner reference stake opposite the first. Loop a string around the second stake and tie it to the nail in the other. Hang a line level at the center of the string and adjust the string at the corner stake to make the string level.

◆ Use the formula on the preceding page to calculate slope, and mark the resulting distance on the corner stake, below the string. Lower the string to the mark, called a grade mark.

◆ Repeat for the other side of the slab.

◆ Connect the grade marks on the corner stakes with a third string to make an end grade line. Use that line and a reference stake near the house to establish a grade line within the slab for each expansion joint required.

3. Adding support stakes.
◆ Mark the grade lines at 2-foot intervals. Directly below each marker, drive a 2-by-2 form-support stake deep enough so you can't pull it out by hand and so the grade line just touches the top of the stake. Place stakes precisely to ensure that corners will be square and the slab sloped correctly.
◆ When all of the support stakes are in place, remove the grade lines and use a handsaw to trim the corner reference stakes to the height marked earlier for the grade lines. Then remove all the boundary-marker strings and stakes; leave only the support stakes and the corner reference stakes.

4. Installing form boards.
◆ Cut a 2-by-4 form board 4 inches longer than the distance from the house to the outer edge of the reference stake. Use more than one if needed, butting the boards.
◆ Set a board against the inside faces of the support stakes, one end against the house. Rest the board on wood blocks so that the top edge is even with the tops of the stakes.
◆ Drive a 2-inch double-headed nail through each end stake into the board, using a maul as an anvil *(above)*. Then nail the board to the intermediate stakes.
◆ Install a form board for the other side of the slab in the same way.
◆ Nail a form board for the end of the slab to its support stakes. Where this board abuts the side boards, toenail the joints with 3-inch common nails.
◆ For each expansion joint, cut a board $\frac{1}{2}$ inch shorter than the distance between the house and the end board. Nail the board to its support stakes on the side of the slab that will be poured first, leaving a $\frac{1}{2}$-inch space at the wall.
◆ Where boards abut *(inset)*, drive a support stake 6 inches to each side of the joint. Nail the boards to the stakes, then nail a strip of $\frac{1}{2}$-inch plywood over the joint.

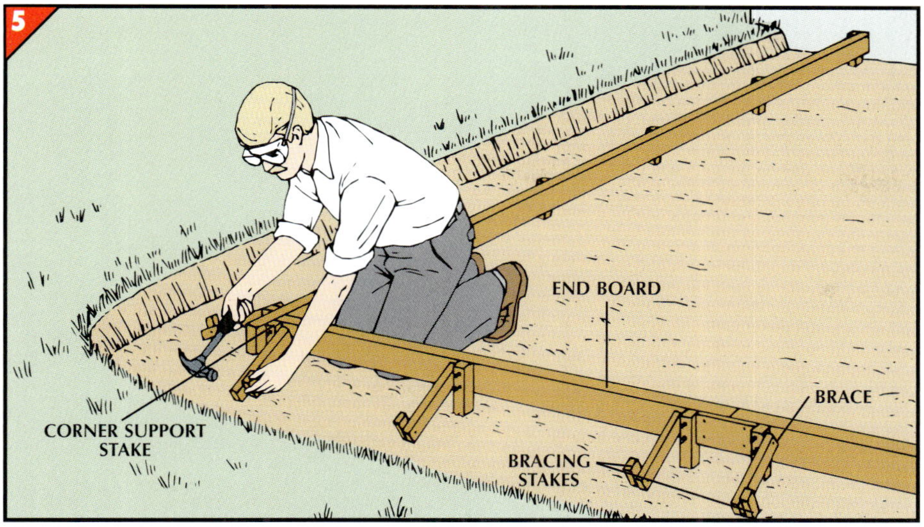

5. Bracing the form boards.

◆ Drive a support stake at the corners where end and side boards meet.
◆ Reinforce each support stake, including those flanking a joint, with a 1-by-2 brace nailed to a stake driven about 1 foot from the form board.
◆ Excavate the slab area along the end board to match the slope of the side form boards, then smooth and tamp.

6. Screeding the gravel.

Pour a layer of $\frac{3}{4}$-inch gravel into each section of the slab, allowing it to spill out under the form boards. With a helper, smooth the gravel by dragging a screed across its surface.

TRICKS OF THE TRADE

To Make a Screed

The function of a screed is to assure a smooth gravel surface and a uniform slab thickness. To make the screed shown here, which is designed for a slab 4 inches thick, cut a 1-by-8 board 2 inches shorter than the distance between forms, and a 2-by-4 board 10 inches longer than this distance. Center the 1-by-8 on the 2-by-4. Offset the 1-by-8 board $\frac{1}{4}$ inch and nail the boards together. To the face of the 1-by-8, toenail two 2-by-2 handles, each 4 feet long and cut at a 30° angle at one end. Brace the handles with 2-by-2s nailed to the top of the 2-by-4.

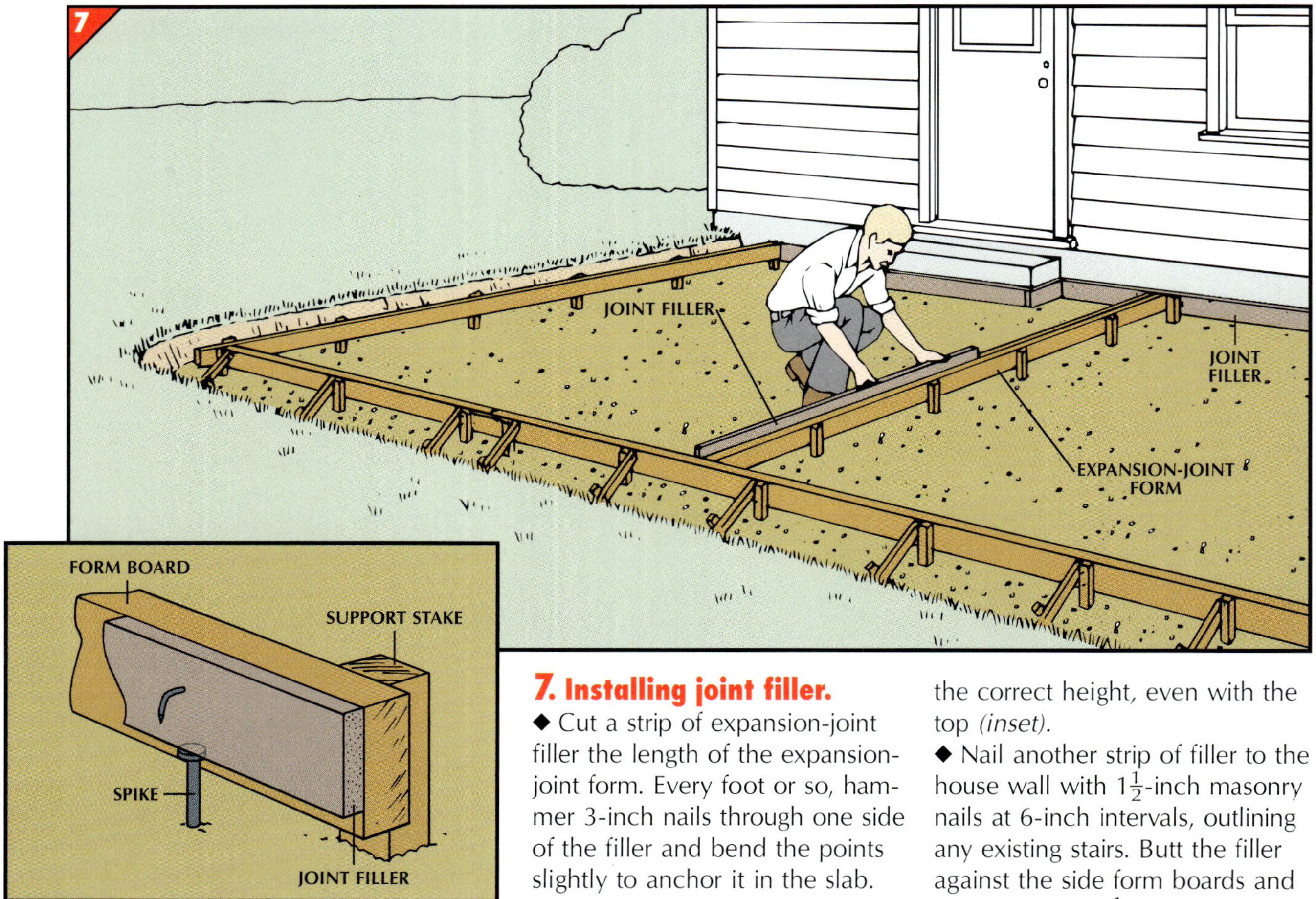

7. Installing joint filler.

◆ Cut a strip of expansion-joint filler the length of the expansion-joint form. Every foot or so, hammer 3-inch nails through one side of the filler and bend the points slightly to anchor it in the slab.

◆ Set the filler against the form *(above)*. Use 6-inch spikes, if necessary, to support the filler at the correct height, even with the top *(inset)*.

◆ Nail another strip of filler to the house wall with $1\frac{1}{2}$-inch masonry nails at 6-inch intervals, outlining any existing stairs. Butt the filler against the side form boards and work it into the $\frac{1}{2}$-inch space between expansion-joint forms and the house.

8. Laying wire mesh.

◆ Wearing gloves, unroll mesh over the gravel. Begin at the outer edge of the slab, and leave 2 inches between the mesh and the form boards. Weigh down the mesh with concrete blocks as you go. When you reach the other side of a section, use wirecutters to trim the mesh 2 inches short of the form board. Then turn the mesh over, and walk on it to flatten it.

◆ Cover the gravel in the section you intend to pour first, allowing panels of mesh to overlap 6 inches. Cut the mesh to fit around steps or other obstacles, then tie panels together with binding wire.

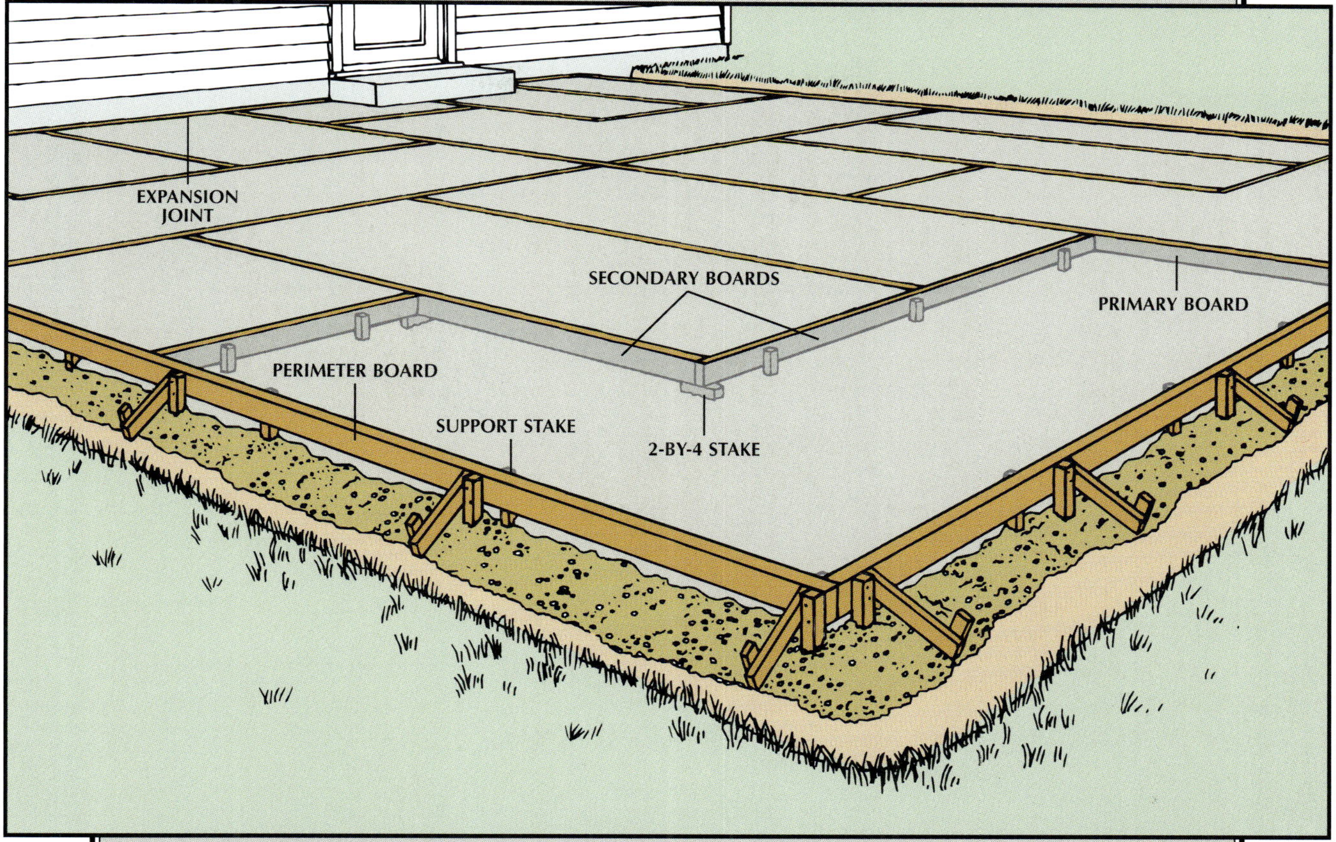

THE APPEAL OF PERMANENT FORM BOARDS

In most instances, form boards become scrap lumber after a slab is poured. A decorative option, however, is to leave them in place as a frame around the slab or, as shown here, to lay out an attractive pattern of interior form boards. For this purpose, pressure-treated or other weather-resistant wood is superior to the pine or spruce used for temporary forms.

Installing permanent form boards follows the same principles used for setting up temporary boards—with a few differences. When laying out the perimeter for such a slab, take into account that the form boards will contribute to its length and width. Set up and brace perimeter form boards as shown on pages 90-91, but drive support stakes for interior boards as well as perimeter boards an inch below the planned surface of the slab so that the concrete will conceal them.

Establish the slope of the slab as shown on page 89. Each interior board that will lie perpendicular to the house needs a grade line. Boards oriented parallel to the house each require a string set up in the same way as an end line *(page 89)*.

Permanent form boards replace expansion joints within the slab but not the one along the house. Boards that cross from one side of the slab to the other are called primary form boards. Next to the house use stakes to secure the ends of primary form boards; nail through perimeter form boards to secure other ends.

Secondary form boards are shorter than the width or length of the patio. Where secondary form boards meet perimeter or primary form boards, they can be face-nailed. Where two secondary boards meet, nail one to the other and toenail both to a 2-by-4 stake driven into the ground under the joint.

Before pouring the slab, drive 3-inch nails halfway into all the form boards to help anchor them in the concrete, and cover their top edges with heavy-duty tape to prevent concrete stains.

CURVED FORMS FOR A ROUNDED SLAB

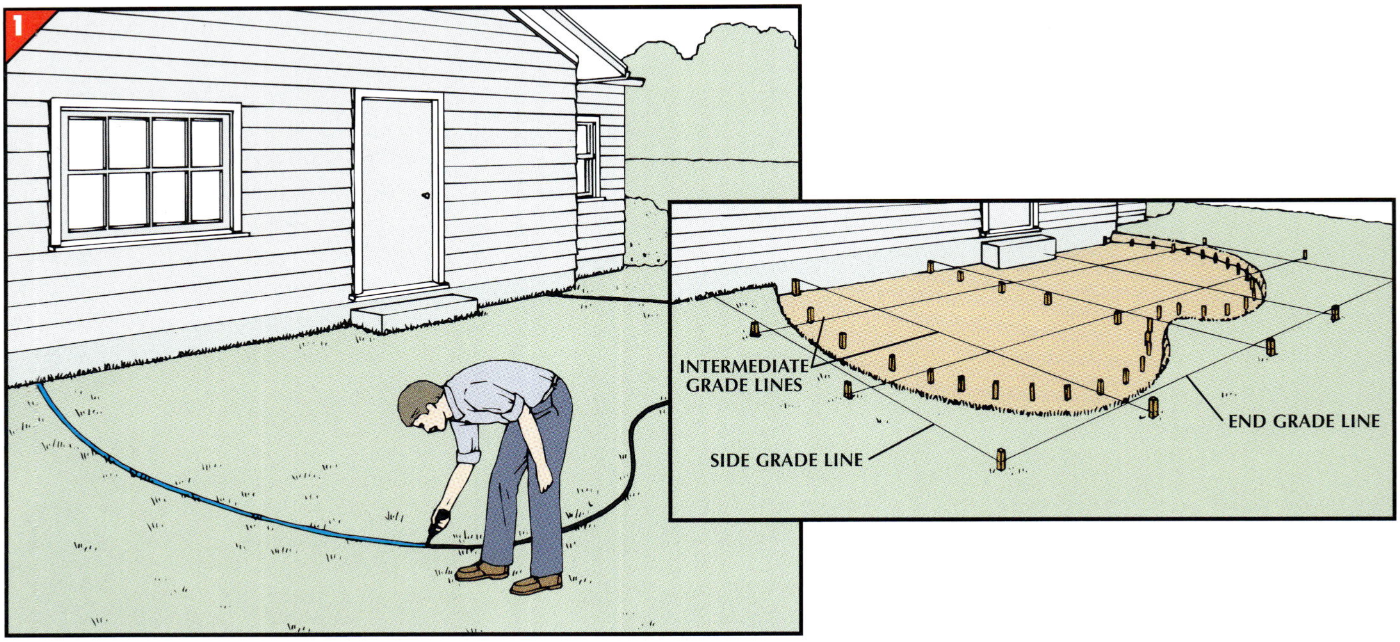

1. Excavating the slab area.

◆ Establish the slab shape with a garden hose, then mark the shape on the ground with powdered chalk.

◆ Remove the hose, and excavate the area a distance 2 feet beyond the chalk line. Dig to a depth equal to the thickness of the drainage bed plus the thickness of the slab. Dig back and forth across the area in parallel rows, then smooth and tamp the soil in the bottom of the excavation.

◆ Establish drainage away from the house, first by setting up boundary lines and grade lines for a rectangle a foot or two larger in each dimension than the slab's maximum length and width *(inset)*.

◆ Tie intermediate grade lines at 3-foot intervals between the side lines, and between the wall of the house and the end line; at the house, tie the strings to masonry nails.

◆ Drive 2-by-2 support stakes into the ground around the slab perimeter, 2 feet in from the edge of the excavation. Space the stakes 2 feet apart along gradual curves, 1 foot apart around sharp curves.

◆ Add support stakes for any interior forms required, spacing them at 2-foot intervals. Set the tops of the stakes even with the strings.

TRICKS OF THE TRADE

Taking the Stiffness Out of Plywood

The rigidity of plywood—layers of wood glued together under pressure—results from orienting the grain in each layer perpendicular to the grain in its neighbors. Yet you can make even $\frac{3}{4}$-inch plywood bend enough to serve as forms for a curved slab. With a circular saw, cut strips about 4 inches wide with the outer grain running lengthwise. Then set the saw for a depth of $\frac{1}{2}$ inch and saw across the strip. Check that the blade cuts through no more than three of the plywood's five layers. Adjust the saw as necessary, then cut grooves across the strip every inch or so.

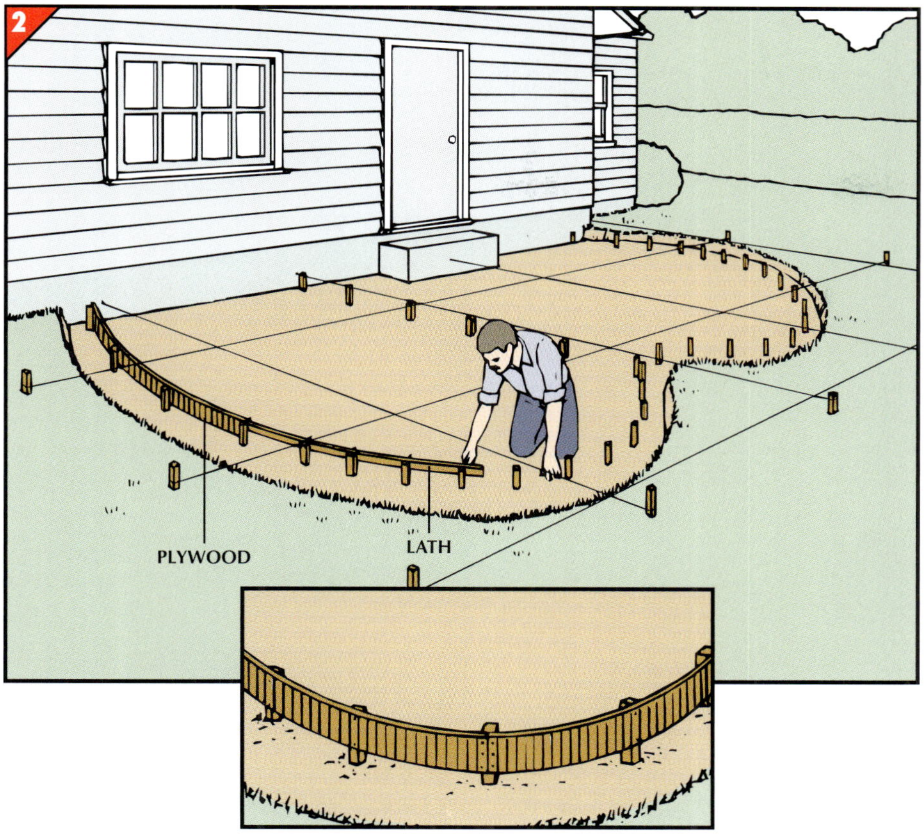

2. Installing form boards.

◆ To measure for curved form boards, first cut a strip of lath 4 to 8 feet long. Tack it to support stakes, even with the tops and butted against the house.

◆ Mark the lath at the midpoint of the support stake nearest the end, then pry off the lath and transfer the mark to a strip of $\frac{3}{4}$-inch plywood cut as wide as the slab depth. Trim the plywood at the mark.

◆ Cut slots in the plywood to make it pliable *(opposite)*, then nail it to the support stakes.

◆ Proceed around the slab perimeter in this fashion, butting sections of plywood at support stakes *(inset)*.

◆ Install expansion-joint forms as necessary *(page 90)*.

3. Sloping the forms.

◆ Work around the curved form, lifting or hammering down the boards and stakes until the top edge of the form just grazes the grading lines. Repeat for the straight forms of the expansion joints.

◆ When both the curved and the straight forms are adjusted, secure the support stakes with braces *(page 91)*.

◆ Correct the depth of the excavation to match the slope of the grade, then spread a gravel drainage bed 4 inches thick.

◆ Install joint filler as shown on page 92.

4. Cutting mesh to fit the form.

◆ Unroll a length of wire mesh over a section of the form, letting it overlap the curve of the form boards where necessary.

◆ Anchor the mesh temporarily with cinder blocks, then cut the mesh along the curve, 2 inches inside the form.

◆ Flatten the mesh either by bending or by removing it from the form and walking it flat.

◆ Cut additional sections of mesh, allowing each to overlap the previous section by 6 inches. Flatten the sections and tie them together with binding wire.

Pouring and Finishing Concrete

The key requirement for pouring and finishing a concrete slab is speed. On a dry, windy day, it may take only three hours for freshly poured concrete to become too stiff to work. For a 10-by-12 slab, two people will need about an hour for the heavy work of pouring, leveling, and smoothing the concrete, plus up to three hours to finish the surface. Until you have some experience, it's best to pour concrete in sections no larger than 120 square feet.

Mixing Your Own: A good source of concrete is a ready-mix company specializing in small loads—unless the slab is far from the street. In that case, haul the concrete in a rented trailer and mixer.

When making concrete yourself, test the mixture's consistency frequently *(below)*. Between checks, add water sparingly—1 cup per cubic foot of concrete at a time.

Planning for the Finish: Smooth and textured finishes to concrete *(pages 98-99)* need no advance preparation, but surfacing with other materials requires forethought. For example, if you intend to apply a pebble-aggregate surface *(page 100)*, you will need a stiffer-than-average concrete mix. Furthermore, you must thoroughly wet the pebbles before pouring the concrete. Order $\frac{1}{3}$ cubic yard of gravel for every 100 square feet of slab.

Redwood rounds *(page 99)*, which are suitable only in dry climates, must be in place before concrete is poured. Positioning them requires cutting openings for them in the slab's mesh reinforcement.

The Process of Curing: After a slab is finished, it must be cured—kept moist and warm for at least a week to allow for the gradual chemical reactions that give concrete its full structural strength. The most common method of curing is to cover the slab with a polyethylene sheet. Colored slabs and pebble-aggregate surfaces are air-cured, however—left uncovered and sprinkled several times a day with water. Wait until the slab has cured to remove the outside forms.

TOOLS

- Concrete mixer
- Shovel
- Rake
- Spade
- 2-by-4 screed
- Bull float
- Ladder
- Mason's trowel
- Edger
- Hand float
- Rectangular trowel
- Convex jointer
- Darby

Concrete Checklist

- When ordering concrete, tell the ready-mix company the dimensions of your slab and whether you intend to apply a pebble-aggregate surface or wish to have it colored.
- If you live in an area subject to freezes and thaws, make sure that an air-entraining agent—a chemical that creates tiny air bubbles in the concrete to prevent cracking—is added to the mix.
- Make arrangements for the ready-mix truck to arrive early; concrete sets more slowly in the cool of the morning.
- Have the truck park on the street, then lay a path of planks for carrying the concrete to the slab in wheelbarrows.
- Transport approximately 1 cubic foot (150 pounds) in a wheelbarrow at a time.

TRICKS OF THE TRADE

Perfect Concrete

Mixing the correct amount of water into concrete is crucial: Too little and a smooth finish on the concrete will be difficult to attain, too much and the material will lack strength and durability. The concrete in the left photograph above, although appearing somewhat dry, is actually just right; light troweling produces a smooth surface. A dash or two more water produces a mudlike mixture that is too wet for use *(above, right)*.

FILLING THE FORMS

1. Adding the concrete.

◆ Support the wire mesh on bricks, and oil the form boards to prevent sticking.

◆ Dump enough concrete into the first form to overfill by $\frac{1}{2}$ inch a 3- to 4-foot-wide section between the form boards, packing each load against the preceding one with a shovel. Use the shovel after each load to push the concrete into form corners and against the joint filler.

◆ Work a flat spade between the forms and the concrete to force the stones in the mix away from the sides. Then jab the spade vertically into the concrete throughout the section, to eliminate air pockets.

◆ If the wire reinforcement sags into the gravel base under the concrete's weight, hook it with a rake and lift it to the middle of the concrete.

2. Screeding the concrete.

◆ As each 3- to 4-foot section is filled, set a screed—a straight 2-by-4, cut 2 feet wider than the width of the form—on edge across the form boards. With the aid of a helper, lift and lower the screed in a chopping motion to force the aggregate down into the concrete.

◆ Then, starting at one end of the filled section, pull the screed across the surface of the concrete, simultaneously sliding it from side to side in a sawlike motion. Tilt the screed toward you as you pull it, so that the bottom of the board acts as a cutting edge.

◆ To level any remaining low spots or bumps, pull the screed across the concrete again, tilting it away from you. In areas around obstacles such as steps or window wells, use a short screed, cut to fit the space.

◆ Fill and level the rest of the form in successive 3- to 4-foot sections.

3. Bull-floating the surface.

◆ To compact and smooth the concrete, first push the float forward, tilting the front edge of the blade upward. Then draw it back, keeping the blade flat against the surface.

◆ Shovel fresh concrete into any remaining depressions. To reach areas beyond arm's length, bridge the wet concrete with a ladder supported on concrete blocks.

◆ Bull-float the surface again.

4. Edging the concrete.

◆ When the concrete is firm enough to hold its shape, run a mason's trowel between the form boards and the outside edge of the slab to separate the top inch of concrete from the wood *(right)*.

◆ Push an edger back and forth along the slot *(far right)*, tilting the leading edge of the tool slightly upward to avoid gouging the concrete. Any deep indentations will be difficult to fill during later finishing steps.

◆ Wait for any surface water to evaporate from the slab before applying the finish.

FINISHING THE SURFACE

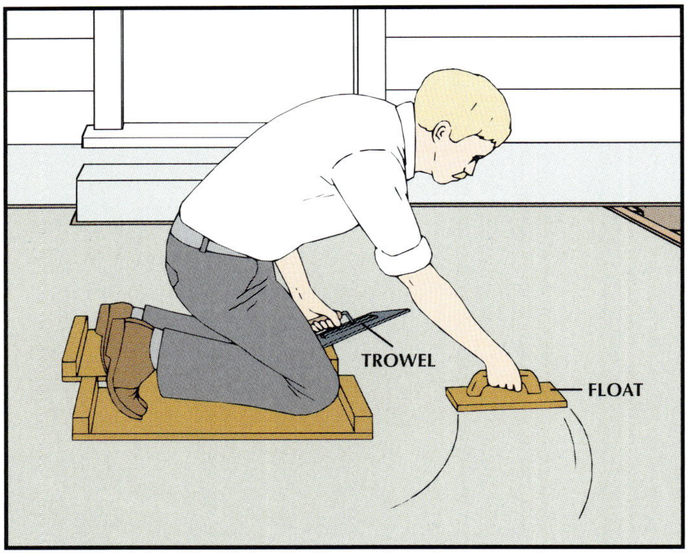

Troweling a smooth finish.

◆ Place a pair of knee boards—1- by 2-foot pieces of $\frac{3}{8}$-inch plywood with 2-by-2 handles nailed at the ends—on the slab. Kneeling on the boards, smooth the concrete with a hand float, holding it flat and sweeping it in overlapping arcs across the surface. Then sweep a rectangular steel trowel, held flat, across the same area. Similarly float and trowel the rest of the slab, moving the knee boards as necessary. *(The concrete will be firm enough to walk on at this stage.)*

◆ After floating and troweling, go over the slab again with the trowel alone, this time tilting the tool slightly. Work the surface until no concrete collects on the trowel and the blade makes a ringing sound indicating that the concrete is too firm to work any further.

◆ Run the edger between the form boards and the edges of the slab *(above)* to restore edging lines.

Brooming a skidproof surface.

Hand-float the concrete and trowel it once *(above)*. Instead of the final troweling, draw a damp, stiff-bristled utility brush across the surface. Either score straight lines at right angles to the forms or move the broom in arcs to produce a curved pattern. If the broom picks up small lumps of concrete, hose down the bristles to clean them; give the slab a few more minutes' drying time before you continue. If you have to press hard to score the concrete, work fast; the concrete will soon be too firm to take a finish.

Creating a flagstone effect.

◆ Immediately after bull-floating the concrete *(page 97)*, score the surface with irregularly spaced grooves, $\frac{1}{2}$- to $\frac{3}{4}$-inch deep, using a convex jointer. Place a ladder across forms as a bridge to reach inaccessible spots.

◆ After surface water has evaporated, hand-float and trowel the surface, then retool the grooves to restore the flagstone pattern to its original clarity.

◆ Brush out the grooves with a dry paintbrush to remove any remaining loose bits of concrete.

COMBINING REDWOOD WITH CONCRETE

1. Installing redwood rounds.

◆ Arrange 4-inch-thick redwood rounds directly on the gravel bed. Cover the top of each round with a sheet of 4-mil polyethylene, fastened with staples; then pour or shovel concrete carefully around each round.

◆ Level the concrete with a 2-by-4 screed cut short enough to fit between the rounds. Smooth the surface with a darby *(above)* instead of a bull float. Hold the darby flat, and move it sideways in a sawing motion to cut off bumps and fill in holes. Run the darby over the slab a second time, sweeping it over the surface in broad arcs.

2. Finishing the edges.

◆ When the concrete is firm enough to hold its shape, run the pointed end of a mason's trowel around the outside of each round to cut a V-shaped groove, $\frac{1}{4}$ inch deep.

◆ Finish the slab with a hand float and a trowel as on page 98. When the concrete has cured, remove the polyethylene covers.

PEBBLES FOR A TOPCOAT

1. Preparing the surface.

◆ Fill the form with concrete as on page 97, Step 1, but pack it even with the tops of the boards rather than above them.

◆ Level the concrete with a screed notched at each end so that its bottom edge rides $\frac{1}{2}$ inch below the tops of the form boards, then bull-float the surface.

◆ Scatter the damp pebbles evenly over the concrete with a shovel. Cover the surface with a single layer of stones, using a ladder bridge, if necessary, to reach inner areas.

2. Embedding the aggregate.

Tap the stones into the concrete with a bull float, forcing them just below the surface. After you have gone over the entire slab with the bull float, press down any stones that are still visible with a hand float, using a ladder bridge, if needed, to reach the interior of the slab. Then run the hand float across the surface as on page 98, covering the stones with a thin, smooth layer of concrete.

3. Exposing the aggregate.

◆ After surface water has evaporated and the concrete is firm enough to resist indentation, brush the surface lightly with a stiff nylon broom to expose the tops of the stones.

◆ While a helper sprays the slab with water, brush it again, uncovering between a quarter and a half of the stones' circumference. If you dislodge any stones, stop brushing and wait until the concrete is a bit firmer before continuing. If the concrete is difficult to wash off, work quickly to expose the aggregate before the surface becomes too stiff.

◆ After exposing the stones, continue to spray the surface until there is no noticeable cement film left on the aggregate. Scrub individual spots missed in the general wash with a scrub brush and a pail of water.

◆ Two to four hours after exposing the aggregate, wash and lightly brush the surface again to remove any cloudy residue from the stones.

A Curved Bench beside a Free-Form Patio

A wood bench is a handsome addendum to any patio, brick or concrete. The design shown here—for a bench shaped to a curved patio—is easily adapted to a rectangular one.

Choose a wood that is sufficiently resistant to decay and insects to be used outdoors. Pressure-treated pine is the least expensive but has a tendency to warp. Cedar, cypress, and redwood stand up well. Left untreated, they weather to a soft, attractive gray.

1. Anchoring posts.

◆ Use a 3-foot length of lath as a guide for chalking posthole marks on the edge of the patio *(right)*. Dig a hole about 7 inches wide, 11 inches long, and 1 foot deep centered on each mark.

◆ Cut a 3-foot-long 4-by-4 post for each hole, and anchor the posts in concrete. Let the concrete set for 48 hours.

◆ With a water level *(page 11)*, mark each post $15\frac{1}{2}$ inches above ground level and trim them to that height.

2. Installing crosspieces.

◆ Cut two $3\frac{1}{2}$-inch by 1-inch notches in the top of each post.

◆ For each notch, cut a 2-by-4 crosspiece, $17\frac{3}{4}$ inches long. Center the crosspieces in the notches and nail them in place with $2\frac{1}{2}$-inch galvanized nails.

◆ Drill two $\frac{3}{8}$-inch holes, diagonally spaced, through the braces and posts. Fasten the crosspieces with 5-inch galvanized carriage bolts—or use brass ones from a marine-supply store.

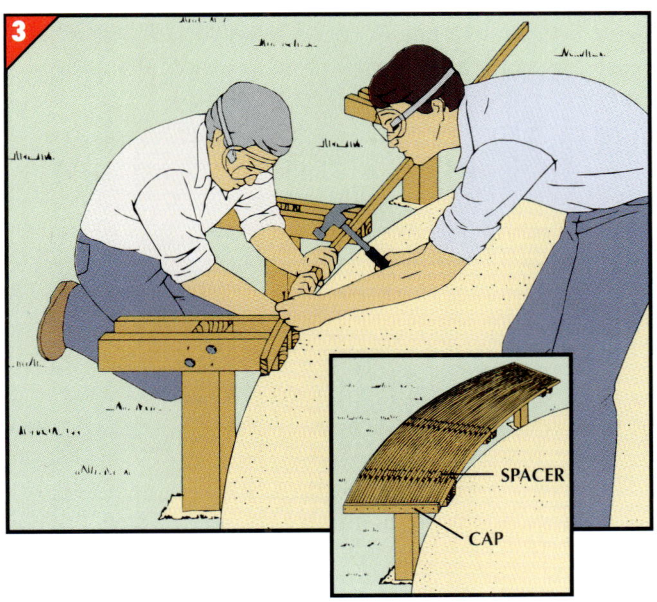

3. Making the seat.

◆ Cut fifteen 1-by-2 slats long enough—at least 7 feet—to overhang the endmost crosspieces. Rip several $\frac{3}{8}$-inch strips from a 2-by-4, and cut them into 5-inch spacers, 42 in all.

◆ Position a slat so that it extends beyond the ends of the crosspieces by about $\frac{1}{4}$ inch *(left)*, and nail it, edge up, to the crosspieces with 3-inch galvanized finishing nails, beginning at the center post. Next, set a spacer on each post, next to the slat. You need not nail the spacers.

◆ Alternate the slats with spacers to cover the crosspieces. Then, using a circular saw, cut off the ends of the slats parallel to the end crosspieces.

◆ Add 1-by-2 caps to the ends of the slats *(inset)*. Fasten the caps to each slat with 2-inch brass or galvanized wood screws.

◆ Reinforce outside slats with a screw driven through them into the spacers behind them.

Brick or Flagstone Set in Mortar

Brick or flagstone set in mortar can transform a drab concrete slab into an attractive focus for relaxing and entertaining. Unless you have recently poured a new slab, test it for soundness before proceeding *(page 122)*. Regardless of results—and no matter how new the concrete—use a metal straightedge to check the entire surface for high and low spots. Bricks and flagstones may rock on high spots and break loose. Water can collect in low spots and cause mortar to deteriorate.

Flatten high spots with a mason's rubbing brick or with a silicon carbide wheel in an electric drill. Break up low spots covering more than 1 square foot with a cold chisel and fill them as you would a hole *(pages 122-123)*.

Estimating Materials: Find the area of the slab. *(For a free-form slab, use the method shown on page 84.)* You will need $4\frac{1}{2}$ paving bricks to 1 square foot. For materials with nonstandard dimensions and for flagstones, consult a dealer. In either case, add about 5 percent for breakage and repair. Some flagstones are soft enough to be cut with a brickset; others are so hard that they must be scored with a masonry blade in a circular saw.

One cubic foot of mortar mix is enough to lay about 35 bricks or 12 square feet of flagstones. Buy additional mix to grout joints between bricks and flagstones.

Laying a Dry Run: Arranging the bricks or stones in a dry run is an essential first step. With bricks, orient the long sides with the slope of the slab. Doing so channels rainwater away from the house. Use a piece of $\frac{1}{2}$-inch plywood to space a row of bricks along two adjacent sides of the slab, trimming bricks as needed *(page 83)* to fill the rows. *(To lay a dry run on a free form, see the advice for tile on page 108.)* Leave the dry run in place as a guide for a string marker.

In a dry run of flagstones, vary the sizes of adjacent stones to avoid long joint lines. Spaces between stones should range from $\frac{1}{2}$ inch to 2 inches wide. Large gaps can be filled with pieces cut from stones that overlap *(page 104)*.

Expansion Joints: Always leave the expansion joint between the slab and the house uncovered. At the end of the job, after the mortar has set, press polyethylene rope into the joint, then cover the rope with self-leveling polysulfide or silicone caulk. If the slab is divided by expansion joints, matching joints are required when veneering with brick but not with flagstones, which can withstand expansion forces that can crack or loosen brick.

A Frame around the Patio: You may want to install edging around brick or flagstone to protect vulnerable corners and cover the sides of the patio. Set pressure-treated 2-by-8s or 2-by-10s in the ground on edge, even with the veneer surface. Metal edging is available for free-form slabs. An application of masonry sealant helps prevent the growth of moss and mildew, which can be unsightly and slippery.

TOOLS

- Mason's rubbing brick
- 2-by-2 stakes
- Mason's cord
- Cold chisel
- Brickset
- Mason's hammer
- 4-pound maul
- Rubber mallet
- Mortar tub
- Hoe
- Mason's trowel
- Pointing trowel
- $\frac{1}{2}$-inch joint filler
- Grout bag
- Wire brush

MATERIALS

- Bricks or flagstones
- Mortar mix
- Chalk
- Muriatic acid
- Masonry sealant

Mortar and Grout

✔ Buy type M mortar, available premixed from building suppliers.
✔ Mix batches no larger than you can use in 10 to 15 minutes, about half a bag.
✔ Heap the dry ingredients in a wheelbarrow or mortar tub and make a depression in the center. Into the depression, gradually pour cold water as recommended by the manufacturer. Stir with a hoe.
✔ Mortar should be just wet enough to slide easily off the hoe. Grout should have the consistency of a thick milkshake. Both must be completely free of lumps.
✔ Before mixing a new batch, scrape or rinse all dried mortar out of the mortar tub.
✔ Moisten both the slab and the veneering materials before beginning work so they will not absorb water from your mortar and grout.

BRICK VENEER FOR A CONCRETE SLAB

1. Setting brick in mortar.

◆ Use a large mason's trowel to spread a $\frac{1}{2}$-inch layer of mortar on the rough face of the first brick in the dry run. Make a shallow groove in the mortar with the point of the trowel.

◆ Set the brick at the edge of the slab and tamp it firmly with the trowel handle to level it. Working one brick at a time, use the $\frac{1}{2}$-inch plywood spacer to position succeeding bricks. Level the bricks before proceeding.

◆ Stake a guide string to align bricks of the second course with the second brick of the dry run. Where a house wall prevents the use of a stake, tie the string to a brick and set it on a scrap of $\frac{1}{2}$-inch plywood.

◆ Level the bricks in each course, then reposition the guide string for the next.

◆ Wait at least 24 hours before proceeding to the next step.

SAFETY TIPS

Use leather-palmed gloves to protect your hands from rough edges of brick or stone. Irritants in mortar and grout call for a dust mask and gloves. Wear goggles when grinding or chipping at a slab, mixing mortar, cutting brick or stone, or when working with muriatic acid.

2. Grouting the joints.

◆ Fill a grout bag with a $\frac{1}{2}$-inch nozzle about two-thirds full and roll the top to squeeze grout into the gaps between bricks. With a $\frac{1}{2}$-inch joint filler, pack the grout into the gaps to a level slightly below the brick surfaces to make a drainage channel. Smooth the grout with the joint filler.

◆ Wait an hour, then remove ragged bits of grout with the trowel. Three hours later, smooth the joints with a wire brush, and hose the patio clean.

◆ Allow the grout to cure for several days. Then remove any grout stains on the bricks with a mild solution of muriatic acid and a wire brush. Hose away the residue.

RANDOM SHAPES FROM FLAGSTONES

1. Laying out a dry run.

◆ Arrange the flagstones on the slab allowing $\frac{1}{2}$- to 2-inch gaps between adjacent stones. Ignore any expansion joints except the one adjacent to the house wall.

◆ Where a stone hangs over the edge of the slab, mark a cutting line on it with chalk, using the edge of the slab as a guide.

◆ Where stones overlap each other, mark one of the stones, allowing space for the mortar joint between them. Cutting lines should be straight; you can approximate a curve with several short cuts.

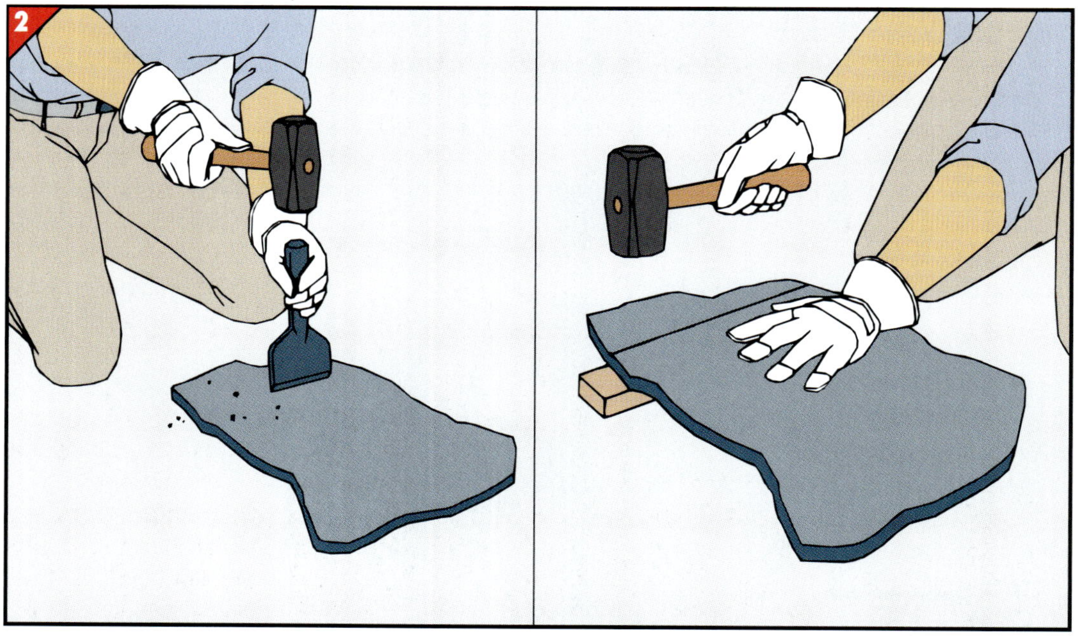

2. Cutting a stone.

◆ Remove marked stones one by one and score each for cutting. To do so, hold a brickset against the chalk line and tap it several times with a maul *(above, left);* then move the brickset along the line and tap again.

◆ For stones that are more than 1 inch thick, score a corresponding line on the other side by extending the first line down the edges of the stone and marking a connecting line on the back.

◆ Rest the stone on a board, with the scored line no more than $\frac{1}{4}$ inch beyond the edge. Then tap the overhang with the maul to snap it off *(above, right).* As each stone is cut, return it to its position on the slab.

3. Laying the stones in mortar.

◆ At a corner or along an edge, set a section of stones about 4 by 4 feet in area next to the slab as they were arranged in the dry run.

◆ Moisten the exposed slab with water, then trowel on a 1-inch-thick mortar bed.

◆ Position the stones on the mortar, seating them with a rubber mallet. Fill any large spaces with pieces of cut stone.

4. Making an even surface.

◆ Examine the flagstones just laid. If a stone sits too high, lift it aside and scoop out some of the mortar with a pointing trowel. If a stone is too low, add mortar and smooth it with the trowel to ensure a good bond.

◆ Finish each section by using a pointing trowel or a tongue depressor to remove any excess mortar that has pushed up between stones. Sponge stray mortar off the stones.

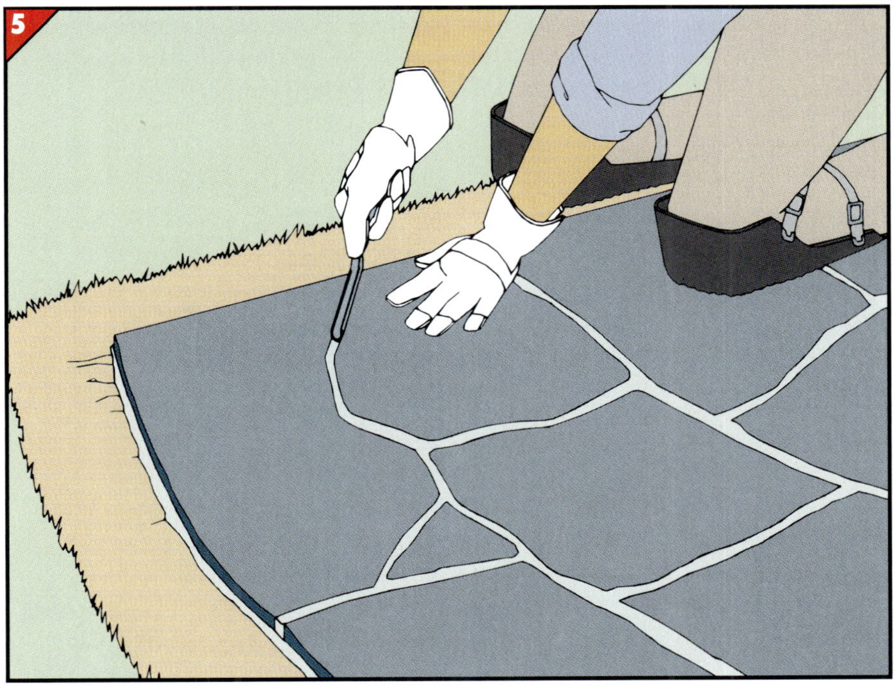

5. Grouting the joints.

◆ After the mortar has cured 24 to 48 hours, trowel grout into the joints. Then use a joint filler to compact the grout to a depth of $\frac{1}{16}$ inch below the stone surface.

◆ Wipe away excess grout with a wet rag within 10 minutes to prevent stains. Do not use muriatic acid; it may discolor flagstone.

◆ To ensure that the wide joints between flagstones cure adequately, mist the stonework with water every four hours for the first day, and allow the grout to cure three more days before walking on the patio.

Paving a Patio with Tile

Hard-fired ceramic-clay tiles set in mortar on a concrete slab offer attractive, durable choices for outdoor patios or at poolside. Any outdoor tile must be frost-proof; purchase tile with an absorption rate of 6 percent or less.

Types of Tile: Quarry tiles have a smooth surface and come in squares, rectangles, hexagons, and octagons of various sizes. Paver tiles are thicker than quarry tiles and are commonly cast in squares and hexagons with a textured surface and rough or rounded edges.

Mosaic tiles, mounted for correct spacing on a 1- or 2-foot-square mesh backing, make fast work of intricate designs. For outdoor use, choose mosaic tiles with a matte glaze so the surface will not be slippery when it is wet.

Preliminary Steps: First, check the slab you intend to tile for flaws *(page 102)*. To estimate the number of tiles you need, calculate the area of the slab *(page 84)*, and purchase tile accordingly.

Laying a Dry Run: Note the position of expansion joints, if any, between sections of slab, and design your tile pattern around them *(page 108)*. Lay a dry run of tile to ensure accurate placement. Plastic spacers or lugs molded into the edges of tiles help position them precisely.

Cutting Tiles: You can cut quarry tiles with the hand tools shown on pages 109 and 110. Buy the microcutter and nippers; rent the more expensive senior cutter.

Tiles more than $\frac{1}{2}$-inch thick require a circular saw with a silicon carbide masonry blade *(page 83)* or an electric tub saw, in which water cools the blade and flushes away ceramic chips and dust. Regardless of the tool you use, always cut ribbed tiles across the ribs.

Latex-Base Mortar: A tiled patio lasts longer and requires less maintenance when the mortar for anchoring the tiles and the grout for filling joints between them are made with a latex tile-setting liquid instead of water. Ceramic-tile grout comes premixed in a variety of colors; a 10-pound bag is enough for about 10 square feet of paver or quarry tile, or 20 square feet of mosaic tile. You can make your own grout by mixing equal parts of Portland cement and fine masonry sand with enough latex liquid to make a thick paste.

When you are ready to lay tiles, dampen the slab and trowel on a thin bed of mortar. Set the tiles in small sections while the mortar is still soft, planning the work so that you do not disturb freshly laid tiles.

Allow the mortar to cure 24 hours before grouting the joints. Do the grouting within the next 24 hours, however, to ensure a solid bond to the mortar.

Preserving Your Patio: To protect tiles and grout from stains, you can seal the finished paving with commercial masonry sealer or a 5 percent silicone solution. You may prefer to seal only the grout, which usually is lighter and more absorbent than the tile and shows stains more readily.

TOOLS

Tile cutters
Mortar tub
Mason's trowel
Notched trowel
Grout float
Caulking gun

MATERIALS

Tile spacers
Mortar/grout mix
Latex tile-setting liquid
Polyethylene-foam rope
Silicone or polysulfide caulk
Masonry sealer

A typical tile.
Outdoor tiles like the textured example above commonly have ribbed backs to improve the bond between mortar and tile. Most tiles are available in a bullnose shape, rounded on one edge or two and used along the perimeter and at the corners of a patio.

SAFETY TIPS

When cutting tile, wear safety goggles and heavy work gloves to protect yourself against chips and sharp edges.

A variety of shapes and colors.
The square tile above, perhaps the most familiar, is just one of many styles available. Six-sided tiles are best used alone *(right),* but 8-sided tiles can be combined with small squares in an octagon-and-dot pattern *(below, middle row, left).* Besides traditional terra cotta, tiles come in many colors and patterns, including a wood-grain finish *(above, far right).*

COMPOSING PATTERNS WITH SHAPED TILES

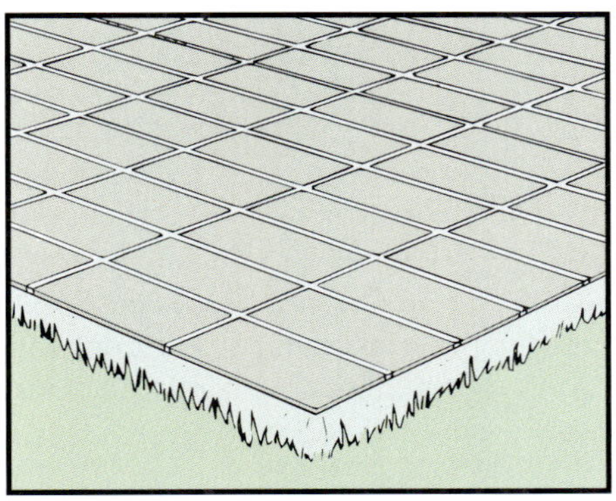

Repeating a single shape.
Some patterns are inherent in the shapes of tiles. At far left is a stacked pattern of rectangular tiles—square ones are also suitable. At left is a honeycomb formed of hexagons; octagons may also be used.

Repeating two shapes.
The octagon-and-dot pattern *(right)* builds automatically with 8-inch octagons and 3-inch squares, or dots. A square-and-picket pattern *(far right)* builds from 8-inch squares surrounded by 3- by 11-inch pickets.

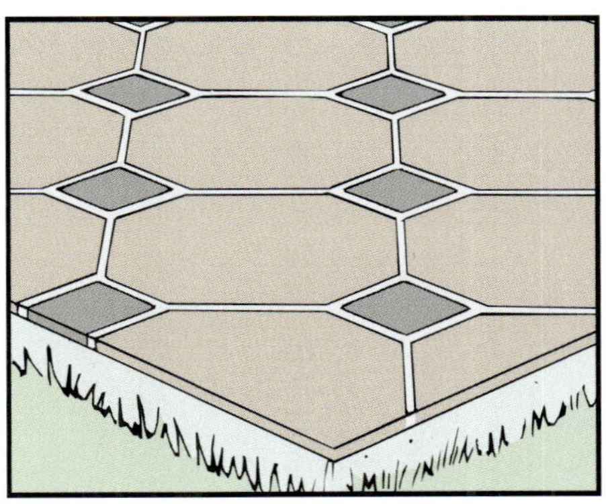

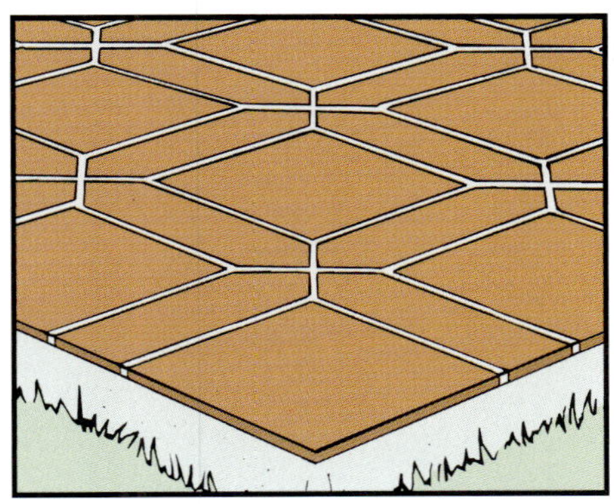

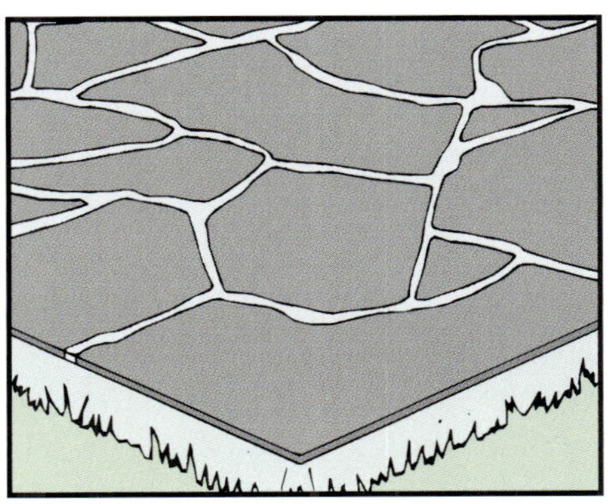

Patterns from many shapes.
Rectangular and square tiles, whose dimensions are multiples of the smallest unit, make a lively pattern with little cutting *(far left).* The rubble pattern is achieved using broken paver tiles with their edges smoothed.

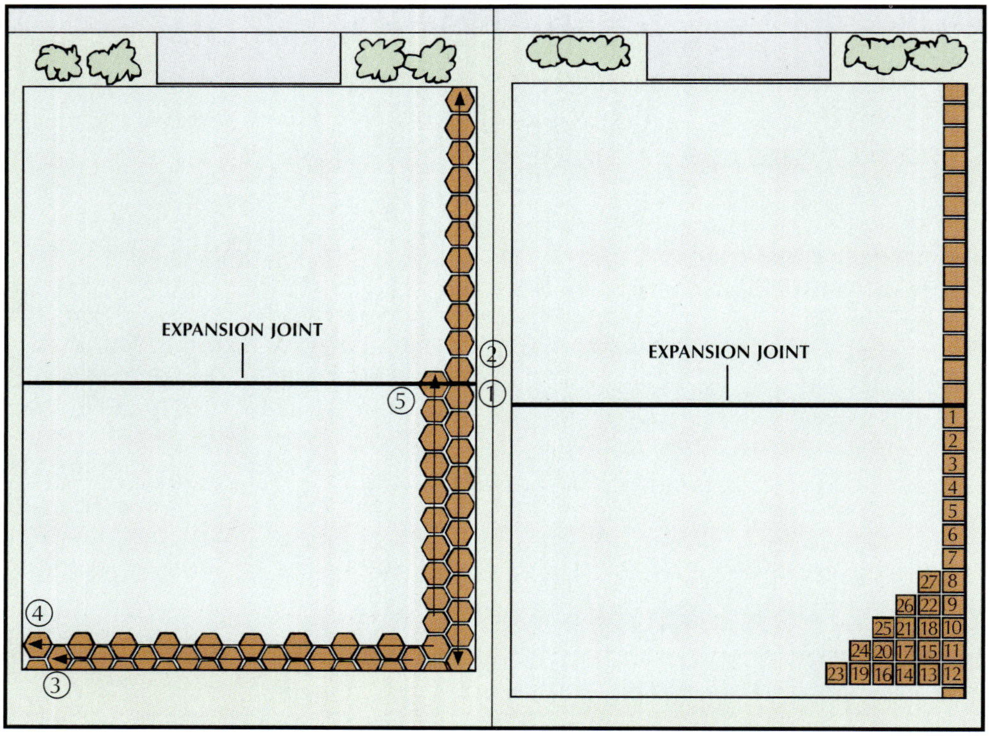

Rectangular slabs.
If there is an expansion joint, begin work there.

◆ For 6- or 8-sided tiles, set the first row to a far corner *(above left, Arrow 1)*, trimming a tile at the end of the row if necessary.
◆ Extend the row toward the house *(Arrow 2)*, leaving a gap at the joint; trim the corner tile as needed.

◆ Using the last full tile nearest the far corner as a guide, set a row of tiles perpendicular to the first, along the edge of the slab *(Arrow 3)*. Alternate tiles may have to be cut.
◆ Set succeeding rows *(Arrows 4 and 5)* in the same manner, letting some tiles bridge the expansion joint,until the entire slab is covered.
◆ Finally, cut tiles to fill in the gaps remaining around the edge.

◆ For square or rectangular tiles in a simple stack pattern, follow the numbers *(above, right)* to set the first row out to a far corner.
◆ There, use the last full tile as the apex of a triangle, and set tiles in diagonal rows until one section of the slab is covered, then proceed with the other section.
◆ Cut tiles to fill any gaps left around the edges.

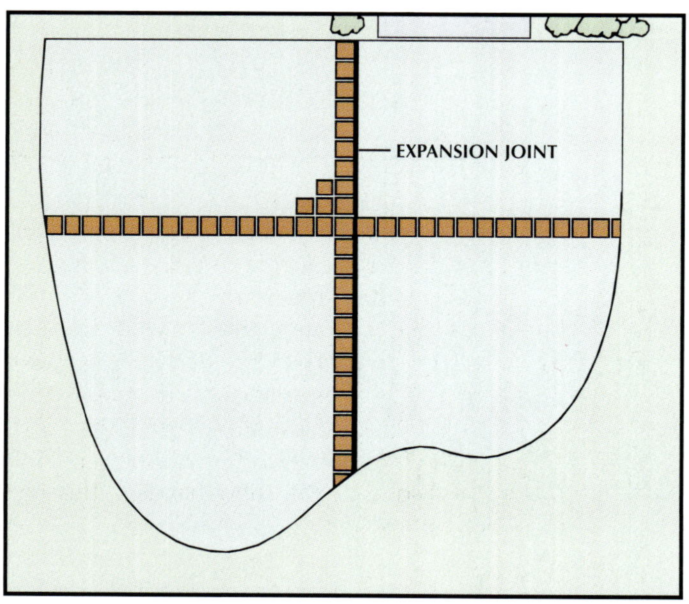

Free-form slabs.
If the shape of the slab is irregular or curved, snap perpendicular chalk lines across its widest dimensions or use expansion joints to divide it into quadrants. Starting at the intersection near the center of the patio, lay tile along each axis toward the edges. Mark tiles for cutting as necessary. Then fill in each quadrant as shown above, right.

Interrupted slabs.

◆ To tile around a tree or pool, first lay a rectangular frame around the obstacle, then fill in the frame as necessary with tiles trimmed to fit. Add an edge of border tiles, if desired.

◆ Divide the slab into quadrants, using a tile at the midpoint of each side of the frame as a reference point.

◆ Lay rows of tiles along the quadrant lines, and fill in each section with parallel rows of tiles. Cut the outermost tile in each row to fit the edge of the slab.

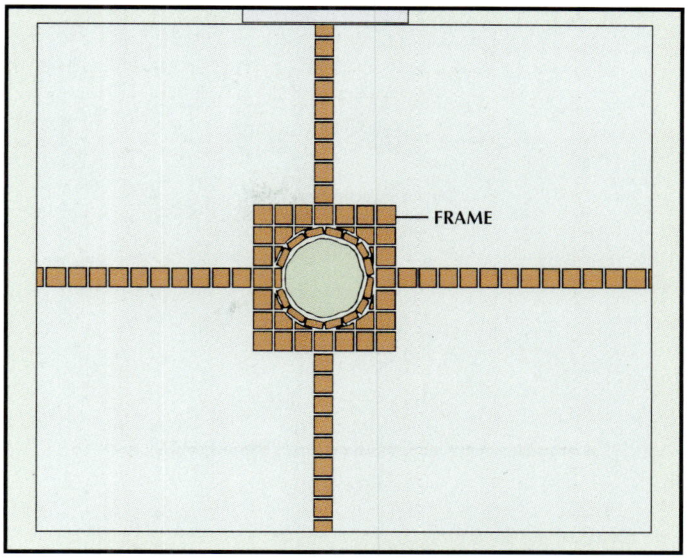

THREE TECHNIQUES FOR CUTTING TILES

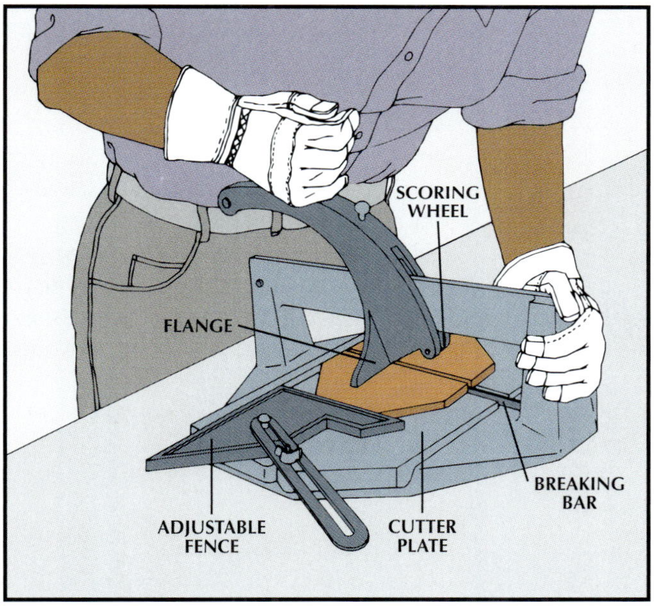

Using a senior cutter.

◆ Place a marked tile on the cutter plate, with the cutting line directly above the breaking bar. Set and lock the adjustable fence to hold the tile firmly in place.

◆ Slide the cutter handle toward you, then lift the handle until the scoring wheel rests on the line. Push the handle forward in one continuous motion, scoring the tile.

◆ Rest the flanges on the tile at its midpoint, then strike the handle sharply with your fist *(above)*, causing the flanges to snap the tile over the breaking bar.

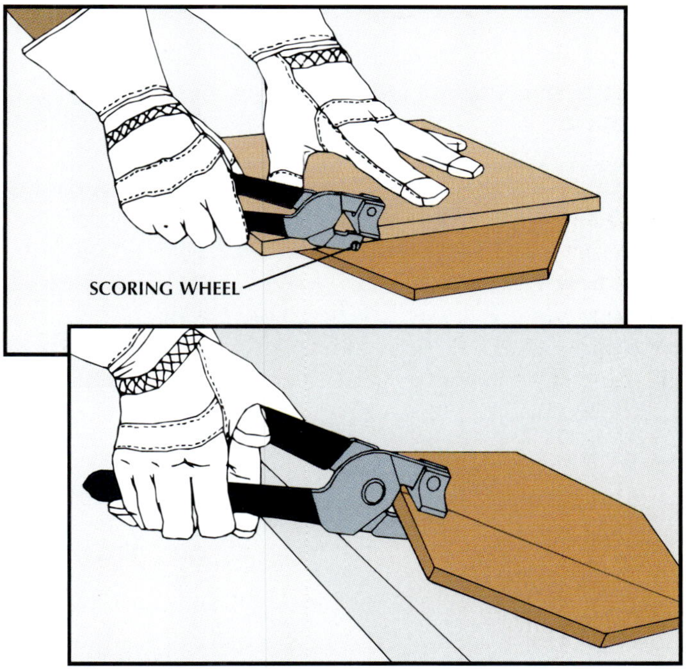

Using a microcutter.

◆ On the tile, draw a cutting line; it may be straight or gently curved. Set the scoring wheel on the line, hold the tile firm, and run the scoring wheel along the line in one continuous motion. For a straight cut, use a plywood scrap or uncut tile as a guide. Follow curves freehand. In either case, score the tile once; a second pass increases the chance of a ragged break.

◆ Center the jaws of the cutter on the scored line *(above)* and squeeze the cutter handles. The tile will snap along the scored line.

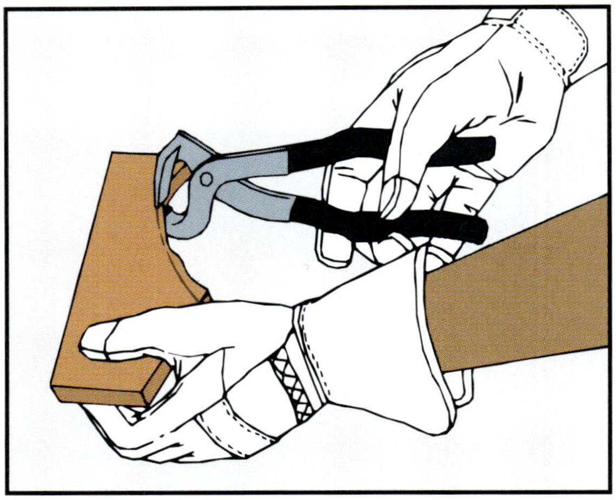

Cutting with tile nippers.

◆ Score a cutting line on the tile followed by a crosshatch pattern in the area to be cut away.

◆ Grasping the tile firmly in one hand, work from the edge toward the cutting line, chipping off small pieces. Hold the nippers with the jaws at an angle to the section of line you are approaching.

◆ When the rough cut is complete, smooth the edges with a piece of brick or a small stone.

LAYING TILES ON MORTAR

1. Applying the mortar bed.

◆ Set dry-run tiles next to the slab, then spray the concrete with water in the area to be tiled first.

◆ Working in sections of 3 square feet or so, spread a thin layer of mortar over the dampened slab with the smooth edge of a rectangular notched-blade trowel. Turn the trowel and draw the notched edge through the mortar, leaving a pattern of uniform ridges. Keep a pointing trowel nearby for removing excess mortar and scraping dripped mortar from the slab. Rinse both trowels often in a bucket of water, to remove mortar before it dries.

2. Laying the tiles.

◆ Hold a tile by its edges and lower it onto the mortar bed with as little sideways motion as possible. Tap the tile with a rubber mallet to seat it firmly.

◆ Unless your tiles are molded with spacer lugs, lay plastic spacers on the mortar at the corners of the tile, then place the second tile against the spacers.

◆ Lay all the full tiles, checking the tiled surface every 4 or 5 tiles for evenness. When laying interlocking tiles near an expansion joint, stand $\frac{3}{8}$-inch furniture dowels—available in bulk at hardware stores or home-improvement centers —between the tiles next to the joint *(inset)*.

◆ Cut tiles for the edge of the slab as needed and mortar them in place.

◆ Allow the mortar to cure for 24 hours.

FILLING JOINTS WITH GROUT

1. Grouting the joints.

◆ If you used plastic spacers between tiles—and they are less than $\frac{1}{4}$ inch below the tiled surface—remove them.

◆ Extract any dowel spacers near an expansion joint and gently fill the gap with strips of rolled newspaper to keep it free of grout.

◆ Place small mounds of grout at intervals along the mortar joints over an area 3- or 4-feet square. Kneeling on a piece of plywood to distribute your weight and avoid dislodging tiles, force the grout between the tiles with a rubber grout float dampened with water. Dip the float in a bucket of water occasionally to keep it wet.

2. Cleaning the tiles.

◆ Let the grout dry for about 10 minutes, but not longer than specified by the manufacturer.

◆ Wipe away any excess grout with a damp sponge, using a light, circular motion. Rinse the sponge often in clean water, but wring it well to avoid saturating the grout or washing the pigment out of colored grout.

◆ Mist the tiled surface with water every 4 hours for the first day, to let the grout cure slowly. After the third day, remove hazy grout residue from the tile surface by buffing with a dry cloth.

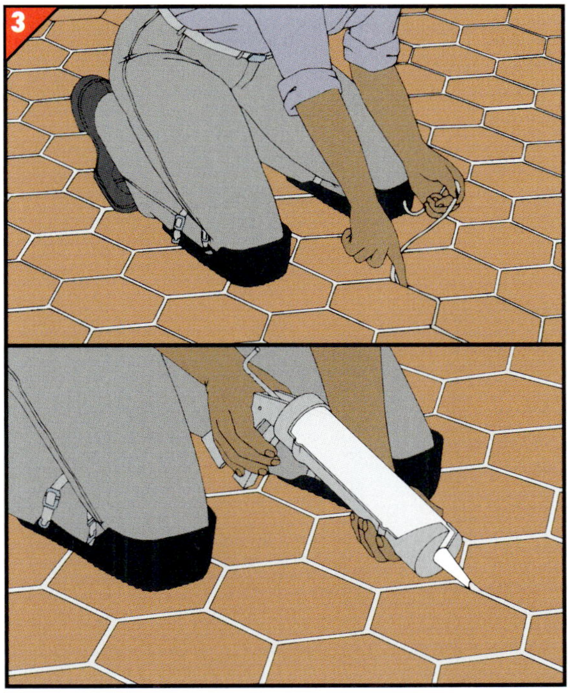

3. Filling the expansion joint.

◆ After the grout has cured, remove the rolled newspaper from the expansion joint and press $\frac{3}{8}$-inch polyethylene-foam rope to the bottom of the gap *(left, top)*.

◆ Fill any space remaining with silicone or polysulfide caulk *(left, bottom)*, wiping excess caulk off the tiles immediately with the solvent recommended by the manufacturer. Let the caulk dry before walking on the tiles.

◆ If you intend to seal the tiles, wait a week or more to allow the grout to dry completely, then apply two coats of sealer.

3 Repairs and Refurbishments

After years of service, even the sturdiest deck, porch, or patio may need restoration. Screens are damaged with surprising ease. Wooden structures eventually begin to deteriorate even if built of rot-resistant lumber, and concrete may crack, admitting water that can crumble a patio. Timely repairs can prevent irreparable damage and ensure continued durability and safety of valued outdoor amenities.

Securing screen to a frame →

Repairing Screens

Although they are tough and durable, screens are often accidentally torn or punctured. Holes up to a few inches across can be patched with the technique shown below, but repairing greater damage—or deterioration from age—requires a new panel of mesh.

Types of Mesh: Replacement screening comes in a variety of widths and mesh sizes in lengths up to 100 feet. Stan‹ ard widths are 24, 36, 48, 60, and 72 inches. The most common mesh size is 16 by 18. Having 16 horizontal filaments per inch and 18 per inch vertically, this mesh is fine enough to keep out most flies and mosquitoes.

Among screening materials, fiberglass and aluminum are the most popular. Aluminum is the more durable choice, but fiberglass is less expensive, is available in more colors, and comes in a densely woven variety called solar screening. This type of mesh blocks up to two-thirds of the sun's rays, making it a good choice for southern and western exposures.

Wood Frames or Aluminum: To replace screening on a wood frame, you'll need shears to cut the mesh, a stiff putty knife to pry molding off the frame, and a staple gun loaded with $\frac{3}{8}$-inch copper-coated staples. If the frame is rotten or broken, build a new one *(page 116)*. To do so you will need a miter box and backsaw to cut the frame pieces, as well as corner clamps to hold the pieces for nailing. To install mesh in an aluminum frame, buy several feet of vinyl cord called screen spline and a tool called a screen-spline roller.

Covering a hole.
- ◆ Cut a piece of matching screening about twice as large as the opening.
- ◆ For aluminum screening, fold opposite sides of the patch to 90° angles, about $\frac{1}{2}$ inch from the edges, as shown at right. Then detach wires to make a fringe *(inset)*.
- ◆ Pass the wires through the screen mesh around the hole and fold them against the screen to hold the patch in place.
- ◆ For fiberglass screening, sew the patch around the edges with nylon monofilament thread.

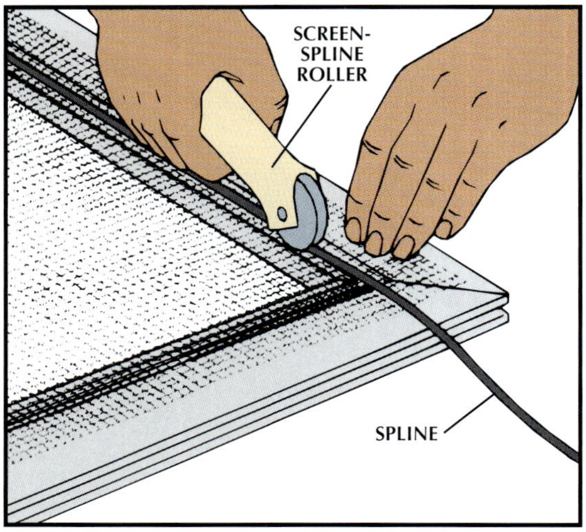

New screen for an aluminum frame.
- ◆ Remove damaged screening by pulling the flexible vinyl spline out of the channel around the edge, and cut a new piece of screening that overlaps the spline channel by 1 inch on each side.
- ◆ If you are using aluminum screening, crease it into the channel with a screen-spline roller. *(Skip this step with fiberglass screening.)*
- ◆ Position a length of new spline over the screening at one end of the frame, and roll the spline and screening into the channel. Trim away excess spline at the corners.
- ◆ Repeat this procedure at the opposite end and then along the sides, pulling the screen tight as you work. When finished, trim the screen along the outer edge of the spline.

Rescreening a wood frame.
◆ Pry off the molding that covers the screen edges and remove the old screening.
◆ Clamp the middle of the frame to boards laid across sawhorses or other supports and push narrow shims under each corner so that the frame is slightly bowed *(right).*
◆ Unroll the screening over the frame, overlapping the ends of the frame by at least 1 inch. Starting at one corner, staple the screening to one end of the frame at 2-inch intervals, $\frac{1}{2}$ inch from the inside edge of the frame.
◆ Pull the screening to remove wrinkles and staple it across the other end. Next, remove the shims and staple the screen to the sides, corner to corner, then use a utility knife to trim the edges about $\frac{1}{2}$ inch from the staples.
◆ If the molding is sound, reinstall it; otherwise, cut new molding *(page 116, Step 1).*

Support for a sagging door.
To stop a screen door from scraping a porch floor or patio as it opens and closes, true the door with a wire-and-turnbuckle stay.
◆ Open a 3-inch turnbuckle to its full extension, and attach a 4-foot length of woven wire to each of its eyes with a wire clamp *(inset).*
◆ Drive $\frac{1}{2}$-inch screw eyes into the corners of the door as shown above and clamp the free ends of the turnbuckle wires to them. Trim excess wire.
◆ Using pliers if needed, tighten the turnbuckle to restore the door to a rectangular shape.

ASSEMBLING A FRAME FOR A SCREEN

1. Mitering the frame corners.
Using a backsaw and miter box, cut each end of four 1-by-2s at a 45° angle as shown above. Make the long edge of each piece $\frac{1}{4}$ inch shorter than the corresponding edge of the opening for the screen.

2. Joining the pieces.

- Secure two adjacent sides of the frame in a corner clamp, then remove one of the sides and apply glue to the end. Reposition it in the clamp.
- Drill two $\frac{1}{16}$-inch pilot holes into the corner *(above)* and drive a 2-inch finishing nail into each. Repeat this procedure to join the other three corners.
- Staple screening to the frame *(page 115)*.

3. Adding the molding.
Cover the staples with $1\frac{3}{8}$-by-$\frac{1}{4}$-inch lattice strips, mitered to match the frame pieces. Align the outer edges of the lattice strips with the outer edges of the frame, and fasten them with $\frac{3}{4}$-inch brads driven near each edge at 6-inch intervals.

Extending the Life of Wood Structures

The major causes of damage to porches and decks are rot and insects. Spongy, discolored wood indicates rot; piles of wood fibers or detached wings signal insect activity. If insects are present, exterminate them before trying any repairs.

Widespread damage may require replacing the entire structure, but in most cases, the affected parts can simply be repaired or replaced. With the exception of porch flooring, which is usually protected by weather-resistant paint, make all repairs with pressure-treated lumber to prevent rot and galvanized nails and hardware to prevent rust.

Using a Jack: Before replacing a post or a column, support the structure above with a screw-operated, telescoping jack. Use a bell jack—a strong, bell-shaped screw jack about 1 foot tall—under a low deck or porch. Before using either type, grease the threads so the jack will operate smoothly.

Periodic Checks: After the repair has been completed, a little routine maintenance can prevent further trouble. If the porch or deck is painted, scrape clean and repaint any blisters or cracked areas as soon as they appear. If the structure is not painted, treat it once a year with a wood preservative. And regular inspections for rot and insect damage will catch any problems before they become severe.

CAUTION *Do not use a hydraulic jack; the weight of a porch or deck may gradually compress the jack.*

SAFETY TIPS *Protect your eyes when hammering nails and when using a circular saw. Wearing earplugs reduces the noise of this tool to a safe level. Wearing a dust mask is advisable when sawing pressure-treated lumber, which contains arsenic compounds as preservatives. And be sure to wash your hands thoroughly after handling pressure-treated wood. Finally, wear a hard hat when handling heavy objects overhead.*

PATCHING A TONGUE-AND-GROOVE FLOOR

1. Chiseling floorboards.

With a 1-inch wood chisel, chip deep grooves across each damaged floorboard on both sides of the damage.

◆ Center the chisel on a joist, with the tool's beveled edge facing the damage. Drive the chisel straight down to cut deep across the board.

◆ Reverse the chisel, move it about $\frac{1}{2}$ inch closer to the damaged area, then drive it toward the first cut, chipping out a groove.

◆ Repeat for each damaged board, staggering the grooves so that adjacent boards are not cut over the same joist.

2. Removing the boards.

◆ With a circular saw set to the thickness of the floorboards, make two parallel cuts down the middle of every damaged board that is longer than damaged boards next to it. Start and stop the saw just short of the chiseled ends, and complete the cuts with a wood chisel.

◆ Use a pry bar to remove first the middle strip, then the tongued side, and finally the grooved side of each board. The remaining boards can be pried out without sawing.

3. Inserting new boards.

◆ Where no floorboard blocks the way, tap a replacement into position with a rubber mallet, fitting the grooved edge over the tongue of the undamaged board next to it.

◆ Drive a $2\frac{1}{2}$-inch finishing nail through the corner of its tongue into the joists below *(inset)*.

◆ Fit as many boards as possible this way. For any pieces that cannot be wedged into place, use the alternative method described in Step 4.

4. Installing the final boards.

◆ Where a neighboring floorboard hinders fitting a replacement, chisel off the lower lip of the new board's grooved edge. Place its tongue in the groove of the adjacent board, and drop its trimmed edge into place *(inset)*, tapping it gently with a rubber mallet to seat it.

◆ Nail the board at each joist with two $2\frac{1}{2}$-inch finishing nails, set at an angle to minimize shifting of the board. Countersink the nails and fill the holes with wood putty.

STRENGTHENING JOISTS

Reinforcing a joist.

To strengthen a weak joist, fit a new joist alongside the existing one, as shown above.

◆ Cut a joist having the same dimensions as the original, then bevel one of its edges to ease installation *(inset)*.

◆ With a helper, rotate the new joist into position atop the beam supporting the deck and fasten it to the ledger board and ribbon board with 7-inch galvanized angle plates held by $1\frac{1}{2}$-inch nails.

◆ Nail the two joists together with $3\frac{1}{2}$-inch nails, staggered top and bottom at 12-inch intervals.

◆ Finally, nail the floorboards to the top edge of the new joist.

TRICKS OF THE TRADE

Cure for a Rickety Deck

A simple diagonal brace adds rigidity to a wobbly deck. With a helper, temporarily tack a 1-by-8 board diagonally across the underside of the deck so that when trimmed to fit it can be nailed to the end joists on both sides of the deck. Mark the top of the board along the end joists, then take the board down and cut along the two lines. Nail the board to the underside of each joist with three $2\frac{1}{2}$-inch galvanized nails.

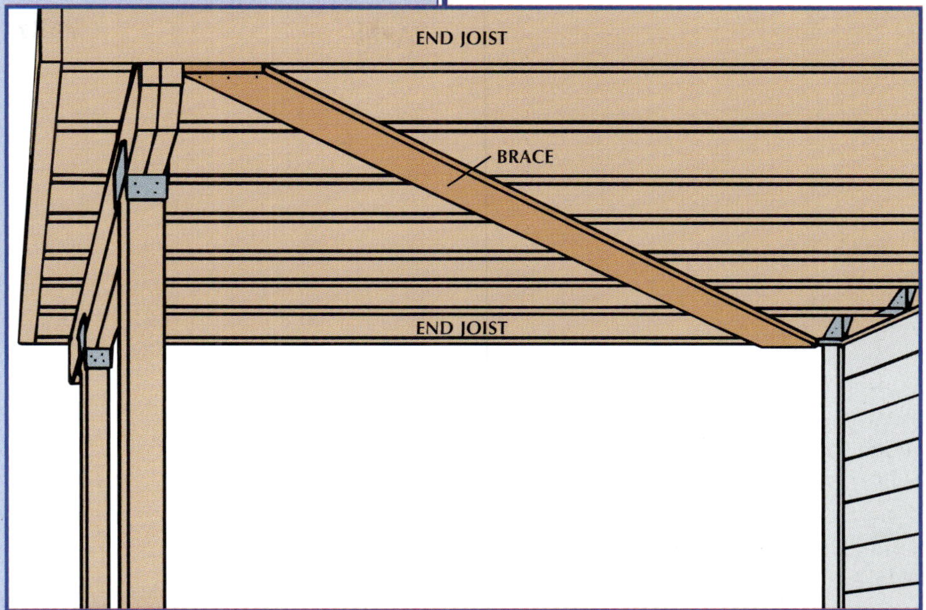

REMOVING PORCH POSTS AND COLUMNS

1. Jacking a porch roof.

◆ Set the jack on a 2-by-12 board and line it up between the roof header and the floor joist nearest the damaged column.

◆ Extend the jack's telescoping tubes so that the top is about 2 inches from the roof header. Lock the tube in place with the steel pins provided.

◆ While a helper holds the jack plumb and steadies a second board atop the jack, extend the jack by turning the screw handle. When the jack is snug against the boards, give the handle a quarter turn—enough for the jack to support the roof without lifting it.

2. Disassembling the support.

◆ To remove a porch post or solid column *(above),* use a handsaw to cut through the post in two places about 1 foot apart. Knock out the middle section with a mallet, and work the top and bottom sections loose. Install a new post using the hardware from the old post.

◆ To remove a hollow column *(above, right),* make two vertical cuts, opposite each other, down the length of the shaft with a circular saw. Then make a horizontal cut around the middle. Pull the two upper sections apart and remove them, staying clear of the capital in case it falls—it may not be nailed to the header.

◆ If the capital is attached to the header, detach it with a pry bar; to free the capital from the post, cut it in two. Remove the two lower shaft sections and the base.

◆ Check the post inside to see if it is damaged, and replace it if necessary. Cover the post with a new shaft, capital, and base.

SALVAGING A DECK SUPPORT

Reusing a ground-level footing.

◆ First, support the deck with a jack set near the damaged post, then cut off the post flush with the top of the footing. Chisel the bottom of the post from the footing.

◆ Fill the resulting cavity with new concrete. Then use a plumb bob to establish the postion of a J bolt, directly under the beam. Push the J bolt into the concrete *(inset).*

◆ When the concrete has cured for 24 to 48 hours, attach a post anchor to the bolt.

◆ Cut a new post to fit between the beam and the post anchor. Nail it to the post anchor and to the beam, using the original hardware if possible.

Building up a buried footing.

◆ To prepare the new footing, support the frame with a jack, dig down to expose the top of the old footing, and cut off the post as close as possible to the footing. Fill the hole with concrete, covering the remnants of the old post by at least 8 inches.

◆ Measure and cut a new post long enough to sink about 1 inch into the new footing, and set it into the concrete.

◆ Hold the post plumb while a helper fastens it at the top. Brace the bottom of the post with scrap lumber to hold it plumb *(inset)*. Allow the concrete to set at least 24 hours before removing the jack.

Splicing a weak post.

When only the upper or lower part of a porch or deck post is rotten, you can splice in a new section instead of replacing the whole post.

◆ Support the deck on a jack and saw through the post just outside the damaged area. Measure and cut a replacement section long enough to sink into a new footing if one is needed *(above)*.

◆ Cut an L-shaped notch, half the thickness of the post and 6 inches long, in the end of the undamaged section, and a matching notch in one end of the replacement section. Clamp the notched sections together and drill three $\frac{3}{8}$-inch holes through the joint, staggering their positions. Counterbore the holes for nuts and washers, then secure the joint with $\frac{3}{8}$-inch carriage bolts.

◆ Attach the other end of the replacement section to the deck or footing.

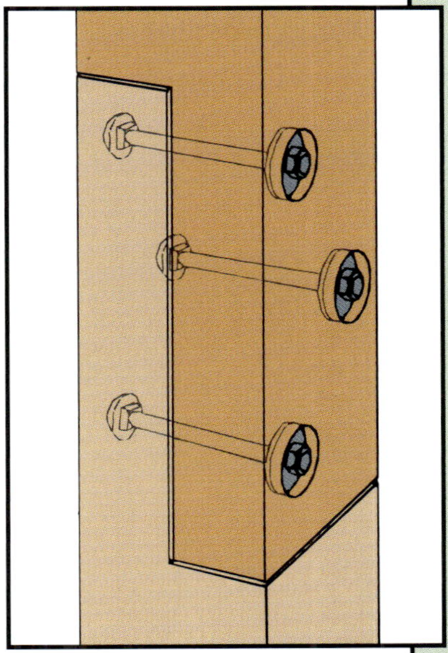

Restoring Damaged Concrete

Holes, pockmarks, and cracks in concrete can usually be filled with patching mortar. The procedure to use depends on the size of the flaw. Cracks and holes less than 1 inch deep can be brushed clean and filled with tough latex or epoxy patching mortar. Epoxy compounds are slightly stronger and more water-resistant than latex ones.

Major Repairs: Larger flaws must be dressed with a cold chisel before patching. Epoxy and latex mortars may be too expensive for filling big cracks and holes. Moreover, they are unsuitable for mending concrete steps *(opposite bottom)*. Instead, use bonding adhesive and prepackaged patching mortar—a dry mix of sand and cement to which you add water.

A Test for Failed Concrete: Such repairs may not suffice if the concrete around a flaw crumbles when chiseled, a possible sign of widespread deterioration. To test for overall soundness, drop a tire iron in several places. A sharp ringing noise indicates firm concrete; a dull thud signals crumbling beneath the surface. Concrete that fails this test is best broken up and rebuilt.

SAFETY TIP

As shown here, wear goggles and gloves when chiseling concrete.

PATCHING A LARGE HOLE OR CRACK

1. Preparing the damaged area.
Chip out the concrete in the damaged area with a cold chisel and a maul to a depth of about $1\frac{1}{2}$ inches. Undercut the edge slightly so that the bottom of the cavity is wider than the top *(inset)*. Clear away the debris, then wet the area with a hose. Blot up excess water with a sponge.

2. Adding the adhesive and mortar.

◆ Brush bonding adhesive evenly around the cavity, and wipe up any spills around the edge of the hole with a rag.

◆ Wait for the adhesive to become tacky—usually from 30 minutes to two hours, depending on the brand—then prepare the sand-and-cement patching mortar according to the manufacturer's instructions. Trowel the mixture into the hole before the bonding adhesive can harden.

3. Smoothing the patch.
Level the surface of the mortar by drawing a wood float back and forth across it several times. Remove excess mortar around the edges of the patch with a trowel; then, before the patch hardens, wipe the edge joint smooth with burlap or a rag. Cover the patch with a towel or a piece of burlap. Keep the cloth moist for a week to be sure that the patch cures completely.

REBUILDING A CRUMBLING STEP CORNER

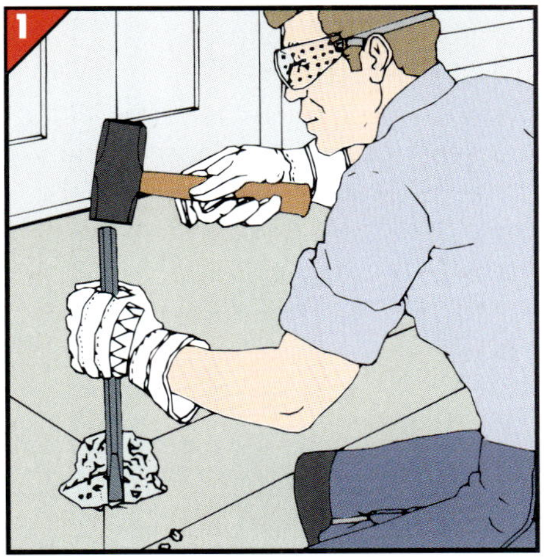

1. Preparing the corner.
◆ Chisel away the damaged corner until you reach solid concrete on all sides, then flatten the bottom of the cavity and undercut the sides slightly. Clear the cavity of debris.
◆ Cut form boards to enclose the corner and contain the mortar. Brace the boards in position, even with the top of the step, and nail their ends together at the corner *(right)*.
◆ Coat the inside of the form boards with motor oil, and paint the cavity with bonding adhesive.

2. Filling in the corner.
◆ After the adhesive has had a chance to become tacky, trowel in sand-and-cement patching mortar and tamp it down to fill the entire hole. As the patch begins to harden, level the surface with a wood float and remove any excess mortar with a trowel.
◆ Cover with burlap and keep the burlap damp for a week.

Fence and Wall Repairs

Even the best-made fence will eventually need repairs. The effects of traffic, weather, and time all take their toll. A few simple fixes, however, can add years to the life of a fence. The commonest problem is rotten wood. Often, most of the board is still sound with only the ends decayed. A quick solution is to support the damaged board with a small block of wood *(below)*. A board with more extensive deterioration can be supported by a sister rail *(opposite, top)*. To ensure your repairs are long-lived, buy pressure-treated wood.

Problematic Posts: A loose post set in soil can often be stabilized by pressing down around the post with a tamping bar. If the post needs added support, bolt on 2-by-4 sister posts *(page 125)*. For a badly damaged post set in soil or concrete, remove and replace the post *(page 126)*.

Brick Wall Repairs: Bricks occasionally need replacement when mortar joints crack or bricks are damaged. A loose brick can usually be worked out of the wall with a pry bar or the end of a cold chisel. A damaged brick may be removed with a cold chisel and a maul. First break the mortar around the brick then split it into pieces small enough to free with a pry bar.

Rebuilding a Stone Wall: While stones have an indefinite lifespan, stone walls need frequent repair. As the stones settle under their own weight and endure stresses such as frost heaves, sections may collapse. Rebuilding a wall is not complicated but does require patience and lots of trial and error. Remove the stones down to the level where the wall is solid; often this means going right down to the ground. When rebuilding the wall, overlap the stones.

TOOLS

Clamps	Screwdriver bit	Shovel
Hammer	File	Posthole digger
Maul	Handsaw	Car jack
Pliers	Circular saw	Stiff-fiber brush
Wrench	Hacksaw	Cold chisel
Screwdriver	Pry bar	Pointing trowel
Electric drill	Tamping bar	Mason's hawk

MATERIALS

2x4s, 2x6s	Galvanized wood screws ($1\frac{1}{2}$", 3" No. 8)	Screw eye ($\frac{1}{2}$")
1" plywood	Carriage bolts ($\frac{3}{8}$"), washers	Turnbuckle and wire cable
Wooden stakes		Concrete blocks
Galvanized common nails (3", $3\frac{1}{2}$")		Gravel

SAFETY TIPS

Wear goggles when drilling, work gloves and goggles to chip out mortar, and gloves when working with wet mortar. Wear gloves when handling pressure-treated wood, which contains arsenic compounds as preservatives; add a dust mask when cutting it.

REINFORCING LOOSE FENCE RAILS

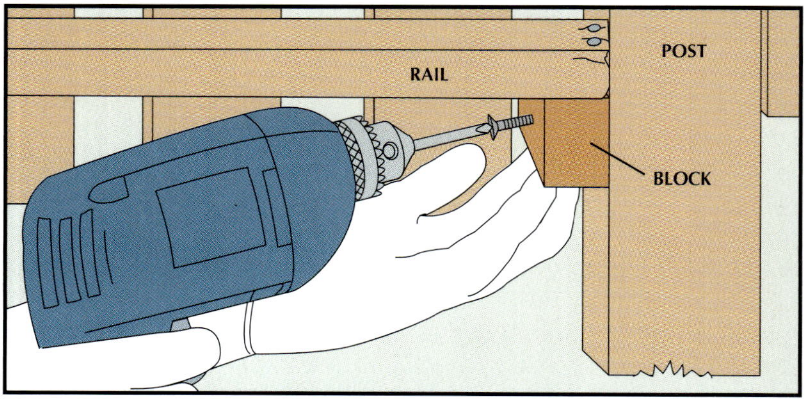

Bracing the end of a rail.

◆ Cut a block the same width as the rail from a 2-by-4.

◆ Drill a pair of $\frac{1}{8}$-inch clearance holes through the block so the screws can pass freely through it.

◆ Hold the piece of wood in place under the rail and screw it to the post with two 3-inch No. 8 galvanized wood screws *(above)*.

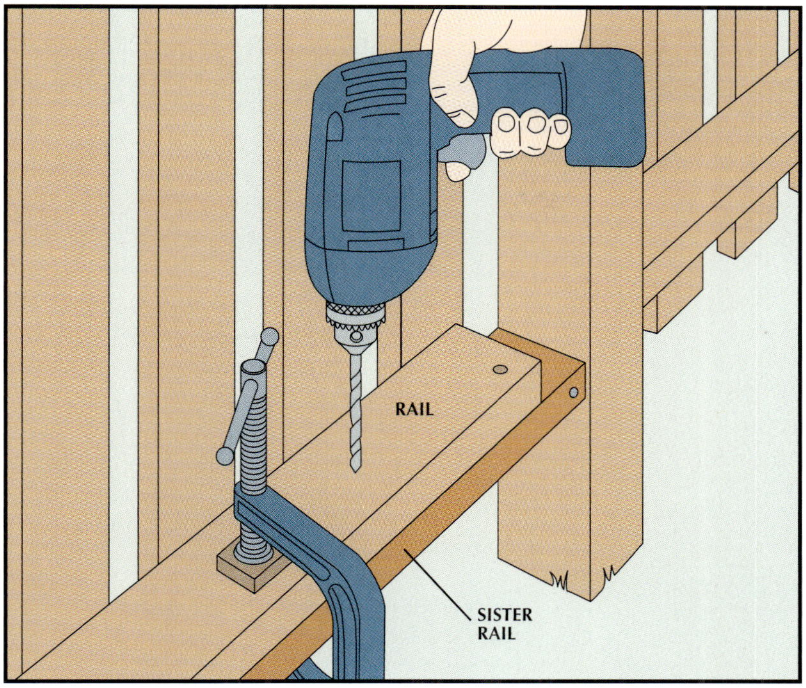

Bracing the length of a rail with a sister rail.

◆ Cut off the damaged part of the rail.

◆ Cut a length of pressure-treated lumber the same size as the rail—commonly 2-by-4—to fit between the two posts.

◆ Position this sister rail underneath the old rail (or above if there is no room below) and clamp it every 12 inches. Toenail the sister to the post on both sides and underneath with $3\frac{1}{2}$-inch galvanized common nails.

◆ Bore a $\frac{3}{8}$-inch hole through both boards every 18 inches, offsetting them as shown *(left)*.

◆ Install $\frac{3}{8}$-inch carriage bolts in the holes, then remove the clamps.

◆ Fill in the gap in the rail with wood; fasten it with 3-inch galvanized nails.

STRENGTHENING A POST

Steadying a post with sister posts.

◆ Cut two pressure-treated 2-by-4s to a length at least half the height of the post to serve as sister posts; saw a 45-degree bevel at one end of each board.

◆ Position a sister post, bevel out, against the fence post.

◆ Place a scrap 2-by-4 against the top of the sister post and drive the post halfway into the ground with a maul *(left)*.

◆ With a circular saw, cut off the top at a 45-degree angle 18 to 24 inches from the ground.

◆ In the same way, position and cut the other sister post on the opposite side.

◆ Bore two holes through the three posts and secure the sister posts with $\frac{3}{8}$-inch carriage bolts.

◆ Trim the bolts with a hacksaw *(inset)* and file off any sharp burrs.

REPLACING A POST

1. Positioning a replacement post.
◆ To indicate the location of the old post before removing it, run a string tautly between the posts on either side of the damaged post.
◆ Tie a marker string to the line on each side of the post *(left)*.

For a corner post, extend a line from both lengths of fence, past the corner post and secure each one to a stake *(inset)*.

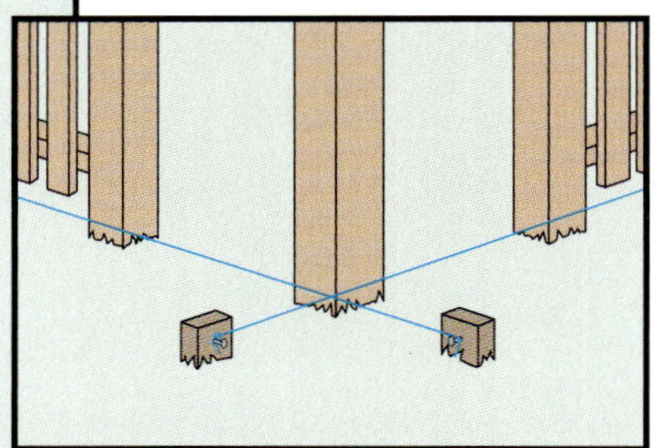

2. Removing the old post.
◆ Remove the rails and fencing on both sides of the post.
◆ Loosen the post and footing, if any, by removing the earth around the post with a shovel and a posthole digger, then rock the post back and forth.
◆ Install the replacement post as you would a new one *(page 134)*, then reinstall the rails and fencing.

If the post is too heavy to be lifted out by one or two people—especially if it is set in concrete—enlist the help of a car jack.
◆ Nail a 12-inch 2-by-4 to the post and nail a 2-by-6 under it, resting one end on the car jack and the other on a pair of concrete blocks *(right)*.
◆ Support the car jack, and with a helper guiding the post, raise it with the jack.

REPAIRING SAGGING GATES

1. Bracing with wood.

◆ Prop a block under the latch side of the gate to hold it in its correct closed position.

◆ Tack a brace the same dimensions as the rails diagonally across the top and bottom rails, and mark cut lines on its back along the rails *(right)*.

◆ Cut the brace at the marks.

◆ Position the brace between the rails, bore clearance and pilot holes *(page 124)* 1 inch from each end *(inset)*, and drive $1\frac{1}{2}$-inch No. 8 galvanized wood screws into the rail.

◆ Also drive a 1-inch screw into every other picket.

◆ If the gate still sags, try correcting it with a wire and turnbuckle stay *(below)*.

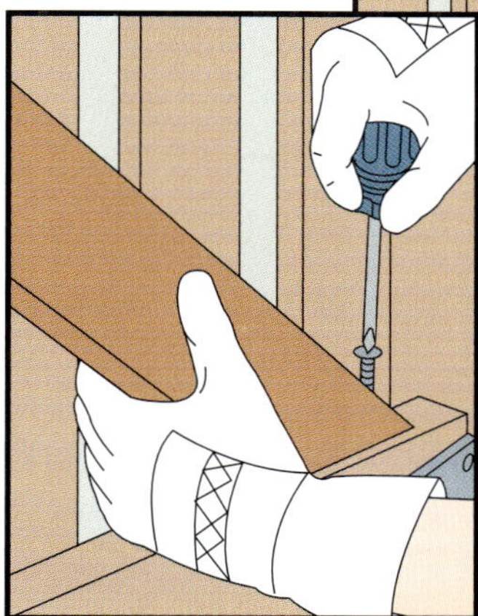

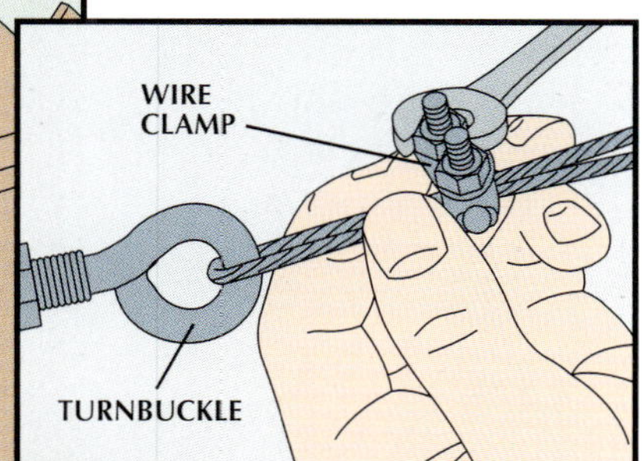

2. Bracing with a wire-and-turnbuckle stay.

◆ Open a 3-inch turnbuckle to its full extension and attach a length of cable to each end with a wire clamp *(inset)*. The cable length will vary with the size of the gate.

◆ Fasten a $\frac{1}{2}$-inch screw eye to the corner of the top rail on the hinge side and the opposite corner of the bot-tom rail as shown, then attach the ends of the turnbuckle wires. Trim any excess wire with pliers.

◆ Tighten the turnbuckle to pull the gate back into square *(left)*.

4 Erecting Fences and Walls

There are many reasons to raise a fence or build a wall, from increasing privacy to discouraging trespassers. The effect can be as imposing as a solid brick wall or as neighborly as that symbol of a quiet suburban home—the picket fence. But no matter what type of structure you decide to erect, there are certain fundamentals that need to be mastered to ensure that it will be both attractive and long-lasting.

Attaching the gate latch →

Creating Terraced Landings

The land surrounding your home may be hilly, making it difficult to find a level spot to erect a structure. Often the solution is to create a terrace by building a retaining wall.

Earth and water exert considerable pressure behind a retaining wall, so you must make your structure strong and provide adequate drainage. Begin by checking your local regulations on drainage (any change in the contour of your land will affect the flow of water) and any other restrictions.

Modular "Stone" Wall: Special concrete wall blocks *(opposite)* create the look of a stone wall in a fraction of the time and are just as strong. Depending on their design, they can be raised to a height of 24 to 48 inches without any anchoring. Each row of blocks is linked to the one above with matching grooves and ledges. The front face of the blocks is usually wider than the back, making it easy to create circular and serpentine walls.

A Palisade of Posts: For a simple retaining wall up to 36 inches high, plant a row of vertical timbers in the ground and spike the timbers together with bars of reinforcing steel *(page 133)*. "Found" materials such as old pier pilings or telephone poles make strong and economical choices for building supplies.

Limitations: The terraces created by these walls are suitable for light-duty demands such as supporting the structures found in Chapter 3. Walls supporting terraces for heavier loads, especially dynamic loads like vehicular traffic, need extra anchoring and should be referred to a structural engineer. Also, walls higher than 36 inches often require a building permit and are best left to a professional.

TOOLS

- Tape measure
- Carpenter's level
- Line level
- Rake
- Shovel
- Square-edged spade
- Pick
- Posthole digger
- Tamping bar
- Rubber mallet
- Maul
- Mason's chisel
- Caulking gun
- Electric drill
- $\frac{3}{8}$" ship-auger bit

MATERIALS

- Stakes
- Posts
- Reinforcing bar ($\frac{3}{8}$")
- Coarse sand
- $\frac{3}{4}$" drainage aggregate
- Gravel
- Concrete retaining wall blocks
- Concrete adhesive
- Landscape filter fabric
- Mason's line

SAFETY TIPS

Protect your eyes with goggles when drilling.

EXCAVATING THE SITE

1. Cutting back the slope.

◆ Working upward from the base of the slope, cut away the earth along the path of the wall with a pick and shovel.

◆ Pitch the excavated soil behind the site of the wall to create a plateau, leaving a drop slightly less than the planned height of the wall.

2. Setting a level base.

◆ Drive stakes to mark the ends of the wall.

◆ Stretch a mason's line between the stakes and level the line with a line level.

◆ With a shovel and rake, level the soil to a uniform distance under the string all along its length.

A MODULAR BLOCK RETAINING WALL

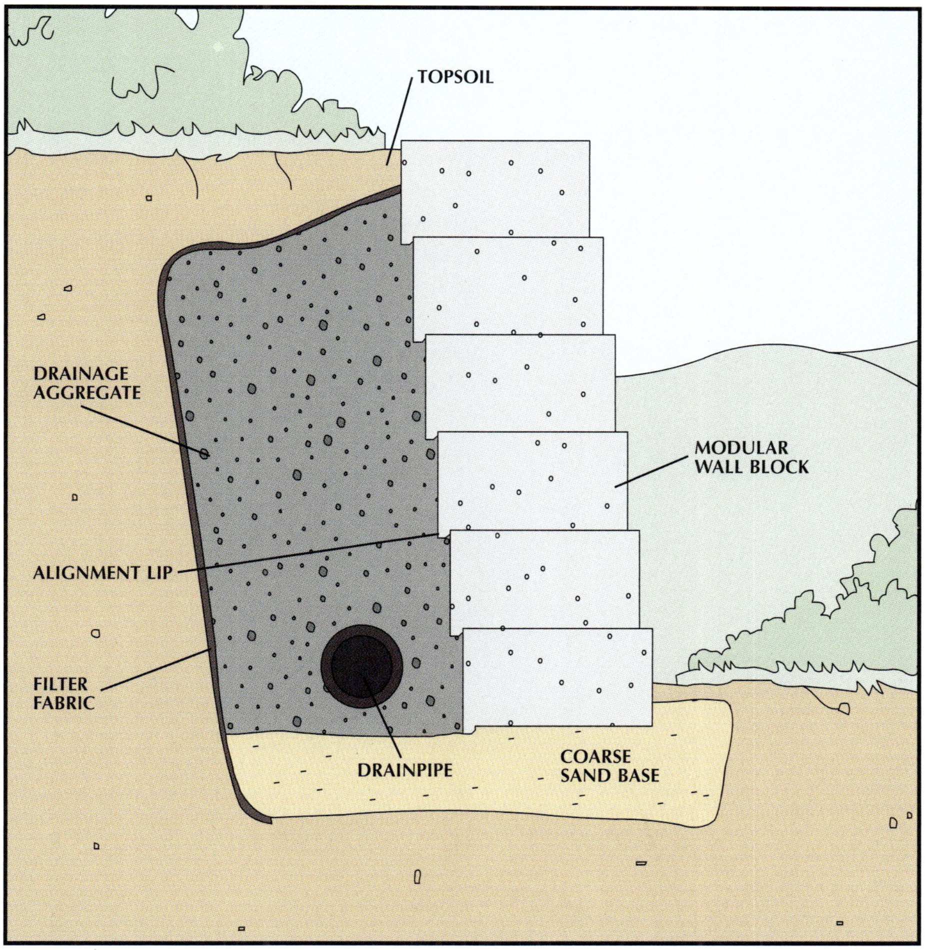

A look behind the wall.
Modular block construction eliminates the threat from frost heaves by preventing the buildup of water behind the wall. The mortarless joints allow water to weep through the wall face. The base of the wall consists of 4 inches of compacted and leveled coarse sand. In soils that drain poorly, a 4-inch perforated drain pipe is installed at the level of the first course. Each course is slightly offset from the one beneath it by alignment lips on the blocks. The wall is backfilled with $\frac{3}{4}$ inch clean drainage aggregate and finished with 3 inches of topsoil. If the soil is very fine, a filter fabric (available at a landscaping supplier) is placed behind the aggregate to keep the backfill clean.

Modular block manufacturers recommend heights to which their walls can be built without reinforcement. Always refer to the manufacturer's height guidelines.

1. Laying the first course.

◆ Dig a shallow trench along the excavated terrace 12 to 18 inches wide and 4 inches deep.

◆ If the soil is very fine, spread a layer of filter fabric on the side of the trench, as shown on page 131. Cut the fabric long enough to fold over the aggregate once the top course of blocks is in place *(Step 3)*.

◆ Spread a 4-inch layer of coarse sand in the trench, then compact and level it.

◆ Arrange the first course of blocks on the base, digging a shallow trench in the sand to accommodate the alignment lips; align the back face of the blocks with the mason's line you set up when excavating the trench *(page 131, Step 2)*. Level each block front to back and side to side *(right)*, making sure adjacent units are flush; a rubber mallet can help to position the blocks.

◆ To cut a block for the ends and corners, first score it with a mason's chisel and maul. Continue striking with the chisel on all four sides until the block splits.

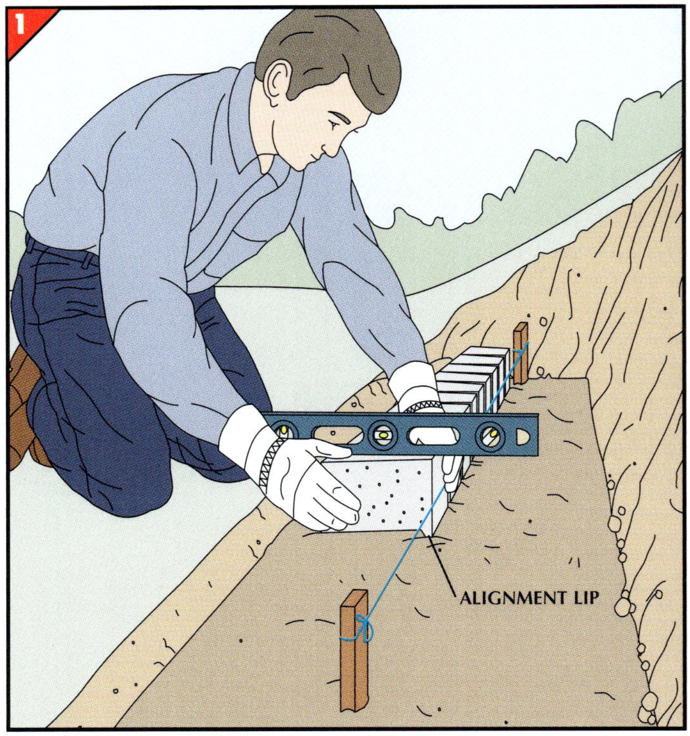

2. Backfilling each row.

◆ To improve drainage from behind the wall, install a 4-inch perforated plastic drain pipe at the level of the first row of stones, as shown on page 131.

◆ Remove the alignment stakes and mason's line, then position the next row of blocks over the first so the alignment lip overhangs the back edge. Overlap the blocks so the joints of the two rows are staggered.

◆ Backfill behind each course with $\frac{3}{4}$-inch drainage aggregate as you proceed *(left)*.

◆ Continue adding rows of stones followed by backfill to reach the necessary height.

3. Securing the top course.

◆ Before you lay each block of the last course, apply two beads of concrete adhesive to the blocks in the previous row *(right)*.

◆ Fold any filter fabric over the aggregate and fill in the last 2 or 3 inches behind the wall with topsoil.

CONSTRUCTING A PALISADE RETAINING WALL

1. Digging the trenches.

◆ Excavate the wall site *(page 130)*.
◆ Dig a trench under the string to a depth equal to the wall height plus 2 inches. Make the trench 4 inches wider than the posts to be used for the wall.
◆ Create a flat, even bearing surface on the downhill face of the trench with a square-edged spade *(photograph)*.
◆ Starting at one end, use a posthole digger to make a hole for a single timber twice the depth of the trench *(left)*.

2. Pinning the wall together.

◆ Set the corner post in its hole, add gravel to fill the hole, and pack the gravel down with a tamping bar *(page 139)*.
◆ Dig a shallow trench for four shorter posts next to the first one, set the second post in the trench, and, with a $\frac{3}{8}$-inch ship-auger bit, drill two holes, one above grade *(right)* and one below, through one timber and into the next. If the wood is hard you may need to rent a $\frac{1}{2}$-inch drill, as shown.
◆ Drive $\frac{3}{8}$-inch reinforcing bars into the holes.
◆ Repeat for each short post, staggering the heights of the holes so the bars do not intersect. Add gravel to hold the posts in place.
◆ When you have laid and pinned four timbers, make another deep hole with the posthole digger; repeat the procedure for every fifth timber.
◆ Fill in the trench with gravel as you go, tamping it down every 4 inches, then fill in the rest of the space between the wall and the retained soil with the soil that was removed.

Setting Fence Posts

The key to an attractive, long-lasting fence is a row of sturdy fence posts, securely anchored and properly aligned and spaced. Posts are the working members of a fence, serving to bear and brace the gates and railings.

There is a wide range of fence post materials, as shown in the box below. Before setting any posts, check your property line and local zoning or building codes, which may determine fence height or setback from the street.

To help protect the top of a fence from rain, cut the post at a 30- to 45-degree angle before setting it, or cover it with a plastic or metal post cap, available at home centers to fit standard post sizes.

Setting Posts Straight and Secure: As a general rule, one-third of the post should be below ground. In relatively stable soil, tamped earth or gravel will hold the post securely. Gateposts and the end and corner posts, which are subjected to greater stress, should be set in concrete wherever possible. If you prefer not to go to the trouble and expense of using concrete, use longer lengths of lumber for these key posts and sink them deeper into the ground.

Avoid leaving holes unattended; set a post in its hole as soon as possible or at least mark the hazard by inserting the post or or a tall stake.

Overcoming Frost Heaves: As freezing water expands under and around posts, it tends to force them up. One solution is to sink the post below the frost line, which varies from region to region. It is generally impractical to sink posts deeper than 3 to $3\frac{1}{2}$ feet. In this case, set the post in concrete; nails partly driven into the post help to hold it to the concrete. For added stability first widen the hole at the base into a bell shape so the surrounding earth holds the concrete in place.

Whether or not you use concrete, always set the base of the post in 6 inches of gravel. The improved drainage reduces the risks of frost heaves and prevents the post bottom from resting in groundwater and rotting. Four ways to set a post are shown on page 138.

TOOLS

- Carpenter's level
- Line level
- Plumb bob
- 1x2 gauge pole
- Hammer
- Maul
- Handsaw
- Mason's trowel
- Shovel
- Garden spade
- Posthole digger
- Tamping bar

MATERIALS

- 1x2
- Wooden stakes
- Common nails ($1\frac{1}{2}$")
- Gravel
- Pre-mixed concrete
- Mason's line

SAFETY TIPS

Wear gloves when handling pressure-treated lumber; add a dust mask when cutting it.

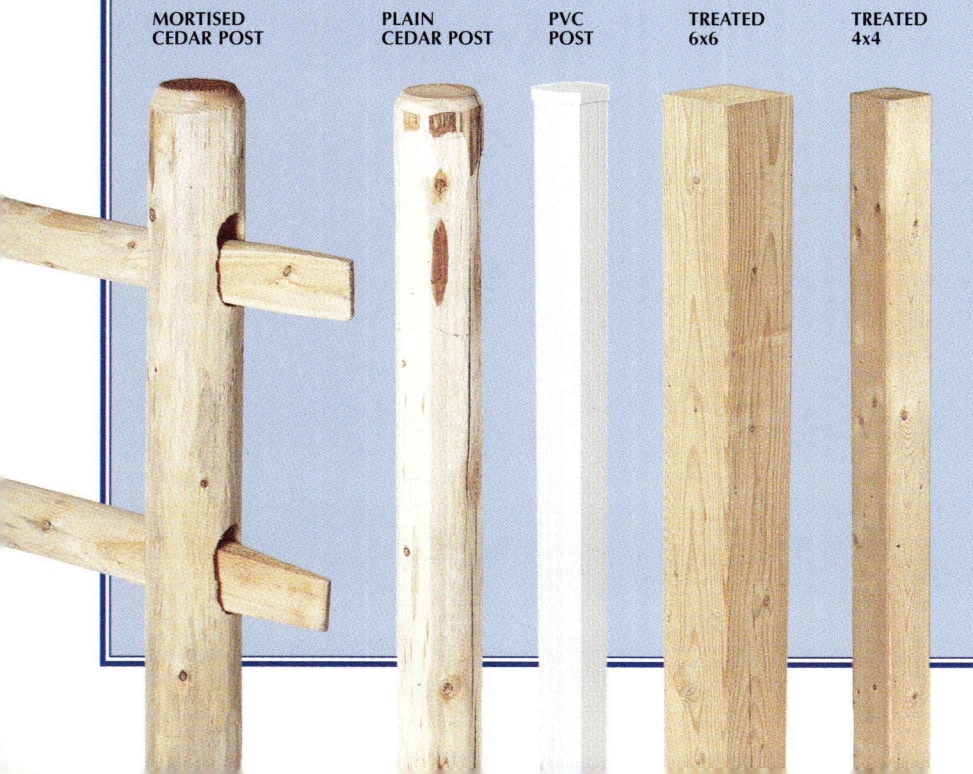

AN ARRAY OF POST MATERIALS

Pressure-treated lumber is one of the most popular choices for fence posts, and with good reason: They are strong, widely available, and last at least 20 years. But there are other sound options. Naturally resistant woods like redwood, red and white cedar, and locust are all good choices if they are available for a good price in your area. They are commonly used for rustic-style fences. PVC posts, although more costly than wood, are attractive and typically guaranteed to last a lifetime.

Most wood fences are best supported by posts no smaller than 4-by-4s, but low picket fences can be anchored with 2-by-4 posts. All corner and gateposts should be 4-by-4s or larger.

LAYING OUT THE POSTS

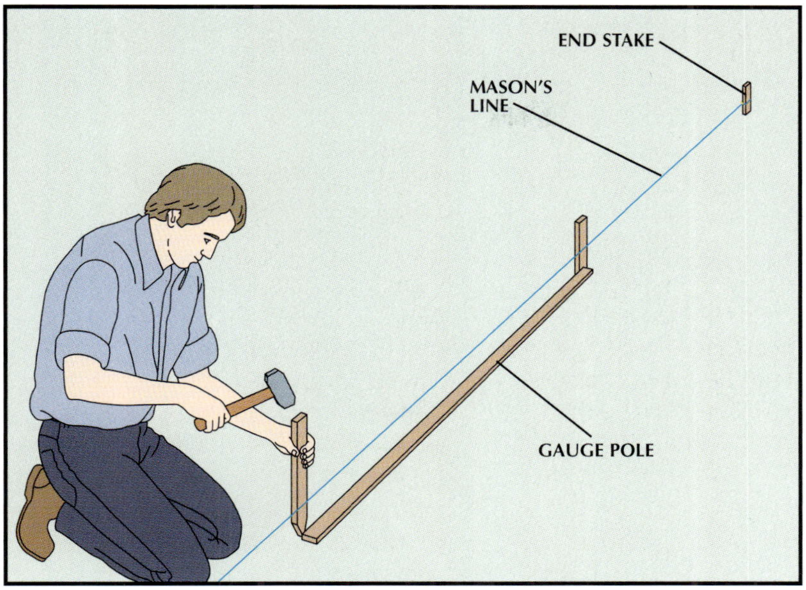

Locating posts on flat ground.

◆ Drive stakes at the locations of the end posts and stretch a mason's line between them.

◆ Measure the distance between the posts and determine the standard lengths of lumber or fencing that will make up the rails of the fence with a minimum of cutting. In general, posts are spaced a maximum of 8 feet apart; this way, a 16-foot length of lumber will span three posts.

◆ Make a gauge pole by cutting a straight 1-by-2 board to the length of the fence sections.

◆ Lay out the post positions with stakes as shown at left. Adjust the intervals for gateposts and to avoid ending the fence with a very short section.

Staking posts on uneven ground.

◆ For a fence with a level top, stretch a mason's line between two end stakes and level it with a line level.

◆ With a helper measuring along the line with a gauge pole, drop a plumb bob from the line to pinpoint each post location on the ground *(right)*. Drive a stake at each one.

For a fence that follows the contours of the ground, drive stakes at the fence ends and at each high and low point in between. Join all the stakes with a mason's line and position the stakes for the remaining posts evenly along the line as shown above.

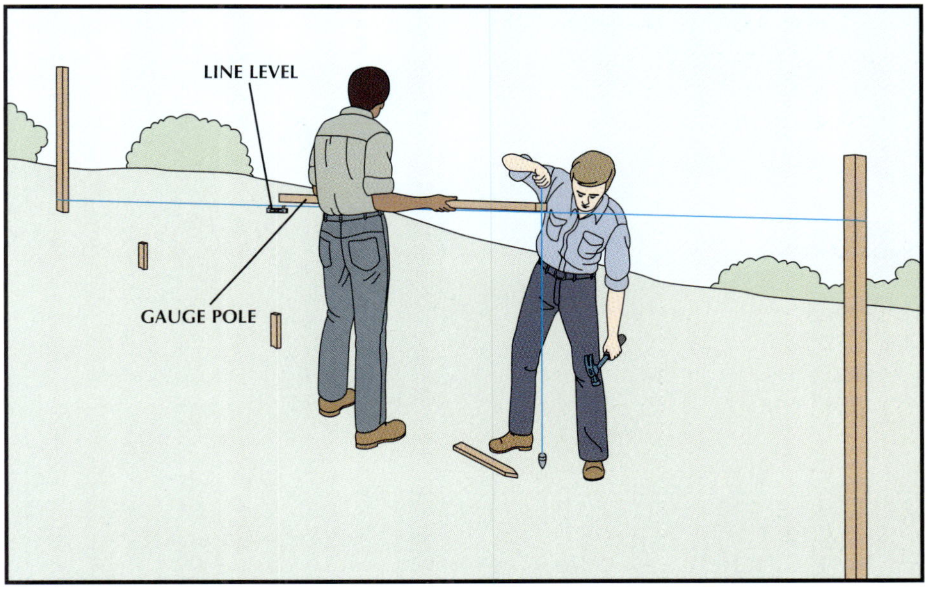

TRICKS OF THE TRADE

Marking a Square Corner

This simple method has been used to lay out right angles for centuries. Drive stakes to establish your first fence line, with one stake at the desired corner point. Attach a mason's line to these two stakes, then tie a marker string to the line at the 3-foot mark. Stretch another line from the corner stake, roughly perpendicular to the first line and secure it to a batter board—a horizontal board nailed to two stakes *(page 208)*. Tie a marker string to this line at the 4-foot mark. Slide this line along the batter board so that the distance between the two marker strings is 5 feet *(right)*. The angle between the two lines will be 90 degrees.

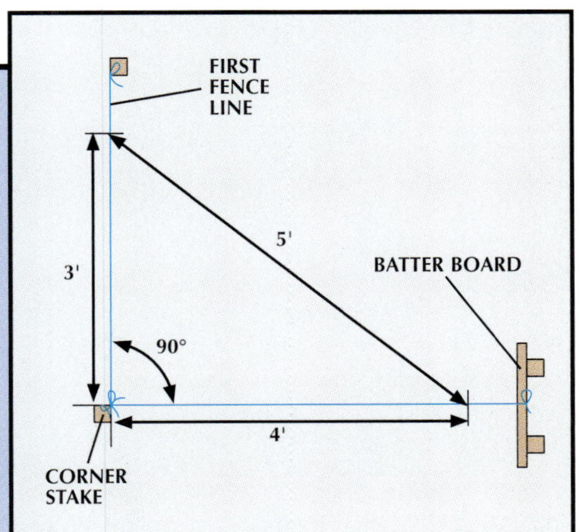

DIGGING POSTHOLES

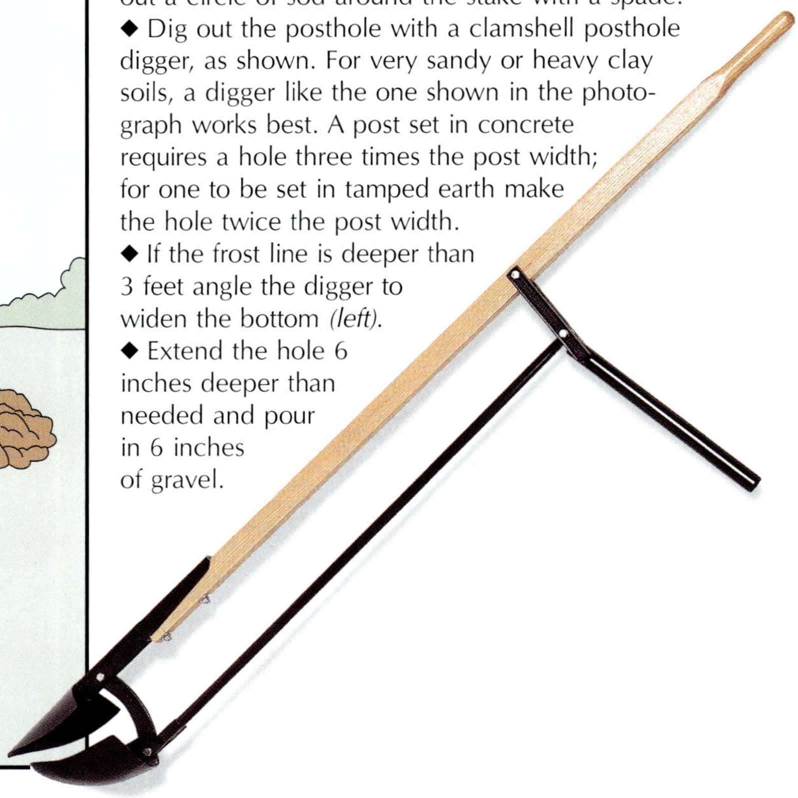

Burrowing a hole with a posthole digger.

◆ Untie the mason's line from the stakes, putting it aside for aligning the posts *(opposite)*. Start the hole by cutting out a circle of sod around the stake with a spade.

◆ Dig out the posthole with a clamshell posthole digger, as shown. For very sandy or heavy clay soils, a digger like the one shown in the photograph works best. A post set in concrete requires a hole three times the post width; for one to be set in tamped earth make the hole twice the post width.

◆ If the frost line is deeper than 3 feet angle the digger to widen the bottom *(left)*.

◆ Extend the hole 6 inches deeper than needed and pour in 6 inches of gravel.

A HOLE DIGGING TIMESAVER

If you are setting 10 or more fence posts, consider renting a power auger. Unless you are working in very rocky or very heavy clay soils it saves both time and effort. The two-person auger at right is less likely to kick out of the hole when it hits a rock than the one-person version.

To use a power auger, mark the posthole depth on the bit with tape and set the machine over the marked position. Start the motor and adjust the speed with the handle-mounted throttle. Guide the machine as the bit pulls it into the ground. After digging 8 to 12 inches, raise the bit to clear the dirt from the hole. If you hit a rock, pry it loose with a digging bar or pick and shovel.

ALIGNING FENCE POSTS

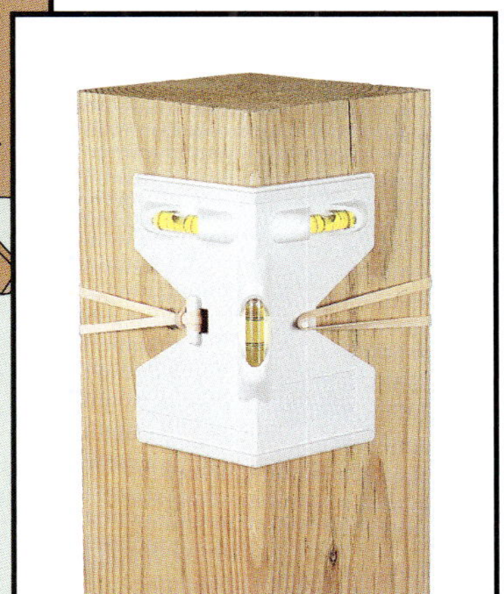

1. Bracing an end or corner post.

◆ Drive two stakes on adjacent sides of the posthole.

◆ Fasten a 1-by-2-inch bracing board to each stake with a single $1\frac{1}{2}$-inch common nail.

◆ Center a post in the hole and use a carpenter's level to plumb one side of the post *(left)*; alternatively, use a special post level *(photograph)*, which will enable you to plumb both directions at once.

◆ Nail the first brace to the post, then check for plumb on the other side and secure the second brace.

2. Aligning intermediate posts.

◆ Attach two lines to the end posts, one near the top and the other close to ground level. For the upper line, make sure that it is attached at exactly the same distance from the top of the posts.

◆ Place an intermediate post in a hole. Add or remove gravel to set the post at the correct height according to the alignment line.

◆ Have a helper align one side of the intermediate post with the two lines, then plumb an adjacent side with a level.

◆ Sight along the top line to check both the post height and the alignment *(right)*; alter alignment by shifting the post base.

ANCHORING POSTS IN THE GROUND

FOUR WAYS TO PLANT A POST

There is no one correct way to secure a fence post. Soil type, intended use, climate, and budget all influence the selection of fillers. The one ingredient common to all methods is a 6-inch base of gravel. This will help prevent water from pooling around the post bottom where it will be drawn into the end grain and hasten decay.

The simplest method is to replace and tamp the soil that was removed to make the hole. This works well if the fence is less than 4 feet high and sitting in well-drained soil, which reduces the risk of frost heave.

There are two practical reasons to bolster a post with concrete: strength and protection from frost heave. If additional strength is needed but frost heave is not a significant threat, then fill the hole halfway with tamped soil and top it with concrete, for a partial concrete collar. If the post only requires protection against frost heave, then pour enough concrete to fill the bottom 8 to 12 inches of the hole, driving nails partway into the post to anchor it to the concrete.

A full concrete collar, extending from the drainage gravel to just above the ground, is definitely the strongest method of setting a post. It protects against frost heave and will render a post strong enough to hang a gate or hold a tall fence.

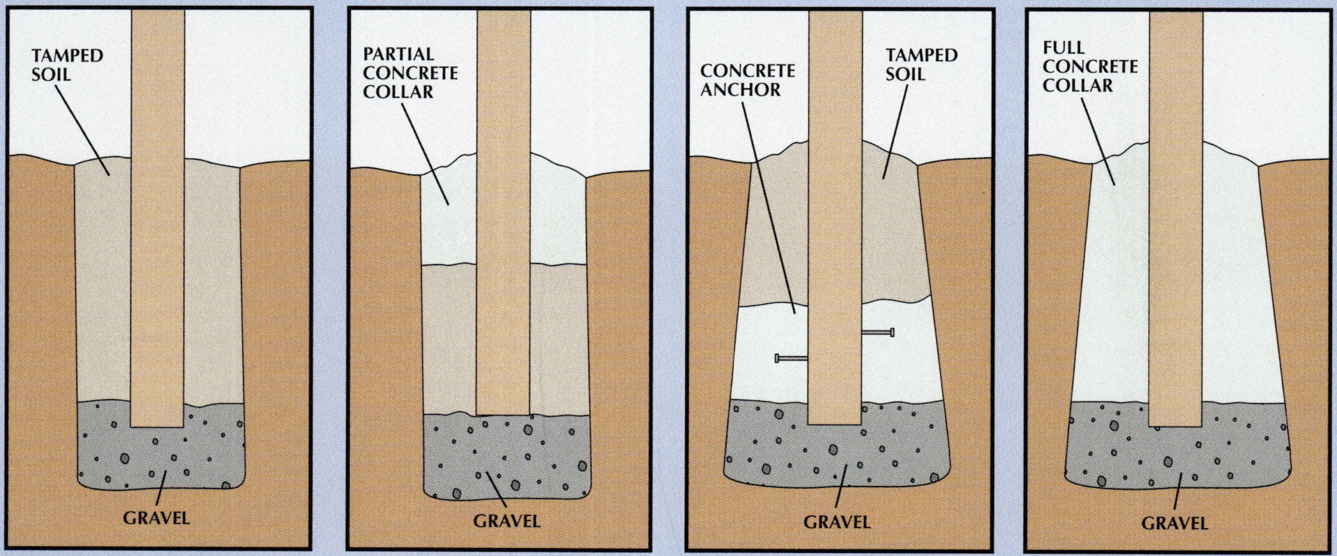

TRICKS OF THE TRADE

Fitting a Hole for a Crooked Post

Unmilled round posts of cedar, locust, or redwood are often curved at their large end. To allow for this, dig the hole to the correct depth; then shape one side to match the curve on the post, allowing the above-ground part of the post to stand plumb. Finally, dig the hole 6 inches deeper, then add 6 inches of gravel for drainage. When the earth is tamped back in place the post will be directly braced against undisturbed soil, providing a secure support.

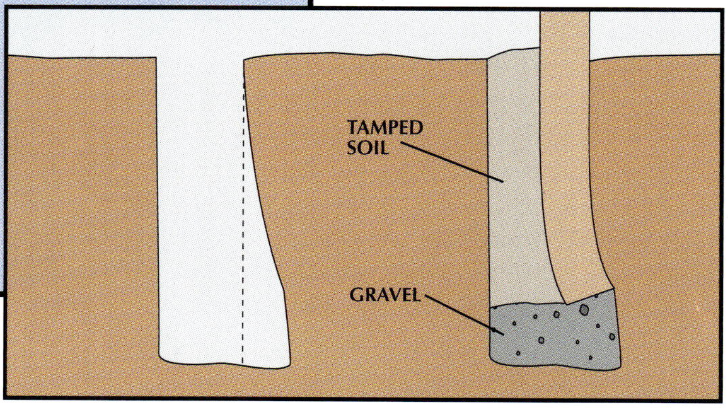

Securing a post in tamped earth.

◆ While a helper holds the post plumb and touching the alignment lines *(page 137)* fill the hole with earth in 3- to 4-inch layers, tamping as you go with the flat end of a tamping bar or a 2-by-4. Make sure you do not inadvertently shift the position of the post.
◆ If you are using only soil, overfill the hole and shape a slope of earth around the post to shed runoff. If you are topping the hole with concrete, simply fill the hole to the appropriate height with tamped earth, leaving room for the concrete *(opposite)*.

Setting a post in concrete.

◆ Ensure that the post is aligned and plumb *(page 137)*.
◆ Prepare a batch of premixed concrete with a square-edged spade according to the manufacturer's directions, then fill the hole.
◆ Agitate the concrete with the shovel to remove any air pockets, but be careful not to knock the post out of position.
◆ Overfill the hole slightly and use a mason's trowel to slope the concrete down from the post to improve runoff.
◆ Allow the concrete to set for 48 hours before removing the braces or attaching the fencing.

If you are only laying down a concrete anchor, pour in about 8 to 12 inches of concrete; usually this amounts to one bag of pre-mixed concrete for each post.

Wooden Fences

Almost every wooden fence is built on a framework of upright posts and connecting rails, or stringers. This simple skeleton can support a range of fences that will meet practically any need. A fence of nothing more than posts and rails makes a clear boundary marker, adapts well to rough or rolling terrain, and covers the most ground with the least lumber. Siding nailed to a post-and-stringer frame can take the shape of a low picket fence to decorate the border of a front yard or of a tall board fence *(page 149)* to ensure privacy or keep children and pets within bounds.

Building Materials: In all of these fence styles, your first concern is the quality of the building materials. Assemble the fence with pressure-treated lumber or naturally decay- and insect-resistant woods, such as cedar or redwood. All are more expensive than construction-grade lumber, but they will last longer. Fasten the elements with hot-dipped galvanized, aluminum, or stainless-steel fasteners, which will not rust and stain the fence.

Post-and-Board Fences: The fence of this type shown on the following pages is made of 1-by lumber, face-nailed to 4-by-4 posts. For a three-rail fence, set the posts 36 to 42 inches high. For a four-rail fence, make the posts 48 to 54 inches high. To protect the top ends of posts from rot, top them with plastic or metal caps or with an angled cap rail.

Picket Fences: This type of fence is built in a wide range of styles. If you cannot find prefabricated pickets you will have to cut your own. A picket fence can be any height but is usually 3 to 4 feet, with 1-by-4 pickets projecting about 6 inches above the top stringer.

The tops of picket fences can be cut into any number of original shapes. The best tool for a relatively short fence is a saber saw or, for mass production, a router equipped with a flush-trimming bit.

Post-and-Rail Fences: With tapered rail ends that fit into mortised posts, these fences are sturdier than post-and-board fences and almost as easy to install. With this fence style, the posts are not all set first—they are placed in their holes as the fence is assembled. Prefabricated mortised posts and tapered stringers are sold by lumber suppliers in a variety of styles. All are assembled like the split-rail fence illustrated on page 148.

TOOLS

- Tape measure
- Carpenter's level
- Combination square
- Carpenter's square
- Clamps
- Hammer
- Maul
- Tamping bar
- Drawknife
- Handsaw
- Circular saw
- Saber saw
- Electric drill
- Screwdriver bit
- $\frac{3}{4}$" spade bit
- Drill guide
- Drill-press stand
- Router and flush-trimming bit

MATERIALS

- Fence posts and rails
- 1x4s, 1x6s
- 2x3s, 2x4s
- Wooden stakes
- Dowels ($\frac{3}{4}$")
- Galvanized common nails ($2\frac{1}{2}$", $3\frac{1}{2}$")
- Galvanized wood screws ($1\frac{1}{4}$" No. 6; $\frac{3}{4}$", $2\frac{1}{2}$" No. 8)
- Angle irons
- Mason's line
- Sandpaper (medium grade)
- Wood glue (exterior)

SAFETY TIPS

Protect your eyes when hammering nails, using a circular saw, or operating a router. Wear gloves when handling pressure-treated lumber, and add a dust mask when cutting it.

A SIMPLE POST-AND-BOARD FENCE

Building a post-and-board fence.

◆ Trim a 1-by-4 or 1-by-6 to extend from a corner or end post to the center of the second line post.

◆ Nail this board to the posts with $2\frac{1}{2}$-inch galvanized common nails.

◆ Trim the board for the next course so it fits from the corner to the center of the first line post, then nail it in place with the aid of a spacer cut to the appropriate length *(above)*. This will result in staggered joints that will make for a more rigid fence.

◆ Work toward the opposite corner, attaching boards cut to span three posts until you need short pieces for ends.

◆ Finally, nail metal or plastic caps onto the posts.

THE FINISHED LOOK OF A CAP RAIL

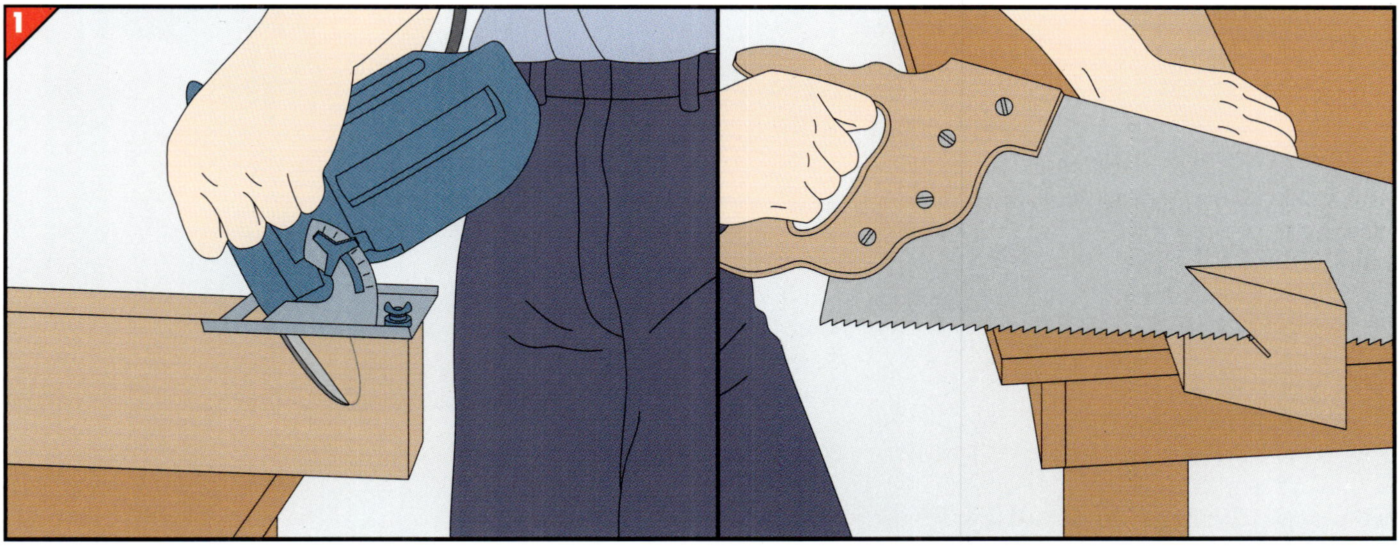

1. Beveling the posts.

Prepare each post for the cap rail by sawing a 30-degree bevel at the post's top end before you set the post in the ground.

◆ Set your circular saw to cut a 30-degree angle across the post about 3 inches from one end *(above, left)*. The saw will cut only partway through and you must finish with a handsaw.

◆ To prepare a corner post, make a second cut at a 30-degree angle across an adjacent side *(above, right)*.

◆ To set the posts, refer to the instructions on pages 134 to 139.

2. Marking the cap rail.

◆ With a helper, hold a 1-by-6 in position on top of a corner post and a line post.
◆ Have the helper set one end of the board at the center of the line post while you mark the underside of the board along the angle of the top of the corner post *(left)*.
◆ Mark the matching cap-rail board to fit across the other angled face of the corner post.
◆ With a combination square, transfer the marks to the other face of each board to facilitate sawing.

3. Cutting the cap rail.

◆ Set your circular saw to cut a 30-degree angle.
◆ Saw the rails along the marks you made in the previous step *(right)*.
◆ Fasten one of the cap rails with $2\frac{1}{2}$-inch galvanized common nails to the corner post and line post, aligning the tops of the rails with the top edges of the beveled posts.
◆ Place the other cap rail in position and test the fit *(below)*. If necessary, trim the board with a block plane.

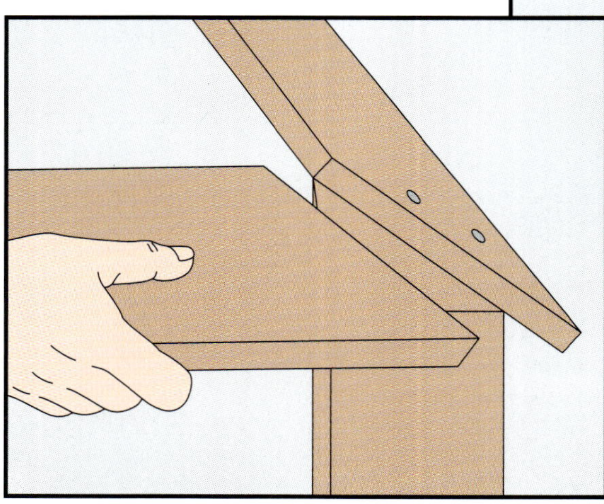

A BASIC PICKET FENCE

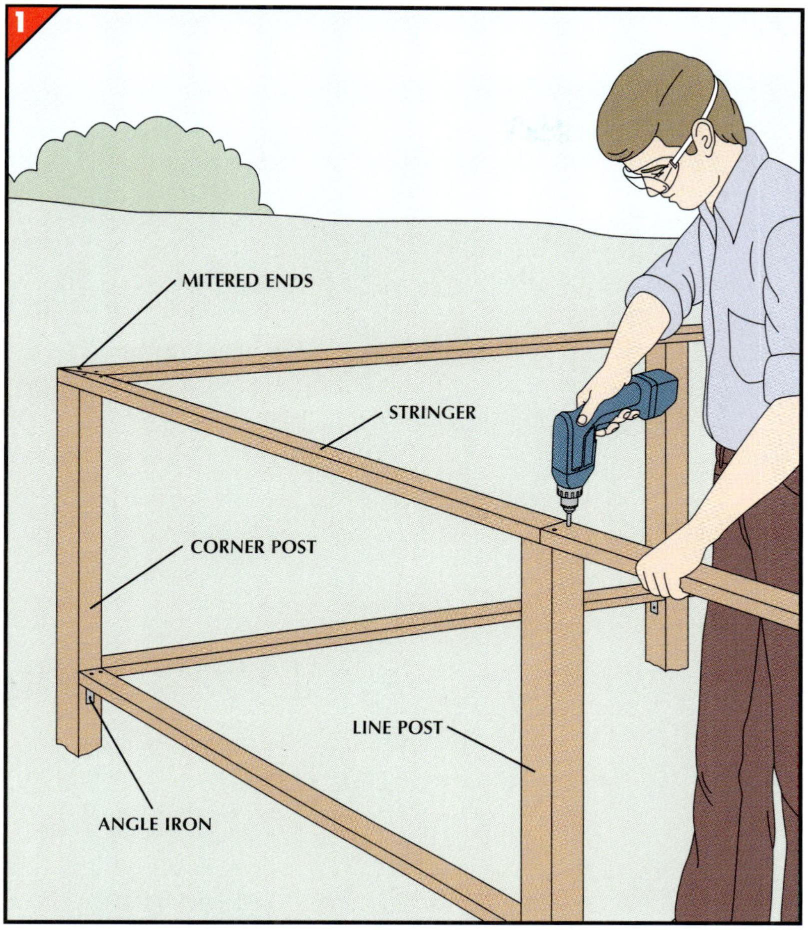

1. Installing the stringers.

Stringers can be installed face down as shown or on edge. The former method is more prone to sag under the weight of the fence while the latter one is more likely to bow from wind pressure.

◆ For the bottom stringers, trim 2-by-4s to fit between each pair of posts and secure an angle iron to each end with $\frac{3}{4}$-inch galvanized No. 8 wood screws.

◆ Attach these stringers to the posts about 8 inches above the ground: Drive screws through the angle iron and toenail the 2-by-4s with $3\frac{1}{2}$-inch galvanized common nails.

◆ Cut the first top stringer to length to stretch from the corner post to the middle of the first line post. Miter one end of the board at 45 degrees so it will match the stringer on the adjoining fence line.

◆ Drill two clearance holes in each end of the stringer, then fasten it to the posts with $2\frac{1}{2}$-inch No. 8 wood screws *(left)*. Continue to install stringers in this way, using long 2-by-4s to span as many posts as possible.

◆ Cut the pattern in the top of your pickets *(below and Step 2)*; if you have purchased precut pickets, go to Step 3.

TEMPLATES FOR PICKET PATTERNS

From the simple rounded shape to more complicated patterns, the gallery below shows just a sample of the possible forms of picket tops you can cut yourself. The first step is to design the pattern on paper. Then transfer it to a 1-by-4 board and cut out the shape with a saber saw. Sand any rough spots. You can use this as a template to draw the pattern on the picket stock before cutting out each one with a saber saw *(page 144)*. A faster method would be to cut the shape out of $\frac{1}{2}$-inch plywood and use it as a router template *(page 145)*.

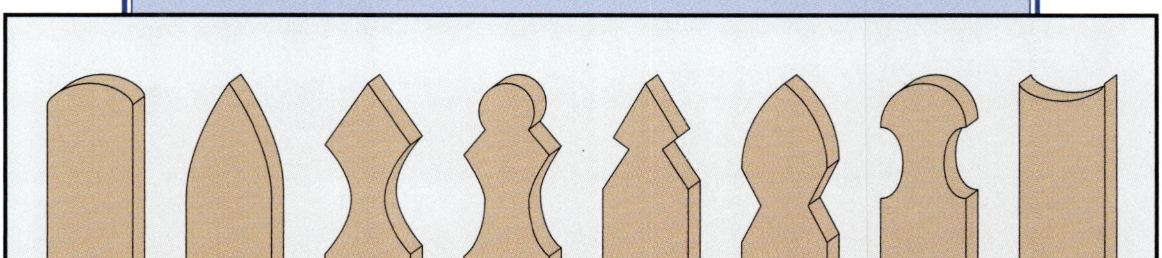

2. Cutting a pattern freehand.

◆ Outline the template pattern onto a picket, then clamp the picket to a work table.

◆ To keep the saber-saw blade from binding in the kerf, make release cuts from the edge of the picket to the tightest turns.

◆ Align the blade with the beginning of the cutting line, then feed the saw into the stock, guiding the tool to keep the blade on line *(right)*.

◆ Smooth any rough spots on the picket with medium-grade sandpaper.

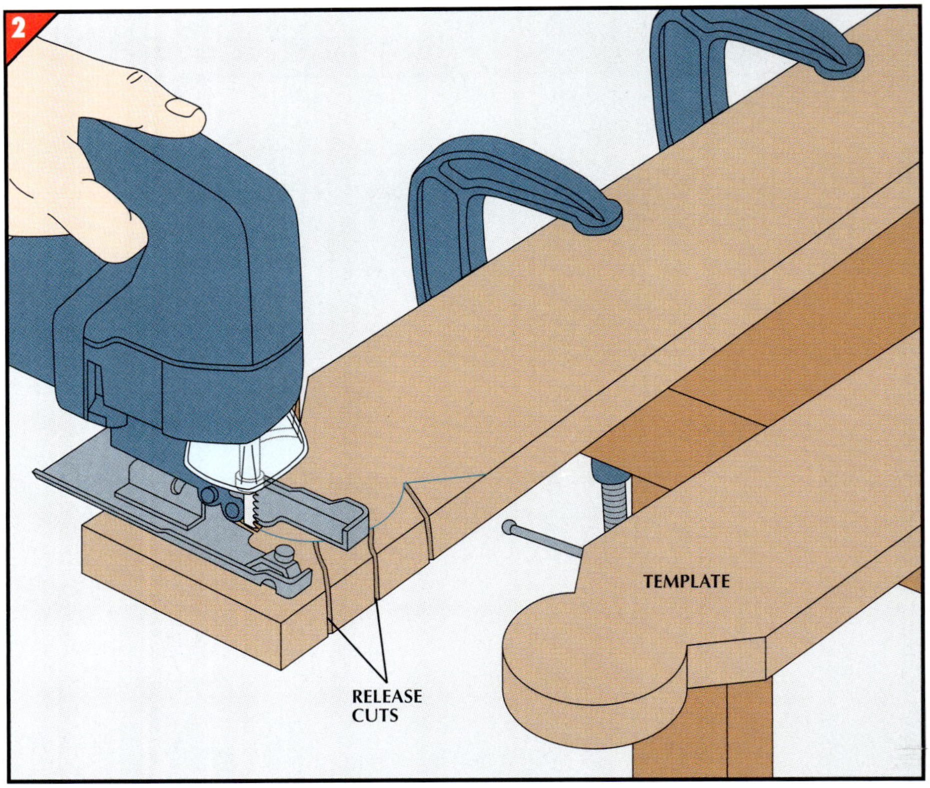

3. Attaching the pickets.

◆ Make a spacer to help you set the height and spacing of the pickets: Cut a piece of scrap wood to the same length as the pickets, then rip it to the desired width of the gap between the pickets. Attach a cleat to the spacer so it will hang from the top stringer at the correct height.

◆ Drill two clearance holes in each picket at the spots where they will contact the stringers.

◆ Set the first picket against the edge of an end post and align its point with the top of the spacer. Plumb the picket with a level and secure it with a $1\frac{1}{4}$-inch No. 6 screw.

◆ Continue in this manner *(above)*, checking with a level every few pickets to make sure they are not straying out of plumb.

SHAPING PICKETS WITH A ROUTER

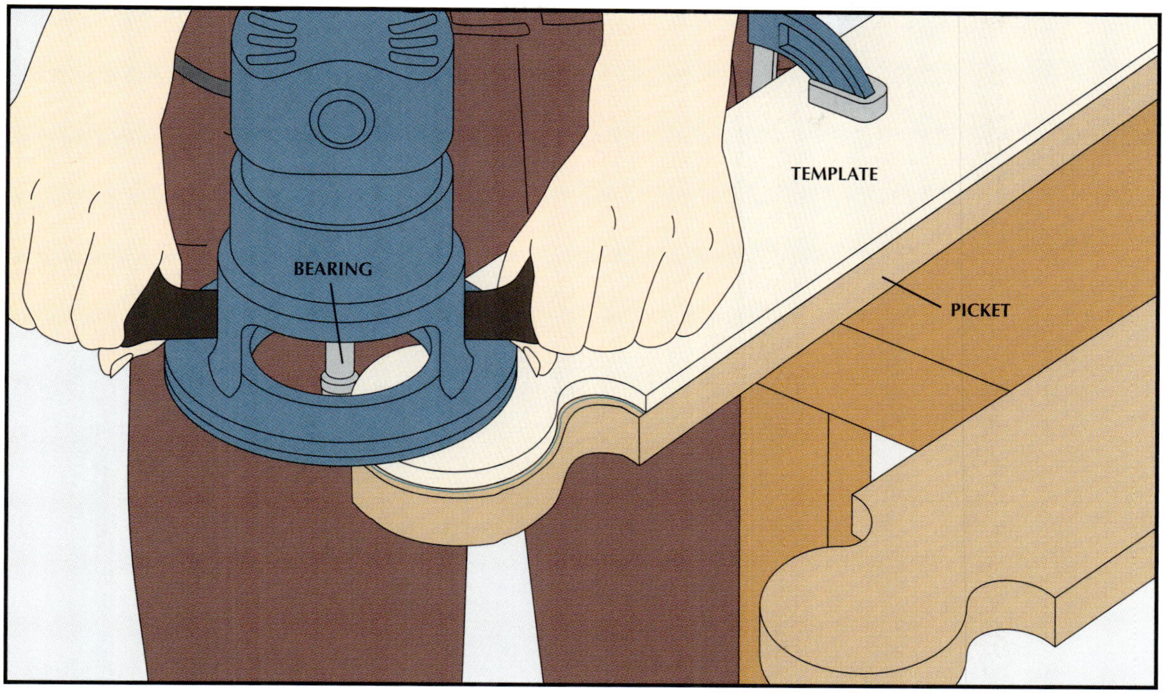

Cutting along the template.

◆ Outline the template *(page 143)* on the picket, then cut out the pattern roughly with a saber saw staying about $\frac{1}{4}$ inch outside the line.

◆ Align the template over the picket stock and clamp the assembly to a work surface.

◆ Fit the router with a top-piloted flush-trimming bit and adjust the cutting depth so the bearing will be in line with the template.

◆ To make the cut, slide the router toward the picket until the bearing touches the template. Move the router around the picket against the direction of bit rotation, keeping the bearing pressed against the template.

A LONG-LASTING ALTERNATIVE: VINYL FENCING

Vinyl fencing offers several advantages over the traditional wooden version, the main one being longevity. Most manufacturers offer at least a 20-year warranty on their fences; some even guarantee them for the life of the original owner. Available in a huge variety of styles, vinyl fencing requires little upkeep. And at the end of its useful life, it is 100 percent recyclable. All these advantages come at a price: vinyl fencing costs aproximately three times as much as a comparable wood fence. However, in the long run, the maintenance-free nature of the product may make it an economical option.

PLAIN PICKETS IN A CURVED PATTERN

1. Building panels of pickets.

Panel frames are built of 2-by-3s so that the pickets will fall flush with the outer face of a 4-by-4 post *(Step 3)*. If you want a stronger frame and do not mind the pickets sticking out a little from the posts, use 2-by-4s.

◆ Build rectangular frames of 2-by-3s to fit between each pair of posts.

◆ For each frame, cut pickets to the length of your longest picket and drill clearance holes where they will cross the stringers. Plan to situate the bottom stringers 8 inches above the ground.

◆ Lay one picket in the middle of the frame and check it for squareness to the stringers with a carpenter's square.

◆ Lay out the remaining pickets evenly spaced, and mark their locations on the frames.

◆ Secure the pickets with $1\frac{1}{4}$-inch No. 6 galvanized wood screws.

2. Marking a curved pattern.

◆ On the first panel, measure down from the top center picket the desired depth of the curve and drive a nail.

◆ Drive two end nails at the top of the picket panel, each a distance from the central nail equal to half the panel length.

◆ Tie a length of mason's line to one end nail, pull it around the central nail, and fasten it to the other end nail. Remove the middle nail.

◆ Keeping the line taut, pull a pencil along it to draw a curve on the picket panel *(above)*.

◆ Mark each panel this way and cut the curves with a saber saw.

3. Installing the panels.

◆ Position a panel between the posts. Rest it on a pair of 4-by-4 blocks so the tallest picket is at the desired height. Clamp the panel to the post at each end.

◆ Drill several clearance holes into the frame then fasten it to the post with $2\frac{1}{2}$-inch No. 8 wood screws *(above)*.

◆ If the panel sags over time, add another 2-by-3 under the top one, positioned on edge with its face against the pickets.

A RACK OF DOWELS

1. Preparing the stringers.

◆ Cut 2-by-3 or 2-by-4 stringers to fit between the posts, clamp each pair together, and mark the positions for $\frac{3}{4}$-inch dowels spaced 3 inches apart.

◆ With a $\frac{3}{4}$-inch spade bit, bore holes through the top stringer and one-third of the way into the bottom one at each marked point. The holes must be straight so make them with a drill press or an electric drill fitted with a drill guide or installed in a drill-press stand *(right)*.

◆ Attach the stringers to vertical members to make a frame, then fasten the frame to the posts *(Step 3, opposite)*.

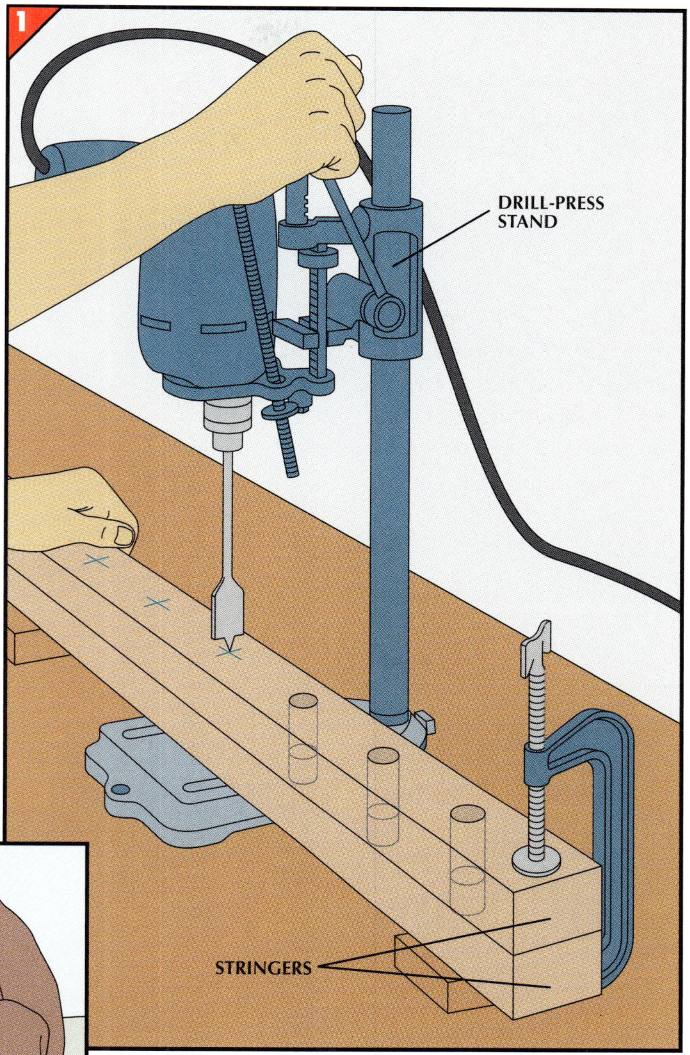

2. Inserting the dowels.

◆ Apply exterior-grade wood glue to the hole in the lower stringer.

◆ Push a $\frac{3}{4}$-inch dowel through the top stringer, resting it in the hole in the bottom stringer *(left)*.

◆ Tap the dowel lightly with a hammer to drive it home.

FITTING TOGETHER A RUSTIC RAIL FENCE

1. Laying a dry run of rails.

◆ Drive stakes for the corner or end posts and string a mason's line between them *(page 135)*.

◆ Lay precut rails on the ground along the fence line, overlapped as in the mortised posts. If the rails do not fit evenly, reposition the stakes, if possible, or cut shorter rails for one or two sections.

◆ Mark the position of each post with a stake *(right)*.

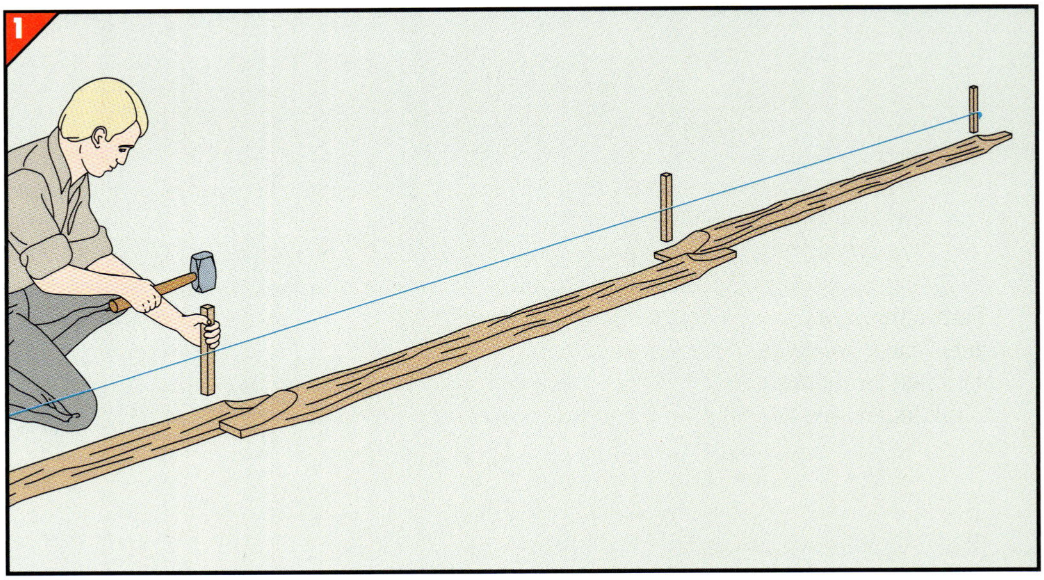

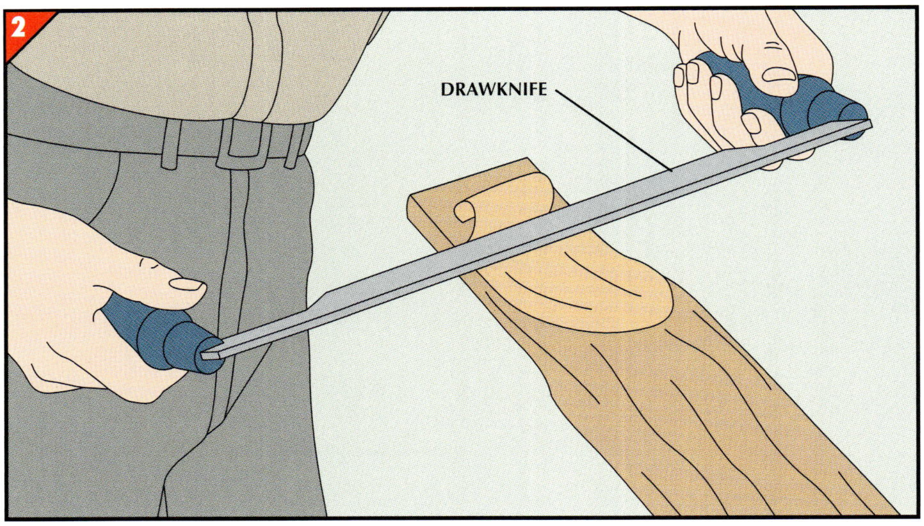

2. Shaping rail ends.

If the rails were cut to fit a shorter section or if a particular rail is misshapen then you will have to retaper it.

◆ Support the rail so the end to be shaped is facing you. Have a helper hold it in place.

◆ With a drawknife taper the end by removing a series of shavings *(left)*.

3. Fitting the rails in place.

◆ Dig the postholes, set a corner post in tamped earth *(page 138)*, and drop the first line post into its hole.

◆ Insert the ends of the rails into the slots of the corner post.

◆ Fit the other ends of the rails into their mortises in the line post *(right)*.

◆ Plumb the post, secure it with tamped earth, and set succeeding sections the same way.

Tall Fences for Privacy

Most privacy fences are built like the picket fences shown on pages 143 to 144. Standard pressure-treated lumber nailed to simple post-and-stringer frames will yield a variety of attractive fences; prefabricated panels can be nailed directly to posts or framed inside posts and stringers.

Tall fences are typically supported on frames of 4-by-4 posts and 2-by-4 stringers. The simplest privacy fence is made of vertical boards or tall narrow slats nailed directly to the top and bottom stringers (and to a middle stringer if the fence is taller than 6 feet). Almost as simple is a fence of horizontal boards or plywood panels face-nailed to the posts and to 2-by-4 studs that are toenailed to the top and bottom stringers 24 to 36 inches apart.

Louvered Fences: Some fences require more sophisticated carpentry. A tall louvered fence, for example, is heavier and more prone to warp than some of the simpler designs; it requires sturdier joints. To build the louvered fence on pages 150 to 151, you will need a router to cut grooves in the posts and the stringers.

Strengthening the Fence: Since the stringers are attached face down, the fence is weaker than if the boards were set on edge. To compensate for this, use the lightest possible materials and reduce the distance between posts to 6 feet or less. Another approach is to screw an extra 2-by-4 on edge underneath one or both of the stringers.

Working with a Router: When routing in tandem with a jig, clamp or nail the jig to the workpiece and make sure the lumber is steady. Keep the router at chest height or below. To make the high cuts in the posts, stand on a stepladder steadied by a helper.

TOOLS

- T-bevel
- Combination square
- Water level
- Clamps
- Hammer
- Screwdriver
- Circular saw
- Router and $\frac{3}{4}$" straight bit
- Paintbrush

MATERIALS

- 1x2s, 1x4s, 1x6s
- 2x4s, 2x6s
- Galvanized common nails (2", $3\frac{1}{2}$")
- Wood screws ($1\frac{1}{4}$" No. 6)
- Wood glue (exterior)
- Wood preservative

SAFETY TIPS

Put on goggles when routing. Wear gloves when handling pressure-treated lumber; add a dust mask when cutting it.

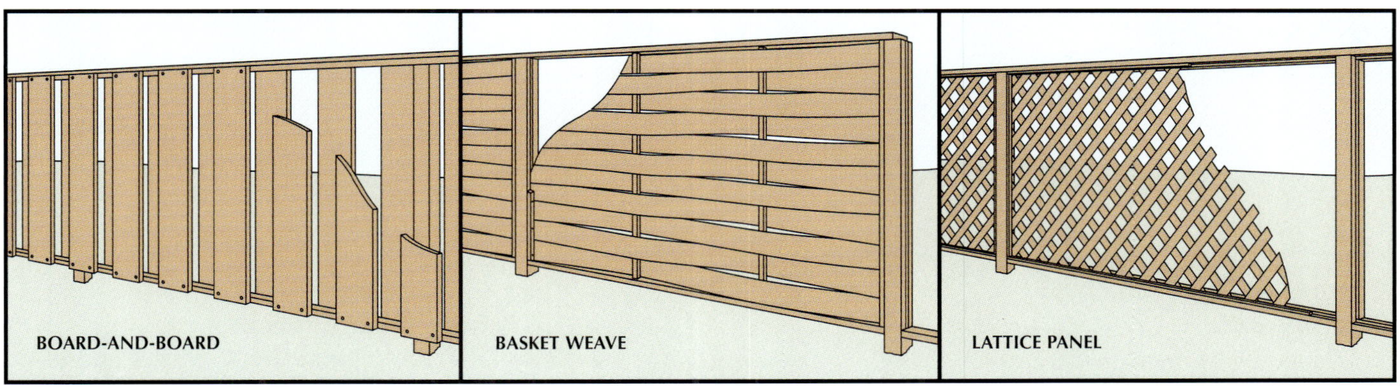

Three screens for your yard. A board-and-board fence admits a breeze and looks good from either side. Vertical boards are nailed to both sides of the frame, separated by less than their own widths. The thin slats ($\frac{1}{2}$-by-6 inch) that make up a basket weave fence are woven around vertical 1-by-1 boards, and fastened in vertical grooves on each post. The boards on one side are positioned opposite the spaces on the other. Ready-made panels in elaborate styles like latticework are mounted against 1-by-2s nailed to the posts and stringers. Instructions for building a latticework panel are on page 185.

A SPECIAL FRAME FOR LOUVERS

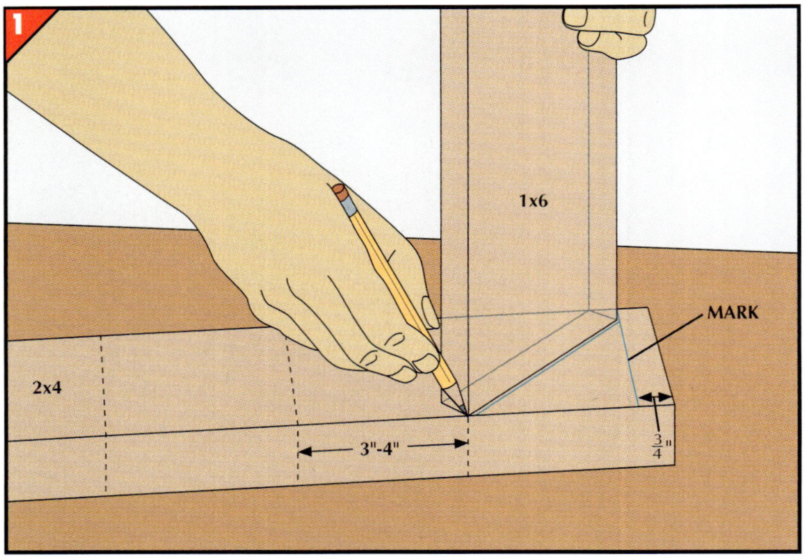

1. Marking a stringer.

◆ Cut two 2-by-4s $1\frac{1}{2}$ inches longer than the distance between two posts.

◆ With a combination square, draw lines across both 2-by-4s, $\frac{3}{4}$ inch in from each end.

◆ Stand a scrap 1-by-6 diagonally across one 2-by-4 so that one corner touches the pencil line and the other touches the stringer edge; trace around the 1-by-6 *(left)*.

◆ Mark the stringer for evenly spaced, overlapping louvers, typically 3 to 4 inches apart, as indicated by the dashed lines in the illustration.

2. Building a jig.

◆ Make the base by transferring the louver angle to a 2-foot-long 2-by-6 with a T-bevel.

◆ Place two 1-by-4s on the base at this angle parallel to each other and separated by the diameter of the router base plate. Fasten them with $1\frac{1}{4}$-inch No. 6 screws.

◆ Fit the router with a $\frac{3}{4}$-inch straight bit, clamp the jig to the bench, and rout a 1-inch-long notch in the jig base *(right)*. For maximum safety, set the bit depth to cut to your final depth of $\frac{1}{2}$ inch in two passes.

◆ Attach another 2-by-6 to the guide separated from the first by the width of the stringer and screw it in place. Notch it as for the other base piece.

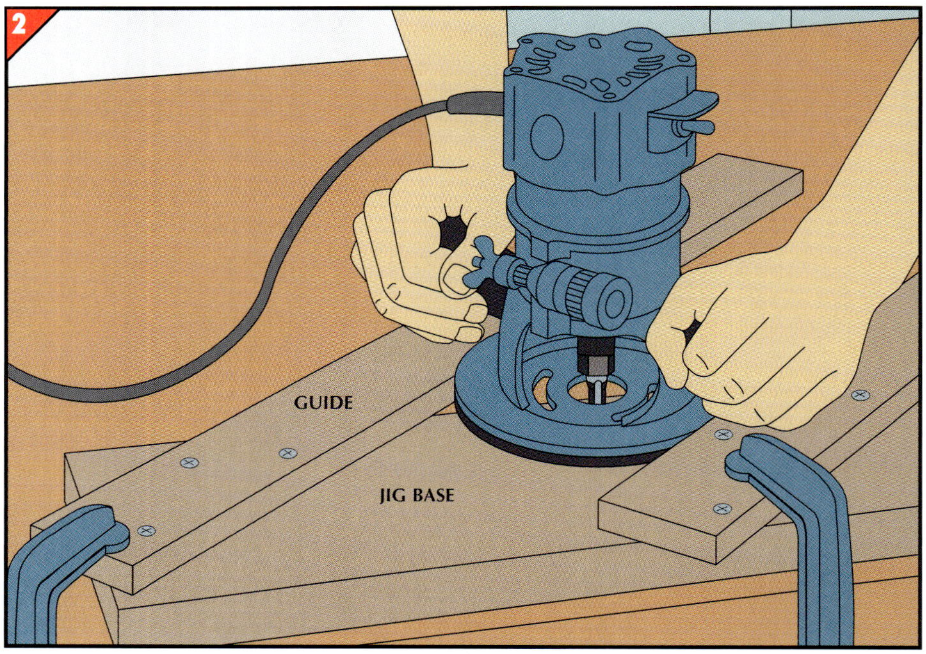

3. Routing the dadoes.

◆ Clamp the marked 2-by-4 stringer and the jig to a bench, aligning the notch in the jig with one of the marks on the stringer *(left)*. Drive a stop screw partway into the stringer to hold it in place.

◆ Cut to your final depth of $\frac{1}{2}$ inch in two passes, moving the router steadily across the stringer until all the dadoes are cut.

◆ Use the grooved stringer as a template to mark the positions of louvers on the second 2-by-4, and rout dadoes in it the same way.

4. Cutting dadoes in the posts.

◆ Mark the positions for the lower edges of the top and bottom stringers on each pair of posts. Use a water level to ensure that the marks are perfectly level.

◆ Construct a two-guide jig as shown, with 1-by-4s for the crosspieces and 1-by-2s for the guides. Attach the guides at right angles to the base pieces and $\frac{3}{4}$ inch farther apart than the diameter of the router base plate.

◆ Set the router's cutting depth to $\frac{3}{4}$ inch and cut a notch in one of the crosspieces by running the tool along one guide and then back along the other.

◆ At each stringer mark on the posts, clamp the jig in place, aligning the lower notch with the mark.

◆ Rout the dadoes in two passes. Set the router's cutting depth to $\frac{3}{8}$ inch for the first pass then increase it to $\frac{3}{4}$ inch for the second. To make each pass, move the router across the post, running it along the lower guide until it hits the notch, then back along the upper guide to make a $1\frac{1}{2}$-inch dado *(right).*

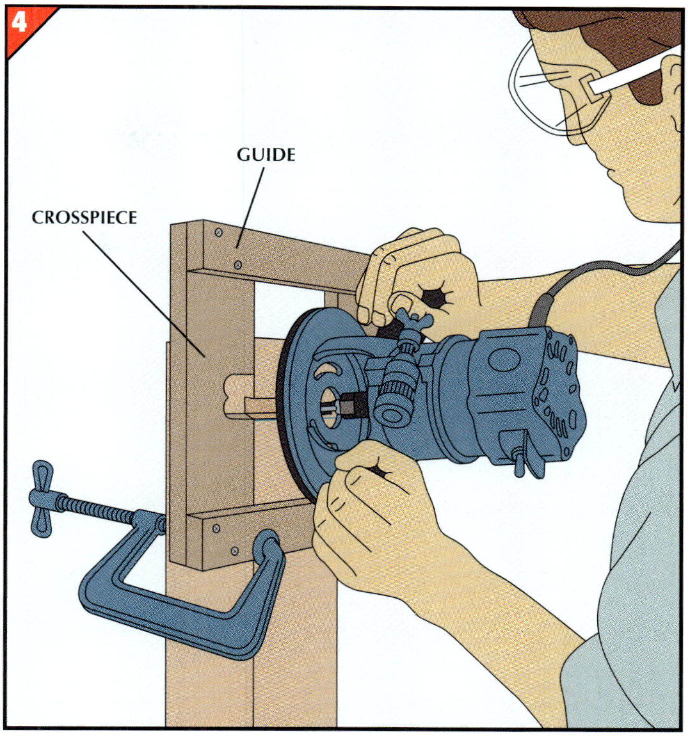

5. Assembling and installing the panel.

◆ Apply wood preservative to the dadoes in the posts and the stringers.

◆ Cut 1-by-6s to length for the louvers.

◆ Partially assemble the louver panel by gluing three louvers into dadoes at one end of the stringers and one near the middle with exterior-grade wood glue; secure them by nailing through the stringers with 2-inch galvanized com mon nails.

◆ Supporting the bottom stringer on boards, lift the panel upright, slip the stringers into the dadoes, and toenail them to the posts with $3\frac{1}{2}$-inch nails.

◆ Install the remaining louvers into their dadoes, securing them with glue at both ends and nails at the top.

Adapting to Uneven Ground

Building a fence that follows the ups and downs of your property often depends on choosing the right style of fence for your land and modifying the design as necessary. A post-and-rail or post-and-board fence *(below)* conforms to any terrain and is best for sharply sloping or rolling ground; a fence with vertical members face-nailed to a post-and-board frame follows the ground almost as well.

Pickets Along the Slope: On rough but relatively level ground, a fence with pickets or slats *(opposite, top)* can smooth out small dips and rises; its bottom follows the earth's contours while the top remains level. For such a fence, buy enough long pickets to fill in the low spots.

Adapting Rectangular Panels: Rectangular-paneled fences are not suited for rough or rolling ground, but they adapt well to steady slopes if built in steps *(opposite, bottom)*. Uniform stepping requires a few calculations, but once the posts are in position, attaching stringers and siding is straightforward.

Normally, the top of each fence section is set level. But on a steep hill this can create the illusion that the section is actually higher on the downhill end. In this case, some fence builders lower the downhill end of the stringer 1 or 2 inches below level until it looks right.

TOOLS

Tape measure
Carpenter's level
Line level or water level
Plumb bob
Clamps
Hammer
Circular saw

MATERIALS

Mason's line

SAFETY TIPS

Wear safety goggles when hammering.

Going up and down hills.

◆ Set posts on each rise and in each depression, then space the remaining posts between them *(page 135)*.
◆ For a post-and-board fence like the one shown, clamp or tack the boards in position against the posts and use a level to make vertical marks on the boards at the post centers wherever two boards meet *(above)*.
◆ Trim the boards at the marked angles.

Before attaching vertical slats or pickets, align them evenly above the top stringer with a spacer *(page 144)* then plumb each one.

Leveling bumps and dips.

◆ Make a spacer as shown on page 144.

◆ To line up pickets on uneven ground, hold each one upside down against the stringers with its shaped top $1\frac{1}{2}$ inches off the ground.

◆ Mark its bottom end even with the top of the spacer *(left),* then trim to the mark.

◆ Install the pickets as you would for a standard picket fence *(page 144).*

TRICKS OF THE TRADE

Scribing the Picket Bottom for a Close Fit

While a picket fence does not have to follow the exact profile of the ground, incorporating this feature is a nice professional touch. Simply trim the pickets to length using the method shown above, but let the pickets touch the ground. Place them in position against the fence, right-side up. Hold a carpenter's pencil on a short piece of scrap 2-by-4 *(left).* Slide the block along the ground to scribe any variation in the terrain on the bottom of the picket. Trim the picket with a saber saw. The gap between the pickets and the ground will be uniform all along the fence.

Stepping down a slope.

◆ Run a level line from the top of the hill to a tall stake at the bottom *(page 135).* The height of the line on the bottom stake is the hill's vertical drop.

◆ Lay out the fence line and mark the post locations as shown on page 135.

◆ Divide the number of fence sections into the total vertical drop to calculate the "stringer drop" from one section to the next.

◆ Set the first post at the top of the hill to the intended fence height, and the rest of the posts to the fence height plus the stringer drop.

◆ Mark the stringer drops on the posts, then attach the stringers *(page 143).*

◆ For a fence with vertical boards, trim each one so its bottom conforms to the slope, the top is even with the top stringer, and there is a $1\frac{1}{2}$-inch gap between the board and the ground *(right).*

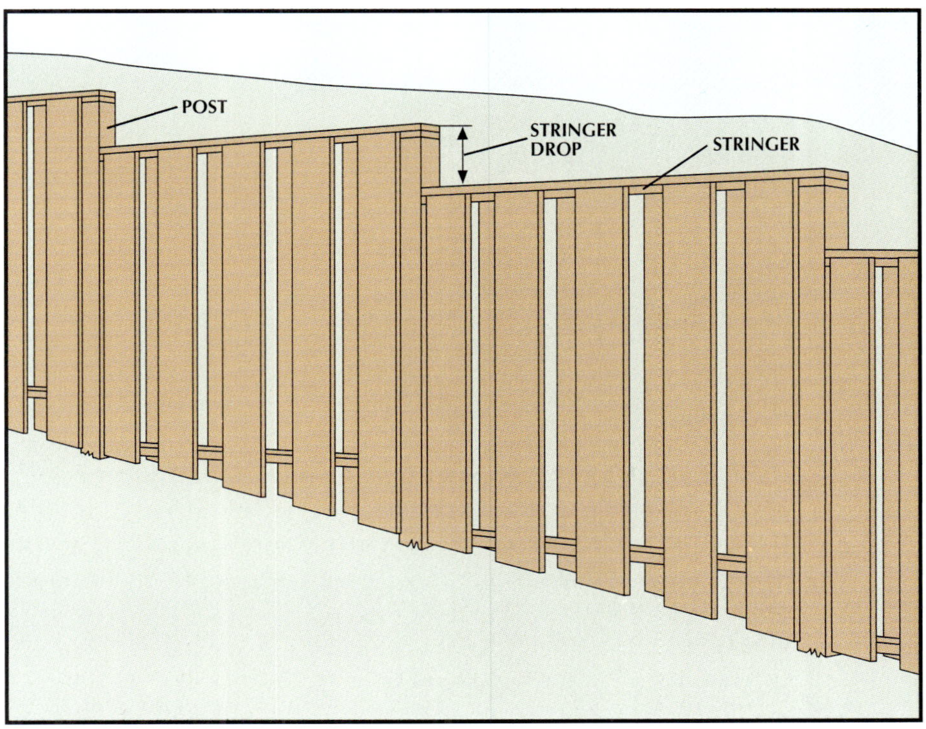

Building Gates

Gates lead a tough life and most show it by eventually sagging, binding, and refusing to latch. But by observing three basic rules you can greatly increase the useful life of your gate.

Gateposts and Braces: The first requirement is a pair of strong, plumb gateposts, set in concrete *(page 138)* to a depth equal to one-half the height of the part aboveground. Space the posts to accommodate the gate width plus a $\frac{1}{2}$-inch clearance for the latch as well as enough clearance for the kind of hinge you plan to install.

The second critical element is a frame that is braced by a diagonal board between the top rail at the latch side and the bottom rail at the hinge side. To provide bottom clearance, hang all gates at least 2 inches above the highest point of ground within the arc of the opening gate.

Hardware: Choose strong hardware, particularly the hinges; weak hinges are the most frequent cause of gate problems. To prevent rusting, use stainless steel or galvanized items.

Among latches, the simplest and most trouble-free is the self-latching type shown opposite; sliding bolts are not recommended because even a slight sag in the gate will throw them out of alignment. A gate spring can be added to automatically close the gate.

TOOLS

- Tape measure
- Carpenter's square
- Hammer
- Screwdriver
- Awl or large nail
- Circular saw
- Electric drill
- Screwdriver bit

MATERIALS

- 1"x1$\frac{1}{2}$" board
- Pressure-treated 2x4s
- Pickets
- Galvanized common nails (3")
- Galvanized wood screws (1$\frac{1}{4}$" No. 6; 1", 4" No. 8)
- Lag screws ($\frac{5}{16}$") and washers
- Gate hinges
- Gate latch

SAFETY TIPS

Wear goggles when drilling. Wear gloves when handling pressure-treated lumber; add a dust mask when cutting.

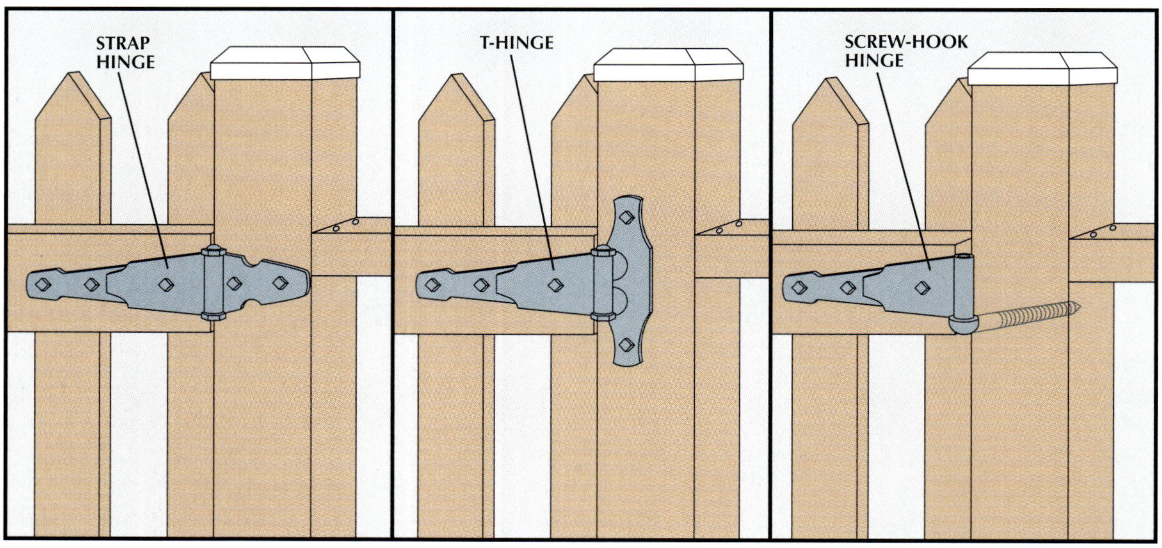

Three types of hinges.
These three styles of hinge attach to the gate with a strap at least 7 inches long but they differ in the way they are secured to the post. The strap- and T-hinges are fastened to the post and gate with lag screws; screw-hook hinges are fixed with screw hooks as shown on page 156 *(Step 3)*. The strap hinge has a post strap running the full width of the post. The T-hinge has at least a 7-inch-high strap, which makes it more stable. The screw-hook hinge is even stronger and makes the gate easy to remove for minor repairs.

MAKING AND HANGING A GATE

1. Assembling the frame.

◆ Cut pressure-treated 2-by-4s the width of the gate for rails.
◆ Position the end pickets so that the gate rails and pickets will align with the fence. Drill clearance holes in the pickets.
◆ Screw the pickets to the rail with $1\frac{1}{4}$-inch No. 6 galvanized wood screws, checking with a carpenter's square to guarantee right angles *(right)*.
◆ For a fence 6 feet tall or more, add a third rail in the middle of the frame.

2. Bracing the gate.

◆ Turn the gate over picket-side down.
◆ Position a 2-by-4 brace on the gate from the top corner on the latch side to the bottom corner on the hinge side. Mark the 2-by-4 to fit between the rails, aligning a straightedge with each rail *(left)*. Cut the brace to length.
◆ Drill two clearance holes through the edge of the brace about 2 inches in from each end, then secure it with 4-inch No. 8 wood screws.
◆ Secure the remaining pickets to the rails and the brace.
◆ Bolt the hinge straps to the ends of the rails with $\frac{5}{16}$-inch lag screws.

3. Hanging the gate.

◆ Set the gate on wood blocks to align it with the fence and, holding the back of the frame flush with the back of the post, mark the post at the bottom of both hinges *(left)*.

◆ Bore a $\frac{1}{2}$-inch-diameter hole in the corner of the post at a 45-degree angle, starting the hole with an awl or large nail so the drill will not slip off the corner. With the hook set at an angle *(inset)* the gate can swing a full 180 degrees without binding against the post.

◆ Drive the screw hooks into the post.

◆ Slip the hinge straps over the screw hooks to hang the gate.

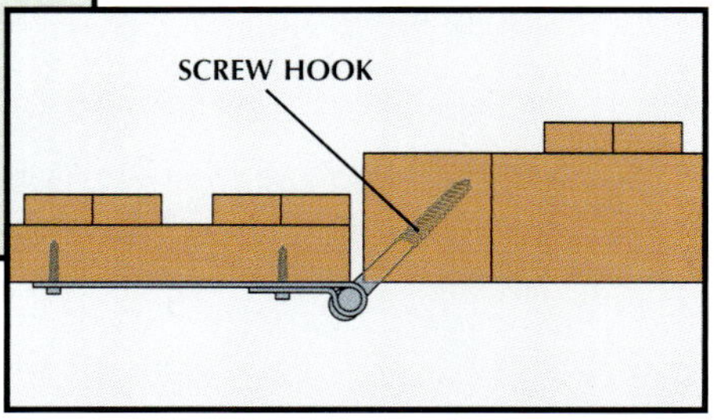

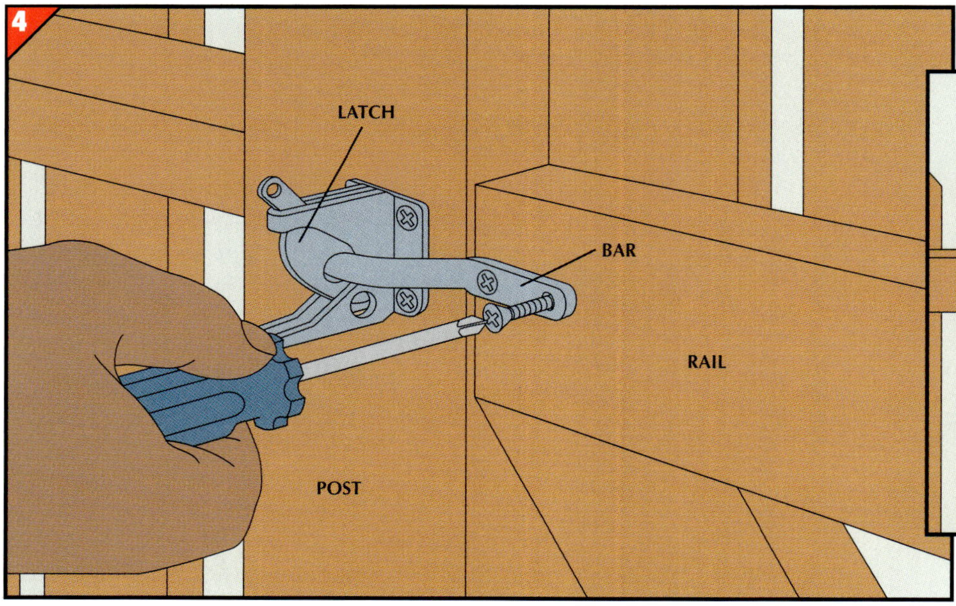

4. Installing a latch and a gate spring.

◆ Position the latch on the post opposite the top rail on the gate. Secure the hardware with 1-inch No. 8 wood screws.

◆ Hold the gate closed and fit the bar in the latch, pressing it against the rail as it would normally sit. Mark the screw holes with a pencil, then drill a pair of pilot holes.

◆ Fasten the bar to the gate with 1-inch wood screws *(above)*.

◆ To make a gate stop, nail a 1-by-1$\frac{1}{2}$ board to the front of the latch post with 3-inch galvanized common nails, positioned so the gate will stop just before the bar strikes the base of the latch. This will keep the latch from bearing the brunt of the force when the gate is closed.

◆ To operate the latch from outside the gate, first bore a hole through the post, then attach a cord to the hole in the latch bar, thread it through the post, and tie a pull ring to the cord on the other side of the post.

If you want to add a gate spring, set it across the gate post and gate in as vertical a position as possible so the movable bracket is on top and tilted to the right. Mark and drill pilot holes, then fasten the spring in place with the screws supplied *(inset)*. Tighten the spring by turning the hex nut at the top clockwise, then fit the metal stop between the nut and bracket to prevent the nut from loosening.

Blocks and Bricks for a Strong High Wall

Because of its solidity and weight, a masonry wall calls for very careful planning. It must sit on soil firm enough to support it, and not block natural drainage. If you have any doubts about the site of your wall, consult your local building authority. In many areas, codes prescribe strict standards for masonry structures more than a few feet high, specifying materials, dimensions, reinforcement, and depths of footings.

Digging Trenches for Footings: The footings must be at least 18 inches below grade and must rest on earth not affected by frost. Before digging, mark the borders of the footing trench and the centerline of the wall with stakes clear of the digging area to fix the marks. In loose soil, you may have to bank the trench walls back from the bed by as much as 45 degrees to keep them from caving in. Keep the bed as level and flat as you can, but do not smooth it off by filling loose earth back in: The footing must rest on undisturbed earth. If the virgin soil at the proper depth is loose, tamp it.

A footing's width and height depend on the thickness of the structure it supports and local soil conditions; consult your building code.

Pouring Concrete Footings: In any but the loosest soil, wooden forms are not needed to contain the concrete poured for a footing. In most soils, widen the trench on one side to allow for smoothing the concrete and laying blocks and mortar from the footing up to the surface *(below, left)*. But if the soil is firm enough to keep the trench walls vertical for their full height, you have a convenient but expensive alternative: You can dig the trench no wider than the footing and fill it with concrete to just below ground level *(below, right)*.

Both types of footing need strengthening with two lines of steel reinforcing bars (rebar) laid along the trench—and both probably need enough concrete for an order from a ready-mix firm. When the truck arrives, have plenty of helpers on hand. Pouring and leveling concrete is heavy work that must be done quickly.

TOOLS

- Tape measure
- 4' level
- Water level
- Hammer
- Maul
- Rebar cutter
- Square-edged shovel

MATERIALS

- 2x4s for floats
- Wooden stakes
- Common nails ($4\frac{1}{2}$")
- Rebar
- Tie wire
- Sand
- Bricks or stones
- Ready-mix concrete
- Polyethylene sheeting

SAFETY TIPS

Check with utility companies about pipe and wire locations before digging a wall's foundation. Wear gloves and a long-sleeved shirt when working with concrete.

Two types of concrete footing. A standard trench *(above, left)* is suitable for most soils. One of its walls is as steep as the firmness of the soil allows; the bottom is squared off to the width and depth of the footing, and above that the trench gets a foot or two wider to create working space. Reinforcing bars are laid, concrete is poured and leveled, then a block foundation is built up to within a few inches of ground level.

A trench dug in very firm soil *(above, right)*, has vertical walls separated by the width of the footing. Reinforcement is laid and the trench is filled with concrete almost to the surface; it needs no block foundation.

POURING A CONCRETE FOOTING

1. Marking the top of the footing.

◆ Dig the trench for the footing *(page 157)*. If you must move a large amount of soil to dig beyond the frost line and you plan to build a high wall more than a dozen feet long, hire a professional. To move a relatively small amount of earth, consider renting a gasoline-powered trencher, which you can operate yourself.

◆ Along the sides of the footing trench, drive 12-inch stakes into the ground in a zigzag pattern every 3 to 4 feet.

◆ Mark the stake at the highest spot in the trench, 8 to 10 inches above the bed.

◆ Mark all the stakes at that height with the help of a water level *(right)*.

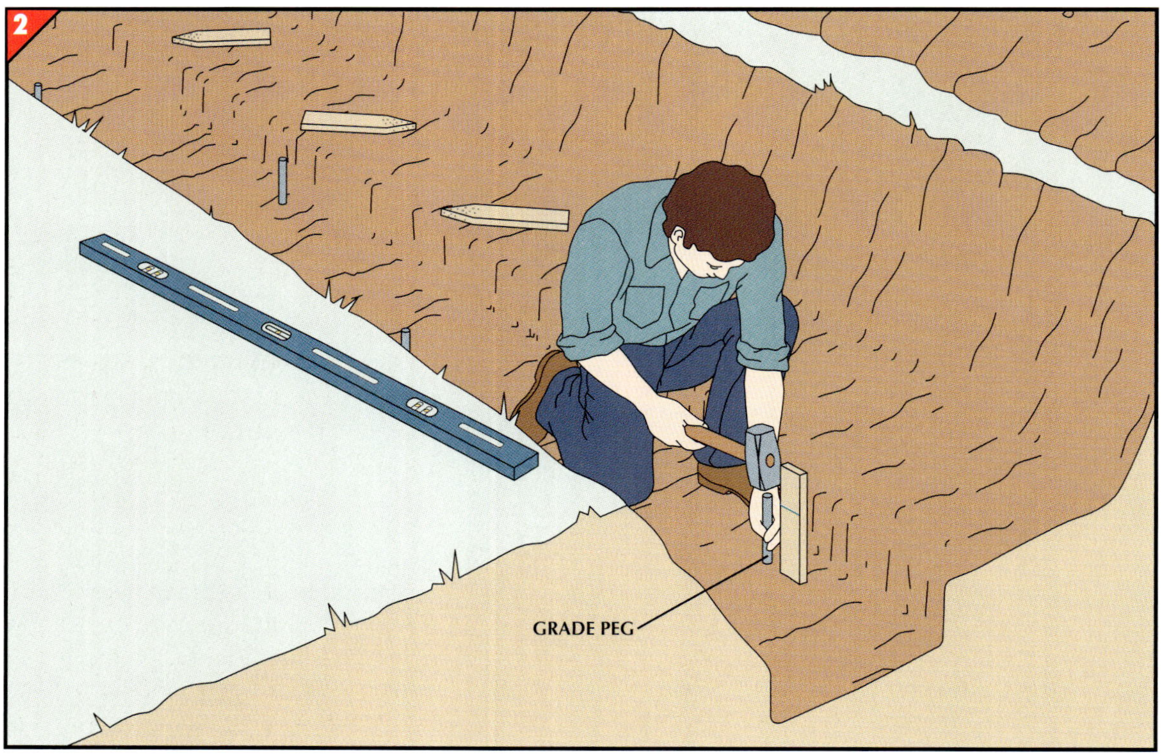

2. Installing grade pegs.

◆ Make grade pegs by cutting a rebar into 18-inch lengths, one for each stake, with a rented rebar cutter.

◆ Drive a peg into the trench bed next to each stake so that the top of the peg is level with the mark on the stake *(above)*. Do not drive the pegs too deep—pulling them up to the correct height will loosen them.

◆ Remove the stakes as you go, filling in the holes they leave with soil.

◆ Check the level of the pegs with a 4-foot level. If any is too high, tap it down.

3. Laying reinforcing bars.

◆ Check your building code for the correct size rebar—usually between No. 4 and No. 8.

◆ Set lengths of rebar in the trench bed alongside each row of grade pegs, supporting the bars 2 to 3 inches above the soil with bricks or stones. Where two bars meet end to end, overlap them 12 to 15 inches. Cut bars to length if necessary with a rebar cutter.

◆ Lash the bars together with tie wire, then tie the bars to the grade pegs.

◆ Once all the bars are in place, remove the bricks or stones.

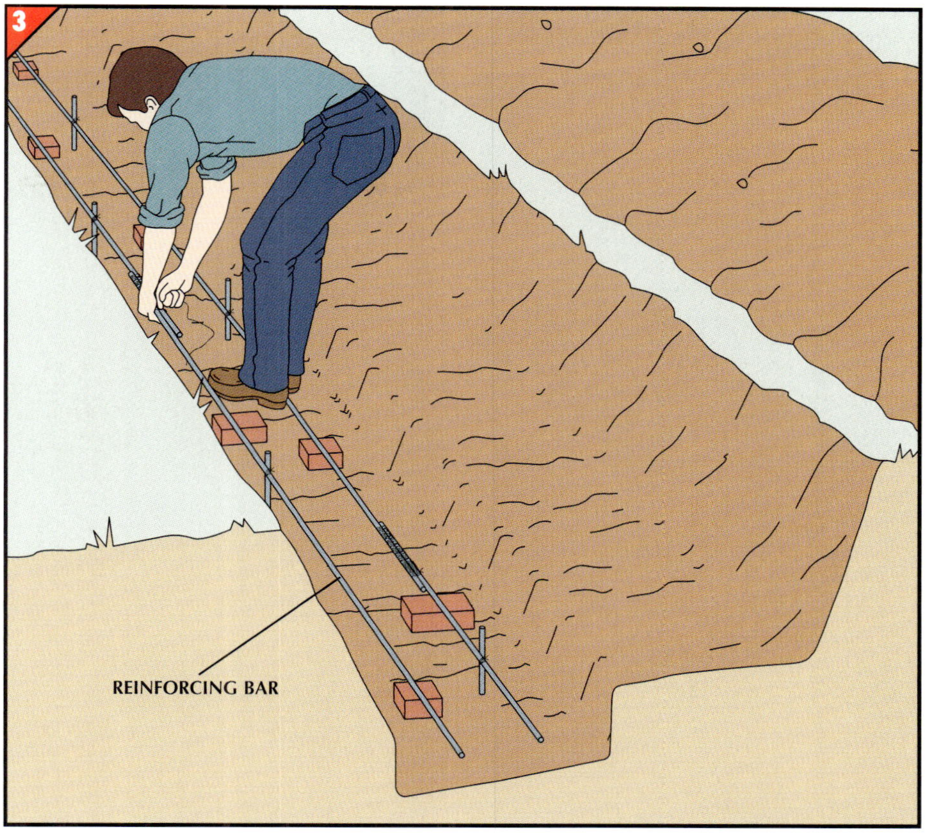

4. Completing the footing.

◆ Working with helpers, pour concrete into the trench, taking care not to dislodge the grade pegs. Spread the concrete with square-edged shovels.

◆ Break up large air pockets in the concrete by pushing a shovel into the mix, again avoiding the grade pegs.

◆ Fill the trench so that the level of the concrete is at least $\frac{1}{2}$ inch above the tops of the grade pegs.

◆ Level the footing with floats fashioned from 2-by-4s nailed together *(left)*. Working on one small area at a time, even out the concrete with a patting motion. Continue, compacting the concrete and spreading it into the corners of the trench until the tops of the grade pegs become visible.

◆ Smooth out the concrete by sweeping the trailing edge of the float across the surface, pulling the float toward you in wide arcs. Again, continue until the tops of the grade pegs and footing are at the same level.

◆ Cover the footing with polyethylene sheeting and let it cure for seven days.

Designing a Wall for Strength and Beauty

Masonry walls need not always present a solid, unvarying face. Bricks and masonry blocks can be laid in patterns to enliven a wall's appearance and in open designs to admit light and air while screening a view.

Building with Blocks and Brick: The decorative block patterns shown opposite feature stacked bond and blocks of standard sizes. Bricks, too, can also be used to make open work, but such walls require a skilled mason to make them structurally sound. An amateur bricklayer, however, can build a solid-brick wall with a decorative pattern based on the interplay of headers (bricks laid crosswise on the wall) and stretchers (bricks laid along the length of the wall), like those shown on page 162. Such designs strengthen an ordinary two-course-thick garden wall, since the headers tie the front and back courses of brick together, performing part of the function of joint reinforcement.

A Two-Color Pattern: Most large brickyards stock many different colors of brick, but to create a simple design, you can use two different colors, one for a background and the other for the pattern *(page 162)*.

To plan the design, draw an outline of a full section of the wall on graph paper. Make the wall an odd number of courses high—the course that serves as a horizontal axis for the design must have an even number of courses above and below it. Find the squares that represent the center brick of the section. Fill in the pattern unit over this center brick, then fill in the rest of the section. You can now tell how many pattern units or parts of units will fit into the section and the wall, and how to begin laying the bricks.

LAYING MASONRY UNITS FOR STRENGTH

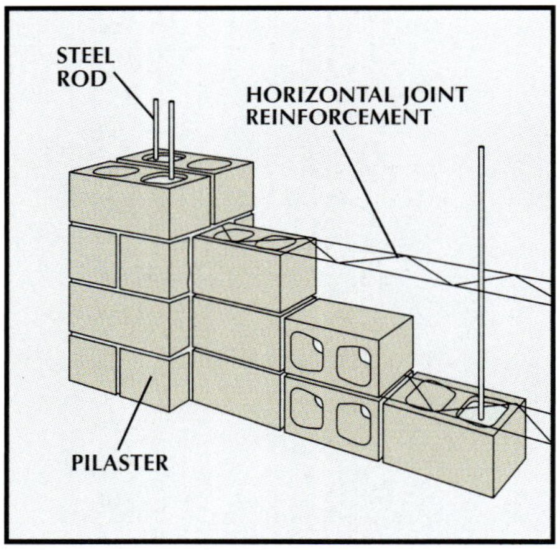

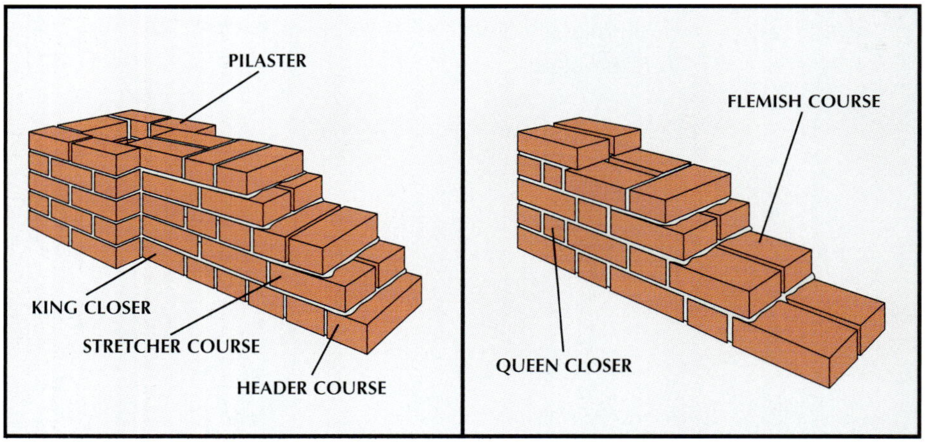

Reinforcing a brick wall

Block walls of stacked bond *(above)* need both horizontal and vertical reinforcement. The pilasters—thick columns built into the wall—bracing this wall are pairs of double-corner blocks knitted to the wall with continuous stretches of joint reinforcement laid after every second course. Steel rods run up through the cores of the blocks of each pilaster and at 4-foot intervals between pilasters; these cores are filled with grout—a mortar thinned with water for filling spaces.

Strengthening a brick wall

Most traditional brick patterns are developed either from English bond *(above, left)*, in which courses of headers and stretchers alternate, or from Flemish bond *(above, right)*, which has alternating headers and stretchers in each course. Variations of these two bricklaying styles produce an enormous range of ornamental patterns, which can be heightened by using bricks of contrasting colors. In either pattern, alternate courses must begin and end with either a quarter brick, called a queen closer, or a three-quarter brick, called a king closer. The odd sizes can be made by setting bricks more or less halfway into a pilaster or by cutting bricks. If you cut queen closers, locate them near—but not at—the end of a course. To save time, cut all the closers before you start laying bricks. Both types of wall can be braced with pilasters every 8 to 10 feet *(page 163)*.

ATTRACTIVE BLOCK WALLS

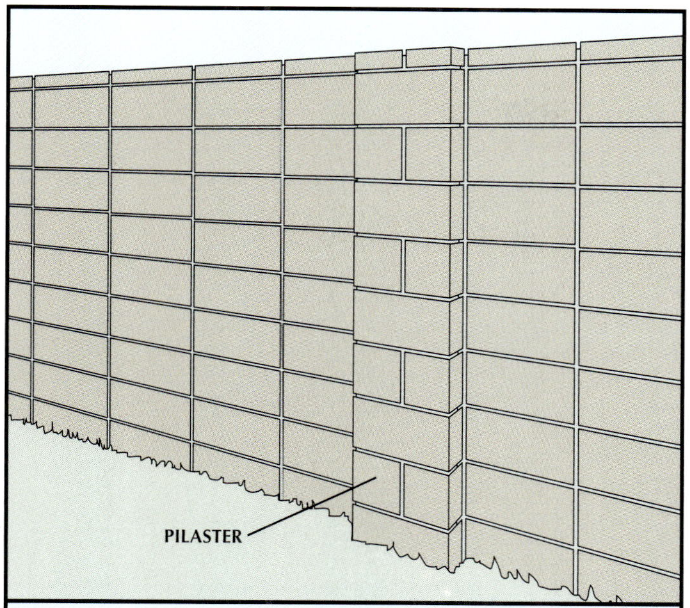

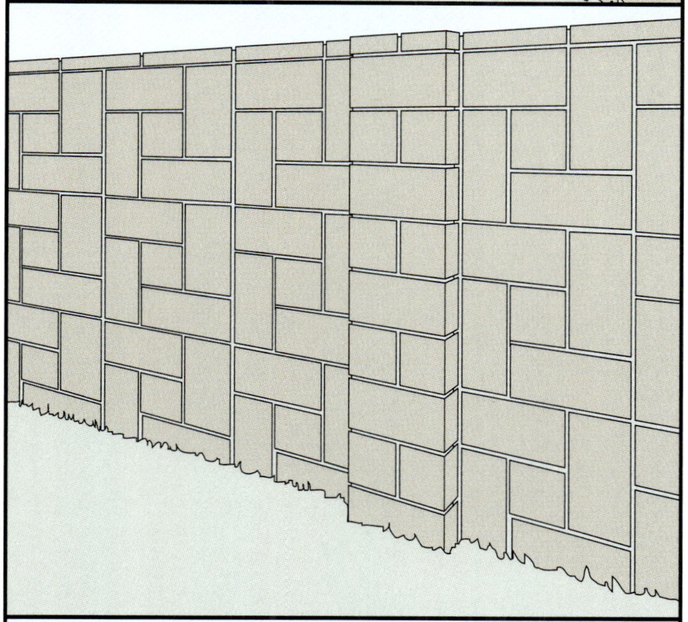

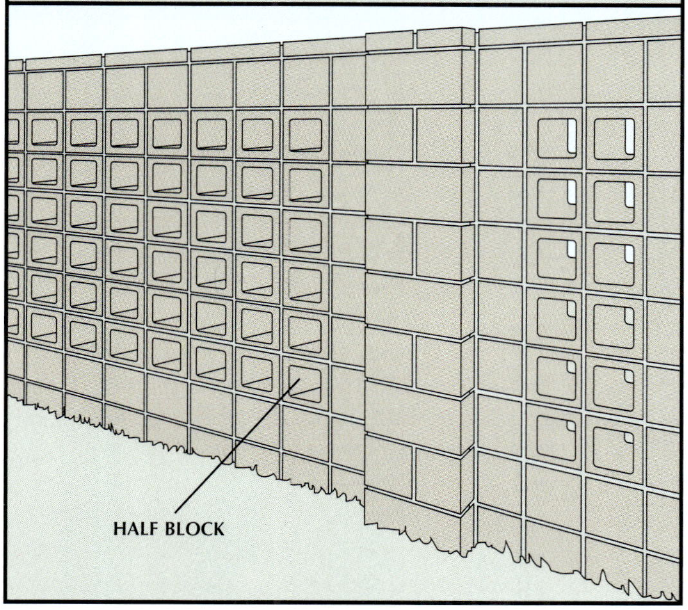

Decorative walls from blocks.
Standard masonry blocks can be arranged to form a number of attractive designs. Despite vertical joints that align, ordinary stretcher blocks in stacked bond *(left, top)* make a surprisingly good-looking wall. Odd sizes give you more complex patterns. A basket-weave pattern *(left, middle)* is made from units of four stretchers and a half block. Half blocks laid on their sides *(left, bottom)* can be arranged in a wide variety of patterns to form openings for light and air.

To allow for vertical reinforcement, the blocks in all these patterns must be laid out so the hollow cores align at least every 4 feet. Work this out on paper before pouring the footing *(page 159)*. When you pour the footing, insert a 4-foot length of reinforcing bar into the concrete at 4-foot intervals. As you raise the wall, fit the blocks over the bar and fill the hollows with grout. For a wall taller than 4 feet, attach extra lengths of reinforcing bar with tie wire. Alternatively, add pilasters to your design every 8 to 10 feet. Install horizontal reinforcement after every second or third course.

HOW MANY BRICKS OR BLOCKS?

To determine the number of standard concrete blocks (8-by-16 inches) required for a wall, multiply the square footage of the wall by 1.125.

A typical brick wall *(page 165)* needs 14 bricks for every square foot of wall face and 90 more for a capped 6-foot pilaster. For a two-color wall, first diagram the pattern on graph paper. Make each course one square high; let two horizontal squares represent a header and four squares a stretcher. Draw enough courses (usually two or three) to show the bond pattern, count the total number of odd-colored bricks, and multiply the figure by the number of pattern repeats you will need for the wall. Double the number of odd-colored stretchers if the pattern must show on both sides of a wall two courses thick; add the odd-colored headers and subtract the total from the number of bricks needed for the wall. Buy 5 percent extra in both colors to allow for breakage.

DESIGNING WITH COLORED BRICKS

English and Flemish variations. Bricks in contrasting colors, and courses with staggered vertical joints, give the traditional bonds shown above a different look. In English cross bond *(top)*, a variation of English bond, the stretcher bricks "cross," or "break joint," overlapping one another by a half brick in succeeding courses. Color emphasizes the pattern: Stretcher courses alternately comprise a single color and two contrasting colors. In Flemish spiral bond *(middle)*, a pattern of diagonal bands is created by the placement of dark headers. Garden wall bond *(bottom)* consists of Flemish courses in which every fourth brick is a header.

Making pattern units. The more complex designs shown above are based on pattern units of a contrasting color called eyes. The fundamental eye *(top)* consists of a single stretcher with headers centered above and below it. Larger eyes are formed by extending the unit by the width of one header in each course, adding headers at the top and bottom and centering the whole on the middle, or axis, course *(middle)*. You can expand the primary unit in this way so that it assumes a diamond shape *(bottom)*.

Combining pattern units. Large wall designs can consist of a number of pattern units defined by colored bricks and arranged in a wall symmetrically. In one widely used design *(above, top)*, eyes abut one another, forming horizontal bands. The bands are emphasized by a course of solid-color stretchers between the rows of eyes. Colored borders made of dark headers can make a simple pattern unit of light-colored bricks into a more complex design *(above, bottom)*.

A Brick Wall on a Block Foundation

A freestanding brick wall more than 4 feet high requires lateral support against wind and climbing children. The 8-inch-wide wall shown on the following pages is reinforced with square pilasters that measure 16 inches per side. The footings are 24 inches wide and 10 inches deep. However, specifications in your area depend on the local building code.

A Concrete Block Foundation: Regardless of the type of wall you are planning aboveground, it is most economical to build from the top of the footing up to ground level with concrete block. Buy standard "stretcher" blocks measuring 8 by 8 by 16 inches. To avoid having to cut the stretchers, you will also need half blocks measuring 8 by 8 by 8 inches. Purchase flat-ended "double-corner" blocks and "partition" blocks measuring 4 by 8 by 16 inches for the pilasters as well. A few inches below ground level, lay the masonry units for the wall itself.

Spacing Pilasters: For ease in positioning pilasters 8 to 10 feet apart, make the length of the wall and the distance between pilasters divisible by 8 inches. Fill the cores of the blocks in the pilasters with grout. For added strength, run two lengths of reinforcing bar down through the cores of the foundation blocks in each pilaster before filling them. No. 4 to No. 8 reinforcing bar is usually required, depending on the local code. Keep in mind that a pilaster is useful as a wall support only if it is perfectly plumb.

Cutting Bricks: With a mason's chisel and a hammer, score a line on the brick at the point where you want it to break. Turn it over and tap the other side a few times. The brick should split on the second or third blow.

TOOLS

Tape measure
Chalk line
Straightedge
4' level
Torpedo level
Shovel
Mortar hoe
Mason's trowel
Mason's blocks and line
Line pins

MATERIALS

1-by board for story pole
Mortar ingredients (Portland cement, lime, masonry sand)
Premixed grout
Concrete blocks
Bricks
Truss-type horizontal joint reinforcement

SAFETY TIPS

Always wear safety goggles when mixing mortar, and long sleeves and gloves when working with mortar and concrete. Wear gloves and safety goggles when cutting bricks.

BUILDING A BLOCK FOUNDATION

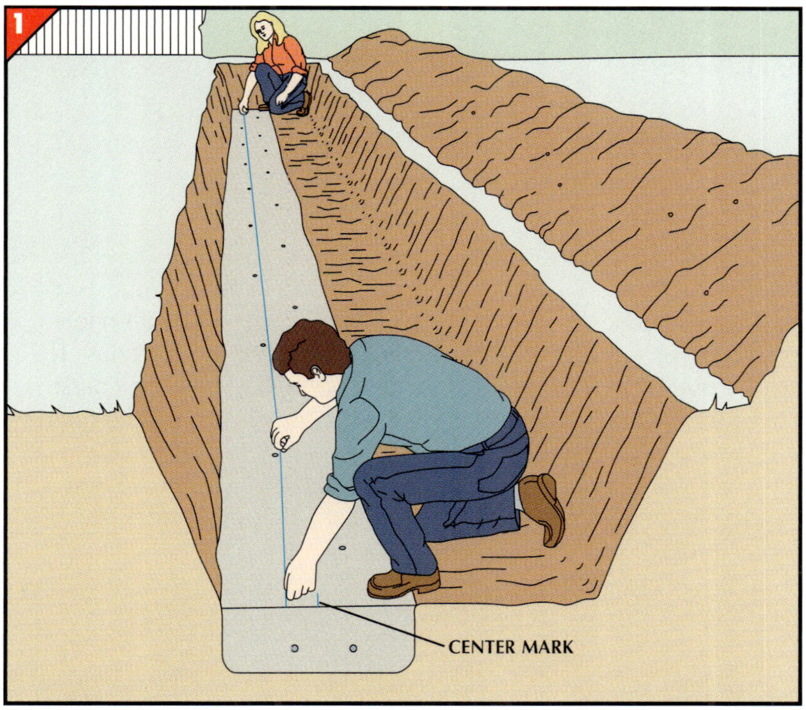

1. Aligning the blocks.

◆ Snap a chalk line 4 inches from the center of the footing to mark the edge of the bottom course of blocks *(left)*; snap a second line 4 inches outside the first for the edge of the pilasters.
◆ Lay a dry run of blocks for the first course, aligning them with the first chalk line. Lay a pair of blocks at the appropriate interval for each pilaster, as shown in Step 3. Leave a $\frac{3}{8}$- to $\frac{1}{2}$-inch gap between the blocks to allow for mortar joints.
◆ If necessary, adjust the thickness of the joints to bring the course to the correct length.
◆ Mark the location of each pilaster on the footing with chalk.

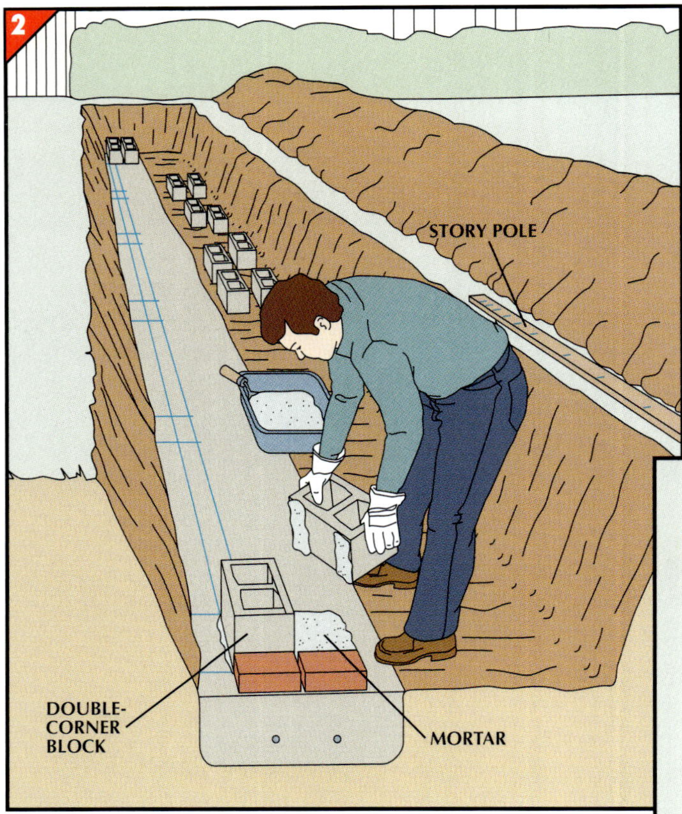

2. Starting the first course.

◆ Prepare a batch of mortar. As you build the wall, spread just enough mortar for one or two blocks at a time with a mason's trowel.

◆ Lay two double-corner blocks side by side in a full mortar bed at one of the end pilaster marks. To gauge how much space to leave between the blocks, set two bricks end to end across the footing, aligning the end of one brick with the second chalk line and leaving $\frac{3}{8}$ inch between the bricks. Lay the blocks so that their outside edges are even with the ends of the bricks *(left)*, leaving about 1 inch between the blocks.

◆ Plumb and level the blocks with a 4-foot level. With a story pole made by marking the desired height of the blocks and the thickness of the mortar bed on a stick, check the block height. Make adjustments if necessary.

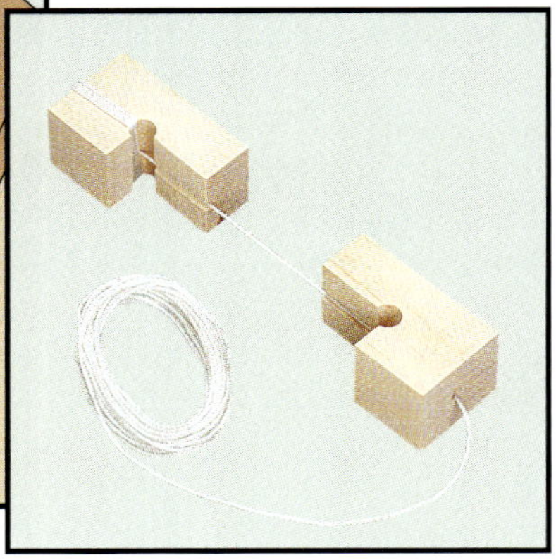

◆ Lay two more double-corner blocks for the other end pilaster, run a mason's line *(photograph)* between the two ends, and lay the other pilaster blocks in position. Fill the cores of the blocks with grout.

PREPARING MORTAR

Mortar holds masonry walls together, sealing out the elements and compensating for variations in the size of the materials. Premixed bags of mortar are useful for small projects, but uneconomical for larger projects like the wall featured here.

Mortar is a mix of Portland cement, lime, sand, and water. The exact formula will vary with local conditions, particularly climate. Check with the code requirements in your area or consult local brick suppliers, masons, or contractors.

To prepare a batch of mortar, combine the dry ingredients in a wheelbarrow with a mortar hoe. Blend in the water—adding just the right amount to obtain a workable mix. To check its consistency, raise a series of ridges in the mortar with a shovel or hoe. If the ridges crumble, the mix is too dry. If they slump, there is too much water.

You can keep a batch of mortar workable for up to two hours by sprinkling water on it as needed and remixing. After two hours, prepare a new batch.

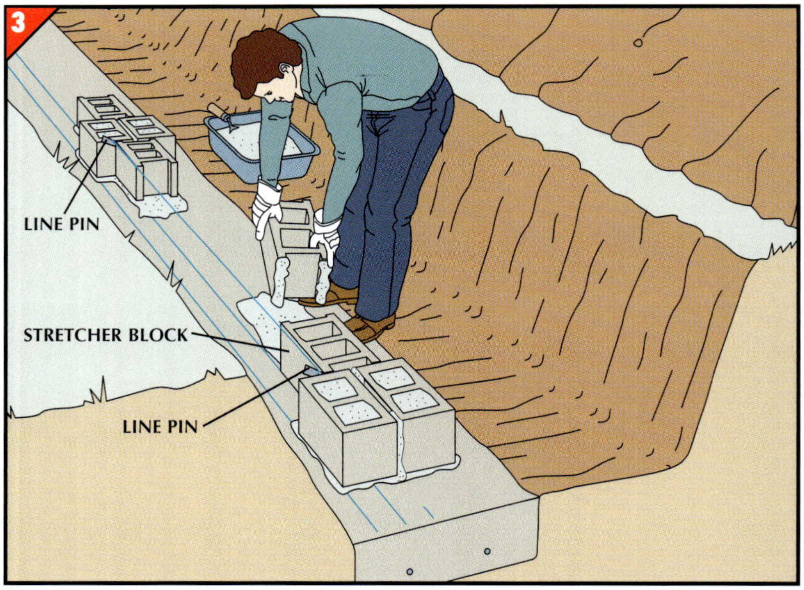

3. Completing the first course.

◆ Lay a stretcher block on the footing against each end pilaster and on both sides of the other pilasters. Center the blocks on the joint between the two pilaster blocks and align them with the inside chalk line.

◆ Once the mortar has begun to set, place a line pin in each joint between the pilasters and the stretcher blocks. Available at masonry suppliers, the pins will anchor a mason's line to align the remaining stretcher blocks along the footing.

◆ Continue laying stretcher blocks *(above)*, completing the first course. Remove the line pins and plug the holes they leave with mortar.

4. Completing the foundation.

◆ Begin the second course with a half block at each end, centering the blocks over the joints between the pilaster blocks. Check the height of the block with your story pole.

◆ Lay a corner block inside each half block, run a mason's line from one end of the wall to the other, and fill in between them with stretcher blocks.

◆ Lay partition blocks at each pilaster, sandwiching the newly laid second-course blocks *(right)*. The partition blocks must be flush with the double-corner blocks beneath them.

◆ Lay the third course as you did the first, but at each pilaster, embed a 15-inch length of truss-type joint reinforcement in the mortar across the wall before laying the blocks.

◆ Once the mortar has set, fill the openings in the blocks at each pilaster with grout so that there is a continuous column of grout from the footing up to a few inches from the top of the third course.

◆ Continuing in this manner, build the foundation to within a few inches of ground level. Check the first block you set in each new course with the story pole.

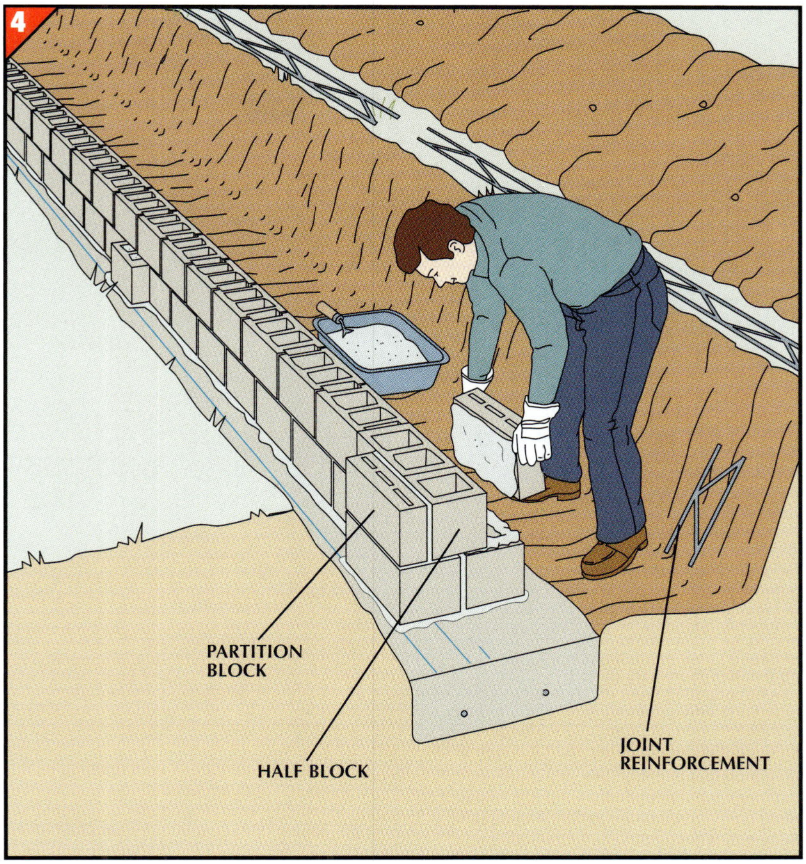

ERECTING A BRICK WALL

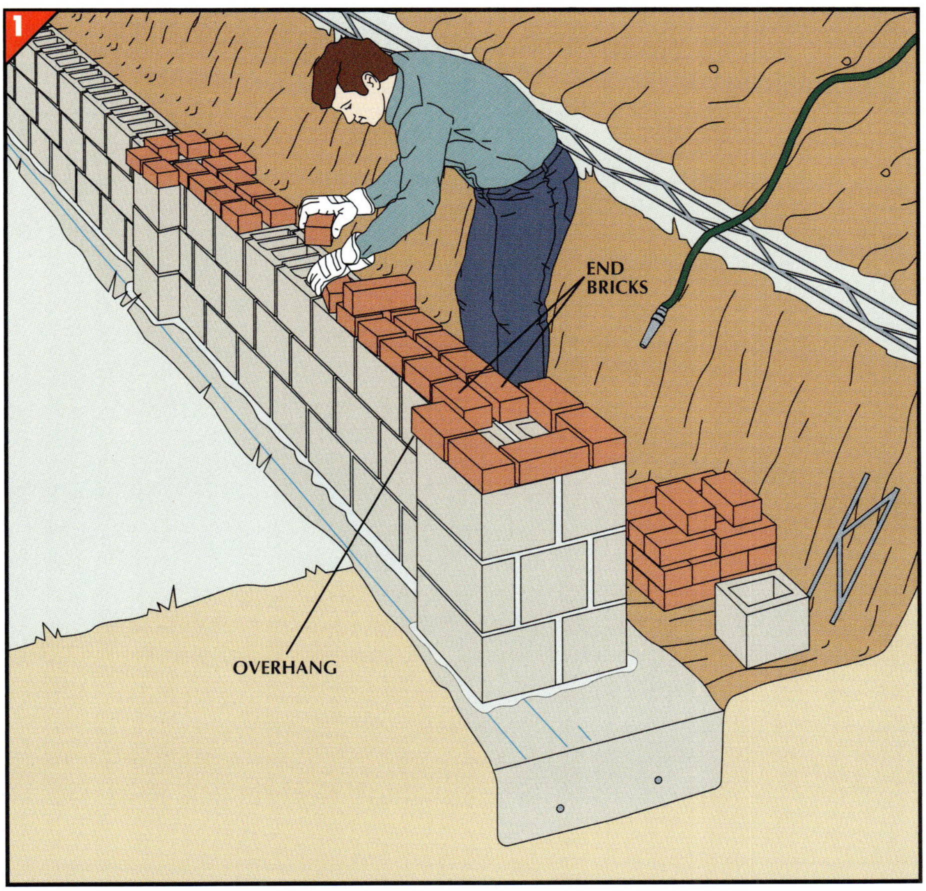

1. Making a dry run.

Lay a dry run of the first course of bricks from pilaster to pilaster to check and adjust their placement.

◆ Lay the bricks in the pattern shown at left, starting with two end bricks set halfway into the core of each pilaster. Leave a gap of about $\frac{1}{2}$ inch between the bricks.

◆ Lay bricks around the perimeter of each pilaster, ensuring they are flush with the outside edges of the pilasters. If the bricks project beyond the blocks, set them so the overhang is all on one side.

◆ Lay the remaining bricks of the run in pairs so their combined width equals the length of a brick *(left)*. Again, locate any overhang on one side of the foundation.

◆ Mark the location of the end bricks on the pilasters, note the gap between bricks, and remove the dry run.

2. Laying the leads.

Start the wall by building a lead—or end structure—six courses high at each end of the wall.

◆ Spread mortar on the tops of the end pilaster blocks and along $2\frac{1}{2}$ feet of the adjoining blocks. Set a 10-foot length of joint reinforcement 1 inch in from the end of the lead.

◆ Following your dry-run pattern, lay a row of bricks around the rim of the pilaster. Lay the end bricks, aligning them with the marks on the pilaster, and add three more pairs of bricks along the wall. Level and plumb each brick with a torpedo level.

◆ Set a half block in the middle of the pilaster.

◆ Begin the second course, altering the pattern so each brick is centered over a vertical joint of the course below. Stop the second course a half-brick's length from the end of the first.

◆ Start the third course, aligning the bricks with those in the first course, but make this row a full brick shorter.

◆ Set a 15-inch length of joint reinforcement across the pilaster *(left)*, then begin three more courses of bricks, staggering the vertical joints between successive courses.

3. Building up the pilasters.

◆ Lay 10-foot lengths of joint reinforcement along the top of the block foundation, overlapping their ends 12 to 15 inches.

◆ At each pilaster between the ends, build six-course double leads—ones that step up from the wall on both sides as described above. To help maintain horizontal alignment, stretch a mason's line between the end pilasters. For vertical alignment, butt a straightedge against the bricks and foundation wall *(right)*, tapping the bricks flush, as necessary.

◆ Fill the cores of the pilaster blocks with grout.

◆ Complete the courses between the pilasters, running a mason's line from line pins stuck in the vertical mortar joints next to the pilasters.

◆ Fill in the soil you dug out for the footing trench and compact it well with a tamper.

4. Extending the wall upward.

◆ Once you have completed six courses of bricks, lay joint reinforcement along the wall. Then, build six-course leads at each pilaster as in Steps 2 and 3.

◆ Grout the lead cores, fill in the courses between the pilasters, and repeat the process, adding joint reinforcement after every sixth course. If you laid one or two courses of brick below grade, four six-course leads will take the wall to 5 feet; an additional three courses plus a cap *(Steps 5 and 6)* will take it to 6 feet.

5. Capping the wall.

◆ Once the wall is 4 inches short of the desired height, lay joint reinforcement along the top, build the pilasters up three more courses, and fill in their cores.

◆ Start with a dry run of rowlocks (bricks laid on edge) along the wall between the pilasters to determine the required thickness of the remaining mortar joints.

◆ Lay the rowlocks in a mortar bed *(above)*.

6. Capping the pilasters.

◆ For each pilaster, cut eight 1-inch-thick pieces of brick, called closers. These serve to widen the two courses that cap the pilasters. Cut the bricks as described on page 163.

◆ Lay the first course of the cap around the rim of the pilaster with full-sized bricks; follow the basic pattern, but ensure the bricks overhang the rim by 1 inch all around. Fit closers in the gaps between the bricks.

◆ Set two bricks in the middle of the pilaster and fill the gaps with mortar.

◆ Alternating the pattern, lay the second cap course flush with the first *(above)*. Set two more bricks in the center.

◆ For the final course, center eight bricks across the pilaster.

5 Buildings for the Backyard

With a few modifications, simple backyard structures can fulfill myriad roles. Some designs, such as the A-frame, are well suited to storage. Others excel at providing comfort and shelter for outdoor living. Whether to afford relief from sunlight, protection from the wind, or a barrier against rain, outdoor structures can be adapted to virtually any climate and situation.

Nailing a post cap to a beam →

Post-and-Beam Structures

Post-and-beam structures are an elegant complement to outdoor living. Built with pressure-treated wood and left without sheathing, the post-and-beam framework can be used as an arbor or a trellis; roofed and sheathed with openwork materials *(page 185)*, it becomes a garden shelter. With weatherproof siding and roofing, the structure can be a workshop, shed, or studio.

Foundations: For an open-roofed structure, a simple concrete slab or set of precast concrete piers is adequate foundation. A closed-roofed structure, particularly one that must bear the weight of snow, requires a turned-down slab *(pages 207-213)* or concrete piers with footings set below the frost line. The latter is similar to the footings for the brick wall except the blocks are built at each post location rather than along the whole outline.

The Posts and Beams: The size of the posts for an unroofed structure is determined by the building's width. Long, narrow structures are easier to build; if the width is less than 8 feet, 4-by-4 redwood or pressure-treated posts suffice. If the structure is wider than 8 feet but less than 12 feet, use 4-by-6 posts. Determining the size of posts for a roofed post-and-beam structure requires more precise calculations and varies from area to area. Consult your local building code.

The size of the beams is determined by the span between posts. The width in inches of a 4-inch beam should equal its span in feet. Thus, a 4-by-6 beam can span distances up to 6 feet, a 4-by-8 up to 8 feet, and so on.

Choosing Rafters: Rafters to bridge the beams can be spaced as far apart as 48 inches in an unroofed structure; use the table below to determine the spacing and lengths of rafters for an open roof. If you plan to roof the structure, the rafters should be set no more than 16 inches apart. Use 2-by-4s for a structure up to 5 feet wide, 2-by-6s for up to 9 feet, 2-by-8s for up to 11 feet and 2-by-10s for up to 14 feet.

Rafter Sizes for an Open Roof

Spacing	Maximum Rafter Length 8 ft.	10 ft.	12 ft.
16 in.	2x4	2x6	2x6
32 in.	2x6	2x8	2x8
48 in.	2x6	2x8	2x8

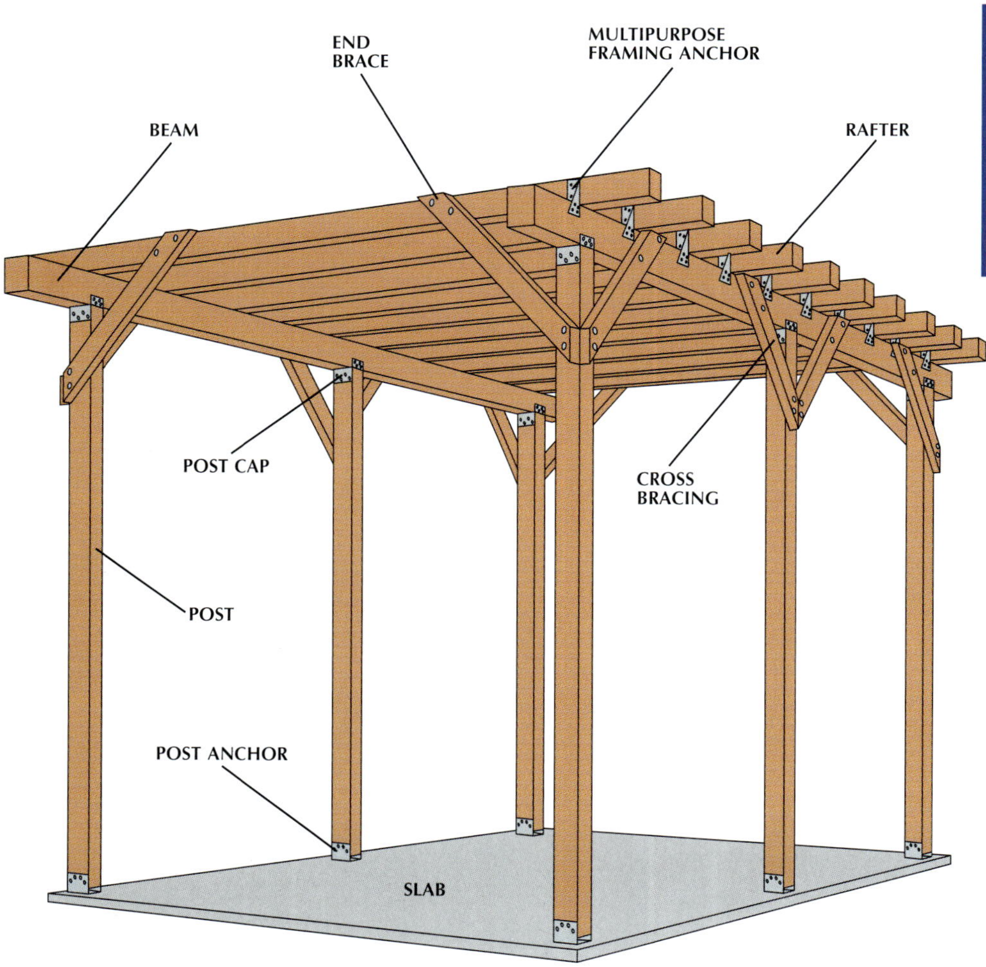

Anatomy of a post-and-beam structure. Metal connectors hold together the basic post-and-beam framework. The posts are attached to post anchors fastened to a concrete slab *(left)* or to precast concrete piers, typically available with a post anchor already embedded. At the tops of the posts, metal post caps secure the beams. Rafters are attached to beams with metal framing anchors. The beam ends overhang the posts below them, and the rafters overhang the beams. Diagonal 2-by-4 cross braces are attached to posts and beams and the end rafters with lag screws.

TOOLS

Tape measure
Carpenter's level
Chalk line
Hammer
Maul
Wrench
Circular saw
Electric drill
$\frac{3}{4}$" masonry bit

MATERIALS

4-by posts
4-by beams
2-by rafters
2x4 braces
Wooden stakes
Common nails ($2\frac{1}{2}$")
Lag screws ($\frac{3}{8}$"x3"; $\frac{1}{2}$"x$3\frac{1}{2}$") and washers
Post anchors and post caps
Framing anchors
Framing-anchor nails ($1\frac{1}{2}$", $2\frac{1}{2}$", $3\frac{1}{2}$")
Lead shield

SAFETY TIPS

Wear goggles when hammering and drilling, and hard hat when working with materials overhead. Put on gloves when handling pressure-treated lumber; add a dust mask when cutting it.

ERECTING POSTS

1. Setting the post anchors.

The U-shaped anchors are bolted to the concrete slab with an offset washer that permits post positions to be shifted slightly for alignment.

◆ Snap chalk lines 2 inches in from each side of the slab.

◆ Place anchors and washers at each post position and mark the location for the lead shield.

◆ Drill a $\frac{3}{4}$-inch hole 4 inches deep at each mark with a masonry bit. Drop a $\frac{3}{4}$-inch lead shield into the hole.

◆ Place the post anchor and washer over the hole, then tighten a $\frac{1}{2}$-inch lag screw into the shield until it is snug but the anchor can still be shifted.

◆ Set a post support inside each anchor.

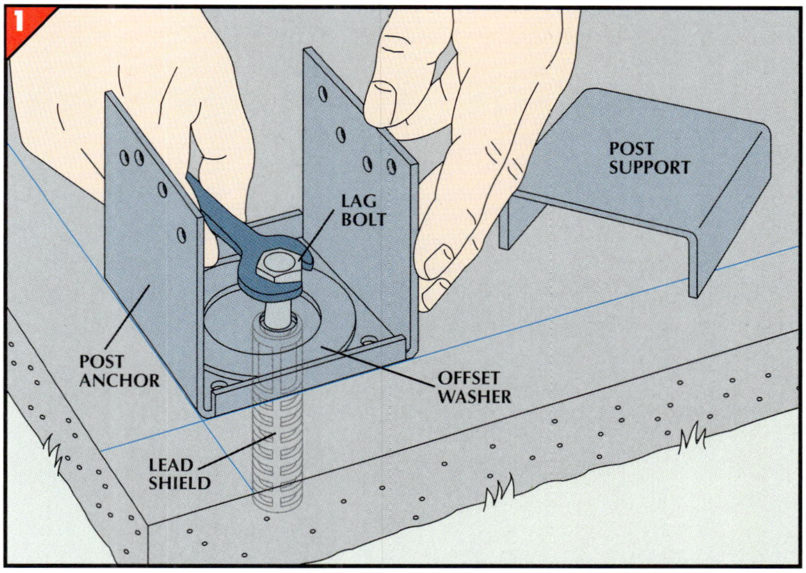

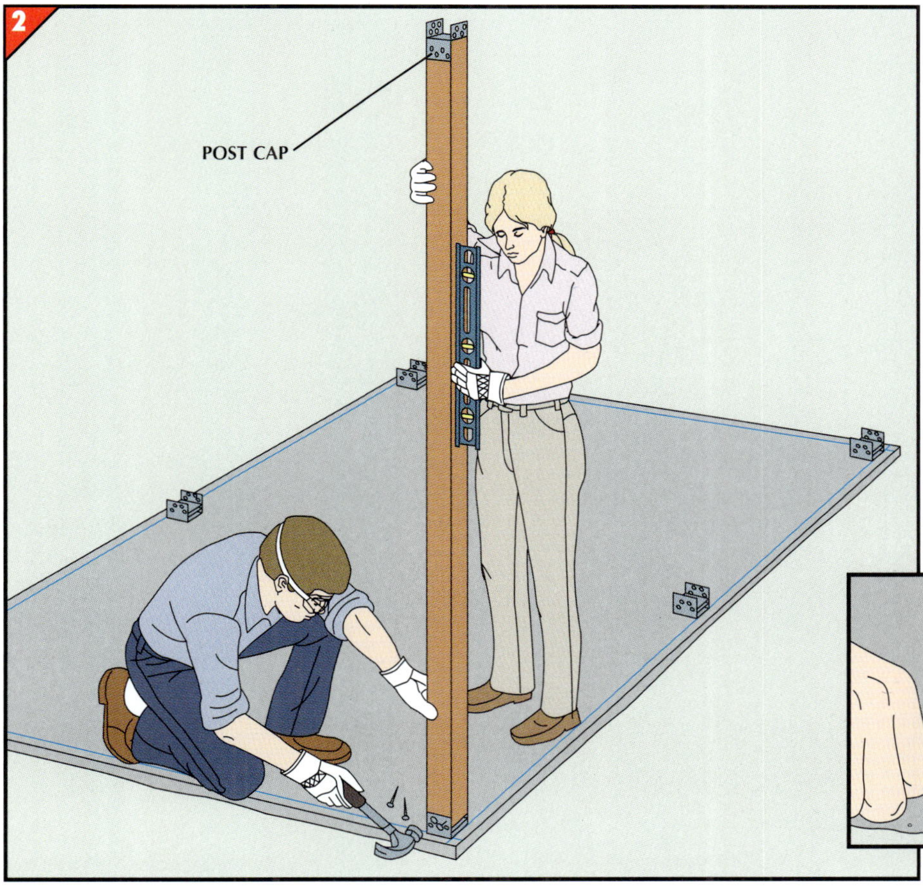

2. Raising the posts.

◆ Install post caps on the top end of the posts with $3\frac{1}{2}$-inch framing-anchor nails. Place a post onto the post anchor.

◆ Have a helper hold the post plumb, checking with a carpenter's level on two adjacent sides.

◆ Secure the bottom of the post to the anchor *(left)*.

◆ Align the outside post edges with the building lines and tighten the lag screw *(inset)*. Repeat for all the other posts.

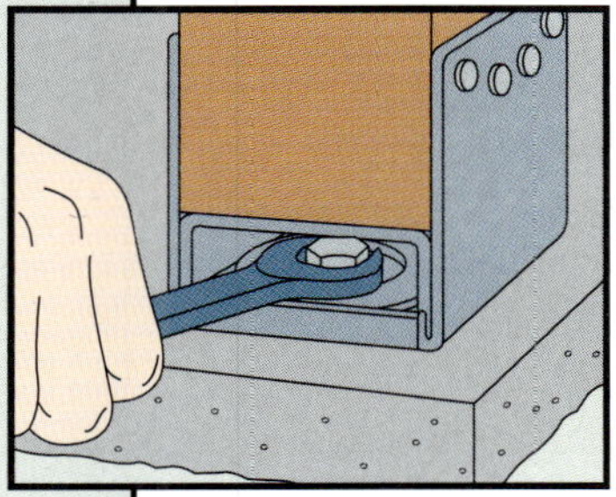

3. Plumbing and bracing the corners.

◆ While a helper holds the corner post plumb—checking with a level—brace the post with 2-by-4s nailed to stakes and to the post at least 20 inches from the top.

◆ Repeat for each corner.

RAISING BEAMS

1. Attaching the beams.

◆ Mark the tops of the beams for rafters, spacing them as desired; refer to the table on page 170 for maximum spacings and spans. Make the first mark to position the outside edge of an end rafter flush with the outside edge of a corner post.

◆ Set each beam in the post caps atop a row of posts, marked-side up, aligning the outermost marks with the outside edges of the corner posts.

◆ Have a helper hold the beam steady while you nail the corner post-cap flanges to the beam with $3\frac{1}{2}$-inch nails designed for connectors.

◆ Plumb the intermediate posts with a level, then nail them to the post-cap flanges *(right)*.

ALTERNATIVE WAYS TO ATTACH POSTS TO BEAMS

Galvanized metal connectors are a strong, utilitarian, and relatively foolproof way to hold the beams to the posts. But there are more attractive solutions, including the three shown at right. The half-lap is the strongest joint, especially with the addition of lag screws. The double beam works by bolting two beams to both sides of the post. The decorative cleat partially conceals a metal post cap connector.

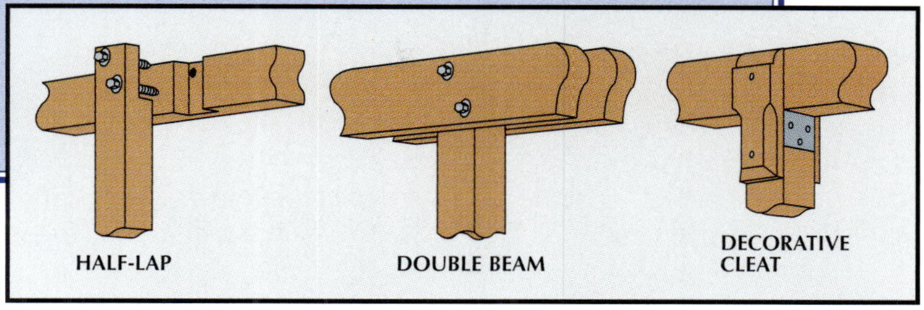

2. Putting up rafters.

◆ Measure and cut the rafters following the table on page 170, adding 24 inches to the total length to give a 12-inch overhang on each side.
◆ Nail a framing anchor to the top of one beam on one side of an end-rafter mark with $2\frac{1}{2}$-inch connector nails.
◆ Nail another anchor on the top of the opposite beam, on one side of the mark.
◆ Make a mark on the side of a rafter 12 inches in from each end, set the rafter against the anchors, and nail it in place with $1\frac{1}{2}$-inch nails *(right)*.
◆ Attach the remaining rafters the same way.

3. Mounting the braces.

The 2-by-4 braces can be cut ahead of time. For most applications cut them at a 45-degree angle at each end and 26 inches in length along their longest edge.
◆ Tack the braces in position so one end is flush with the top of the beam and the other is aligned with the center line of the post. (For the end post align the lower end of the brace with the outside edge of the post.)
◆ Drill a $\frac{1}{4}$-inch-diameter pilot hole through the brace and into the beam or post *(left)*.
◆ Secure the braces with $\frac{3}{8}$-by-3-inch lag screws and washers, driving the screws in with a socket wrench.
◆ Attach the end braces similarly, but position the higher end flush with the top of the rafter, as shown on page 170. This will mean cutting longer pieces than the standard cross braces.
◆ Remove the temporary nails and bracing.

Erecting Sloping Roofs

For small-scale post-and-beam structures, roof rafters can be measured and marked in position. Lumber sizes given in this section are guidelines; consult the building code in your area for possible variations. For an open roof like the ones shown on page 187, buy pressure-treated wood for all the parts.

A Shed Roof: This type of roof is defined as one that slopes because one side of the structure is built higher than the other. To calculate how much higher, start with the desired roof pitch, which in the example below is 1-in-12 (or 1 inch of rise for every foot of roof width). In this method, the 2-by-6 rafters butt against the crossbeam on the high side, but one-half their width ($2\frac{5}{8}$ inches) fits into notches cut in the lower crossbeam. You will need to add this amount to the high side, or subtract it from the low side, when building the sides.

A Gable Roof: In this type of roof, the rafters rest on beams and meet at a 1-by-8 ridge beam, which forms the peak of the roof. This type of roof is easier to lay out than the shed because the sides are built at the same height. A simple marking guide *(page 176)* will enable you to mark the rafters accurately with no calculation or guesswork.

Bracing with Collar Ties: Both types of roof suffer an inherent weakness. Since the rafters meet the beams at an angle, their weight and the loads they bear tend to push the sides outward. This can be overcome with collar ties. Brace a shed roof by attaching 2-by-6 collar ties to each pair of end posts, as shown on page 187, with $\frac{3}{8}$-by-$3\frac{1}{2}$-inch lag screws. For gable roofs, which are more prone to spreading, join every third pair of rafters with a collar tie *(page 177)*.

A SHED ROOF

1. Marking the rafters.

- Make rafter marks 16 inches on center on the crossbeams.
- Snap a chalk line down the middle of a rafter board. With a helper, align the board so its top is flush with the top of the upper crossbeam and the chalk line touches the top edge of the lower crossbeam.
- Tack the rafter to the upper crossbeam, and outline the edges of the lower crossbeam for a bird's-mouth cut, a notch that fits the rafter snugly to the crossbeam.
- Mark the rafter along the inner face of the upper crossbeam for the ridge cut, the cut that fits the rafter to the upper crossbeam.
- With a level, mark a vertical overhang cut on the end of the rafter.

TOOLS

Tape measure
Carpenter's level
Chalk line
1x2, 1x8, 2x6 for marking guide
Hammer
Hand saw or saber saw
Circular saw
Electric drill

MATERIALS

1x2s, 1x4s
1x8 ridge beam
2x6 rafters and collar ties
Galvanized common nails (3", $3\frac{1}{2}$")
Lag screws ($\frac{3}{8}$"x$3\frac{1}{2}$")
Multipurpose framing anchors and nails ($1\frac{1}{2}$", $2\frac{1}{2}$")

SAFETY TIPS

Wear goggles when nailing and a hard hat when handling materials overhead. Put on gloves when handling pressure-treated wood; add a dust mask when cutting it.

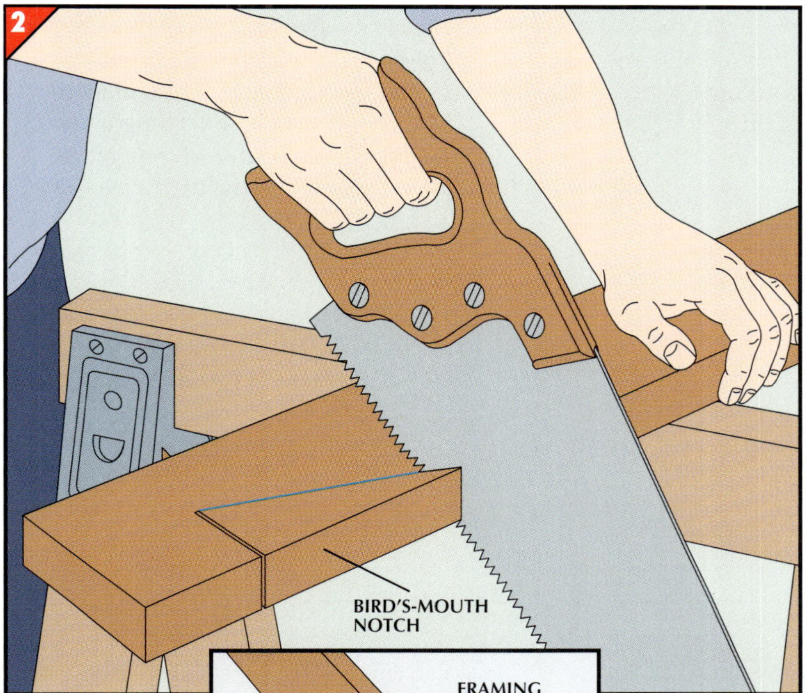

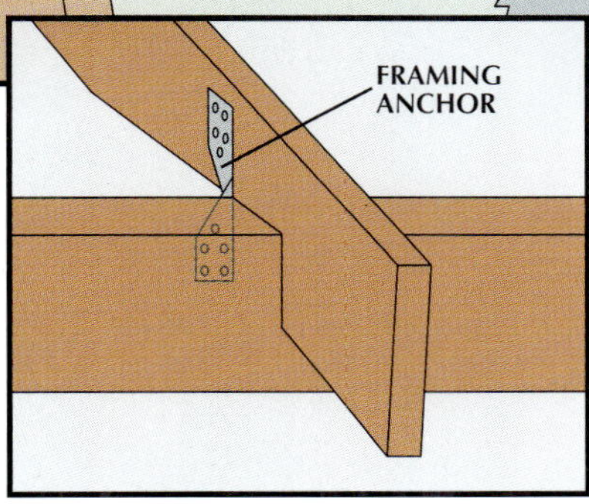

2. Cutting and installing the rafters.

◆ Support the rafter on a pair of saw horses and cut along the marked lines with a hand saw *(left)* or a saber saw.
◆ Mark out the remaining rafters, using the cut rafter as a template.
◆ To raise the rafters, toenail them with $3\frac{1}{2}$-inch galvanized common nails to the upper and lower crossbeam at the marked spots.
◆ For additional support, secure each rafter to the lower beam with a multipurpose framing anchor *(inset)* with the nails recommended by the manufacturer.

CUSTOM CUTS FOR RAFTER ENDS

These six patterns are common choices for adding a decorative touch to the plain ends of open-structure rafters. Enlarge the pattern you plan to use on graph paper and transfer it to a rafter. Cut out the patterns with a saber saw, then smooth the shape with medium-grit sandpaper. Another approach is to make a template of the pattern on $\frac{1}{2}$-inch plywood. You can then cut the rafter ends using the pattern-routing method shown on page 145.

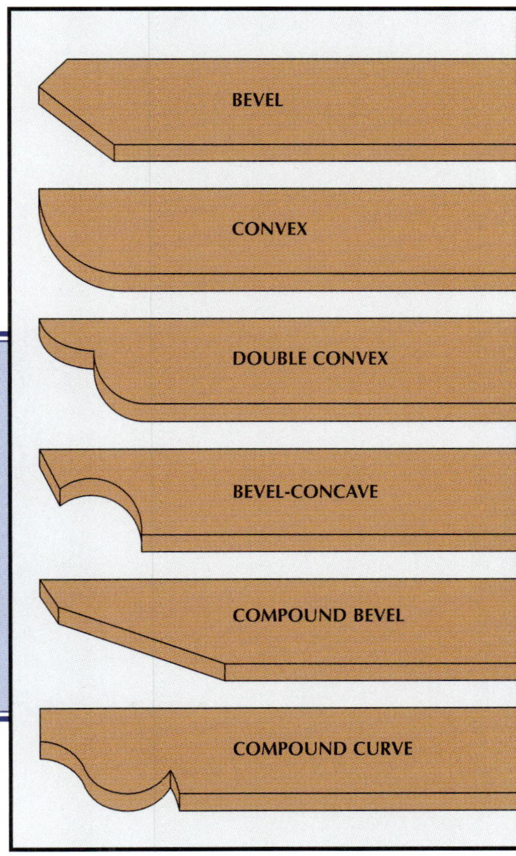

A GABLE ROOF

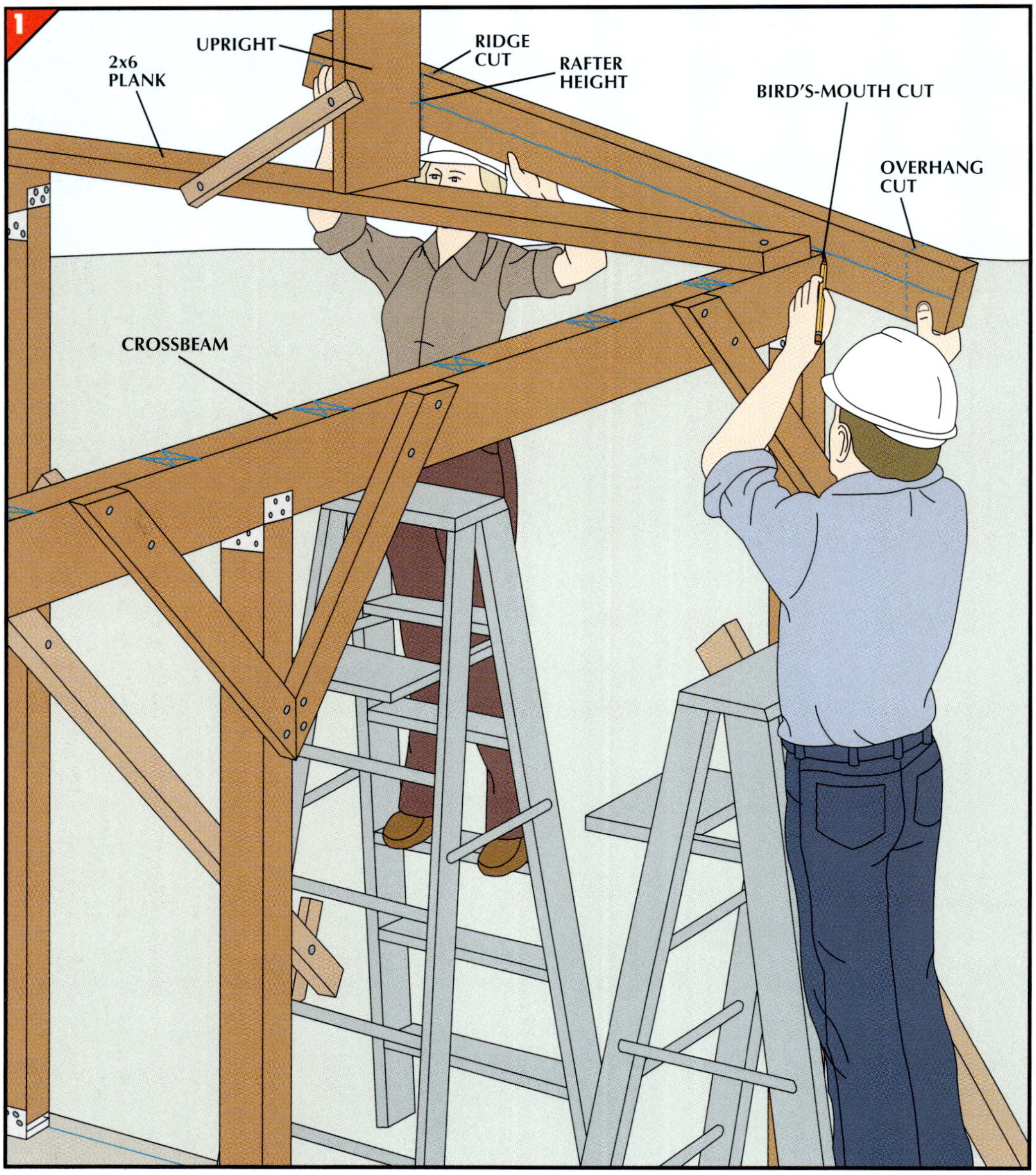

1. Marking rafters for a gable roof.

◆ Construct a marking guide by attaching a 1-by-8 upright to the center of a 2-by-6 plank long enough to span the structure. Secure the upright at 90 degrees to the plank with a 1-by-2 brace. Mark the desired height of the peak on the upright.
◆ Set the marking guide on the crossbeams, $1\frac{1}{2}$ inches in from the edge, with the upright centered between the sides. Tack the guide in place.
◆ Check that the upright is plumb and adjust the brace as needed.
◆ Snap a chalk line at the center of a rafter board and position the board against the guide as shown *(left)*.
◆ Mark the bird's-mouth cut, the ridge cut, and, with a level, the overhang cut *(page 174)*. Remove the marking guide.
◆ Cut the bird's-mouth *(page 175)*, ridge, and overhang, then mark and cut the other rafters using the first one as a template.

2. Assembling the frame.

◆ Cut a 1-by-8 ridge beam to the same length as the crossbeams and mark it for rafters every 16 inches.
◆ On one side of the beam, fasten a rafter to each end, nailing through the beam into the end of the rafter with three 3-inch galvanized common nails.
◆ Toenail rafters to the opposite side of the beam *(right)*.

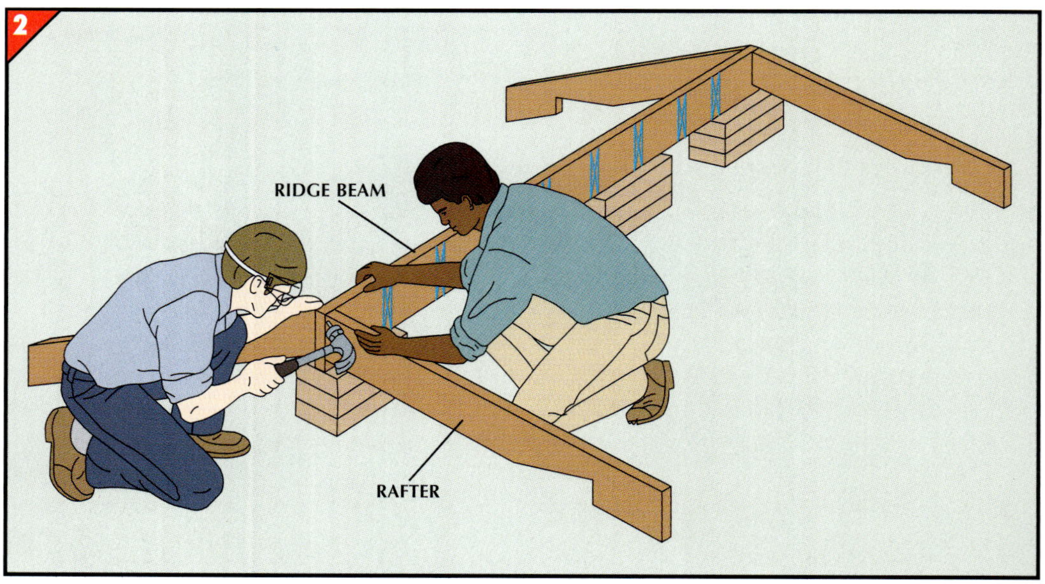

3. Positioning the frame.

◆ Brace the end rafters temporarily with 1-by-4s nailed across them.
◆ With three helpers, lift the frame into place, setting the bird's-mouth cuts onto the crossbeams.
◆ If necessary, remove the temporary bracing so you can adjust the fit of the rafters, and replace it when they are correctly positioned.
◆ Toenail the rafters to the crossbeam with $3\frac{1}{2}$-inch common nails.
◆ To strengthen the rafter-and-beam joints, add framing anchors with the nails suggested by the manufacturer.

4. Fitting the collar ties.

◆ Set a 2-by-6 equal to the width of the structure atop the crossbeams and against a pair of end rafters, and mark it along the top of the rafters *(left)*.
◆ Cut the board at the marks and use it as a template for the other collar ties.
◆ Nail the collar ties to the end rafters with six 3-inch common nails.
◆ Mount the rest of the rafters, nailing a precut collar beam to every third pair of rafters as you go; then remove the temporary bracing.

Constructing a Gazebo

The gazebo is an open post-and-beam structure, usually with five, six, or eight sides and a peaked roof. The version shown here is six-sided, and can be built up to 15 feet in diameter—a larger gazebo requires collar ties to connect opposing rafters; the collar ties are fastened to the bottom end of the rafters *(page 177)*.

A gazebo is best built with pressure-treated lumber. It can be left open or covered with woven reed or bamboo *(pages 190 and 191)*, with fiberglass or aluminum screening *(page 193)*, or with lattice *(page 188)*.

A gazebo's foundation can often be as simple as concrete blocks or 6-by-6 wooden blocks set under the corner of the platform. If the site is uneven, embed the blocks in the earth. Before beginning, always check local building codes; some may require a more substantial footing.

TOOLS

Carpenter's level
Water level
Hammer
Handsaw
Circular saw
Saber saw
Shovel

MATERIALS

1x1s, 1x3s, 2x4s, 2x6s, 4x4s
$\frac{5}{8}$" exterior-grade plywood
Concrete blocks
Gravel
Galvanized common nails ($1\frac{3}{4}$", 2", 3", $3\frac{1}{4}$", $3\frac{1}{2}$")
Galvanized wood screws ($\frac{3}{4}$" No. 8)
Angle irons (2")
Truss plates (1", 3", 4") and recommended nails
Wood glue (exterior)

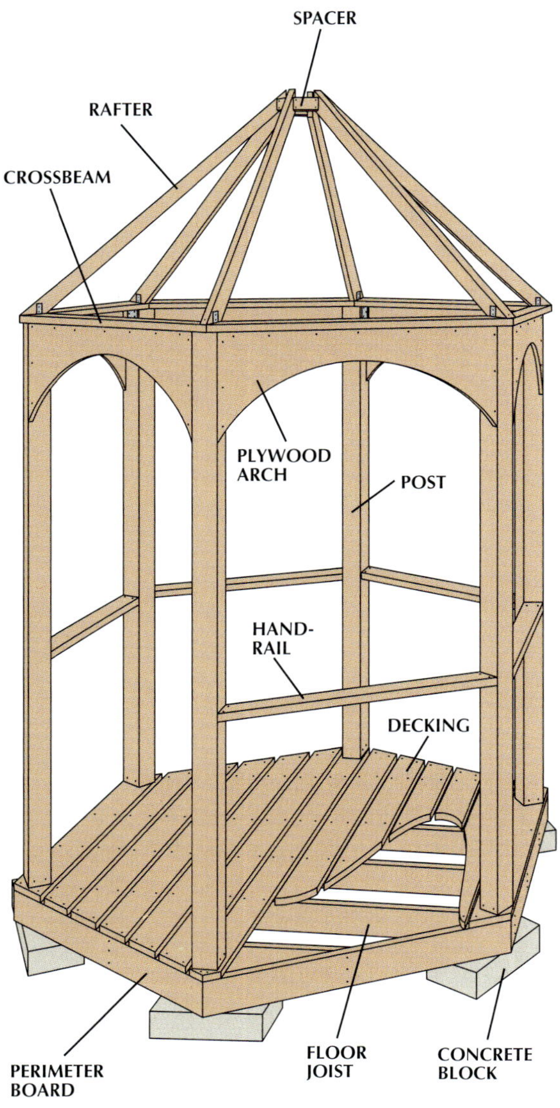

Anatomy of a hexagonal gazebo.
Six 4-by-4 posts toenailed to a wood platform and secured to the beam-and-rafter unit that forms the roof provide the uprights of this post-and-beam structure. The gazebo platform consists of perimeter boards, joists, and decking—all made from 2-by-6s. Six crossbeams, five handrails (all 2-by-4s), and six plywood arches give the structure lateral rigidity. The 2-by-6 roof rafters are nailed at their bases to the crossbeams and attached at their peaks to 2-by-4 spacers. The entire structure rests on concrete blocks.

JOINING GAZEBO RAFTERS

Even if gazebo rafters are cut accurately to length and angle, assembling them can be a juggling act. Commercial roof peak rafter ties *(below)* take much of the guesswork out of the job by allowing the ends of the rafters to be sawn square. The ties are flexible enough to accommodate different pitch roofs.

Gazebo connectors are also available to fasten rafters to crossbeams; others are designed to join the perimeter boards at the correct angle without requiring miter cuts.

CUTTING PARTS FOR DIFFERENT-SHAPED GAZEBOS

The lengths of the perimeter boards and crossbeams are determined by the number of sides of the gazebo, and by its overall size. Base your calculations on a circle whose area is about equal to the floor area of the gazebo you plan to build. If your gazebo will be hexagonal, its sides must be the same length as the circle's radius; for a pentagon, multiply the radius by 1.25; for an octagon, multiply the radius by .75.

Cut the perimeter boards to length and miter their ends to an angle of 30 degrees for a hexagon, 36 degrees for a pentagon, or $22\frac{1}{2}$ degrees for an octagon. Cut the spacers (the boards that separate the rafters) the same way.

BUILDING A HEXAGONAL GAZEBO

1. Making the base.

◆ Cut the perimeter boards to length with a circular saw, then set the blade to 30 degrees and bevel the ends.

◆ Assemble the perimeter boards *(right)*, using exterior-grade wood glue on their ends and toenailing the ends together with $3\frac{1}{4}$-inch galvanized common nails.

◆ Reinforce the inside joints of the assembled base with 4-inch metal truss plates bent to fit the inside angle of the joints *(inset)*. Fasten the plates with the nails recommended by the manufacturer.

◆ Prepare the crossbeams as you did the perimeter boards, but with 1-inch truss plates on their inside corners. Put them aside until you prepare the rafters *(page 180, Step 4)*.

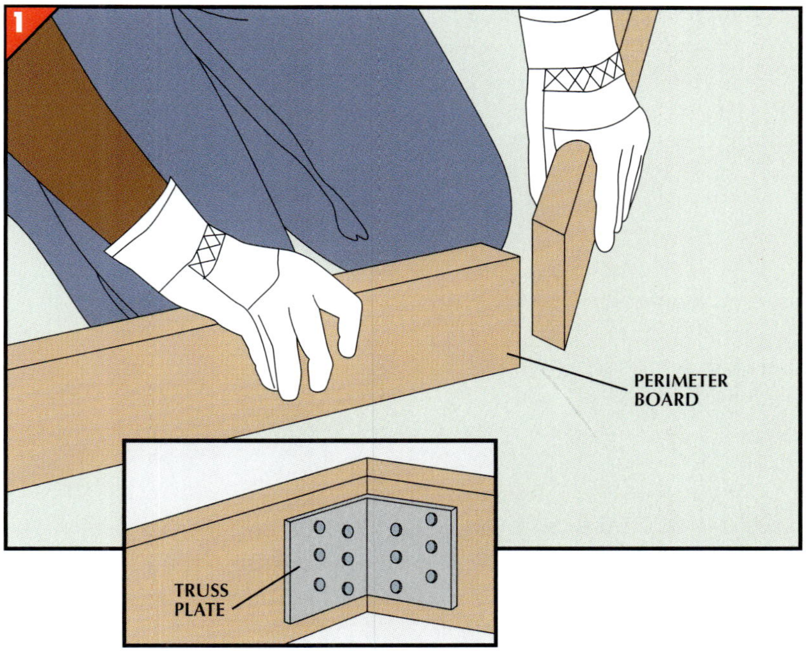

2. Putting in floor joists.

◆ Nail 2-by-6 joists, aligned on 16-inch centers, to the gazebo base with $3\frac{1}{2}$-inch nails. Cut the joist ends at an angle, as necessary, to match the angle of the perimeter boards.

◆ Fasten decking boards at right angles to the joists with 3-inch nails, and trim the protruding edges of the boards with a circular saw *(page 196, Step 3)*.

◆ Place six masonry blocks on the ground or on a bed of gravel to serve as supports for the gazebo base. Check their heights with a water level, adjusting them as necessary, then place the completed base on the blocks.

3. Raising the posts.

◆ Mark the posts to the correct height, then cut them with a circular saw, completing the cuts with a handsaw.
◆ Toenail the first post to the deck with $3\frac{1}{2}$-inch nails, driving them in partway to keep the post from slipping.
◆ Plumb and brace the first post *(page 137)*, then drive the nails home *(left)*.
◆ Erect, plumb, and secure the remaining posts, bracing each one to the adjacent one with temporary 1-by-3 stiffeners, as shown opposite.

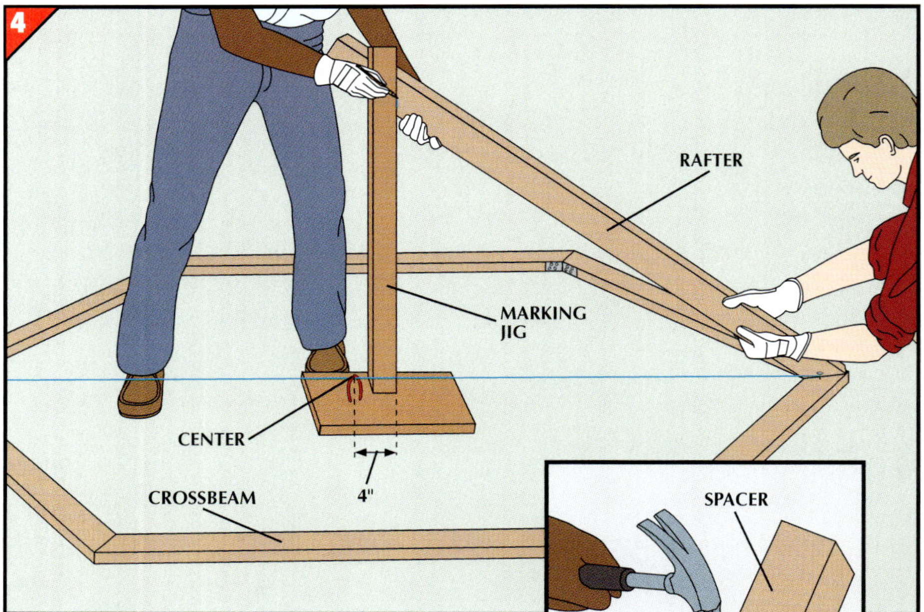

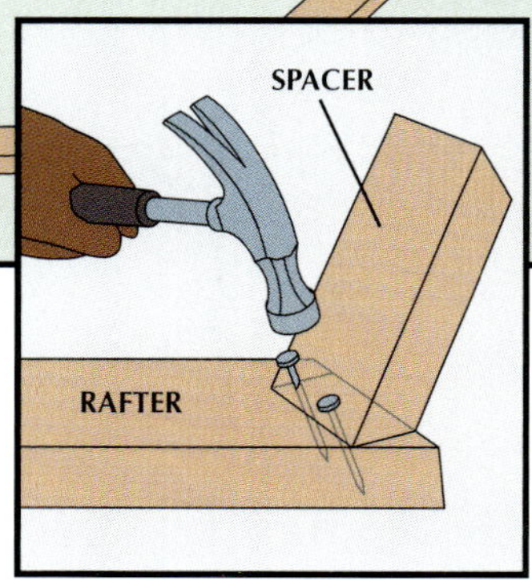

4. Preparing the rafters.

With a 2-by-6 long enough for a rafter, make a rafter to use as a template.
◆ Mark and cut one end of the 2-by-6 to match the pitch of the roof.
◆ Stretch a string from opposite corners of the crossbeam assembly and mark the middle of the string.
◆ Make a marking jig by fastening a 2-by-4 to a plywood base. Position the jig against the string with its outside edge 4 inches from the center.
◆ Place the 2-by-6 against the crossbeam and the jig, mark it *(right)* and trim it.
◆ Using this rafter as a template, cut five more rafters.
◆ Cut six $4\frac{1}{4}$-inch spacers from a 2-by-4, angling their ends at 30 degrees. Toenail a spacer to each rafter with $3\frac{1}{4}$-inch nails *(inset)*.

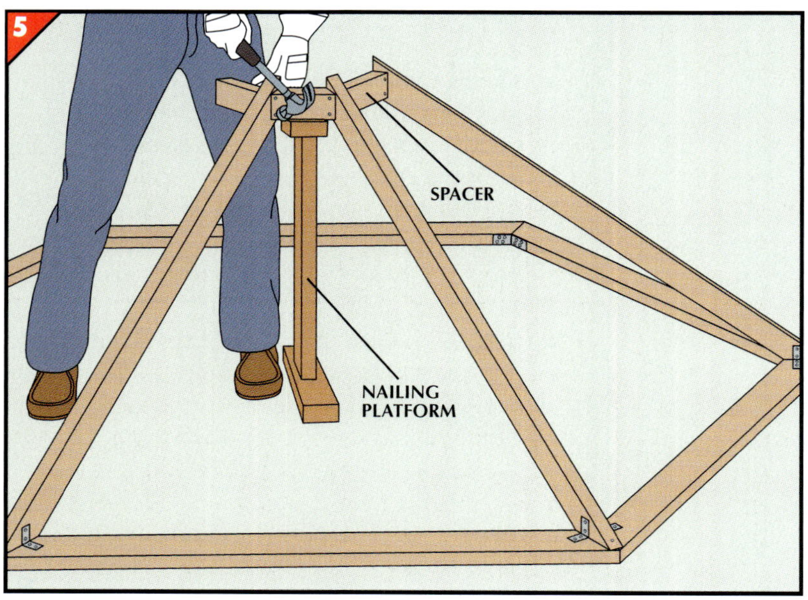

5. Assembling the roof frame.

◆ Position the bottom of a rafter over a joint of the crossbeam roof base. Toenail the rafter with a 3-inch nail and secure the connection with 2-inch angle irons and $\frac{3}{4}$-inch galvanized No. 8 wood screws.
◆ Attach a second rafter and its spacer the same way, then toenail the free end of the first spacer to the open side of the second rafter. To facilitate nailing, slip a temporary platform—made with 2-by-4s—under the spacers and brace the rafter with a leg *(left)*.
◆ Add the remaining rafters and spacers the same way.

6. Positioning the roof frame.
Lifting the roof into place is much easier and safer with two rented scaffolds.

◆ Have two helpers hand the roof up to you and another person standing on the scaffolds.

◆ Carefully walk the roof into place; position it with the outer edges of the crossbeams resting on the corners of the posts.

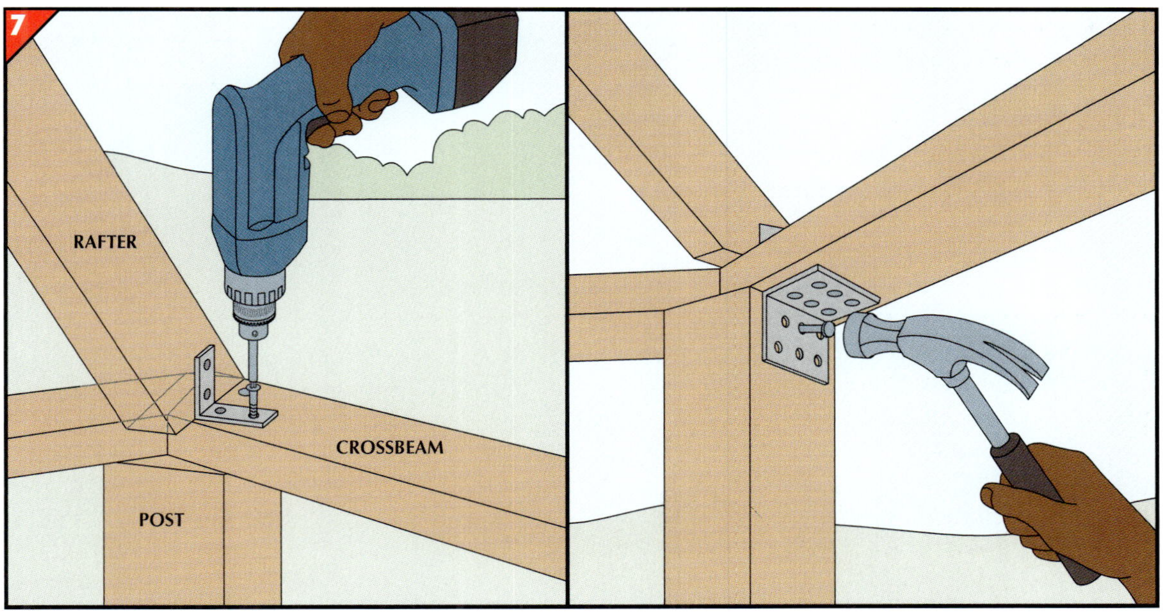

7. Fastening the roof.
◆ Drive a $3\frac{1}{2}$-inch nail through each crossbeam and into the top of each post, then strengthen each joint with a 2-inch angle iron and $\frac{3}{4}$-inch screws *(above, left)*.

◆ Secure a 3-inch metal truss plate under the crossbeams to both sides of each post *(above, right)*.

◆ Cut the handrails from 2-by-4s, mitering the ends at 30 degrees. Toenail them to the posts with $3\frac{1}{4}$-inch nails; reinforce with angle irons.

◆ Cut plywood arches *(page 178)* with a saber saw, beveling the ends at 30 degrees. Fasten 1-by-1 nailing strips to the undersides of the crossbeams with 2-inch nails and secure the arches in place with $1\frac{3}{4}$-inch nails.

Building a Tree House

Children love tree houses of all shapes and sizes, from simple platforms to elaborate hideaways with doors and windows.

Designing a Tree House: Tree-house platforms are typically attached to strong limbs of a low-branching tree, atop horizontal crossbeams. The design has to suit the plant—a tree with three main branches going off at angles is easiest to work with. In the absence of a suitable tree, a tree-house platform can be anchored to posts. Buy pressure-treated lumber for building your tree house.

Tree-house Safety: Even the most carefully built tree houses are subject to unusual stress, and their height is a hazard. Make sure that the tree and its branches are sufficiently stout to bear the weight. A tree house made for small children should be no higher than 8 to 10 feet off the ground, and located within sight of the main dwelling. Guard rails at least 3 feet high around the sides of any elevated structure are a mandatory feature. And to cushion the shock of an accidental fall, rake the ground beneath the structure free of rocks, then line it with 2 or 3 inches of sawdust, wood chips, or pine needles.

Before attaching a platform frame to a tree, inspect all the branches that you will nail into to ensure that the tree wood is free from rot. Once the tree house is in place, check periodically to make sure that high winds or tree growth have not weakened any braces supporting the platform. Do not skimp on nails; the fasteners will not hurt the tree.

TOOLS

Tape measure
Carpenter's level
Hammer
Wrench
Circular saw
Electric drill

MATERIALS

1x6s, 2x2s, 2x4s, 2x6s, 4x4s
Pulley
$\frac{1}{2}$"-diameter rope
Galvanized common nails (3", $3\frac{1}{2}$", 4")
Lag screws ($\frac{3}{8}$"x$3\frac{1}{2}$") and washers

SAFETY TIPS

Wear goggles when nailing and a hard hat when handling materials above your head. Put on gloves when handling pressure-treated wood; add a dust mask when cutting it.

A structure nailed to branches. A typical tree-house platform, attached to a tree that has strong, spreading limbs, rests on 2-by-6 crossbeams nailed between the branches. The platform is a framed deck of 1-by-6s laid atop 2-by-6 joists. It is braced with 2-by-4s attached to the tree and to the deck frame. Include a guardrail of 2-by-4s with 4-by-4s at the corners and enclose the open spaces between the rails and the deck with 2-by-2 pickets spaced no more than 4 inches apart.

A small roofed structure sheathed with plywood is erected over part of the deck, while a rope ladder (or boards nailed to the tree trunk) gives access to a trap door cut in the deck.

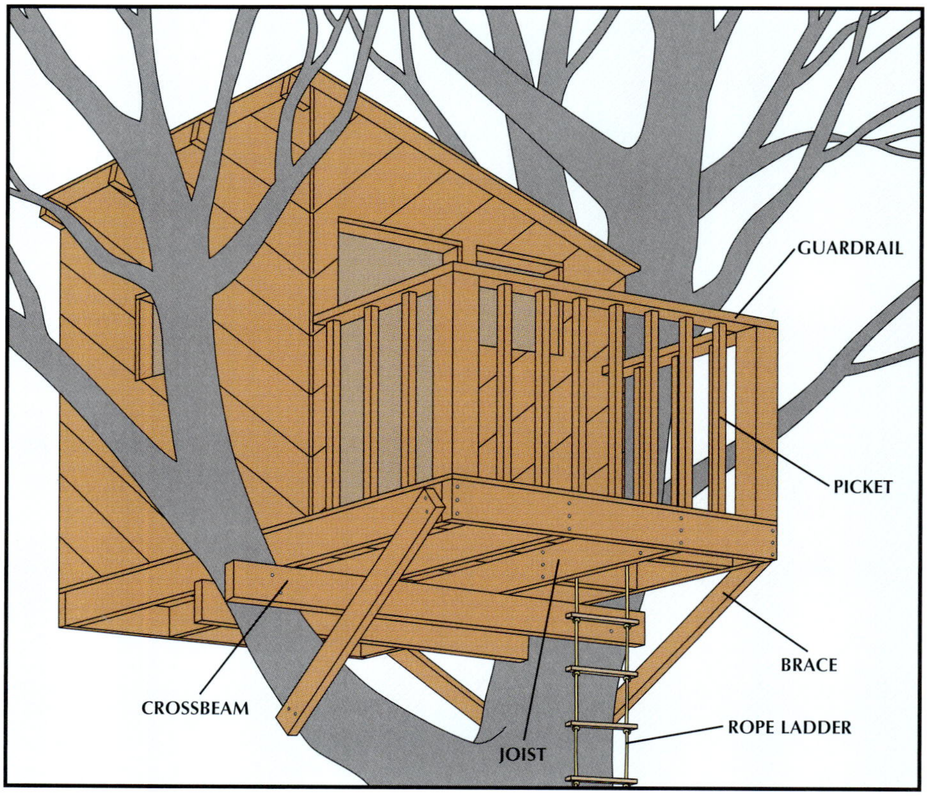

HOISTING AND SECURING THE PLATFORM

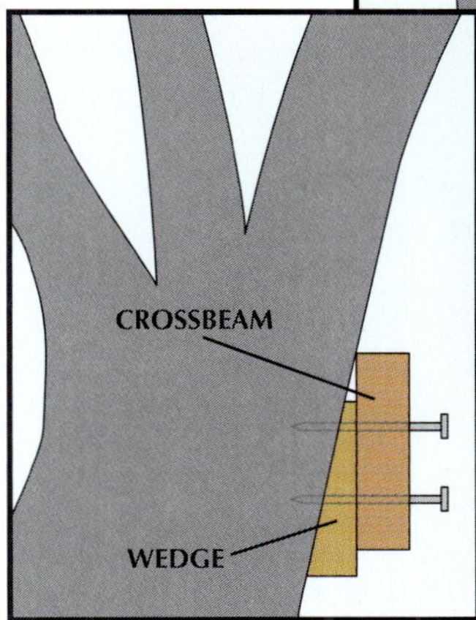

1. Installing the crossbeams.

Once you have selected a site for the platform, work with a helper to attach two or three 2-by-6 horizontal crossbeams to the tree *(right)*.

◆ Place wedges between the crossbeams and the branches, if necessary, to ensure that the beams will provide a level surface for the platform *(inset)*.

◆ Fasten the crossbeams with 4-inch galvanized common nails, driving them into the tree at the same height and level with each other.

2. Making and raising the platform.

◆ Build the platform, adapting the design shown on page 196 to fit the tree. Install 2-by-6 headers between the joists as shown on page 184 to frame the opening for the trap door.

◆ Cut the decking to fit around the opening and fasten it in place—except for one end board so the platform can be hoisted into the tree.

◆ Secure a pulley to a stout branch above the crossbeams with $\frac{1}{2}$-inch rope. Tightly wrap the rope around the branch several times so it will not slip sideways.

◆ Looping a length of $\frac{1}{2}$-inch rope around one platform frame member and through the pulley, hoist the platform up to the crossbeams, guided by two helpers.

◆ Set the platform on the crossbeams, toenail it in place with $3\frac{1}{2}$-inch nails, and install the last deck board.

3. Bracing the platform.
Working from a ladder with its top rung butted squarely against a scrap 2-by-4 nailed to a branch, nail at least three diagonal 2-by-4 braces to the platform frame and the tree with 4-inch nails.

To provide good nailing surfaces for the braces or to bridge gaps, slide a wedge between a brace and branch as for the crossbeams *(page 183, Step 1)*. To avoid having to toenail a brace directly to a branch, fasten a 2-by-4 cleat to the branch, and face-nail the brace to the end of the cleat.

A DECK BUILT AROUND A TREE

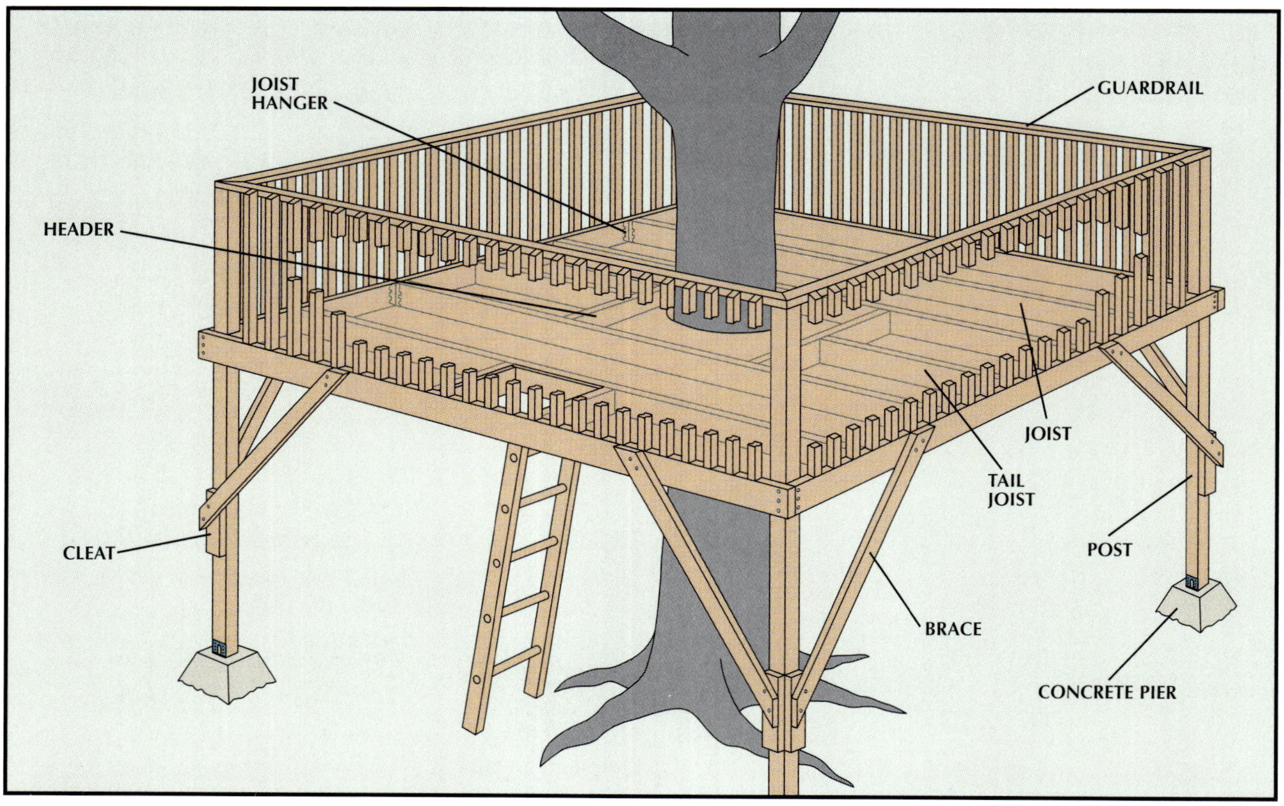

A freestanding platform.
For trees with high-branching trunks, build an elevated deck supported by 4-by-4 posts anchored to concrete piers and long enough to serve as guardrail supports.

◆ Make the platform *(pages 195-196)*. If the tree is wider than the gap between joists, omit one or more joists and attach headers and shortened "tail" joists.

◆ Fasten 2-by-4 cleats to the posts with $3\frac{1}{2}$-inch galvanized common nails. Attach braces from the posts to the frame with $\frac{3}{8}$-by-$3\frac{1}{2}$-inch lag screws. Then nail 2-by-6 decking to the joists with 3-inch nails.

◆ Fasten 2-by-4 guardrails to the posts with $3\frac{1}{2}$-inch nails, then add 2-by-2 pickets, leaving no more than 4 inches between them.

A Range of Coverings for Roofs and Sides

Selecting roofing and siding for an outdoor project depends on the design and intended use of the structure. Storage sheds are best sheathed in weatherproof materials, whereas lawn pavilions and shade houses can be left virtually open—although lattice can be added for privacy or shade. Hybrid designs, such as a waterproof roof with open sides or an open roof with solid sides, expand the range of choices.

Roofing Materials: Outdoor structures can be enclosed in much the same manner as houses. Rainproof options range from traditional shingle or clapboard to inexpensive, quick-to-install roll roofing.

Each of these choices is applied over a base of plywood sheathing. A simpler alternative is corrugated plastic paneling.

For an open roof, leave the rafters, with decorative end cuts *(page 175)*, unprotected, or nail crosspieces between them *(page 187)*. To provide more shade, you can cover the rafters with latticework or rows of slats, lattice, or shade cloth.

Siding Materials: You can install these same materials, along with bamboo shades, as siding for an outdoor structure. Or, cover open walls with screening to let in light and air—and exclude insects.

TOOLS

- Tape measure
- Combination square
- Hammer
- Utility knife
- Handsaw
- Circular saw
- Mason's trowel
- Broom

MATERIALS

- 1x1s, 1x2s, 2x4s
- $\frac{1}{2}$" plywood
- Molding ($\frac{1}{2}$"x1")
- Galvanized common nails ($2\frac{1}{4}$", $2\frac{1}{2}$", 3", $3\frac{1}{2}$")
- Galvanized finishing nails (2")
- Galvanized roofing nails ($1\frac{1}{4}$")
- Roll roofing
- Roofing cement
- Lattice

SAFETY TIPS

Wear safety goggles when nailing and a hard hat when working overhead. Put on gloves when handling pressure-treated wood; add a dust mask when handling it.

A RAFT OF ROOFING MATERIALS

The materials shown at right are all appropriate choices for a waterproof roof. Cedar shakes and shingles are rustic and traditional, and typically last 20 to 25 years. Asphalt shingles are probably easier to install, with a lifespan of 15 to 20 years depending on their weight. Corrugated panels (whether of fiberglass or steel) have the advantage of not needing a sheathing underlayment. Translucent panels seal out the elements, but do admit a certain amount of light.

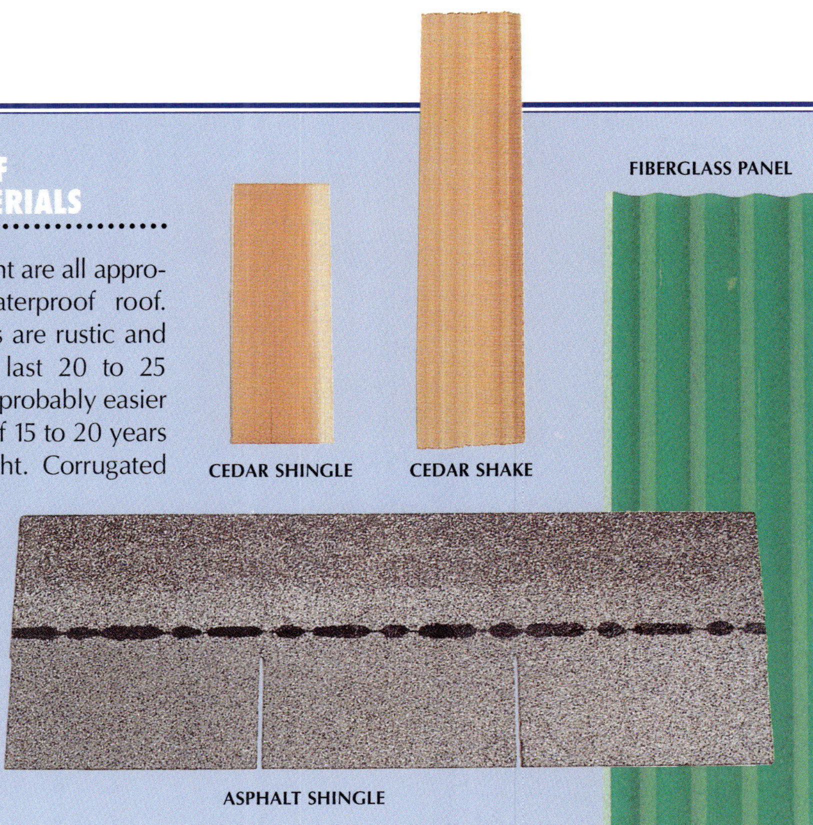

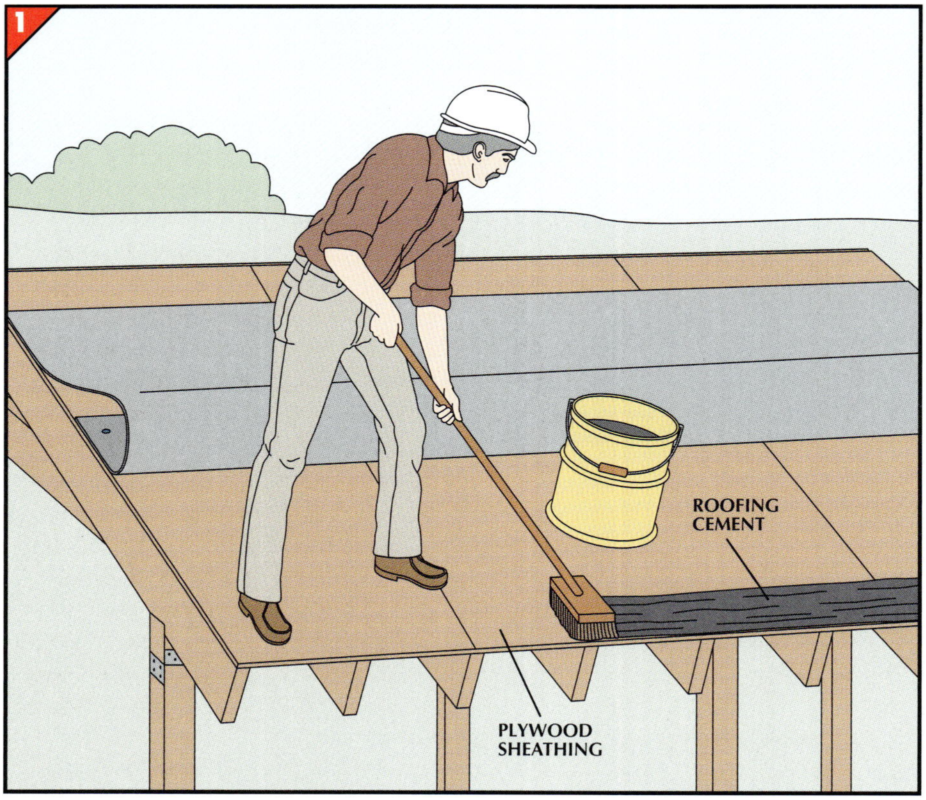

1. Setting roll roofing.

◆ Nail $\frac{1}{2}$-inch plywood sheathing to the rafters, driving $2\frac{1}{2}$-inch common nails at 6-inch intervals.

◆ With $1\frac{1}{4}$-inch roofing nails, fasten the upper edge of a strip of roll roofing to the sheathing so that the lower edge projects beyond the eave by $\frac{1}{2}$ inch. Fold the roofing up and spread a 12-inch-wide strip of roofing cement on the sheathing along the eave *(left)*.

◆ Press the strip firmly in place and nail its lower edge down.

◆ Work your way up the roof, lapping each new strip over the one in place by 4 inches. On a gable roof, trim the last strips even with the ridge, cutting with a utility knife, then set ridge pieces *(Step 2)*. On a shed roof, lap the last strip over the eave by 5 inches and fasten it to the crossbeam.

2. Covering the ridge.

Cut pieces of roll roofing 12 by 36 inches and cement them along the ridge *(right)*. Overlap the ends of the pieces by 6 inches. After pressing down each piece, nail it to the sheathing within 6 inches of the end. Then set the next piece, concealing the nailheads.

OPEN ROOFING FOR LIGHT AND SHADE

Nailing down slats.

◆ To provide a safe working platform on the roof, fasten a 2-by-4 toeboard along one edge of a plywood sheet, then tack the sheet to the rafters with 3-inch common nails.

◆ Starting at the roof peak, nail 1-by-2 slats across the rafters with $2\frac{1}{4}$-inch galvanized common nails. To ensure the slats are parallel and evenly spaced, fit a spare slat between the piece you are nailling down and the last one installed *(left)*.

◆ Move the platform as you work your way to the eaves; finish the job from a ladder.

Creating an egg-crate design.

◆ With a tape measure and combination square, mark locations for crosspieces on the rafters. A staggered pattern, as shown, makes for an eye-catching design.

◆ Cut the crosspieces from boards of the same dimensions as the rafters and face-nail the pieces to the rafters with $3\frac{1}{2}$-inch galvanized common nails.

HANGING LATTICE SIDING

THE ALLURE OF LATTICE

An attractive roofing or siding option that does not impede airflow, lattice enhances the quality of outdoor living. Overhead, the overlapping strips partially deflect the sun's rays while leaving a view of the sky intact. In the garden, lattice can also serve as a support for climbing plants, creating a living wall.

Lattice is not difficult to make, but the process is tedious. It is much easier to buy 4-by-8-foot ready-made sheets. The most economical and widely available choice is wooden lattice *(left)*. Made from cedar or a pressure-treated wood, it is attractive and long lasting, but fairly fragile. More expensive—and more durable—is PVC lattice *(right)*. Not only is this synthetic material nearly unbreakable, it will also look new for a long time. Some manufacturers offer a lifetime guarantee with their PVC products.

Installing lattice.

◆ Attach 1-by-1 or 1-by-2 nailing strips around the inside of the frame with $2\frac{1}{2}$-inch galvanized common nails.

◆ Trim the lattice to fit within the frame and secure it with 1-inch strips of molding and 2-inch galvanized finishing nails *(left)*. For a finished look, miter the ends of the molding strips.

Lightweight Sheathing Materials

Outdoor structures meant only for warm weather can be graced with a wide range of lightweight and inexpensive roofing and siding materials. Bamboo, woven reed, shade cloth, and corrugated plastic are suitable for structures like trellises and tree houses because they require minimal support and are attached quickly.

Shade cloth is particularly suitable for sheltering shade-loving plants. It is available in a variety of weaves that admit different amounts of light. Woven reed and bamboo are normally employed to cover outdoor living spaces.

Shade Cloth: The easiest of these materials to install is shade cloth made of synthetic fiber; the polypropylene type is durable and lightweight. Shade cloth must be specially ordered through a nursery or garden shop, which will cut it to size, reinforce the sides, and install grommets to your specifications. Order the cloth so the finished size is 2 inches less all around than your roof *(below)*. Ask for reinforced edges and No. 2 brass grommets.

Corrugated Panels: Corrugated plastic panels are more difficult to install. Furring strips must first be nailed to the rafters and special filler strips attached at the top and bottom—but they do provide rain protection. They should be installed on a roof with a minimum pitch of 1 inch to 1 foot or, in a snowfall area, a pitch of at least 3 inches to 1 foot.

Make sure that any wood you purchase to mount your sheathing is pressure-treated.

TOOLS

- Hammer
- Pliers
- Heavy-duty shears
- Circular saw
- Abrasive blade
- Electric drill
- Heavy-duty stapler
- Handsaw
- Wire cutters

MATERIALS

- 1x1s, 2x2s
- Lumber for fascia, cross supports
- Galvanized common nails (2", $3\frac{1}{2}$")
- Roofing nails ($1\frac{3}{4}$") with rubber washers
- Galvanized wood screws (3" No. 8)
- Screw eyes (2")
- Galvanized wire

SAFETY TIPS

Wear goggles when drilling, hammering, or stapling. Wear gloves when handling pressure-treated wood; add a dust mask when cutting it.

A SHADE CLOTH COVER

Lacing a shade cloth

◆ Install 2-inch screw eyes at the corners of the roof, stretch the cloth across its opening, and tie the corner grommets to the screw eyes with good-quality nylon cord.
◆ Position screw eyes around the perimeter of the roof, aligning them with the grommets in the cloth.
◆ Tie one end of a length of cord to a corner screw eye and lace the other end through the grommet at the same corner. Continue feeding the cord through all the screw eyes and grommets on one side of the roof, tightening the cord just enough to remove the slack *(left)*.
◆ Lace the opposite side the same way, working with a helper to tighten the cord on both sides and keep the fabric centered on the roof. Tie the cord to the last corner screw eye.
◆ Lace the remaining sides the same way.

ROOFING WITH WOVEN REED

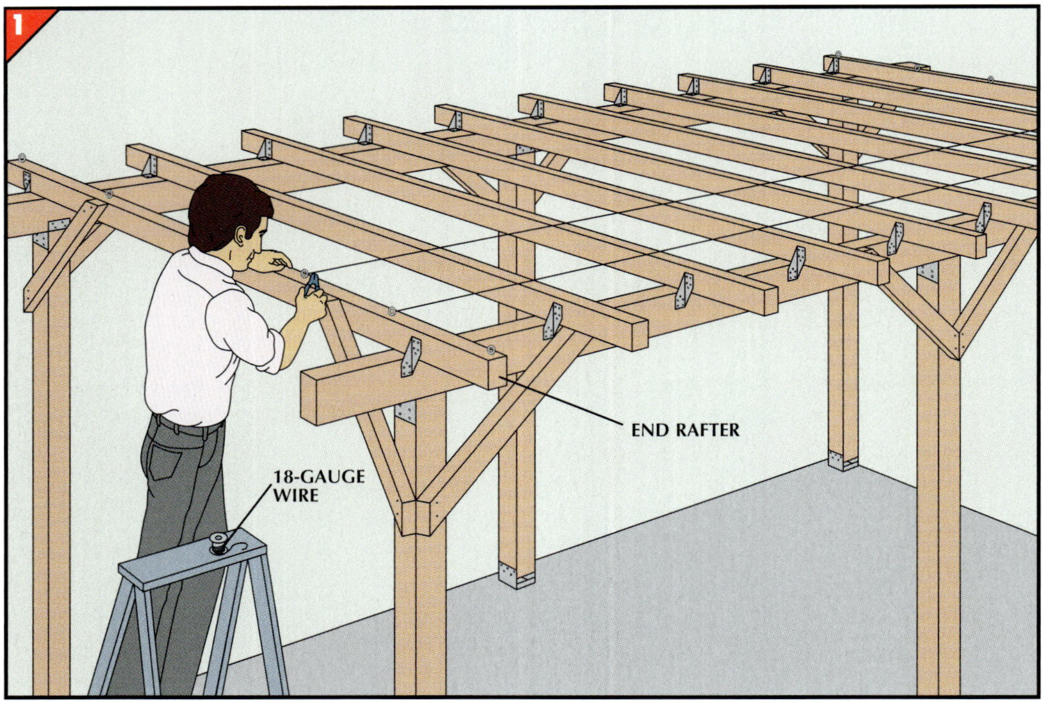

1. Wiring the frame.

◆ Place 2-inch screw eyes about every 20 inches along the tops of the end rafters, making sure opposite screw eyes align.

◆ With pliers, secure a length of galvanized 18-gauge wire to each screw eye on one end rafter.

◆ Stretch the wires across the roof and pull them taut. Secure each length to the screw eye on the opposite rafter *(left)*.

2. Securing the reed.

◆ Set the woven reed panels on your wire frame, overlapping them by at least 2 inches or more. Trim the panels to size with heavy-duty shears, if necessary.

◆ Place 1-by-1s along the seams between the panels. At every second rafter, fasten the 1-by-1s to the panels with 22-gauge wire threaded through the reeds and around the wire frame *(above)*.

FASTENING WOVEN REED SIDING

1. Preparing the frame.
Build a frame of 2-by-2s to support the reed panels.
◆ Position 2-by-2s against the posts; on the end posts, set them flush with the outside edges *(inset)*, but run them down the center of the remaining posts. After drilling clearance holes, fasten the 2-by-2s in place with 3-inch galvanized No. 8 wood screws.
◆ Cut three more 2-by-2s to fit across the top, middle, and bottom of each opening formed by the 2-by-2s on the posts. Drill two clearance holes at each end of the boards.
◆ Holding a 2-by-2 in position, screw it to the posts *(above)*.

2. Attaching the woven reed siding.
◆ Cut the woven reed so it will sit flush with the outside edges of the frame you installed in Step 1.
◆ With a helper holding the reed in position, staple the top corner to the frame *(above)*. Drive staples at 6-inch intervals around the reed, keeping it square as you go.

BAMBOO AND REED SHADES

Bamboo and reed shades hung from beams can be raised for airiness and lowered for privacy. Available from home decorating centers, the shades typically are screwed to the beams, positioned so they hang in front of the openings between posts. These products also provide protection against moderate wind and rain. In tempestuous weather, however, it is advisable to roll the shades up.

A TRANSLUCENT RAINPROOF ROOF

1. Attaching filler strips.

◆ Install a fascia board the same dimensions as the rafters to the lower ends of the rafters with $3\frac{1}{2}$-inch galvanized common nails. Fasten cross supports between the rafters at 3-foot intervals.

◆ Nail scalloped wooden filler strips across the tops of the fascia board and cross supports with 2-inch nails *(right)*. To ensure that the plastic panels fit properly, keep the filler strips aligned.

◆ Cut half-round filler strips to fit on the rafters between the scalloped filler strips and fasten them in place.

2. Installing the panels.

◆ Trim the panels to length with a circular saw equipped with an abrasive blade.

◆ Working on a calm, windless day, position a panel on the roof so one end overlaps the fascia board and one edge overlaps an edge of the roof.

◆ Drill holes $\frac{1}{16}$ inch larger than $1\frac{3}{4}$-inch washered roofing nails *(photograph)* through the panels' crowns. Starting at the outside edge *(above)*, drill through every second crown at 12- to 15-inch intervals along the fascia, cross supports, and the upper crossbeam. Do not drill through the last crown on the inside edge.

◆ Nail the panel to the filler strips. If you are sheathing a gable roof, add a ridge piece to the peak before driving the top row of nails.

◆ Position the next panel, overlapping the first one by one ridge. Align the bottom ends of the panels, and drill nail holes through both pieces at the same time.

◆ Lift the second panel, apply the adhesive supplied to the underside of the last ridge of the first panel, and drive the nails.

◆ Install the remaining panels the same way, maintaining the same overlap throughout the procedure.

Screening for an Outdoor Structure

Covering an outdoor structure with screening is an attractive compromise between openness to the outdoors and protection from the elements. Screens let air circulate but bar insects and, to some extent, soften the glare of sunlight. Moreover, they are simple and inexpensive to assemble, and they fulfill their role for years without requiring maintenance.

Types of Screening: Most screening is either aluminum or fiberglass. Aluminum screens corrode in salt air, but resist tearing better than fiberglass and are easier to pull taut. Both materials come in packaged rolls in widths up to 48 inches and lengths up to 72 inches. Longer pieces can be cut to order by most building-supply dealers.

Installing Screening: The easiest way to attach screening is to staple it to the wood framing of a wall or roof. Have a helper hold the screen taut at one end as you drive the staples. Then nail molding over the edges of the screening to cover the staples. A stronger and more permanent solution is a special screening system like the one shown on page 194.

Frames for Screens: Another option involves fastening screening to a frame that can be attached to and easily removed from the structure, much like a window screen. These frames can be made of 1-by-4s, but aluminum ones, constructed from special channeling and connectors, are simpler to build.

Sections of aluminum screen frame, designed to be cut to size and snapped together over right-angle fasteners, are available in lengths up to 8 feet. They generally come with a spline—a length of rubber or vinyl tubing that clamps the screening inside a groove along the edges of a frame. To set the spline into the frame, you need a screen-spline roller, available from screening suppliers. The maximum size for a screening frame, whether wood or metal, is 4 feet by 8 feet. For larger areas, build several frames and install them in tandem.

TOOLS

- Hand stapler
- Hammer
- Screwdriver
- Utility knife
- Heavy-duty shears or tin snips
- Hacksaw
- C-clamps
- Screen-spline roller

MATERIALS

- 1x1s
- 1x4s
- $\frac{3}{4}$" quarter-round molding
- Galvanized finishing nails ($1\frac{1}{2}$")
- Aluminum or fiberglass screening
- Aluminum screen frame and fasteners
- Screen spline
- Turn buttons

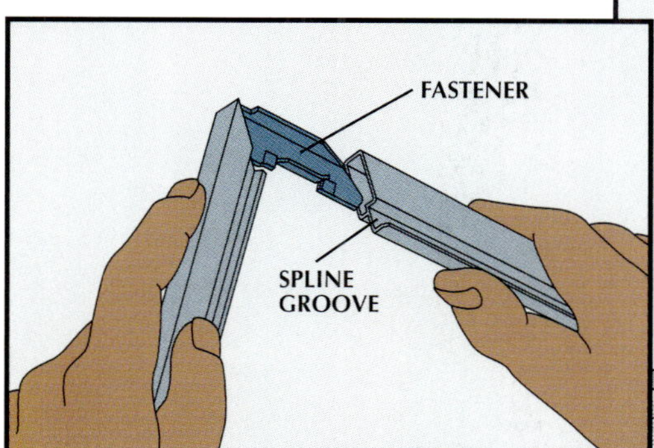

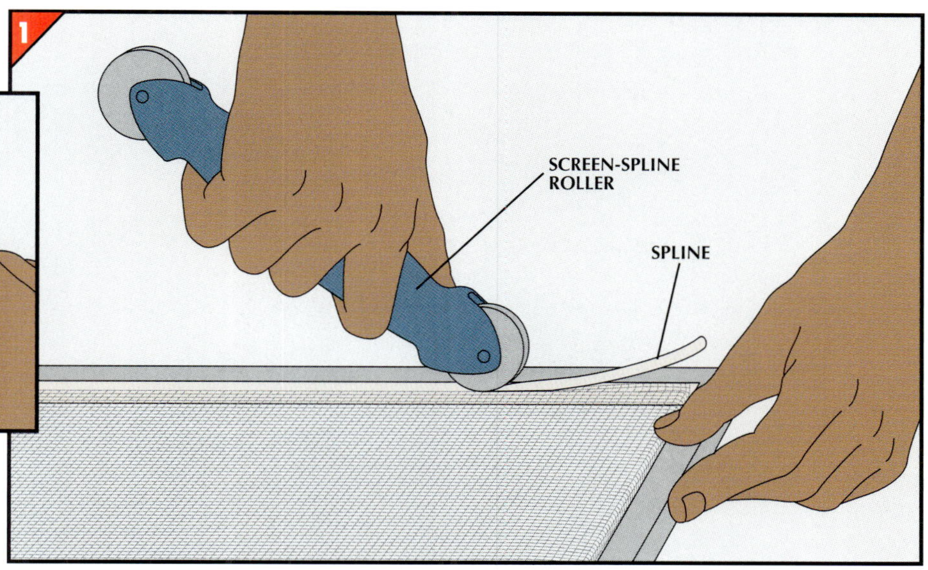

1. Making a screen frame.

◆ Miter the ends of each frame section at 45 degrees with a hacksaw. To form the corners of the frame, slip mating ends over a right-angle fastener *(inset)*.

◆ Cut the screening slightly larger than the frame with heavy-duty shears or tin snips, slicing the corners at 45 degrees to prevent bunching. With a helper holding the screen in place, crease the screen into the frame grooves with the convex wheel of a spline roller.

◆ Secure the screening to one side of the frame with C-clamps, protecting it with wood pads.

◆ Pull the screen taut to the opposite side and secure it, pressing the screen-spline into the groove with the concave wheel of the roller *(above)*.

◆ Secure the remaining sides the same way, then trim the excess screening with a utility knife.

2. Hanging the screen.

The screen is held in its opening by $\frac{3}{4}$-inch quarter-round molding or 1-by-1 strips coupled with turn buttons.

◆ Attach the molding or strips with $1\frac{1}{2}$-inch galvanized finishing nails so the frame will be flush with the inside or outside of opening.

◆ To lock the frame in place, install turn buttons, screwing them to the edges of the structure *(inset)*.

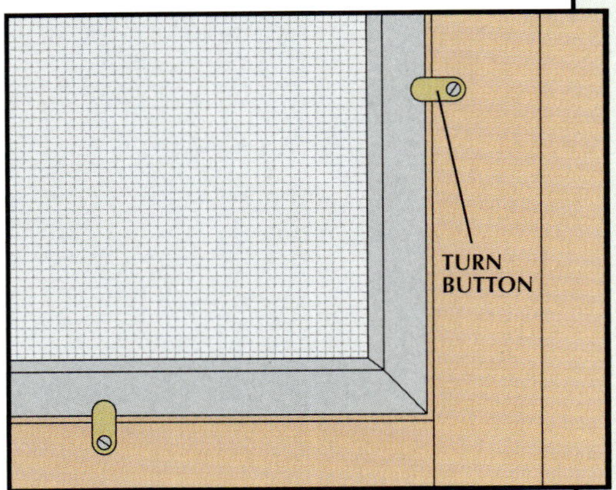

SCREENING THAT COMES FRAMED

Convenient and readily available, screening systems combine the advantages of two screen installation methods. Like screening frames, they are held in grooves by screen-splines, facilitating removal for repairs or tightening. But since they are attached directly to the framing of the structure, they maximize the screen area.

The system is quite simple. A base with two grooves is screwed to the framing. Screening is secured with standard screen-splines, then a cover is snapped in place.

The base and cover for the style shown come in strips that can be cut with a pair of heavy-duty shears.

Wooden Floors for Comfort

Some structures—A-frames, tree houses, and gazebos—depend on floors for support. Others (like the post-and-beam structure shown below) do not need floors because they rest on a concrete slab or below-ground footings. But you can cover bare ground with gravel or sand. To provide a dry and ventilated surface for walking or for storage, a wood floor may be desirable.

Two Types of Floor: For a permanent floor, build an understructure as shown. For a removable floor, build portable deck modules, called duckboards, which rest on the ground or on a slab.

Make the deck surface from pressure-treated 2-by-4s or 2-by-6s spaced $\frac{1}{8}$ inch apart for good drainage. The boards are normally nailed to 2-by-6 or 2-by-8 joists spaced 16 inches on center.

If any of the floorboards is cupped, install it hollow-side down to help prevent water from pool ing on the floor.

TOOLS

Tape measure
Chalk line
Hammer
Wrench
Handsaw
Circular saw
1x3 guide
Electric drill

MATERIALS

2x4 or 2x6 floorboards
2x6 or 2x8 beams and joists
Plywood cleats ($\frac{3}{4}$")
Galvanized common nails ($2\frac{1}{2}$", 3", $3\frac{1}{2}$")
Lag screws ($\frac{3}{8}$"x$3\frac{1}{2}$") and washers
Joist hangers and nails

SAFETY TIPS

Wear goggles when sawing or hammering. Wear gloves when handling pressure-treated wood; add a dust mask when cutting it.

LAYING A PERMANENT WOOD FLOOR

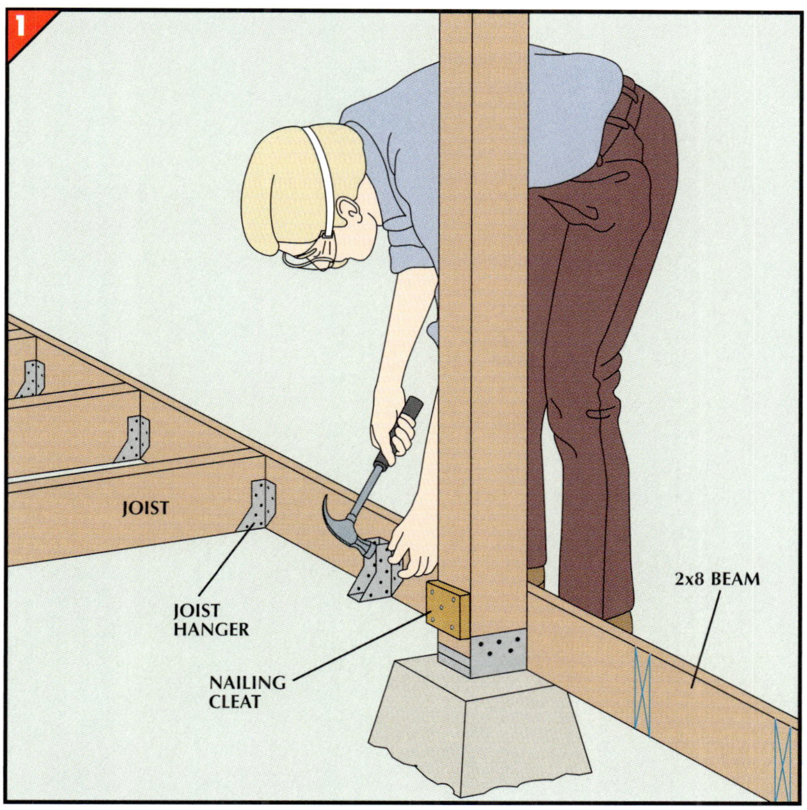

1. Building the understructure.

- Attach 2-by-8 beams to the outsides of the posts with $\frac{3}{8}$-by-$3\frac{1}{2}$-inch lag screws.
- Mark joist positions every 16 inches along the beams.
- With $2\frac{1}{2}$-inch galvanized common nails, attach $\frac{3}{4}$-inch plywood nailing cleats to the posts level with the beams so the cleats will support the deck boards.
- Secure joist hangers to the beams with joist hanger nails *(left)*, then attach the joists to the hangers.
- From joist lumber cut bridging boards to fit between joists. Fasten the bridging with $3\frac{1}{2}$-inch nails, offsetting the boards for ease of nailing.

2. Fastening the floorboards.

◆ Notch floorboards with a handsaw, as necessary, to fit around the posts.
◆ Fasten the first row of boards flush with the beam edge and extending at least 2 inches beyond the understructure, driving two 3-inch nails at each joist position.
◆ Nail down the rest of the floor, spacing boards $\frac{1}{8}$ inch apart. Extend each row at least 2 inches beyond the understructure. Center any end-to-end joints between boards over a joist.
◆ To ensure the edge of the last board is flush with the beam, adjust the spacing between the last 3 feet of boards *(right)*—or trim $\frac{1}{4}$ inch off the edge of one or more boards—as necessary.

3. Trimming the board ends.

◆ Mark the ends of the boards with a chalk line.
◆ Align the blade of your circular saw with the chalk line, butt a 1-by-3 against the base plate, and tack the strip to the deck boards as a cutting guide.
◆ Trim the first 12 inches with a handsaw—the power saw's motor will keep the blade from reaching any closer to the post—then cut along the chalk line with a circular saw *(left)* until the saw contacts the far post. Keep the saw base plate flush against the cutting guide throughout.
◆ Finish the job with a handsaw.

PUTTING TOGETHER A PORTABLE PLATFORM

Making duckboard decking.

◆ Measure the length and width of your structure and calculate the quantity and size of duckboards you will need. The usual size is around 3 to 4 foot square.
◆ Build an understructure by butt-nailing pressure-treated 2-by-4s with $3\frac{1}{2}$-inch nails.
◆ Face-nail 2-by-6 boards onto the frame, spacing them $\frac{1}{4}$ inch apart.
◆ Adjust spacing of the last few boards so that the outermost board fits the end of the frame precisely.

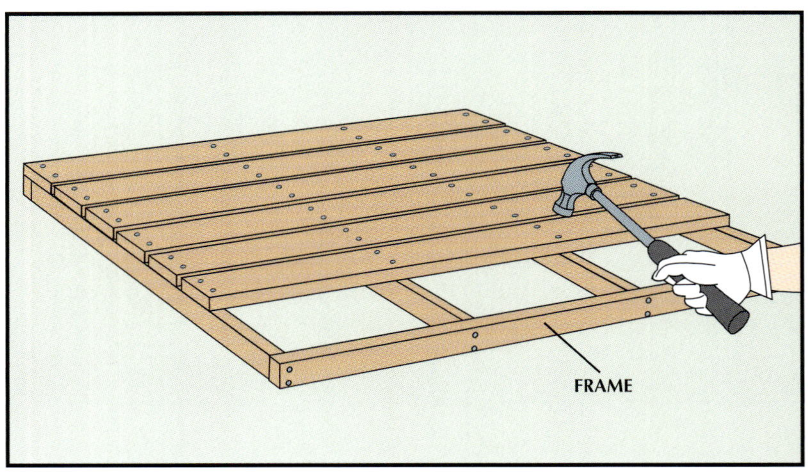

A Tree Bench

This bench is a tree hugger's delight. As a secluded place for reading or reflection, it can double as a stand for potted plants or even serve as a picnic table. Its hexagonal design blends well with almost any architectural setting.

Planning Construction: Try to situate a tree bench on fairly level ground. On a slope, one side will be too close to the ground while the opposite side will be too high.

The bench shown below features an opening of 19 inches, easily fitting a tree about 1 foot in diameter or smaller. You can enlarge the opening in 1-inch increments simply by making the seat boards $\frac{9}{16}$ inch longer. Bear in mind that the lengths of the spokes and seat supports remain the same.

Building the Bench: Construct the bench in two halves using pressure-treated wood, then assemble it on site around the tree. Level the bench by trial and error. Set it in place and dig earth from under high spots or shim the legs above low spots with flagstones.

TOOLS

Tape measure
T-bevel
Protractor
Straightedge
Hammer
C-clamps
Handsaw
Circular saw
Electric drill

MATERIALS

1x2s, 1x4s
2x2s, 2x4s, 2x6s
4x4s
$\frac{3}{4}$" plywood
Common nails ($1\frac{1}{4}$")
Galvanized common nails (2", 3")
Galvanized finishing nails (2", 3")
Galvanized wood screws ($2\frac{3}{4}$", 3" No. 8)
Post anchors

SAFETY TIPS

Wear goggles when hammering or operating a power saw. Wear gloves when handling pressure-treated wood; add a dust mask when cutting it.

Anatomy of a tree bench

The bench shown at right consists of six wedges that form a hexagon around a tree. Each wedge is made from seven pieces: three 2-by-6 seat boards, two 2-by-2 supports, a 1-by-4 trim piece, and a 1-by-4 faceplate. All the parts have both ends sawn at a 60-degree angle. The bench is supported by 4-by-4 posts.

In the diagram, the length of the seat boards refers to their longest edge.

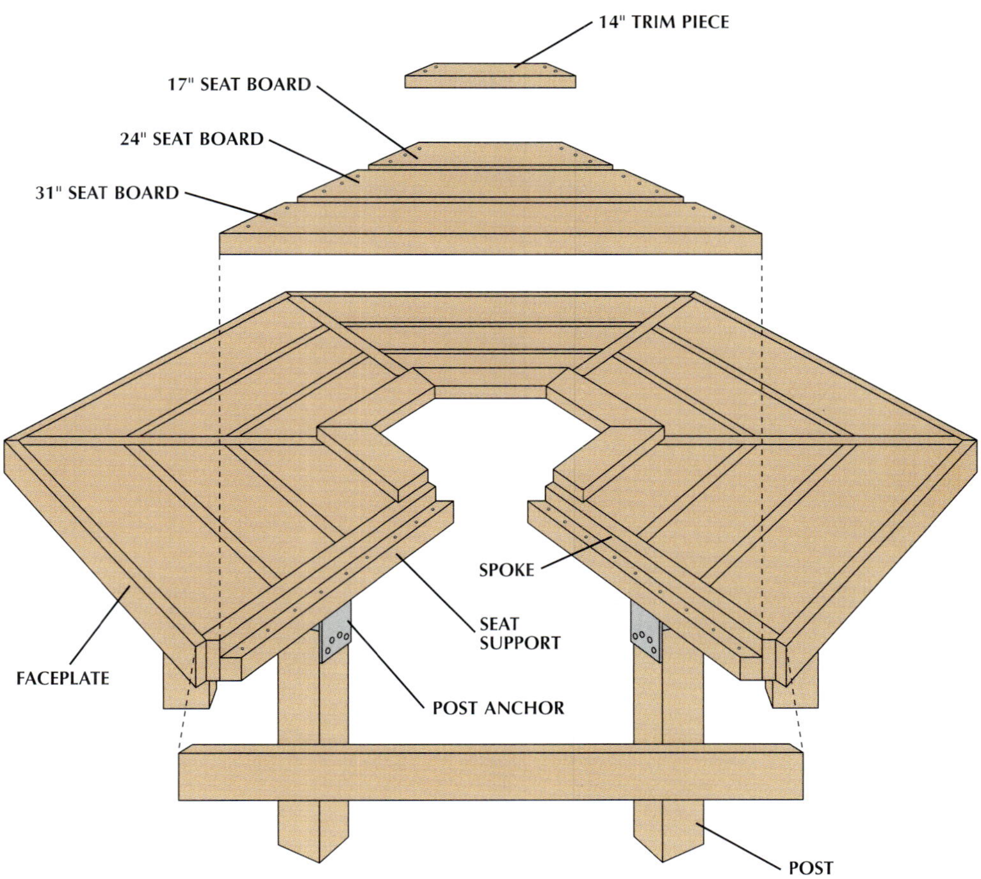

CUTTING THE SEAT BOARDS

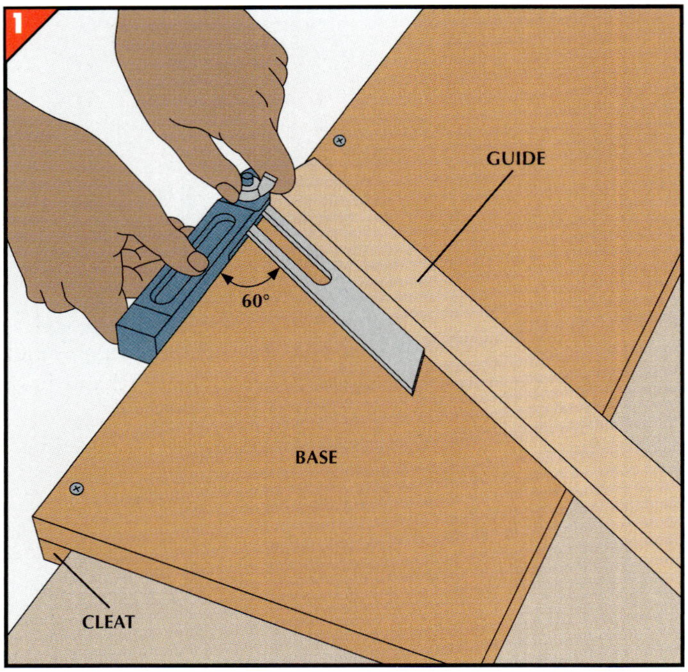

1. Making the cutting jig.

Make a cutting jig by securing a 1-by-2 guide to a $\frac{3}{4}$-inch plywood base at least 9 inches wide and 30 inches long.

◆ Attach a 1-by-2 cleat along the underside of the base, flush with the longer edge.

◆ Set a T-bevel to 60 degrees, then set it on the base with the apex of the angle 10 inches from one end.

◆ Place a 12-inch-long 1-by-2 against the bevel *(left)*.

◆ Holding the guide firmly in position, tack it to the base with $1\frac{1}{4}$-inch common nails.

◆ Clamp the base to a work surface with its end extending past the edge. Run a circular saw along the guide to trim the end of the base.

2. Mitering one end of the seat boards.

◆ Sandwich a 2-by-6 between the jig and a scrap board, and clamp the assembly to a work surface so that one edge of the 2-by-6 is flush against the cleat.

◆ Adjust the cutting depth of your circular saw so the blade will cut into but not through the scrap board.

◆ Riding the saw base plate along the 1-by-2 guide, trim one end of the seat board *(right)*.

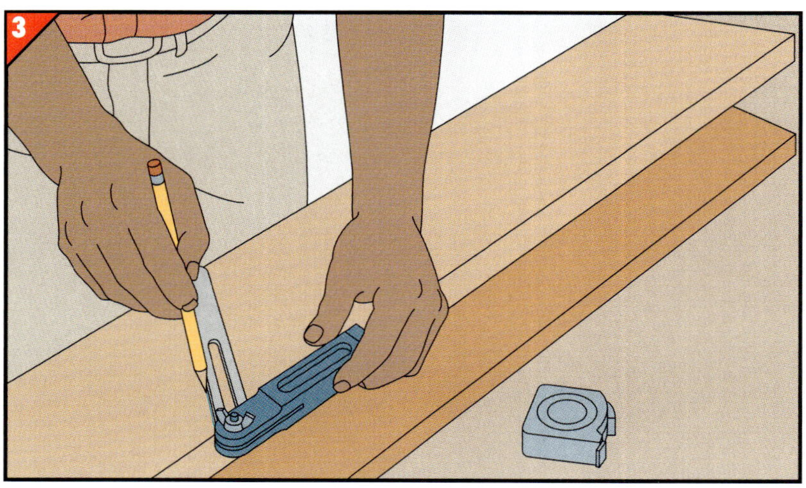

3. Marking and cutting the other ends.

◆ Remove the jig and turn the 2-by-6 over.

◆ Measuring along the board's long edge, mark the length of the seat board, guided by a T-bevel to maintain the 60-degree angle *(left)*.

◆ Repeat the cut described in Step 1 to trim the other end of the seat board.

BUILDING BENCH SECTIONS

1. Assembling sections.

◆ Lay out the three boards that form a seat, leaving a $\frac{3}{4}$-inch gap between them.
◆ Cut two 2-by-2 seat supports to length, angling their front ends at 60 degrees.
◆ Mark lines $\frac{7}{8}$ inch in from the ends of each seatboard and start six 3-inch galvanized finishing nails into each seat board along the marked lines *(left)*.
◆ Starting with the longest piece, nail the seat boards to the seat supports. Maintain the $\frac{3}{4}$-inch gap between the seat boards and position them so they are flush with the supports along the sides and at the front.

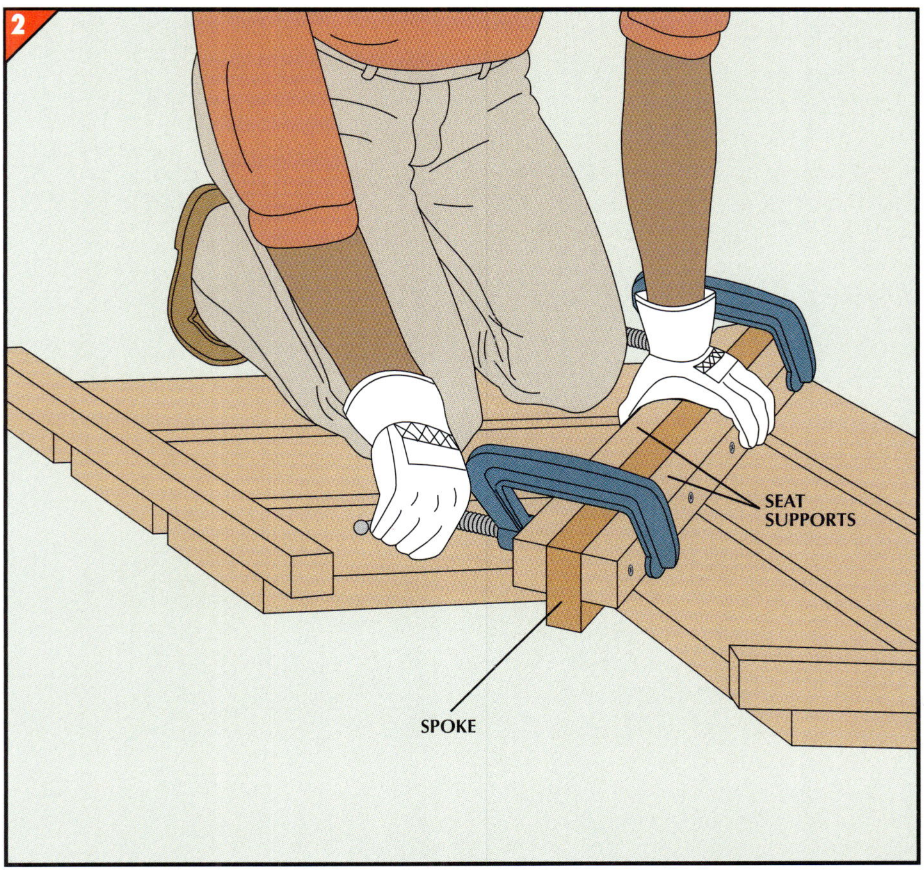

2. Joining seat sections.

◆ Drill clearance holes through the seat supports.
◆ To fashion the spokes, cut six 2-by-4s slightly longer than the width of the seat sections.
◆ Place two sections face-down on a flat surface and clamp a spoke between adjoining seat supports, aligning the ends of the spoke and supports at the back of the seat *(right)*.
◆ Fasten the supports to the spoke with $2\frac{3}{4}$-inch No. 8 galvanized wood screws.
◆ Continue joining seat sections with spokes until half the bench is assembled. Build the other half this way.

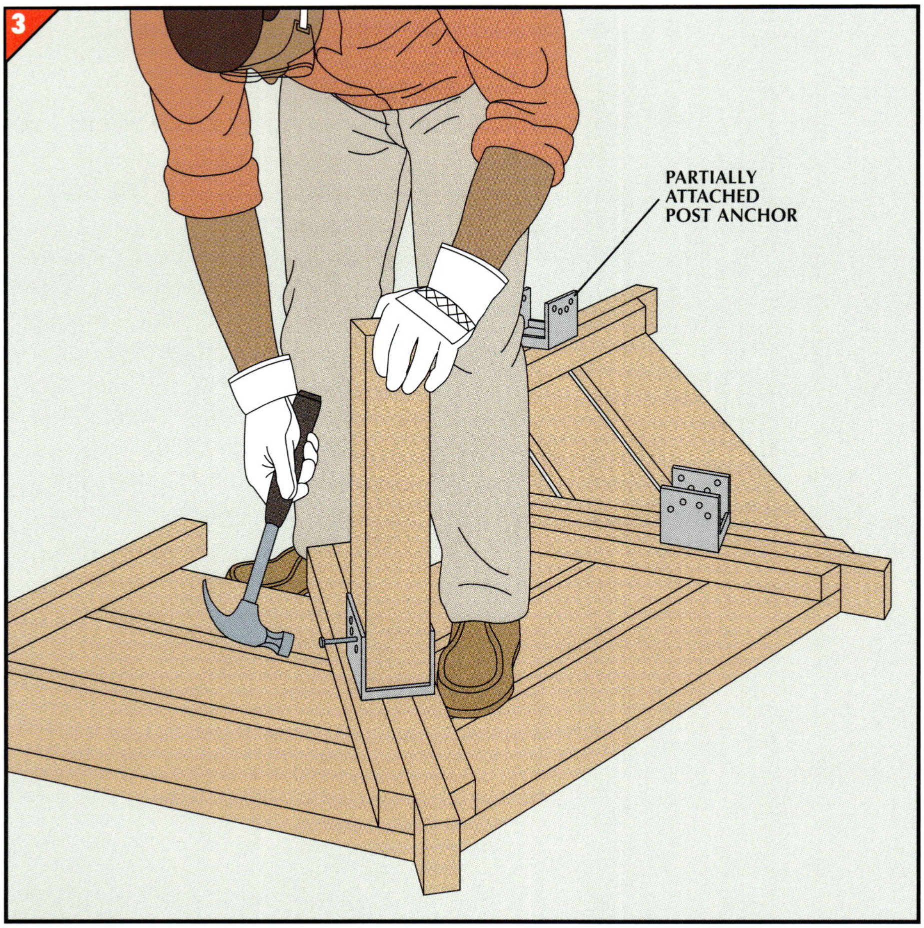

3. Attaching the posts.

◆ Attach post anchors to the seat supports with 3-inch galvanized common nails, centering the anchors on the spokes 15 inches from the inside end of the seat. The anchors at the edges of the bench section can only be secured to one seat support for now.

◆ Cut six 15-inch-long 4-by-4s for posts.

◆ Nail a post to each anchor that has been fastened to both of its seat supports. Hold the post upright as you drive the nails *(left)*. Install the remaining posts after you join the bench halves.

ASSEMBLING THE BENCH

1. Joining the bench halves.

◆ Position the two halves around the tree, align the sections, and clamp them together.

◆ Fasten the bench sections together with 3-inch galvanized No. 8 screws.

◆ Finish attaching the partially fastened post anchors and nail the remaining posts to their anchors *(right)*.

2. Attaching the trim pieces.

◆ Measure the distance between the centers of two adjoining spokes and cut the six trim pieces to this measurement, mitering their ends at 60 degrees. Arrange the boards around the inside of the bench.

◆ Mark the outside edge of each piece on the bench *(left)* to help you reposition the boards for nailing.

◆ Attach each trim board with 2-inch galvanized common nails.

3. Trimming the spokes.

◆ With a straightedge, extend a line from the outside edge of the seat across the top of each spoke, forming V-shaped cutting lines.

◆ Trim the ends of the spokes with a handsaw, cutting along the marked lines *(right)*.

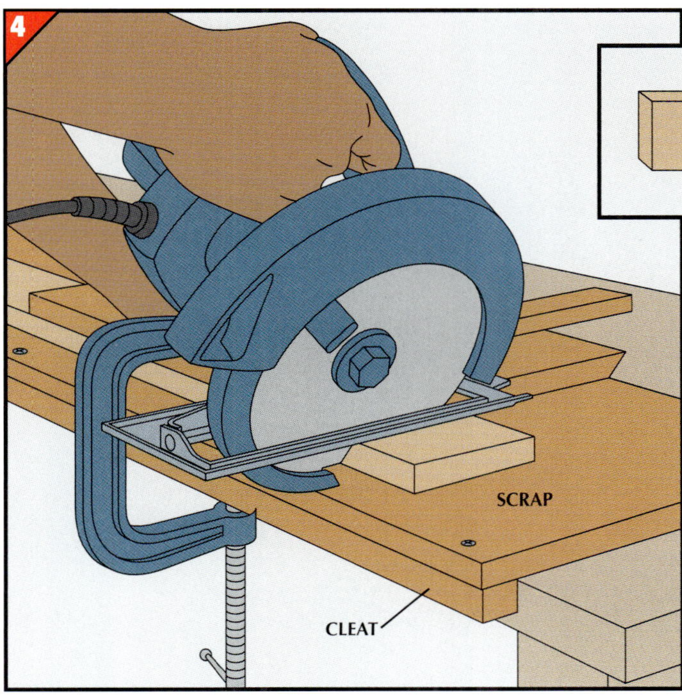

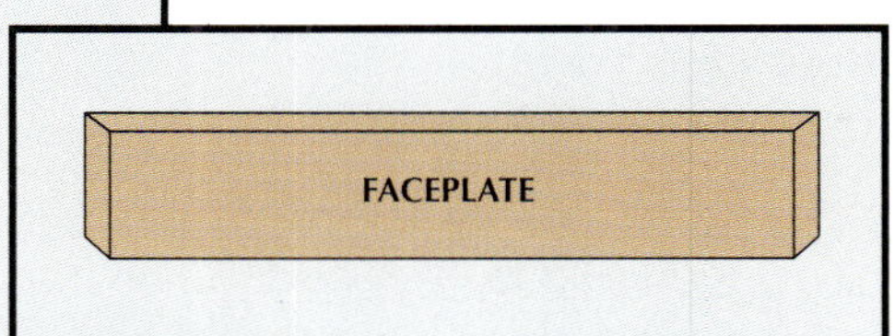

4. Installing the faceplates.

◆ Determine the length of the faceplates by measuring the distance between spoke ends.

◆ Adapt the instructions on page 198 to build a 90-degree-angle cutting guide.

◆ Adjust the cutting angle of a circular saw to cut a 60-degree bevel.

◆ Cut the faceplates as you did the seat supports *(left)*, clamping 1-by-4s in the guide and riding the circular saw base plate along the guide strip. Make sure the ends are beveled as in the inset.

◆ Fasten the faceplates to the seat supports, spoke ends, and seat boards with 2-inch galvanized finishing nails.

Building a Cold Frame for Seedlings

Cold frames are miniature greenhouses for seedlings. By shielding tender plants from spring frosts while permitting the sun to warm the air and soil beneath its hinged glass or plastic top, a cold frame lets keen gardeners get a jump on the growing season.

Building the Frame: For the cold frame's top, recycle an old storm window or build a frame of 2-by-2s with a plastic "window." Make the cold frame from either rot-resistant or pressure-treated wood. For the latter, check that the preservative employed is safe for plants.

Slope the side walls of the frame from a height of 12 inches at the back to $5\frac{1}{2}$ inches in front. Paint the interior of the frame white so it will reflect the sunlight and heat. Install a prop to hold the top open during hot spells—a temperature above 70 degrees inside the frame could harm the seedlings.

Positioning the Frame: Situate the frame so the window faces south and slants toward the noon sun. To prevent the frame from losing heat on frosty nights, drape a tarpaulin over it in the evening or pile leaves or straw around it.

TOOLS

- Tape measure
- Combination square
- C-clamps
- Maul
- Shovel
- Jack plane
- Circular saw or saber saw
- Electric drill
- Screwdriver bit

MATERIALS

- 1x2s
- 2x2s, 2x6s, 2x12s
- Storm window
- $\frac{1}{2}$" dowels
- Galvanized wood screws (3" No. 8)
- Butt hinges
- Wood glue (exterior)

SAFETY TIPS

Wear gloves when handling pressure-treated wood; add a dust mask when cutting it.

1. Preparing the frame pieces.

◆ For a side piece mark a line along the length of a 2-by-12 $5\frac{1}{2}$ inches from one edge. Set a window sash on the board as shown so that one corner touches the line and the other extends $\frac{1}{4}$ inch beyond the board's corner. Run a pencil along the edge of the sash to mark the slope *(right)*.

◆ To indicate the front end of the side piece, make a mark across the board through the point where the two lines intersect.

◆ Secure the board to a work surface, then cut at the slope and the front end marks with a circular saw or saber saw.

◆ Using this as a template, mark and cut the other side.

◆ For the back and front pieces, cut a 2-by-12 and a 2-by-6 3 inches shorter than the length of the window sash.

2. Assembling the frame.

◆ Fasten the side pieces to the front and back with 3-inch galvanized No. 8 wood screws.
◆ Plane the top edges of the front and back pieces to match the side slope.
◆ To anchor the frame in the ground, dig a 2-inch trench in the soil, sink the frame in place, then drive 2-by-2 stakes (12-inch stakes at the front and 18-inch stakes at the back) at the inside corners with a maul *(left)*. Screw the frame to the stakes.
◆ Attach the sash to the back of the frame with butt hinges.

GETTING THE MOST FROM A GREENHOUSE KIT

The easiest, most economical way to grace your property with a full-scale greenhouse is to buy one in kit form. Kit models range from compact units, 4 feet by 6 feet, to structures that enclose areas as large as 1,000 square feet.

The least expensive greenhouse kits contain parts of lightweight aluminum and rest on a frame of pressure-treated 4-by-4s. This type of greenhouse is covered with a plastic film and is often regarded as temporary.

More expensive greenhouses are often permanent, secured with appropriate foundations and relying on tempered glass instead of plastic coverings. These structures are often equipped with some form of automatic climate control and ventilation.

Almost all greenhouses need devices to keep the temperature within a limited range. Greenhouse manufacturers and garden-supply stores sell heaters, coolers, and automatic ventilators, but you can keep heating and cooling costs down by locating your greenhouse with its long axis running east and west, ideally underneath a large deciduous tree. This will keep it cool in the summer but give it full winter sunlight, when the leaves have fallen and the sun is low.

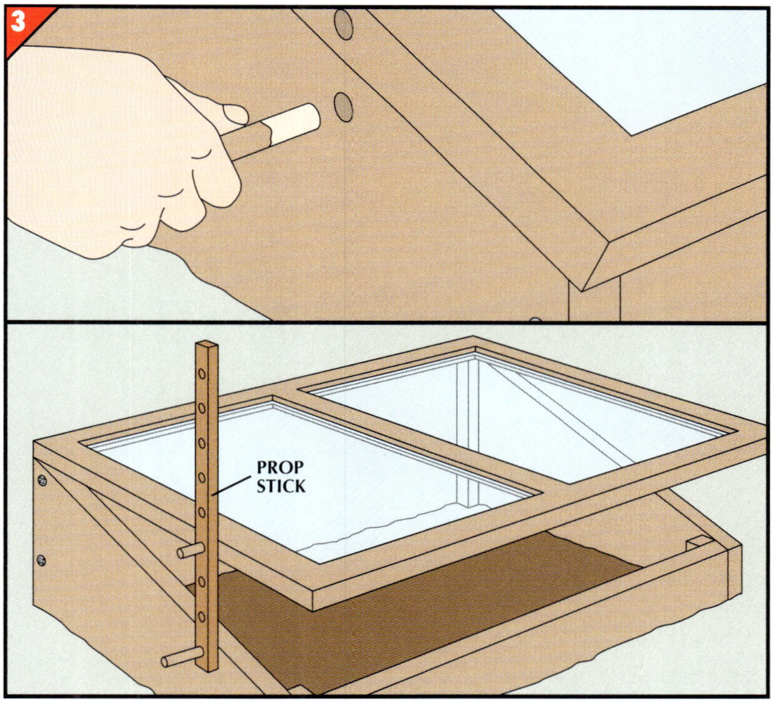

3. Rigging prop sticks.

◆ Bore a $\frac{1}{2}$-inch diameter hole into each edge of the sash about 8 inches from the front of the frame. To avoid drilling into the glass or plastic, make the holes no deeper than $\frac{1}{2}$ inch. Bore holes directly below these through the frame sides.
◆ Glue a $\frac{1}{2}$-inch-diameter dowel into each hole *(above, top)*.
◆ Make two prop sticks from 24-inch-long 1-by-2s, drilling a row of $\frac{9}{16}$-inch holes through them at 2-inch intervals.
◆ Slip the sticks over the dowels to hold the sash open as desired *(above, bottom)*.

6 A Roomy All-Purpose Outbuilding

The building featured in this chapter can be adapted for many uses. In its simplest form, it can serve as a convenient place to store yard and garden tools. Incorporate a door and a concrete floor in your design to upgrade the structure into a two-car garage. Add a few windows for sunlight and fresh air to transform this simple building into a studio or workshop.

Attaching a batter board to a stake →

A Versatile Structure

Large outbuildings like the one shown below can serve as garages, storage areas, studios, workshops, or some combination of all of these. Almost any purpose can be accommodated except living quarters. Each use, however, has requirements that should be considered early in the planning process.

A garage needs a driveway, walkways, a main entrance, and perhaps a side door. The floor must be sloped for drainage. For garden storage, include a door that provides easy access to the garden. A studio or shop should have windows, and possibly a loft for storage. If you need electricity and water, consult your local utility companies about preparing the structure for their installation.

Planning the Construction: Draw a floor plan of the building on a map of your property to ensure it is located at least as far from the house and the property lines as local codes require. Then sketch front and side views of the building on graph paper to determine whether the building will harmonize with the main house and surrounding property. You will probably need a building permit. Bring along your diagrams and sketches, and be prepared to describe the type of foundation, wall construction, and roof design that you propose. Some localities require a soil test to determine whether it will support the proposed structure. And set up an inspection schedule well in advance so that work will not be delayed.

CAUTION *Before excavating, establish the locations of underground obstacles such as electric, water, and sewer lines, and dry wells, septic tanks, and cesspools.*

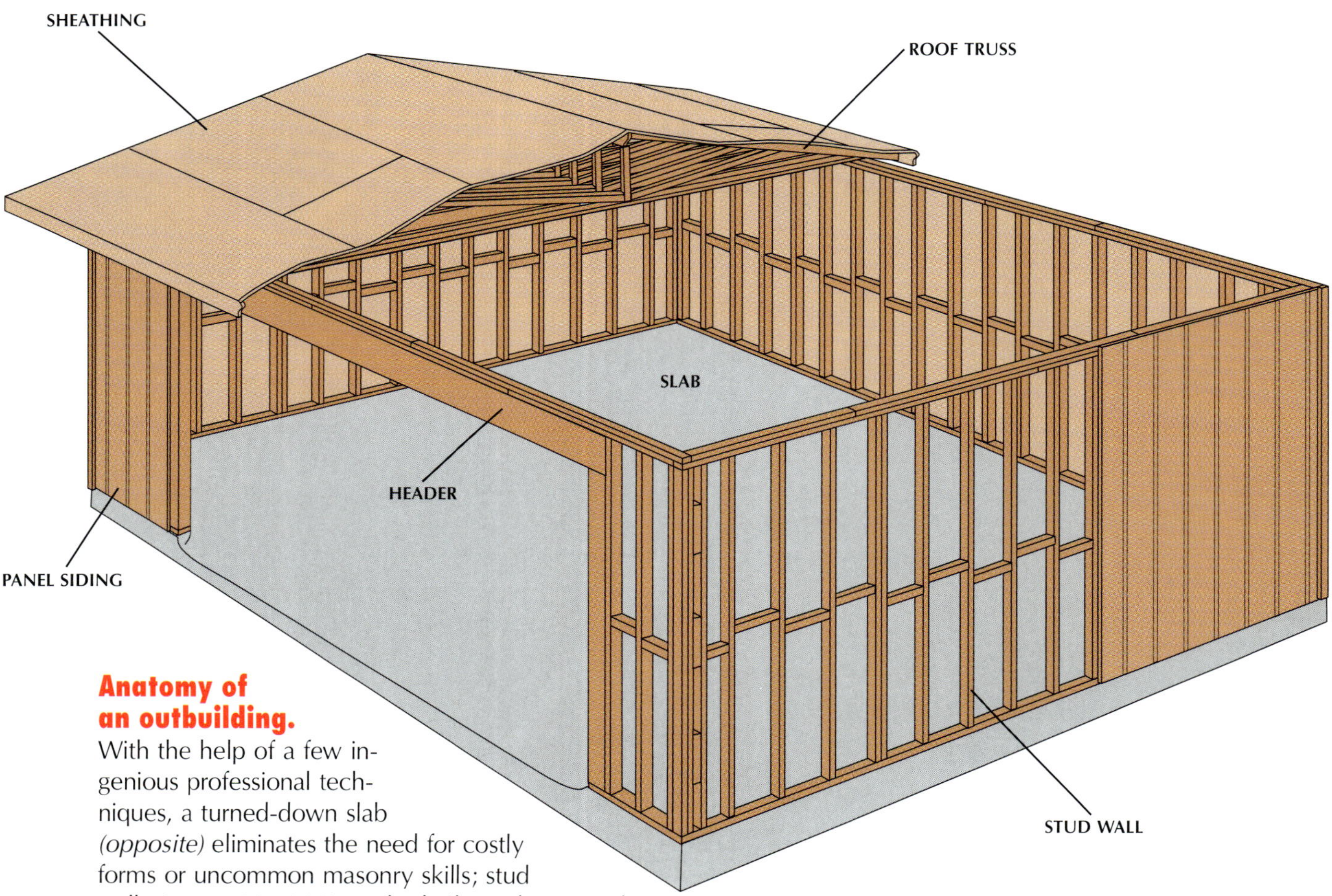

Anatomy of an outbuilding. With the help of a few ingenious professional techniques, a turned-down slab *(opposite)* eliminates the need for costly forms or uncommon masonry skills; stud walls *(pages 214-218)* can be built on the ground and erected as units; and prefabricated trusses *(page 220)*, which require no tricky rafter cuts or a ridge beam, make the installation of a sloping roof a simple assembly process.

Laying a Concrete Slab Foundation

For a sizable building, the simplest base is a turned-down slab—a concrete slab with its edges set in trenches. The rim serves the same function as poured footings or a foundation wall of concrete block.

The turned-down slab has its limitations, however. It requires trenches little wider than a shovel blade, but deep enough to meet footing requirements for your area—which may be impossible in regions where frost penetrates deeper than 2 feet. The concrete in the trenches must be reinforced by rebar; check your building code for the correct size. If your local building department advises against a turned-down slab, use a deep concrete footing like those described on pages 157 and 163.

Preparing for Construction: Plan an expedient route for the heavy trucks bringing in materials and concrete. On the job itself, save time and work more effectively with rented professional tools. A transit level enables you to establish lines and angles quickly and accurately. A power tamper helps compact the soil before the concrete is poured; a power troweler speeds the job of finishing the concrete.

Creating a Slant: The structure shown on these pages has a sloped floor. The forms are installed level, then a long notch is cut out along the door opening to lower it 1 inch for every 8 feet from the back wall. While the concrete is still wet, it can be shaped to slope toward the door.

TOOLS

Tape measure
Carpenter's level
Water level
Transit level
Hammer
Maul
Handsaw
Circular saw
Rebar cutter
Electric drill
Shovels
Power tamper
Mason's hoe
Bull float
Power troweler

MATERIALS

1x2s, 1x6s
2x4s, 2x8s
$\frac{5}{8}$" plywood
Common nails (2", 3")
Anchor bolts, ($\frac{1}{2}$"x12"), washers, nuts
Rebar
Tie wire
Reinforcing mesh (6"x6" 10-gauge)
Gravel
Bricks
Ready-mix concrete
Polyethylene sheeting
String

SAFETY TIPS

Wear goggles when nailing and a long-sleeved shirt, gloves, and rubber boots when working with concrete. Wear gloves when handling pressure-treated wood; add a dust mask when cutting it.

SETTING UP BATTER BOARDS

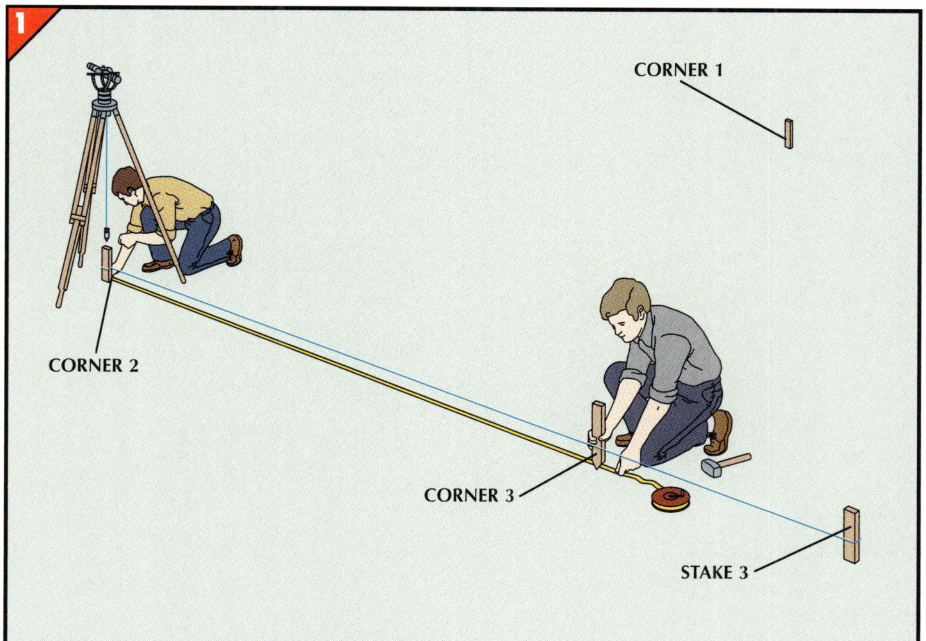

1. Finding the building lines.

◆ Drive stakes to mark two adjacent corners of the slab.
◆ Centering a transit level over one of the stakes, set a third stake at a right angle to the first two.
◆ From the stake under the transit level, string a line to the third stake. Measure the desired distance along the line with a tape measure to mark the third corner *(left)*.
◆ Drive a stake at your mark, set the transit above the stake, and repeat the operation to locate the fourth corner.
◆ Run a string boundary about 4 inches off the ground around all the corner stakes.

2. Building batter boards.

At each corner of the slab, set up a batter board to which you can anchor the string boundary.

◆ Drive three 2-by-4 stakes about 2 feet outside the strings so they form a right angle at the corner.

◆ Fasten 1-by-6 boards to the outside faces of the stakes with 2-inch nails so the top edges of the boards are about 10 inches above the ground. Double-headed nails *(photograph)* simplify later disassembly of batter boards and forms, because they are easy to pull out; a maul or a brick makes a solid backing for nailing *(right)*.

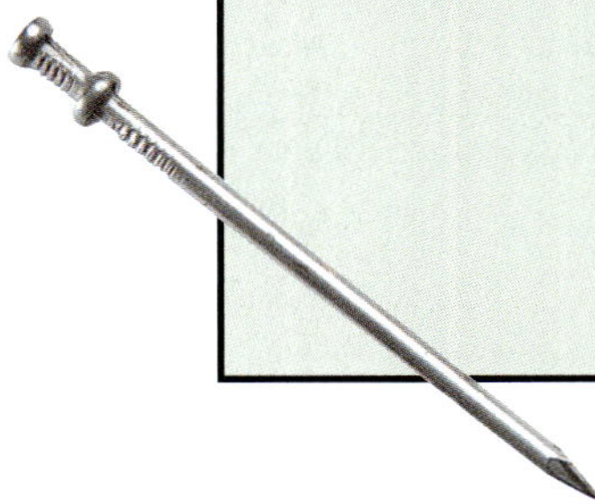

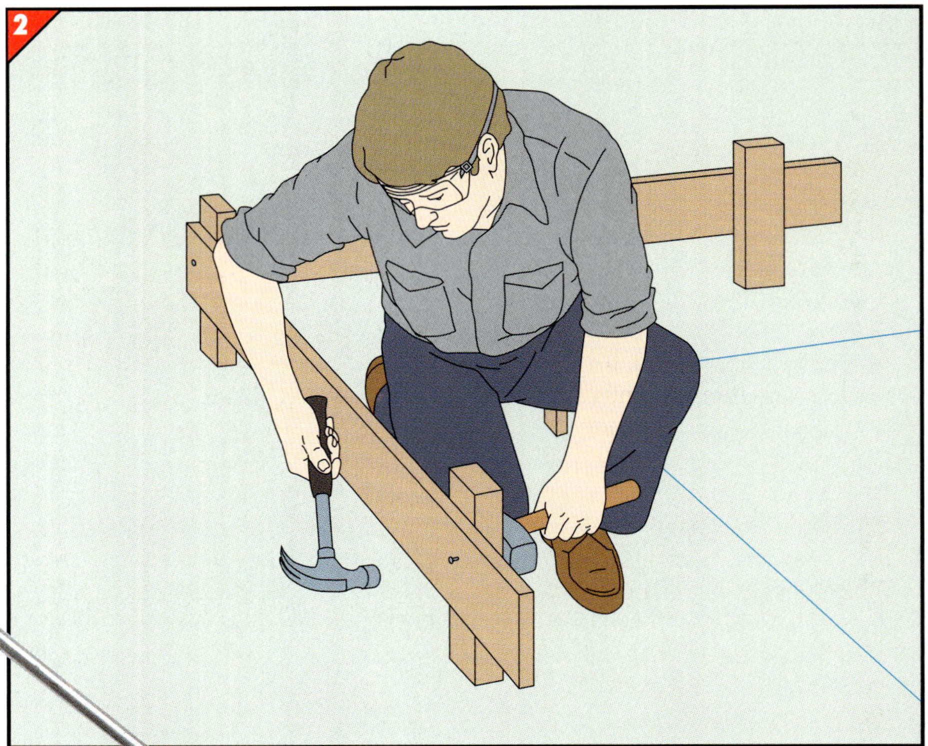

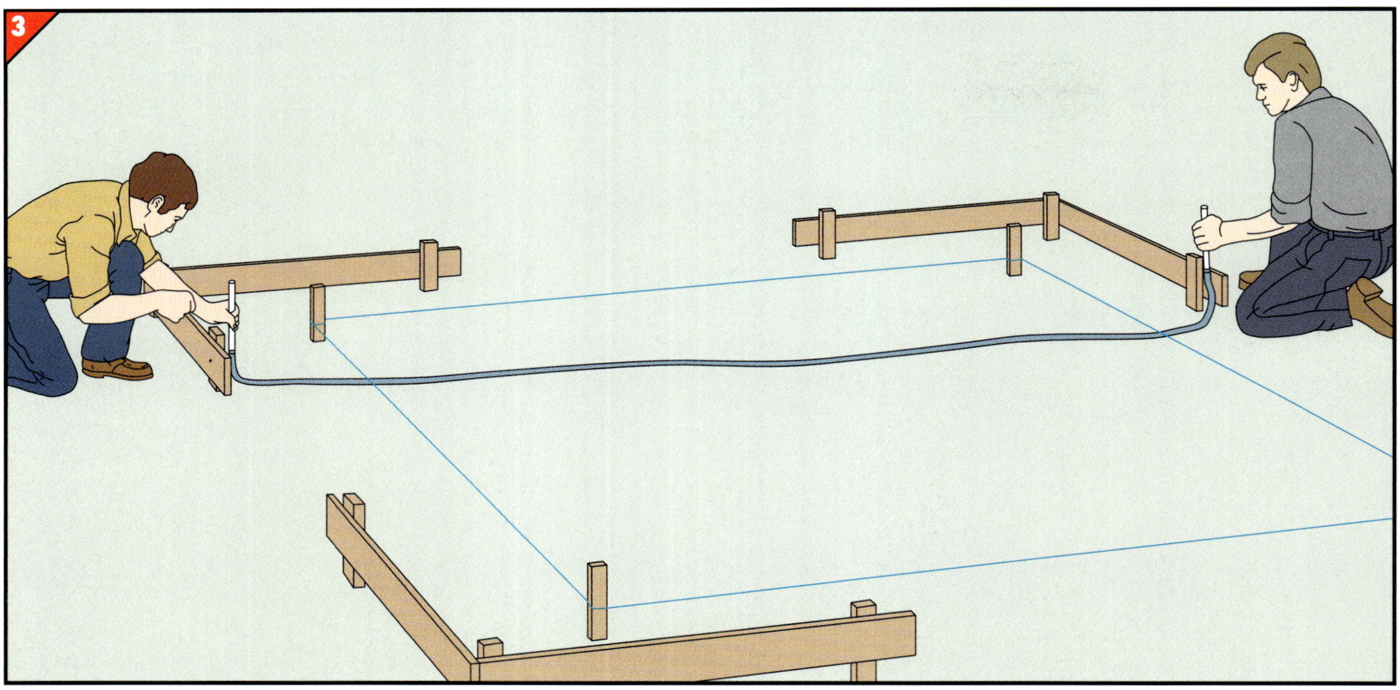

3. Leveling the batter boards.

◆ With a water level, determine which set of batter boards is the lowest *(above)*; this will be your reference set. Check whether both boards of the set are at the same height: Lay a carpenter's level across the boards' top edges and, if necessary, drive down the stake on the high side.

◆ Keeping one end of the water level against one reference batter board, level the other three sets. Then level both boards of each set with the help of the carpenter's level.

◆ String lines between the batter boards directly above the lines attached to the corner stakes, then remove the corner stakes and their strings.

If the ground between the batter boards and the new lines is uneven, smooth high spots and fill depressions with clean 1-inch gravel so that no point is less than 8 inches below the tops of the batter boards. Compact the soil thoroughly with a power tamper.

LAYING OUT THE FORMS

1. Placing and leveling forms.

◆ Make the forms for the slab from 2-by-8s, fastening three 2-by-4 stakes to the outside face of each board with 3-inch common nails. Attach the stakes so they are at least 6 inches from the board ends, except at the corners of the slab, where they must be flush.

◆ Starting at a corner, position a form with its inside face flush with the string line. Drive the stakes into the ground *(right)* so the top of the form is even with the line.

◆ Continue placing the forms, nailing them together at the corners; elsewhere, butt them end-to-end, reinforcing the seams with $\frac{5}{8}$-inch plywood backing fastened with 2-inch nails.

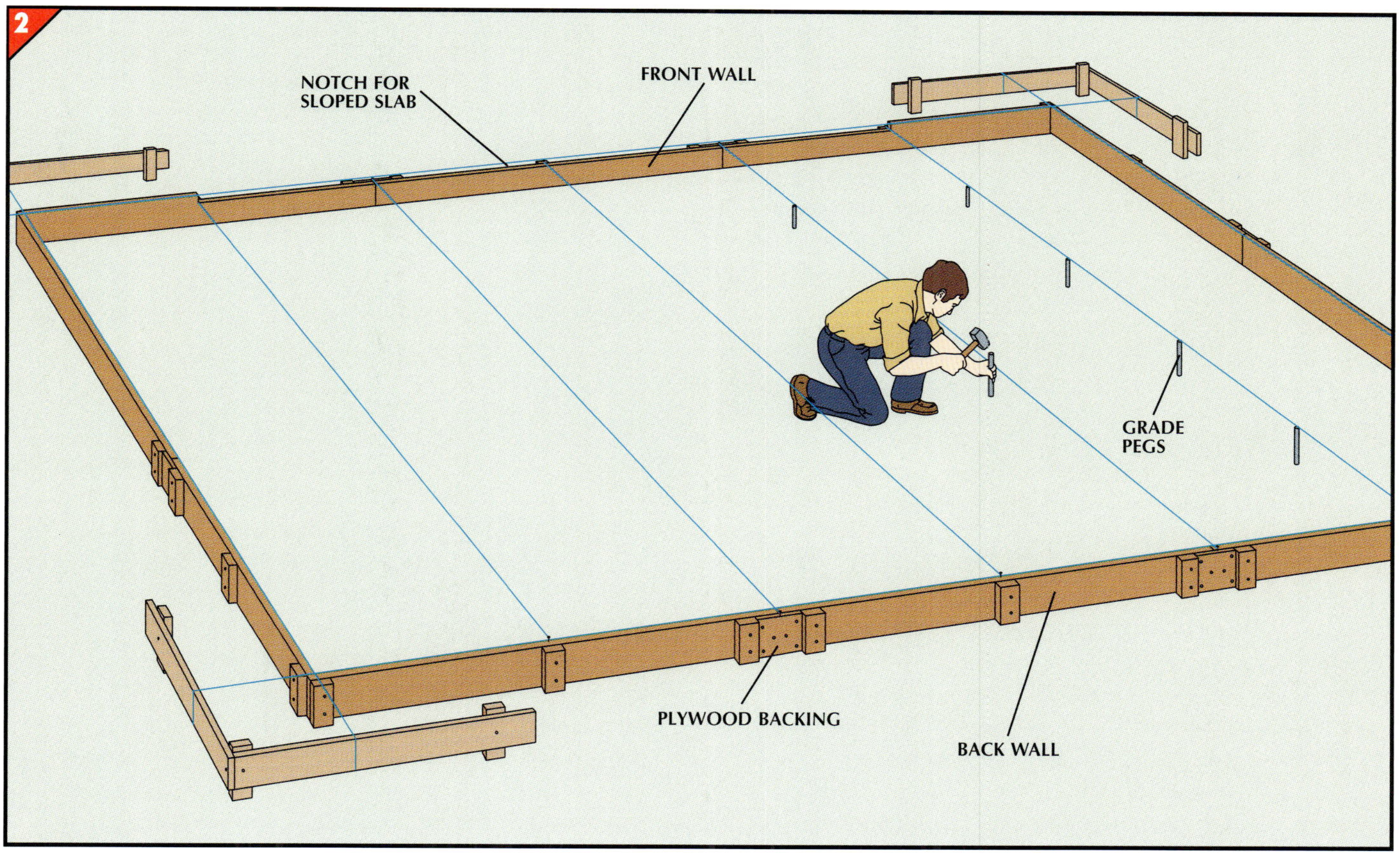

2. Setting grade stakes.

◆ For a sloping floor, mark the door opening on the forms and notch their top edges between the marks. Make the notch 1 inch deep for every foot between the front and back walls.

◆ String lines between the back- and front-wall form boards every 4 feet.

◆ To make grade pegs, drive lengths of rebar along the strings 4 feet apart so the tops of the spikes are level with the strings. Remove the strings.

3. Bracing the forms.

◆ Drive a 2-by-4 bracing stake into the ground 12 inches behind each form stake.

◆ Fasten two 1-by-2 braces between each bracing stake and form stake *(right)*.

4. Digging the trenches.

◆ Beginning 5 inches inside the inner lip of the trench, slope the lip at a 45-degree angle *(above)*.

◆ To prevent concrete from leaking out between the forms and the ground, pack a layer of dirt or gravel against the forms where they meet the ground.

5. Bending lengths of rebar.
In preparation for Step 6, bend four lengths of rebar to turn each corner of the trench. To do so, slide a length of rigid plumbing pipe over the end of a rod, step on the rod, and gradually pull the pipe toward you.

6. Laying the rebar.

◆ Every 4 feet along the trench bottom, drive a pair of rebar spikes into the ground 5 inches apart so their tops are 5 inches below the top of the form.

◆ Fasten horizontal rebars to the vertical ones with tie wire about $2\frac{1}{2}$ inches from the trench bottom, overlapping the ends by at least 15 inches. At the corners, lay lengths of bent rebar.

◆ Attach a second course of horizontal rebar 1 inch from the tops of the vertical ones.

◆ Spread a 3-inch layer of clean 1-inch gravel over the floor site, but avoid getting gravel in the trench. Cover the gravel with sheets of 4-mil polyethylene followed by 6-inch by 6-inch 10-gauge mesh supported on bricks and extending to the inside edge of the trench.

CASTING THE SLAB

1. Pouring the concrete.

◆ Cut lengths of pressure-treated 2-by-4s to fit around the perimeter of the slab as sole plates. Starting 12 inches from the board ends and at 5-foot intervals in between, bore $\frac{5}{8}$-inch holes through the pieces.

◆ Pour the concrete, filling the trenches first. Work with a square-edged shovel to break up air pockets in the trenches and push the concrete against the forms.

◆ Pour the concrete over the rest of the slab and spread it with a mason's hoe.

◆ Meanwhile, have a helper level the surface and create the slope toward the door opening with a screed of 2-by-4s so the slab is even with the tops of the forms and grade pegs. Have another helper smooth the entire slab, including the slope, with a bull float.

2. Bolting the sole plates to the slab.

◆ Fit $\frac{1}{2}$-by-12-inch anchor bolts through each hole in the sole plates and install a washer and nut.

◆ Set the plates on the wet concrete, $\frac{3}{8}$ inch in from the forms with the threaded end of the bolts facing up. Do not place sole plates across the door opening.

◆ Tap the bolts into the concrete with a hammer *(right)*.

◆ Cover the slab with polyethylene sheeting. Let the concrete cure for seven days, then remove the forms.

FINISHING A FLAT SLAB

Smoothing the surface.

A flat slab can be finished to a very smooth surface with a power troweler. This technique cannot be used on a slab with a sloped surface.

◆ Wait until the concrete is hard enough to walk on without sinking more than $\frac{1}{4}$ inch. Remove the polyethylene sheeting from the slab.

◆ Set the troweler's blades flat against the slab and run the machine over the surface. Then, angle the blades upward and smooth the surface again.

◆ Sprinkle the slab with water, replace the sheeting, and let the concrete cure for the remainder of the curing period before removing the forms.

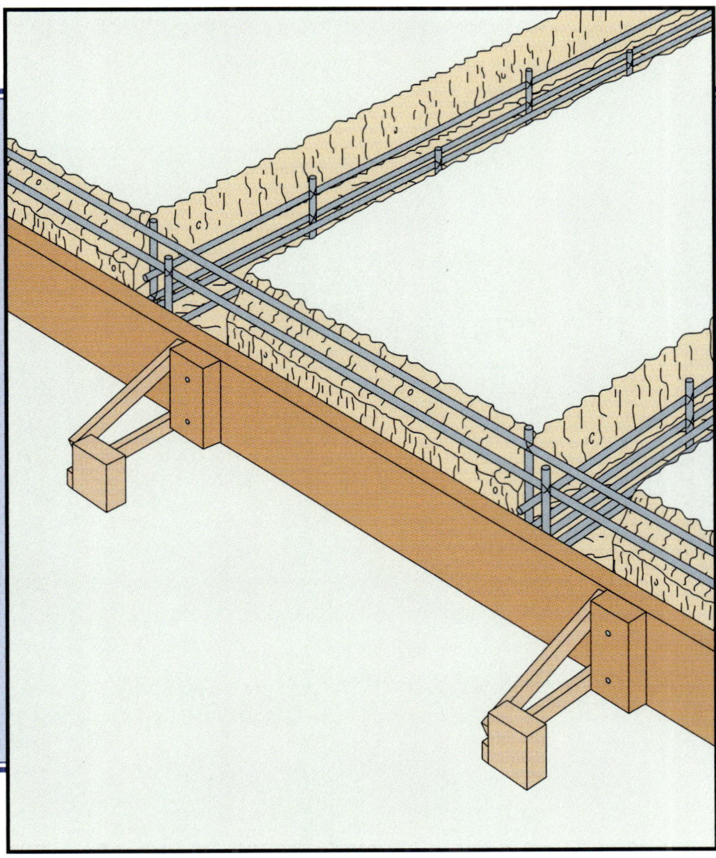

GRADE BEAMS: STIFFENERS FOR A CONCRETE FLOOR

Concrete is a strong building material, but if a slab is poured on marshy soil, clay, or a site that has been leveled with fill, it may settle and eventually crack. In such situations, professional masons often support a slab with grade beams—trenches filled with concrete and reinforcing steel. The grade beams shown at left are the type generally used with a turned-down slab. The trenches are 8 inches wide and deep, and spaced at 4-foot intervals between the perimeter trenches. First, two $\frac{1}{2}$-inch rebars are wired to vertical rods about 3 inches from the trench bottoms and to rebars in the rim trenches. Two more rebars are attached to the vertical rods 2 inches from the top. Next, the concrete is poured, filling all the trenches then forming the slab.

Adding Sturdy Walls

Stud walls provide a sturdy framework suitable for any structure, from a shed to a garage. The method is simple: Evenly spaced studs are nailed to top plates, then the walls are tilted upright in sections and the studs are toenailed to sole plates.

Header Beams: At each door or window opening, the roof load is carried by a horizontal header supported at its ends by posts or studs. For most headers, a board-and-plywood sandwich $3\frac{1}{2}$ inches thick and up to $11\frac{1}{2}$ inches wide is generally appropriate. Check your code requirements. Wider spans like the garage door opening shown below may require an engineered wood such as laminated veneer lumber (LVL). A wood dealer can tell you the required size; two pieces of LVL can be fastened together to create a thicker beam.

Following a Plan: Draw a set of plans to show the building inspector when you apply for a permit and for reference as you work. Start by drawing a simple floor plan on graph paper; indicate the overall dimensions of the structure, the distance between the center of each opening and the nearest corner of the building, and the size of each rough opening (usually specified by the manufacturer of the finished door or window). Then draw head-on views of the walls that have openings; indicate the height of the walls, the height and span of each opening and the sizes of the studs, posts, and headers that will support the roof.

Use the plan to determine exactly what materials you need when you order lumber. Studs—generally 2-by-4s cut 8 feet long at the sawmill—are usually spaced 16 inches apart. The 2-by-4 top plates should be straight pieces of structural-grade lumber at least 14 feet long.

Bracing the Walls: Plumb the walls accurately and brace them firmly. The temporary braces must hold the entire structure rigid while the roof trusses are put in. When the roof has been sheathed, remove the braces one by one as you apply the wall sheathing.

TOOLS

Tape measure
Carpenter's square
Carpenter's level
Plumb bob
Hammer
Chisel
Mallet
Circular saw

MATERIALS

2x4s
4x4s
LVL
Common nails (3", $3\frac{1}{2}$")

SAFETY TIPS

Wear goggles when nailing or cutting with a circular saw.

Anatomy of stud-wall framing.
In the structure shown at right, the studs are nailed to the bottom layer of the top plates then to the sole plates. The second layer of the top plates ties the walls together at the corners and at the joints in the first layer. Temporary diagonal bracing holds the walls and corners plumb. The long span of the garage door is bridged with an LVL beam supported by 4-by-4 posts. Horizontal 2-by-4 fire stops nailed between the studs are required in some areas; they add rigidity to the structure and provide a nailing surface for exterior sheathing.

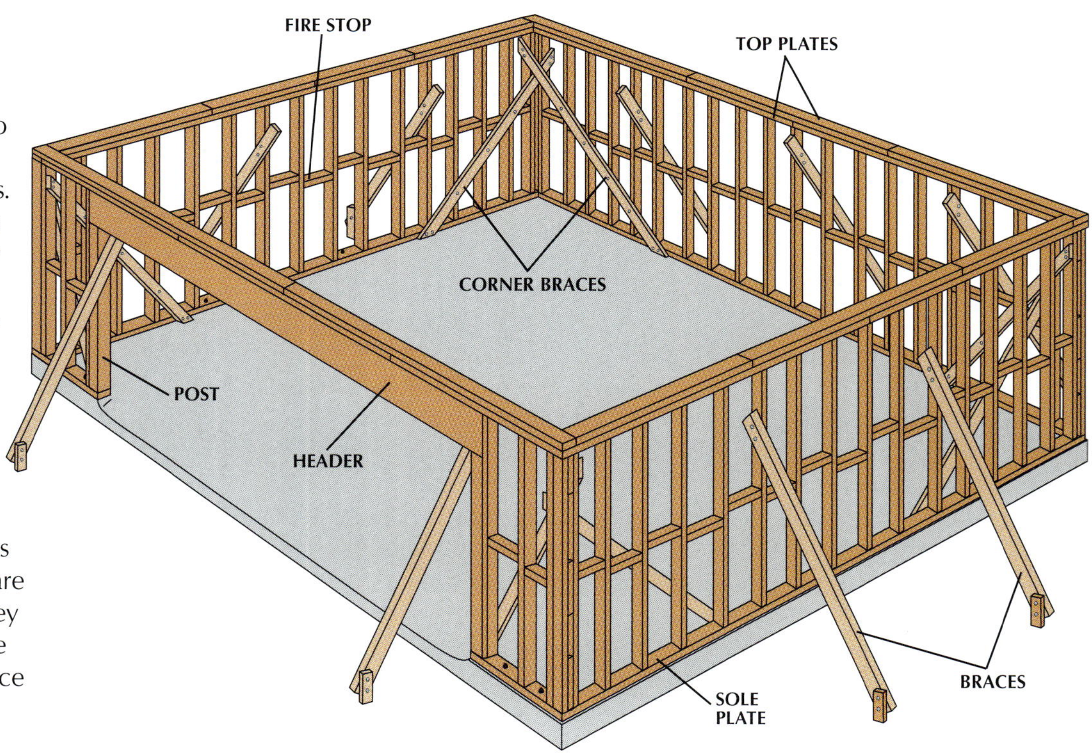

PREPARING THE SOLE AND TOP PLATES

1. Marking the studs on the sole plates.

◆ Drive a nail into the sole plate of a side wall $15\frac{1}{4}$ inches from the outside of the back wall.

◆ Holding the tongue of a carpenter's square across the sole plate at the nail, run a pencil along both edges of the tongue, outlining the first stud location.

◆ Hook a long tape measure on the nail and outline the next stud 16 inches from the first, while a helper holds the tape taut *(above)*.

◆ Mark the remaining stud locations at 16-inch intervals on all the sole plates. On each side of the garage door opening, mark the 4-by-4 posts.

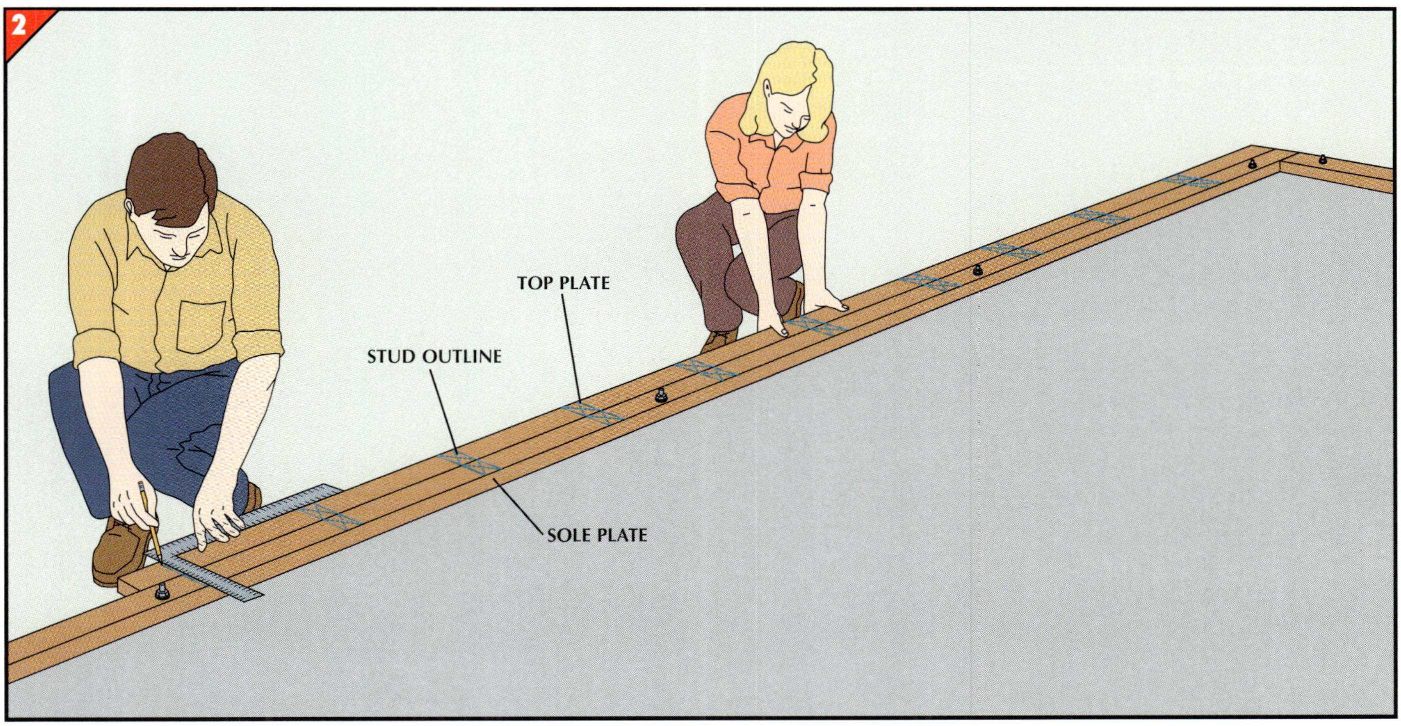

2. Marking the top plates.

◆ Working with a helper, butt a top plate against the sole plate with the ends flush at a corner.

◆ Transfer the stud outlines from the sole plates to the top plates with a carpenter's square *(above)*.

◆ With a circular saw, trim the ends of top plates in the middle of stud outlines to ensure that seams in the plate are centered over a stud.

◆ Make sure that sections of the top plate abutting a corner are at least 8 feet long and perfectly aligned with the end of the sole plate.

RAISING THE WALLS

1. Nailing studs to the top plate.

Build and raise the back and side walls *(Steps 1-3)* then the front one *(Step 4)*.

◆ Lay studs on edge on the slab—one for each outline on the sole plate—and position a top plate along the tops.

◆ Stand on the stud and top plate, align the stud with its outline, and drive two $3\frac{1}{2}$-inch common nails through the plate into the stud. If a stud aligns with a seam in the top plate, center the joint on the stud, and angle the nails toward its middle.

◆ For a stud that lines up with an anchor bolt in the sole plate, notch the stud with a chisel to fit over the bolt.

2. Preparing corner posts.

◆ For each corner, sandwich three, evenly spaced 18-inch-long 2-by-4s between two studs and fasten the assembly together with $3\frac{1}{2}$-inch nails *(left)*, making a corner post.

◆ Nail the post to the end of one of the top plates at each corner *(inset)*.

3. Erecting the walls.

◆ With one helper for every 8 feet of wall, tilt one wall upright.

◆ Set the studs on their marks on the sole plate and brace the wall with long 2-by-4s at 6-foot intervals *(page 172, Step 3)*, keeping the wall roughly vertical with a carpenter's level.

◆ Toenail each stud to the bottom plate with 3-inch nails, driving two fasteners from one side of the stud and one from the other.

◆ At each corner, face-nail the outside stud of one wall to the corner post of the adjoining wall, tying them together.

4. Fashioning the front wall.

◆ Assemble the front-wall sections on either side of the door, nailing studs to top-plate sections that extend over the door opening by at least 3 feet.
◆ Cut two 4-by-4 posts to the height of the wall studs, less the height of the header for the door opening.
◆ Fasten a stud along the inside edge of each post with $3\frac{1}{2}$-inch nails spaced 10 inches apart in a zigzag pattern *(right)*.
◆ Erect and brace the front wall sections as you did the other walls.

ALIGNING THE FRAMEWORK

1. Plumbing the corners.

◆ Hang a plumb bob from the top plate near a corner so the tip of the bob is slightly above the bottom plate.
◆ Make a corner brace by mitering the ends of a long 2-by-4 at 45-degree angles. With a 3-inch common nail, secure the brace to the last stud of the wall being plumbed so one mitered end is flush with the outside edge of the stud.
◆ With one helper supporting the wall and another eyeing the plumb bob, remove the exterior bracing you set up when raising the wall *(page 216, Step 3)*. Have your helper tilt the wall so that the plumb bob aligns with the edge of the sole plate, then face-nail the brace to the sole plate of the adjoining wall, holding its bottom end against the slab *(left)*.
◆ Plumb the other walls the same way.

2. Straightening the walls.

◆ Nail a 2-by-4 block to the inside edge of the top plate at each end of one wall.
◆ Drive a nail into one end of each block and stretch a string tautly between the nails and across the face of each block.
◆ Working on a stepladder near the middle of the wall, hold a scrap 2-by-4 between the string and the top plate. If there is a gap between the string and the board, or if the board pushes out the string, have one helper tilt the wall as necessary while another reinstalls exterior bracing to hold the wall in position *(left)*.
◆ Straighten the other walls this way.

3. Completing the top plate.

To reinforce the corners, arrange the second top-plate layer so the boards overlap as shown on page 214.
◆ Position a 2-by-4 over the first top-plate layer, aligning one end with the outside edge of the adjoining wall. Cut the other end so it is at least 4 feet from a joint in the first layer.
◆ Nail the second top-plate board to the lower one with $3\frac{1}{2}$-inch common nails spaced every 8 inches in a zigzag pattern. At the corners, drive two nails where the top layer overlaps the bottom one of the adjoining wall *(right)*.
◆ Continue nailing the second top-plate layer around the perimeter, except over the door opening where the header must be installed first *(opposite)*.
◆ Nail the corner braces to every stud they cross with 3-inch nails.

BRIDGING THE DOOR OPENING

1. Building the header.

◆ For a span over 8 feet, cut a length of LVL lumber to fit between the studs at the edges of the door opening.

◆ For a double header, you can nail two lengths of LVL together face to face, staggering $3\frac{1}{2}$-inch common nails along both sides at 10-inch intervals *(right)*. Or, order an LSL (laminated structural lumber) beam *(photograph)* as required for your span.

For a span up to 8 feet, build a header from a pair of 2-by-12s with a strip of $\frac{1}{2}$-inch plywood of the same width and length sandwiched between them. Nail the header as you would a doubled LVL beam, adding construction adhesive to the surfaces that will be in contact.

2. Lifting the header into place.

◆ With one helper for every 5 feet of header length, lift the header and slide it onto the posts at the edges of the door opening. Although the typical header is a manageable load for four people, as shown above, you can rent a hoist to make the job easier.

◆ Have your helpers hold the ends of the header in place while you fasten it to the studs adjoining the posts, the posts themselves, and the top-plate sections with $3\frac{1}{2}$-inch nails.

◆ Finish installing the lower top-plate layer, then nail the upper top-plate layer over the door opening.

Ready-Made Trusses to Support the Roof

The most rapid and economical way to frame the roof of a rectangular structure is to install prefabricated trusses. In addition to eliminating the need for heavy structural joists and rafters, trusses save you from having to cut rafters at complex angles and erecting a ridge beam.

Truss Parts: Trusses typically consist of three chords—the pieces that form the triangular shape—and webs that fit between the chords to support the top chords and transfer stress to the bottom chord and to the exterior bearing walls. The corners of a truss are joined with metal gussets.

Purchasing Trusses: When ordering trusses, specify the span between the exterior walls, the length of the overhang, and the type of end cut—plumb or square—you desire. Also specify the pitch of the roof. The standard pitch for trusses spaced at 24-inch intervals is 4 inches to 1 foot, but local codes in areas with heavy snowfall may require a greater pitch or more closely spaced trusses. Consult your local building code for this information.

Installing the Framing: Trusses rely on sheathing for stability. In areas with little snow, $\frac{3}{8}$-inch plywood is acceptable. In others, $\frac{1}{2}$- to $\frac{5}{8}$-inch may be required. Check the code. In either case, bolster the joints with plywood sheathing clips *(page 226)*.

You will need at least three helpers to lift, roll, and secure the trusses. When lifting the trusses, carry them in a vertical position with one helper at each end. Trusses can be damaged easily if mishandled.

The final step involves weatherproofing and adding ventilation.

TOOLS

- Tape measure
- Carpenter's square
- Chalk line
- Carpenter's level
- Hammer
- Maul
- Handsaw
- Circular saw
- Saber saw

MATERIALS

- 1x6s, 2x4s
- Plywood sheathing
- Plywood panel siding
- Prefabricated roof trusses
- Common nails ($2\frac{1}{2}$", 3", $3\frac{1}{2}$")
- Galvanized common nails ($2\frac{1}{2}$", $3\frac{1}{4}$", $3\frac{1}{2}$")
- Plywood sheathing clips
- String

SAFETY TIPS

Wear safety goggles when driving nails or cutting with a circular saw. Put on a hard hat when working overhead. To position and secure trusses, rent two 6-foot scaffolds.

A RANGE OF TRUSS STYLES

Truss construction is largely dictated by local conditions. Queen is a common style, but Howe might be found in an area with high snowfall. If you plan to build a catwalk above the bottom chords for storage, order trusses without a center web, such as the Fink. You will need two gable end trusses with webs spaced 16 inches apart for attaching the sheathing. Because these trusses rest on a wall, their webs can be modified to create framing for a ventilation opening *(page 223)*. A truss manufacturer or distributor will suggest the right trusses for your project.

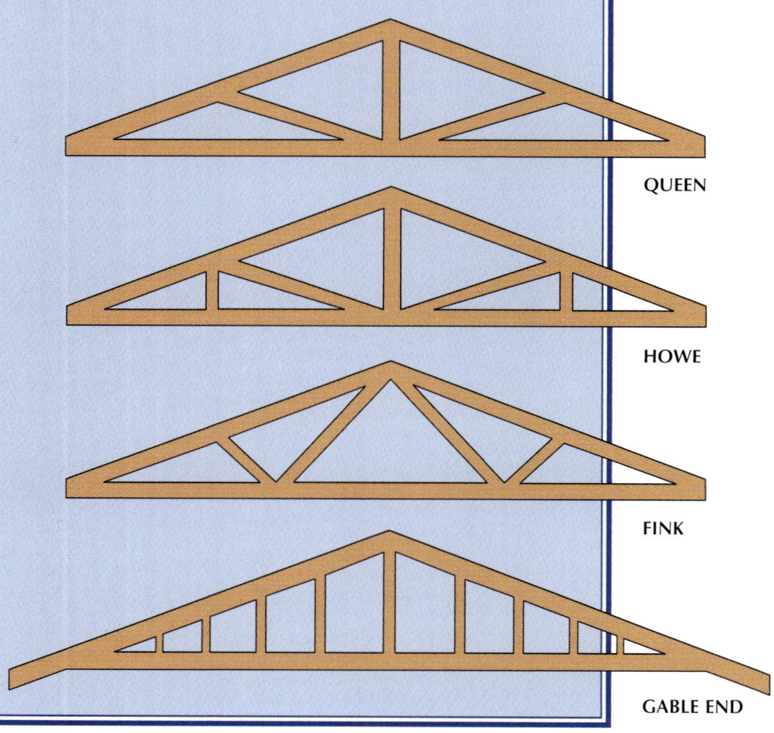

PREPARING THE WALLS FOR TRUSSES

1. Marking the truss locations.

◆ If required by your building code, add 2-by-4 fire stops, staggering their heights so you can face-nail them to the studs with $3\frac{1}{2}$-inch common nails.

◆ Standing on a scaffold, measure $24\frac{3}{4}$ inches from a side wall and mark a line across the front wall's top plate with a carpenter's square. Mark a second line $1\frac{1}{2}$ inches away to outline the truss location.

◆ Outline the remaining truss positions on 24-inch centers, using the first mark as a starting point *(left)*.

◆ Repeat the process to lay out truss locations on the back wall.

2. Laying out the overhang.

To assist in positioning the trusses, set up a layout line along the front wall. To do so:

◆ Nail a 2-by-4 to the outside face of each side wall top plate with $3\frac{1}{2}$-inch common nails so the tops of the board and the top plate are flush. Attach the board so it projects beyond the truss overhang by a few inches.

◆ Mark the overhang on each 2-by-4, then tie a string tautly between the marks *(above)*.

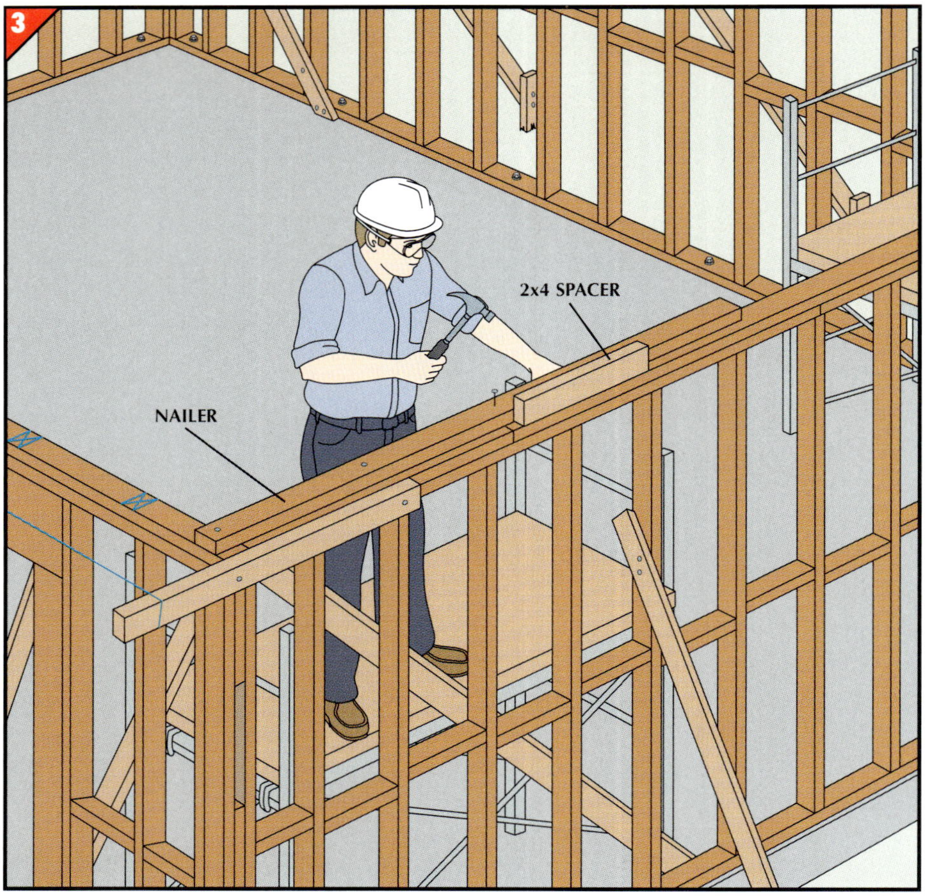

3. Fastening the nailers.

Secure boards to the side-wall top plates as nailing surfaces for the bottom chords of the end trusses.

◆ Attach 2-by-4 nailers to the top plates with 3-inch nails; hold a 2-by-4 spacer on edge on the top plate while fastening to offset the front edges of the nailer and top plate by $1\frac{1}{2}$ inches *(left)*.

◆ Trim the nailers flush with the front and back walls.

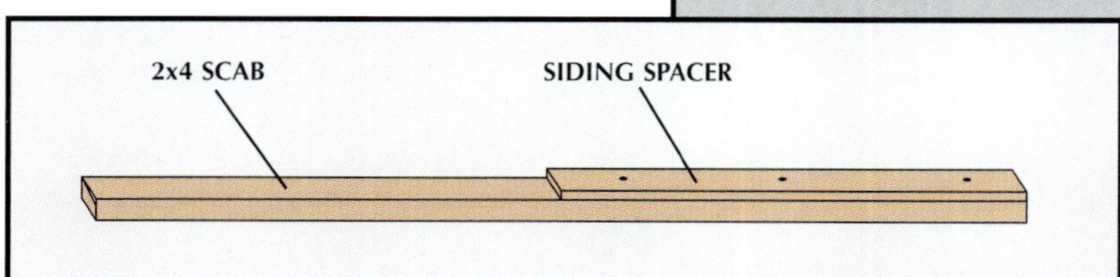

4. Erecting the scabs.

◆ Prepare four 8-foot-long 2-by-4 braces—or "scabs"—to align and hold the end trusses even with the edge of the top plates. Since siding is applied to end trusses before they are raised, attach a 4-foot strip of siding to each scab as a spacer *(inset)*.

◆ Attach two scabs to each side wall with 3-inch common nails *(right)*. Position the scabs about one-third of the way in from the front and back walls; set their height so the top end of the siding spacer is flush with the top plate of the wall.

5. Sheathing the end trusses.

◆ Install framing in the end trusses for a vent.

◆ Set an end truss on the ground and lay a 4-by-8 sheet of plywood siding on it, aligning a corner of the sheet with the heel—or bottom corner—at one end of the truss.

◆ Snap a chalk line across the siding in line with the top chord of the truss *(above)*, then cut the siding along the line.

◆ Nail the cut section of siding to the truss with galvanized box nails long enough to penetrate 1 inch into the truss.

◆ Fasten siding to the rest of the truss the same way, then cut the vent opening with a saber saw.

RAISING THE ROOF

1. Hoisting an end truss.

◆ With two helpers, carry an end truss upside down into the building. Then, standing on a scaffold, lift one end until the top chord rests on the top plate of one side wall *(left)*.

◆ With your helpers on another scaffold, pivot the other end of the truss onto the opposite side wall top plate.

2. Installing the end truss.

◆ Have a helper wedge a 2-by-4 into the peak of the truss and tilt it upright *(right)*. With another helper on the scaffold, guide the truss so the bottom chord settles between the nailer and the scabs.

◆ Align the front-wall end of the truss with the overhang line along the front wall.

◆ On a ladder outside the building, nail the scabs to the top chord of the truss and drive a $3\frac{1}{2}$-inch galvanized common nail through the siding and the bottom chord of the truss into the nailer every 16 inches.

3. Plumbing the end truss.

◆ Support the end truss with a 16-foot-long 2-by-4 brace, nailing one end of the brace to the vent opening framing and the other to a 2-by-4 stake driven into the ground about 8 feet from the wall.

◆ Loosen the scabs and position a carpenter's level against the top and bottom chords of the end truss. Meanwhile, have a helper reposition the brace on the stake so that the end truss is plumb *(above)*.

TRICKS OF THE TRADE

A Truss Pole

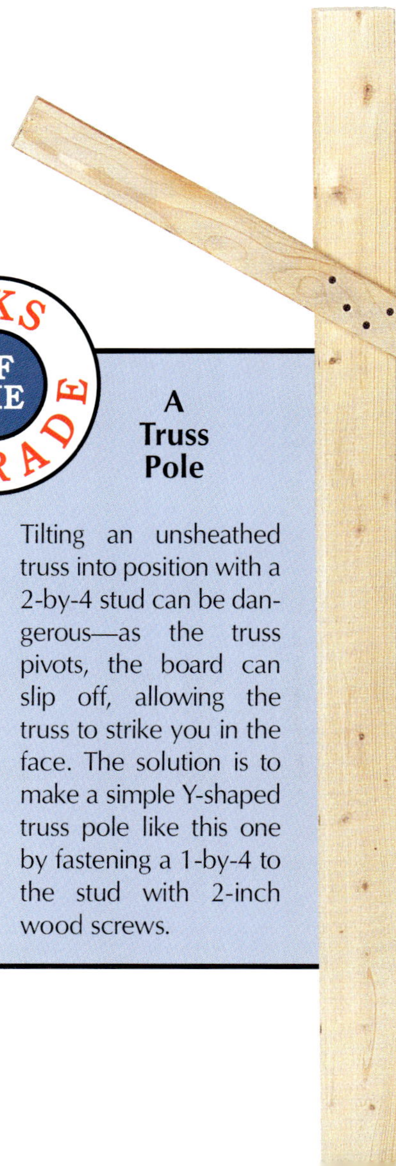

Tilting an unsheathed truss into position with a 2-by-4 stud can be dangerous—as the truss pivots, the board can slip off, allowing the truss to strike you in the face. The solution is to make a simple Y-shaped truss pole like this one by fastening a 1-by-4 to the stud with 2-inch wood screws.

4. Installing truss bracing.

◆ Tilt the second truss into position over its outlines on the top plates and align an end with the overhang line.

◆ Toenail the truss to the top plates with $3\frac{1}{4}$-inch galvanized common nails. Attach a multipurpose framing anchor *(photograph)* to each end of the truss with the nails recommended by the manufacturer.

◆ Outline the truss spacing on an 8-foot-long 1-by-6 brace for each side of the ridge and fasten one end of the brace to the end truss with two $2\frac{1}{2}$-inch nails. Aligning the truss with the first outline, nail the brace to the top chord *(left)*. Repeat on the other side of the ridge.

5. Raising the remaining trusses.

◆ Position and brace the rest of the trusses except the last four. Install more braces as needed, fastening them to trusses already in place *(right)*.

◆ Install the remaining end truss.

◆ Tilt the last three trusses up to the roof before positioning any of them. Then position and brace them one at a time.

6. Sheathing the trusses.

◆ Set up the scaffolds along the side walls. With a helper, snap chalk lines along the top chords of the trusses 4 and 8 feet from the overhang as guidelines for laying plywood sheathing.

◆ Align the top edge of a 4-by-8 sheet of sheathing with the chalk line and center it over the fifth truss.

◆ As a helper slips a plywood clip *(photograph)* onto the top edge of the sheathing between each truss, secure the sheet with $2\frac{1}{2}$-inch galvanized common nails every 6 inches along the top chords *(right)*.

◆ After sheathing the bottom 4 feet of the roof, remove the braces fastened to the trusses and cover the next 4 feet, starting the row with a half-sheet in order to stagger the joints from the bottom row.

◆ Before installing the last row of sheets, trim their top edges so the sheathing stops 1 inch short of the ridge. Cover the other side of the trusses the same way.

7. Stabilizing the bottom chords.

On each side of the ridge, support the bottom chords of the trusses with the bracing you removed in Step 6. Position a brace across the trusses and, holding the chord in line with its outline, attach the brace to the truss with two $2\frac{1}{2}$-inch nails *(left)*.

If your area experiences high wind, diagonal bracing may be required; check the local building code.

Siding with Plywood

Plywood siding is sturdy, economical, and easy to install. Designed to face the elements, it comes in various lengths—but 8 feet is most common—and in a variety of textures and patterns. It is also available with shiplap edges that mesh with adjoining panels.

If your studs are 24 inches apart, make sure the paneling is the thicker kind designed for this spacing. When ordering the paneling, ask your supplier for Z-flashing to fit between the end-truss siding and the wall siding.

TOOLS

- Caulking gun
- Hammer
- Tin snips
- Circular saw

MATERIALS

- 1x3s, 1x4s
- Plywood siding panels
- Z-flashing
- Exterior caulk
- Galvanized box nails
- Galvanized finishing nails ($2\frac{1}{4}$")

SAFETY TIPS

Wear goggles when nailing.

1. Fastening the first panel.

◆ Starting at a corner, apply exterior caulk to the stud surfaces that will contact the first panel.

◆ Slip one flange of a piece of Z-flashing behind the sheathing that covers the end truss, then ease the first siding panel behind the other flange *(inset)*.

◆ Secure the panel to the studs with galvanized box nails long enough to penetrate the studs by 1 inch. Space the fasteners 6 inches apart along the starting stud and at 12-inch intervals along the other studs. Rather than driving nails through the lapped edge of the panel, apply caulk along the lap *(right)*.

2. Finishing the job.

◆ Install the next panel so its lapped edge meshes with the first. Avoiding the joint, nail the edge of the second panel to the stud *(left)*; this will leave the first panel free to expand.

◆ Install the rest of the siding this way. Trim the corner panels and Z-flashing as needed using tin snips to cut the flashing.

◆ Cover the exposed edges of the siding at the corners with 1-by-3s and 1-by-4s fastened with $2\frac{1}{4}$-inch galvanized finishing nails *(inset)*.

7 Landscaping Plans and Preliminaries

Whether considering planting a single shrub or remaking your entire yard, successful landscaping begins with a well-thought-out plan. Besides forecasting results, it can show where improvements are needed. Then, armed with the proper tools, you can level uneven ground, grade or terrace slopes, correct faulty drainage, and enrich soil in preparation for making your landscaping plan a reality.

A design based on circular shapes →

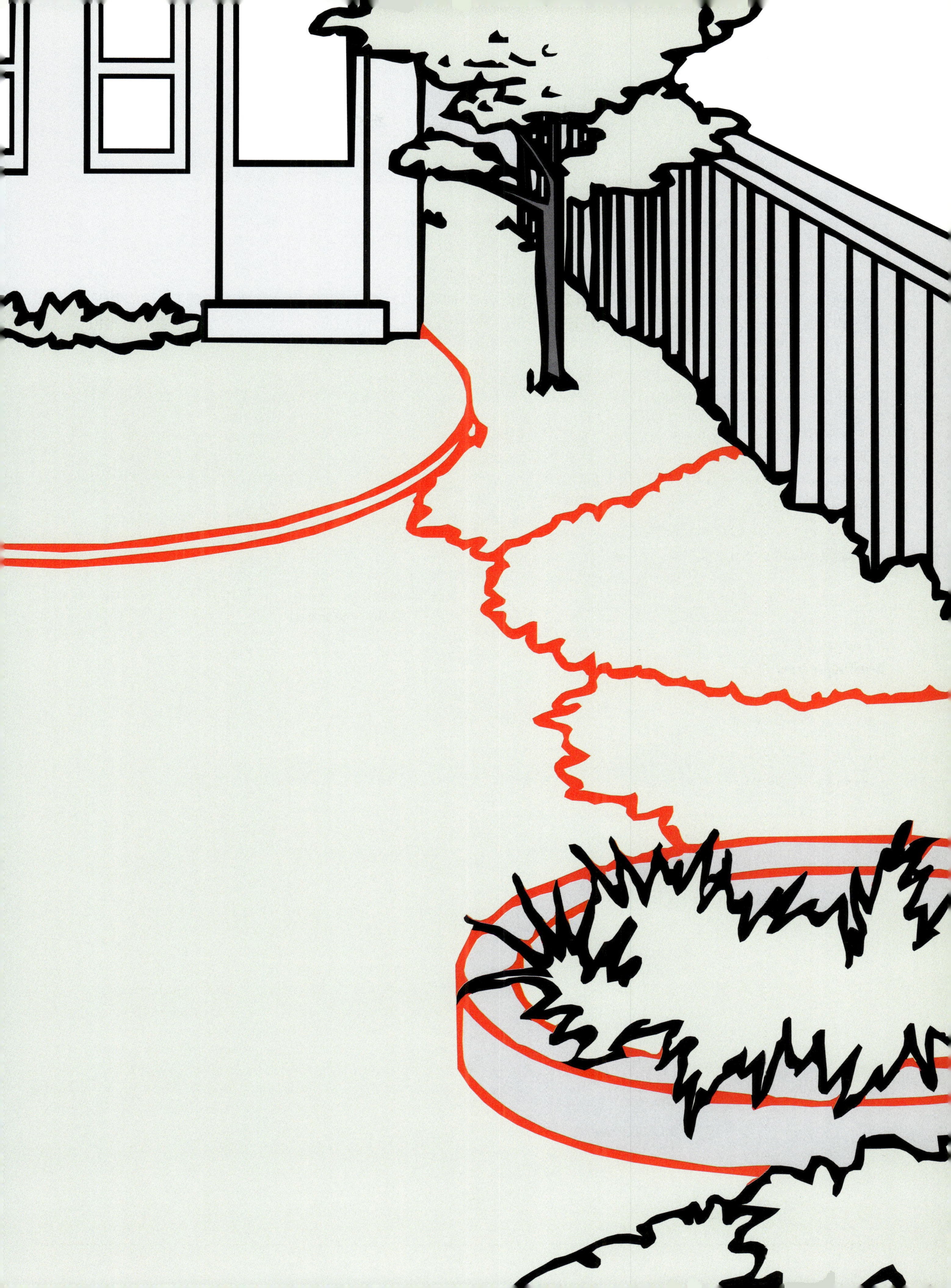

Caring for Landscaping Tools

A collection of gardening equipment represents a big investment and should be treated accordingly. Proper storage and maintenance will prolong the life of your tools. Moreover, simple repairs can often restore broken or aging equipment to full usefulness.

Basic Care: Tools should be kept indoors in a place free of rust-producing moisture; before putting them away, clean them and wipe them dry. Protect cutting tools against corrosion with a light application of household oil. Sharpen blades when they become dull. Carefully clean chemical sprayers after each use.

Easy Repairs: Typical troubles with a garden hose are treatable through surgery. If the hose develops a leak, remove the damaged section and make a splice with a mending kit; if a coupling is corroded or loose, cut it off and clamp a new one in place *(opposite)*. A tool with a broken handle can also be salvaged in almost all cases; replacement handles are generally available.

On shovels, rakes, hoes, and other lightweight garden tools, the new handle slides into a metal sleeve and is fastened with screws. The heads of heavy tools such as axes, sledgehammers, and mattocks have a collar that accommodates a thicker handle, and the repair also involves some extra steps *(page 233)*.

CAUTION *Before removing a lawnmower blade to sharpen it, be sure to disconnect the motor's ignition wire from the spark plug to prevent inadvertent starting.*

TOOLS

- Electric drill
- Flat file
- Grinding stone drill attachment
- Hammer
- Knife
- Screwdriver
- Small sledgehammer
- Whetstone

SAFETY TIPS

Wear gloves when cleaning any part of a sprayer, and wear goggles when sharpening metal blades and when hammering tool heads onto new handles.

SHARPENING PRUNING SHEARS AND MOWER BLADES

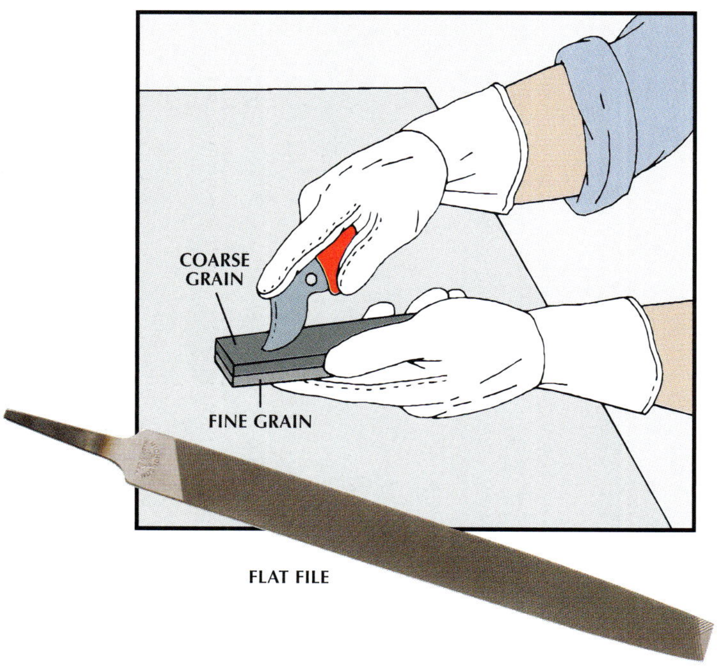

Honing a pair of shears.

◆ Disassemble the shears by removing the hinge bolt.
◆ Put a few drops of light household oil or water on a whetstone's coarse side. Hold the beveled edge of the blade flush against the stone *(left)* and, starting at the tip, grind in small circles until the blade's edge is keen.
◆ Smooth the beveled edge by honing it on the whetstone's fine side with the same grinding motion. Reassemble the shears.
◆ You can also use a flat file *(photograph)* to sharpen shears: File the blade as described on the opposite page for a lawnmower blade.

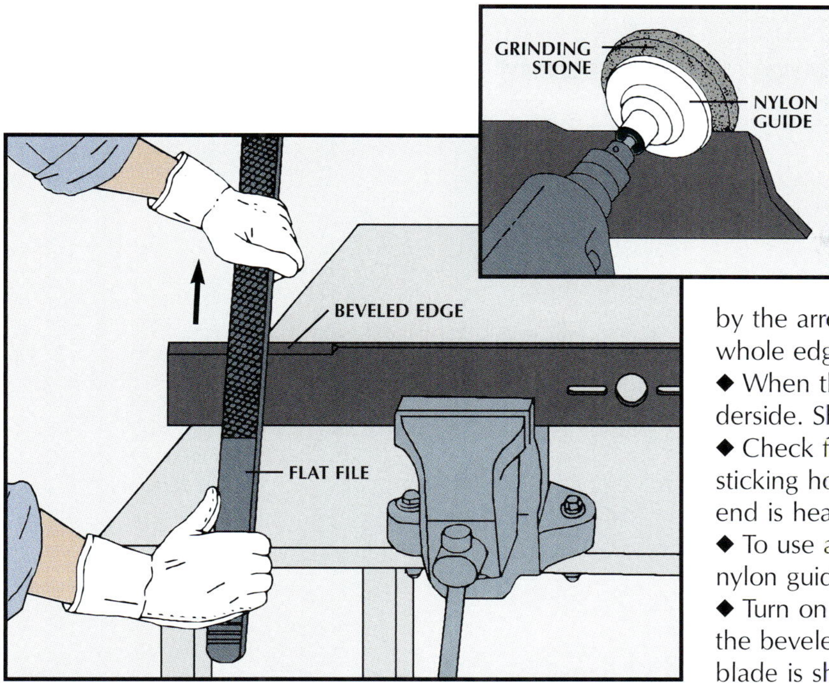

A keen edge for a lawnmower blade.

◆ Secure the blade in a vise. Lay a flat file flush with the beveled cutting edge *(left)*, and file in the direction indicated by the arrow; do not pull back. File evenly along the whole edge.
◆ When the edge looks shiny, file the burr off the underside. Sharpen the blade's other end the same way.
◆ Check for balance by hanging the blade on a nail sticking horizontally out of your workbench. If one end is heavier, sharpen it until the blade balances.
◆ To use a grinding stone drill attachment, place the nylon guide against the blade's underside *(inset)*.
◆ Turn on the drill and, holding the stone against the beveled edge, move it back and forth until the blade is sharp.

MENDING A HOSE

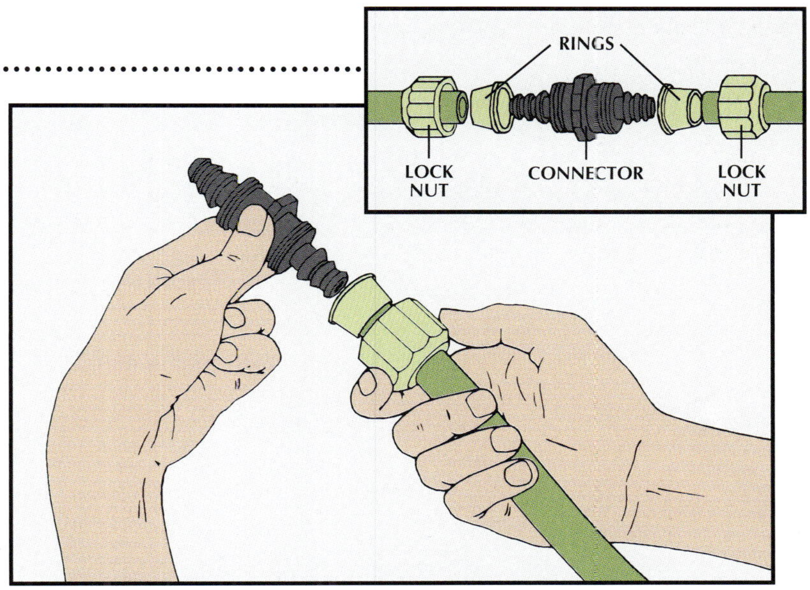

A splice to fix a leak.

◆ Cut out the leaking section of the hose. Soak the cut ends in hot water to soften the vinyl.
◆ Slip a lock nut from the mending kit over one cut end, with the nut's threads facing out toward the cut.
◆ Put a ring over the same end, then push the connector into the hose as far as it can go *(right)*. Slide the lock nut over the ring, and tighten the nut securely to the connector by hand.
◆ Repeat on the other end of the hose.

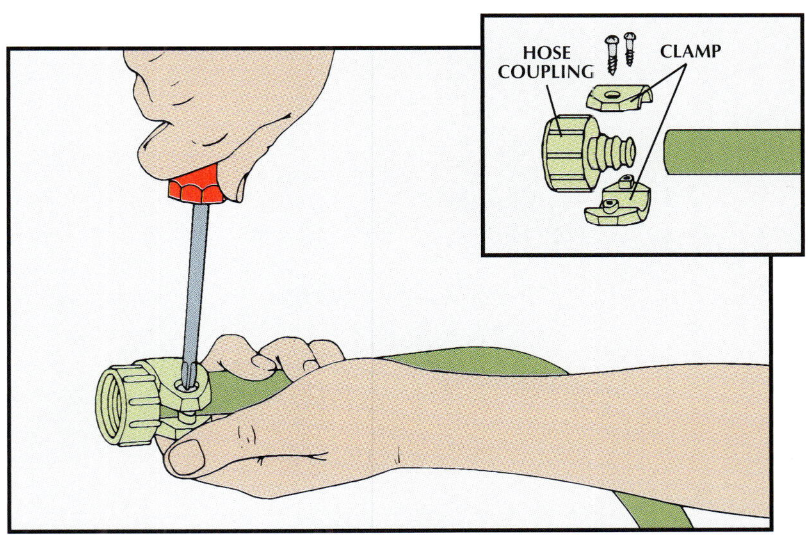

A new coupling for a hose end.

◆ Cut off the defective coupling. Push the new coupling into the cut end of the hose as far as it will go.
◆ Place the clamp halves around the hose at the base of the coupling, and screw the halves together to tighten the clamp *(right)*.

FLUSHING OUT A GARDEN-HOSE SPRAYER

Back-flushing the sprayer head.

◆ Remove the container from the sprayer head, leaving the head attached to the garden hose.

◆ Turn the control valve of the sprayer to ON, and cover the outlet hole with a finger *(right)*. Run water through the hose; the water will flush back through the sprayer and out of the suction tube, washing away chemical residues. Catch the water and residues in a separate container.

◆ Remove your finger from the outlet hole, and run water through the sprayer in the normal direction; if the hole is clogged, clear it with stiff wire.

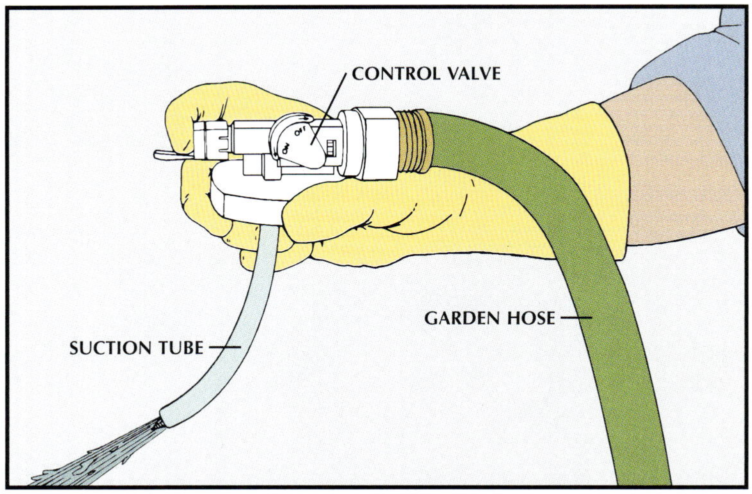

KEEPING A CANISTER SPRAYER CLEAN

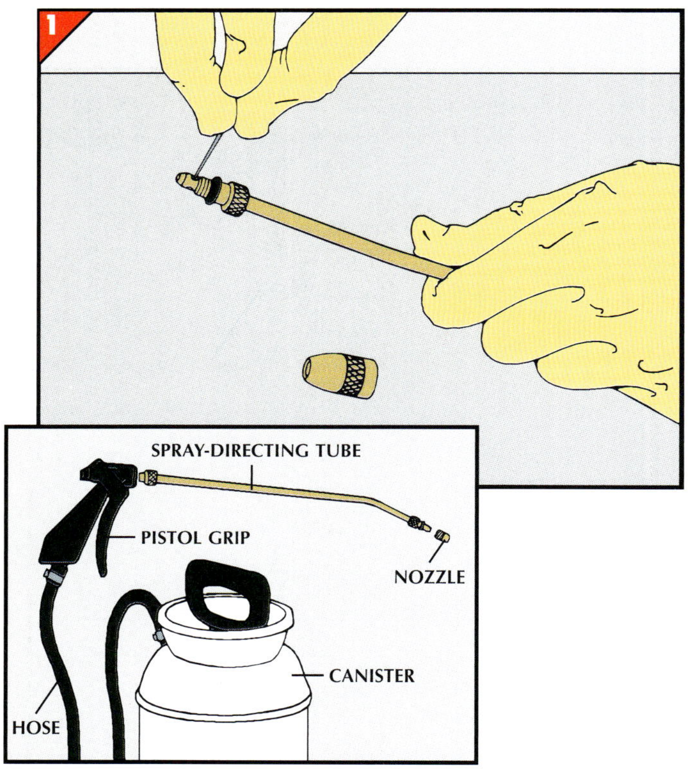

1. Clearing the outlet holes.

◆ Unscrew the spray-directing tube from the pistol grip, and remove the nozzle from the end of the tube.

◆ With a stiff wire, clear any residue from the outlet holes at the end of the tube *(above)*.

CAUTION

Handling Chemicals Safely

When cleaning sprayers, dump all rinse water into a separate container. Wrap paper around any wire and swabs used in the cleaning. Take the waste materials to your area's toxic waste pickup or disposal facility. Do not pour chemical wastes down the drain.

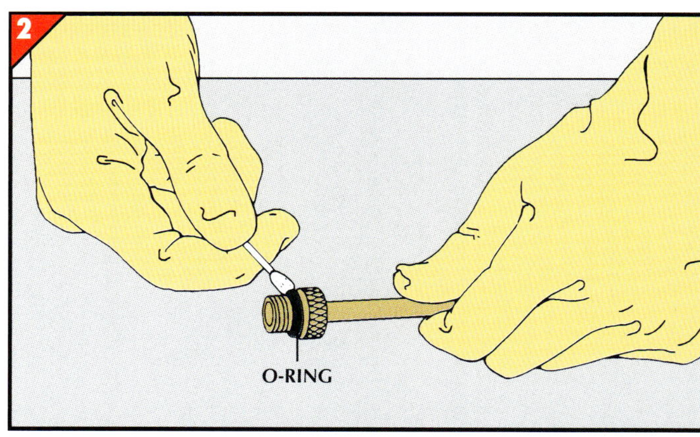

2. Completing the cleaning.

◆ Wipe the inside of the nozzle and the threads at the ends of the spray-directing tube with moistened cotton-tipped swabs until the cotton comes away clean.

◆ Lubricate the nozzle and threads with a swab dipped in household oil.

◆ With the swab, oil the O-rings at each end of the tube *(above)* to prevent sticking and maintain sealing power.

◆ Reassemble the sprayer and fill the canister with water. Spray the water to flush the hose and pistol grip.

A NEW HANDLE FOR A LARGE TOOL

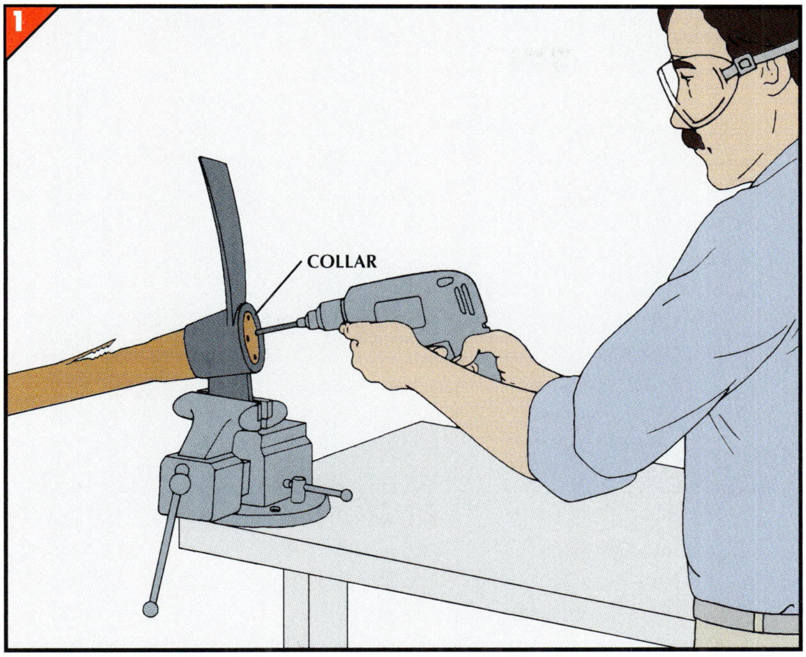

1. Removing a damaged handle.

◆ Secure the head of a large tool, such as the mattock shown at left, in a heavy vise.
◆ With a $\frac{1}{4}$-inch bit, drill four deep holes into the wood at the top of the handle as close as possible to the collar.
◆ Remove the tool from the vise, and tap the head with a small sledgehammer, driving it down toward the narrow part of the handle. If the head remains stuck, drill additional holes and tap harder.

2. Setting the new handle in place.

◆ Slip the mattock head onto the new handle.
◆ Drive the head into position with a small sledgehammer, forcing it over the wide section at the top of the handle *(above);* alternate the hammer blows from one side of the collar to the other to keep the head level.
◆ Set the mattock head in warm water overnight to swell the wood.

3. Making a tight fit.

◆ Let the wood dry. With a hammer, drive a $\frac{1}{2}$-inch metal wedge—available at hardware stores—into the top of the handle across the grain of the wood *(above).* This should press the wood firmly against the collar.
◆ If the head of the tool is even slightly loose on the handle, drive additional wedges perpendicular to the first until the head is absolutely secure.

How to Be Your Own Landscape Designer

Like any major home-improvement project, landscaping calls for advance planning. Even a small lot is surprisingly flexible and warrants a systematic weighing of the design options that are available.

Making a Map: Begin by creating a map of your property—the more detailed the better *(page 238)*. Include such factors as pleasing views and existing plantings. Note the locations of underground obstacles such as electric, water, and sewer lines, or dry wells, septic tanks, and cesspools; they will prevent or limit digging in certain areas.

Planning the New Yard: Look at your lot as a whole and list all the important intended uses of your outdoor space—relaxation, storage, gardening, and so on. To some extent, the orientation of the house on the lot will define these areas: Traditionally, the house divides the lot into an approach area in the front yard; a private living area in the back; and an out-of-the-way service area, perhaps at the side of the house, for a set of trash cans or a toolshed. You may want to distinguish other areas—for games or work, say—and perhaps set them off with their own design elements.

Adding Design Touches: Once you have outlined these areas, experiment on paper with the look of each one, keeping in mind the design principles explained at right and on the following two pages. At this stage, think of plantings in terms of their general visual attributes *(below)* and such basic characteristics as whether they are evergreen or deciduous, flowering or nonflowering. Consider physical comfort in your planning. Hedges and fences can screen an area from the street or neighboring houses. A strategically placed tree will filter light or create shade and can lower the temperature on a patio by 15° to 20° F. A row of evergreen shrubs will shelter a walkway from winter winds. Choosing the specific plants that meet your criteria is the last step in the design process *(see appendix, pages 346-360)*.

Visual Building Blocks

Each tree and shrub in a landscape has a number of visual attributes—shape, color, texture, scale (or size), proportions (the relationship between vertical and horizontal dimensions), and intensity of color. As you plan your design, picture how the visual qualities of the individual plantings will blend or contrast and how each tree or shrub might contribute to an overall feeling.

Design elements need to be considered not just individually but also in combinations. Terms such as *symmetry* or *balance* refer to their joint effects on the eye and mind.

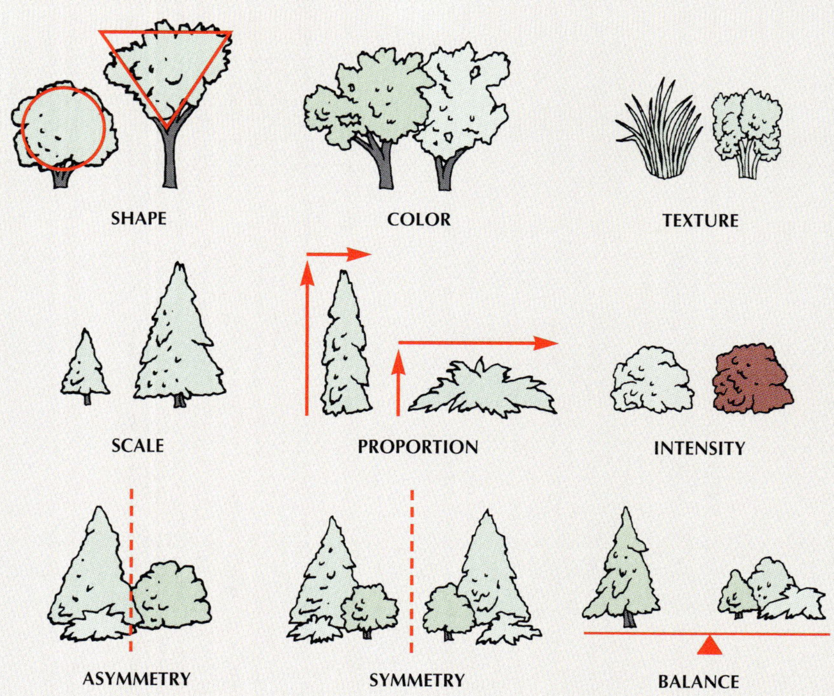

A RANGE OF EFFECTS

Unity.
Arrange the elements of your yard to create a unified picture—one in which the viewer's eye travels easily over the various elements, seeing them as parts of a whole. At right, two different borders of trees and shrubs both have a harmonious effect: In the top arrangement, the various sizes and shapes blend together casually; at bottom, the pattern of small and large plantings has a more formal unity.

Focal point.
An element that attracts the eye is a focal point; it may be a door, bench, garden pool, arbor, specimen plant, or sculpture. Focal points are often at one end of a central axis, as at top left. The symmetrically planted flowers and shrubs accentuate the walk and draw the viewer's attention to the focal point—the front door.

Another way to highlight an element is to place it in an area where it stands out; this can be off-center, as with the bench at bottom left. The shape of the garden leads the eye to the bench—the focal point for this view.

Balance.
All landscape elements have a visual "weight." Good designs often balance their elements—large and small, light and dark, coarse and fine, dense and open—around a central point. In the asymmetrically balanced view at right, each side is different but the weights are similar: the group of shrubs balance the tall tree. A simpler route to balance would be through symmetry, designing a yard so that its two sides almost mirror each other.

Rhythm.
The repeated use of similar patterns or shapes creates a visual rhythm by drawing the eye from one area to the next. Here, the outlined elements—the rectangular paving blocks, the planting beds, and the two trees along one side of the yard—provide a pleasant sense of movement.

Contrast.
Alterations in materials, plants, textures, or lines can enliven a design. In this example, the stone path adds a new texture, and its curving shape breaks up the yard's straight lines. The vine-covered screen provides some variety because it contrasts with the rest of the fencing, and the different shapes of the trees also add interest.

Designing with geometry.
Geometrical arrangements of plantings and paving can play a major role in a landscape design. In the top example at left, rectangles and squares *(highlighted)* reflect and extend the straight architectural lines of the house. Curves *(middle)* do the opposite, posing a strong and intriguing contrast to the house lines. Triangles *(bottom)* direct the eye to a focal point—here, the expanse of lawn in the center.

1. Mapping the site.

◆ On a sheet of graph paper, draw a map of your lot to scale. Then add a floor plan of the house's ground floor.
◆ Indicate good and bad views both from the windows of the house and from points within the yard; also note views into neighboring yards.
◆ Draw in existing trees, shrubs, flower beds, downspouts, and underground utilities; label steep banks, level areas, and spots with good drainage.
◆ Show the sun's morning, midday, and afternoon positions, as well as the direction of summer and winter winds.

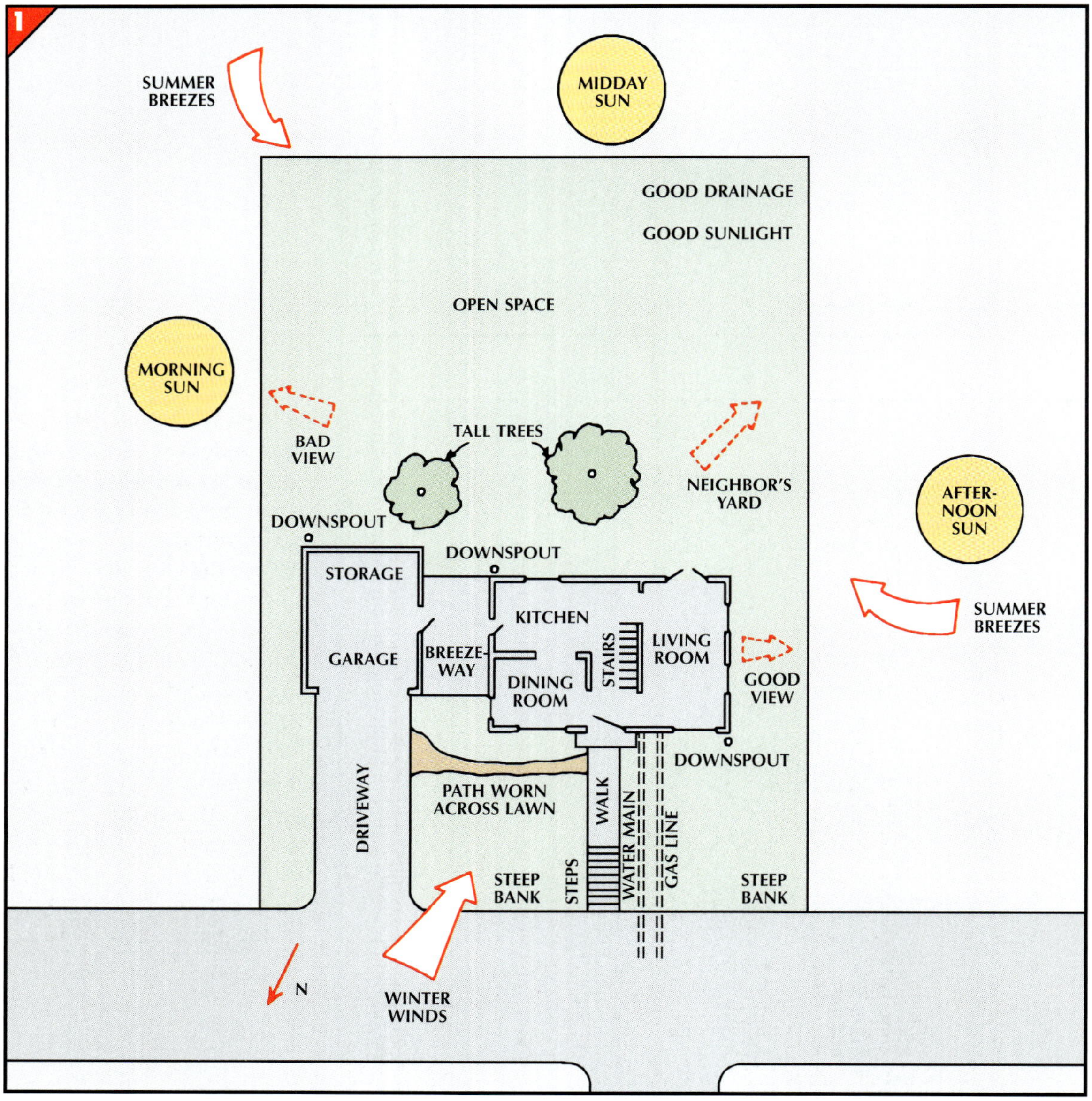

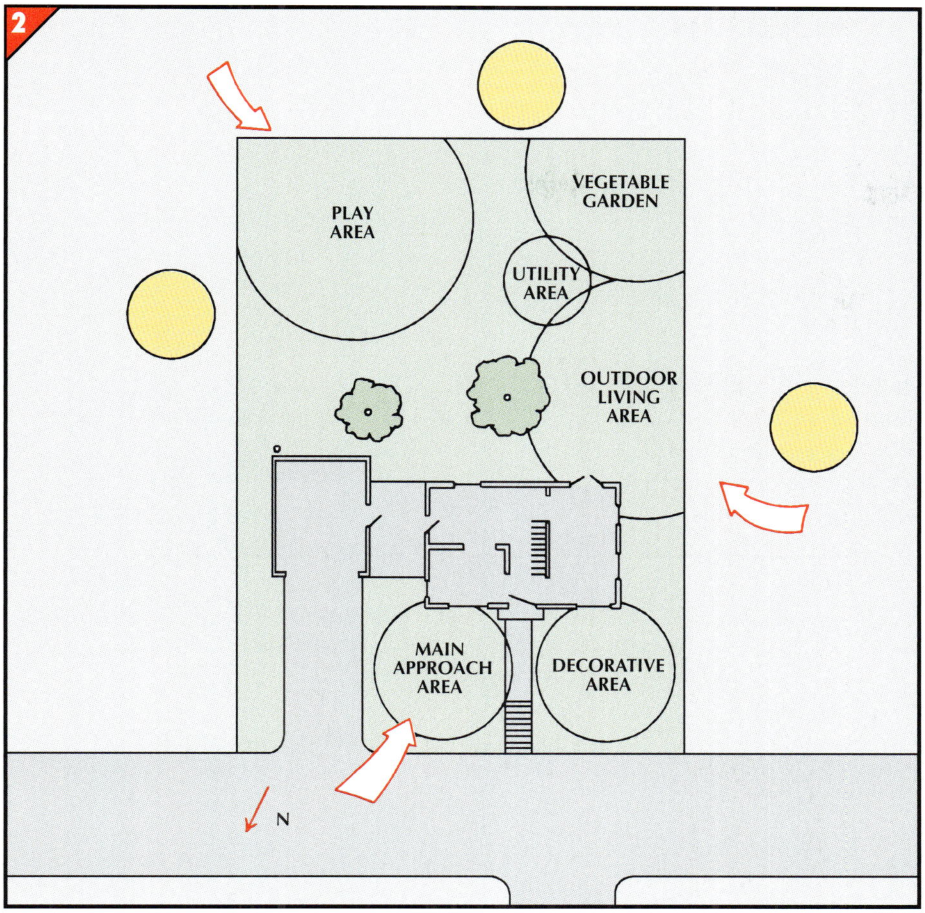

2. Outlining use areas.

◆ Tape tracing paper over the lot map and outline some use areas for the major sections of your yard.

◆ In the plan at left, the lawn near the driveway is designated as the main approach area; a path has already been worn there. The plan calls for decorative plantings that will screen the street view from inside the house. The space behind the living room is defined as an outdoor living area. A well-drained, sunny corner of the yard is envisioned as a vegetable garden, with an adjacent utility area for tool storage.

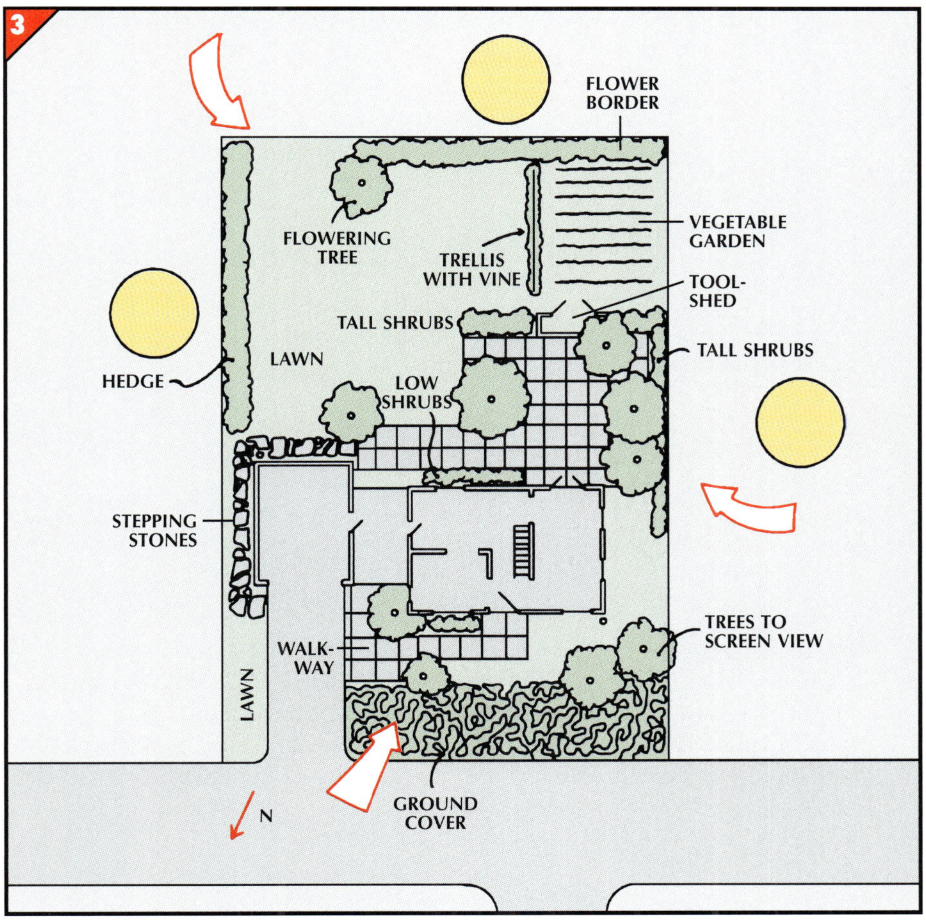

3. Experimenting with designs.

◆ Put a fresh sheet of tracing paper over your map, and experiment with designs for each of your circles on the previous map.

◆ Try to think of two or three different options for each area, remembering that you can remove things as well as add them. In the example at left, the old front steps are gone; instead, a paved walkway runs from the driveway to the front door. Decorative ground cover replaces hard-to-mow grass on the bank facing the street. In the backyard, the outdoor living area becomes a paved patio, and new shade trees and a high hedge block the afternoon sun and the neighbor's yard.

Leveling the Ground

Many landscaping projects require that the contours of uneven ground be smoothed. Gardens, pools, patios, and playgrounds, for example, all need a level tract. Lawns, too, are more attractive and easier to maintain if they are relatively flat. Although some earth-moving jobs are extensive enough to warrant the hiring of an excavating company, a surprising amount of earth can be moved by hand, in short sessions of digging and hauling.

Clearing Away Obstacles: Stones, stumps, logs, and other large debris must be removed before a site can be leveled. If a rock is too massive to be moved by the technique that is shown on page 241, either call in professional excavators or modify your landscape design to incorporate it—as the centerpiece of a rock garden, for example.

Don't try digging out a large tree stump by hand. Rather, rent a stump grinder; burn the stump with a special chemical solution sold in garden-supply centers; or cut the stump off just below ground level, cover it with dirt, and let it decompose naturally.

Grading the Land: If a plot of land is perfectly flat, water will pool there during a rain. To ensure that water drains properly, grade the site so that it drops at least 1 inch vertically for every 4 horizontal feet. Make sure that the grade slopes away from the house.

If different parts of your yard slope in different directions, wait for a steady, heavy rain and observe the natural drainage patterns for an hour or so. Then establish the right grade for each part of the yard by the string-and-grid method described on pages 242-243.

Filling In Low Spots: If you purchase earth to top off a grade, buy topsoil—a mix of earth and fertilizers from which stones, wood chips, and other debris have been removed—rather than fill, which often contains dense chunks of clay as well as rocks. A cubic yard of soil will cover 300 square feet of ground to a depth of 1 inch.

Protecting Your Back: To avoid back injuries, lift heavy loads as much as possible with the muscles of your arms and legs. As a further precaution, wear a lower-back support—either a weightlifter's belt or a back-saver brace of the kind used by furniture movers.

TOOLS

- Spade
- Garden rake
- Metal rod or digging bar
- Sod cutter
- Line level
- Wooden stakes and string

MANAGING HEAVY LOADS WITHOUT STRAIN

The right way to wield a spade.
◆ Standing upright, set your foot atop the blade of the spade and force it deep into the earth.
◆ Place your hands in the positions that are shown in the second picture above, and push the top of the handle down, using the tool as a lever to dislodge the soil.
◆ Flex your knees and slide your lower hand down the handle for better leverage. Keeping your back as straight as possible, use your arms and legs to lift and pitch the soil *(third and fourth pictures)*.

A two-hand lift.

◆ Holding your torso erect, squat as close as possible to the load to be lifted *(left picture).*

◆ Keep the load close to your body and stand up slowly, using your legs—not your back—for lifting force *(middle).*

◆ To lessen strain on your back, hold the load close to your waist *(right).* When you turn, move your entire body, without twisting your torso.

A one-hand lift.

◆ Bending your knees slightly and keeping your back straight, lean forward from the waist to reach the load.

◆ Using your legs for lifting power and keeping your shoulders level, raise your body upright to lift the load. Extend your free arm for balance.

Clearing logs from a site.

◆ With a sturdy, rigid rod or digging bar, maneuver the log onto a roller—a smooth, cylindrical piece of wood or a section of iron pipe.

◆ Tie a rope around the forward end of the log. Pull the log slowly over the roller, slipping additional rollers under the forward end to keep the log supported. As each roller comes free at the back, move it to the front.

Moving a rock.

◆ With a rod or digging bar, lever a heavy stone—up to 100 pounds—onto a sheet of heavy canvas or burlap.

◆ Grasp the cloth firmly at both corners of one end, and use your arm and leg muscles to drag the rock from the site.

LEVELING AND GRADING A PLOT OF LAND

1. Skimming sod from the surface.
With a sod cutter, remove the sod in strips from the area that will be leveled. If you intend to relay the sod on the plot after grading, gently roll up the strips, move them off the site, and unroll them again. Keep the sod well watered until you are ready for replanting.

2. Leveling ridges and depressions.
Working when the soil is neither wet nor dry but slightly moist, transfer the dirt from obvious high spots in the plot to low spots. After you drop each spadeful, use the blade's end to break up compacted soil into chunks 1 inch across or less.

3. Setting a slope with stakes and strings.
◆ Drive stakes at the four corners of the plot. The stakes at the lowest corners (generally farthest from the house) should be tall enough to roughly match the level of the highest corners' stakes.
◆ Tie a string to one of the higher-corner stakes and stretch it along the side of the plot to the lower-corner stake opposite. As a helper checks a line level *(photograph)* hung from the string, raise or lower the string as necessary to level it.
◆ Mark the lower stake at the level of the string. Move the string down the stake to set the desired slope *(page 240)*. Tie the string in place there.
◆ Repeat the procedure on the other side of the plot, then complete the boundary by tying leveled strings between the stakes at the top and the bottom of the plot.

LINE LEVEL

4. Laying out a grid.

◆ Drive stakes at 6-foot intervals just outside the strings that mark the boundaries of the plot.
◆ Create a grid over the area by tying a string between each opposite pair of stakes, setting the string at the level of the boundary strings. Make sure that the grid strings are taut.

5. Grading the surface.

◆ Working in one 6-foot square at a time, use a heavy rake to break up the soil to the consistency of coarse sand and spread it parallel to the plane of the string grid.
◆ Smooth the plot with the flat top side of the rake. Remove the stakes and strings.

Correcting Faulty Drainage

Professional landscapers define drainage as a two-stage process—the flow of water across the ground according to grade and the subsequent seepage of the water into the soil. In the first stage, rainwater can create problems in several ways: It can erode steep ground; it may flow to low areas and leave them soggy long after the rain has stopped; or it may pool around a house and perhaps find its way through the foundation.

A Low-Cost Fix for a Wet Basement: If a high water table or some other unseen problem is causing a wet basement, drainage professionals will have to be called in—but first check to see if the situation is simply a result of faulty surface drainage. In a 10-foot-wide zone around the house, the grade should drop at least 1 vertical inch for every horizontal foot.

Correct any insufficiency in the grade, and at the same time, use flexible plastic pipe to extend your gutter downspouts so that rainwater is channeled away from the house. Depending on the slope of your yard, the extension can end either in an underground dry well that traps and slowly disperses the water *(right)* or in a simple culvert that drains it away.

Managing Hill Runoff: To keep rainwater from collecting at the base of a gentle slope, divert the flow by constructing berms and swales—low earthen dams and shallow trenches *(opposite, bottom)*. For steeper slopes, the solution may be to terrace the land and build a retaining wall *(pages 246-249)*.

TOOLS
- Line level
- Sod cutter
- Spade
- Tamper
- Tape measure

MATERIALS
- Wooden stakes and string
- Flexible nonperforated drainpipe
- Downspout adapter
- Splash block
- Topsoil
- Gravel

DIVERTING WATER FROM THE FOUNDATION

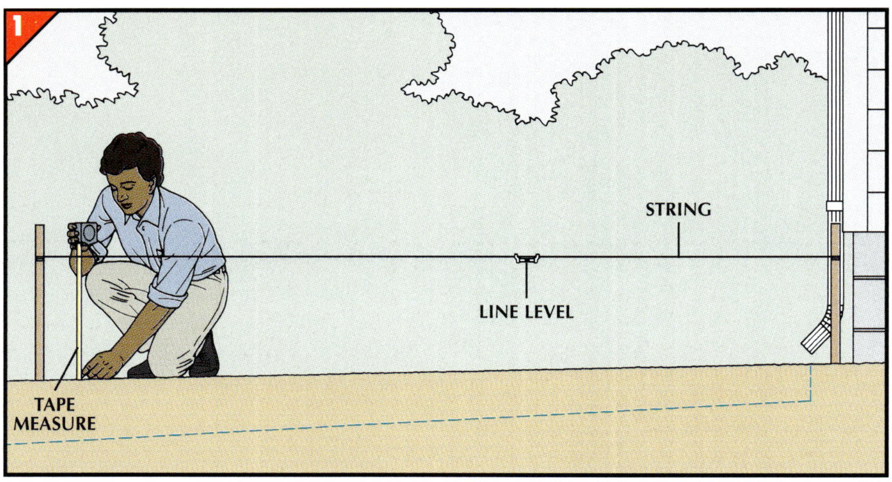

1. Checking the grade.

◆ Drive a stake next to the house and another one 10 feet away from the foundation. Tie a string between them and level it with a line level. Measure from the string to the ground at 1-foot intervals to calculate the grade. Move the stakes and repeat at other points along one side of the house.

◆ In any area where the grade drops less than 1 vertical inch for each horizonal foot, strip the sod *(page 242)* and remove any shrubs *(page 328)*.

◆ Dig a trench for the downspout extension; the trench should be 8 inches wide, a minimum of 10 feet long, and at least 6 inches deep at the downspout. It should also slope 1 inch per foot *(dashed lines, above)*.

2. Extending the downspout.

◆ Attach an adapter to the end of the downspout.

◆ Lay flexible nonperforated drainpipe in the trench and connect it to the adapter. The pipe must lie flat along the bottom of the trench without any dips or humps. Remove or add dirt under the pipe as necessary.

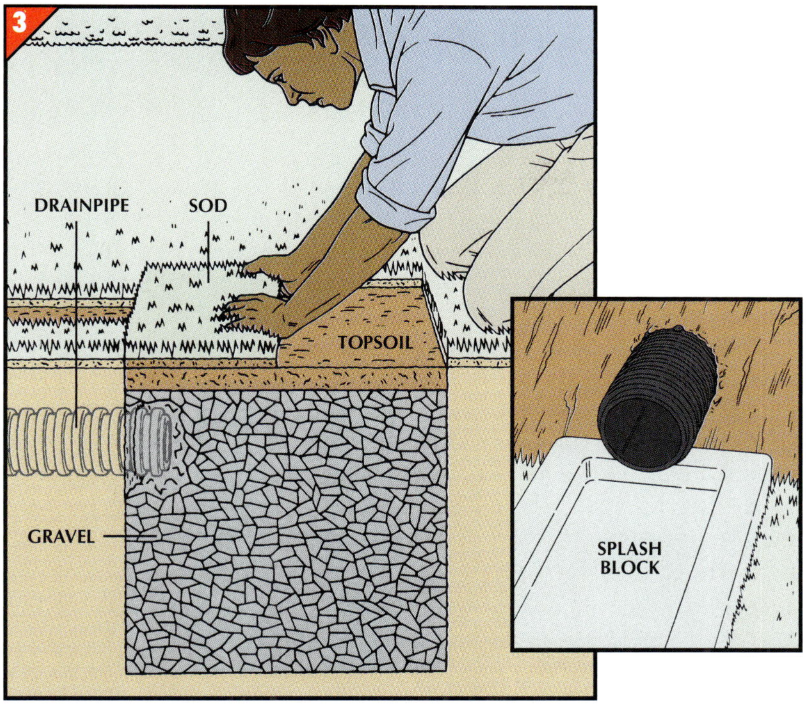

3. Making a dry well.

◆ At the end of the drainpipe trench, skim the sod from a $2\frac{1}{2}$-foot-square area and set it aside. Then dig a hole about 3 feet deep.

◆ Pull the flexible drainpipe so that the lip protrudes a few inches over the hole. Fill in the trench with topsoil and tamp it down.

◆ Fill the hole with gravel to a point about 1 inch above the top of the pipe. Add topsoil and replace the sod *(above)*.

◆ If the trench ends on a slope, lead the pipe out of the hill and onto a splash block *(inset)*. The block will prevent erosion at the outlet point.

4. Correcting the grade.

◆ When the drainpipe extension is complete, correct any improper grade around the house. If you are piling dirt higher against the foundation, first treat the masonry with a waterproofing sealant. The soil level must remain at least 6 inches below wooden siding in order to keep termites out.

◆ Use a tamper to pack the soil firmly.

CONTROLLING RUNOFF ON A GENTLE SLOPE

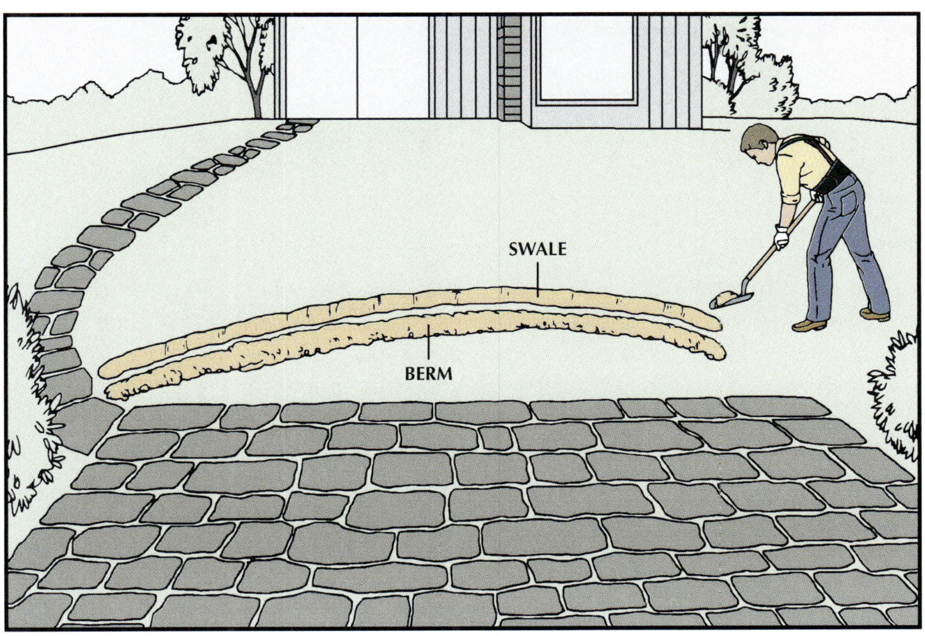

Creating berms and swales.

◆ Dig a trench, or swale, about 3 inches deep and at least twice that wide across the slope above the area you wish to protect. Create a berm by piling the leftover soil into a gently rounded mound below the swale, then tamp it down.

◆ Lay sod *(page 298)* on the berm and the swale or plant a ground cover *(page 299)*.

A Timber Retaining Wall

Terracing slopes with timber retaining walls not only solves erosion problems but can also add to the visual appeal of yards and gardens. Because earth and water create tremendous pressures behind a retaining wall, you must make the structure strong and provide for adequate drainage.

The design described at right and on the following pages meets these requirements; moreover, it is easy to build, presents a trim face unmarked by nails or fasteners, and in most localities requires no building permit. This design, however, is not suitable for walls that are more than 3 feet high; they call for both a permit and the services of a structural engineer. If you have a long, steep slope, consider terracing it at intervals with two or more 3-foot walls.

Choosing the Material: Wooden retaining walls can be made of any timbers that have been treated to resist rot and termites. Railroad ties were once the material of choice, but they have fallen out of favor because the wood is treated with the preservative creosote, which is poisonous to many plants.

Pressure-treated 6- by 6-inch timbers of poplar or pine, either rough- or smooth-sawed, are excellent alternatives. They are treated with environmentally safe preservatives and come in convenient 8-foot lengths, which can be cut as needed with a chain saw *(box, below)*.

Where to Place the Wall: If you build the wall near the bottom of the slope, as is the case here, you will need to add fill dirt behind it. Alternatively, you can excavate higher up, erect the wall against the slope's face, and cart away the leftover dirt. The first option increases your level yard space above the wall; the second, below it.

CAUTION *Before excavating, establish the locations of possible underground obstacles such as dry wells, septic tanks, and cesspools, and electric, water, and sewer lines.*

TOOLS

- Line level
- Shovel
- Hand- or gas-powered tamper
- Carpenter's level
- Chain saw
- Heavy-duty drill with a $\frac{3}{8}$-inch bit 18 inches long
- Long-handled sledgehammer

MATERIALS

- Wooden stakes and string
- Gravel
- 6-by-6 pressure-treated timbers of poplar or pine
- Galvanized screen and nails
- $\frac{3}{8}$-inch reinforcing steel bars 42 inches long
- $\frac{3}{8}$-inch galvanized spikes 12 inches long
- 4-inch perforated drain tile

Using a Chain Saw Safely

Be sure the cutting teeth are sharp and the chain is at the proper tension: You should never be able to pull it more than $\frac{1}{8}$ inch away from the bar. Steady the timbers on solid supports for sawing, and chalk cutting lines on the timbers as guides. Wear goggles to protect your eyes from flying woodchips. Brace the saw firmly on the ground before starting it, and hold the saw with both hands when cutting. Because pressure-treated lumber contains pesticides, wear a dust mask when sawing it and wash your hands thoroughly afterward.

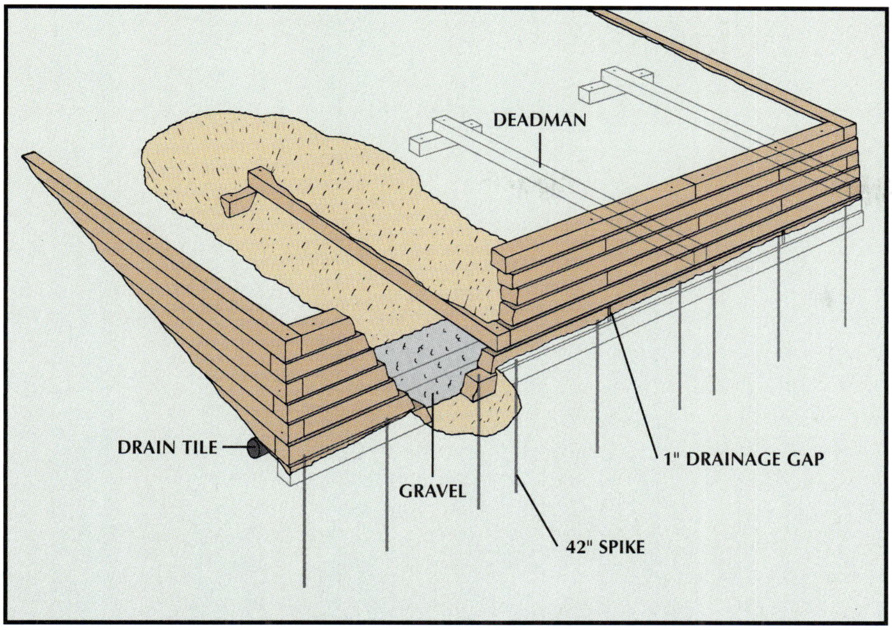

Anatomy of a retaining wall.
The bottom course in this 3-foot retaining wall is set in a trench and anchored by 42-inch-long bars of $\frac{3}{8}$-inch reinforcing steel, or rebar. Successive courses are secured with 12-inch galvanized spikes. Several features help the wall withstand the pressure of earth and water behind it. Each course is staggered $\frac{1}{2}$ inch toward the slope. Reinforcing timbers—deadmen–run 8 feet back into the hillside and rest on 1-foot-long timber crossplates anchored with 42-inch spikes. Sidewalls are built up on the corner deadmen and connected to the wall by interlocked corners. Four-inch perforated drain tile buried in gravel and 1-inch gaps between adjacent timbers in the second course provide escape routes for the water behind the wall.

PREPARING THE SITE

1. Marking the wall trench.

◆ Drive 5-foot stakes at the points you have chosen for the corners of the wall. Tie a line between the stakes, and level it with a line level.
◆ Measure to find the point where the line is farthest from ground level *(right)*. This is the lowest grade point; mark it with a stake.
◆ Drop a plumb line every 4 feet along the line, and drive stakes at these points to mark the outer edge of the wall. Transfer the line from the 5-foot stakes to the lower stakes.

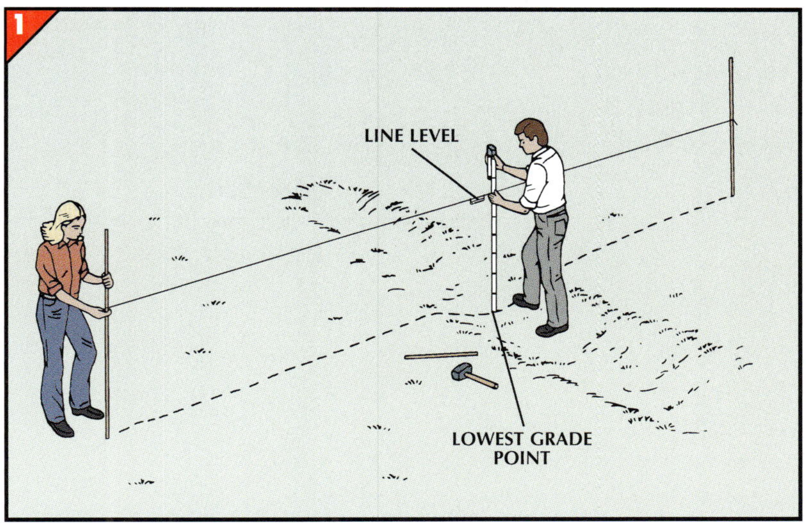

2. Digging the trench.

◆ Starting at the lowest grade point and working out to the corner stakes, dig a level-bottomed trench that is 1 foot deep at the lowest grade point and 1 foot wide along its full length.
◆ Spread a 6-inch layer of gravel in the trench and tamp it down. Check the base of the trench with a carpenter's level. Remove the stakes.
◆ Lay the timbers for the first course in the trench. Their tops should be even with ground level at the lowest grade point.
◆ To lay out deadman trenches, start at one corner and use the squaring method on page 256 to stretch an 8-foot line at right angles to the wall; drive a stake at the end of the line. Repeat at the other corner and at 6-foot intervals in between.

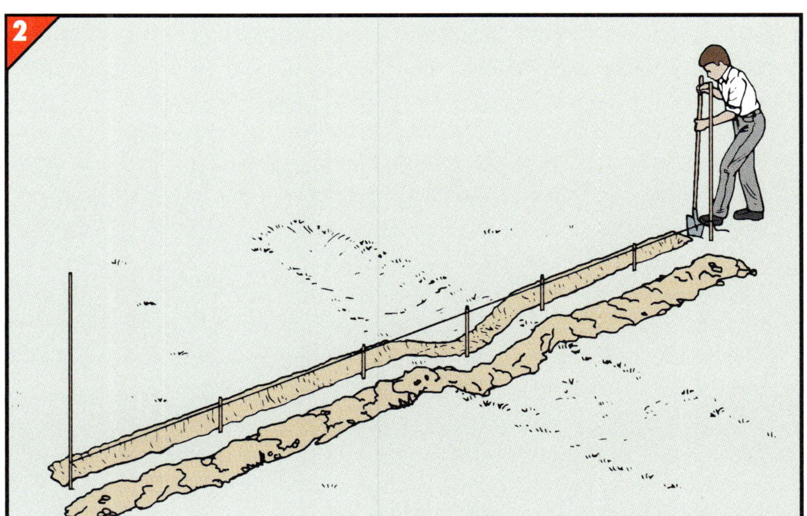

BUILDING THE WALL

1. Securing the first two courses.

◆ At the center of each timber and 6 inches from each end, drill vertical holes completely through, using the $\frac{3}{8}$-inch bit. Then drive 42-inch spikes through the holes and into the ground with a sledgehammer *(right)*.

◆ Lay the second course so that the joints between timbers do not coincide with those of the first. Set the second course $\frac{1}{2}$ inch closer to the hillside, and leave 1-inch gaps between timbers to serve as drainage holes.

◆ Drill three holes through each timber, and drive 12-inch spikes through the holes to pin the first two courses together.

2. Bracing the wall.

◆ For the deadmen, dig trenches—their bottoms level with the top of the second course—back to the stakes.

◆ Across the ends of the deadman trenches, dig crossplate trenches 3 feet long and 6 inches deeper than the deadman trenches at that point.

◆ Lay the crossplates in place, then set the deadmen on top of them so their other ends rest on the second course, $\frac{1}{2}$ inch back from the front face. Drill pilot holes and drive 42-inch spikes through the deadmen and the crossplates and into the ground. Drive 12-inch spikes through the deadmen into the second course.

◆ For the third course of the wall, cut timbers to fit between the deadmen—making sure that the joints don't align with those of the second course—and secure them with spikes.

3. Laying a drainage run.

◆ On the back of the wall, nail pieces of galvanized screen over the drainage gaps in the second course of timbers.
◆ Shovel a bed of gravel behind the wall, leaving enough space to run a length of 4-inch perforated drain tile along the top of the bed and under the deadmen *(below)*. Then add another 6 inches of gravel.

4. Interlocking the corners.

◆ After completing the fourth course of timbers, lay a sidewall timber at each end of the wall and secure it to the corner deadman with 12-inch spikes.
◆ Lay another sidewall timber atop the first so that its end is set back $\frac{1}{2}$ inch from the face of the fourth course. Secure it with spikes.
◆ Fit the timbers for the fifth course between the sidewall timbers, fastening them with spikes.
◆ Continue laying the front and sidewall courses in this manner, making sure to offset the timber joints between courses and stagger each course $\frac{1}{2}$ inch closer to the hillside. Then drill horizontal holes through the corner deadmen and those sidewall courses that extend to the front of the wall, and drive 12-inch spikes to secure the corners *(right)*.
◆ Spread a 4-inch layer of soil behind the wall and tamp it with a hand- or gas-powered tamper. Spread and tamp additional 4-inch layers until the fill is level with the top of the wall.

Preparing Soil for Planting

All soils are composed primarily of mineral particles, ranging in size from fine, dense clay to medium-size silt to coarse, loose sand. The proportions of these ingredients—along with decayed vegetable and animal matter, known as humus—determine the texture and quality of the soil. Soil that has too much clay in it retains water almost indefinitely, causing problems with drainage. Sandy soil dries too quickly and allows nutrients to leach out.

The best garden soil is called loam and is a balance of clay, silt, and sand, with plenty of humus to help hold the mineral particles together and aid in the retention of moisture. Crumbly in texture, loam has plentiful spaces to let both air and excess water pass through, while nutrients are retained. Humus keeps the soil fertile and makes the soil easy to work.

Proper texture is only one requirement of good garden soil. In addition, the soil must contain nutrients necessary for plant growth, and it should be neither too acidic nor too alkaline—conditions that impair the ability of roots to extract the nutrients from the soil.

A Soil Diagnosis: With a few simple tests, you can evaluate your soil's texture and chemical composition. The water test shown at right can gauge the need for texture-improving organic amendments. Peat moss and dehydrated manure are two widely used amendments, but the best of all is compost; it adds nutrients as well as improving soil structure—and you can make it in your backyard *(page 253)*.

For chemical tests, use an inexpensive soil-test kit, available at garden centers. Most of these kits contain an array of test vials and chemicals, along with charts for interpreting the results. There are tests for nitrogen, phosphorus, potassium, and—most important of all—the degree of acidity or alkalinity, known as pH.

Getting the Correct pH: The scale that measures pH runs from 0 to 14. Neutral soil has a pH of 7. Above 7, soil is increasingly alkaline; below 7, it is increasingly acid. Most plants grow best in slightly acid soil, with a pH level between 6 and 7; consult the appendix *(pages 346-360)* for plant preferences.

To reduce acidity, add dolomitic limestone, which includes magnesium, an essential nutrient. In light, sandy soil, 4 pounds per every 100 square feet will raise the pH by .5; add 20 percent to this formula for loamy soil and 30 percent in heavy, clayey soil.

Excess alkalinity is corrected by adding sulfur—either pure ground sulfur, iron sulfate, or aluminum sulfate. Pure sulfur acts more slowly than the others but lasts longer; iron sulfate puts iron in the soil, producing lush, dark foliage; aluminum sulfate must be used cautiously because too much aluminum can be harmful to plants.

To reduce the alkalinity in 100 square feet of sandy soil by a pH interval of .5 to 1, use 3 to 5 pounds of iron or aluminum sulfate, or $\frac{1}{2}$ to $\frac{3}{4}$ pound of ground sulfur; use $1\frac{1}{2}$ times as much in loamy soil, 4 times as much in clayey soil.

When and How to Enrich the Soil: Add amendments to your soil 4 to 6 months before planting, to give them time to become thoroughly incorporated. Mix in organic amendments by tilling the soil *(page 252)*. Broadcast dolomitic limestone or sulfur on the surface, then rake it into the top few inches.

For a small area, you can do the tilling with a spade and spading fork *(page 252)*. To till a large area quickly and easily, rent a power tiller. A model that has the tines set behind the engine is more stable and generally preferable for a beginner; a model with tines mounted on the front is more maneuverable in tight places.

Do not till soggy soil; it will break up into large, heavy clods that can dry as hard as rocks. A good time for tilling is generally 3 days after a rain, when the soil is neither too wet nor so dry that the job creates annoying dust.

TOOLS

- Spade
- Bucket
- Trowel
- Ruler
- Test kit
- Tarp
- Spading fork
- Power tiller

MATERIALS

- Manure
- Peat moss
- Compost
- Dolomitic limestone
- Sulfur

ANALYZING TEXTURE AND CHEMISTRY

1. Gathering samples.

◆ At several different spots within the area you intend to plant, dig holes about 6 inches wide and 6 to 9 inches deep.

◆ Slice a thin wedge of soil from the wall of each hole *(above)*. Wearing gloves so that your hands do not affect soil chemistry, remove sod and any small stones or roots from the samples, then mix them all together in a plastic bucket with the spade or a trowel.

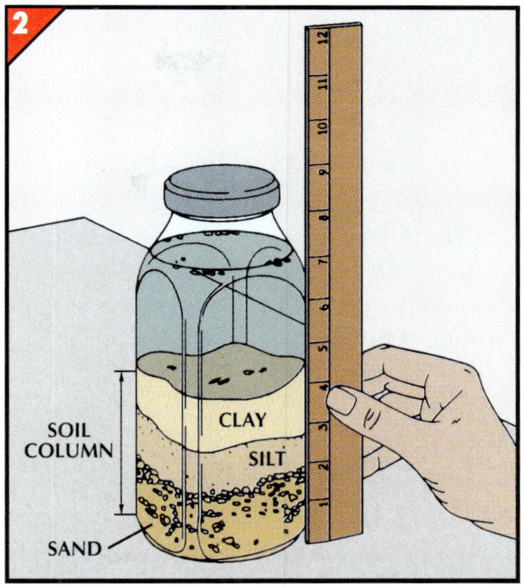

2. A water test for texture.

◆ Fill a quart bottle half full with water and add soil until the bottle is nearly full. Cap the bottle, shake it well, then wait for the soil particles to settle in layers—from 3 hours to a day.

◆ Measure the thickness of each layer—clay on top, silt in the middle, and sand on the bottom—and divide it by the total height of the soil column to get each component's percentage.

◆ When you adjust your soil's texture with organic amendments *(page 252)*, add about 2 or 3 inches of peat moss, manure, or compost if the soil is less than 25 percent silt or more than 25 percent clay. For soil that is more than 30 percent sand, add twice as much.

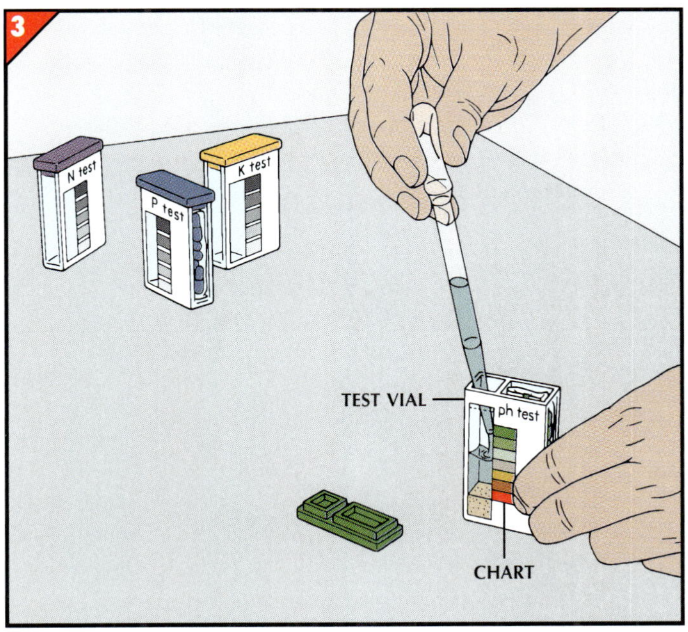

3. Testing the pH level.

◆ Fill the pH test chamber of a soil test kit to the correct mark with soil and add the amount of chemical called for in the kit's directions.

◆ Using an eyedropper, fill the chamber with water up to the indicated line *(left)*. Cap the chamber and shake it to mix the soil and the liquid thoroughly.

◆ After the soil particles settle, compare the color of the remaining solution with the kit's color chart. The closest match of colors indicates your soil's pH level.

MODIFYING SOIL TO IMPROVE IT

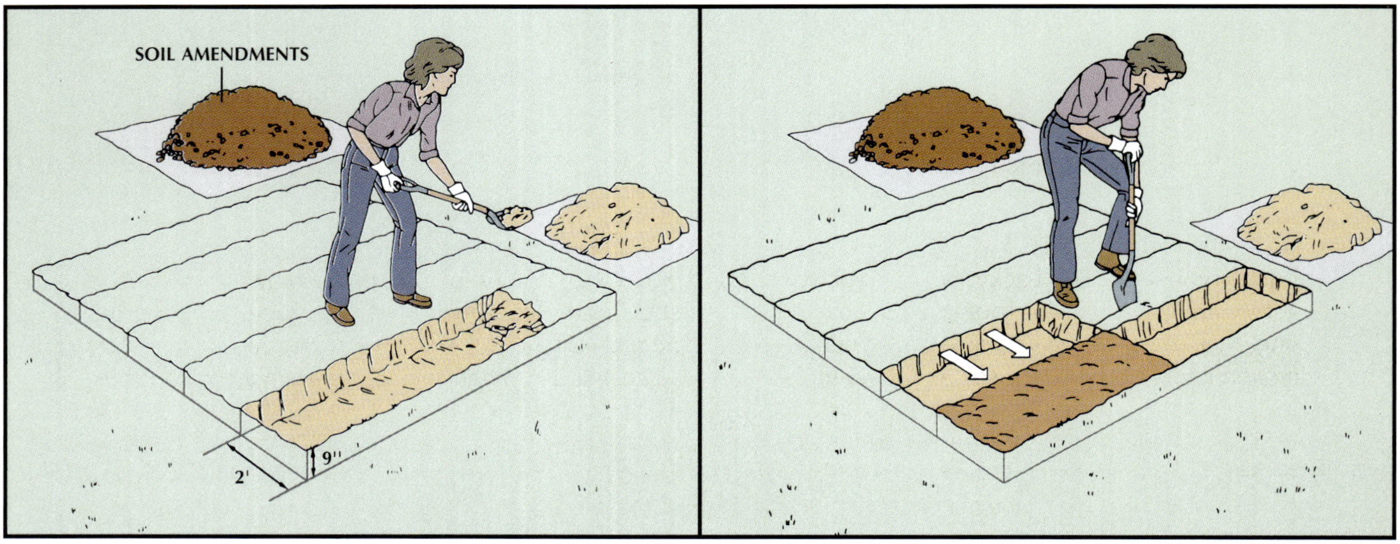

Turning the soil by hand.

◆ With the point of a spade, outline the area to be worked and divide it into sections 2 feet wide.

◆ Dig out the soil from an end section to the full depth of the spade (6 to 9 inches), depositing the soil on a plastic sheet or tarp *(above, left)*. Then fill this trench with soil from the adjacent section *(above, right)*.

◆ Spread the desired organic soil amendments *(Step 2, page 251)* on the first section and work them in with a spading fork.

◆ Transfer the top 9 inches of soil from the third section to fill up the second, and add amendments. Continue in this way until you reach the last section. Fill the last trench with the original soil from the first section.

Operating a power tiller.

◆ Put the tiller in neutral, position it at one corner of the planting area, and set the tines to the correct depth—from 3 inches for heavy, clayey soil to 8 inches for sandy soil.

◆ Start the engine, shift into forward, and guide the machine along one side of the bed. Make a broad turn at the far end, and work back in the opposite direction, creating a U-shaped area of tilled soil.

◆ Continue back and forth until you reach the end, then reverse directions and repeat the pattern in the untilled strips *(inset)*. If your soil is very heavy, set the tines at 6 inches and till again.

◆ Spread the desired amount of organic soil amendments *(Step 2, page 251)* on top of the soil. Set the tines at maximum depth and till in a direction perpendicular to the first set of lines to work in the amendments. If the tiller bucks excessively, go more slowly and raise the tines slightly.

THE COMPOST PILE: FREE FERTILIZER FROM THROWAWAYS

Making compost is somewhat like setting up a fertilizer factory in your own backyard. The workers in the factory are billions of microorganisms—bacteria and fungi that convert organic waste from your yard and kitchen into a nutrient-rich soil amendment.

A Suitable Container: If organic matter is simply heaped in a pile, the composting process can take up to a year. But if you place the materials in bins that distribute heat and moisture evenly, you will have usable compost in just 3 or 4 weeks. The most efficient composting system uses three bins: one for fresh organic material, one for half-decomposed matter, and one for the finished product. You can buy bins —plastic barrels, for example—or you can make them.

One easy-to-build arrangement is shown below. These bins are 4 feet high and 3 feet square. No floor is necessary. The vertical posts, set into the ground for stability, are 2-by-4s. Grooves cut into the front posts with a router or circular saw allow 1-by-6 slats to slide in and out for easy turning of the compost.

Air circulation around the pile is very important. Here, the front slats are held apart by screws that are driven into one side of the boards. The sides and backs of the bins are heavy-gauge wire screening, held in place by 1-by-6 boards nailed to the top and bottom of the posts.

The Ingredients: To start a compost pile, you need equal proportions of so-called "browns" (shredded sticks, sawdust, and leaves) and "greens" (grass and hedge clippings, garden refuse, and vegetable scraps). Other organic materials, such as wood ashes, fruit peels, crushed eggshells, and coffee grounds, are also helpful. Do not include diseased plants, invasive weeds, pet droppings, or cooked scraps, which will attract vermin.

Place 6 inches of coarse brown material on the bottom. Then add an inch of commercial manure to provide food for the microorganisms, followed by 6 inches of green material, another inch of manure, and an inch of soil. Water until damp, then keep stacking layers in the same sequence and proportions until the bin is full.

Cooking the Pile: Leave the pile alone for a few days, then start turning it with a spading fork several times a week to speed decomposition. After a couple of weeks, shift part of the pile to the next bin, and add fresh kitchen and yard waste to the first; layering does not matter now.

Water both bins occasionally to keep the piles moist. In another 2 weeks, the compost in the second bin should be dark and crumbly; store it in the third bin until ready for use.

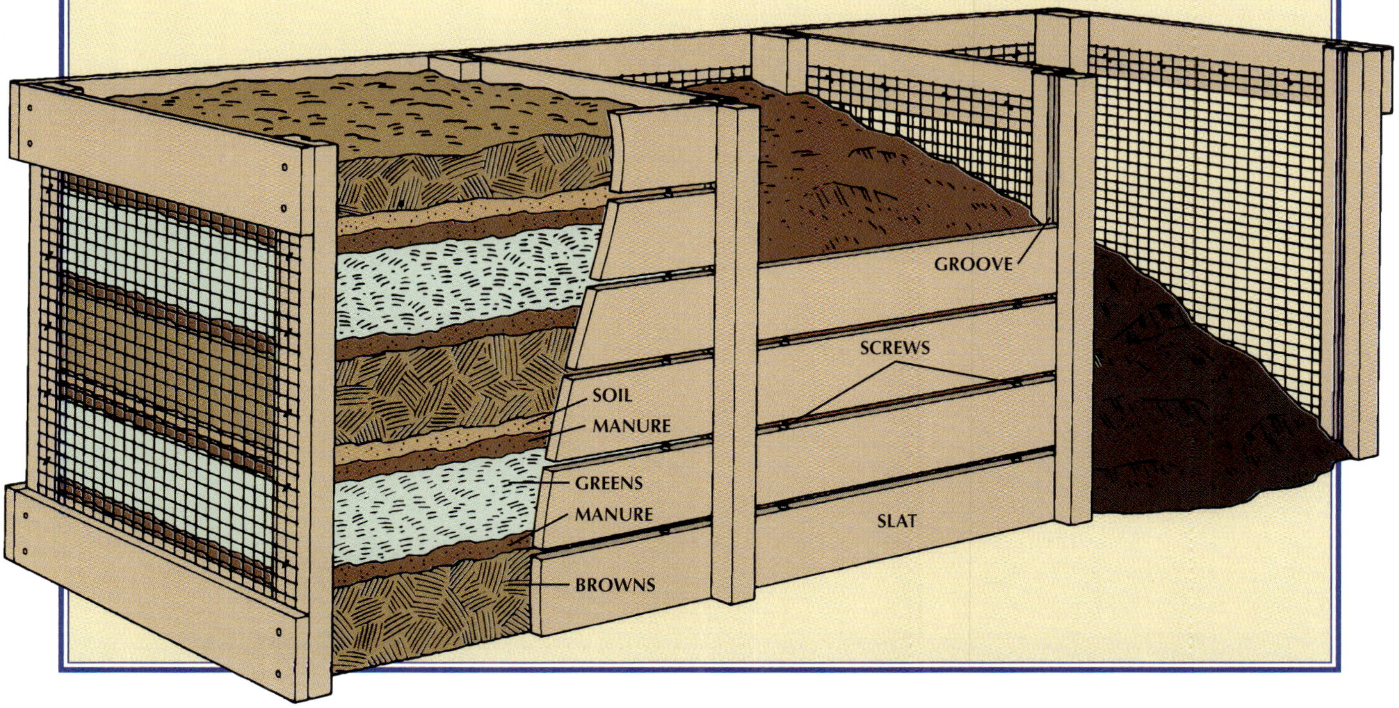

8 Special Touches for Your Yard

A carpet of green, punctuated by trees and shrubs, supplies almost everything needed for a well-landscaped yard. Yet a constructed element or two in the plan can make for an appealing finale. An addition as simple as a new flower bed or as ambitious as a garden pool can showcase favorite varieties or establish a fresh vantage point from which to appreciate the fruits of your landscaping labors.

Assembling a flower box →

Settings for Flowers or Shrubs

Clearly defined areas set aside for flowers or shrubs are part of any landscaping plan. Beds for such plantings can be dug into the ground or boldly raised above the surrounding terrain.

The Simple Approach: Locate ground-level beds in an area of your yard with good drainage. Apart from properly prepared soil, the only requirement for the bed is a barrier of edging to keep out grass and weeds.

Plastic edging comes in 20-foot rolls and includes a coupler for joining sections. Purchase plastic stakes separately to anchor the edging to the ground.

Aluminum edging in a choice of colors is sold in 16-foot lengths. It is molded with flanges and grooves for joining sections and comes with one anchor stake for each 4 feet of edging.

Both metal and plastic edgings bend easily, making them especially suitable for irregularly shaped beds. Right-angle couplers are also available for installing both kinds of edging around a bed with corners that are square. However, rectangular beds are also ideally suited to the mortarless brick edging shown on page 258. Whatever edging you choose for a rectangular bed, use the triangulation method *(below)* to lay out square corners.

Raised Beds: In locations with poor drainage or crossed by large tree roots, a ground-level bed is impractical. The solution is an aboveground bed of soil framed by walls between 12 inches and 24 inches high.

Among the materials suitable for building a raised bed are stone and brick, but pressure-treated timbers are by far the easiest to work with *(pages 258-259)*. After you have assembled the walls, fill the frame of the bed with amended soil and compost *(pages 250-253)*.

TOOLS

- Garden spade
- Mattock
- Edging tool
- Circular saw
- Sawhorses
- Carpenter's level
- Maul
- Electric drill
- $\frac{1}{4}$-inch and $\frac{3}{8}$-inch auger bits

MATERIALS

- Garden hose
- Stakes and string
- Edging
- Chalk
- 6-by-6 pressure-treated timbers
- Mason's cord
- $\frac{3}{8}$- by 24-inch reinforcing rods
- 10-inch galvanized spikes

SAFETY TIPS

Gloves protect your hands during spadework. Wear a back brace to reduce the risk of injury when digging.

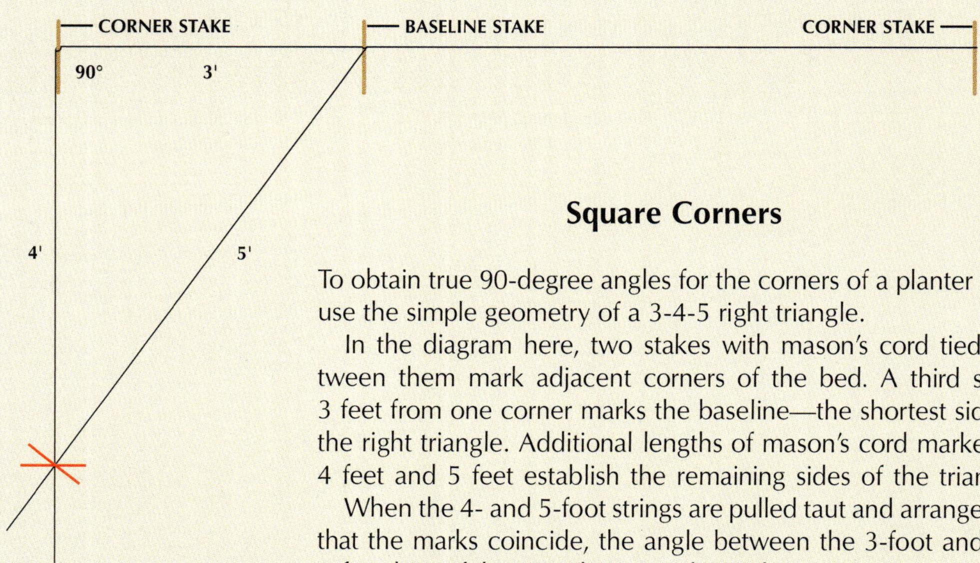

Square Corners

To obtain true 90-degree angles for the corners of a planter bed, use the simple geometry of a 3-4-5 right triangle.

In the diagram here, two stakes with mason's cord tied between them mark adjacent corners of the bed. A third stake 3 feet from one corner marks the baseline—the shortest side of the right triangle. Additional lengths of mason's cord marked at 4 feet and 5 feet establish the remaining sides of the triangle.

When the 4- and 5-foot strings are pulled taut and arranged so that the marks coincide, the angle between the 3-foot and the 4-foot legs of the triangle is exactly 90 degrees.

MAKING A GROUND-LEVEL BED

1. Outlining the bed.

◆ For a curved bed, lay out a garden hose in the desired shape; for a bed with straight sides, use stakes and string.
◆ Stand outside the bed and place the blade of a garden spade against the inside edge of the hose or string. Holding the shaft at a slight angle, push the blade 4 to 6 inches deep *(left)*.
◆ Cut along the outline of the bed in the same manner to make a continuous slit in the turf.

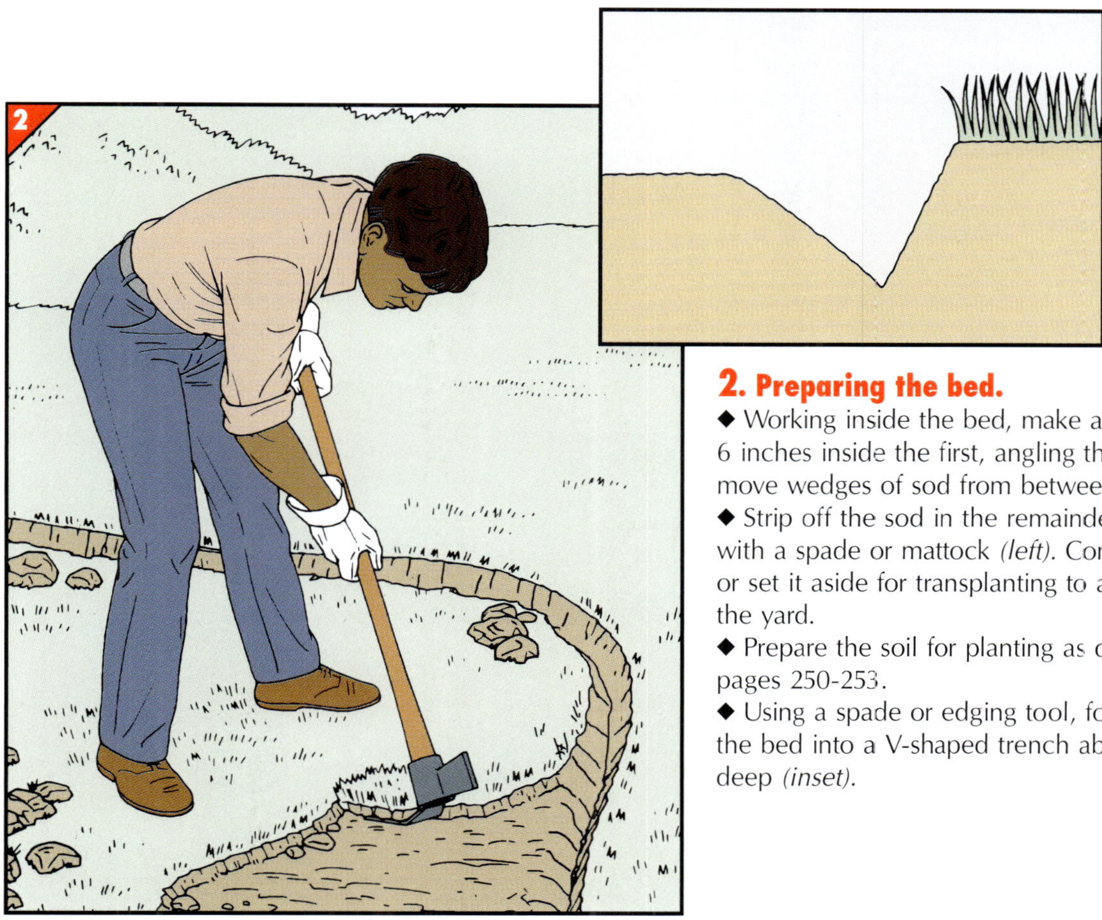

2. Preparing the bed.

◆ Working inside the bed, make a second cut 6 inches inside the first, angling the spade to remove wedges of sod from between the two cuts.
◆ Strip off the sod in the remainder of the bed with a spade or mattock *(left)*. Compost the sod, or set it aside for transplanting to another part of the yard.
◆ Prepare the soil for planting as described on pages 250-253.
◆ Using a spade or edging tool, form the edge of the bed into a V-shaped trench about 4 inches deep *(inset)*.

EDGING CHOICES

Plastic.

◆ Unroll the edging and lay it flat for an hour.

◆ Meanwhile, deepen the trench with a garden trowel to leave only the hose-shaped rim of the edging exposed.

◆ Bend the edging to match the trench contours and set it in place. To link edging sections, insert a plastic coupler halfway into the upper rim of one section, then slide the next section onto the coupler *(right)*.

◆ To anchor the edging, drive plastic stakes through the barb molded into the bottom. Place the point of the stake at the barb and, to assure a 45-degree angle, hold the beveled tip against the edging *(photograph)*. Position stakes at the ends of the edging, the joints, and at 4-foot intervals between them.

◆ Backfill the trench and tamp on both sides of the edging until only the rim can be seen.

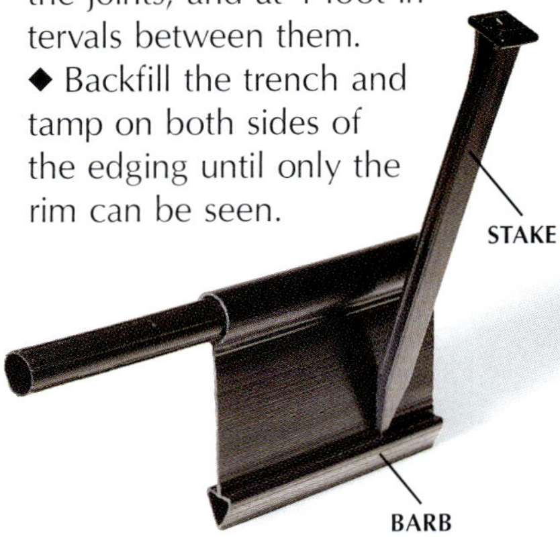

Aluminum.

◆ Deepen the trench to leave $\frac{1}{2}$ inch of the edging above ground level.

◆ Stand the edging alongside the bed and gently bend it to match the curves of the trench.

◆ To join lengths of edging, align the flanges at the top and bottom of one section with matching grooves in the other *(photograph)*. Push the pieces together, overlapping them at least 2 inches.

◆ To shorten the edging, increase the overlap at joints or disassemble sections for trimming with a hacksaw.

◆ Set the edging in the trench, and secure it at 4-foot intervals. To do so, hook the 12-inch aluminum stakes over the top of the edging and pound them into the ground.

◆ Backfill and tamp on both sides of the edging.

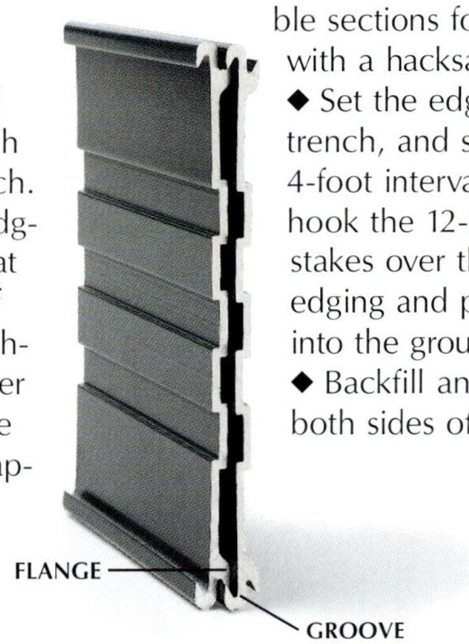

Brick.

◆ Widen the bottom of the trench with a mattock blade to a depth of about 5 inches. Tamp the trench bottom with the end of a 2-by-4.

◆ About 3 inches above the center of the trench, stretch a string between two stakes.

◆ Set a brick in one corner of the trench to prop a row of bricks set at an angle in the trench along one side of the bed. Place the bricks so that their top edges touch the string *(right)*.

◆ Brick the bed's other sides in the same fashion.

CONSTRUCTING A RAISED BED

1. Measuring and cutting timbers.

◆ Lay timbers to be cut across a pair of sturdy sawhorses. Mark each timber one timber-width ($5\frac{1}{2}$ inches for a 6-by-6) shorter than the exterior dimensions of the bed you plan to build. If the sides of the bed are more than one timber in length, plan your cutting to stagger joints from course to course.

◆ Fully extend the blade of a circular saw. Make one pass through the timber, then turn it over and make a second pass to complete the cut *(right)*.

2. Anchoring the base.

◆ Dig a trench 2 inches deep with a mattock or spade and lay the bottom course of timbers in the trench.

◆ With a carpenter's level, check that the timbers are level, adjusting the depth of the trench as needed to make them so.

◆ Drill $\frac{3}{8}$-inch pilot holes for reinforcing rods, 6 to 8 inches from both ends of all four timbers.

◆ With a maul, drive a 24-inch length of $\frac{3}{8}$-inch reinforcing rod through each hole and into the ground, marking rod locations on the fronts of the timbers in chalk.

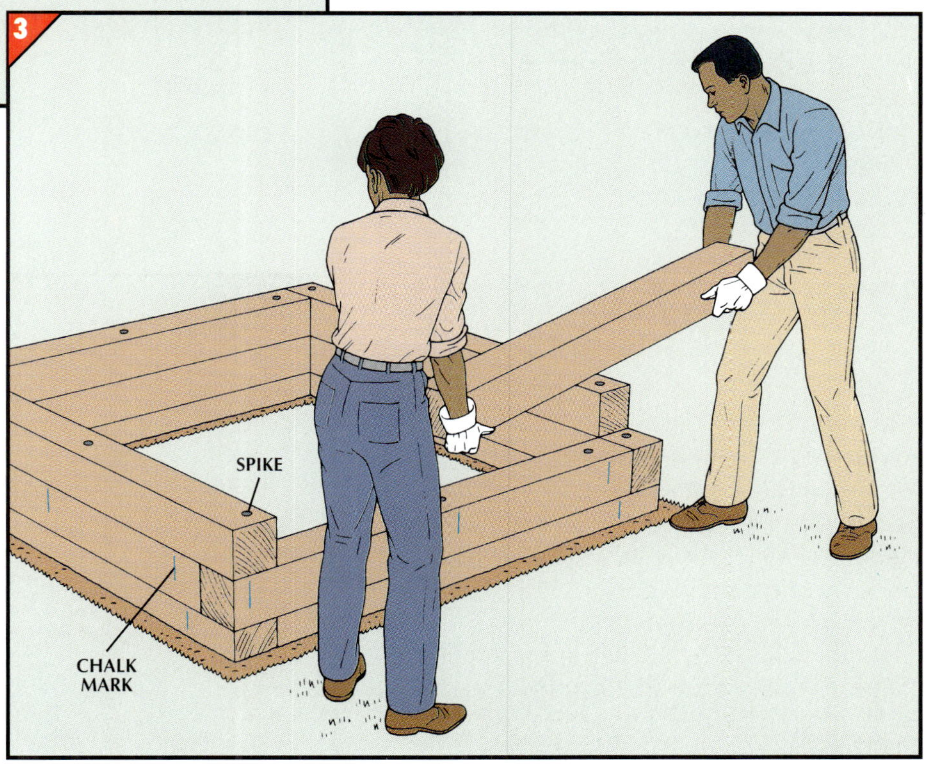

3. Adding the upper courses.

◆ Lay the remaining timber courses, constructing corners as shown at right.

◆ For each course, drill a $\frac{1}{4}$-inch pilot hole, 6 inches deep, at all four corners, about 1 inch from timber centerlines. In addition, drill a hole midway along every timber and 6 to 8 inches from the end that is not in the corner. Make sure that no hole coincides with a chalk mark on the course below.

◆ Drive 10-inch galvanized spikes into the holes, then mark the spike positions with chalk on the front of all but the top course.

Decorative Wooden Containers for Plants

Wooden containers, as landscape elements, not only sustain small parcels of greenery on a deck or on a patio, but they are visually appealing in their own right. The easy-to-build flower box that is shown below requires only two board sizes for the frame and two sizes for the trim. You can readily adapt the instructions on this and the following pages to make a container of any length you wish. The modular design of the freestanding planter with optional benches that is shown on pages 91 to 93 allows you to use your imagination to fill a space of just about any size or shape.

Treating the Wood: Because the chemicals in pressure-treated wood can harm many plants, buy ordinary lumber for planters and flower boxes. Countersink the heads of all finishing nails and plug the holes with waterproof wood putty, then paint or stain the wood to seal it. Before filling a container with soil for planting, cover the bottom with galvanized screening and 1 to 2 inches of gravel.

TOOLS

- Combination square
- Circular saw
- Hammer
- Plane
- Clamps
- Saber saw
- Electric drill with $\frac{1}{16}$-, $\frac{1}{8}$-, and $\frac{3}{4}$-inch bits
- Caulk gun
- Backsaw and miter box

MATERIALS FOR FLOWER BOX

- 1-by-6
- 1-by-8
- 1-by-2
- 1-by-3
- Caulk
- $1\frac{1}{4}$- and 2-inch galvanized finishing nails
- Waterproof wood putty

MATERIALS FOR PLANTER

- 2-by-4s
- 2-by-2s
- $2\frac{1}{2}$-inch galvanized common nails
- $2\frac{1}{2}$-inch galvanized finishing nails
- $2\frac{1}{2}$-inch galvanized wood screws
- $\frac{3}{8}$-inch plywood for spacers

Anatomy of a flower box.
This attractive flower box has angled sides that not only add to its appeal but help prevent the weight of plants and damp soil from pushing out the bottom, which has holes bored through it to promote drainage. Trim around the top serves as a handle for lifting the box. Stands raise the box from the surface of a deck or patio, or allow it to be set atop a 2-by-6 deck railing.

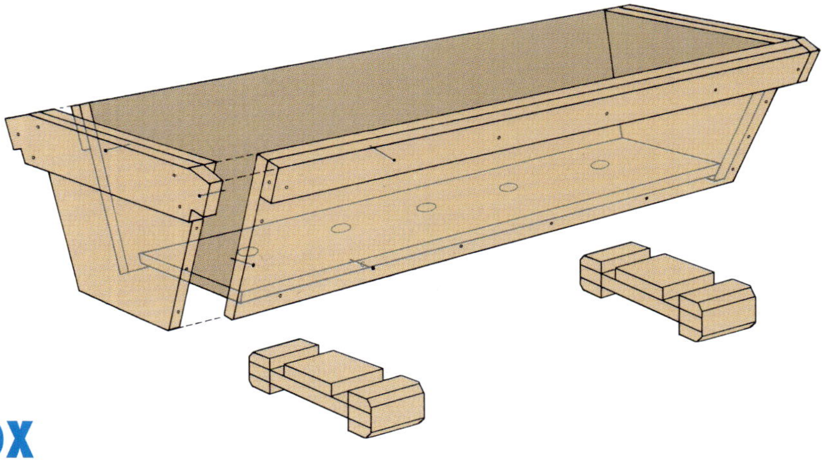

BUILDING A FLOWER BOX

1. Cutting out the pieces.

- To mark the end pieces, draw a baseline with a combination square 1 inch from the end of a 1-by-8. Along one edge, mark the board 9 inches and $13\frac{1}{2}$ inches from the line.
- On the opposite edge, mark the board $2\frac{1}{4}$ inches, $6\frac{3}{4}$ inches, and $15\frac{3}{4}$ inches from the line.
- Join the marks on each side with three straight lines as shown at right, and saw along the center of the lines.
- Place one end piece on top of the other and sand the edges as necessary to make the ends identical.
- Cut the two side pieces to the desired length from a 1-by-8.
- From a 1-by-6, cut the bottom $1\frac{1}{2}$ inches shorter than the sides.

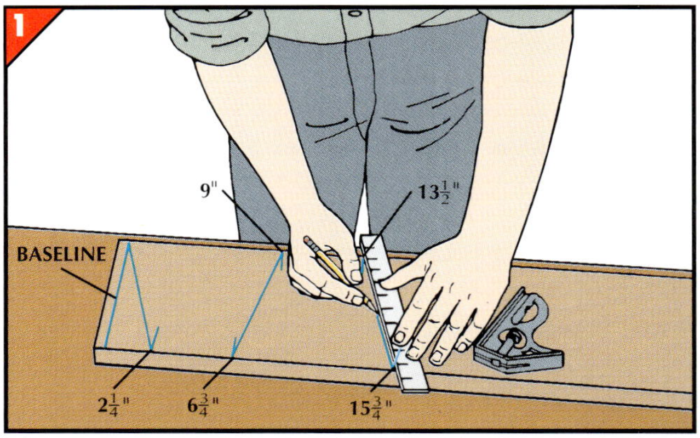

2. Attaching the sides to the ends.

◆ With a $\frac{1}{16}$-inch bit, drill four evenly spaced pilot holes along a line $\frac{3}{8}$ inch from each end of each side piece. Place a 2-inch galvanized finishing nail in each hole.

◆ Spread glue sparingly on one edge of an end piece. Place the end piece top down on the floor with one corner against a wall for support. Mate a side piece to the end piece, and drive the four nails as shown at right.

◆ Repeat the process for the remaining three joints between the end pieces and the sides.

3. Shaping the bottom.

With a plane, bevel the edges of the bottom to fit between the sides:

◆ First, draw lines the length of the board $\frac{1}{4}$ inch in from each side edge, and then draw diagonal lines across the ends of the board as shown in the inset.

◆ Clamp the bottom to a work surface with the marked side up, protecting the board with scraps of wood.

◆ Plane both edges to the pencil lines, then check the fit of the bottom against the sides of the box. Plane or sand the bottom as needed to match the bevel to the slant of the sides.

◆ With the bottom out of the box, drill $\frac{3}{4}$-inch drainage holes along the center of the board, 3 inches from each end and about 7 inches apart.

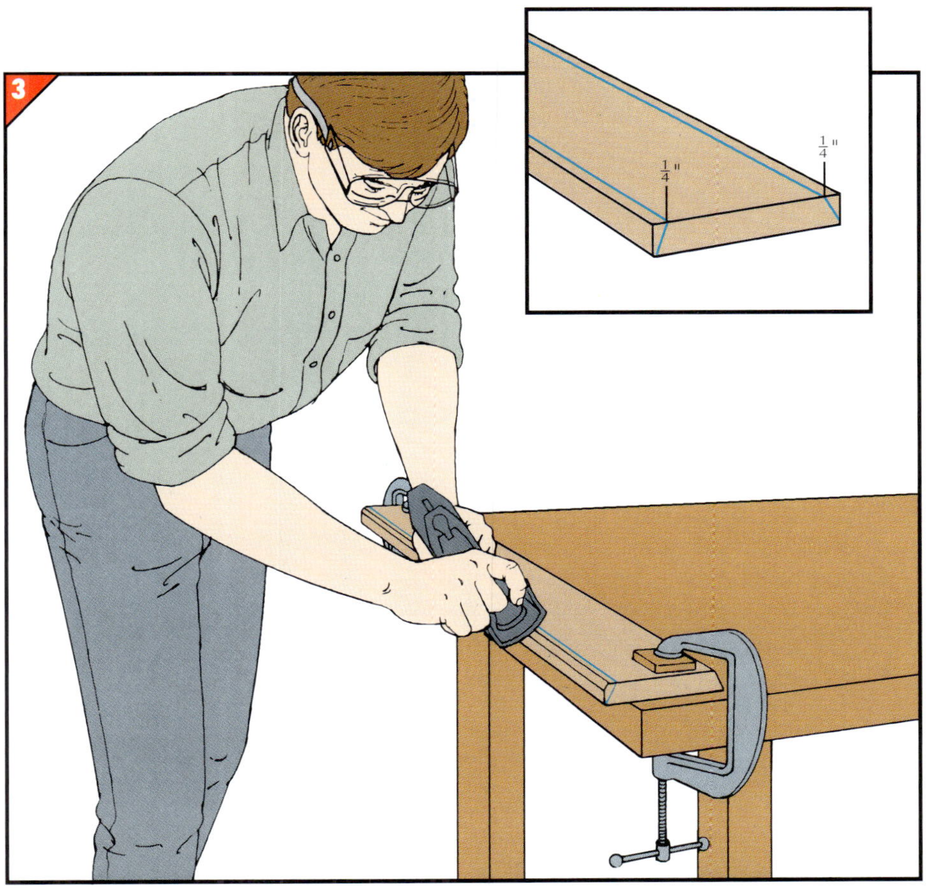

4. Attaching the bottom.

◆ Put the bottom in the box, then measure the distance between the top of the box and the bottom *(near right)*.

◆ Add $\frac{3}{8}$ inch to this measurement and mark both sides of the box at both ends *(far right)*. Remove the bottom and connect the marks with straight lines.

◆ Along the lines, drill $\frac{1}{16}$-inch pilot holes through the sides, 6 inches apart.

◆ Spread glue sparingly along the beveled edges of the bottom, place it in the box, and drive 2-inch galvanized finishing nails through the pilot holes and into the bottom.

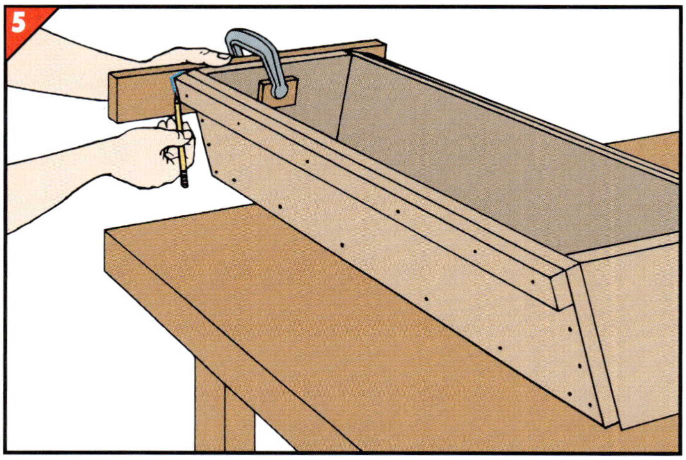

5. Trimming the top.

◆ Cut two pieces of 1-by-2 the length of the sides; drill $\frac{1}{16}$-inch pilot holes through them, 6 inches apart.

◆ Glue and nail the side trim flush with the tops and ends of the sides with $1\frac{1}{4}$-inch galvanized finishing nails. Sand the trim flush with the ends of the box.

◆ For the end trim, clamp a piece of 1-by-3 to the box *(left)*, and trace the shape of the box on the back of the 1-by-3. Unclamp it and cut along the lines with a saber saw. Make a similar piece for the other end.

◆ Drill $\frac{1}{16}$-inch pilot holes in each end trim piece as shown in the anatomy drawing on page 88, then glue and nail the trim to the ends of the box.

◆ Sand the trim to smooth and make the edges flush with the box's contours.

6. Building the stands.

Two stands are sufficient for boxes less than three feet long; build a third stand for longer versions.

◆ For each stand, cut pieces $4\frac{1}{2}$ inches long and 9 inches long from a piece of 1-by-4.

◆ Cut a 15-inch length of 1-by-2 and lightly bevel one edge with a plane. Then cut four $3\frac{1}{2}$-inch pieces from the 1-by-2.

◆ To test the fit, assemble the stands on the floor as shown at right and set the box on them. Sand the ends of the shorter 1-by-4s if necessary to make the box sit firmly.

◆ Glue and nail all the pieces to the longer 1-by-4s.

PLANTERS WITH BENCHES

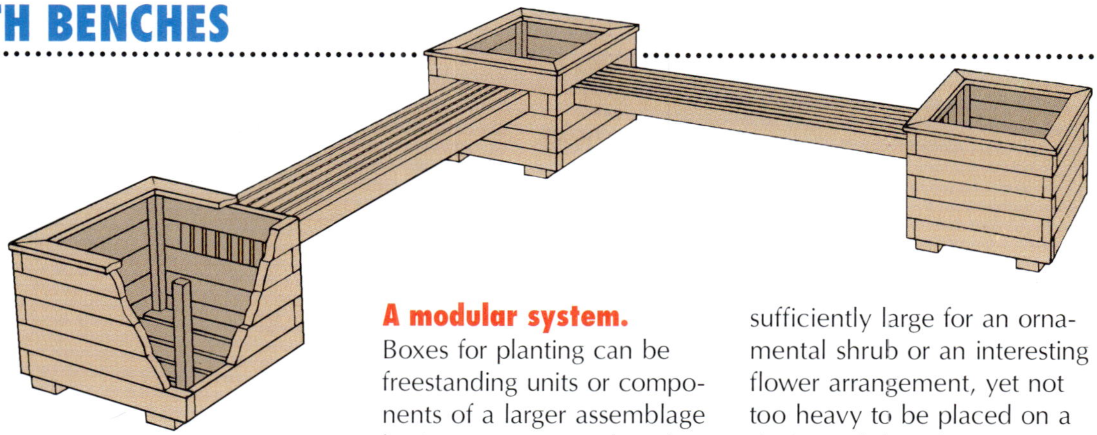

A modular system.
Boxes for planting can be freestanding units or components of a larger assemblage having one or more benches. A box consists of five courses of 2-by-4s with a 2-by-2 brace in each corner and a cap of mitered 2-by-4s. These dimensions yield a planter sufficiently large for an ornamental shrub or an interesting flower arrangement, yet not too heavy to be placed on a deck. Each bench uses seven 2-by-4s, up to 8 feet long. Because the presence of benches affects box construction, plan the unit before you begin building it.

1. Building the base.

◆ Cut four 2-foot lengths of 2-by-4 and set them on edge to form a square. For best results, orient the end grain of the pieces as shown in the photo at right.

◆ With a $\frac{1}{8}$-inch bit, drill two pilot holes through the face of each 2-by-4 where it overlaps the adjacent piece, then fasten each corner with $2\frac{1}{2}$-inch galvanized nails.

◆ For the feet, cut two 2-by-4s, $25\frac{3}{4}$ inches long. Drill two pilot holes at each end of the feet, then lay them across the frame, about 2 inches in from the edges. Square the frame and nail the feet in place.

◆ Cut five pieces of 2-by-4, $22\frac{1}{4}$ inches long. Turn the structure over and nail the 2-by-4s to the feet as shown above, leaving uniform drainage spaces between the boards.

TRICKS OF THE TRADE

A Jig for Cutting 2-by-4s

For a planter that looks professionally built, it is essential that all the 2-by-4 pieces be exactly the same length. If you don't have a table saw, you can achieve the results with a circular saw and the jig shown below.

A 2-by-6 at least 6 feet long serves as the base. Near one end, screw a piece of 2-by-2 to act as an end stop. A little more than 2 feet from the end stop, screw an 18-inch 2-by-2 to the base, flush against the edge, as a side stop. Mark a 2-by-4 with a cut line 2 feet from one end, and set the board against the side and end stops. Place the blade of your saw at the cut line, then set a piece of $\frac{3}{4}$-inch plywood alongside the saw's baseplate. Put the saw aside and screw the plywood to the side stop as a saw guide.

To use the jig, set your saw for a 2-inch depth. Slide a 2-by-4 against the stops, place the saw baseplate against the guide, and cut through.

2. Putting the box together.

◆ For the corner braces, cut four 16-inch lengths of 2-by-2.

◆ Hold a brace firmly in one corner of the base and drill $\frac{1}{8}$-inch pilot holes through the 2-by-2 and into the 2-by-4s at the corner, offsetting the holes so they do not meet. Attach the brace with $2\frac{1}{2}$-inch galvanized screws. Repeat at the other corners.

◆ Assemble the second course as you did the frame for the base, and slip it over the braces, forming the corner-joint pattern shown at left. Drill pilot holes and screw the corner braces to this course.

3. Finishing the box.

For boxes without benches, repeat the preceding step to add the remaining three courses. However, if your plan includes benches, stop after the third course and build the fourth course as shown here—three-sided to support one bench end or two-sided to support the ends of two benches.

◆ Nail a two- or three-sided course together, as called for. Lay it on the third course, and screw the corner braces to it. Set the fifth course in place, supporting it with a scrap piece of 2-by-4 in the case of a two-sided fourth course *(inset)*. Screw the corner braces to the fifth course.

◆ For the cap, cut four lengths of 2-by-4, $26\frac{1}{2}$ inches long, then miter the ends with a backsaw and a miter box. Nail the cap pieces to the fifth course with finishing nails, set the heads, and hide the holes with waterproof wood putty.

ADDING THE BENCHES

1. Fitting bench slats.

◆ Place the boxes in their final locations with open sides of the fourth course facing each other.

◆ Measure the distance between the interior faces of the boxes, and cut seven 2-by-4 slats to that length.

◆ Insert the slats on edge into the space in the fourth course so that the ends are flush with the interior faces of the boxes *(above)*.

◆ Place $\frac{3}{8}$-inch spacers—plywood works well—between the slats at both ends of the bench *(inset)*, then center the bench in the fourth course.

2. Completing the fourth course.

◆ Measure the gap between the bench and the inside edge of the fourth course *(left)*, and cut a 2-by-4 filler to match. Fit the filler into the gap, then nail through the fourth course into the end of the filler to secure it. (You need not anchor the filler to the bench.)

◆ On the other side of the bench, slide a piece of 2-by-4 into the gap and against the bench. Mark a trim line on the board using the outside of the box as a guide, then cut the filler and nail it in place.

Support for Climbing Plants

Flowering or fruit-bearing plants gracefully climbing a wooden framework bring a three-dimensional touch to your landscape design. Along an exterior wall, a trellis can give plants maximum exposure to the sun, shield them from extreme weather, or provide privacy for a pool or a patio. Freestanding post-and-beam arbors control and support heavy, spreading vines like grapes and wisteria and at the same time add a touch of classic design.

The Proper Location: Mount lightweight wood or plastic trellises at least 2 inches from the house with wooden spacers. The gap lets air circulate and helps prevent vines from attaching themselves to the wall. Erect sturdier trellises intended for bushy plants at least 6 inches from the wall.

If you want an arbor that is big enough to walk under, build it at least 4 feet wide and 7 feet high, with beams and rafters overhanging the corner posts at least 1 foot on all sides. Choose a site for the arbor that is level and use the squaring method described on page 256 to locate the corner posts.

Build to Last: Trellises and arbors must be strong enough to support mature plants in full bloom and to withstand the worst weather your region offers.

Rot-resistant redwood or cedar are excellent choices for trellises and arbors. Neither requires painting or sealing as ordinary pine does. And unlike pressure-treated lumber, they contain no preservatives harmful to some plants. No matter what material you choose, assemble the structure with corrosion-resistant galvanized nails and other hardware.

TOOLS

- Screwdriver
- Carpenter's level
- Hammer
- Saw
- Spade or post-hole digger
- Adjustable wrench
- Stepladders

MATERIALS

- 4-by-4 posts
- 2-by-4s
- 1-by-2s, -6s, and -8s
- $\frac{1}{4}$-by-2 lath
- Hooks and eyes
- Strap hinges
- 6-inch carriage bolts, washers, and nuts
- Galvanized nails
- Galvanized rafter ties

TWO VARIETIES OF TRELLIS

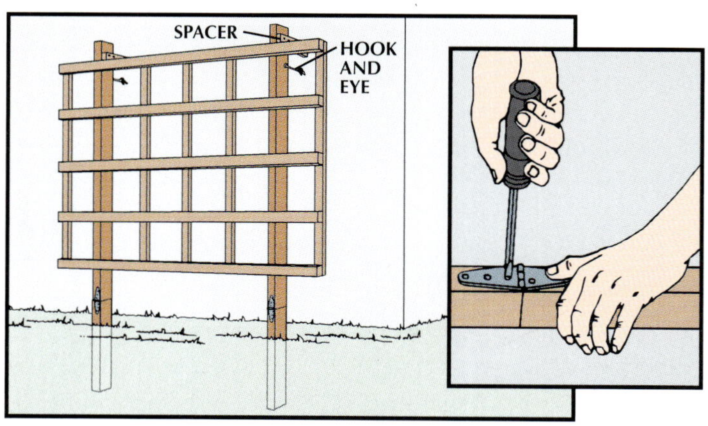

Choosing a trellis.
A simple trellis starts with a pair of 2-by-4 uprights, located parallel to a wall or at right angles to it and set at least 2 feet into the ground.

A trellis to support light vines *(above, left)* begins as a rectangular frame of 2-by-4s nailed to the posts, flush with the tops. The frame should be 1 foot shorter than the height of the posts and at least 2 feet wider than the distance between them. You can weave $\frac{1}{4}$- by 2-inch lath into a uniform grid *(inset)* or buy basket weave lattice and cut it to fit the frame.

For heavier vines, a grid of 1-by-2s (with the posts serving as two of the verticals) provides sturdy support *(above, right)*. Spacers that are made of 1-by-2s and sets of hooks and eyes hold the trellis 6 inches from the wall. You can cut and hinge the posts *(inset)* about 6 inches from the ground to permit tipping the trellis outward for pruning the vines or painting the house.

A POST-AND-BEAM ARBOR

1. Setting the posts.

◆ For each 4-by-4 corner post, dig a hole 3 feet deep with a spade or posthole digger. In soft or sandy soil, place a flat stone or brick at the bottom of each hole.
◆ Stand a post in the center of a hole with the sides aligned to the rectangular layout. While a helper uses a level to hold the post vertical *(left),* tamp soil around the post with a 2-by-4 in successive layers a few inches deep until the hole is filled.
◆ To keep the post plumb, temporarily nail two braces to the post and to stakes in the ground.
◆ When the first post is in place, stand the other posts alongside it one at a time and mark them at the height of the first. Turn the posts over, then set and brace them in the remaining holes to the depth marked.

2. Mounting the beams.

◆ Measure and cut four 1-by-8s for the beams. With a helper, lift a board even with the top of one pair of posts, the ends extending equally. Fasten the board to one post with a nail, then level the board and nail it to the other post. Mount a second on the posts' opposite sides.
◆ Drill two $\frac{1}{2}$-inch holes through the boards and post, 1 inch from post and board edges *(inset).* Insert 6-inch carriage bolts and secure with flat washers and nuts.
◆ To complete the beam, cut $7\frac{1}{2}$-inch-long spacers from 4-by-4 post lumber. Nail the spacers between the boards at 12- to 18-inch intervals, flush with the top and bottom edges.
◆ Build a similar beam on the other two posts.

3. Installing the rafters.

◆ Measure and mark rafter positions on top of the beams at 18- to 24-inch intervals, then cut 1-by-6 boards for the rafters.
◆ Set each rafter on edge across the beams, aligned with the marks and overhanging the beams equally on each side. Toenail the rafters to the beams *(right),* or use galvanized rafter ties *(inset).* To prevent splits from occurring when toenailing along the edge of a board, drill pilot holes at the correct angle slightly smaller than the diameter of the nails.

Walls of Greenery from Vines

Among vines, there are eager climbers and reluctant ones. You can coax up plants such as climbing rose, which despite its name is not a natural climber, by carefully weaving their stems through a supporting trellis or by tying their stems with string or wire to a support.

However, the classic climbers are a different matter. Provided modest assistance, they will ascend a wall with little further attention. You can buy vines in flats and plant them as you would ground covers *(pages 299-300)*, or you can carefully detach established vines from their support as shown at right and move them to a new location.

Ivy and Brick Walls: Climbing ivy and other clingers *(below)* may compromise weak mortar in a brick wall, allowing moisture to penetrate and weaken the wall's structural integrity. Perform this test: Scratch a key against the joint. If the mortar does not scrape off or crumble, your wall can support the growth.

Caring for Climbers: Periodic pruning will keep vines bushy and robust. Climbers are generally less vulnerable to pests and disease than are low-growing plants. An occasional hosing down of the leaves helps to discourage insects. But vines are susceptible to heat scorch and drought stress from excessive evaporation from the leaves. Water them more often than low-growing varieties. Many vines tolerate frost poorly. Check with a nursery for varieties suitable to your climate.

Three ways vines hold on. Clingers, such as English ivy and Virginia creeper *(above, left)*, anchor themselves even to vertical surfaces with adhesive disks, tiny hooks, or rootlets. Moisture at anchor points can damage wood siding. Stem twiners *(center)* encircle downspouts, trellises, wires, and strings. Some, such as Hall's Japanese honeysuckle, wrap their stems counterclockwise; others, like Dutchman's pipe, twine in a clockwise direction. Tendril twiners, including plants like the sweet pea *(right)* and trumpet vine, extend threadlike spirals that wrap tightly around a thin support, such as a wire fence. Some tendril twiners also wind their stems around the support.

EASY UPKEEP FOR CLIMBERS

Thinning a climber. Prune a climbing plant in summer to improve air circulation and to permit new growth to strengthen the plant before the autumn frost. Clip and disentangle enough large stems (up to $1\frac{1}{4}$ inches in diameter) near ground level to allow light to reach all the inner branches. Prune other areas of the plant selectively, removing unhealthy stems without damaging sound ones.

Encouraging new growth.

To induce lateral buds to sprout new shoots where leaves might otherwise appear, prune stems just above the buds.

In general, vines that flower in the spring bloom on the previous year's growth; prune them after they bloom to give the new growth time to strengthen before winter. Those that flower in late summer or fall bloom on the current year's growth and are best pruned in late autumn when the plant is dormant or in early spring before any new growth appears.

Detaching vines from their support.

When transplanting a clinger, tug gently near the adhesive disks, hooks, or rootlets that grip a wall *(near right)*. Unravel the tendrils or unhook the leaf stalks of a twiner that attaches to a string or wire *(far right)*. When unwinding the stems or tendrils, note whether they grow clockwise or counterclockwise, then wrap them in the appropriate direction around supports at the new location.

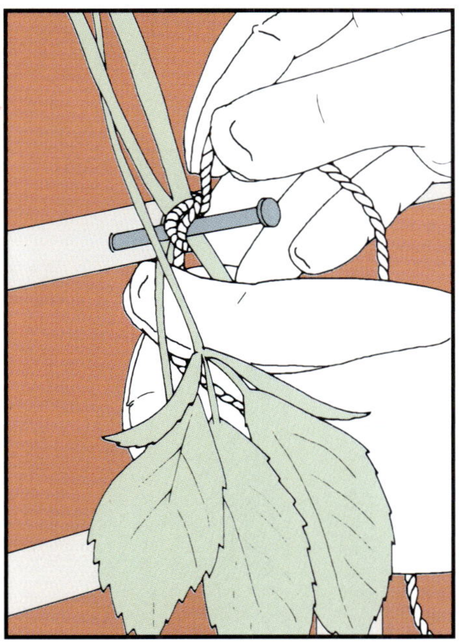

Tethering newly planted vines.

To secure a clinging vine to a brick wall, hammer masonry nails into the mortar joints at 2-foot intervals. Loosely tie the stems of the plant to the nails with string or twist ties *(left)*.

For twiners, stretch string or wire between two nails to provide vertical supports for new growth to climb. Secure the plant stem loosely to the support.

Check the plant periodically, trimming back any yellowed or wilted leaves near the top. When the plant can support itself, remove the strings or ties.

Creating Walkways for a Yard

Aesthetically, a walkway can draw the eye to a focal point in the yard. Practically, it can prevent a much trodden path from becoming a sea of mud after rain or snow. Timbered terraces or steps in a walkway not only tame modestly undulating terrain but also can protect a footpath from erosion.

Stepping Stones: For seldom or occasionally traveled routes, flagstones, thin precast concrete slabs, or other kinds of stepping stone can make an attractive walkway. Choose elements that are 18 inches to 24 inches across. Lay rectangular slabs in pairs to form squares, as shown below.

Loose Pavings: For pathways that get more frequent use, a path of pine needles, bark mulch, or gravel is more suitable. Moreover, loose paving is easier and less expensive to build with than is concrete or brick. Spreading plastic sheeting called landscaping fabric under the paving keeps weeds at bay, and an edging of bricks prevents the paving material from washing into the lawn. Make the path at least 4 feet across, wide enough for two people to walk abreast.

Dealing with Slopes: For gentle inclines, construct a series of terraces called ramps. Set pressure-treated 6-by-8s into the slope and spread loose paving material between them. The distance between timbers can vary from 4 feet to 10 feet; generally, the steeper the slope, the closer together the timbers should be set. Whatever the distance, keep it uniform to help reduce the risk of stumbles.

On slopes too steep for ramps, timber steps make an attractive alternative. They require a hill that allows a tread depth of 11 inches or more *(page 273, Step 1)*. A steeper hill would demand an impractical amount of excavation.

Before beginning, check local building codes; in some jurisdictions, stairways of more than four steps require a handrail.

TOOLS

Edge cutter	Electric drill with $\frac{1}{2}$-inch bit
Spade	4-pound maul
Sod cutter	Tamper
Garden rake	Sledgehammer
Line level	

MATERIALS

Stepping stones	$\frac{1}{2}$-inch steel reinforcing rods
Sand	$\frac{3}{8}$-inch galvanized spikes
Stakes and string	6-by-6 and 6-by-8 pressure-treated timbers
Landscaping fabric	
Bricks	
Loose paving	

SAFETY TIPS

Gloves protect your hands during spadework, and a back brace can reduce the risk of injury when digging. Wear goggles whenever you use a hammer.

A CHAIN OF STEPPING STONES

1. Laying out the stones.
◆ Position the stepping stones along the proposed pathway. Adjust them as necessary so that they fall naturally underfoot as you walk the path.
◆ Cut around the stones with an edge cutter *(left)*, then set the stones aside. Remove the sod with a spade, digging $\frac{1}{2}$ inch deeper than the thickness of the stepping stones.

2. Tapping the stones down.
◆ Spread $\frac{1}{2}$ inch of sand in each hole, then place the stones on the sand.
◆ Tap the stones into place with the butt of a hammer *(left)* to bring the tops level with the ground.

PATHS OF GRAVEL OR MULCH

1. Digging the path.
◆ Lay out a straight path with strings and stakes; for a curved path, use a rope or garden hose. Strip the sod between the marks with a sod cutter, then remove 2 or 3 inches of soil with a spade. Smooth the path with a rake.
◆ Dig edging trenches 2 inches wide and 2 inches deeper than the path.
◆ Spread landscaping fabric across the path and into the edging trenches *(above)* to curb weed growth.

2. Edging the path with brick.
◆ Place bricks on end in the trenches on either side *(inset)*. Pack soil behind and under the bricks as needed to align the tops just above grass level.
◆ Fill the path with loose material, then level it with a rake *(above)*.

TERRACES FOR A GENTLE SLOPE

1. Setting the timbers.

◆ Drill three $\frac{1}{2}$-inch pilot holes through the narrow face of a 6-by-8 timber, one in the center and the others 6 inches from each end.

◆ At the bottom of the slope, dig a trench 2 inches deep and set the timber in it *(right)*. Save the displaced soil to use for fill.

◆ With a 4-pound maul, drive 24-inch reinforcing rods through the pilot holes to anchor the timber.

◆ Working up the slope, anchor a timber in a 2-inch-deep trench at each timber location.

2. Making the ramps.

◆ Distribute the dirt from each trench along the uphill side of the corresponding timber. Tamp the loose fill *(right)*, retaining a slight slope to the ramp to aid drainage.

◆ Uphill from each timber, spread a layer of loose paving. Keep the top of the layer below the top of the timber, and extend it up the slope to the next timber.

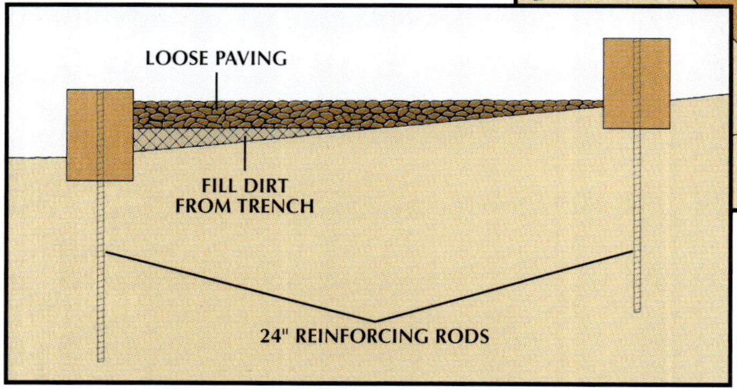

BUILDING TIMBER STEPS

1. Measuring rise and run.

◆ Drive vertical stakes at the top and bottom of the incline. Tie a string to the upper stake at ground level.

◆ Hold the string against the lower stake, and level it with a line level. Mark the lower stake at the string *(right)*, then measure the total rise, that is, the distance in inches between the mark and the ground.

◆ Divide the length of the rise by $5\frac{1}{2}$ inches—the thickness of a 6-by-6 timber—to determine the number of steps. Round a fraction to the nearest whole number.

◆ Next, measure the horizontal distance between the stakes to get total run. Divide the run by the number of steps to find tread depth.

2. Anchoring the first step.

◆ To make the steps, cut 6-by-6 timbers to the desired width of the stairway. Nail two timbers together with two 10-inch galvanized spikes. Nail additional timbers to one or both sides of the first two to make a step of the correct tread depth, allowing for an overlap of at least 2 inches between steps. Make as many steps as needed for the stairway.

◆ In the front timber of each step, drill three $\frac{1}{2}$-inch pilot holes, one in the center and the others 6 inches from each end.

◆ Working uphill from the stake driven at the bottom of the slope in Step 1, excavate a flat area large enough for the step. Secure the step with 24-inch reinforcing rods as shown above.

3. Installing the second step.

◆ Excavate an area above the first step large enough for the second one and set it in place. With light blows from a sledgehammer *(above)*, adjust the position of the second step to the desired tread depth and step overlap.

◆ Next, drill three $\frac{1}{2}$-inch pilot holes through the steps where they overlap. Drive reinforcing rods through the two steps and into the ground.

◆ Continue overlapping and securing the steps to the top of the slope.

A Pool and Water Garden

Creating a pool and water garden is a big undertaking, but the reward—a dramatic focal point for your yard and a habitat for fish and exotic plants—is substantial. Furthermore, once the pool is completed, upkeep is not any more strenuous than for a traditional flower bed.

New Materials to Line the Pool: Garden pools once were made either of one-piece rigid fiberglass or poured concrete. Nowadays the material of choice is polyvinyl chloride (PVC) plastic or a synthetic rubber called EPDM. With a life of a decade or more, these pliable membranes conform to any pool shape, from geometric to a free-form outline that is meant to mimic a natural pond.

Pool liners are available in a variety of thicknesses; 45 mils (a mil is $\frac{1}{1,000}$ inch) should be sufficient for a backyard pool. When you purchase the liner, it will come folded and boxed and is ready to set in the excavation.

Choosing the Proper Site: Since the banks of the pool must be level all around, select a location on nearly flat terrain. To ensure sunlight for plants and fish, avoid placing the pool directly under a tree.

Some jurisdictions require a fence around pools, usually if they are more than 18 inches deep. Check your local building codes before you break ground.

Finishing Touches: To protect the liner from direct sunlight where it extends above the water line, trim the pool with a coping of flat, thin landscaping stones that overhang the edge. Unless you expect the pool area to receive heavy foot traffic, there is no need to set the stones in mortar.

A pump and fountain not only add a decorative touch to your pool but also will prevent insects from breeding on the pool's surface by keeping the water in motion. Select a fountain head and length of plastic piping in order to create the spray effect that you desire on the surface of the pool.

To power the pump, tap an electrical circuit in the house and extend it to the pool with UF (underground feeder) cable of the same gauge as that of the house circuit. Protect against shock with an outlet containing a ground-fault circuit interrupter (GFCI) *(pages 278-279)*. Alternatively, have an electrician run a new circuit protected by a GFCI in the service panel.

Flora and Fauna: Before stocking a pool, treat the water with a liquid dechlorinating agent available from pool suppliers. Since plants in containers need shallow water, either dig the pool with a 9-inch shelf around the perimeter or stand the containers on concrete blocks.

CAUTION *Before excavating, note the locations of underground obstacles—electric, water, and sewer lines, or dry wells, septic tanks, and cesspools.*

TOOLS

- Tape measure
- Powdered chalk
- Shovel
- Wheelbarrow
- Edge cutter
- Spade
- Carpenter's level
- Garden rake
- Scissors
- Push broom
- Electric drill

MATERIALS

- Ropes or hoses
- Lengths of 2-by-4
- Sand
- Pool liner
- Landscaping stones
- Dechlorinating agent
- 10-inch galvanized spikes
- UF electrical cable
- Conduit, nipple, elbow, and bushings
- LB fitting
- Metal strap
- Concrete block
- Outdoor outlet box
- GFCI receptacle

Length/Width of Pool		2 x Depth of Pool				Length/Width of Liner
________	+	________	+	4	=	________ feet

Calculating liner dimensions.
Use the length and width of your pool in feet with the formula above to determine the size liner required. Apply the formula twice, once to find liner length and again for the width. Ignore any shelf you have planned for the pool perimeter; it does not affect the results.

EXCAVATING THE POOL

1. Marking the dimensions.

◆ Outline the shape of your pool on the ground with a rope or hose. Then lay a second rope or hose 1 foot outside the first to mark the strip of sod to be removed for a stone coping.

◆ Measure across the pool outline at its longest and widest points *(right),* then use the formula on page 274 to calculate the size of the liner you need.

◆ Squeeze powdered chalk from a chalk bottle along both markers, then lift them away.

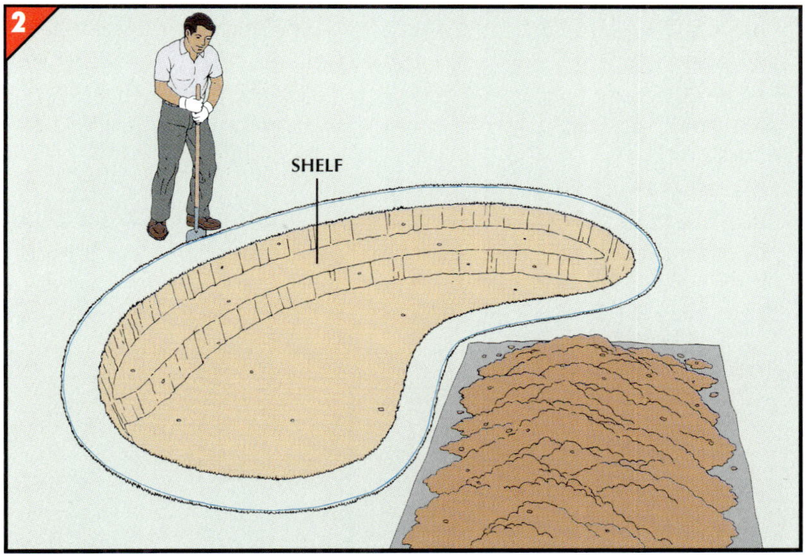

2. Preparing the hole.

◆ Starting at the center of the pool outline, excavate to the desired depth—plus 2 inches for a layer of sand on the bottom. For a shelf, leave a ledge 1 foot wide about 9 inches below ground level. At the pool perimeter, slope the sides of the hole and any shelf about 20 degrees.

◆ Cut along the sod line with an edge cutter *(left),* then remove the sod inside the line with a spade.

3. Leveling the banks.

◆ Rest the ends of a 2-by-4 on opposite banks, inside the sod line.

◆ Level the board, if necessary, by removing soil from the higher bank. Mark the banks under the 2-by-4 with chalk.

◆ Leaving one end of the board on one of the marks, set the other end on the bank at a third point. Add or remove soil there to level the board, then mark that spot with chalk.

◆ Repeat this procedure to level several other points along the banks, always keeping one end of the 2-by-4 on a point that you have already leveled.

◆ Add or remove soil between these points to bring the entire bank to the same height.

4. Checking the depth.

◆ For a level pool bottom, mark the desired depth on a scrap of wood to use as a guide. If the pool will have a shelf, add a second mark to the depth guide 9 inches below the first.

◆ Lay a 2-by-4 across the excavation and hold the depth guide vertically against the 2-by-4 *(left),* checking at several points for high and low spots. Use the 9-inch mark at the shelves. Add or remove soil to level the shelves and the bottom.

◆ Repeat at various points that span the hole.

5. Preparing the bottom.

Shovel sand into the hole to cushion the pool liner. With a garden rake, spread the sand across the bottom in an even layer 2 inches thick. Do not sand the shelf.

LAYING OUT A PLASTIC OR RUBBER LINER

1. Spreading the liner.

◆ Place the liner in the hole and begin unfolding it, working toward the banks.

◆ With a helper, contour the liner over shelves and up the sides *(left).* Avoid overlapping folds in the liner and make sure it covers the sod line.

◆ Temporarily anchor the liner with coping stones set at several places around the edge.

◆ Fill the pool with a garden hose. Shifting anchor stones as necessary, smooth the liner so that the rising water presses it flat against the sides.

◆ Add dechlorinating agent according to the manufacturer's directions.

2. Securing the liner.

◆ When the pool is full, trim the liner along the sod line with a pair of scissors *(right)*.

◆ To permanently anchor the liner use a hammer to drive 10-inch galvanized spikes into the banks 4 inches inside the sod line, every 2 feet around the perimeter.

3. Laying the coping.

◆ Place the pump in the pool and run the power cord onto the bank where you plan to install the outlet.

◆ Spread 2 inches of damp sand between the sod line and the pool edge.

◆ Set the coping stones in the sand around the perimeter of the pool so that they extend at least 1 inch over the edge *(below)*, protecting the liner from deterioration caused by sunlight.

◆ Sweep sand into the gaps between stones with the push broom.

ELECTRICITY FOR A PUMP AND FOUNTAIN

1. An exit from the house.

◆ Dig a trench from your house to the receptacle location. Make the trench 6 inches deep if you plan to install rigid metal conduit for the electrical cable; otherwise make it 12 inches deep. Widen the trench near the pool to fit a concrete block.

◆ Drill a $\frac{7}{8}$-inch hole through the house siding and floor framing to accommodate a $\frac{1}{2}$-inch-diameter nipple, a short length of threaded conduit.

◆ To the back of an LB fitting, a small box used to direct cable toward the trench, screw a nipple long enough to extend into the basement or crawlspace *(left)*.

◆ To the other end of the LB fitting, fit a length of conduit that reaches at least 6 inches into the trench. Screw a plastic bushing to the bottom of the conduit.

◆ Push the nipple through the hole into the house and secure the conduit to the foundation with a metal strap.

◆ Inside the house, screw a bushing onto the nipple.

2. Making connections.

◆ Remove the cover plate and gasket of the LB fitting.

◆ Thread UF cable up the conduit and into the LB fitting, then push it through the nipple *(left)*.

◆ At a convenient location inside the house, install a box for a single-pole switch. Run the UF cable to the box, then continue the circuit with indoor (NM) cable, preferably to an existing receptacle.

◆ At the switch, connect black wires to the switch terminals, white wires to each other, and ground wires to the switch and box (if it is metal) by means of jumper wires and wire caps.

Replace the LB fitting's gasket and cover plate, and caulk the joint between fitting and house.

3. Installing the outlet box.

◆ Run cable to the end of the trench.

◆ Screw a bushing to one end of a 12-inch nipple; onto the other, thread an elbow connector. Then cut an 18-inch length of conduit; connect the threaded end to the elbow and the other end to a fitting called a threadless connector *(inset)*.

◆ Thread the cable through this assembly, set it in the trench, and lower a concrete block over it.

◆ Slip a weatherproof outlet box over the cable end and screw it to the threadless connector *(right)*.

◆ Pack soil mixed with stones around the conduit within the concrete block to prevent wobbling, then fill the trench.

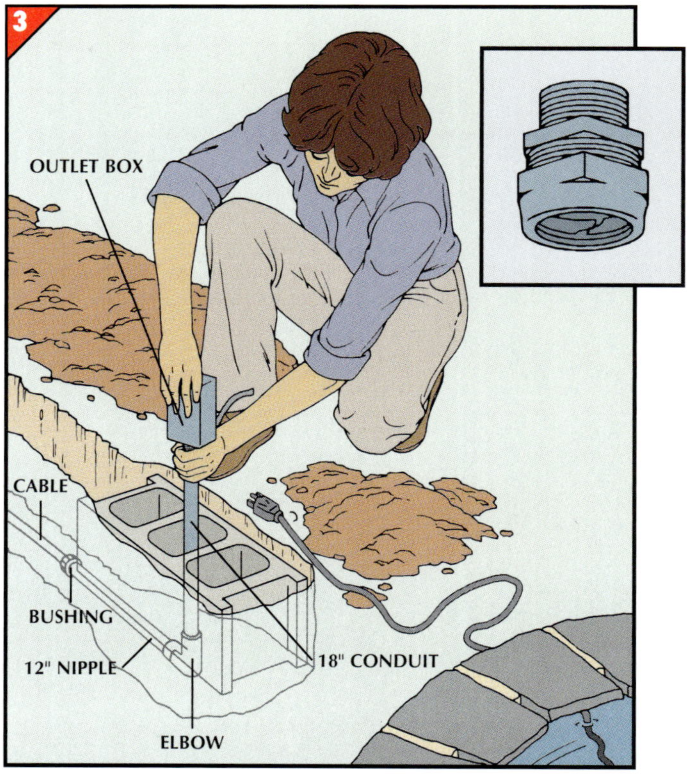

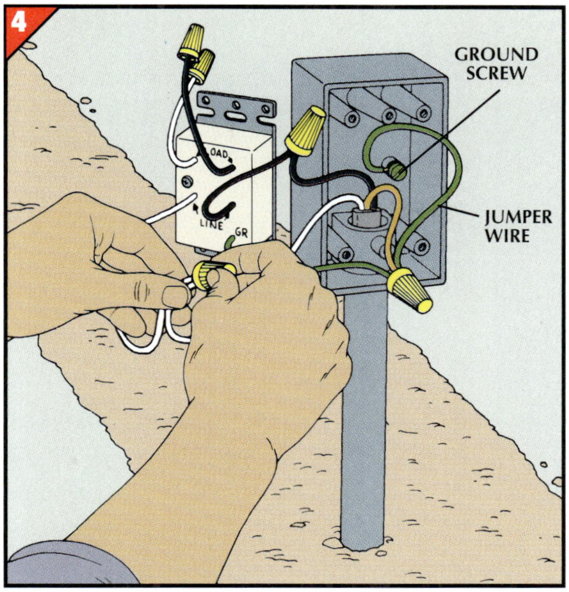

4. Connecting a GFCI receptacle.

◆ Cover both GFCI leads marked LOAD with wire caps.

◆ Connect the black and white wires in the cable to the GFCI wires of corresponding colors marked LINE *(left)*.

◆ Attach a jumper wire to the ground screw in the box and join the jumper to cable and GFCI ground wires.

◆ Fold all the wires into the box, screw the outlet in place, and attach a weatherproof GFCI cover.

◆ In the house, turn off power to the receptacle where you intend to tap a circuit. Connect the wires in the new cable to those in the box there, black to black, white to white, and ground to ground.

◆ After screwing the receptacle to the box, restore power, and then plug in the pump.

Maintaining a Healthy Pool

Fish and plants work together to keep your pool clean and attractive. Aquatic plants provide oxygen and food for the fish, which in turn help keep the water clear by feeding on algae.

Periodic Cleaning: Drain your pool and scrub the liner every 3 to 4 years, or after an inch of silt has built up on the bottom. To empty the pool, lift out the plant containers, replace the fountain attachment on the pump with a hose leading outside the pool, then turn on the pump.

When about 6 inches of water remain, remove the fish with a net and place them in a clean plastic container (a new trash can works nicely) with water from the pool. Finish draining the pool, then disconnect the hose and put the pump in the fish container. Run the pump; doing so provides oxygen for the fish. Place the fish and plants in a shaded area.

Gently scrub the liner with a nylon-bristle broom, then use a wet-or-dry vacuum to suck the silt from the pool. Refill the pool and dechlorinate the water. When the pool temperature rises to within 5° of the water temperature in the container, net the fish into the pool and return plants to the shelf.

Winterizing a Pool: When the pool's water temperature drops to 45° F., trim plants to a height of 3 inches and move them from the shelf to the bottom of the pool.

Fish can survive the winter without food, but not without oxygen that enters the water through the surface. In regions with mild winters, water circulation from the pump may prevent the pool from freezing. Should the surface freeze over, however, you must cut in the ice an opening of at least 1 square foot. In extremely cold areas, an electric pond deicer can keep a corner of a pool ice free.

9 Growing a Carpet of Green

For many, landscaping begins and ends with the lawn—and for good reason. There is no escaping a continuous regimen of lawn upkeep throughout the growing season. A less burdensome alternative is to plant a low-maintenance ground cover such as ivy or periwinkle. Whatever your choice, this chapter holds the keys to a verdant backdrop for your house that will retain its beauty year after year.

Planting a lawn with plugs →

Maintaining a Healthy Lawn

Expanses of weed-free, perfectly groomed grass do not occur naturally; they require careful attention and consistent care. Along with the routine demands of mowing and watering, other periodic tasks such as fertilizing, aerating, and dethatching are also necessary to keep the grass green and healthy.

Cutting the Grass: There are a wide variety of mowers available; choose the one that best suits your needs. Sharpen the blade yearly *(page 230)* and keep the lawn free of debris that might dull the blade or be thrown out of the mower's chute. Before starting the engine, adjust the cutting height *(page 284)*. Recommended mowing heights for the most common lawn grasses are given in the chart on pages 348-349.

Lawn clippings can be bagged, but short clippings left on the lawn decompose to a natural fertilizer. Modern mulching mowers, which have a special blade and a fully enclosed deck, chop clippings fine to speed decomposition; you may be able to convert an older mower to work like a mulcher.

For a finished appearance, crop around posts and other hard-to-reach areas with a power trimmer, and use an edger to cut a small, narrow trench along flower beds and sidewalks *(page 285)*.

Providing Water and Food: In summer, when high heat and lower rainfall slow the growth of grass, you will mow your lawn less often but water it more. A thorough watering—perhaps once a week—is preferable to frequent light waterings, which can inhibit the growth of deep roots. Control the amount of water the lawn receives by setting your sprinkler for the correct intensity and area.

Grass does not, of course, live by water alone. To replace soil nutrients, fertilizers must be added. The timing depends on the type of grass, as indicated in the grasses chart. Always sweep excess fertilizer from sidewalks and driveways onto the lawn to prevent runoff into storm drains.

Controlling Weeds: Even in the best-kept lawn, a few weeds are inevitable and must be dug up or destroyed with a selective herbicide that kills weeds without harming grass. Some weed-killers wither parts of the plant they touch. Others are systemic: they are absorbed into the plant, destroying even the roots. Weed-killers can be applied directly to isolated weeds or they can be sprayed over an entire area that is badly infested *(pages 290-291)*.

Most large garden centers carry water-soluble, environmentally safe dyes that when mixed with herbicides in the sprayer help ensure even coverage. Rain or watering soon washes the dye away.

Stimulating Growth: Despite careful watering and fertilizing, a lawn may still deteriorate if thatch—a matted layer of dead grass—becomes too thick, strangling new growth. Strip it off with a thatch rake or a power dethatcher *(page 292)*; both devices cut slits through the tightly woven barrier so it can easily be raked away.

The soil in heavily used backyards or play areas can become so compacted that grass roots cannot penetrate it. An aerator *(page 293)*, which extracts small plugs of earth to loosen compacted soil, may be needed as often as every 2 years. Periodic aeration also helps prevent thatch buildup.

Compost is an excellent soil amendment, or additive, when raked into the holes left by the aerator. Contact your local extension service to see if composted municipal sludge is available in your area.

CAUTION *Before repairing or adjusting power lawn-care equipment, always unplug an electrically powered machine, or if it has a gasoline engine, disconnect the spark plug wire.*

TOOLS

Tape measure
Screwdriver
Weeding fork
Spading fork
Garden rake
Hoe
Garden trowel
Thatch rake or power dethatcher
Grass rake
Aerating fork or power aerator

MATERIALS

Lawn fertilizer
Grass seed
Weed-killer
Stakes
String
Peat moss
Composted municipal sludge
Straw or wood fiber mulch
Chain-link fencing

SAFETY TIPS

When using lawn-care machinery, wear sturdy leather shoes (preferably steel-tipped), long pants, goggles, and gloves. Also protect your ears when operating loud gasoline-powered machines. Wear gloves when using hand tools to dig or rake.

EQUIPMENT FOR MOWING AND TRIMMING

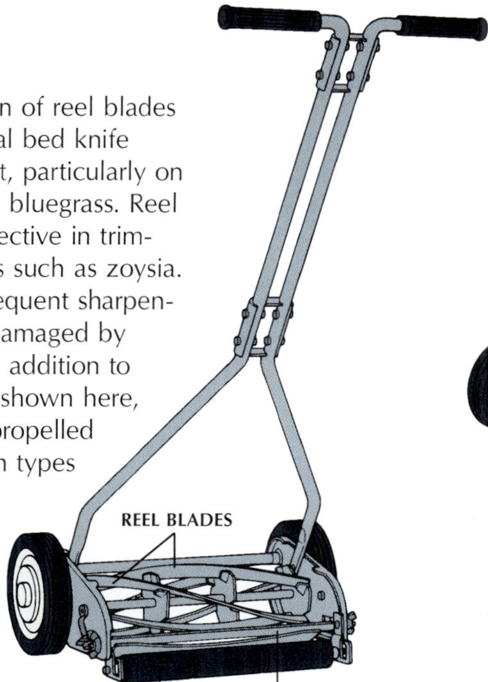

A reel mower.
The scissoring action of reel blades against a fixed metal bed knife makes a smooth cut, particularly on thin grasses such as bluegrass. Reel mowers are less effective in trimming denser grasses such as zoysia. The blades need frequent sharpening and are easily damaged by twigs or pebbles. In addition to the manual mower shown here, there are also self-propelled power models. Both types are best suited for small, level lawns.

The versatile rotary mower.
A walk-behind mower like the one shown above cuts a clean swath through any type of grass and allows you to bag your clippings, discharge them, or mulch them. Similar features are available in riding mowers, which may be worth their extra cost for lawns larger than $\frac{1}{2}$ acre. Essential to mulching is a mulching blade *(photograph)*, which is specially curved to lift and slice the grass repeatedly over a long cutting edge.

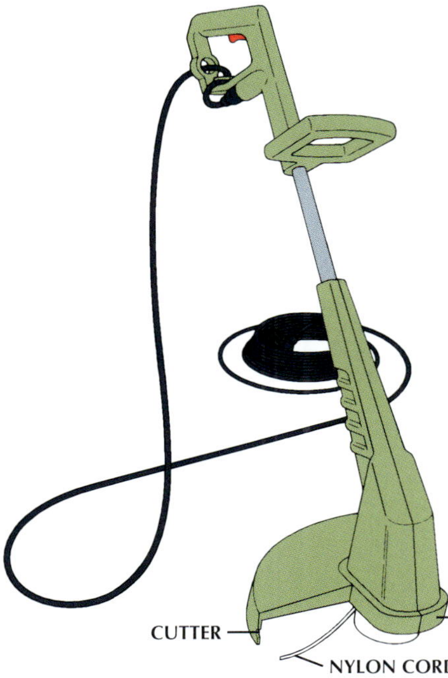

A power trimmer.
Available in gas, plug-in, or battery-powered models, this tool is handy for cropping grass around posts and other obstacles to lawn mowers. A rotating nylon cord lops off grass with a whipping action. Cord frayed through use is replaced from a reel in the cutting head, which when tapped on the ground releases a length of fresh cord. A cutter on the safety guard trims the cord to the correct length.

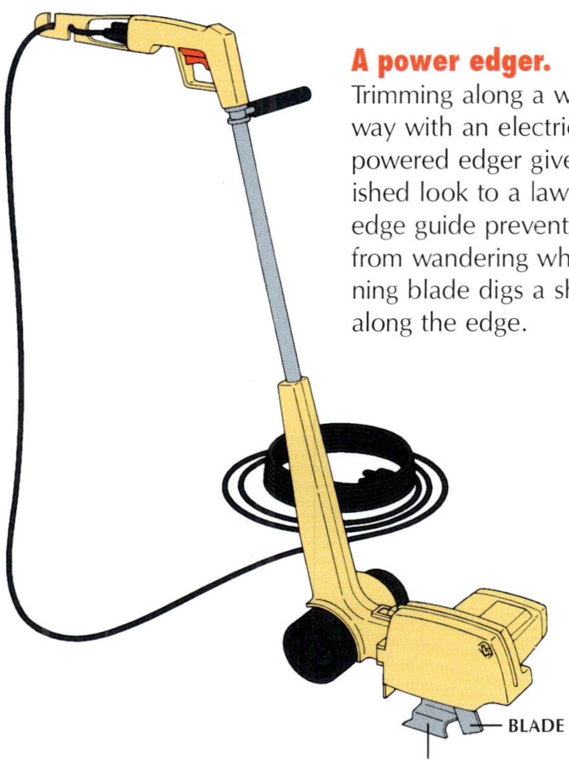

A power edger.
Trimming along a walk or driveway with an electric or gasoline-powered edger gives a neat, finished look to a lawn. A metal edge guide prevents the machine from wandering while the spinning blade digs a shallow trench along the edge.

1. Setting the mower blade height.

◆ Roll the lawn mower onto a driveway or sidewalk and detach the spark plug wire. (Unplug electric models.)
◆ Reach into the discharge chute and rotate the blade so that one end is toward you, then measure the distance from the blade to the ground.
◆ Move the height-adjustment levers *(right),* raising or lowering the deck to achieve the desired blade height—usually between 1 and 2 inches.

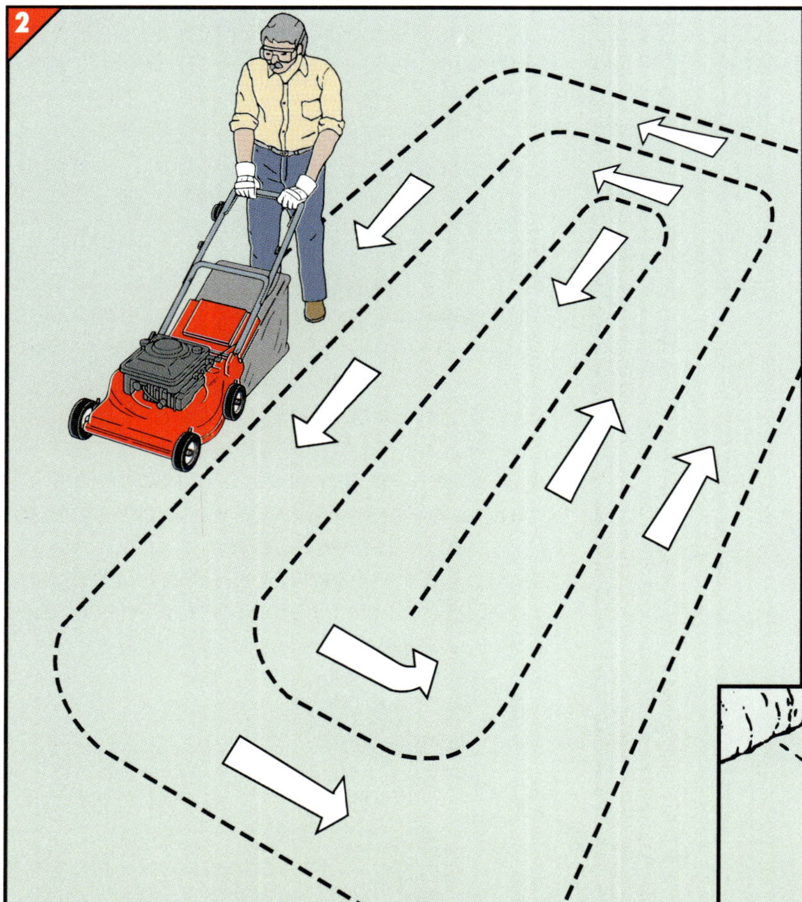

2. Mowing on level lawns and slopes.

On a level lawn, the choice of mowing pattern is up to you. But whether you cut in parallel strips up and down the lawn or in an elongated spiral as shown at left, remember that mowing affects the direction in which grass grows and leans. To prevent stripes in the lawn, change the direction of the pattern each time you mow.

To mow safely on a hillside *(inset),* begin at the top of the slope, and guide a walk-behind power mower across it in parallel lines. With a riding mower, drive up and down the slope for the best stability.

3. Trimming around obstacles.

Hold the power trimmer's cutting head parallel to the ground, an inch or so above the soil, and swing the cutter back and forth in smooth passes, working toward the obstacle.

4. Cutting a clean edge.

For short lengths of edging along sidewalks, driveways, and flower beds, a manual rotary edger may be sufficient, but for bigger jobs, use a power edger *(left)*.

◆ If the blade of your edger is adjustable, set it to the desired depth. Then position the edger so the wheels are on the hard surface.

◆ Turn on the machine and walk at a steady pace, pressing the guide against the edge of the pavement or border.

CHOOSING THE RIGHT SPRINKLER

An oscillating sprinkler.
Driven by water pressure from a garden hose, an oscillating sprinkler provides an even dousing of a rectangular area of grass. The perforated, curved crosspiece swings back and forth through all or part of an arc; controls at the base of the crosspiece set the sprinkler to water all of the lawn, the center alone, or either half *(shaded areas, left)*.

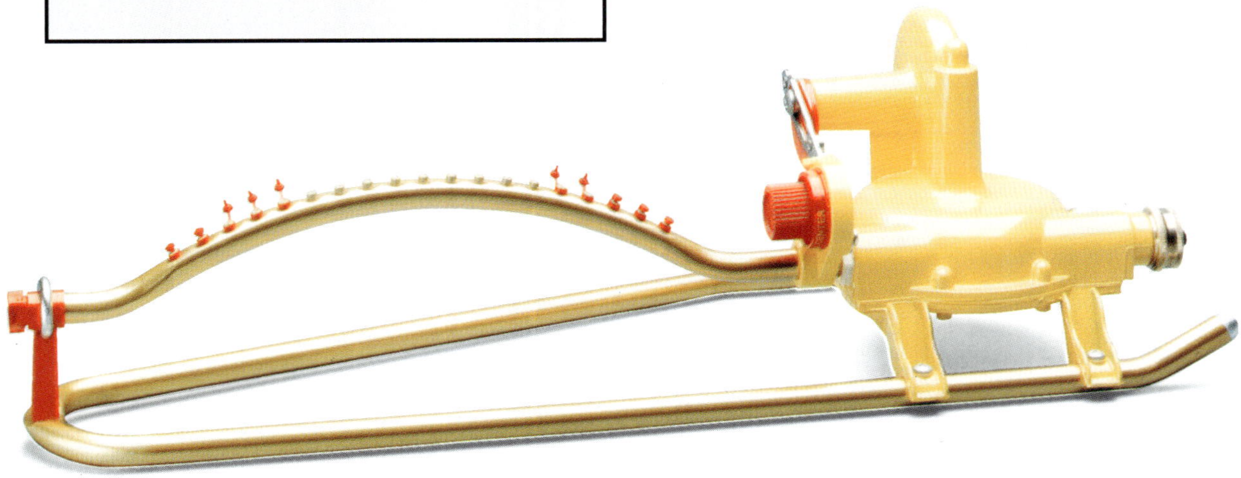

TRICKS OF THE TRADE

Testing Your Sprinkler Coverage

To check the quantity and distribution of water from your sprinkler, set several shallow containers, such as empty tuna cans, throughout the area to be watered, then run the sprinkler for an hour at the same time of day you water the lawn. You should expect to collect 1 inch of water in an hour, and the amounts of water in each can should be almost equal.

Test for water penetration by pushing a screwdriver tip into the lawn 24 hours after watering it. If you encounter resistance before the tip reaches a depth of 6 inches, water the lawn longer.

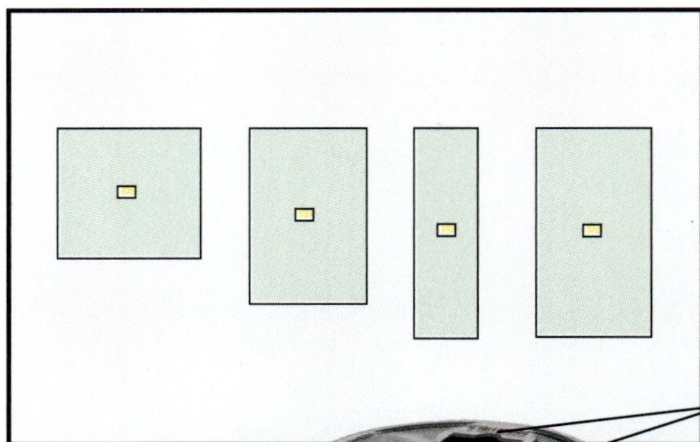

A turret sprinkler.
Multiple sprinkler heads on the turret spray rectangular patterns of different lengths and widths. Compared with an oscillator, a turret sprinkler provides a dousing that is quick, heavy, and somewhat uneven.

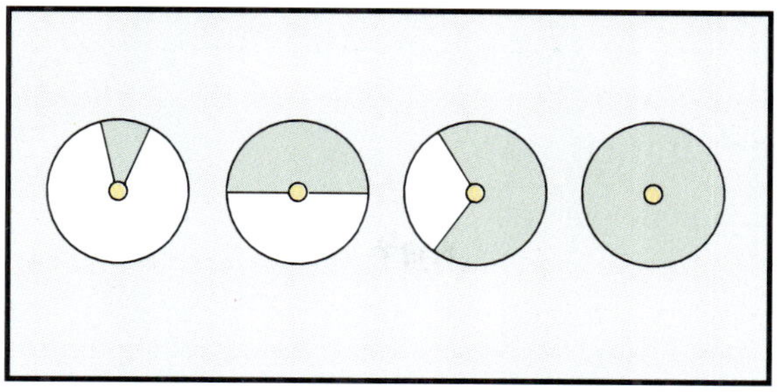

A pulsating sprinkler.
The head of this sprinkler waters grass in a circular pattern that can be adjusted from a narrow wedge to a full circle. The sprinkler head is constantly in motion to prevent water from pooling, and the stream can be varied from a fine spray for small areas to a heavy, longer-range jet.

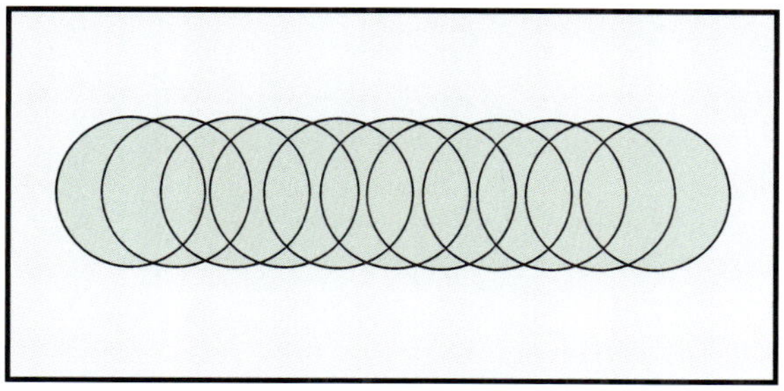

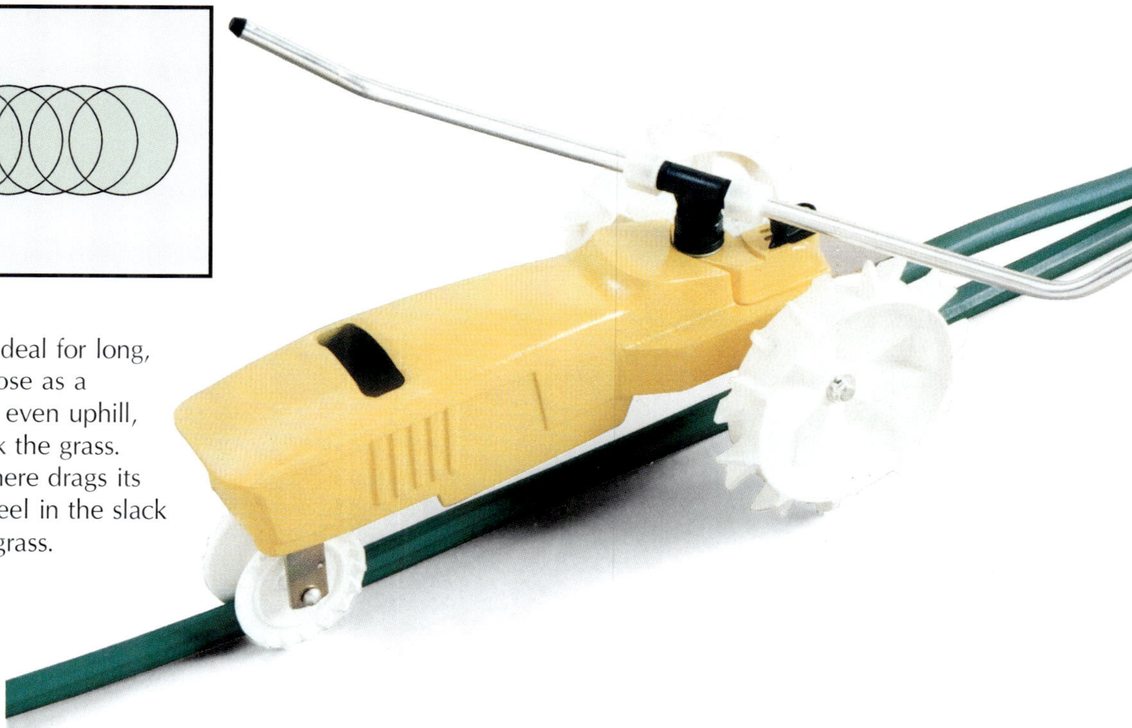

A traveling sprinkler.
This self-propelled sprinkler is ideal for long, narrow lawns. Using its own hose as a track, it creeps along the route even uphill, while the spinning nozzles soak the grass. The traveling sprinkler shown here drags its hose behind it; other models reel in the slack hose as they move across the grass.

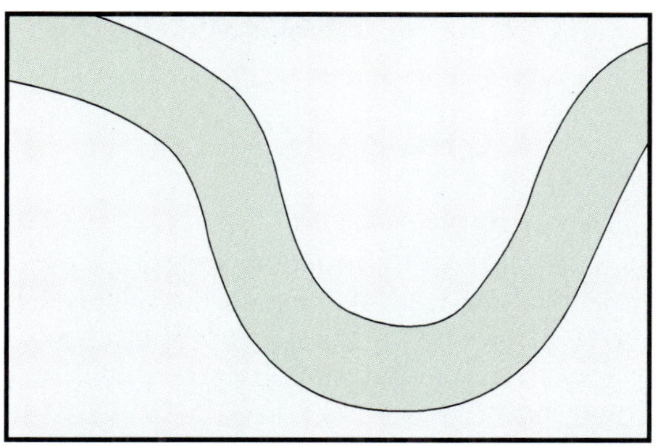

A sprinkler hose.
Tiny holes along the top of the hose provide a fine, soaking mist. The flexible hose is especially suited for very narrow areas. It can also be laid to match an irregular plot's contours *(left)*.

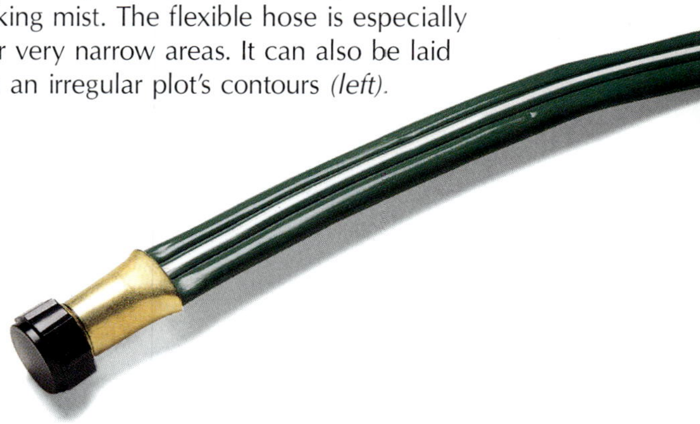

APPLYING FERTILIZER

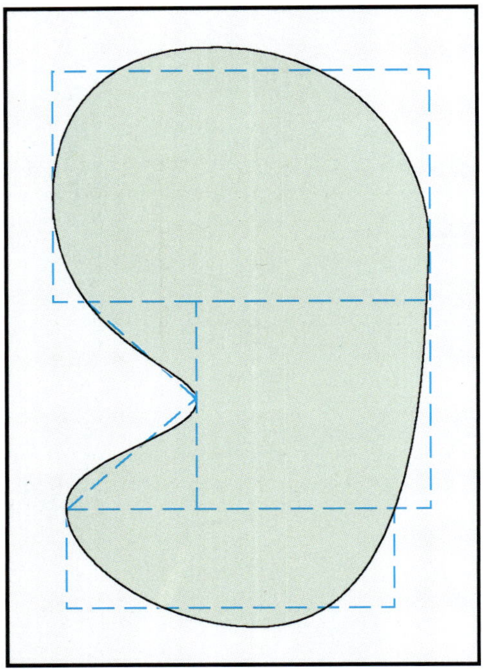

Calculating the quantity.

◆ To determine how much fertilizer you need for your lawn, divide the grassy area into rough geometric shapes such as rectangles, circles, and triangles *(above).*

◆ Calculate the area of each section, then add those figures together. Small areas outside the lawn that happen to be included in this estimate tend to compensate for grassy patches that are left out.

Using a trough spreader.

◆ Set the spreader gauge according to the instructions on the fertilizer package.

◆ At a corner of the lawn, open the trough with the release lever and immediately start walking at an even, moderate pace along one side of the lawn. Close the trough when you reach the far end to avoid burning the grass with excess fertilizer.

◆ Turn the spreader around and position it so that the next row touches but does not overlap the first. Open the trough and run the second row, then make two similar rows at the opposite end of the lawn *(inset).*

◆ Fill in the remaining area by running rows perpendicular to the end rows, being careful not to overlap the fertilizer at any point.

What to Look for in a Fertilizer

Lawn fertilizers come in liquid, pellet, and granular form, with labels that rate the nitrogen, phosphorus, and potassium content according to a three-number code. For example, one common rating, 10-6-4, indicates that 10 percent of the fertilizer bulk is nitrogen, 6 percent phosphorus, and 4 percent potassium. Make a soil test *(page 251)* annually to check for deficiency in any of these three minerals. If the soil is found wanting in one of them, use fertilizer with a higher proportion of the mineral in short supply.

Liquid fertilizer is easy to apply, but the nutrients leach through the soil quickly, necessitating frequent reapplication. Although time-release pellets last 6 months or more, they are costly and slow acting. The more common choice is dry granular fertilizer because it is quick, reliable, and relatively inexpensive.

Using a broadcast spreader.

◆ Calibrate the spreader according to the fertilizer directions, then, beginning at a corner of the lawn, push the spreader at a steady pace that scatters fertilizer 3 or 4 feet to each side.

◆ Work up and down the lawn in wide parallel sweeps. To ensure full coverage near the edges of the path where the fertilizer falls less densely, overlap the rows by about 1 foot. Approach corners and boundaries close enough to give them full coverage.

◆ Repeat the pattern at a right angle to the original rows *(inset)*.

CAUTION

Fertilizers, weed-killers, and other chemicals can be harmful if they come in contact with the skin. Read the labels carefully and follow their recommendations. In addition to long pants and a long-sleeved shirt, it is advisable to wear rubber gloves and eye protection. A dust mask traps particles of dry fertilizers.

SPOT TREATMENTS FOR ISOLATED WEEDS

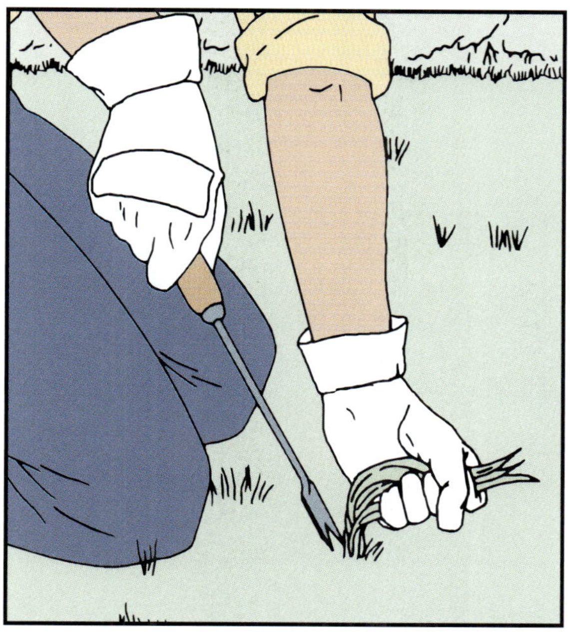

A weeding fork.

◆ If the soil around the weed is hard, soften it by watering over a period of days.

◆ Grasp the runners or leaves in one hand; with the other, push a weeding fork 3 or 4 inches into the earth alongside the main root. For an unusually stubborn weed, dig the fork all the way around it, trying not to tear the leaves or break the roots.

◆ Lever the fork in the surrounding soil to work the roots free, then pull up lightly on the bunched leaves to remove the weed with its roots intact.

◆ Sprinkle a few grass seeds in the hole that has been left by the weed.

A trigger sprayer.
◆ Hold the bottle of weed-killer above the weed, and spray directly onto the center of the plant, coating the leaves and main stem.
◆ Allow 2 to 4 weeks for the weed to shrivel and die, then remove it.

Weed-Killer Checklist

✓ Unless an area is badly infested with weeds, spot-treat individual plants rather than treating the entire area.
✓ Spray weed-killers on calm, still days.
✓ To expose the greatest surface area of the weed to the weed-killer, postpone mowing until at least 2 days after applying the chemical.
✓ Keep clippings from grass that has been treated with weed-killers out of mulch or compost used in gardens or around shrubs. Residual chemicals may harm other plants.
✓ Observe the cautions noted on page 289.

SPRAYING WEED-KILLER OVER A LARGE AREA

Using a pressurized sprayer.
◆ Along one end of the weed-infested area, mark off a 3-yard strip with a pair of staked parallel strings.
◆ Build up pressure in the sprayer with a few strokes of the hand pump, then spray the area between the strings, holding the wand about 12 inches above the lawn and moving it quickly and steadily for a light, even coverage.
◆ Move one of the strings to mark off an adjoining strip, and treat this area in the same way.
◆ Continue spraying strips until you have covered the entire area.

Using a garden-hose sprayer.

◆ Read the weed-killer's label to see how many square feet one jarful will cover, mark off that area with string and stakes, then run a string down the middle to divide it in half.

◆ Fill the sprayer jar with the weed-killer-and-water mixture specified in the label instructions; then screw the sprayer nozzle onto a garden hose and attach the jar to the nozzle.

◆ Turn on the hose and start the flow of weed-killer by covering the air-siphon hole with your thumb or by depressing the trigger, depending on your model.

◆ Spray half the weed-killer evenly on one side of the string, then apply the remainder on the other side.

RESEEDING A BARE PATCH

1. Preparing the soil.

◆ Turn the soil in the plot with a spading fork, digging 5 or 6 inches deep.

◆ Remove 3 inches of soil and work the remainder to break up clods.

◆ Dust the area lightly with lawn fertilizer and add a 3-inch layer of composted municipal sludge or peat moss, then use the spading fork to mix it thoroughly with the underlying soil.

◆ Make the soil even with the surrounding earth by tamping it down with your foot. If necessary, adjust the soil level, either by removing mix or by adding and tamping down more made from the 3 inches of soil removed from the area.

◆ Smooth the surface of the soil with the back of a garden rake.

2. Reseeding the patch.

◆ With your thumb and forefinger, sprinkle grass seeds $\frac{1}{8}$ inch apart over the patch *(right)*.

◆ Work the seeds into the top $\frac{1}{8}$ inch of soil mix with a garden rake, then tamp the soil lightly with the back of a hoe.

◆ Cover the patch with a thin layer of straw—half the soil should show through—to protect the seeds from birds and wind, and lightly mist the area with a garden hose.

CUTTING THROUGH LAYERS OF THATCH

1. Checking for thatch buildup.

◆ Pierce the lawn with a garden trowel and pull the slit open to expose the layers of grass, roots, and soil *(left)*.

◆ Check for a matted layer of densely intertwined roots and dead grass between the green blades and the soil *(inset)*. If this layer is thicker than $\frac{1}{2}$ inch, dethatch the lawn.

2. Dethatching the lawn.

For a small plot, work in rows about 2 feet wide with a thatch rake *(above, left)*. Hold the rake at a 30-degree angle and press the teeth through the thatch. Pull the rake through the grass to dislodge the thatch.

◆ For large areas, rent a self-propelled power dethatcher *(above, right)*. At the center of the lawn, pull the height lever to lower the blades into the thatch, then turn the adjustment knob until the blades barely penetrate the soil.

◆ Engage the clutch, then run the machine over the lawn. Follow the pattern used for mowing *(page 284)*, but do not overlap the rows.

◆ Remove the thatch with a flexible grass rake.

BREAKING UP COMPACTED SOIL

1. Aerating the lawn.

◆ Mow the lawn and saturate the ground with a sprinkler a day in advance of when you plan to aerate.

◆ For a small lawn, thrust an aerating fork with three or four tines *(below, left)* into the ground at 6-inch intervals; try to penetrate to a depth of at least 3 inches. If the soil is too compacted, make a shallower pass, resoak the lawn, and try again.

◆ Work along one boundary, and then back and forth parallel to this line, leaving the extracted cores scattered on the ground.

For large areas, rent a power aerator *(below, right)*.

◆ Beginning at the center of the lawn, start the aerator's engine and warm it up with the clutch disengaged.

◆ Engage the clutch to start the corer drum, and guide the aerator in the pattern that is used for mowing, but do not overlap rows.

◆ In particularly hard soil you may need to increase penetration either by adding water to the corer drum or by attaching weights, if they were provided, or both.

2. Crumbling the cores.

For a small area, use the back of a garden rake to break up the cores *(left)* and spread a $\frac{1}{2}$-inch layer of composted municipal sludge or other soil amendment over the area, filling the core holes. Water the lawn thoroughly.

For larger lawns, drag a section of chain-link fencing across the lawn—either by hand or attached to a lawn tractor—to break up the cores.

Growing a New Lawn

Whether establishing a new lawn on an empty lot or replacing an old one that is terminally choked with weeds, you must start the job from scratch. Although not complicated, the process requires careful planning and hard work.

Choosing the Right Grass: The type of grass you plant depends largely upon the local climate. Cool-season grasses, so called because they grow rapidly in the cool temperatures of spring and autumn while languishing in the warm months of a relatively short summer, do well in northern climates. Warm-season grasses, which are more suited to southern climates, flourish in the heat of a long summer and are dormant in cool months. In regions with wide variations of temperature, a mixture of grasses gives the best results.

Check the grass chart on pages 348 and 349 for other characteristics such as color, texture, and drought tolerance that you should consider when choosing a grass.

Selecting a Planting Method: How you plant your new lawn depends primarily upon the kind of grass you plan to grow and on how quickly you want the lawn to be established.

Seeding *(right)* is the least expensive way to start a lawn and offers the greatest choice of grasses. It is also the slowest because the plants must sprout before they can begin to spread and fill in the lawn. Planting alternatives for warm-season grasses and for sterile hybrids, which produce no seeds, are sprigging *(page 296)* and plugging *(page 297)*. Sprigs and plugs generally fill in faster than a seeded lawn and, in the meantime, are less fragile. In both cases, the sparsely planted mature plants send out new shoots that fill the gaps in between.

The quickest—and most expensive—way to a new lawn is sodding, in which long strips of fully developed turf are set on bare ground *(page 298)*. Lay sod within 36 hours of its harvest, and have your plot ready before the delivery date. For large lawns, consider having the sod delivered in installments so it does not dry out before planting.

Preparing the Site: No matter which planting method you choose, you must carefully prepare the planting bed *(below)*. Before replacing a weed-infested lawn, apply a systemic herbicide formulated to kill all plant life. Follow the manufacturer's instructions, allowing the chemical to dissipate before replanting. Use a sod cutter to remove the old turf, and prepare and smooth the bed *(below and at right)*.

TOOLS

Sod cutter
Tiller
Garden rake
Lawn roller
Hopper
Mechanical spreader
Grass rake
Garden hoe
Grass plugger
Tamper

MATERIALS

Straw
$3\frac{1}{2}$-inch nails
2-by-4, 8 feet long
2-by-2, 6 feet long
Two 1-by-2s, 3 feet long

PREPARING THE BED

1. Smoothing the soil.

◆ Till the lawn bed, then rake it, removing stones and other debris.
◆ Check the grading and drainage around the house *(pages 244-245)* and in the rest of the yard *(pages 240-243)*, and make corrections if necessary.
◆ Test the soil and add amendments as needed *(pages 250-252)*; work them into the soil thoroughly.
◆ Rake the soil again to remove any remaining debris.

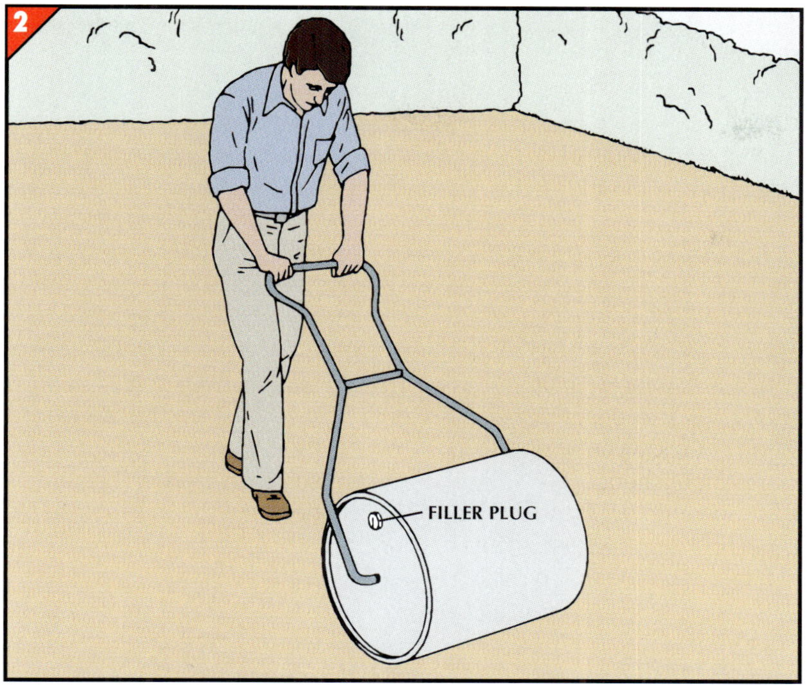

2. Firming the soil.

◆ Remove the filler plug on the barrel of a lawn roller and fill the barrel halfway with water in order to increase the roller's weight.
◆ Push the roller in parallel rows across the lawn bed to flatten it, then roll the area again, perpendicular to the first pass.
◆ Fill in any low spots revealed by rolling, rake the fill smooth, then roll the entire bed again.

NEW GRASS FROM SEED

1. Sowing seed with a hopper.

◆ Measure the correct quantity of seed for the entire area *(chart, pages 348-349)*, then divide it into two equal portions. Do not try to speed growth by using more than the recommended quantity of seed.
◆ Walk slowly over the plot in parallel lines, scattering seed from the hopper by turning the crank steadily until you have covered the entire area once with half the seed; then, walking in rows at right angles to the first direction, sow the other half of the seed. For even coverage over a large area, use a mechanical spreader *(pages 288-289)*, following the same sowing pattern.
◆ Rake the area lightly with a grass rake to mix the seed into the soil, then roll it with a half-filled roller to ensure good contact between the seed and soil.

2. Covering and watering.

◆ Scatter clean straw over the seedbed, covering it so that half the soil can be seen beneath the straw.

◆ Mist the bed just enough to soak the soil without forming puddles or rivulets.

◆ Keep the soil dark with moisture until the seeds germinate—about 2 to 3 weeks, depending on the type of grass and the growing conditions—then water once a day until the seedlings are $\frac{1}{2}$ inch tall. Thereafter, water as frequently as necessary to prevent the lawn from drying out.

◆ Do not mow or walk on the new grass until it is 3 inches high; at that point, either rake off the straw or leave it to decompose into the soil.

STARTING A LAWN WITH SPRIGS

1. Furrowing the soil.

◆ After preparing the bed *(pages 294-295),* soak it with water and let it seep in for 24 hours.

◆ With the corner of a garden-hoe blade, cut a series of straight furrows 3 to 4 inches deep and 6 to 12 inches apart.

GRASS SPRIG

2. Setting the sprigs.

◆ Place sprigs in each furrow at 6- to 12-inch intervals, slanting them upward from the bottom of a furrow to the top of one side *(right).* The closer they are planted, the faster the lawn will fill in.

◆ Press soil gently around the roots with your hands, leaving some blades of each sprig protruding above the ground.

◆ Smooth the soil and level it around the sprigs.

◆ When you have planted all of the sprigs, keep the lawn moist until they have rooted, then water them as you would a mature lawn.

PLANTING WITH PLUGS

1. Cutting holes for planting.

◆ Prepare the soil bed *(pages 294-295)*, soak it thoroughly, and let the water seep in for 24 hours before planting.

◆ Mark the placement of each plug hole, spacing them as recommended for your grass type.

◆ Use a grass plugger, available at a nursery or garden center, to make the holes. Press the foot bar down until it touches the ground, then twist the handle a quarter-turn. Lift the plugger, extracting a core of soil, then deposit the core on the ground.

A Spacing Tool for Plugs

Grass plugs should be planted in even rows 12 to 18 inches apart. You can mark a precise planting grid on your lot with the homemade spacing tool shown above. To make one, drive $3\frac{1}{2}$-inch nails through a 2-by-4 at whatever interval you have chosen, then attach a 6-foot-long 2-by-2, braced with two 3-foot-long 1-by-2s, to serve as a handle. Drag the tool the length of the plot to scratch parallel lines in the soil; pull it across the plot to complete the grid. Plant a plug at each intersection.

2. Planting the plugs.

◆ Fill the holes with water; allow it to drain completely.

◆ If your plugs are square *(photograph)*, round them gently with your hands to fit the holes. Then insert one plug in each hole.

◆ With the ball of your foot, step gently on each plug to bring it even with the surrounding soil.

◆ Break up the extracted soil cores with a garden rake. Using a grass rake, smooth the ground between plugs, erasing any footprints.

◆ Water the area daily for 2 weeks, then water every other day for a month until the plugs have rooted.

◆ Once the plugs are established, water and mow the lawn regularly to stimulate growth.

GRASS PLUG

INSTANT GREEN FROM ROLLS OF SOD

1. Laying the sod.

◆ Prepare the bed as directed on pages 294 and 295, making it 1 inch lower than any adjoining walkways, driveways, or patios.

◆ Wet the soil thoroughly a day or 2 before laying the sod, and keep the soil bed moist but not muddy while laying the rolls.

◆ Lay the first course of sod along a straight pavement or a staked string to provide a uniform edge. Unroll sod gently to avoid breaking off corners and edges. If a section feels uneven, roll it up and relevel the ground beneath it.

◆ For later courses, kneel on a piece of plywood or planking laid across the new sod to avoid creating depressions. Butt the sod rolls together as tightly as possible, staggering joints between them as shown above.

◆ At the end of a row, cut excess with a sharp knife *(inset),* and use these pieces to fill oddly shaped areas around the perimeter of your lot.

2. Establishing root contact.

◆ Tamp the sod firmly against the soil bed; alternatively, roll the turf with an empty lawn roller.

◆ Water the new sod every day for 2 weeks; small pieces at the ends of rows may dry out more quickly than full sections and need more frequent watering. After 2 weeks, try to lift a piece of sod by the grass blades; if it has rooted, the blades will tear and you can begin watering less frequently. Otherwise, retamp the piece, continue watering daily, and test again in a few more days.

Planting Ground Cover

Ground covers are excellent problem solvers. Many flourish in deep shade where grasses won't grow. Their wide range of color, foliage, and flowers can break up the monotony of open spaces or form a transition between low grasses and tall shrubs. And planting a hillside with ground cover eliminates the hazards of mowing on a slope, yet still prevents erosion.

Planting: Some ground covers can be grown from seed, but most are propagated either as cuttings taken from established plants or by dividing large plants into smaller ones, as described on pages 301-303. You can use these methods yourself if you have access to a patch of ground cover either in your own yard or that of a cooperative neighbor. Alternatively, ground covers are sold as immature plants in lots of 50 or more temporarily rooted in a shallow tray called a flat.

The chart on pages 350-351 provides a selection of ground cover plants including information on their special requirements. Consult your nursery about the number of plants of a particular variety you will need to cover a given area. And before planting, mulch the area with a layer of shredded pine bark to help keep weeds at bay. Even so, expect to weed often during the first year.

Coping with Slopes: To prevent the rain from washing newly planted ground cover down an erosion-prone slope, you must stabilize the soil long enough for the ground cover to spread out. Jute netting, a loosely woven, biodegradable material, works especially well *(page 301)*. It does not restrict plant growth or prevent water and nutrients from reaching the roots. Within 6 to 9 months the netting starts to disintegrate, disappearing completely in about 2 years.

Controlling Expansion: After ground covers have become established, they may run rampant. Keep varieties that spread by surface runners in check by pruning. Cut the runner with pruning shears no closer than three or four nodes—points where leaves attach to the stem—from the main stem. A species that widens its coverage by means of the root system can be temporarily contained by cutting the roots along the border of the bed *(page 303)*, but for a more permanent solution, install edging *(page 258)*. Whenever ground cover begins to pop up in a lawn or flower bed, weed it out immediately before it grows beyond control.

TOOLS

Garden trowel
Hammer
3-inch masonry trowel
Hand fork
Spade
Weeding fork

MATERIALS

Mulch
Jute netting
Sod staples
Flat
Plant hormone powder
Rooting medium
Sheet of glass or clear plastic

A TECHNIQUE FOR PLANTING

1. Separating the plants.
◆ Remove no more than half a dozen plants and rooting medium from the flat. Separate the plants with your fingers *(above)*, taking care not to injure the roots.
◆ Set the plants in the ground immediately *(overleaf)*.

2. Setting the plants.

◆ To prepare a planting hole, push a garden trowel through the mulch and into the soil, then pull it toward you, opening a small pocket in the ground.

◆ Holding the soil back with the trowel, set a plant in the pocket, with about $\frac{1}{4}$ inch of its stem below ground level *(left)*.

◆ With the trowel, gently push the displaced soil back into the pocket.

3. Tamping the soil.

◆ Smooth the soil and mulch with your fingers, patting the mulch down around the stem, forming a slight depression to catch and hold moisture *(inset)*.

◆ Set in the remaining plants, and water them for at least half an hour with a lawn sprinkler or with a hose set for a fine mist. Continue to water the new plants every other day for a month.

STABILIZING A SLOPE

Bracing plants with jute netting.

◆ Strip away any sod, grade the slope if necessary *(pages 242-243)*, and prepare the soil for planting *(pages 250-252)*.

◆ Working uphill from the bottom of the slope, unroll strips of jute netting *(photograph)* across the incline. Overlap the strips 8 inches and secure them with sod staples *(above)*. Cover the area with an inch of mulch.

◆ With a 3-inch masonry trowel, dig holes for the plants, in staggered rows to prevent water from washing straight down the hill.

◆ After setting the plants, mold a basin around the lower side of each stem with your hand to prevent runoff. Then water as described on page 300, Step 3.

PROPAGATION BY CUTTINGS

1. Obtaining a cutting.

◆ Cut a 3- to 6-inch length from a main stem or an entire side stem of a well-established plant. The stem should contain three to five nodes.

◆ With a small sharp knife, make a clean, slanting cut slightly below the nodes *(right)*.

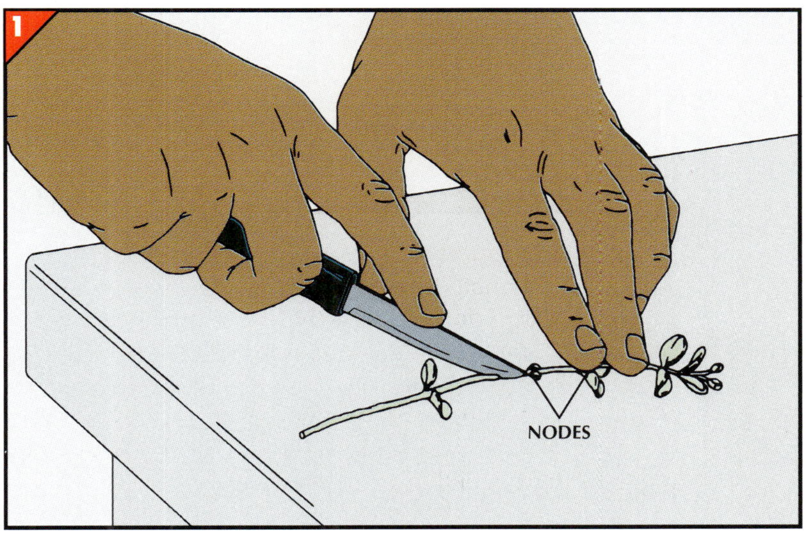

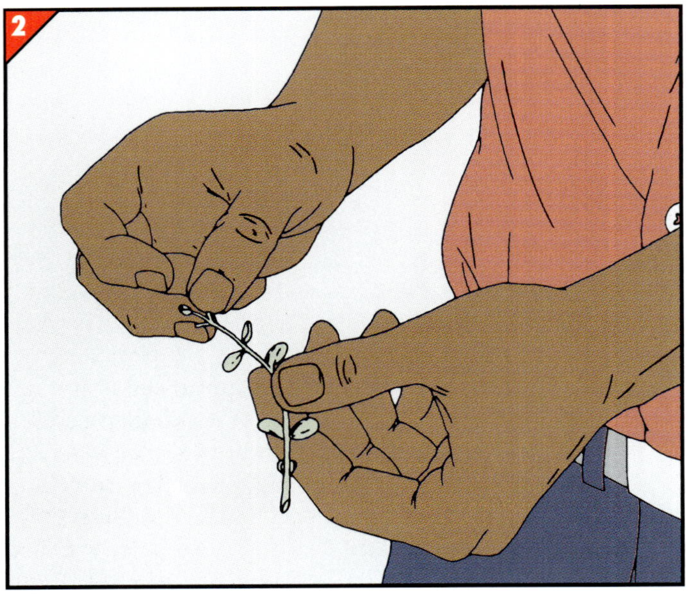

2. Preparing the cutting for planting.

◆ Pinch off any flowers or seed heads from the stem *(left);* if allowed to remain, they will divert nutrients away from the roots that will form on the cutting.
◆ Trim the leaves from the bottom of the cutting so that no foliage will be buried in the planting.
◆ Allow the cut end of the stem to dry out slightly; if the leaves begin to wilt, place them on a damp towel.

3. Planting the cuttings.

◆ Fill a flat with a moistened rooting medium, such as a combination of sand and peat moss in equal parts, to about an inch from the top.
◆ With a stick or a pencil, poke holes in the medium just deep enough to cover two or three nodes on the cuttings.
◆ Dip the end of each cutting into plant hormone powder, available at nurseries or garden-supply outlets, to encourage root growth. Set the cutting in a hole and tamp rooting medium down around it.
◆ After planting all the cuttings, water the entire flat gently but thoroughly.
◆ Cover the flat with a sheet of glass or clear plastic to protect the young plants until they can survive outdoors.
◆ Keep them in a warm room and out of direct sunlight. When new leaves appear, the cuttings are ready to be transplanted *(page 300).*

MULTIPLICATION BY DIVISION

1. Uprooting the plants.

◆ Water the plants well a couple of days before you divide them to soften the ground.
◆ Using a hand fork or a spading fork, dig around a clump of plants containing 8 to 12 new plants.
◆ Raise the clump and guide the roots away from the fork with your free hand *(right).*

2. Separating the plants.

◆ Shake or rinse enough soil from the clump to reveal the roots, then carefully pull apart individual plants *(left).*

◆ After discarding any wilted or yellowed plants, return two or three of the stems to the original hole, then set the rest in a new hole and water them thoroughly.

CONTROLLING THE SPREAD OF GROUND COVERS

Countering an invasion.

For deep-rooting plants—pachysandra and ivy, for example—slice straight down into the soil along the edge of the ground cover bed with a sharp spade, penetrating to the full depth of the plants' roots, usually about 6 to 8 inches *(right).*

If ground cover begins to pop up in a lawn or flower bed, remove it by hand with a weeding fork. Hold the base of the ground cover with one hand as you push the blade down into the soil alongside the root *(far right),* then lever the plant out of the ground.

Outdoor Faucets and Fixtures

Extending water lines outside your house can pay rich dividends in convenience: A new line may serve a faucet called a sillcock on an exterior wall *(opposite)*, a yard hydrant near a flower garden *(page 313)*, or a sprinkler system *(pages 314-319)*. Most such additions call for no more than basic pipe fitting skills *(pages 304-306)* and some digging of trenches.

Pipe Material: Polyethylene (PE) pipe and polyvinyl chloride (PVC) pipe are both good choices for outdoor extensions of a plumbing system: They are inexpensive, durable, and easy to work with. PE pipe, which is flexible and sold in long rolls, may require fewer fittings than rigid PVC pipe; however, its fittings are inserted into the pipe and will reduce water flow somewhat.

Because both types of plastic pipe deteriorate in direct sunlight, any portion of the run that is aboveground should be covered by two coats of latex paint or enclosed.

Tapping the Household Supply: As the water source for an outdoor line, select a cold-water supply pipe close to the extension's exit point from the house—preferably a pipe in the basement, minimizing problems of access. If the extension will have a run of more than 300 feet or will serve numerous outlets, use 1-inch pipe. Otherwise, match the extension to the size of the indoor pipe—most likely $\frac{1}{2}$ or $\frac{3}{4}$ inch.

Cold-Weather Safeguards: Some outdoor fittings are specifically designed to cope with freezing temperatures. In the absence of such protection, however, outdoor plumbing may burst in cold weather unless you include a valve that allows water to be drained out before winter arrives. In many cases, this valve can be located in the basement *(pages 309 and 311)*. If such a handy arrangement is not possible, you will need an exterior valve that permits the extension pipe to be flushed by air pressure *(page 312)*.

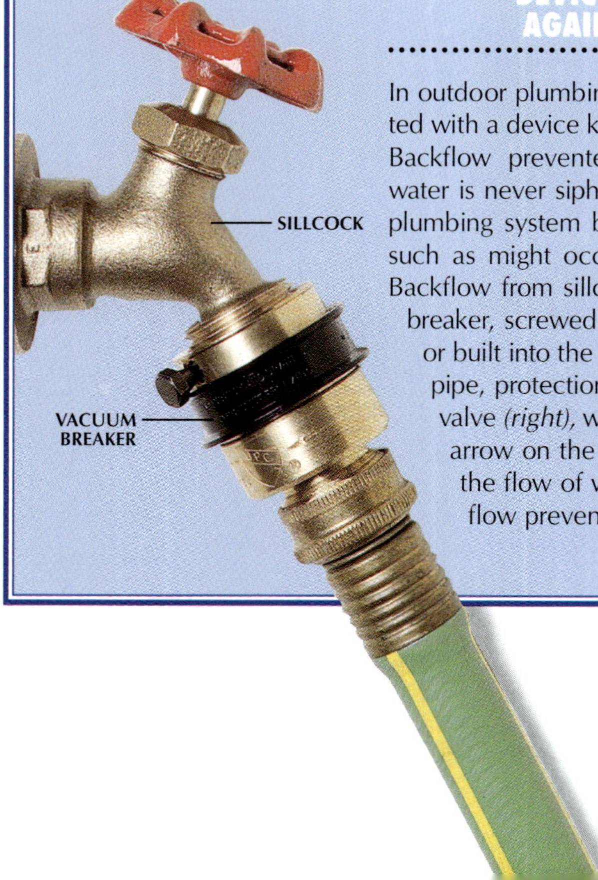

DEVICES THAT GUARD AGAINST BACKFLOW

In outdoor plumbing, any supply line must be fitted with a device known as a backflow preventer. Backflow preventers ensure that contaminated water is never siphoned back into the household plumbing system by a sudden drop in pressure, such as might occur if a supply main ruptures. Backflow from sillcocks is blocked by a vacuum breaker, screwed onto the sillcock threads (left) or built into the fitting *(page 327)*. On a supply pipe, protection is conferred by a dual check valve *(right)*, which must be installed with the arrow on the valve going in the direction of the flow of water. Replace or service backflow preventers every 5 years.

TOOLS

Drill
Spade bit
Star drill
Maul (4-lb)
Screwdriver
Hammer
Tube cutter
Hacksaw
Plumber's sandcloth
Flat file
Round file
Fitting brush
Flux brush
Propane torch and striker
Flameproof pad
Shovel
Plastic sheeting
Garden hose
Carpenter's level
Pipe cutter
Adjustable wrench
Measuring stick

MATERIALS

Silicone caulk
Plumbing-sealant tape
Pipe, fittings, and adapters (copper or plastic)
Plastic pipe primer and cement
Paste flux
Applicator brushes
Solder
Miter box
Wooden stakes
String

SAFETY TIPS

Wear gloves and safety goggles to solder copper supply pipe. When digging, gloves and a back brace help prevent injury.

INSTALLING A SILLCOCK

1. Boring a hole for the pipe.

For an ordinary sillcock, the supply pipe should pass through the wall horizontally. For a freezeproof sillcock *(page 309)*, the hole should slope slightly downward toward the outside.

◆ On a wood wall *(left)*, bore the hole just above the masonry foundation with a spade bit and, if necessary, an extension. Make the hole just large enough for the pipe.

◆ For masonry, use a star drill. Set the point on a horizontal strip of mortar or at the center of a cinder block, and strike the drill with a 4-pound maul, turning the point a few degrees between blows. Make the hole diameter 1 inch larger than the pipe to accommodate a sleeve *(pages 311-312)*.

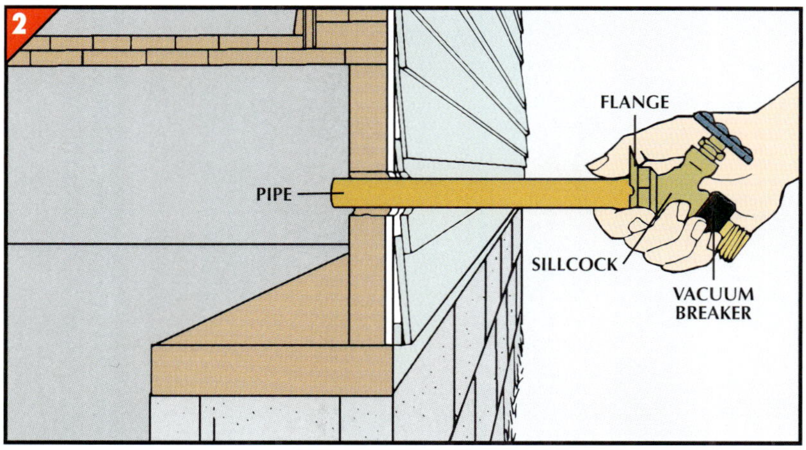

2. Assembling the sillcock.

◆ Screw a vacuum breaker onto the sillcock. Attach the sillcock to a pipe 3 inches longer than the thickness of the wall, using an adapter, if necessary. A freezeproof sillcock does not require a separate pipe, but must have a stem at least 2 inches longer than the wall thickness.

◆ For masonry walls, run the pipe through a sleeve *(pages 311-312)* to prevent corrosion and damage to the pipe.

◆ Insert the assembly into the hole and screw the flange to the wall, using anchors, if necessary. Fill any gaps with silicone caulk.

***Installing a Sillcock* continues on page 309**

Pipe-fitting Fundamentals

To bring water outdoors, extend a cold-water line to a convenient exit point using the techniques shown here, which presume copper pipe indoors. If your house has plastic pipe, cut into the line as shown below for copper, then cement the extension together as explained on page 308.

TAPPING A COPPER SUPPLY LINE

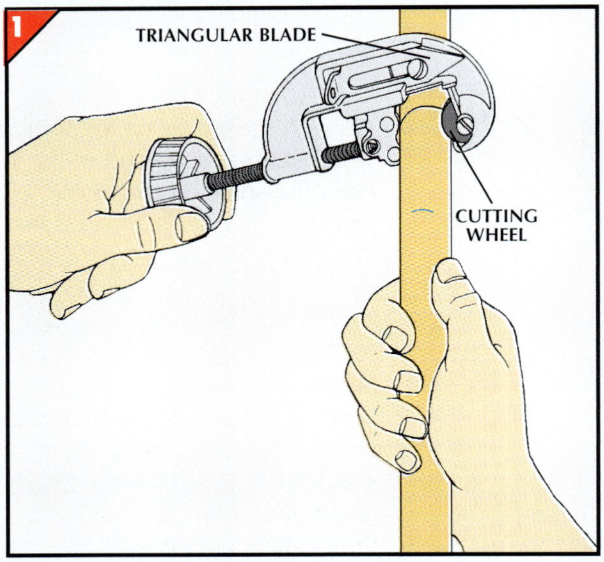

1. Using a cutter.

Although a hacksaw may be needed to open a hard-to-reach section of copper pipe, use a tube cutter if possible.

◆ Mark the pipe at the shoulders molded into a T.

◆ Slide the cutter onto the pipe and turn the knob until the cutting wheel bites into the copper, but no further.

◆ Turn the cutter once around, retighten the knob, and continue turning and tightening. Once the pipe is severed, loosen the knob, and cut pipe at the second mark.

◆ With the cutter's triangular blade, ream out the burr inside the standing pipe. Remove the ridge on the outside with a file. (For a hacksaw cut, remove the inner burr with a round file.)

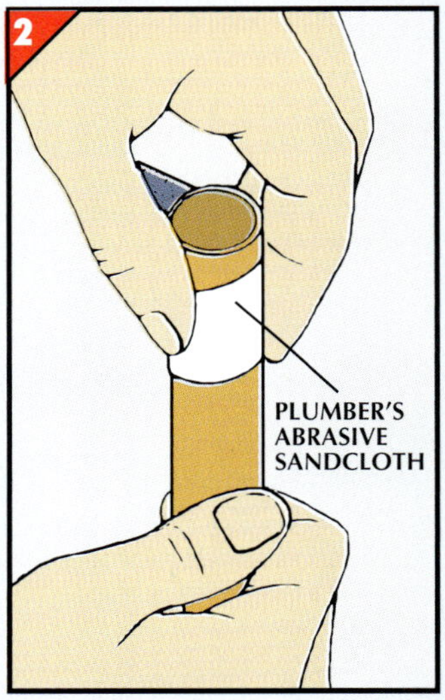

2. Preparing the cut ends.

◆ With a piece of plumber's sandcloth—not a file or steel wool—clean the cut pipe ends to a distance slightly greater than the depth of fittings that you will use to connect them. Rub until the surface is bright.

◆ Scour the inner surfaces of the T's three sockets with a wire fitting brush. Once the surfaces of the fittings and pipes have been cleaned, do not touch them: Even a fingerprint will weaken the joint.

TRICKS OF THE TRADE

Dos and Don'ts of Soldering

Well-soldered joints *(below, left)* are achieved by careful handling of flux and solder. Spread the coat of flux thinly and evenly. Excessive residue can cause corrosion; too little flux will create gaps in the bond between solder and copper. Do not overheat the fitting or direct the flame into the socket: If the flux burns—indicated by a brownish black coloring—the bond will be imperfect. Never direct the flame at the solder, and be sure to remove the solder as soon as capillary action sucks it around the full circumference of the joint. If solder drips, it has been overheated or overapplied, and the capillary action will fail. Thick, irregular globs of solder at the edges of sweated joints are a sign of a bad job *(below, right)*.

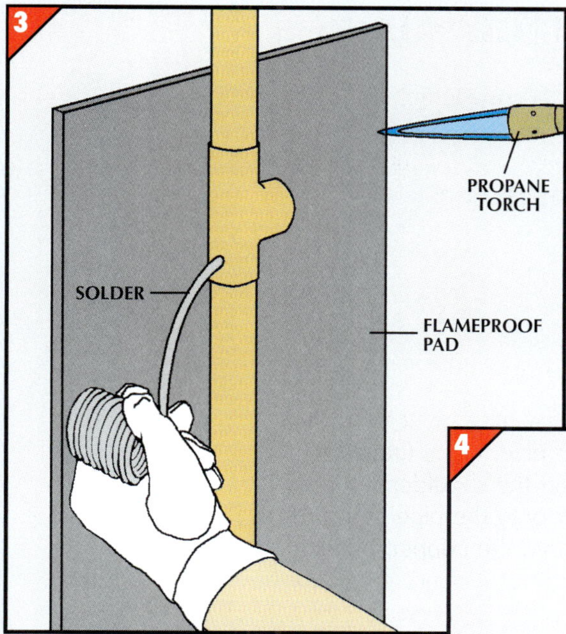

3. Assembling and heating a joint.

◆ Brush a light coat of flux over the cleaned surfaces, place the T between the ends of the supply pipe, and twist the fitting a quarter-turn.
◆ Place a flameproof pad in back of the joint.
◆ Light the torch with a striker. Holding the tip of the flame perpendicular to the metal and about a half-inch away, play it over the fitting and nearby pipe.
◆ From time to time, touch solder to the fitting *(left)*. When the solder melts on contact, turn the flame aside to avoid burning off the flux, which enables the solder to flow smoothly.

4. Soldering the joint.

◆ Touch the solder tip to the pipe where it enters one end of the T. Keep the solder at that point while the capillary action of the flux draws molten solder into the fitting to seal the connection.
◆ Remove the solder from the joint when a bead of metal completely seals the rim.
◆ Wipe away excess with a clean cloth, leaving a shiny surface.
◆ Solder the other end of the fitting in the same way, reheating the joint as needed.

SWITCHING FROM COPPER TO PLASTIC

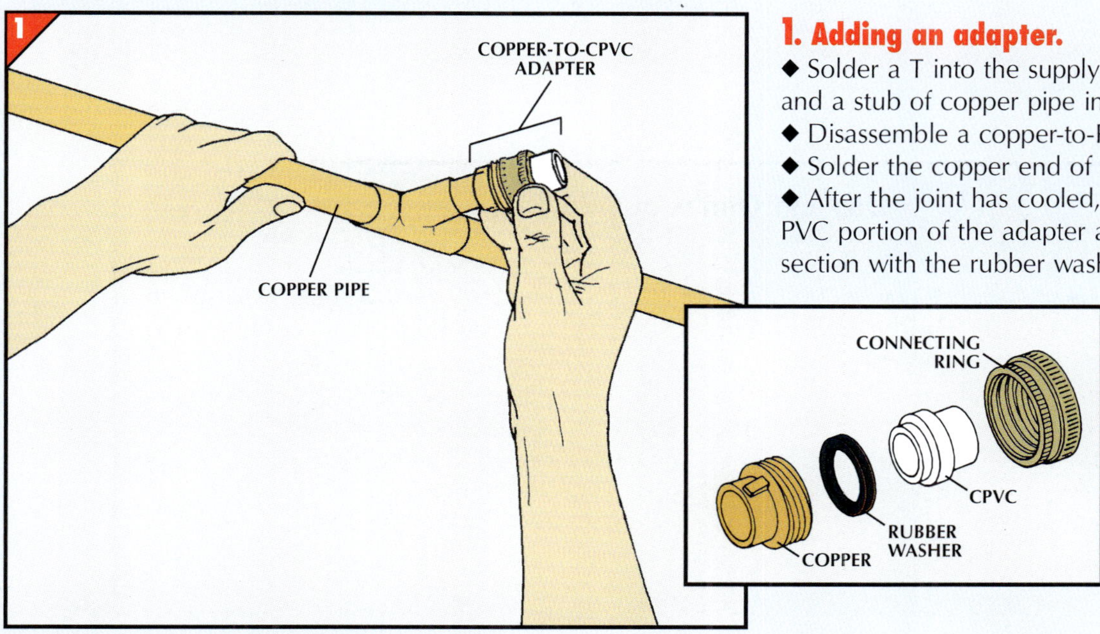

1. Adding an adapter.

◆ Solder a T into the supply line *(page 306)* and a stub of copper pipe into the T.
◆ Disassemble a copper-to-PVC adapter *(inset)*.
◆ Solder the copper end of the adapter to the T.
◆ After the joint has cooled, position the threaded PVC portion of the adapter against the copper section with the rubber washer between them.
◆ Slide the connecting ring over the PVC portion of the adapter and hand-tighten it *(left)*.
◆ With an adjustable wrench, tighten the fittings just beyond hand tight.

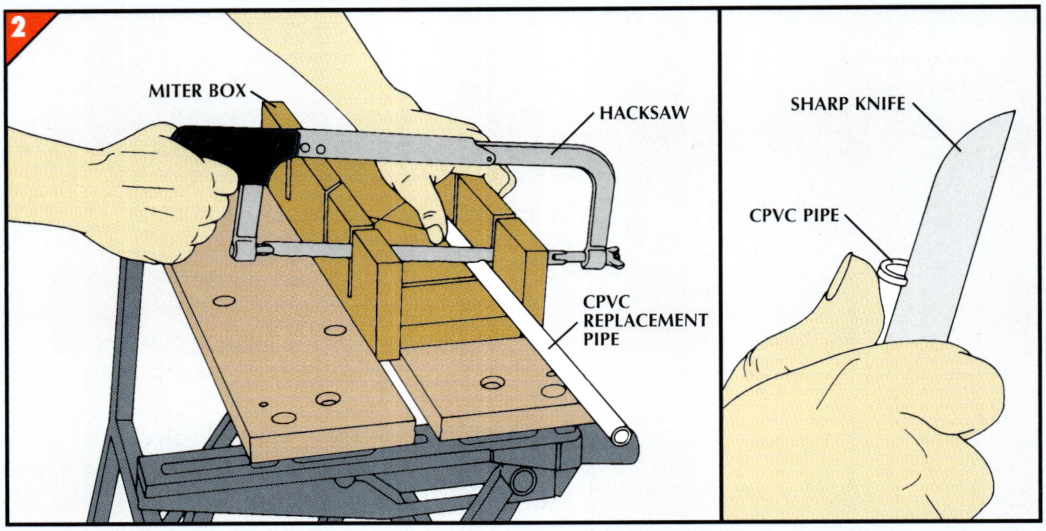

2. Cutting PVC pipe.

◆ Cut PVC pipe with a tube cutter or a hacksaw. If you use a hacksaw, place the pipe in a miter box and brace it with your thumb as you make the cut *(above).*

◆ Ream the ends of the pipe and bevel the edges inside and out with a sharp knife. Doing so aids water flow and improves the welding action of the primer and cement solvents.

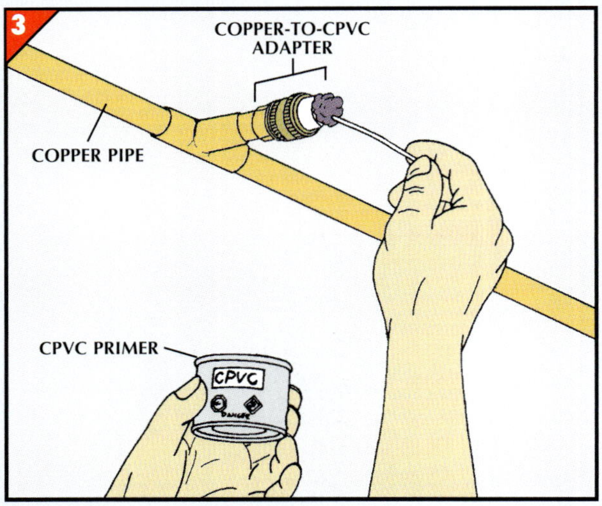

3. Priming and cementing the joint.

Work as quickly as possible with PVC cement. It sets in less than 30 seconds.

◆ With an applicator or clean cloth, apply a coat of primer inside the adapter socket *(left)* and to the outside pipe surface that will be fitted into the socket.

◆ With a second applicator, spread a coat of CPVC cement over the primed surfaces at the end of the PVC pipe.

◆ Spread a light coat of cement inside the adapter socket.

4. Fitting the extension pipe.

◆ Working rapidly, push one end of the PVC pipe into the socket, give the pipe a quarter-turn to evenly distribute the cement inside the socket, then hold the pipe securely for about 10 seconds.

◆ Wipe away any excess cement with a clean, dry cloth. Do not run water in the pipe until the cement has cured (about 2 hours at temperatures above 60°F).

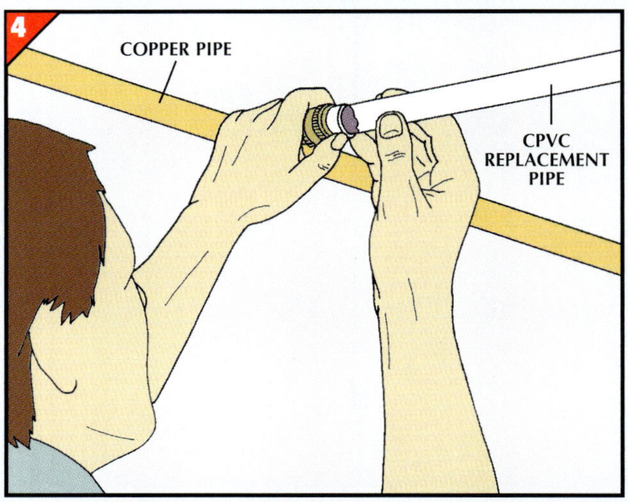

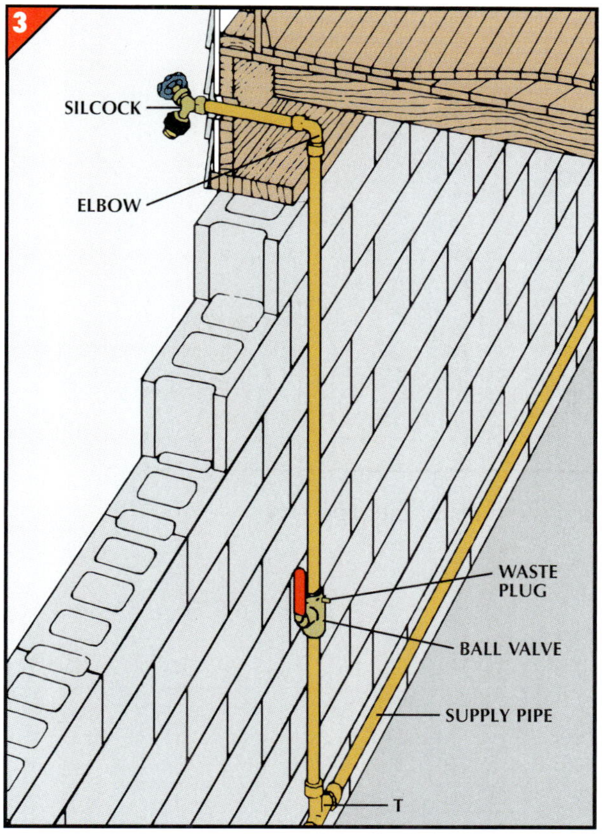

3. Tapping a basement supply line.

◆ Insert a T fitting in a convenient supply pipe (pages 306-308), add a short section of pipe, and install a ball valve with a waste plug, orienting the valve so that the waste plug is on the side nearest the sillcock.

◆ Attach an elbow to the end of the sillcock pipe, and connect the elbow to the valve.

◆ Finish the job by caulking any gaps around the hole on the basement side of the wall.

To drain the line, close the ball valve, open the outdoor faucet, and then open the valve's waste plug.

AN ICE-THWARTING OUTDOOR FAUCET

A freezeproof sillcock has all the parts of a standard stem faucet, but its elongated body allows the stem to stop the flow of water inside the house, where the temperature is above freezing. Because the sillcock is installed sloping slightly downward toward the outside, water drains out when the valve is closed. Choose a model with a built-in vacuum breaker; adding a screw-on breaker could prevent proper draining.

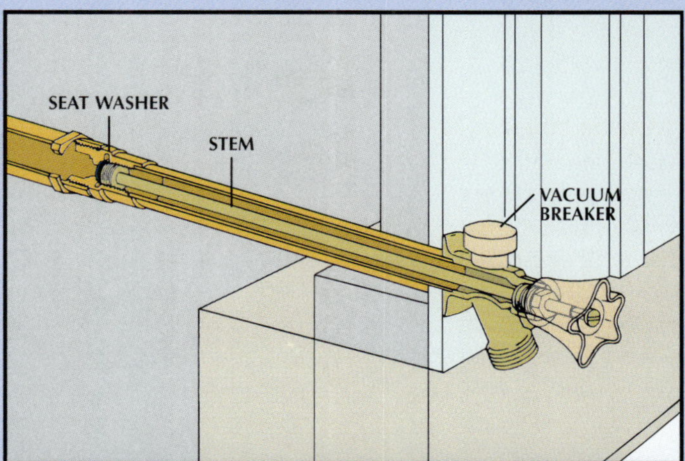

AN UNDERGROUND ROUTE TO A YARD OUTLET

1. Staking out a trench.

◆ Drive a stake into the ground at the location for the yard outlet, and another stake at the wall where the supply pipe will exit the house. Tie a string between the two stakes.

◆ With a flat shovel, make two parallel grooves about 3 inches to the left and the right of the string, pushing the blade down about 2 inches into the ground.

◆ Remove the string and stakes. Use the shovel to divide the sod between the grooves into segments 5 or 6 feet long. Spread a plastic sheet next to one of the grooves.

◆ Push the shovel under the sod at the corner of a segment and work it up and down to free the roots. Repeat along the rest of the segment, then lift the sod carpet and place it on the plastic sheet.

CAUTION *Before excavating, confirm that your trench will not encounter electric, water, or sewer lines—or other underground obstacles such as dry wells, septic tanks, and cesspools.*

2. Digging the trench.

◆ Spread a large plastic sheet or a tarpaulin on the ground.

◆ Working in from the sides of the cleared area, dig a V-shaped trench about 1 foot deep, piling the loose soil on the plastic sheet.

◆ For a freezeproof hydrant *(page 313),* dig the trench to a depth below the frostline in your area.

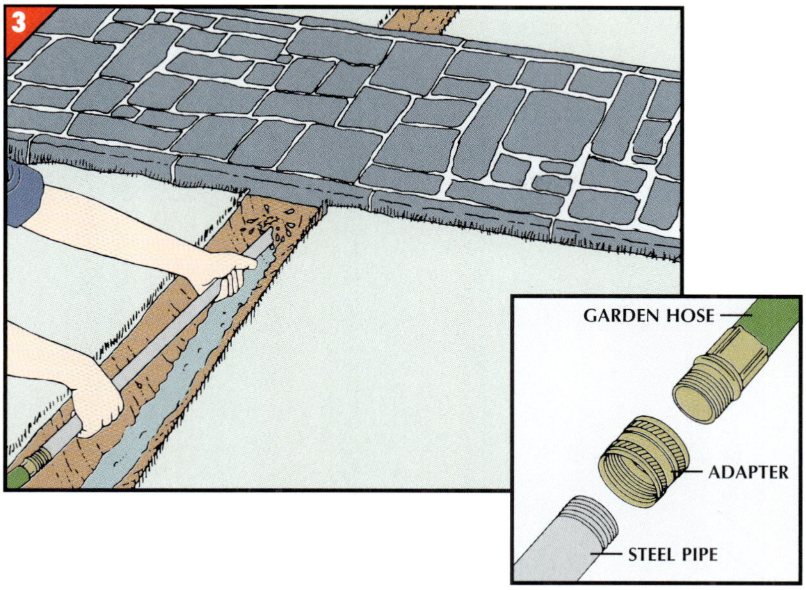

3. Tunneling under a paved walk.

◆ Have a 3-foot length of $\frac{3}{4}$-inch steel pipe threaded at one end, and join it to a garden hose with an adapter *(inset)*.

◆ Turn the water on full force and stick the end of the steel pipe into the ground under the walk, using the pipe as a water-pressure pick to loosen the earth. The stream of water should be strong enough to keep the open end of the pipe clear and to sweep away loose earth.

◆ When you reach the middle of the walk, cross to the other side and work from there to complete the tunnel.

TWO TACTICS FOR WINTERTIME DRAINING

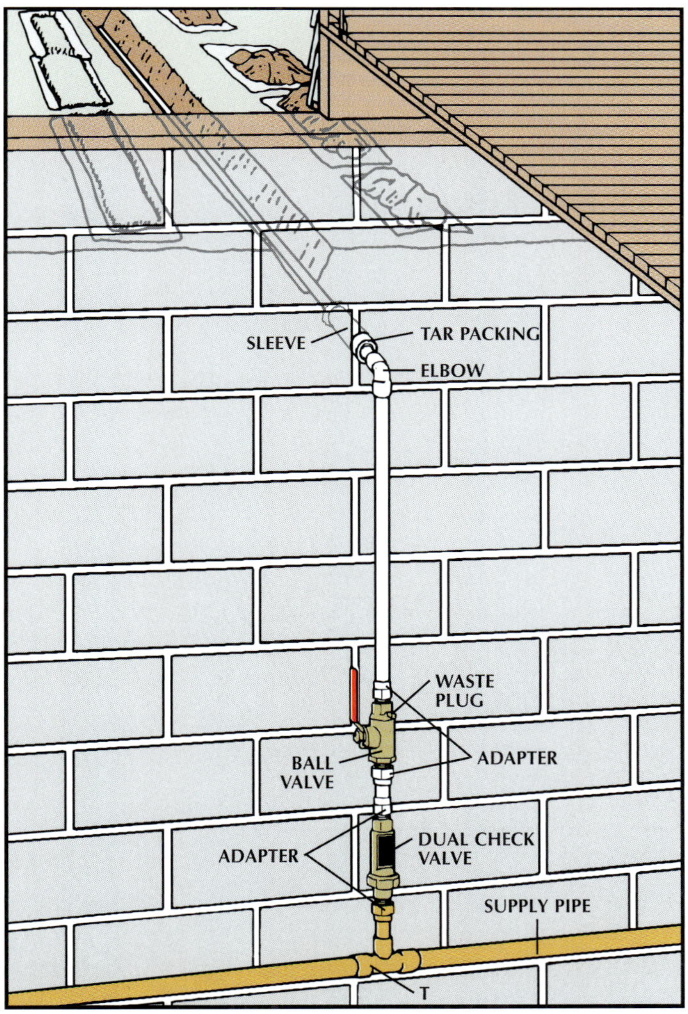

A drain in the basement.

If the ground outside your house is level or slopes slightly downward toward the house, you can tap water for a yard hydrant from a basement supply line and also drain the system from there.

◆ Bore a hole through the wall *(page 305)* at the bottom of the trench, sloping it slightly downward into the basement.

◆ Make a sleeve from a PVC pipe 1 inch larger in diameter than the supply pipe and slightly longer than the wall thickness. Insert the sleeve in the exit hole.

◆ Run pipe from the end of the trench through the sleeve. With a carpenter's level, make sure that the pipe is pitched slightly downward toward the house along its entire length. If necessary, give it the proper pitch by propping it up with fragments of brick or stone at 6-foot intervals, then shoring up the pipe between the fragments with loose earth.

◆ Attach an elbow to the pipe.

◆ Insert a T fitting in the supply pipe *(pages 306-307)*, followed by a short length of pipe.

◆ Install a dual check-valve backflow preventer *(page 304)*, and add another short length of pipe

◆ Install a ball valve with a waste plug, orienting the valve with the plug toward the outside.

◆ Run a pipe from the valve to the elbow.

◆ Seal the sleeve by packing the space around the pipe with tar.

TRICKS OF THE TRADE

A Watertight Connection through a Wall

To seal an underground hole through masonry, fill gaps around the sleeve with the material used to patch concrete swimming pools. Made predominantly of Portland cement, this material doesn't shrink when it dries and can solidify even under water. It is generally available at swimming pool supply stores.

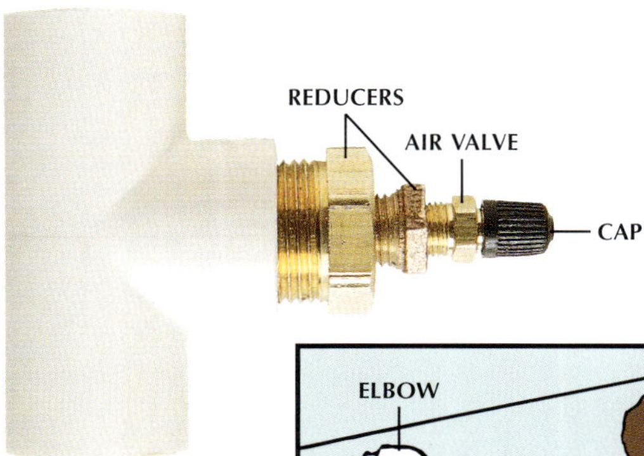

Purging a line with air.

If your house has no basement or the lawn slopes away from the foundation, a yard hydrant requires a different supply and drainage arrangement.

◆ As the water source, choose a supply pipe near an outside wall and install a T, a dual check valve, and a ball valve as on page 311.

◆ Bore a hole in the wall *(page 305)*, run pipe from the valve through the wall, and attach an elbow followed by a short length of pipe.

◆ Add a T with a threaded outlet, then extend another section of pipe to the bottom of the trench.

◆ Attach an elbow and run pipe from the elbow to the yard hydrant.

◆ Screw reducers onto the threaded T until the opening fits a $\frac{1}{8}$-inch air stem valve *(photograph)*.

◆ To drain the pipe for winter, hook a bicycle pump or an air compressor to the air valve and flush the water out through the open yard outlet, keeping the pressure below 60 pounds.

ADDING A YARD HYDRANT

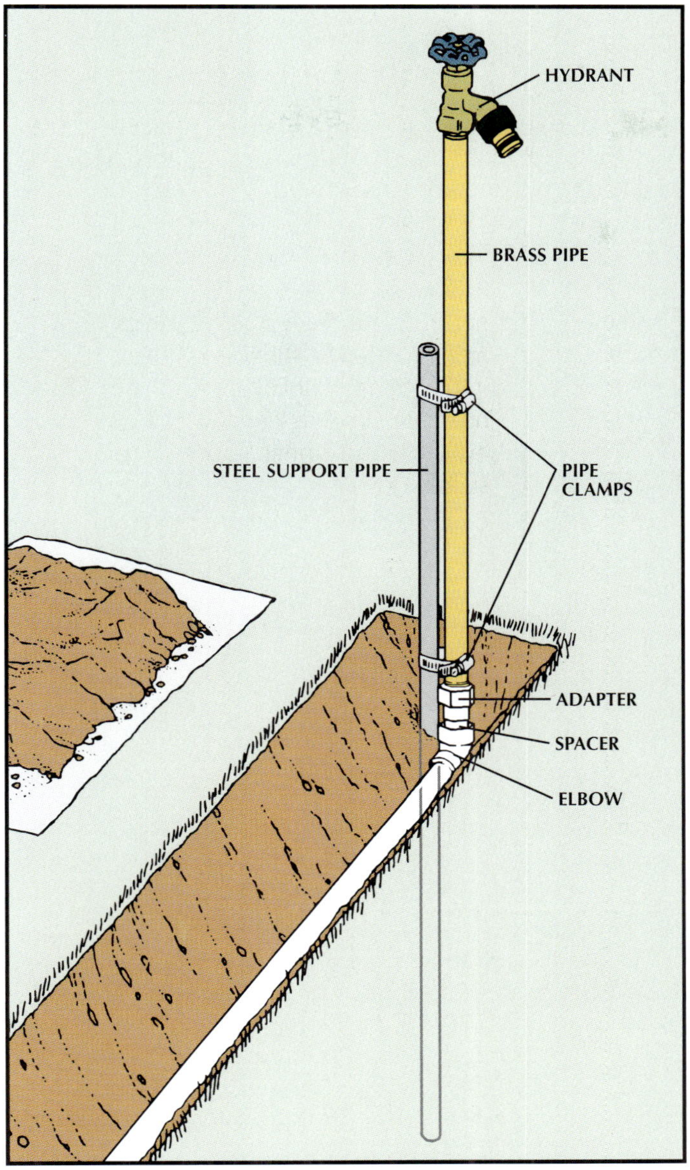

Bracing the hydrant.

◆ Cut a 40-inch-long support from a $\frac{3}{4}$-inch steel pipe. At the far end of the pipe in the trench, drive this steel pipe about 2 feet into the earth with a sledgehammer.

◆ For the vertical riser, use a brass pipe threaded at both ends. Attach an elbow to the end of the pipe in the trench, and add a short spacer. Using plumbing-sealant tape, attach a threaded adapter to one end of the brass pipe, then glue the adapter to the spacer on the elbow.

◆ Strap the two vertical pipes together with stainless-steel pipe clamps and turn on the water briefly to flush dirt from the supply pipe.

◆ Wrap plumbing-sealant tape around the threads of the brass pipe and screw the hydrant to the pipe. Turn on the water to test for leaks before filling the trench.

FREEZEPROOF YARD HYDRANTS

Freezeproof yard hydrants—functional year-round—come in two basic types: ground-level *(left)* and freestanding *(right)*. Both have a valve that lets water drain into the ground from the stem when the hydrant closes. To install a freezeproof hydrant, dig the trench for the supply pipe deeper than the frostline in your area. At the end of the trench, dig a drainage pit at least 8 inches deeper than the trench and add 8 inches of gravel at the bottom. Connect the supply pipe to the freezeproof hydrant in the same manner for an ordinary yard hydrant *(above)*.

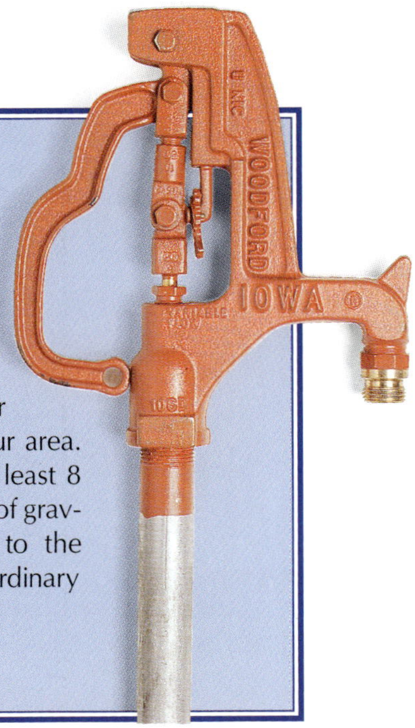

An Underground Sprinkler System

Few homeowners enjoy dragging a sprinkler around the yard to water the lawn in summer. Fortunately, a fully automated alternative is available—a sprinkler system buried in the ground and controlled from a timing box in the basement.

In response to timer commands, electrically operated valves open, and water pressure in the system causes sprinkler heads to rise above the grass and create overlapping umbrellas of spray. At the end of the watering period, the heads sink back into the ground. To deviate from a preset watering program, you can manually override the system's automatic controls.

A Tailor-Made Plan: Most distributors and manufacturers of sprinkler parts will make a blueprint of a system tailored to your home if you agree to buy their components. The designer needs a rough scale map of your house and yard, showing grass, flowers, and bushes; areas of sunlight or shade; the location of large trees or other obstacles; and whether your soil is sandy, rocky, or compact.

In order to recommend the appropriate type and size of pipe, the designer must also know the water pressure in your supply lines. (To measure the pressure, open the main shutoff valve fully and close all other valves in the house. Next screw a pressure gauge, available at hardware stores, to an outdoor faucet and open it all the way.)

Rigid PVC pipe is the usual choice for a sprinkler system, although polyethylene (PE) pipe may be preferred in some cases *(page 319)*.

Winterizing: In cold climates, all exterior pipes must be drained to prevent their bursting. Typically, two special valves are required—one outdoors for flushing the sprinkler network by air pressure, and one inside the house to drain water from the supply line that leads to the control valves.

TOOLS

Straight-edged shovel
Hacksaw or PVC cutting tool

MATERIALS

Graph paper for scale map
Stakes and string
Sprinkler heads
Control valves with anti-backflow protection
Sprinkler timer
PVC pipes and fittings

A three-zone sprinkler system.
This sprinkler system illustrates common situations: a sunny front lawn, a tree-shaded side lawn, and a flower garden. Separate supply lines feed three networks of pipe, called circuits, that serve the watering zones; electric control valves *(numbered squares)* are clustered near the exit of the main supply pipe from the basement. The pipe layout between the control valves and sprinkler heads is shown in green, yellow, and blue, with the pipe diameters indicated for each run. The flower garden at the top is watered by simple pop-up spray heads (triangles), the two lawns by impulse pop-ups (circles). When in operation, these heads spray water in the patterns indicated by large half and quarter circles. Each pattern overlaps others by about 60 percent to provide more uniform coverage.

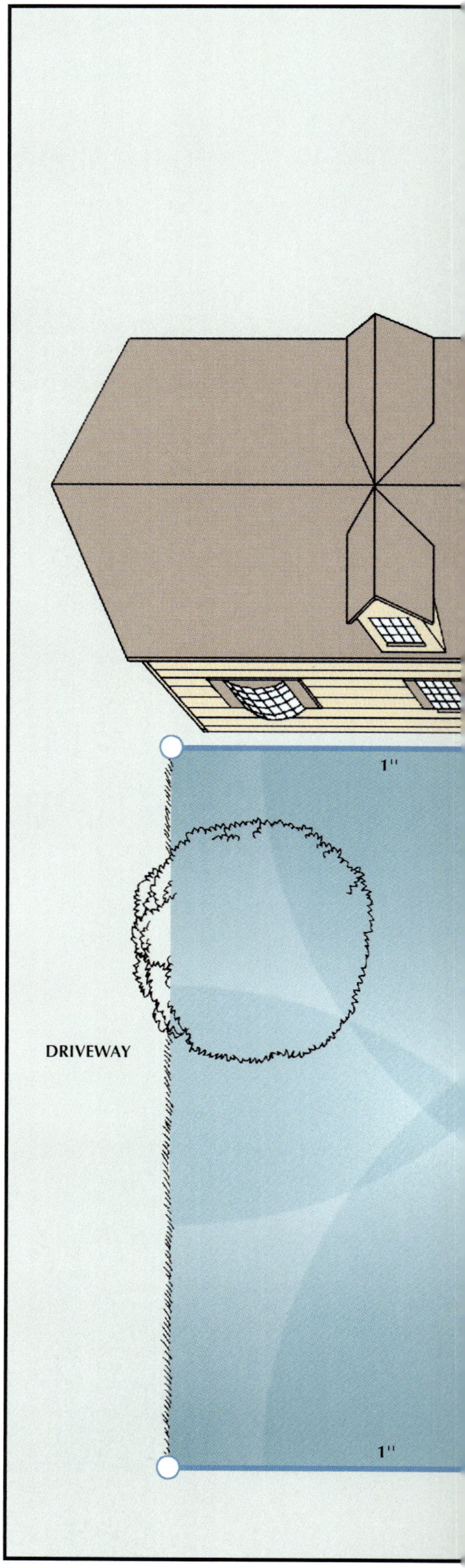

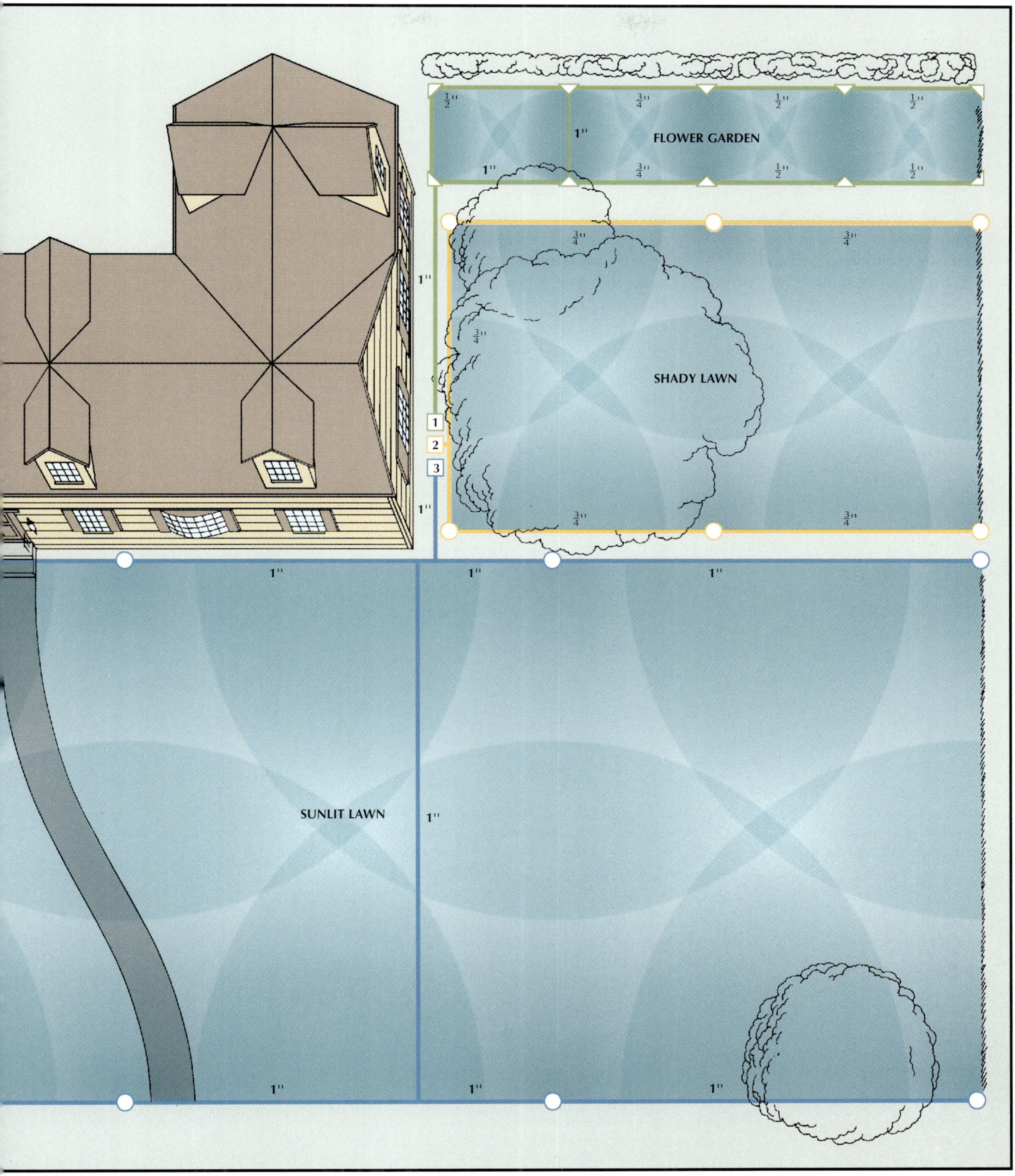
FLOWER GARDEN
SHADY LAWN
SUNLIT LAWN
1
2
3

POP-UP SPRAY

PLASTIC POP-UP IMPULSE

BRASS POP-UP IMPULSE

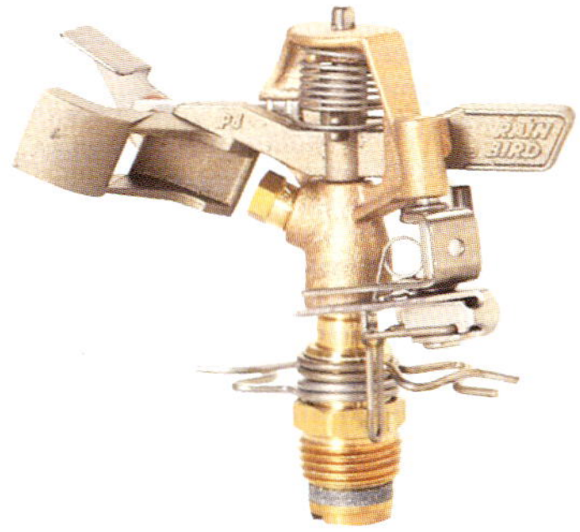

BRASS STANDING IMPULSE

PLASTIC STANDING IMPULSE

A gallery of sprinkler heads. Spray sprinkler heads are used to send a steady shower of water over a small-to-medium area. Impulse heads shoot out long jets of water from a rotating nozzle on medium-to-large areas. Both are available with working parts of brass or plastic and come in "pop-up" or "standing" versions. A pop-up head serves for a traveled area. When the control valve is opened, water pressure forces a piston in the sprinkler head upward; gravity or a spring within the head brings it down again when the water is shut off. A standing version is permanently raised aboveground in an out-of-the-way location—along the perimeter of the yard, for example.

INSTALLING THE CONTROLS

1. Connecting the control valves.

◆ Tap a basement supply line and fit the extension pipe with a ball valve with a waste *(page 311)*. Drill the extension pipe's exit hole so it has a slight inward slope. Run the control-valve wires and pipe through the hole.

◆ Install an elbow on the extension pipe *(right)*, then attach a vertical pipe and another elbow. Add a pipe with a T attached. Add a similar length and T for a two-circuit system, and so on.

◆ Clamp the assembly to the house, sloping it slightly toward the elbow.

◆ Into each T, insert a riser long enough to raise the control valve at least 6 inches above the ground. Install the valve on the riser.

◆ In cold climates, attach a $\frac{1}{8}$-inch air stem valve on the vertical pipe *(page 312)*. Before winter, close the ball valve in the basement and use an air compressor at the air stem valve to flush water out of the sprinkler networks. Open the waste on the ball valve to drain remaining water.

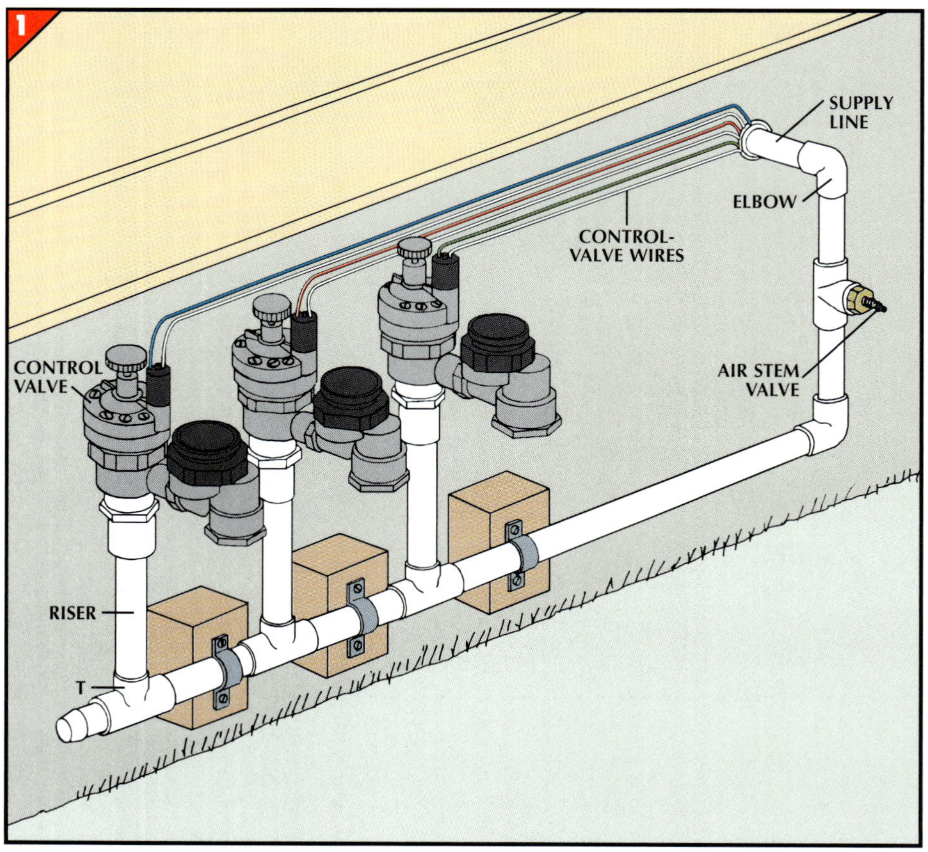

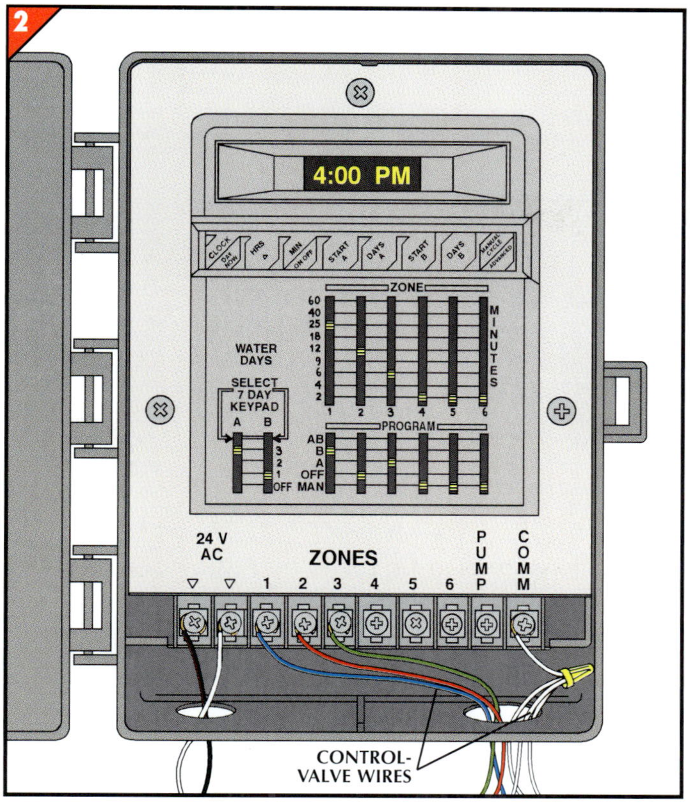

2. Wiring the timer.

◆ Affix the control box to the basement wall near the point where the control-valve wires enter from the outside.

◆ Thread either of the two wires from each valve through the right-hand hole below the terminals. Connect the valve wires to the terminals by matching the terminal and valve numbers. (The power line for the control box should already be attached to the terminals marked 24 V AC.)

◆ Thread the remaining valve wires into the box and, using a wire cap, join them to each other and to a short length of wire of the same kind and size; connect this wire to the terminal marked COMM (common).

◆ Switch the main box control to OFF. Plug the control box cord into an electrical outlet. Set the control box to your desired schedule, according to the manufacturer's specifications.

ADDING PIPES AND SPRINKLER HEADS

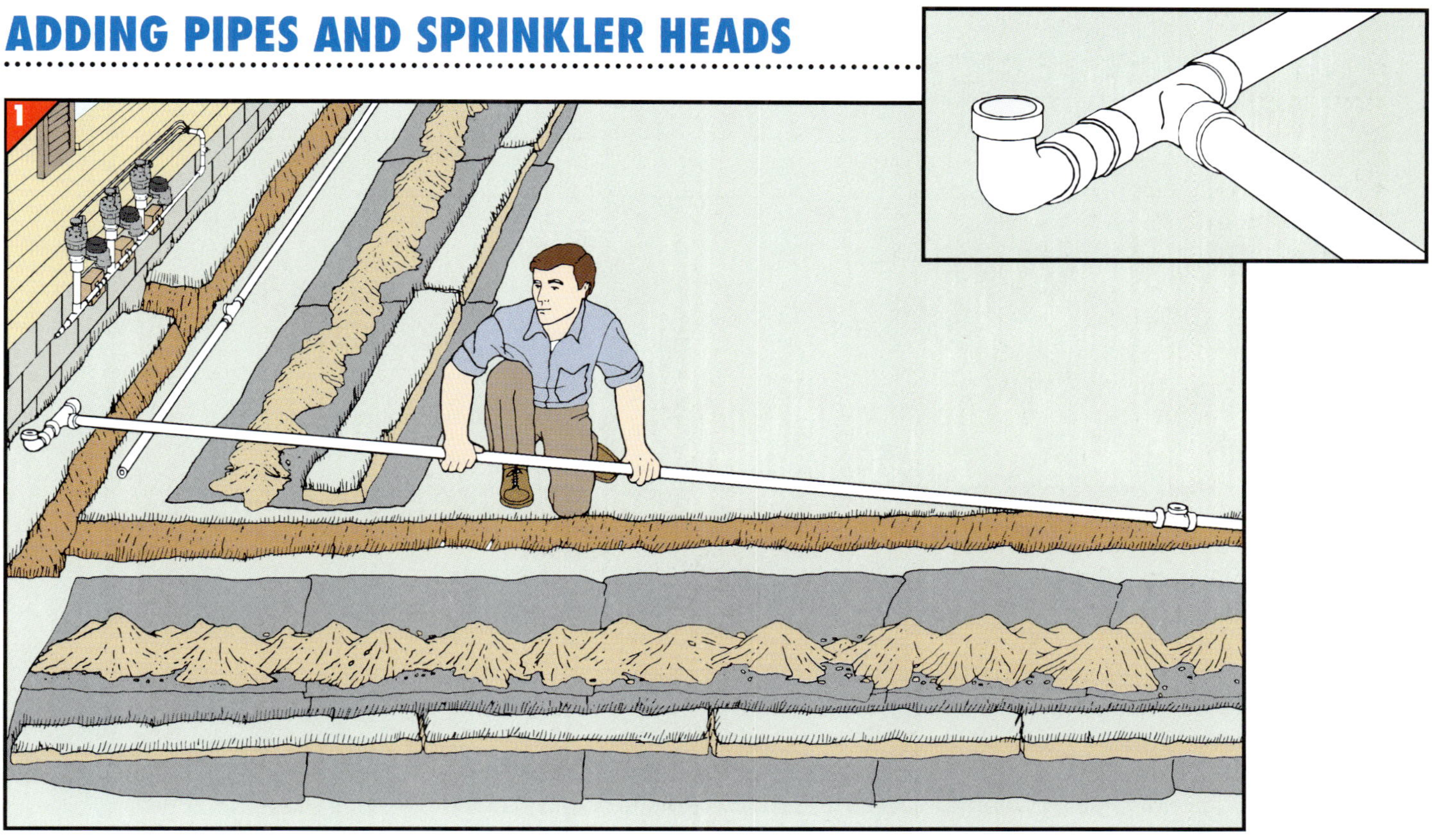

1. Running the pipe.

◆ Working with one circuit at a time, drive stakes into the ground where the sprinkler heads will be. Stretch strings in between as guides to dig straight trenches for the pipe *(page 310)*.

◆ Assemble straight sections of pipe and install fittings: an elbow for a sprinkler head at the end of a pipe; a T for a head in a straight run of pipe or for the addition of two pipes; and a T-and-elbow combination, linked by a short spacer, for a head at the corner *(inset)*.

◆ Set each completed run of pipe into the trench and connect the runs inside the trench. Connect the pipe network to its control valve.

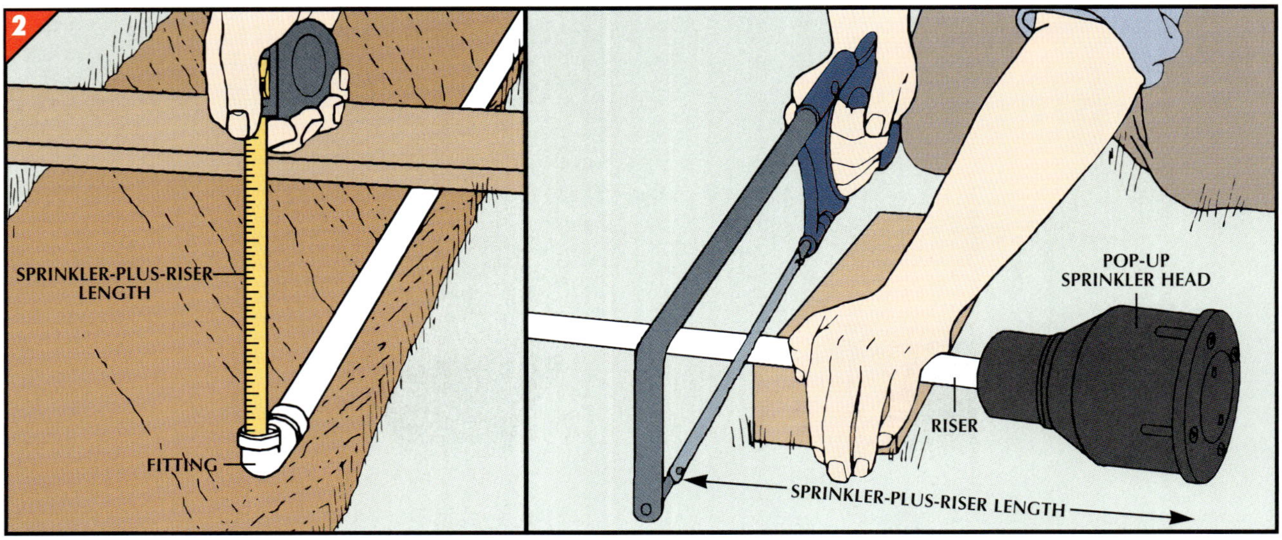

2. Connecting the sprinkler heads.

Pop-up sprinkler heads should be installed so that their tops are flush with the ground.

◆ Set a straight board across the top of the trench over a sprinkler fitting and measure the distance from the board to the inside of the fitting *(above, left)*. This is the length of the sprinkler head with its attached riser.

◆ Attach a sprinkler head to an adapter and a section of pipe. Measuring down from the top of the head, cut the pipe to give the sprinkler-plus-riser length measured *(above, right)*. Repeat this procedure with all other heads.

◆ Finally, flush out the pipes and then install the head assemblies.

3. Testing the system.

◆ With the pipes still exposed in the trenches, open the control valve for a few minutes to check for leaks in the pipes and observe the spray patterns of the heads.

◆ If a head sprays an oval pattern rather than a circle, the riser beneath is not vertical; drive a short vertical stake into the trench next to the riser and, with heavy wire, tie the riser to the stake so that it is tight *(above)*.

◆ If a head sprays in the wrong direction, twist it on the riser to correct the aim.

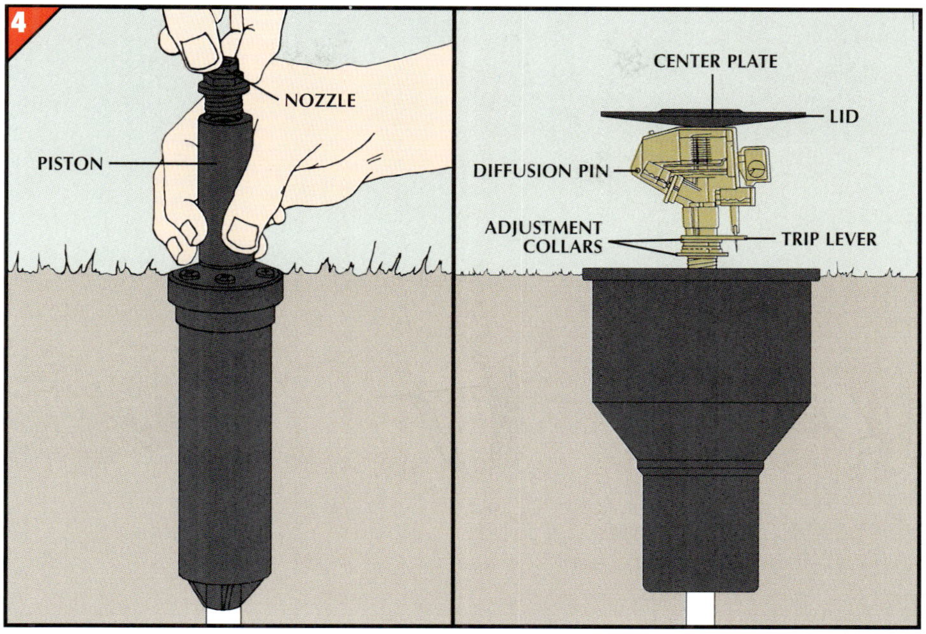

4. Adjusting the spray.

To change the pattern or trajectory of the water from a pop-up spray head *(above, left),* pull the piston out and hold it with one hand while unscrewing the nozzle with the other; reverse the procedure to install a new nozzle.

With an impulse head *(above, right),* pry off the center plate, then pull out the cotter pin below to release the entire lid, providing access to the controls below. To water any area less than a full circle, slide the adjustment collars from side to side with the trip lever in the down position. For full-circle coverage, flip the trip lever up. To adjust the distance and dispersion of the spray, screw the diffusion pin in or out of the water stream.

THE POLYETHYLENE OPTION

Flexible polyethylene plastic pipe may be best for a sprinkler system if the yard is irregularly shaped or if the pipe must follow a winding course. Sold in long rolls, it is easy to cut with a sharp knife or a specialized ratchet cutter. (Do not cut with a sawing motion.) Fittings for polyethylene, unlike those for rigid PVC, are inserted inside the pipe and reduce water flow; if you choose PE pipe, buy it one standard pipe size larger than the diameter recommended for PVC. It is better to use PVC pipe to connect the basement supply line to the control valves, since that pipe is under constant pressure.

10 Shrubs and Trees

Shrubs and trees create a variety of visual delights, but they have practical uses, too. Trees can shade a deck or patio; shrubs can serve as a living privacy fence, a border to walkways and flower beds, or a windscreen. Planting—or transplanting—shrubs and trees is not difficult, and with regular pruning and fertilizing, they will provide a lifetime of enjoyment.

Pruning a broken stem →

Landscaping with Shrubs

Shrubs are surely the most versatile of landscape elements. With a little training or trimming, they can add a variety of shapes and textures to the yard *(below)*.

Basic Shrub Care: Throughout the spring and summer, give shrubs a long, slow watering every 2 weeks —every 7 to 10 days during dry spells. Fertilize them no later than the spring growth spurt; later applications stimulate new growth that will suffer in winter.

Spread shredded pine bark or other organic mulch around shrubs to insulate the roots against heat and cold, and to inhibit weeds. Renew mulch in the spring and fall.

The Value of Pruning: Few tasks are more important than pruning. It eliminates damaged and diseased wood as well as crossing branches, which can abrade each other and leave the plant open to infection. Pruning also encourages new growth and boosts flower and fruit production. Finally, pruning keeps the shrub in bounds and shapes it.

Prune shrubs several times a year. In the spring, remove winter damage and do light trimming. Wait to prune shrubs such as azaleas, which flower on old wood, until the blossoms have wilted. Most other shrubs can be pruned through the winter and up to midspring—or in summer after flowering.

Summer calls for biweekly shapings and trimmings. After the shrubs have flowered, snip off one third of the older stems at ground level, so that each plant renews itself every 3 years or so.

Winterizing: Some shrubs need protection from wind, cold, and snow. A local nursery can tell you which plants need help through the winter. Effective methods of protecting shrubs are shown on page 327. For the best results, winterize shrubs before the first hard freeze.

Heavy, wet snow is especially damaging to evergreens. After a storm, dislodge snow gently, taking care not to snap the branches.

TOOLS

- Pruning shears
- Loppers
- Pruning saw
- Hedge trimmer
- Hedge shears
- Action hoe
- Sprinkler extension
- Sprinkler hose
- Staple gun
- Saw
- Hammer

MATERIALS

- Mulch
- Fertilizer
- Burlap
- Twine
- 2-by-3s
- 1-by-4s
- 3-inch nails
- Stakes and string

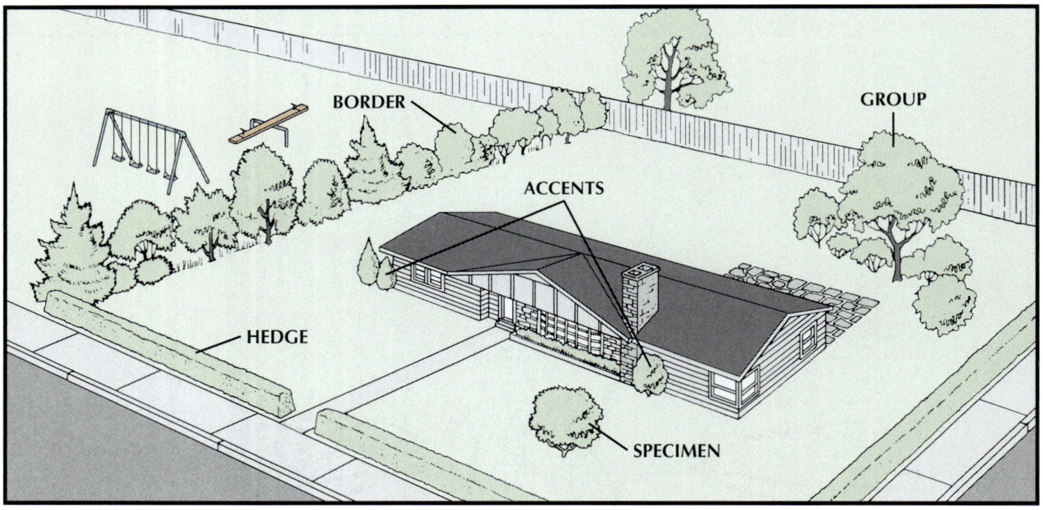

Using shrubs in a landscape. Depending on where they are planted and how they are combined, shrubs offer many landscaping options. Besides their visual appeal, shrubs can be living fences or screens for trash bins and compost heaps. In deciding what shrubs to plant and where, consider how they will look in relation to the house, as well as how they appear from indoors. Landscape architects call a single free-standing shrub selected for its color, shape, or seasonal blossoms a specimen. Several shrubs differing in sizes and colors, perhaps combined with a tree, are known as a group. Shrubs strategically located to contrast with or complement an architectural feature are called accents. A closely spaced row of a single species forms a hedge, useful to define property lines and preserve privacy. A combination of trees and shrubs becomes an informal border, offering diverse and contrasting colors and textures.

Pruning to promote growth.

◆ To encourage a new branch *(dashed lines)* in a sparse area of a shrub, grasp a branch just below a lateral bud—that is, a bud pointing outward from the side of the branch.

◆ Hold a pair of pruning shears at a 45-degree angle and sever the branch about $\frac{1}{4}$ inch above the bud, taking care not to damage it *(inset)*.

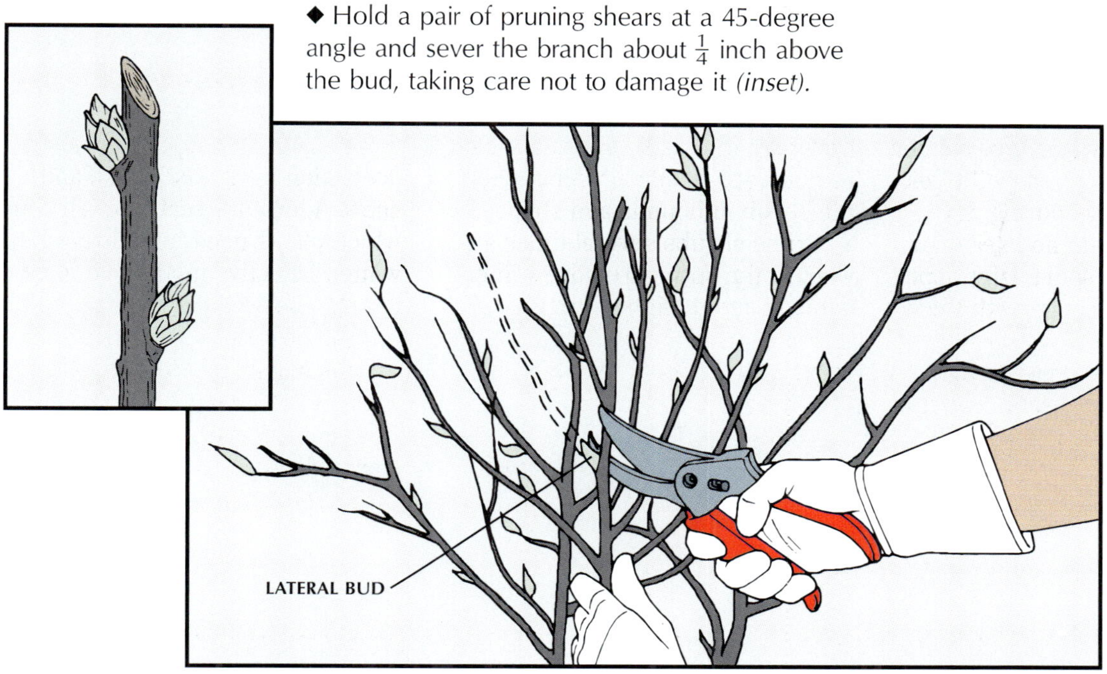

Removing damaged wood.

◆ Cut back a broken or diseased branch to healthy wood, either at a point just beyond a lateral bud or flush with the nearest healthy stem *(left)*.

◆ After cutting branches from a diseased shrub, clean blades of shears or saw with alcohol to avoid infecting other plants.

Thinning for health and light.

◆ After the growing season each year, trim and shape the shrub's outer branches. Remove completely any branches that are weak or misshapen, or that cross other branches. Prune individual branches at a main stem, and main stems near the ground *(right)*.

◆ Then, to let sunlight reach new buds and foliage next spring, cut away up to one third of the oldest stems.

The right way to prune roses.

◆ Every fall—after the last bloom but well before the first frost—cut away deadwood, small shoots, and crossing branches. Then cut back every main branch by a third of its length *(above, left)*.

◆ In the spring, cut away any stems damaged by winter weather. Then prune all healthy branches back to the point where their stems are at least $\frac{3}{8}$ inch thick *(above, right)*. The spring pruning should leave a compact, bowl-shaped bush.

◆ During the growing season, regularly trim away all dead and damaged wood, as well as small branches.

Trimming hedges.

For a formal hedge, stretch a level string taut between posts at the ends of the hedge as a cutting guide. To speed the work, use an electric or battery-operated hedge trimmer held at the height of the string. Draw the trimmer across the hedge top, taking care not to poke the tip of the tool into the hedge. Alternatively, use hedge shears as shown in the inset. If any long shoots are growing into a gap in the hedge, cut the shoots back with pruning shears to stimulate thick growth that will fill the hole.

Shape an informal, relatively irregular hedge as you would a shrub, using pruning shears and trying to create a natural, feathery appearance; take special care to prune out any branches that have grown faster than the others.

Trim both formal and informal hedges narrower at the top than at the bottom, to permit sunlight to reach the base of the hedge. After trimming a hedge, shake it to dislodge the clippings, then rake them away.

ROUTINE CARE TO KEEP SHRUBS HEALTHY

Stirring up the soil.

Cultivating the soil around a shrub bed makes weeding easier and watering more effective. Use an action hoe *(left)* to loosen weeds and break up compacted soil.

◆ Push the hoe blade about 2 inches into the earth—shallower if it catches the roots of a shrub—and work it back and forth parallel to the surface.

◆ After weeding the bed, use the hoe again to smooth the soil before watering or applying mulch.

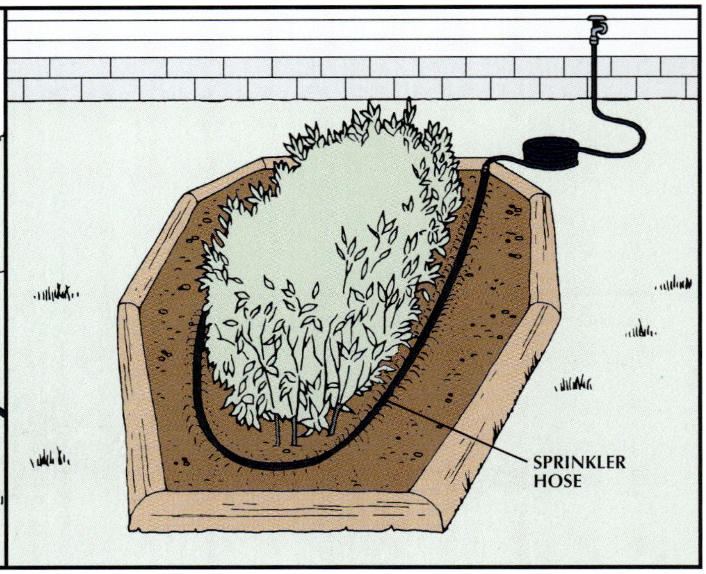

Getting water to the roots.
The best way to water specimens and small groups is with a sprinkler extension *(above, left)*. This wandlike device with a fine-spray nozzle allows you to direct water at the base of a shrub. For larger groups and hedges, surround the bed with a sprinkler hose *(above, right)*. Water shrubs for at least 10 minutes or until the soil is thoroughly saturated. Puddles on the ground indicate overwatering, which can damage the roots; stop watering immediately.

Spreading mulch.
Twice a year, rake away old mulch from around shrubs and replace it with fresh material. In spring, spread an even layer of dense material, such as woodchips or ground-up bark, about 2 inches thick. Use only aged mulch—new chips and bark leach valuable nitrogen from the soil—and keep it away from stems; moisture in the mulch could encourage fungus, insect infestation, and root rot.

Before the first frost, insulate the bed with 3 inches of pine needles or oak leaves.

COUNTERMEASURES AGAINST THE COLD

Protection from wind and snow.
Before the first frost, cover low-growing shrubs with evergreen branches *(below, left)* or spread a double thickness of burlap over them and peg it to the ground.

To shield taller shrubs that are exposed to the full force of the wind, build a shelter of stakes and burlap to the full height of the shrub *(center)*. First, drive several stakes in a tight circle all around the plant, then staple the burlap to the stakes.

Wind twine around evergreens to prevent heavy, wet snow from weighing down the branches and breaking them. Loop the twine around the bottom of the shrub, then wrap it tightly enough to hold the branches upright *(right)*. At the top, tie the twine into another loop.

Shelter under an eave.
A sloping shelter on a frame of 2-by-3s prevents snow that slides off a roof from damaging shrubs next to a house.

◆ Cut a pair of pointed 2-by-3 posts at least 2 feet longer than the height of the shrubs and drive them a foot or more into the ground next to the house. In front of the shrubs, drive posts 1 foot shorter than the posts erected next to the wall.

◆ Fasten 2-by-3 crossbars to each pair of posts, then nail a canopy of 1-by-4s on the crossbars as shown at left.

Putting Shrubs in New Places

Often, as a landscaping plan evolves and matures, the need to discard or transplant old shrubs and to plant new ones arises. Techniques for accomplishing these tasks are shown on these and the following pages.

Timing and Preparation: Moving an old shrub—or planting a new one—is best done in early spring or fall. A few days before transplanting a shrub, water it generously to soften the soil around its roots, then proceed as shown on the next page. Have a tarpaulin on hand to help move the shrub easily, and plastic sheeting to keep soil off the lawn.

Buying from a Nursery: Except for some flowering shrubs—rhododendron and laurel, for example—which can be propagated through a technique called layering *(page 333)*—new shrubs come most often from nurseries. The plants come in three forms: rooted in a ball of soil and wrapped in burlap; grown and rooted in plastic containers; and with bare roots.

Selecting Healthy Plants: Choose shrubs suited to your climate and soil conditions *(pages 356-359)* and check their condition carefully. Sound, undamaged bark and bright foliage on well-shaped branches spaced evenly around the stem are signs of a hardy specimen. Reject plants that have broken branches, bruised bark, or pale leaves, or those that are growing in dry soil.

Ask a nursery worker to show you the roots of container-grown plants. Look for a thick profusion of roots at the rootball's bottom; reject a shrub with roots that coil around the rootball or protrude from the top—sure signs of being potbound. In a healthy burlapped shrub, the rootball has a firm, solid feeling, with moist soil and no weeds. Bare-root stock should be undamaged, clean smelling, and uniform in color.

Plant shrubs immediately if possible, or store them in shade and keep the roots moist; if you cannot plant a bare-rooted shrub within a week, bury it in a shallow trench and keep it watered until you can plant it permanently.

TOOLS

- Pruning shears
- Mattock
- Spade
- Digging bar
- Garden fork
- Garden trowel

MATERIALS

- Plastic sheeting
- Twine
- Tarpaulin
- Burlap
- Peat moss
- Sand
- Fertilizer
- Rooting powder

SAFETY TIPS

Shrubs are heavy; lift with the arms and legs and wear a back brace to reduce risk of back strain. Gloves protect your hands during spade work.

DISCARDING AN UNWANTED PLANT

1. Digging out the roots.

◆ Cut off most of the shrub's outer branches with pruning shears and trim main stems to a length of 2 or 3 feet.
◆ With a mattock, dig a trench around the shrub 1 foot or more from the stem and extending down through the root system.
◆ Undercut the shrub with a spade or digging bar to sever all the roots, then pull out the shrub by the trunk.

2. Refilling the hole.

◆ Knock the soil off the roots and into the hole with a spade or garden fork. If the plant is diseased, spread plastic sheeting in the hole to collect the soil and dispose of it away from the yard and garden.

◆ Refill the hole with soil and tamp it firmly. Add more soil to form a loose mound 4 to 6 inches high; the soil will settle in a few months, leaving the area level.

RELOCATING A SHRUB

1. Defining the rootball.

◆ Wrap the plant with twine to gather the branches into a compact bundle.

◆ Score the ground with the point of a shovel or spade to mark a circle roughly the diameter of the wrapped plant; this defines the size of the rootball. Make another circle about 9 inches outside the first.

2. Cutting out the rootball.

◆ Lay a canvas tarpaulin or sheet of heavy plastic next to the outside circle to receive the soil.

◆ Dig out the soil between the two circles to the depth of the shrub's main roots, usually about 18 inches. Undercut the rootball all around the plant with the spade or shovel, freeing it.

3. Wrapping the rootball.

◆ Cut a square sheet of natural-fiber, biodegradable burlap about 3 times the diameter of the rootball and place it next to the hole; do not use synthetic fabric or plastic.

◆ Push against one side of the rootball to tip the shrub on its side and stuff at least half of the burlap under the tilted rootball *(left, top)*. For large shrubs, consider enlisting a helper.

◆ Tip the ball toward the opposite side of the hole, then pull the burlap from under the ball *(left, bottom)*, roughly centering the ball on the burlap square. Lift the edges of the burlap and tie them securely around the stem with twine.

4. Pulling out the shrub.

◆ Set a sheet of canvas or heavy plastic next to the hole and lift the shrub onto the sheet. You may need a helper to assist in moving medium-sized or larger shrubs.

◆ Carry or slide the shrub on the sheet to its new location. Before replanting, unwrap the branches but leave the rootball in the burlap. Cut away any broken branches and prune the shrub by about a third to compensate for any roots lost through digging it up.

◆ Refill the old hole with soil.

PLANTING A BALLED AND BURLAPPED SHRUB

1. Digging the hole.
At the new location, dig a circular hole about twice as wide and half again as deep as the rootball. Pile the soil on a plastic or canvas sheet next to the hole.

2. Conditioning the soil.
Add peat moss and other amendments to the soil that was removed. Blend the soil and other materials thoroughly, keeping the mixture on the sheet and off grass or ground cover.

Soil recipes: For loamy soil, add one part peat moss to two parts soil; for clay soil, add one part peat moss and one part sand to one part soil. For sandy soil, mix equal amounts of peat moss and soil. To any of these mixtures, add slow-release fertilizer in the amount recommended on the package.

3. Making a base for the shrub.
Shovel a layer of the conditioned soil into the hole and compact it with your feet or a tamper. Repeat the process, partially filling the hole to a depth about 2 inches shallower than the height of the rootball.

4. Positioning the shrub.

◆ Set the shrub in the hole, adjusting the bottom as needed to make the main stem vertical. Lay a straight stick across the hole to make sure the top of the rootball is about 2 inches above ground level. If the shrub sits too high or too low, lift it out of the hole and add or remove conditioned soil to bring the shrub to the right height.

◆ Add soil mixture to the hole around the rootball, tamping as you go, until the hole is two-thirds full. Then loosen the burlap and spread it over the soil mixture *(inset).*

◆ Fill the hole with water, and let it seep into the ground. Then add soil mixture to about 1 inch above ground level and tamp it down firmly.

5. Forming a basin of soil.

◆ Build a soil dam about 4 inches high around the planting hole to catch water for the shrub. Fill this basin with water and let it seep into the soil.

◆ Spread a 2-inch layer of mulch or bark chips around the shrub. Cover the basin walls but stop 2 inches short of the main stem. Keep the soil moist around the transplanted shrub for the first few months, but do not overwater.

PROPAGATING SHRUBS BY LAYERING

1. Wounding the branch.

◆ In early spring, bend a healthy lower branch to touch the ground about 12 inches from the tip and dig a bowl-shaped hole about 6 inches deep there.

◆ Bend the branch into the hole. Where it touches the center of the hole, slit the branch diagonally about halfway through with a sharp knife and wedge a twig in the cut *(inset)*. Sprinkle the wound with rooting powder, a synthetic hormone available at garden centers.

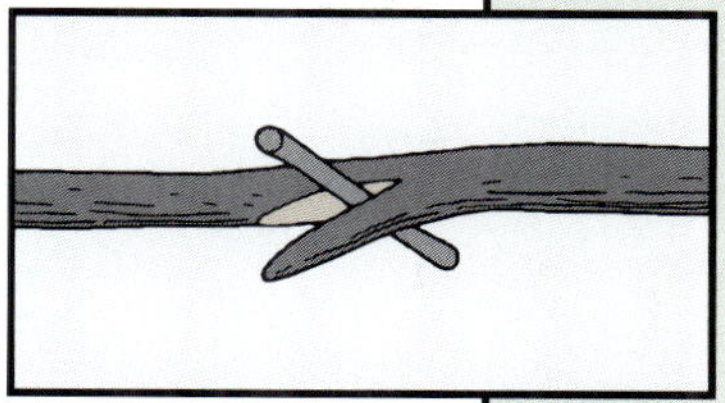

2. Anchoring the branch.

◆ Mix enough topsoil, peat moss, and sand, in equal parts, to fill the hole. then put about one fourth of the mixture into the hole.

◆ Bend the branch back into the hole with the cut facing down and cover it with soil mix. Anchor the branch with a pair of crossed sticks *(right)*, and fill the hole with the remaining soil mix, making sure that 6 inches of the branch protrude above ground level.

◆ Water the soil mix thoroughly and set a rock over the crossed sticks to hold them in place.

3. Separating the new shrub.

◆ Do not disturb the branch until next spring, then dig it up. Pull away some soil to see if roots have developed at the cut. If three to five roots are present, sever the branch to free the new plant from the old one *(left)*; if not, rebury the branch and check again in the fall.

◆ After detaching the branch, push gently on the rootball to slant the roots in the opposite direction from the tip. Plant the newly propagated shrub as you would any other, tilting the rootball so that the top of the plant points upward.

Keeping Trees in Good Health

Like the houses they protect and adorn, trees need regular care, sometimes by professionals. You can perform the routine chores of low-level pruning, fertilizing, and pest control, but tasks such as bracing limbs with guy wires, or climbing to a high perch to cut them off, should be left to a specialist.

The Right Way to Prune: Judicious pruning can improve a tree's health. But because each cut wounds the tree, you can also do harm if you prune carelessly.

A tree walls off a wounded area with cells and chemical barriers that keep disease-causing organisms from invading healthy tissue. These guardians develop at the base of each branch in a swollen area called the branch collar.

Part of the collar is destroyed by pruning a branch flush to the trunk, a method favored in the past; the wound closes slowly, if at all. Cutting too far from the trunk is also a poor practice, since the stub is too far from the source of protective cells. To close properly, cuts must be made at a precise angle, just outside the collar *(opposite)*. Leave the wound untreated, or apply a thin coat of asphalt-based tree paint. Other paints retard closure.

Do your pruning in late winter or early spring, before the buds open. Prune flowering trees just after the blooms fade, and remove any broken or diseased branches from all trees immediately.

Feeding Trees: To maintain normal growth, trees need a variety of nutrients, often provided in the form of fertilizer. Among the most effective fertilizers are organic materials such as cottonseed meal, bone meal, or blood meal.

Fertilizer works best when it is spread on the ground or injected as a liquid *(pages 338-339)*. You can also spray liquid fertilizer onto a tree's leaves *(page 340)*, or hammer fertilizer spikes around the drip line *(page 338)*. However, if the drip line is 30 inches or less from the trunk, do not use spikes.

The best time to apply fertilizer is in late autumn, when all the leaves have fallen and trees begin storing nutrients for the winter. You can also fertilize in early spring; for flowering trees, wait until they begin to bloom.

Whatever season you choose, avoid overuse of fertilizer. One or two applications a year is enough for young trees, and once every 3 to 5 years for mature ones.

Safe Pest Control: If a tree looks sickly or harbors bugs you do not recognize, call your local extension service for a diagnosis. The prescription is likely to be a spray-on chemical, which must be handled with care. You can safely spray a tree up to 25 feet tall with the equipment shown on page 340. Hire a professional to treat larger trees.

Before you start, check local laws governing chemical spraying and study the instructions on the package label. Some pesticides must be mixed with water; dilute them exactly as directed. Wear protective clothing and keep children and pets out of the area.

If you prefer a nontoxic treatment, try dormant oil, a commercial mixture of mineral oil and water. Sprayed on a tree in early spring before leaves emerge, it coats and smothers aphids, scales, and mites, even before they hatch from eggs. Read the directions on the label carefully. Although harmless to humans, the oil can damage evergreens and certain species of beech, birch, and maple.

Another nontoxic approach is biological control, using a pest's natural enemies. A single ladybug, for example, can eat four dozen aphids a day, while a bacterium called Bt attacks gypsy-moth and other caterpillars but is harmless to other organisms. Ask your nursery operator or extension agent about pest fighters indigenous to your area.

TOOLS

Pruning shears
Lopping shears
Pole shears
Pruning saw
Broadcast or trough spreader
Root-zone injector
Spray canister
Garden-hose sprayer

MATERIALS

Dry fertilizer
Tree spikes
Fertilizer cartridges
Liquid fertilizer
Pesticide

SAFETY TIPS

Wear gloves when handling fertilizers. Add goggles when cutting tree branches. Follow manufacturer's instructions precisely when spraying pesticides. Depending on toxicity, you may need to don not only gloves and goggles but boots, long sleeves, and a dust mask or cartridge respirator, as well.

THE ART OF PRUNING

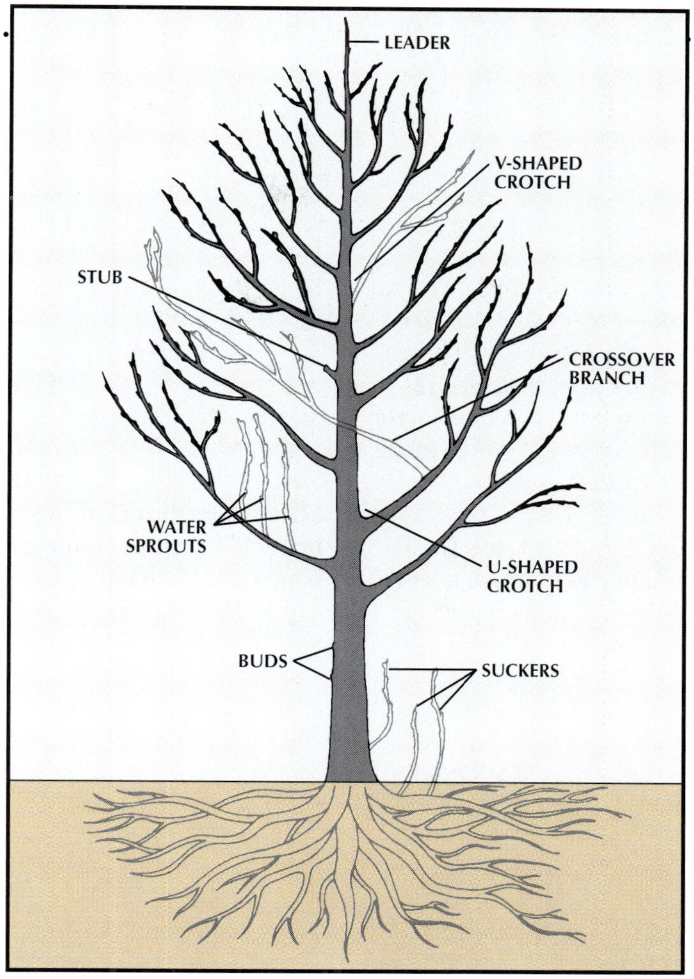

The basic guidelines.
Well-formed young trees have a straight central branch, or leader, extending from the top; the main limbs have U-shaped crotches evenly distributed around the trunk at least a foot apart vertically. To maintain this strong, balanced framework, prune away any undesirable features:

- ◆ Remove branches having a tight, V-shaped crotch, which makes a weak joint.
- ◆ Cut off suckers or water sprouts—which can grow anywhere on a tree and have no lateral branches—as well as any buds from which new suckers and water sprouts might grow.
- ◆ Dispose of branch stubs, dead or broken limbs, and small branches that grow toward the trunk or across larger limbs; crossover growth can damage the trunk and other branches by rubbing against them.
- ◆ Periodically thin inner branches of mature trees to admit light. On deciduous trees, remove low limbs that keep you from walking under the tree. Leave the lower limbs on evergreens in place.

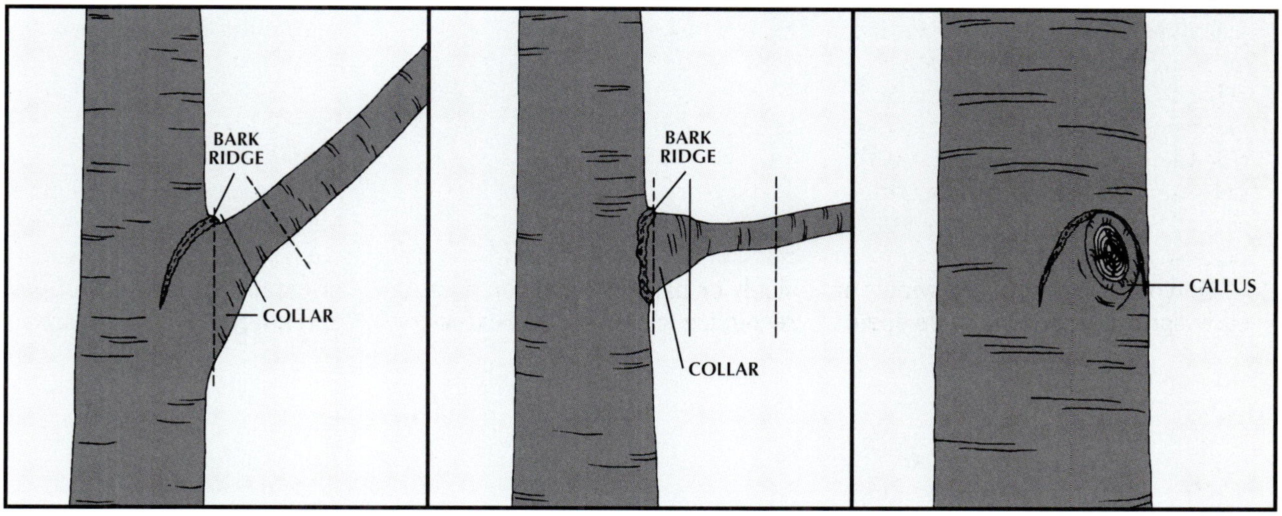

Proper pruning cuts.
Two features of a branch govern the position and angle of a pruning cut—the thick collar at the base of the branch and the dark ridge in the bark of the parent branch or trunk.

On mature deciduous trees, trim branches off square near the collar *(solid line, above left).* Do not cut into the collar or the ridge, and do not leave a stub *(dotted lines).* A branch on a very young deciduous tree or an evergreen may have a large collar and a bark ridge that encircles the base *(above, center).* Prune just outside the collar and parallel to the bark ridge *(solid line),* neither leaving a stub nor cutting into the ridge or the collar *(dotted lines).*

In a year or so, a hard callus should form at the edge of the wound *(above, right),* later closing over the cut.

THREE TOOLS FOR SMALL BRANCHES

Shearing small sprouts.
Use pruning shears to sever buds and small branches that are up to $\frac{1}{4}$ inch thick. Cut as close to the trunk as you can without damaging the bark.

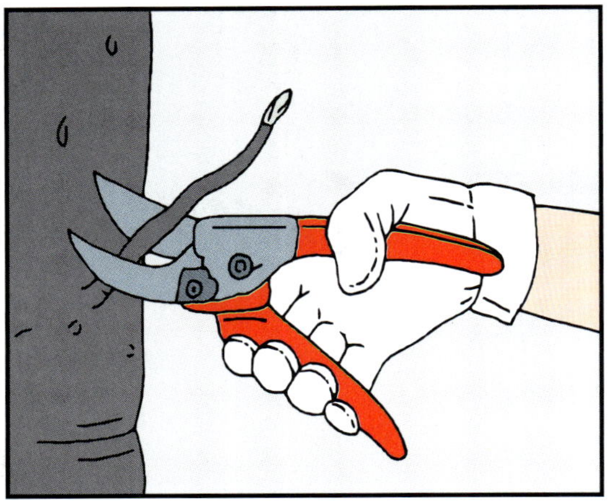

Cutting off small branches.
To remove a branch up to 1 inch thick, set the cutting blade of a pair of lopping shears on top of the limb, with the side of the blade against the trunk or supporting branch. Angle the lower blade away from the bark ridge and the collar, and bring the handles of the shears together in a single smooth motion. Do not twist the shears or use them to tear the branch from the tree. If the shears do not make a clean cut on the first attempt, sharpen them *(page 230)* or switch to a saw.

Extendable shears.
Pole shears can cut branches as big as 1 inch in diameter and reach branches up to 15 feet overhead. The pole consists of a telescoping plastic or wooden shaft. A cutting blade under a stationary hook is operated by a cord that runs through a pulley to increase leverage *(photograph).*

◆ Place the hook over the base of the branch in the position shown on page 335. Wrap the cord once around the pole to keep the shaft from bowing, and pull the cord sharply. Cut close enough to the branch collar so no stub remains.
◆ If the severed branch hangs in the tree, pull it down with the head of the shears, taking care not to break other branches.

SAWING OFF A LIMB

1. Removing the branch.

◆ When cutting a branch that is up to 3 inches thick, first trim off any secondary limbs. This will serve to lighten the branch and keep it from catching in the tree as it falls.

◆ Use a pruning saw to cut halfway through the bottom of the branch, about a foot from the trunk; this cut will stop bark from tearing loose when the branch falls.

◆ About an inch outside the first cut, saw through the branch from the top. When this second cut is halfway through the branch, the limb will snap off, leaving a stub.

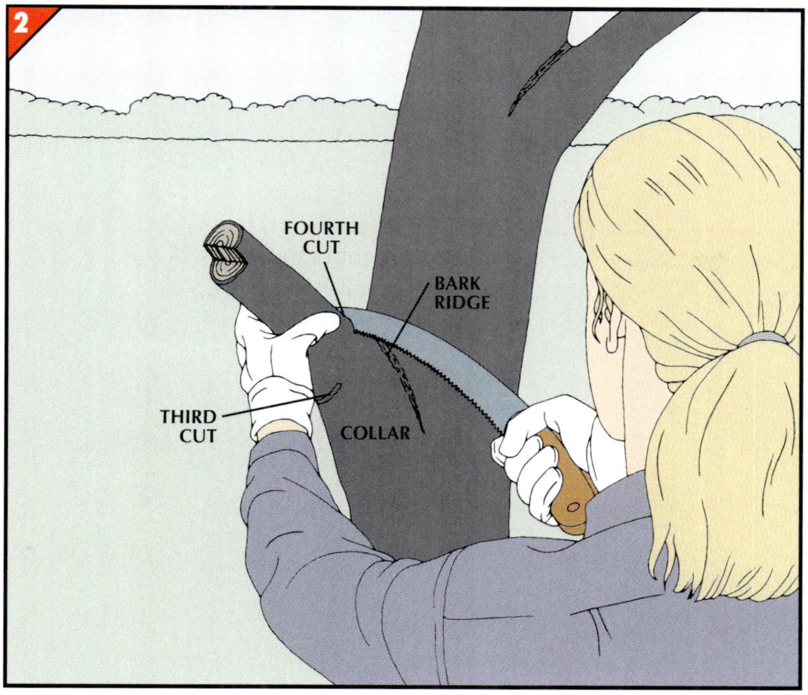

2. Trimming the stub.

◆ For the third cut, saw 1 inch into the underside of the stub, just outside the branch collar and at a right angle to the stub.

◆ Make the fourth cut at the crotch of the stub, just outside the bark ridge at the base of the stub *(left)*. Support the stub with one hand and saw downward to meet the third cut.

FEEDING ROOTS FROM THE SURFACE

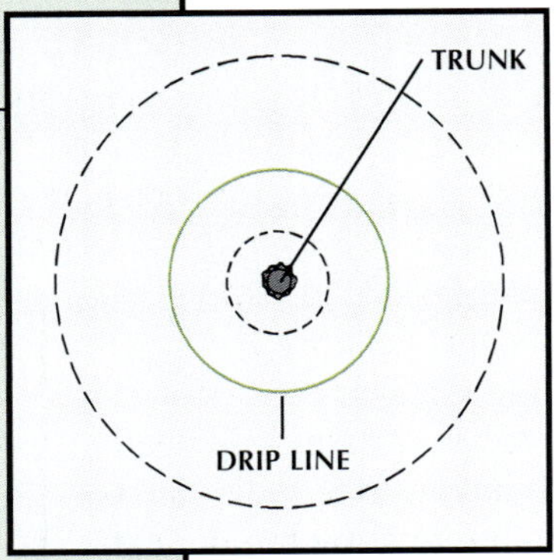

Mapping for surface fertilizer.

◆ Lay a string or garden hose around the tree at the drip line, which is directly below the tree's outermost leaves.

◆ Mark a second circle about two-thirds of the way in from the drip line to the center, but not less than 5 feet from the trunk. Mark a third circle about twice the drip-line distance from the trunk *(inset).*

◆ Using a broadcast or trough spreader, spread tree fertilizer over the area between the inner- and outermost circles.

Placing tree spikes.

◆ Mark the drip line of your tree as for surface fertilizer, above.

◆ For each inch of trunk diameter, drive a spike into the ground along the drip line. Space the spikes evenly, and while hammering, shield the tops with the protective plastic cap provided.

INJECTING FERTILIZER BY WATER PRESSURE

1. Preparing a root-zone injector.

◆ Along the tree's drip line *(opposite),* mark spots for an injection every 2 to 3 feet. For a tree having a trunk more than 4 inches in diameter and widespread branches, mark a second circle halfway to the trunk and plot injector locations along it *(inset).*

◆ Consult the fertilizer box for the number of fertilizer cartridges needed for each inch of tree trunk diameter. Divide the total by the number of injection points to get the number of cartridges per injection.

◆ Load the root-zone injector for one injection by unscrewing the reservoir cap and dropping in water-soluble fertilizer cartridges. If the reservoir is too small for all of them at one time, replenish the supply as the fertilizer dissolves.

2. Using the injector.

◆ Close the water-flow control valve and connect a garden hose to the injector.

◆ Turn the water on to a medium flow, and open the control valve on the injector just enough to permit water to trickle out of the tube.

◆ Slowly push the tube into the soil, twisting it back and forth until it reaches a depth of 6 to 8 inches. In hard ground, allow the water to soften the dirt and ease the way.

◆ For trees with shallow roots, set the control valve halfway between OFF and HALF ON; for more deeply rooted trees, set it to HALF ON; for very large, well-established trees, start at HALF ON, then turn the valve to ON after the first minute. Leave the injector in place until the fertilizer has dissolved, then turn the water off, pull out the tube, and move to the next injection spot.

A HAND-PUMPED SPRAYER FOR SMALL JOBS

A pressurized canister.

◆ To fill the canister, remove the pump assembly. Pour liquid fertilizer or pesticide into a small amount of water in the canister, then add the rest of the water needed to dilute the chemical. Mix powdered chemicals thoroughly with the full measure of water in a bucket before pouring it into the canister.

◆ Screw in the pump, and vigorously raise and lower the handle several times to pressurize the tank. Aim the nozzle upward and squeeze the pistol grip to saturate the undersides of leaves. Adjust the fineness of the spray, if necessary, by turning the nozzle tip, and repressurize the tank whenever the spray weakens.

USING A GARDEN-HOSE SPRAYER

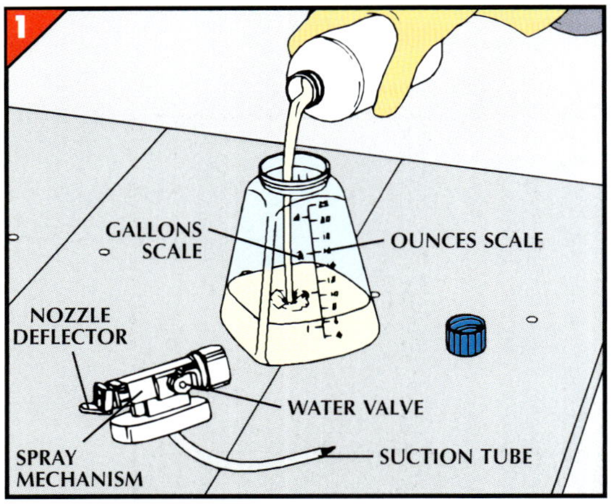

1. Filling the sprayer.

◆ Pour concentrated liquid fertilizer or pesticide into the reservoir, using the ounces scale on its side to measure the desired amount.

◆ Add water slowly while watching the gallons scale, stopping when the mixture reaches the level that matches the amount of spray solution you need.

◆ Screw on the spray mechanism, close the water valve, and gently shake the sprayer.

2. Using the sprayer.

Connect the sprayer to a garden hose and open the spigot. With the sprayer pointed at the tree, open the water valve; when spraying dormant oil, saturate both the trunk and the limbs. To control the force of the spray, turn the garden-hose spigot. Direct the spray upward with the nozzle deflector. Doing so allows you to keep the sprayer level enough for the suction tube to siphon chemicals into the spray.

How to Move a Tree

A tree's size, weight, and stability make it seem a permanent part of the landscape, but there are times when it is necessary to move a tree. Small or young trees, for example, may need to be temporarily stored out of the way of construction projects. And some trees should be permanently moved away from areas with poor drainage, unfavorable soil conditions, or extreme wind. Mature trees in good health can also be relocated to fit a new landscape plan.

A Matter of Size: In general, those trees up to 10 feet tall with trunks up to 3 inches thick can be moved with relative ease and can be expected to thrive after the experience. Larger trees, however, are unwieldy and are more vulnerable to shock; the job of moving them should be evaluated—and usually performed—by a professional.

Planning Ahead: The best time to move a deciduous tree is late autumn or early spring, when the tree is dormant. An evergreen can be moved at any time. Several months to a year in advance, cut about half of the horizontal roots, but not the vertical taproot. Make these cuts in three 60-degree arcs 24 to 30 inches from the trunk *(Step 1, below)*.

Pruning the tree *(pages 334-337)* in advance lessens the danger of shock by allowing new feeder roots time to form before the tree is moved. To compensate for the lost root capacity, however, prune away about a third of the branches.

TOOLS

Spade
Shovel
Rake

MATERIALS

Burlap
Twine
Mulch

SAFETY TIPS

Wear work gloves when digging and a back brace to reduce the chance of injury when moving heavy objects such as trees.

1. Pruning the roots.
Using a spade with a well-sharpened blade, sever the roots in a circle 24 to 30 inches wide around the trunk, recutting roots where they were pruned in advance. Push the blade into the ground at about a 30-degree angle toward the trunk *(dotted line)*, so that the rootball will taper.

2. Uprooting the tree.

◆ Excavate an access trench, 18 inches deep, around the rootball.

◆ Thrust the blade of a spade—the long-handled variety works best—under the tree to sever the taproot and any other uncut roots *(above)*.

◆ With a helper, lift the tree by the rootball and place it on a square of burlap. Removing a tree with low branches may be easier if you work the burlap under the rootball before lifting the tree from the hole *(page 330)*.

3. Bagging the rootball.

◆ Draw the burlap up around the ball on all sides, twisting the excess around the trunk.

◆ Run twine around the ball in several directions, tilting the tree to get the string under it.

◆ When you have bound the rootball into a neat package, wrap the twine around the trunk several times and tie it off.

4. Storing the tree.

If you can replant the tree within a week, set it in a shady spot, cover the rootball with mulch, and water it.

To store a tree for longer periods, dig a hole about half the rootball depth in a shady area, protected from wind. Tip the rootball into the hole and cover it with a 6-inch layer of mulch *(left)*. Keep the rootball moist.

The Right Way to Plant a Tree

Trees are available for planting in three forms: balled and burlapped, container grown, or bare rooted. Before buying any young tree, however, use the charts on pages 352 to 355 to find out which species thrive in your area. Prepare a soil mixture for the planting hole as you would for a shrub *(page 331)*.

Planting a Tree: Bare-rooted trees, usually sold by mail-order nurseries, are generally smaller, younger, and less expensive than the others. Start such trees in the early spring, within a day or two of their arrival. The technique for setting a bare-rooted tree into the ground appears on the next page.

You can plant container-grown and balled and burlapped trees at any time of the year. A balled and burlapped tree is planted exactly as a similarly packaged shrub *(pages 331-332)*—as is a container-grown tree, once you have slipped the plastic pot from around the rootball as described below.

Care after Planting: Unless the tree has been container grown or pruned at the nursery, cut away about one-third of the branches *(pages 334-337)*. Wrap a plastic tree protector around the base of the trunk to prevent damage to the lower bark *(page 344)*.

Brace or guy trees in areas where high winds or playing children may loosen their roots *(page 345)*. Never tie braces or guy wires taut; root systems strengthen faster when a tree can sway gently in the wind. Guying kits are available at garden centers. You can assemble a tree brace yourself using galvanized wire and pieces of old garden hose.

Finally, water a newly planted tree well; it needs the equivalent of an inch of rainfall a week during the growing season.

TOOLS

Utility knife
Pruning shears
Spade
4-pound maul

MATERIALS

Tree protector
2-by-2 stakes
Cloth strips
Old garden hose
Galvanized wire

CONTAINER-GROWN SPECIMENS

Trees from plastic pots.

◆ Slide the pot off the rootball, tapping or flexing the sides of the pot as necessary to loosen it.
◆ If the tree you buy has circling roots *(right)*, gently unwind them. Cut off large curling and matted roots with pruning shears.
◆ With a utility knife or sharp kitchen knife, score the rootball 1 inch deep from top to bottom in four or five locations that are evenly spaced *(inset)*.
◆ Plant the tree as shown for shrubs on pages 331-332.

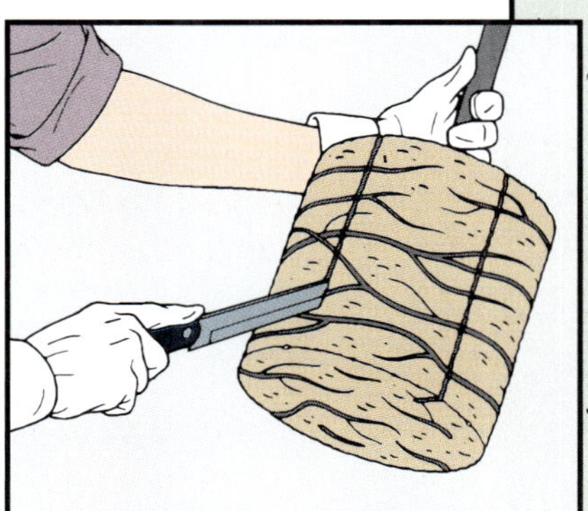

TREES WITH BARE ROOTS

1. Positioning the roots.

◆ Dig a planting hole *(page 331)* about one and a half times as deep as the length of the tree's longest root; make the hole about as wide as it is deep.

◆ Pile soil in the center of the hole, then gently spread the tree roots over the mound. With a straight board as a guide *(above),* adjust the mound so the soil-level mark on the tree trunk falls no lower than ground level.

2. Filling in around the roots.

◆ Holding the tree vertically, scoop soil into the hole. Pack the soil gently but firmly around the roots to eliminate air pockets.

◆ Fill the hole two-thirds with soil, one-third with water. After the water has seeped away, add soil to ground level. Build a soil basin as shown in Step 5 on page 332, fill it with water, then mulch.

CARING FOR RECENT TRANSPLANTS

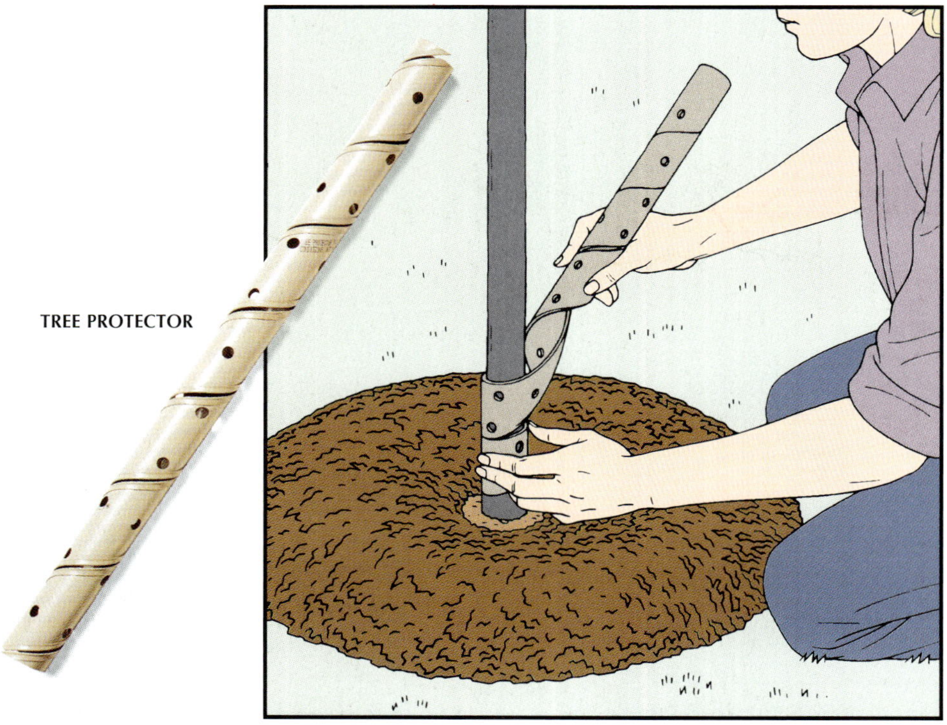

Protecting tender bark.

◆ Push back the soil at the tree trunk's base to a depth of about 2 inches.

◆ Coil a plastic tree protector around the trunk *(left).* After installing the protector, slide it to the base of the tree. Replace the loosened soil.

◆ Tree protectors are designed to expand as the plant grows. At least once a year, check the protector for binding and loosen it as needed. Remove the protector after 2 to 3 years.

Bracing small trees.

◆ For a trunk less than 3 inches thick, position a pair of 6-foot, 2-by-2 stakes next to the planting hole. With a 4-pound maul, drive them at least 18 inches into the ground.

◆ Tie one end of a cloth strip near the top of one post. Loop the cloth once around the trunk, leaving about 1 inch of slack. Tie the other end of the cloth to the second post, again leaving an inch of slack.

◆ Remove the bracing when the tree is firmly rooted—no later than a year after planting.

Guying a tree.

◆ For trunks 3 inches or more in diameter, drive three notched stakes into the ground outside the planting hole.

◆ Thread the end of a guy wire through a 1-foot-long length of garden hose. Loop the hose around the trunk above a branch, then twist the wire around itself to secure the hose to the tree. Tie the other end of the wire to the notch in a stake.

◆ Add two more guy wires, then adjust all three of them to allow the tree to sway slightly.

Appendix

Every grass, plant, tree, and shrub has characteristics that best suit it to one environment or another. The charts beginning on page 348, coded to appropriate climatic zone maps, highlight important factors to consider when deciding what to plant. Consult the checklist on the opposite page to schedule planting and landscape maintenance throughout the year.

YEAR-ROUND YARD CARE

A landscaped yard requires constant attention to stay healthy and beautiful, and each season calls for its own set of chores. Because climates vary widely in the United States, the calendar is an unreliable guide to the seasons. Changes in temperature, soil conditions, and plant appearance are more trustworthy indicators.

The last hard frost marks the beginning of spring, when bulbs begin to put out shoots and perennials unfurl new leaves and stems. Rising soil temperature is a signal for preemptive weed control. Agricultural extension agencies monitor soil temperatures and can tell you other ways they affect landscaping in your area.

Many flowering shrubs bloom in mid-spring, but rosebuds announce the arrival of summer. In northern climes, cooler nighttime temperatures and falling leaves signal the start of autumn. The first few killing frosts are a prelude to winter, when most plants are dormant and require little more than protection from ice and snow.

A Checklist of Seasonal Chores

EARLY SPRING

✔ Remove protective coverings from shrubs and plants. Remove old mulch or mix it into the soil and lay new mulch; start pruning shrubs, trees, and roses.

✔ Rake leaves from the lawn and ground covers. Reseed bare spots in the lawn, spread fertilizer, and water it. Cut grass as low as recommended *(page 348)*, and begin crab grass control by applying a preemergent weed-killer.

✔ Fertilize ground covers, and cut away any stringy top growth.

✔ Spray trees and shrubs with a dormant-oil spray for pest control.

MIDSPRING

✔ Cut the grass to a medium height; weed both lawn and garden weekly.

✔ When the soil is moist and easy to work, you can plant or transplant most trees and shrubs.

✔ Edge plant beds; start a vegetable garden.

LATE SPRING

✔ Prune shrubs that do not flower or that will flower in late summer or fall. Prune spring-blooming shrubs after they have lost their blossoms.

✔ Check the lawn periodically to see if the soil needs more or less water.

EARLY SUMMER

✔ Apply pesticides as needed to control fungus, insects, disease, and scale on any plants that have these afflictions. Continue spraying or dusting roses once a week until the growing season ends.

✔ If you have a pool, this is a good time to plant delicate water flowers, such as water lilies and lotuses.

MIDSUMMER

✔ Keep all plants watered well—especially any trees and shrubs planted in the spring—to prevent sunscorched leaves.

✔ Weed flower beds and shrub beds.

✔ Cut grass about 1 inch longer than its springtime length, to prevent burnout.

LATE SUMMER

✔ Start a new lawn or renovate an old one.

✔ Examine plants for possible iron deficiency: If you see yellow leaves with dark green veins, feed the plants with an iron-rich fertilizer.

EARLY FALL

✔ Aerate and dethatch the lawn; cut it shorter and at less frequent intervals.

✔ Dig up and move evergreen shrubs and trees or plant new ones. Wait until the leaves fall before moving deciduous plants.

✔ Plant bare-rooted roses. Water new plants regularly and mulch them lightly to deter weeds.

✔ Fall is an excellent time to start a compost pile; use yard waste such as vegetable tops, dead or dying annuals, and fallen leaves.

✔ Deep-feed tree roots.

LATE FALL

✔ Clear leaves from lawns and ground covers. Rake up pine needles and spread them as mulch for shrubs.

✔ Give roses, trees, and hedges a final pruning.

✔ Renew or replenish mulch on all shrubs. Break up any old, compacted mulch to allow air and water to reach the roots.

✔ Add dead plants from the vegetable garden to the compost pile. Spread manure or compost in the garden, then turn the soil.

✔ Until freezing temperatures set in, water plants well one morning a week to give them moisture to weather the winter.

EARLY WINTER

✔ Cover low shrubs with evergreen clippings; wrap medium-sized shrubs with burlap. Build a shelter over the plants that are near your house, to shield the branches from snow sliding off the roof *(page 327)*.

✔ Trim hollies and other broad-leaved evergreens.

✔ Rake leaves from lawns and flower beds.

MIDWINTER

✔ Check and repair protective coverings often and, after each snowstorm, gently shake the snow from shrub branches.

✔ Take care not to shovel snow onto plants bordering walks and driveways.

✔ After bad storms, cut broken shrub and tree branches. On mild days, finish pruning trees and shrubs that flowered in the late summer and fall.

GRASSES FOR ANY CLIMATE

This chart divides grasses into northern (cool season) and southern (warm season) varieties, each listed by common English name followed by botanical name. Details in the chart include: areas in which each grass grows best, keyed to the map on the facing page; the optimal range of soil pH *(pages 250-251)*; the planting methods and preferred planting seasons; the amount of seed in pounds needed to sow an area of 1,000 square feet; and the ideal mowing height. The last column lists important attributes and the maintenance requirements of each variety.

Northern grasses	ZONES	SOIL PH	PLANTING	SEEDING DENSITY	MOWING HEIGHT	CHARACTERISTICS
Bent grass; colonial, creeping, red top, velvet AGROSTIS	3	5.3-7.5	seed, sprig, sod in fall	1.5-2	$\frac{3}{4}$ inch	*Thick, fine texture; shiny green; grows in cool, humid climates; needs constant maintenance; water frequently, fertilize every month; dethatch yearly*
Bluegrass; Canada, Kentucky, rough-stalk POA	1-3	6.0-7.5	seed, sod in fall or early spring	2-4	2-2$\frac{1}{2}$ inches	*Dense, rich green, fine-textured turf; drought resistant and semidormant in warm weather; Kentucky bluegrass also grows in Zone 4*
Fescue; red, tall FESTUCA	2-5 (tall); 1-3 (red)	5.3-7.5	seed, sod in fall or early spring	6-10	2-3 inches	*Tall is tough, medium-textured turf, red is fine textured, shade tolerant; forms clumps if too sparsely sown; very low maintenance*
Ryegrass; annual, perennial LOLIUM	2-4	5.5-8.0	seed in late fall	6-8	1$\frac{1}{2}$-2 inches	*Fast-growing, light green annual; good for overseeding southern grasses before winter in Zones 5 and 6*
Wheatgrass; crested, western AGROPYRON	2, 4	6.0-8.5	seed in fall or early spring	1-2	2-3 inches	*Bluish green bunches; dormant in summer and tolerant of drought; avoid overwatering and over-fertilizing*

Southern grasses	ZONE(S)	SOIL PH	PLANTING	SEEDING DENSITY	MOWING HEIGHT	CHARACTERISTICS
Bahia grass PASPALUM	6	5.0-6.5	seed, sod in spring	4-6	2$\frac{1}{2}$-3 inches	*Light green, extremely coarse, drought resistant*
Bermuda grass CYNODON	4-6	5.2-7.0	seed, sprig, plug, sod in late spring or summer	2-3	$\frac{1}{2}$-1$\frac{1}{2}$ inches	*Dense, lush, quick spreading; dark green to bluish, depending on hybrid; dethatch each spring*
Blue grama grass BOUTELOUA	2, 4, 5	6.0-8.5	seed in early spring	1-2	2-2$\frac{1}{2}$ inches	*Drought-resistant, small, grayish leaves, which form low tufts*
Buffalo grass BUCHLOE	2, 4, 5	6.0-8.5	seed, plug, sod in spring or summer	3-6	1-2$\frac{1}{2}$ inches	*Rugged, slow-growing, grayish blades, which make a very smooth-textured lawn; may be left unmowed*

KENTUCKY BLUEGRASS

WESTERN WHEATGRASS

BERMUDA GRASS

BUFFALO GRASS

ZOYSIA

Southern, ***continued***	ZONES	SOIL PH	PLANTING	SEEDING DENSITY	MOWING HEIGHT	CHARACTERISTICS
Carpet grass AXONOPUS	6	4.7-7.0	seed, sprig, plug, sod in spring or early summer	1.5-2.5	1-2 inches	*Rugged, though spotty, light green turf; survives with little maintenance in acidic, sandy, and poorly drained soil and in wet locations*
Centipede grass EREMOCHLOA	4-6	4.0-6.0	seed, sprig, plug, sod in spring or early summer	4-6	2 inches	*Slow, low-growing, low-maintenance grass with yellowish, coarse leaves*
St. Augustine grass STENOTAPHRUM	6	6.0-7.0	seed, sprig, plug in spring or early summer	2-3	1-2 inches	*Coarse, dense, low-growing, bluish turf; dethatch yearly*
Zoysia **Also called Manila, Mascarene, Japanese, Korean lawn grass** ZOYSIA	2-6	5.5-7.0	seed, plug, sod in spring or early summer	2-3	$\frac{1}{2}$-$1\frac{1}{2}$ inches	*Dense, slow-growing turf, ranging from coarse grayish to fine moss green. Infrequent watering and fertilizing.*

A MAP OF GRASS ZONES

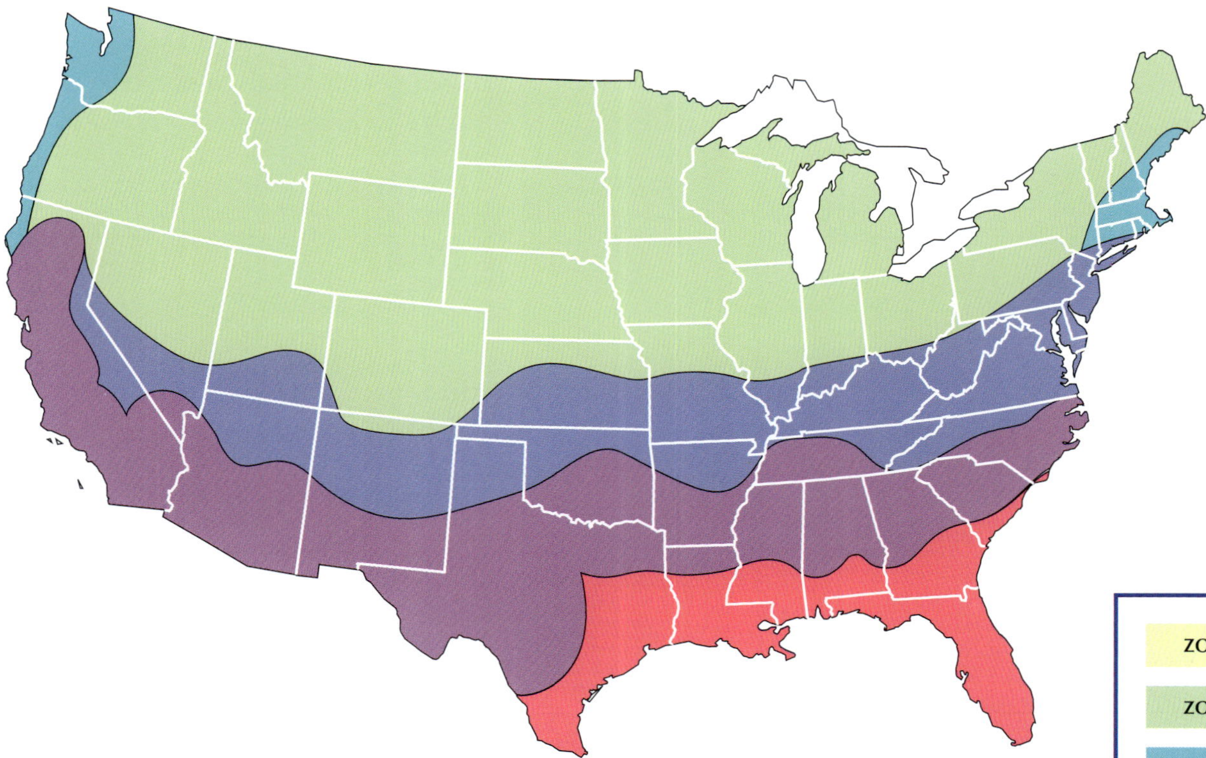

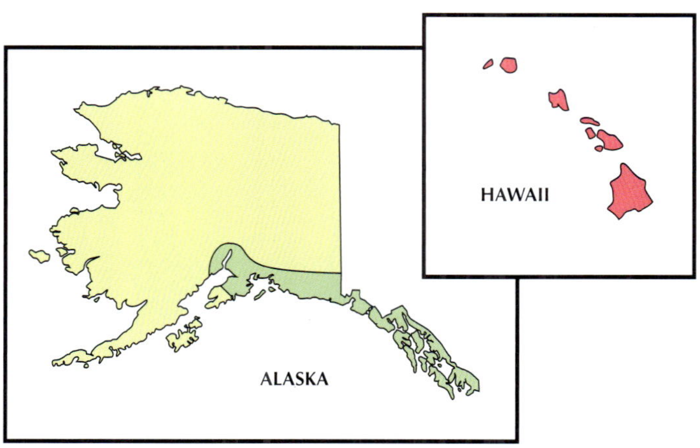

Where grasses grow best.
For the purpose of choosing a grass for a lawn, the United States is divided into six climatic zones. The boundaries of these regions are drawn according to environmental factors that are critical to grass health, primarily minimum winter and maximum summer temperatures and annual rainfall. Northern grasses generally do well in Zones 1 through 4; southern grasses generally prefer Zones 4, 5, and 6.

GROUND COVERS

This chart lists more than three dozen common ground covers by their English and Latin names, grouped according to foliage type—evergreen, deciduous, or semievergreen (plants that keep their leaves only where winters are mild). The zones in which each plant thrives, listed in the second column, are keyed to the map that appears on page 360. Semievergreen plants flourish widely but are green year round only in Zones 8 to 11. Plant height and methods of propagation are listed in the third and fourth columns. The last column notes a variety of special characteristics, such as ground covers that are well suited to slopes or rock gardens and any special light or soil requirements. All of the plants have green foliage and all flower or fruit, unless otherwise noted.

Evergreen	ZONES	HEIGHT	PROPAGATION	SPECIAL CHARACTERISTICS
Bearberry ARCTOSTAPHYLOS UVA-URSI	2-11	8-16"	layering	*Good on slopes; easy maintenance; dry soil*
Candytuft, evergreen IBERIS SEMPERVIRENS	3-11	8-16"	cuttings, division	*Easy maintenance; full sun*
Carmel creeper CEANOTHUS GRISEUS HORIZONTALIS	7-11	over 16"	cuttings	*Good for slopes; full sun*
Coyote brush BACCHARIS PILULARIS	8-11	over 16"	cuttings	*Good for slopes; rapid growth; easy maintenance; full sun*
Daisy, trailing African OSTEOPERMUM FRUTICOSUM	9-11	over 16"	cuttings	*Good for slopes; rapid growth; easy maintenance; full sun; gray-green color*
Dichondra DICHONDRA REPENS	9-11	under 8"	division	*Good for rock gardens; rapid growth; easy maintenance; no flower or fruit*
Geranium, strawberry SAXIFRAGA STOLONIFERA	8-11	under 8"	division, layering	*Rapid growth; easy maintenance; moist soil; partial shade*
Grape, dwarf holly MAHONIA REPENS	5-10	over 16"	cuttings, division	*Good for slopes; rapid growth; easy maintenance; moist soil*
Heath, spring ERICA CARNEA	5-11	over 16"	division, layering	*Good for slopes; moist soil*
Heather, Scotch CALLUNA VULGARIS	4-10	over 16"	cuttings, division	*Good for slopes; easy maintenance; moist soil*
Ivy, English HEDERA HELIX	5-11	under 8"	cuttings	*Good for slopes, rock gardens; rapid growth; easy maintenance; moist soil; vine with no flower or fruit*
Juniper, Wilton carpet JUNIPERUS HORIZONTALIS WILTONII	2-11	under 8"	cuttings	*Good for slopes; easy maintenance; partial shade; no flower or fruit*
Lilyturf, creeping LIRIOPE SPICATA	4-11	8-16"	division	*Easy maintenance*
Pachysandra, Japanese PACHYSANDRA TERMINALIS	4-9	8-16"	cuttings, division	*Good for slopes; rapid growth; easy maintenance; moist soil*
Periwinkle, common VINCA MINOR	4-11	under 8"	cuttings, division	*Vine that is good for slopes; rapid growth; easy maintenance; moist soil; partial shade*
Plum, Green Carpet Natal CARISSA GRANDIFLORA	10-11	8-16"	cuttings	*Moist soil*
Sandwort, moss ARENARIA VERNA SATUREJA	2-11	under 8"	division	*Good for slopes; rapid growth; moist soil*
Snow-in-summer CERASTIUM TOMENTOSUM	2-11	under 8"	cuttings, division	*Good for rock gardens; rapid growth; easy maintenance; full sun; gray-green color*

EVERGREEN CANDYTUFT

TRAILING AFRICAN DAISY

SPRING HEATH

ENGLISH IVY

JAPANESE PACHYSANDRA

Evergreen, *continued*	ZONES	HEIGHT	PROPAGATION	SPECIAL CHARACTERISTICS
Strawberry, sand FRAGARIA CHILOENSIS	8-11	8-16"	cuttings	*Rapid growth; easy maintenance; full sun*
Thrift, common ARMERIA MARITIMA	2-11	8-16"	division	*Good for rock gardens; full sun*
Thyme, wild THYMUS SERPYLLUM	3-11	under 8"	division	*Rapid growth; easy maintenance; dry soil; full sun*
Yarrow, woolly ACHILLEA TOMENTOSA	2-11	8-16"	cuttings, division	*Good for rock gardens; rapid growth; easy maintenance; dry soil; full sun; gray-green color*
Yew, spreading English TAXUS BACCATA	5-11	over 16"	cuttings, layering	*Easy maintenance; moist soil; no flower or fruit*

Deciduous	ZONES	HEIGHT	PROPAGATION	SPECIAL CHARACTERISTICS
Artemesia, Silver Mound ARTEMESIA SCHMIDTIANA	3-11	8-16"	cuttings, division	*Easy maintenance; full sun; gray-green color*
Catmint, mauve NEPETA MUSSINII	4-11	8-16"	cuttings	*Rapid growth; easy maintenance; full sun; gray-green color*
Epimedium EPIMEDIUM GRANDIFLORUM	3-8	8-16"	division	*Easy maintenance; moist soil; partial shade*
Lily of the valley CONVALLARIA MAJALIS	3-7	8-16"	cuttings	*Easy maintenance; moist soil; partial shade*
Rose, Max Graf ROSA 'MAX GRAF'	5-11	over 16"	cuttings, layering	*Easy maintenance; full sun*
Vetch, crown CORONILLA VARIA	3-11	over 16"	division	*Good for slopes; rapid growth; easy maintenance*
Woodruff GALIUM ODORATUM	4-11	8-16"	division	*Rapid growth; easy maintenance; moist soil; partial shade*

Semievergreen	ZONES	HEIGHT	PROPAGATION	SPECIAL CHARACTERISTICS
Baby's-tears SOLEIROLIA SOLEIROLII	9-11	under 8"	cuttings, division	*Rapid growth; easy maintenance; moist soil; partial shade; no flower or fruit*
Bugleweed AJUGA REPTANS	3-11	under 8"	division	*Rapid growth; easy maintenance; moist soil*
Chamomile CHAMAEMELUM NOBILE	3-11	under 8"	division	*Easy maintenance*
Fescue, blue FESTUCA OVINA GLAUCA	3-9	under 8"	division	*Rapid growth; dry soil; full sun; no flower or fruit*
Mint, Corsican MENTHA REQUIENII	6-11	under 8"	division	*Good for rock gardens; rapid growth; moist soil; full sun*
Mondo grass OPHIOPOGON JAPONICUS	8-11	under 8"	division	*Easy maintenance; moist soil*
Phlox, moss PHLOX SUBULATA	3-9	under 8"	cuttings, division	*Good for rock gardens; rapid growth; easy maintenance; full sun*
Rose, memorial ROSA WICHURAIANA	5-11	8-16″	cuttings, layering	*Vine that is good for slopes; rapid growth; easy maintenance; full sun*
St.-John's-wort, Aaron's beard HYPERICUM CALYCINUM	6-11	8-16"	cuttings, division	*Good for slopes; rapid growth; easy maintenance*

MAUVE CATMINT

SILVER MOUND ARTEMESIA

MOSS PHLOX

MONDO GRASS

CHAMOMILE

YARD AND GARDEN TREES

This chart lists 83 small and medium-sized ornamental trees suitable for a garden, patio, or yard; 54 are deciduous, 14 are narrow-leafed evergreens, and 15 are broad-leafed evergreens.

The first column gives the common English names of each tree in alphabetical order, followed by the botanical name; the second lists the geographical zone or zones in which each tree grows best *(map, page 360)*. The third column gives the approximate height of a mature tree. Growth rates for trees vary, from less than 12 inches annually (slow), to 1 to 2 feet per year (moderate), to 3 feet or more a year (fast).

Tree shapes sometimes differ within a single species, as listed in the Shape column. The Special Characteristics column includes other qualities, such as striking leaf color or unusual bark, which make trees distinctive; here, too, variations exist within a species. Also noted in this column are soil and sun requirements, and whether a tree produces flowers, fruit, or seeds.

Inquire at a local nursery about trees that are native to your area; these species will flourish, because they have adapted to local conditions.

Deciduous	ZONES	HEIGHT	GROWTH RATE	SHAPE	SPECIAL CHARACTERISTICS
Ash, European mountain SORBUS AUCUPARIA	3-7	over 25 ft.	fast	spreading	*Full sun; flowers; fruit or seeds; colorful leaves*
Ash, Modesto FRAXINUS VELUTINA GLABRA	5-11	over 25 ft.	fast	spreading	*Dry, alkaline soil; full sun; colorful leaves*
Ash, Moraine FRAXINUS HOLOTRICHA 'MORAINE'	5-11	over 25 ft.	fast	columnar, rounded	*Full sun*
Bauhinia, Buddhist BAUHINIA VARIEGATA	10	to 25 ft.	fast	rounded, spreading	*Moist, acidic soil; full sun; flowers; fruit or seeds*
Birch, European white BETULA PENDULA	2-7	over 25 ft.	fast	weeping, conical	*Moist soil; full sun; colorful leaves, attractive bark*
Catalpa, common CATALPA BIGNONIOIDES	5-11	over 25 ft.	fast	rounded	*Flowers; fruit or seeds*
Cherry, double-flowered mazzard PRUNUS AVIUM PLENA	3-8	over 25 ft.	fast	conical	*Full sun; flowers*
Cherry, Higan PRUNUS SUBHIRTELLA	4-9	to 25 ft.	fast	weeping	*Full sun; flowers*
Cherry, paperbark PRUNUS SERRULA	5-6	to 25 ft.	fast	rounded	*Full sun; flowers; fruit or seeds; attractive bark*
Cherry, Yoshino PRUNUS YEDOENSIS	5-8	over 25 ft.	fast	spreading	*Full sun; flowers*
Chestnut, Chinese CASTANEA MOLLISSIMA	4-9	over 25 ft.	fast	spreading	*Acidic soil; full sun; flowers; fruit or seeds; colorful leaves*
Chinaberry MELIA AZEDARACH	7-11	over 25 ft.	fast	rounded	*Alkaline soil; full sun; flowers; fruit or seeds*
Crab apple, Arnold MALUS ARNOLDIANA	4-10	to 25 ft.	moderate	rounded	*Moist, acidic soil; full sun; flowers; fruit or seeds*
Crab apple, Dolgo MALUS 'DOLGO'	3-10	over 25 ft.	moderate	spreading	*Moist, acidic soil; full sun; flowers; fruit or seeds*
Crab apple, Flame MALUS 'FLAME'	2-10	to 25 ft.	moderate	rounded	*Moist, acidic soil; full sun; flowers; fruit or seeds*
Crab apple, Red Jade MALUS 'RED JADE'	4-10	to 25 ft.	moderate	weeping	*Moist, acidic soil; full sun; flowers; fruit or seeds*

EUROPEAN MOUNTAIN ASH

COMMON CATALPA

YOSHINO CHERRY

RED JADE CRAB APPLE

FLOWERING DOGWOOD

Deciduous, *continued*	ZONES	HEIGHT	GROWTH RATE	SHAPE	SPECIAL CHARACTERISTICS
Crab apple, Zumi MALUS ZUMI CALOCARPA	5-10	to 25 ft.	moderate	conical	*Moist, acidic soil; full sun; flowers; fruit or seeds*
Dogwood, flowering CORNUS FLORIDA	5-8	to 25 ft.	moderate	rounded, weeping, spreading	*Moist, acidic soil; full sun; flowers; fruit or seeds; colorful leaves, attractive bark*
Dogwood, Kousa CORNUS KOUSA	4-8	to 25 ft.	moderate	spreading	*Moist, acidic soil; full sun; flowers; fruit or seeds; colorful leaves*
Franklinia FRANKLINIA ALATAMAHA	5-9	to 25 ft.	slow	conical	*Moist, acidic soil; full sun; flowers; colorful leaves*
Fringe tree CHIONANTHUS VIRGINICUS	3-9	to 25 ft.	slow	rounded	*Moist soil; flowers; fruit or seeds; colorful leaves*
Golden-rain tree KOELREUTERIA PANICULATA	5-9	to 25 ft.	fast	rounded	*Alkaline soil; full sun; flowers*
Golden shower CASSIA FISTULA	10-11	to 25 ft.	fast	rounded	*Flowers; fruit or seeds*
Hawthorn, Toba CRATAEGUS MORDENENSIS 'TOBA'	3-10	to 25 ft.	slow	rounded	*Full sun; flowers; fruit or seeds*
Hawthorn, Washington CRATAEGUS PHAENOPYRUM	3-8	over 25 ft.	slow	conical	*Full sun; flowers; fruit or seeds; colorful leaves*
Hop hornbeam, American OSTRYA VIRGINIANA	3-9	over 25 ft.	slow	conical	*Moist soil; flowers; fruit or seeds; colorful leaves*
Hornbeam, European CARPINUS BETULUS	4-8	over 25 ft.	slow	rounded, conical	*Full sun; colorful leaves, attractive bark*
Jacaranda, sharp-leaved JACARANDA ACUTIFOLIA	10-11	over 25 ft.	fast	spreading	*Acidic soil; full sun; flowers; fruit or seeds; attractive bark*
Jerusalem thorn PARKINSONIA ACULEATA	9-11	to 25 ft.	fast	spreading	*Full sun; flowers; fruit or seeds*
Jujube ZIZIPHUS JUJUBA	6-11	to 25 ft.	moderate	spreading	*Alkaline soil; flowers; fruit or seeds*
Katsura tree CERCIDIPHYLLUM JAPONICUM	4-8	over 25 ft.	fast	spreading, conical	*Moist soil; full sun; colorful leaves*
Laburnum, Waterer LABURNUM WATERERI	5-7	to 25 ft.	moderate	rounded	*Moist soil; light shade; flowers*
Lilac, Japanese tree SYRINGA RETICULATA	3-7	to 25 ft.	moderate	spreading	*Moist soil; full sun; flowers*
Locust, Idaho ROBINIA 'IDAHO'	3-11	over 25 ft.	fast	conical	*Dry, alkaline soil; full sun; flowers*
Magnolia, saucer MAGNOLIA SOULANGIANA	4-11	to 25 ft.	moderate	spreading	*Moist, acidic soil; flowers; fruit or seeds; colorful leaves, attractive bark*
Maple, Amur ACER GINNALA	2-8	to 25 ft.	fast	rounded	*Flowers; fruit or seeds; colorful leaves*
Maple, Japanese ACER PALMATUM	5-8	to 25 ft.	slow	rounded	*Moist soil; light shade; colorful leaves*
Maple, paperbark ACER GRISEUM	4-8	to 25 ft.	slow	rounded	*Full sun; colorful leaves, attractive bark*
Maple, vine ACER CIRCINATUM	5-10	to 25 ft.	moderate	spreading	*Moist soil; light shade; flowers; fruit or seeds; colorful leaves*

FRINGE TREE

WASHINGTON HAWTHORN

KATSURA TREE

SAUCER MAGNOLIA

JAPANESE MAPLE

Deciduous, *continued*	ZONES	HEIGHT	GROWTH RATE	SHAPE	SPECIAL CHARACTERISTICS
Mesquite, honey PROSOPIS GLANDULOSA	8-10	over 25 ft.	fast	conical	*Dry, alkaline soil; full sun; flowers; fruit or seeds; attractive bark*
Oak, California black QUERCUS KELLOGGII	7-10	over 25 ft.	moderate	spreading	*Acidic soil; full sun; fruit or seeds; colorful leaves*
Olive, Russian ELAEAGNUS ANGUSTIFOLIA	2-7	to 25 ft.	fast	rounded	*Full sun; flowers; fruit or seeds; colorful leaves, attractive bark*
Parasol tree, Chinese FIRMIANA SIMPLEX	7-11	over 25 ft.	fast	conical	*Moist soil; full sun; flowers; fruit or seeds; attractive bark*
Pear, Bradford PYRUS CALLERYANA 'BRADFORD'	5-9	over 25 ft.	moderate	conical	*Full sun; flowers; fruit or seeds; colorful leaves*
Pistache, Chinese PISTACIA CHINENSIS	6-9	over 25 ft.	fast	rounded	*Alkaline soil; full sun; fruit or seeds; colorful leaves*
Plum, Pissard PRUNUS CERASIFERA ATROPURPUREA	4-8	to 25 ft.	fast	rounded	*Full sun; flowers; fruit or seeds; colorful leaves*
Poinciana, royal DELONIX REGIA	10-11	over 25 ft.	fast	spreading	*Full sun; flowers; fruit or seeds*
Redbud, eastern CERCIS CANADENSIS	3-9	over 25 ft.	moderate	rounded, spreading	*Moist soil; flowers; fruit or seeds; colorful leaves*
Serviceberry, apple AMELANCHIER GRANDIFLORA	4-9	to 25 ft.	fast	rounded	*Moist soil; flowers; colorful leaves*
Silver bell, Carolina HALESIA CAROLINA	4-8	to 25 ft.	slow	rounded, conical	*Moist, acidic soil; flowers; colorful leaves*
Snowbell, Japanese STYRAX JAPONICUS	5-8	to 25 ft.	slow	spreading	*Moist soil; flowers; colorful leaves*
Sorrel tree OXYDENDRUM ARBOREUM	4-9	to 25 ft.	slow	conical	*Moist, acidic soil; full sun; flowers; fruit or seeds; colorful leaves*
Tallow tree, Chinese SAPIUM SEBIFERUM	7-10	over 25 ft.	fast	spreading	*Full sun; fruit or seeds; colorful leaves*
Walnut, Hinds black JUGLANS HINDSII	8-10	over 25 ft.	fast	rounded	*Full sun; fruit or seeds*

Narrow-Leaved Evergreen	ZONES	HEIGHT	GROWTH RATE	SHAPE	SPECIAL CHARACTERISTICS
Arborvitae, Douglas THUJA OCCIDENTALIS DOUGLASII AUREA	2-11	to 25 ft.	fast	conical	*Moist soil; full sun*
Cedar, California incense CALOCEDRUS DECURRENS	5-11	over 25 ft.	fast	conical	*Moist soil; fruit or seeds; attractive bark*
Cedar, Japanese CRYPTOMERIA JAPONICA	5-11	over 25 ft.	fast	conical	*Moist, acidic soil; full sun; fruit or seeds; colorful leaves, attractive bark*
Cypress, Italian CUPRESSUS SEMPERVIRENS STRICTA	7-9	over 25 ft.	fast	columnar	*Dry soil; full sun; fruit or seeds; colorful leaves*
Cypress, moss sawara, false CHAMAECYPARIS PISIFERA SQUARROSA	4-8	over 25 ft.	moderate	conical	*Moist soil; full sun*
Fir, China CUNNINGHAMIA LANCEOLATA	6-9	to 25 ft.	fast	conical	*Acidic soil; fruit or seeds; colorful leaves, attractive bark*
Juniper, blue column JUNIPERUS CHINENSIS COLUMNARIS	3-9	to 25 ft.	moderate	conical	*Dry soil; full sun*

CALIFORNIA BLACK OAK

RUSSIAN OLIVE

PISSARD PLUM

JAPANESE CEDAR

FALSE MOSS SAWARA CYPRESS

Narrow-Leaved, *continued*	ZONES	HEIGHT	GROWTH RATE	SHAPE	SPECIAL CHARACTERISTICS
Pine, Japanese black PINUS THUNBERGIANA	5-11	over 25 ft.	fast	spreading, conical	*Dry soil; full sun; fruit or seeds*
Pine, Norfolk Island ARAUCARIA HETEROPHYLLA	7-11	over 25 ft.	fast	conical	*Moist, acidic soil; full sun; fruit or seeds*
Pine, Tanyosho PINUS DENSIFLORA UMBRACULIFERA	3-7	to 25 ft.	slow	spreading	*Dry soil; full sun; fruit or seeds; colorful leaves*
Pine, umbrella SCIADOPITYS VERTICILLATA	4-11	to 25 ft.	slow	conical	*Moist, alkaline soil; full sun; fruit or seeds*
Podocarpus yew PODOCARPUS MACROPHYLLUS	8-11	to 25 ft.	moderate	columnar	*Moist soil; light shade; colorful leaves*
Spruce, Serbian PICEA OMORIKA	4-7	over 25 ft.	slow	conical	*Full sun; fruit or seeds*
Yew, Irish TAXUS BACCATA STRICTA	5-11	to 25 ft.	slow	columnar, conical	*Acidic soil; fruit or seeds; colorful leaves*

Broad-Leaved Evergreen	ZONES	HEIGHT	GROWTH RATE	SHAPE	SPECIAL CHARACTERISTICS
Ash, shamel FRAXINUS UHDEI 'MAJESTIC BEAUTY'	9-11	over 25 ft.	fast	spreading	*Moist, alkaline soil; full sun*
Camphor tree CINNAMOMUM CAMPHORA	9-11	over 25 ft.	moderate	spreading	*Flowers; fruit or seeds; colorful leaves*
Cootamundra wattle ACACIA BAILEYANA	10-11	to 25 ft.	fast	rounded	*Dry soil; full sun; flowers; colorful leaves*
Elm, Chinese ULMUS PARVIFOLIA	4-11	over 25 ft.	fast	weeping	*Full sun*
Holly, English ILEX AQUIFOLIUM	6-10	over 25 ft.	slow	rounded	*Acidic soil; full sun; fruit or seeds; colorful leaves*
Horsetail beefwood CASUARINA EQUISETIFOLIA	9-11	over 25 ft.	fast	conical	*Fruit or seeds*
Laurel LAURUS NOBILIS	6-11	to 25 ft.	slow	conical	*Fruit or seeds*
Loquat ERIOBOTRYA JAPONICA	8-11	to 25 ft.	fast	spreading	*Moist soil; flowers; fruit or seeds; colorful leaves*
Oleander NERIUM OLEANDER	8-11	to 25 ft.	moderate	rounded	*Moist soil; full sun; flowers*
Olive, common OLEA EUROPAEA	9-11	to 25 ft.	moderate	rounded	*Dry soil; full sun; flowers; fruit or seeds; attractive bark*
Orange, sweet CITRUS SINENSIS	9-11	to 25 ft.	moderate	rounded	*Moist soil; full sun; flowers; fruit or seeds*
Osmanthus, holly OSMANTHUS HETEROPHYLLUS	7-11	to 25 ft.	fast	rounded	*Dry soil; light shade; flowers*
Pepper tree, California SCHINUS MOLLE	9-11	over 25 ft.	moderate	weeping	*Full sun; flowers; fruit or seeds*
Photinia, Fraser PHOTINIA FRASERI	8-11	to 25 ft.	moderate	spreading	*Flowers; fruit or seeds; colorful leaves*
Pineapple guava FEIJOA SELLOWIANA	8-11	to 25 ft.	fast	rounded	*Moist soil; flowers; fruit or seeds; colorful leaves*

JAPANESE BLACK PINE

ENGLISH HOLLY

OLEANDER

SWEET ORANGE

PINEAPPLE GUAVA

GARDEN SHRUBS

This chart lists 58 flowering shrubs by their common English names, followed by their botanical names. The numbered zones in which each shrub can be grown are keyed to the map on page 360. In the chart's third column the approximate height for each variety is listed. Colored circles in the fourth column indicate the range of flower colors usually produced by each shrub or its relatives. To the right of the colors is the shrub's blooming season. The Special Characteristics column contains uses to which the plant is well suited—a hedge or a ground cover, for example; its soil and sun preferences; and the presence of fruit, attractive foliage, or a pleasant fragrance.

Flowering	ZONES	HEIGHT	FLOWER COLORS	BLOOMING SEASON	SPECIAL CHARACTERISTICS
Acacia, rose ROBINIA HISPIDA	5-9	to 6 ft.	pink, red	spring-summer	*Ground cover; full sun*
Almond, flowering PRUNUS TRILOBA	5-9	over 6 ft.	pink, red	spring	*Full sun; fruit; attractive foliage*
Azalea, catawba RHODODENDRON CATAWBIENSE	3-10	over 6 ft.	pink, red, blue, purple	spring	*Moist, acidic soil; shade*
Azalea, Exbury hybrid RHODODENDRON	5-8	to 6 ft.	white, yellow, orange, pink, red	summer	*Moist, acidic soil; attractive foliage*
Azalea, flame RHODODENDRON CALENDULACEUM	4-10	to 6 ft.	yellow, orange, pink, red	summer	*Moist, acidic soil*
Azalea, pinxter-bloom RHODODENDRON NUDIFLORUM	3-8	to 6 ft.	white, pink, red	spring	*Moist, acidic soil*
Barberry, Japanese BERBERIS THUNBERGII	4-10	over 6 ft.	yellow, orange	spring	*Hedge; fruit*
Barberry, Mentor BERBERIS MENTORENSIS	5-10	over 6 ft.	yellow, orange	spring	*Hedge; fruit*
Beauty-bush KOLKWITZIA AMABILIS	4-9	over 6 ft.	pink, red	spring	*Fruit; attractive foliage*
Broom, hybrid CYTISUS HYBRIDS	6-11	any	white, yellow, orange, pink, red, blue, purple	spring	*Full sun; fragrant*
Buckeye, bottlebrush AESCULUS PARVIFLORA	4-10	over 6 ft.	white	summer	*Attractive foliage*
Butterfly bush, fountain BUDDLEIA ALTERNIFOLIA	5-11	over 6 ft.	blue, purple	spring-summer	*Full sun; attractive foliage; fragrant*
Cherry, Cornelian CORNUS MAS	4-8	over 6 ft.	yellow, orange	spring	*Fruit; attractive foliage*
Cherry, western sand PRUNUS BESSEYI	3-6	over 6 ft.	white	spring	*Full sun; fruit*
Chokeberry, black ARONIA MELANOCARPA	4-10	under 3 ft.	white, pink, red	spring	*Fruit; attractive foliage*
Chokeberry, brilliant ARONIA ARBUTIFOLIA BRILLIANTISSIMA	4-10	over 6 ft.	white, pink, red	spring	*Fruit; attractive foliage*
Cinquefoil, bush POTENTILLA FRUTICOSA	2-9	to 6 ft.	white, yellow, orange	summer-fall	*Full sun*

EXBURY HYBRID AZALEA

JAPANESE BARBERRY

HYBRID BROOM

CORNELIAN CHERRY

BUSH CINQUEFOIL

Flowering, *continued*	ZONES	HEIGHT	FLOWER COLORS	BLOOMING SEASON	SPECIAL CHARACTERISTICS
Cotoneaster, early COTONEASTER ADPRESSUS	4-11	under 3 ft.	pink, red	summer	*Full sun; fruit; attractive foliage*
Cotoneaster, horizontal COTONEASTER HORIZONTALIS	5-11	under 3 ft.	pink, red, blue, purple	summer	*Ground cover; full sun; attractive foliage*
Cotoneaster, Sungari COTONEASTER RACEMIFLORUS	3-11	over 6 ft.	white	summer	*Full sun; fruit; attractive foliage*
Crape myrtle LAGERSTROEMIA INDICA	7-10	over 6 ft.	white, pink, red, blue, purple	summer	*Hedge; moist soil; full sun; attractive foliage*
Daphne, February DAPHNE MEZEREUM	4-9	under 3 ft.	pink, red	spring	*Fruit; fragrant*
Deutzia, slender DEUTZIA GRACILIS	4-9	to 6 ft.	white	spring	*Hedge*
Enkianthus, redvein ENKIANTHUS CAMPANULATUS	4-9	over 6 ft.	white	spring	*Moist, acidic soil; attractive foliage*
Forsythia, border FORSYTHIA INTERMEDIA	5-9	over 6 ft.	yellow, orange	spring	*Hedge*
Hazelnut, curly CORYLUS AVELLANA CONTORTA	4-9	over 6 ft.	yellow, orange	spring	*Attractive foliage*
Honeysuckle, Amur LONICERA MAACKII	2-9	over 6 ft.	white	spring	*Fruit; fragrant*
Honeysuckle, Tatarian LONICERA TATARICA	3-9	over 6 ft.	white, pink, red	spring	*Fruit*
Honeysuckle, winter LONICERA FRAGRANTISSIMA	5-9	to 6 ft.	white	spring	*Fruit; fragrant*
Hydrangea, peegee HYDRANGEA PANICULATA	4-9	over 6 ft.	white, pink, red	summer-fall	*Moist soil*
Jasmine, winter JASMINUM NUDIFLORUM	6-9	over 6 ft.	yellow, orange	spring	*Full sun*
Kerria KERRIA JAPONICA	4-9	to 6 ft.	yellow, orange	spring-summer-fall	*Attractive foliage*
Lilac, common SYRINGA VULGARIS	3-7	over 6 ft.	white, yellow, orange, pink, red, blue, purple	spring	*Fragrant*
Mock orange, Lemoine PHILADELPHUS LEMOINEI	5-9	to 6 ft.	white	summer	*Fragrant*
Olive, Russian ELAEAGNUS ANGUSTIFOLIA	2-9	over 6 ft.	yellow, orange	summer	*Hedge; full sun; fruit; attractive foliage; fragrant*
Pearlbush, common EXOCHORDA RACEMOSA	5-9	over 6 ft.	white	spring	*Full sun*
Photinia, Oriental PHOTINIA VILLOSA	4-8	over 6 ft.	white	spring	*Fruit; attractive foliage*
Plum, beach PRUNUS MARITIMA	3-7	to 6 ft.	white	spring	*Full sun; fruit*
Privet, Amur LIGUSTRUM AMURENSE	3-9	over 6 ft.	white	summer	*Hedge; fruit*

HORIZONTAL COTONEASTER

CRAPE MYRTLE

KERRIA

COMMON LILAC

LEMOINE MOCK ORANGE

Flowering, *continued*	ZONES	HEIGHT	FLOWER COLORS	BLOOMING SEASON	SPECIAL CHARACTERISTICS
Privet, Regel LIGUSTRUM OBTUSIFOLIUM	3-9	to 6 ft.	white	summer	*Hedge; fruit*
Privet, vicary golden LIGUSTRUM VICARYI	4-9	over 6 ft.	white	summer	*Hedge; fruit; attractive foliage*
Pussy willow SALIX DISCOLOR	2-9	over 6 ft.	white	spring	*Moist soil; full sun*
Quince, hybrid flowering CHAENOMELES HYBRIDS	6-10	to 6 ft.	white, pink, red	spring	*Hedge; full sun*
Rose, Japanese ROSA RUGOSA	2-10	to 6 ft.	white, pink, red	summer-fall	*Full sun; fruit; attractive foliage; fragrant*
Snowberry SYMPHORICARPOS ALBUS	3-9	to 6 ft.	pink, red	summer	*Hedge; fruit*
Spirea, bridal-wreath SPIRAEA PRUNIFOLIA	4-10	over 6 ft.	white	spring	*Hedge; attractive foliage*
Spirea, Bumalda SPIRAEA BUMALDA	5-10	under 3 ft.	pink, red	summer	*Attractive foliage*
Spirea, Ural false SORBARIA SORBIFOLIA	2-8	to 6 ft.	white	summer	*Moist soil*
Spirea, Vanhoutte SPIRAEA VANHOUTTEI	4-10	to 6 ft.	white	spring	*Hedge*
Summer-sweet CLETHRA ALNIFOLIA	3-10	to 6 ft.	white	summer	*Moist, acidic soil; attractive foliage; fragrant*
Sweet shrub CALYCANTHUS FLORIDUS	4-10	to 6 ft.	pink, red	spring	*Moist soil; attractive foliage; fragrant*
Tamarisk, five-stamened TAMARIX PENTANDRA	2-11	over 6 ft.	pink, red	summer	*Sun; attractive foliage*
Viburnum, fragrant snowball VIBURNUM CARLCEPHALUM	5-9	over 6 ft.	white	spring	*Hedge; fruit; attractive foliage; fragrant*
Viburnum, Marie's double file VIBURNUM PLICATUM	5-9	over 6 ft.	white	spring	*Hedge; fruit; attractive foliage*
Viburnum, Siebold VIBURNUM SIEBOLDII	4-9	over 6 ft.	white	spring	*Fruit; attractive foliage*
Weigela, hybrid WEIGELA	5-9	to 6 ft.	white, pink, red	spring	
Winter hazel, fragrant CORYLOPSIS GLABRESCENS	5-9	over 6 ft.	yellow, orange	spring	*Moist, acidic soil; attractive foliage; fragrant*
Witch hazel, Chinese HAMAMELIS MOLLIS	5-9	over 6 ft.	yellow, orange	spring	*Moist soil; attractive foliage; fragrant*

PUSSY WILLOW

MARIE'S DOUBLE FILE VIBURNUM

HYBRID FLOWERING QUINCE

HYBRID WEIGELA

CHINESE WITCH HAZEL

This chart lists 20 evergreen shrubs by their common names, then by their botanical names. The numbered zones in which each shrub can be grown refer to the map on page 360. Special characteristics and growing conditions are mentioned in the last column; these include specific uses, such as a lawn specimen, hedge, screen, or ground cover; soil requirements; and whether the plant produces fruit, berries, or flowers.

Evergreen	ZONES	HEIGHT	FOLIAGE COLOR	SPECIAL CHARACTERISTICS
Arbor vitae, Berckman's golden PLATYCLADUS ORIENTALIS	7-11	to 6 ft.	green, yellow-green	*Hedge, screen; moist soil*
Bearberry, 'Point Reyes' ARCTOSTAPHYLOS UVA-URSI 'POINT REYES'	2-11	under 1 ft.	dark green	*Ground cover; dry, acidic soil; fruits or berries; pink-red flowers*
Box, edging BUXUS SEMPERVIRENS SUFFRUTICOSA	5-6	to 3 ft.	blue-green	*Lawn specimen; hedge; moist soil*
Camellia, common CAMELLIA JAPONICA	7-11	to 10 ft.	dark green	*Lawn specimen, hedge; moist, acidic soil; pink-red flowers*
Cypress, false slender hinoki CHAMAECYPARIS OBTUSA	4-8	to 6 ft.	dark green	*Lawn specimen; moist soil*
Cypress, false thread sawara CHAMAECYPARIS PISIFERA	4-8	to 10 ft.	green	*Lawn specimen; moist soil*
Fire thorn, Laland PYRACANTHA COCCINEA	5-11	to 10 ft.	dark green	*Hedge; fruits or berries; white flowers*
Grape, Oregon holly MAHONIA AQUIFOLIUM	4-8	to 6 ft.	green	*Fruits or berries; yellow-orange flowers*
Holly, American ILEX OPACA	5-9	to 10 ft.	green	*Hedge; acidic soil; fruits or berries*
Holly, Burford ILEX CORNUTA	6-9	to 10 ft.	green	*Hedge; acidic soil; fruits or berries*
Holly, Japanese ILEX CRENATA	5-7	to 10 ft.	dark green	*Hedge; acidic soil; fruits or berries*
Juniper, Gold Coast JUNIPERUS CHINENSIS AUREA	3-11	to 3 ft.	yellow-green	*Lawn specimen, ground cover*
Juniper, tamarix JUNIPERUS SABINA	3-11	to 3 ft.	blue-green	*Ground cover*
Juniper, Wilton carpet JUNIPERUS HORIZONTALIS	3-11	under 1 ft.	blue-green	*Ground cover*
Laurel, mountain KALMIA LATIFOLIA	4-9	to 10 ft.	dark green	*Lawn specimen; moist, acidic soil; pink-red flowers*
Nandina NANDINA DOMESTICA	6-11	to 6 ft.	green	*Moist soil; fruits or berries; white flowers*
Pine, Mugo PINUS MUGO	2-8	to 3 ft.	dark green	*Lawn specimen, hedge, ground cover*
Spruce, dwarf Alberta PICEA GLAUCA	2-6	to 10 ft.	blue-green	*Lawn specimen, hedge, screen*
Tea tree LEPTOSPERMUM SCOPARIUM	9-11	to 10 ft.	green	*Hedge; acidic soil; pink-red flowers*
Yew, spreading English TAXUS BACCATA REPANDENS	5-11	to 6 ft.	dark green	*Lawn specimen, hedge; acidic soil*

GOLD COAST JUNIPER

LALAND FIRE THORN

MOUNTAIN LAUREL

DWARF ALBERTA SPRUCE

TEA TREE

A MAP OF MINIMUM TEMPERATURES

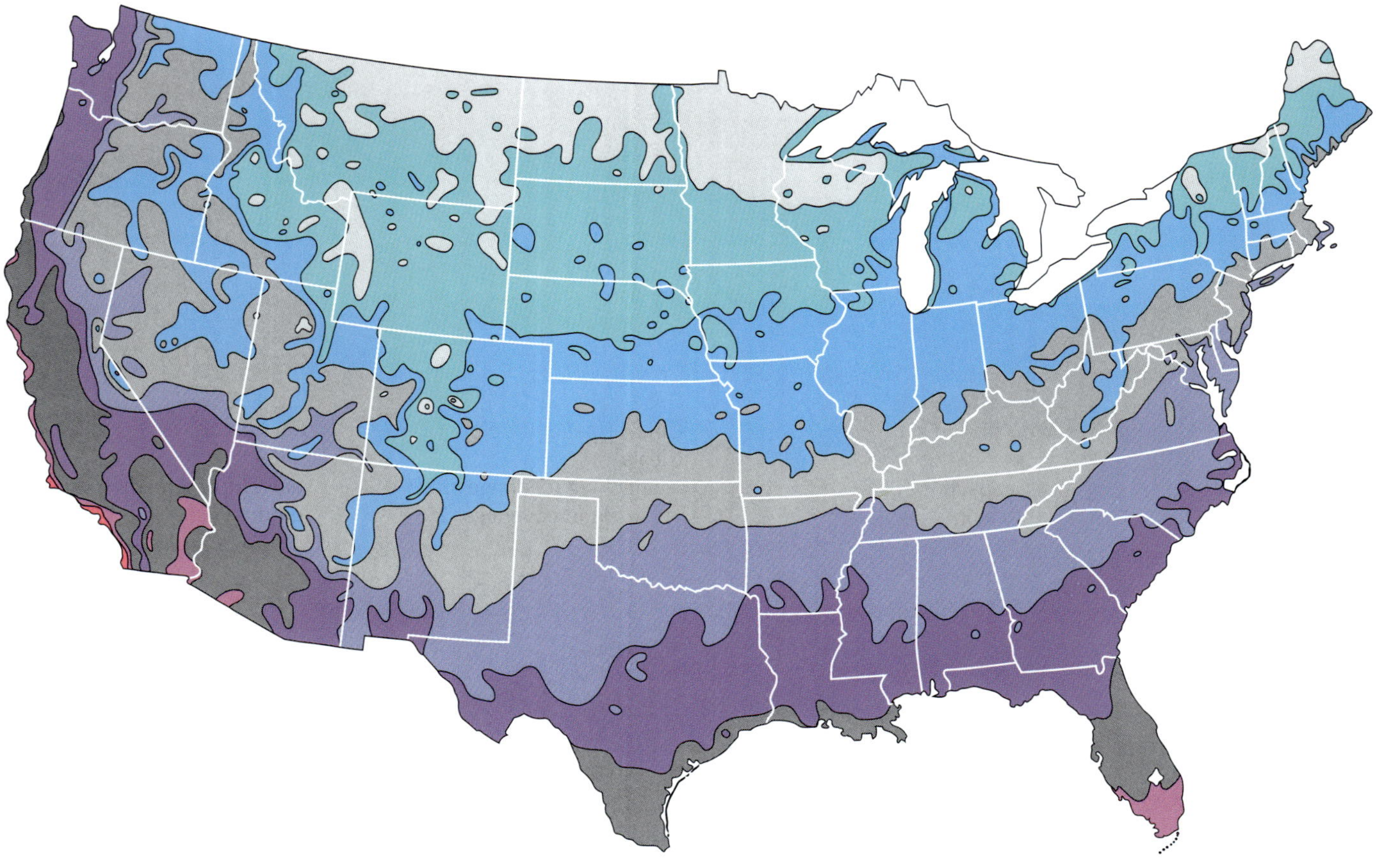

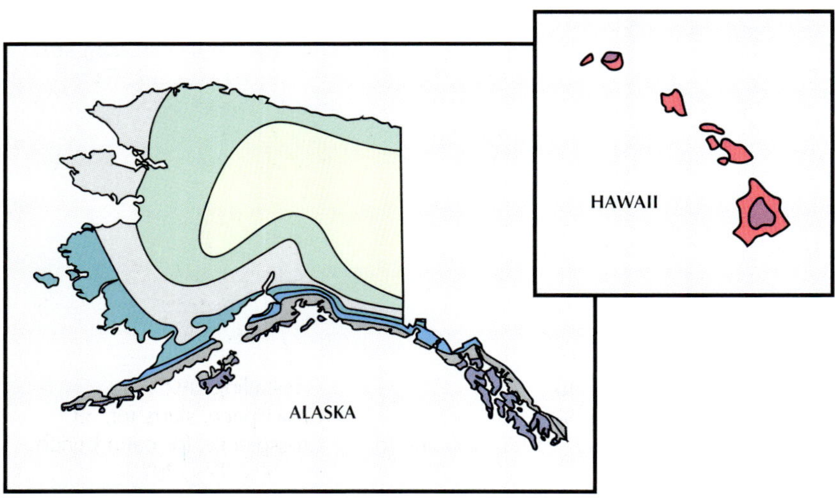

ZONE 1	BELOW -50° F.
ZONE 2	-50° TO -40°
ZONE 3	-40° TO -30°
ZONE 4	-30° TO -20°
ZONE 5	-20° TO -10°
ZONE 6	-10° TO 0°
ZONE 7	0° TO 10°
ZONE 8	10° TO 20°
ZONE 9	20° TO 30°
ZONE 10	30° TO 40°
ZONE 11	ABOVE 40°

Plants and winter cold.

Successful landscaping depends upon a choice of plants that thrive on the land they adorn. Since soil conditions and moisture levels can usually be altered artificially, limitations on where plants will flourish depend largely upon the severity of winter cold. This map devised by the U.S. Department of Agriculture divides the United States into 11 numbered and colored zones, each distinguished by an average minimum winter temperature. Use the charts of ground covers *(pages 350-351) and* flowering shrubs *(pages 356-357)* with this map to select plants that will grow best in your area.

INDEX

E

F

G

S

PICTURE CREDITS

Illustrators: James Anderson, Jack Arthur, Terry Atkinson, Gilles Baeuchemin, George Bell, Michael Blais, Frederic F. Bigio from B-C Graphics, Laszlo Bodrogi, Adolph E. Brotman, Roger C. Essley, Nicholas Fasciano, Charles Forsythe, Gerry Gallagher, Donald Gates, Adisai Hemintranont from Sai Graphics, William J. Hennessy Jr. from A & W Graphics, Elsie J. Henning, Walter Hilmers Jr., Fred Holz, Fil Hunter, John Jones, Arezou Katoozian from A & W Graphics, Al Ketter, Dick Lee, Peter McGinn, Joan S. McGurren, Gerard Mariscalchi, John Martinez, Jennifer and John Massey, Robert Paquet, Eduino J. Pereira, Jacques Perrault, Jaques Proulx, Graham Sayles, Michael Secrist, Ray Skibinski, Snowden Associates, Inc., Jeff Swarts, Stephen Turner, Vantage Art, Inc., Stephen R. Wagner, Walter Hilmers Studios, Whitman Studio, Inc.

Photographers: (Credits from left to right are separated by semicolons, from top to bottom by dashes) 14: Fil Hunter. 15: Renée Comet. 27: Pamela Harper. 61, 80: Renée Comet. 91: Rick McCleary. 94: Renée Comet. 96: Rick McCleary. 106–107: Renée Comet. 133: Robert Chartier. 134: Robert Chartier. 136: Robert Chartier. 137: Robert Chartier. 145: Lifetime Fence. 164: Robert Chartier. 178: Simpson Strong-Tie. 185, 188: Robert Chartier. 194: Screen Tight. 192: Robert Chartier. 208: Robert Chartier. 219: Robert Chartier. 224: Robert Chartier. 225–226: Robert Chartier. 304, 307, 312, 313: Renée Comet. 316: Rain Bird®. 319: Renée Comet. 230, 242: Renée Comet. 283: The Toro Company. 286: L. R. Nelson Corporation. 287: L. R. Nelson Corporation (2)—Renée Comet. 296, 297, 301, 336, 358, 263: Renée Comet. 279: Ronnie Luttrell. 348: Doug Brede. 350: Jerry Pavia; Joanne Pavia; Jerry Pavia; Joanne Pavia; Jerry Pavia. 351: Jerry Pavia. 352: Joanne Pavia; Jerry Pavia (4). 353: Jerry Pavia (2); Joanne Pavia (2); Jerry Pavia. 354: Joanne Pavia (3); Jerry Pavia (2). 355: Jerry Pavia (3); Joanne Pavia; Jerry Pavia. 356, 357: Jerry Pavia. 358: Joanne Pavia (2); Jerry Pavia (3). 359: Joanne Pavia; Jerry Pavia (4).

ACKNOWLEDGMENTS

The editors also wish to thank the following individuals and institutions:
Les and Barbara Allison, Washington, D.C.; Anthony Forest Products, El Dorado, Ark.; Christopher Baldwin, Middleburg, Va.; Joe Beben, Fairfax County Department of Environmental Management, Public Utilities Branch, Fairfax, Va.; Birchall & Associates Inc., Mississauga, Ont.; Bowa Builders, Arlington, Va.; BPCO, Lasalle, Que.; Doug Brede, Jacklin Seed Company, Post Falls, Idaho; Cedar Shake and Shingle Bureau, Bellevue, Wash.; Christopher's Glen Echo Hardware, Glen Echo, Md.; CMT Tools, Oldsmar, Fla.; Jeff Cox, Kenwood, Calif.; Howard R. Crum and Virginia Crum, Lilypons Water Gardens, Buckeystown, Md.; Ashley Crumpton, Chapel Hill, N.C.; Geoff and Meg Dawson, Washington, D.C.; Delta International Machinery/Porter-Cable, Guelph, Ont.; DeWalt Industrial Tool Company Inc., Richmond Hill, Ont.; DeWitt Company, Sikeston, Mo.; Garant Tools, St. François, Que.; Joan L. Gregory, Vienna, Va.; Kenny Haddaway and Bob Hill, Belmont Power Equipment, Newington, Va.; Reed Harper, Summitville Fairfax Inc., Alexandria, Va.; Hechinger, Gardening Department, Alexandria, Va.; Ben Hoenich, Glen-Gery Brick, Wyomissing, Pa.; Home Depot, Gardening Department, Alexandria, Va.; Independent Nail Company, Taunton, Mass.; Gerald W. Klancer, Woodbridge, Va.; Lanark Cedar, Carleton Place, Ont.; Laser Tools, Little Rock, Ark.; Lifetime Fence, Fair Oaks, Calif.; Mary Levine, Tile Promotion Board, Jupiter, Fla.; John Lewett and Mike Mayeux, J. L. Tree Service, Fairfax, Va.; Macklanburg-Duncan, Oklahoma City; Merrifield Garden Center, Merrifield, Va.; National Concrete Masonry Association, Herndon, Va.; Naturalistic Gardens, Sudbury, Mass.; Northwestern Steel and Wire, Sterling, Ill.; William T. Patton Sr., Turf Center Lawns, Inc., Silver Spring, Md.; Plastics Research, Flint, Mich.; Portland Cement Association, Skokie, Ill.; PVC Lumber Systems, Montreal, Que.; Louise S. Roberts, Chevy Chase, Md.; Alvin Sacks, Bethesda, Md.; Screen Tight, Georgetown, S.C.; Sequentia, Strongsville, Ohio; Seven Corners Rentals, Falls Church, Va.; Simpson Strong-Tie, Pleasanton, Calif.; Scott and Dibby Smith, Arlington, Va.; Stanley Tool Works, New Britain, Conn.; Pam Underhill, Landscape, Arlington, Va.; Versa-lok, St. Paul, Minn.; Russell Whitt, Silver Spring, Md.; David Yost, Virginia Cooperative Extension, Fairfax, Va.

COMPLETE GUIDE TO OUTDOOR PROJECTS
Editor: Lee Hassig
Marketing Director: James Gillespie

Art Director: Kathleen Mallow
Associate Editor/Research and Writing: Karen Sweet
Marketing Manager: Wells Spence
Picture Coordinator: Lisa Groseclose

Special Contributors: John Drummond (illustration); William Graves, Craig Hower, Marvin Shultz, Eileen Wentland (digital illustration); Janet Barnes Syring (composition); Jennifer Rushing-Schurr (index).

Cover photography: Jay Graham. Deck design by Gary Marsh. Cover design by Vasken Guiragossian.

Back cover photography: Mark Rutherford

SUNSET BOOKS

10 9 8 7 6 5 4 3 2 1
First printing January 2003

ISBN 0-376-00522-X
Library of Congress Control Number: 2002117077
Printed in the United States.